wetter LOUDER Stickier

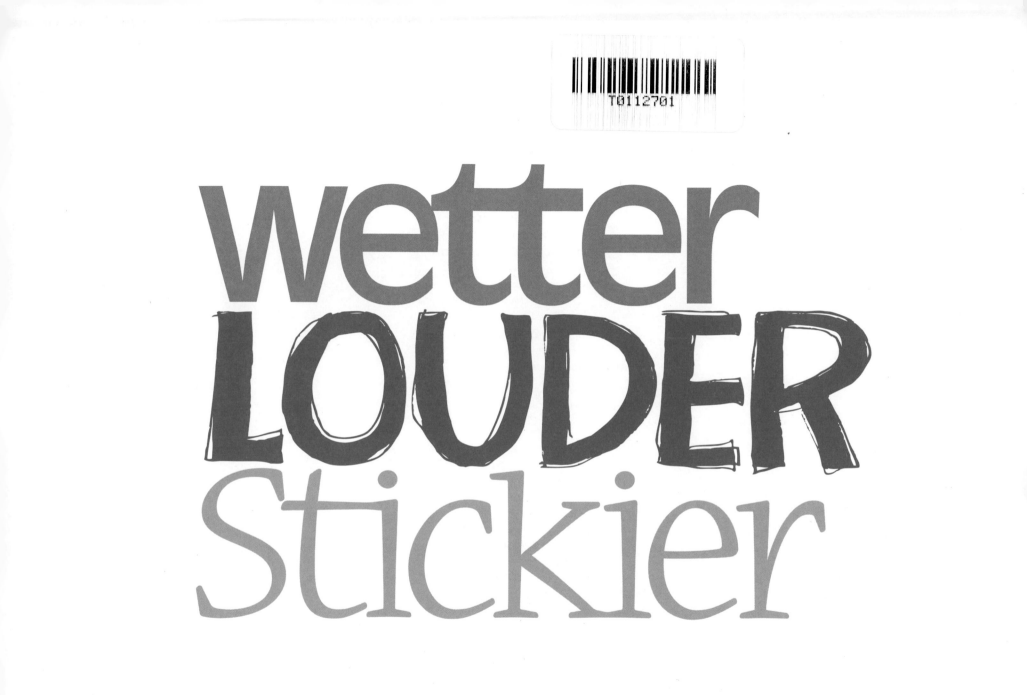

Other Baby Blues® Books from Andrews McMeel Publishing

Guess Who Didn't Take a Nap?
I Thought Labor Ended When the Baby Was Born
We Are Experiencing Parental Difficulties . . . Please Stand By
Night of the Living Dad
I Saw Elvis in My Ultrasound
One More and We're Outnumbered!
Check, Please . . .
threats, bribes & videotape
If I'm a Stay-at-Home Mom, Why Am I Always in the Car?
Lift and Separate
I Shouldn't Have to Scream More Than Once!
Motherhood Is Not for Wimps
Baby Blues®: Unplugged
Dad to the Bone
Never a Dry Moment
Two Plus One Is Enough
Playdate: Category 5
Our Server Is Down
Something Chocolate This Way Comes
Briefcase Full of Baby Blues®
Night Shift
The Day Phonics Kicked In
My Space
The Natural Disorder of Things
We Were Here First
Ambushed! In the Family Room
Cut!
Eat, Cry, Poop
Scribbles at an Exhibition
Bedlam

Treasuries

The Super-Absorbent Biodegradable Family-Size Baby Blues®
Baby Blues®: Ten Years and Still in Diapers
Butt-Naked Baby Blues®
Wall-to-Wall Baby Blues®
Driving Under the Influence of Children
Framed!
X-Treme Parenting
BBXX: Baby Blues: Decades 1 and 2

Gift Book

It's a Boy
It's a Girl

wetter LOUDER Stickier

Scrapbook

NO. 31

rick kirkman
jerry scott

Andrews McMeel
Publishing

Kansas City • Sydney • London

To Abbey. Happy 21st year, kiddo, from your very proud dad
—JS

To The Gann Clann: Becca, Jeff, Jillian and Allison.
—RK

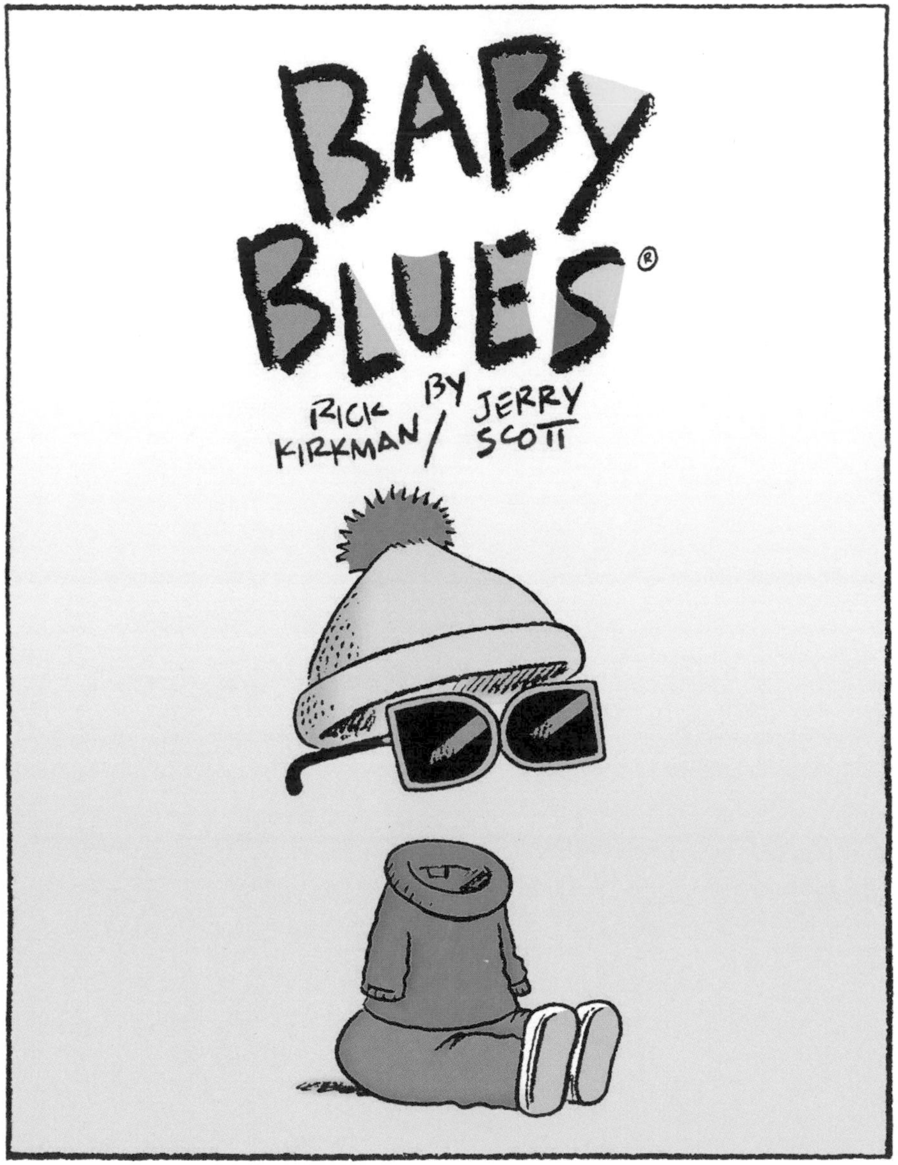
BABY BLUES®
BY
RICK KIRKMAN / JERRY SCOTT

Rick: The title panel has a little nod to the 1933 version of *The Invisible Man*. I gave Zoe's shades the shape of those worn by Claude Rains in the movie.

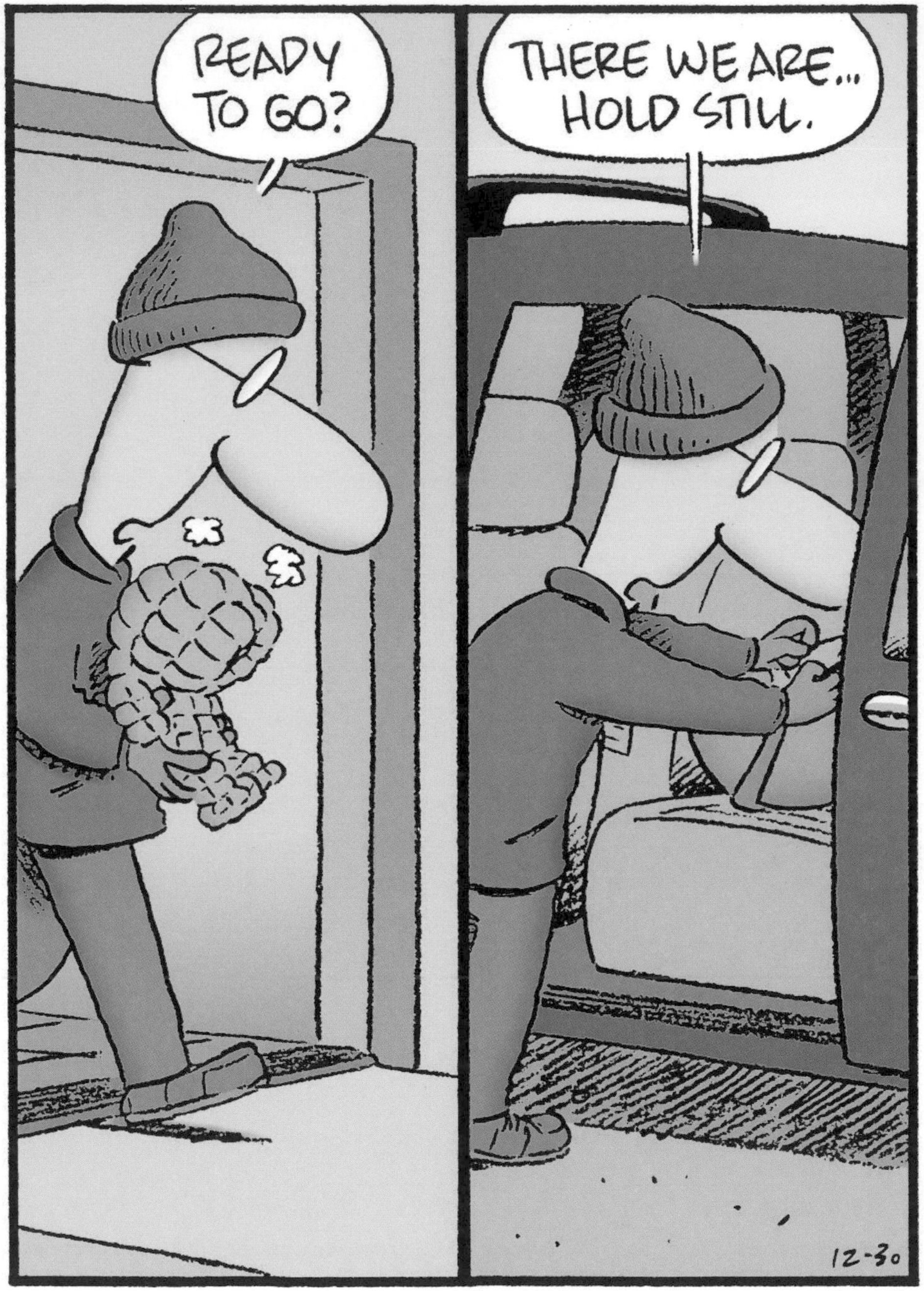
READY TO GO?
THERE WE ARE... HOLD STILL.
12-30

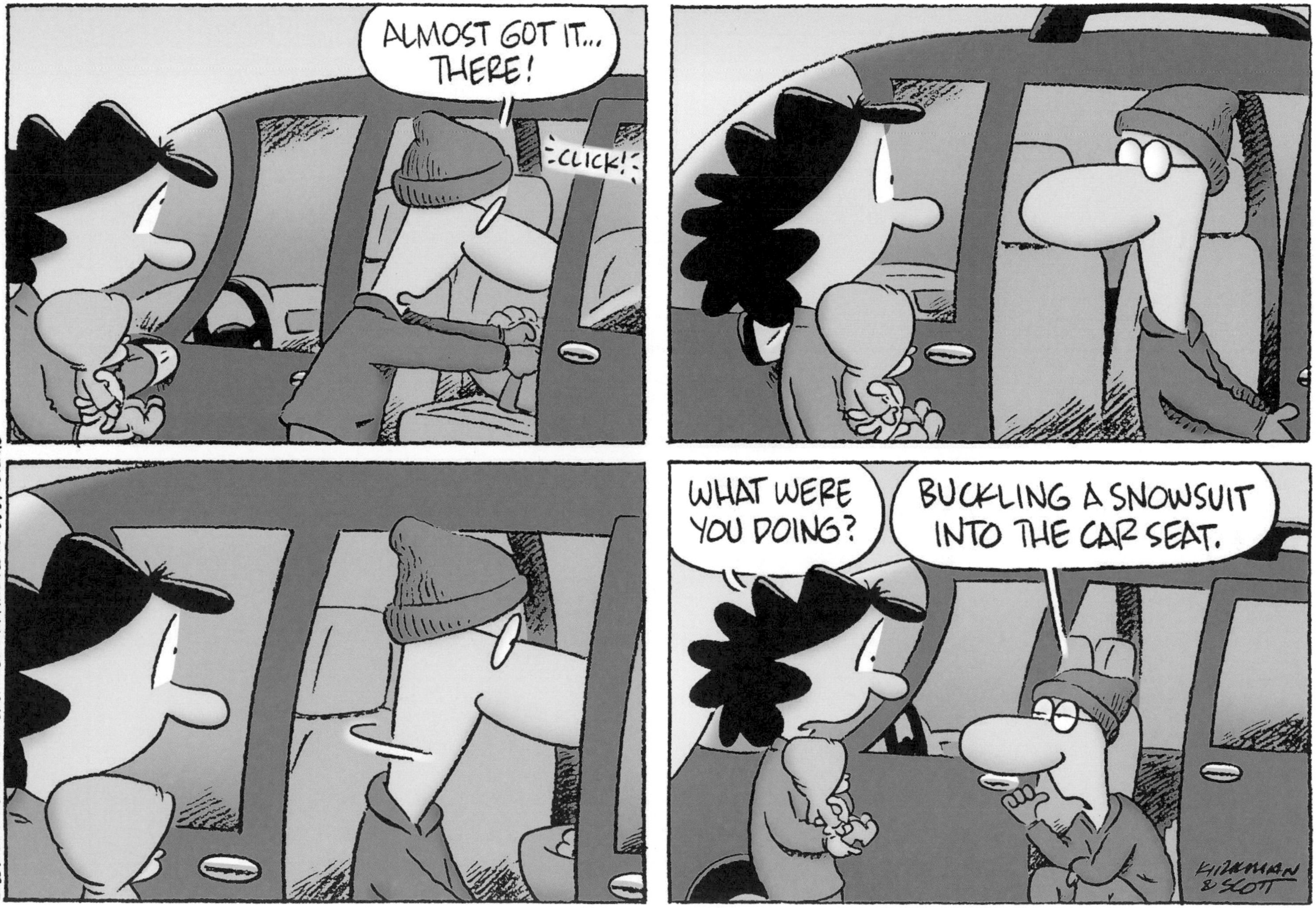
ALMOST GOT IT... THERE!
CLICK!
WHAT WERE YOU DOING?
BUCKLING A SNOWSUIT INTO THE CAR SEAT.
KIRKMAN & SCOTT

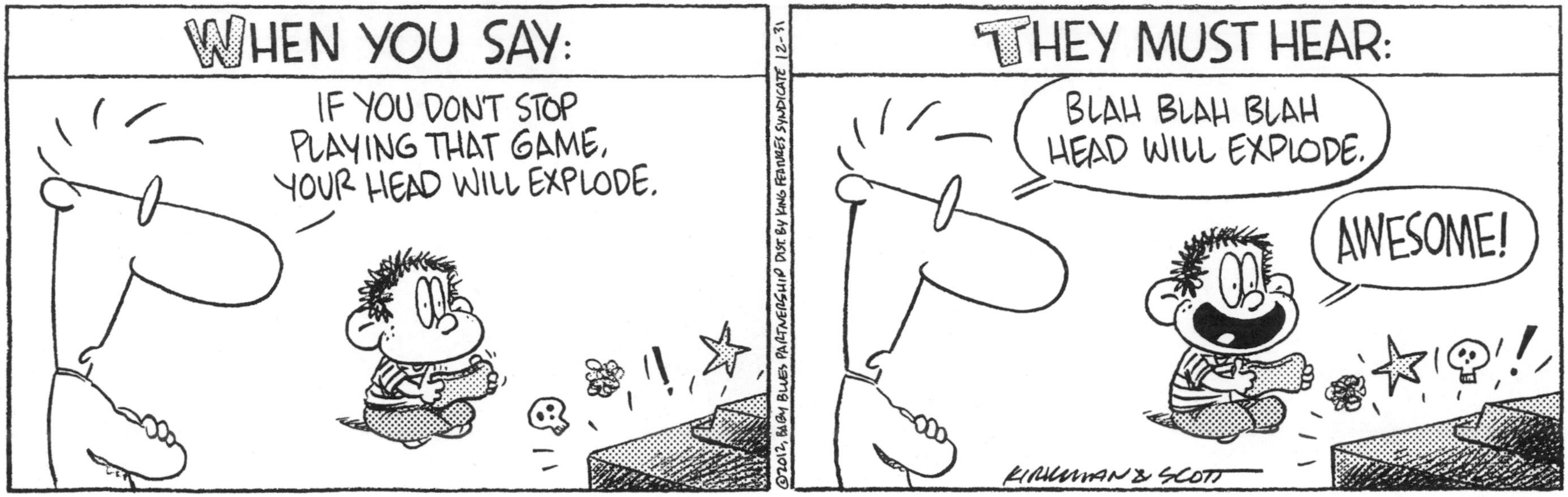
WHEN YOU SAY:
IF YOU DON'T STOP PLAYING THAT GAME, YOUR HEAD WILL EXPLODE.
THEY MUST HEAR:
BLAH BLAH BLAH HEAD WILL EXPLODE.
AWESOME!
©2012, BABY BLUES PARTNERSHIP DIST. BY KING FEATURES SYNDICATE 12-31
KIRKMAN & SCOTT

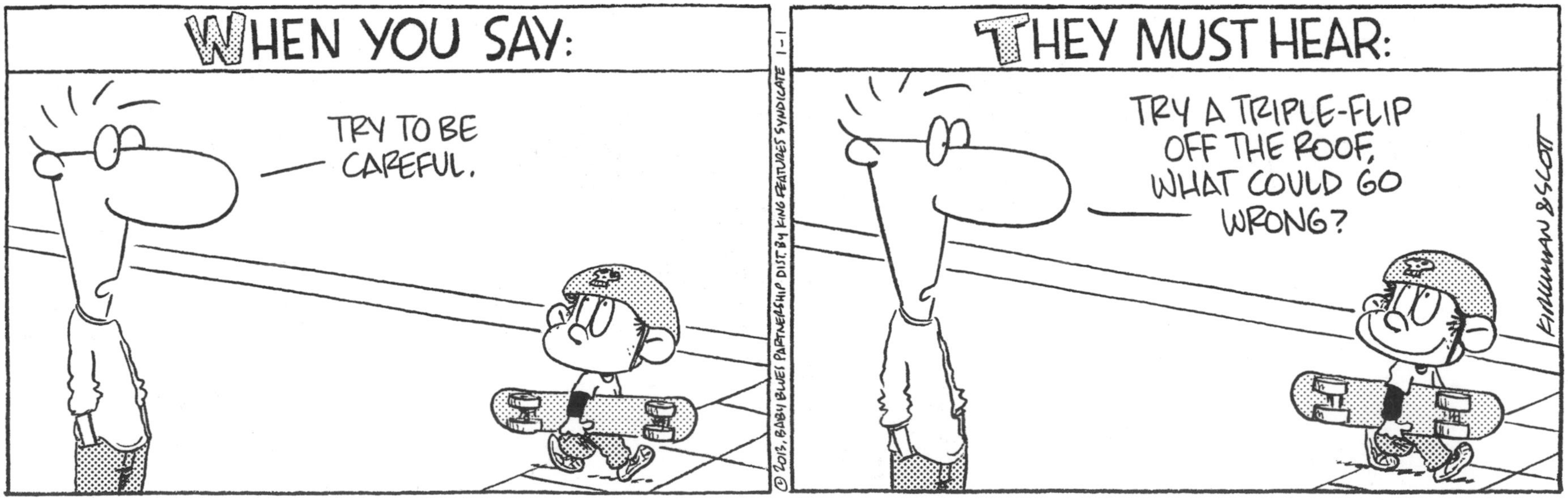
WHEN YOU SAY:
TRY TO BE CAREFUL.
THEY MUST HEAR:
TRY A TRIPLE-FLIP OFF THE ROOF, WHAT COULD GO WRONG?
©2013, BABY BLUES PARTNERSHIP DIST. BY KING FEATURES SYNDICATE 1-1
KIRKMAN & SCOTT

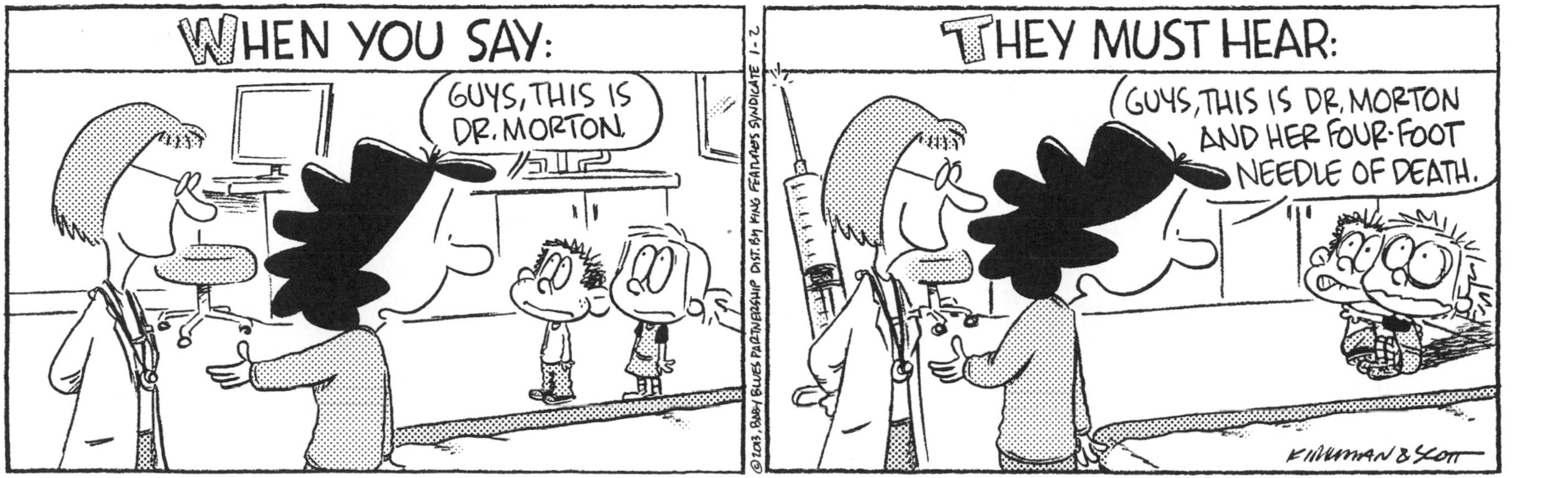
WHEN YOU SAY:
GUYS, THIS IS DR. MORTON.
THEY MUST HEAR:
GUYS, THIS IS DR. MORTON AND HER FOUR-FOOT NEEDLE OF DEATH.
©2013, BABY BLUES PARTNERSHIP DIST. BY KING FEATURES SYNDICATE 1-2
KIRKMAN & SCOTT

Jerry: My dentist is Dr. Morton, but he's a dude, so this is a totally fictional strip. Except for his four-foot needle of death. That's real.

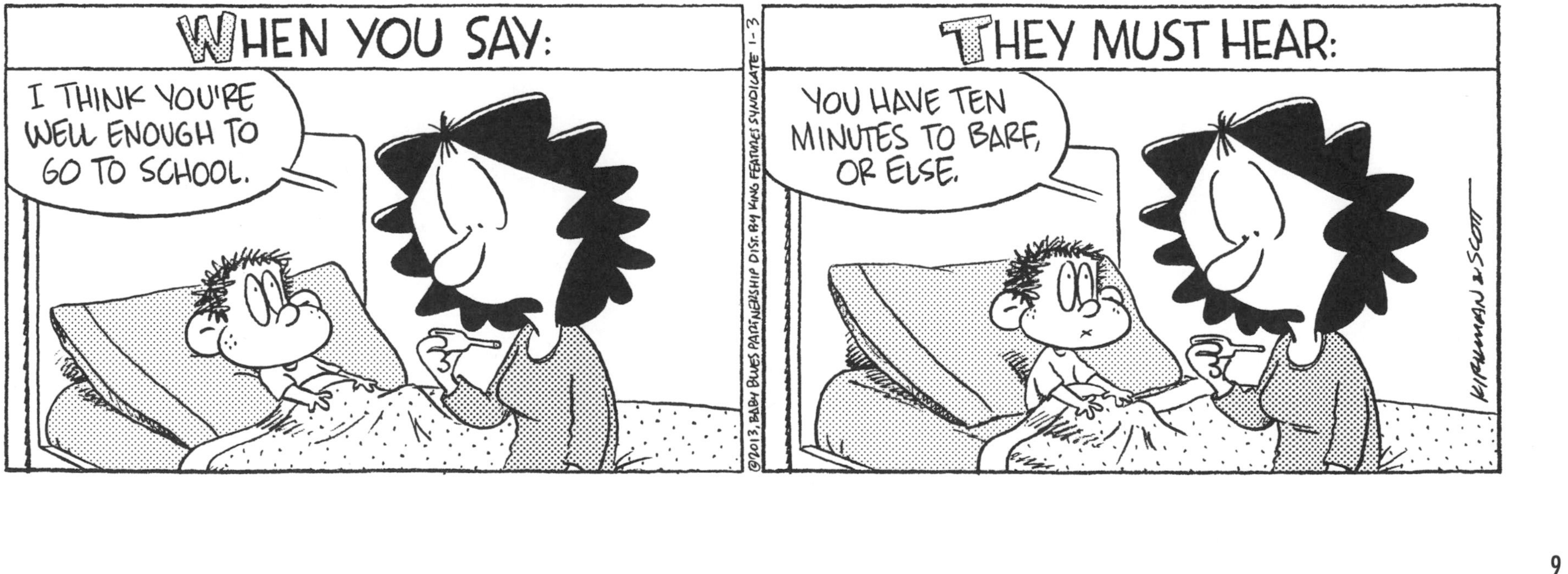
WHEN YOU SAY:
I THINK YOU'RE WELL ENOUGH TO GO TO SCHOOL.
THEY MUST HEAR:
YOU HAVE TEN MINUTES TO BARF, OR ELSE.
©2013, BABY BLUES PARTNERSHIP DIST. BY KING FEATURES SYNDICATE 1-3
KIRKMAN & SCOTT

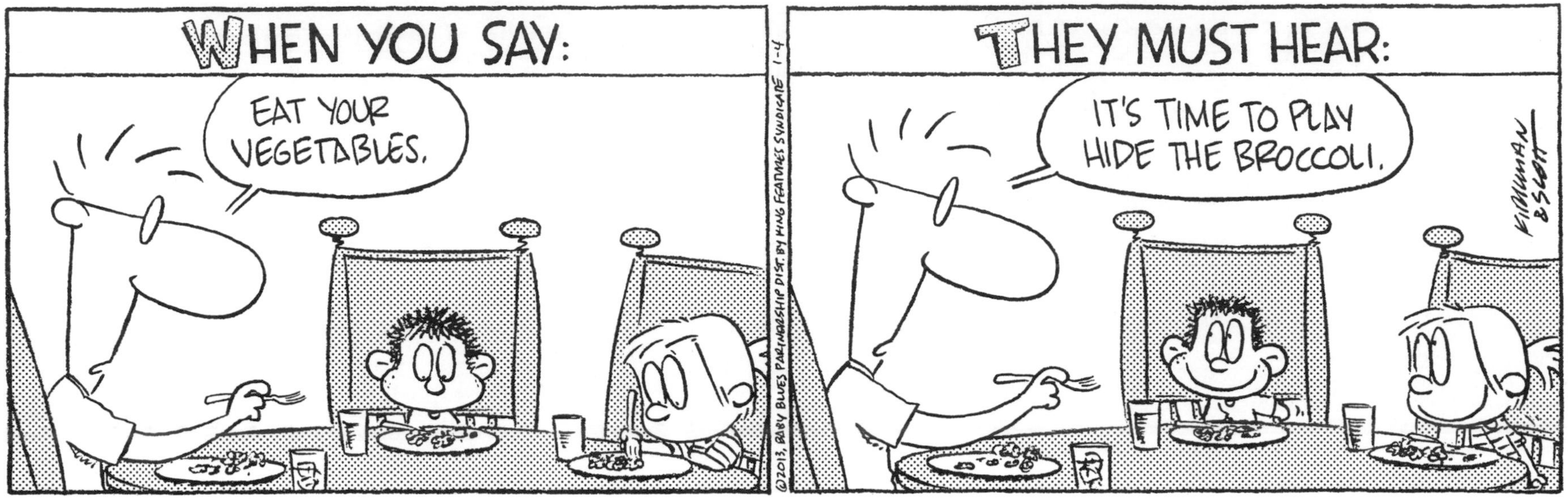
WHEN YOU SAY:
EAT YOUR VEGETABLES.
THEY MUST HEAR:
IT'S TIME TO PLAY HIDE THE BROCCOLI.
KIRKMAN & SCOTT
©2013, BABY BLUES PARTNERSHIP DIST. BY KING FEATURES SYNDICATE 1-4

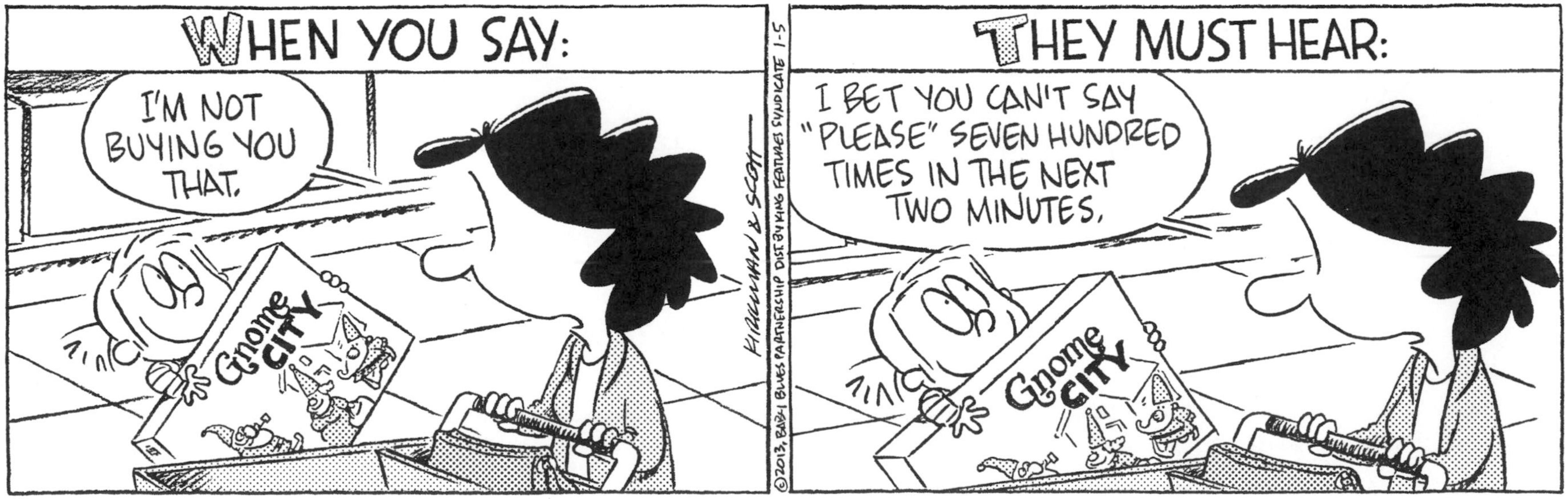
WHEN YOU SAY:
I'M NOT BUYING YOU THAT.
Gnome CITY
KIRKMAN & SCOTT
THEY MUST HEAR:
I BET YOU CAN'T SAY "PLEASE" SEVEN HUNDRED TIMES IN THE NEXT TWO MINUTES.
Gnome CITY
©2013, BABY BLUES PARTNERSHIP DIST. BY KING FEATURES SYNDICATE 1-5

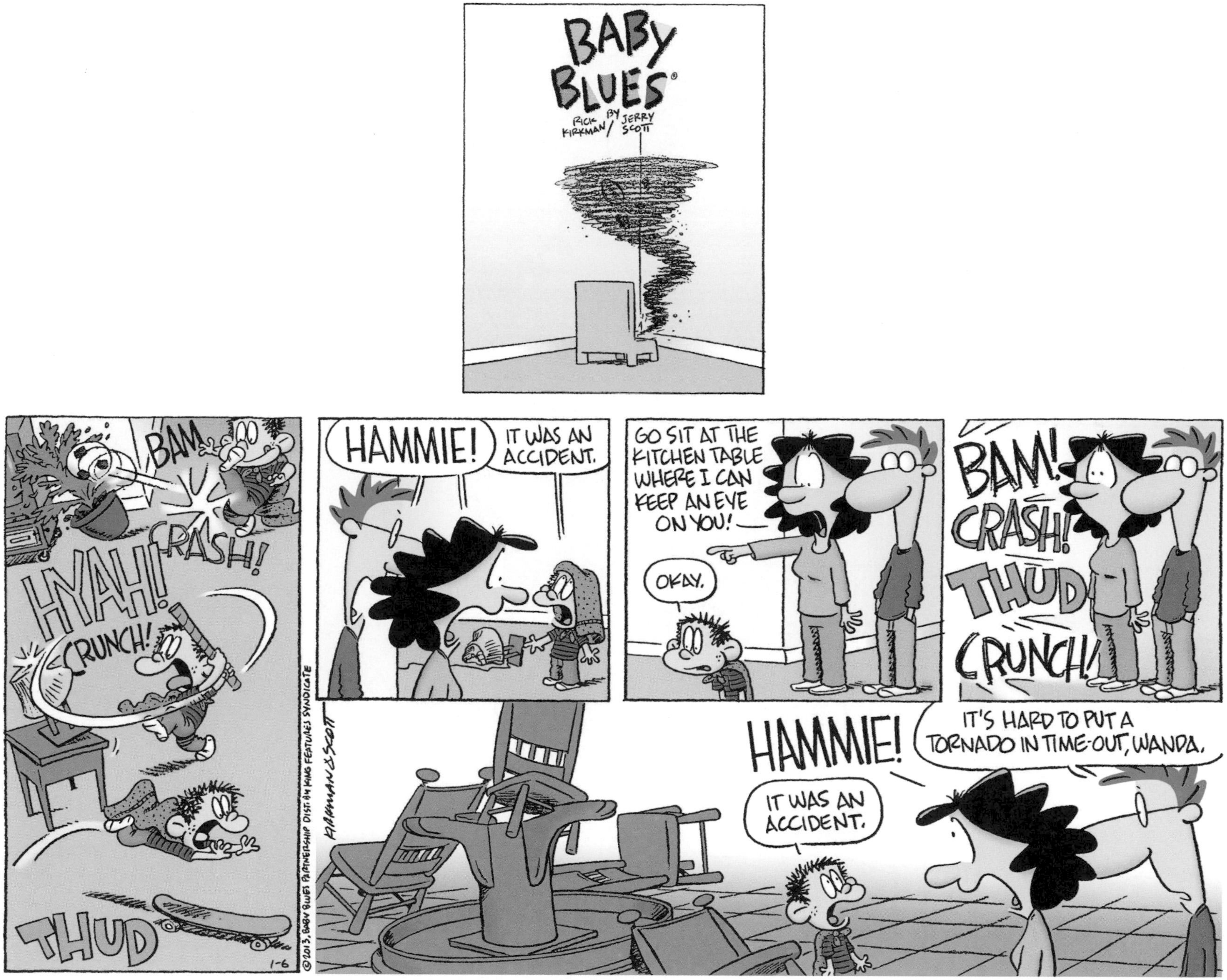
BABY BLUES®
BY RICK KIRKMAN / JERRY SCOTT
BAM
CRASH!
HYAH!
CRUNCH!
THUD
1-6
©2013, BABY BLUES PARTNERSHIP DIST. BY KING FEATURES SYNDICATE
KIRKMAN & SCOTT
HAMMIE!
IT WAS AN ACCIDENT.
GO SIT AT THE KITCHEN TABLE WHERE I CAN KEEP AN EYE ON YOU!
OKAY.
BAM!
CRASH!
THUD
CRUNCH!
HAMMIE!
IT WAS AN ACCIDENT.
IT'S HARD TO PUT A TORNADO IN TIME-OUT, WANDA.

Rick: I love drawing panels with a lot of action, and you can do more sometimes by compressing a lot of action into one panel.

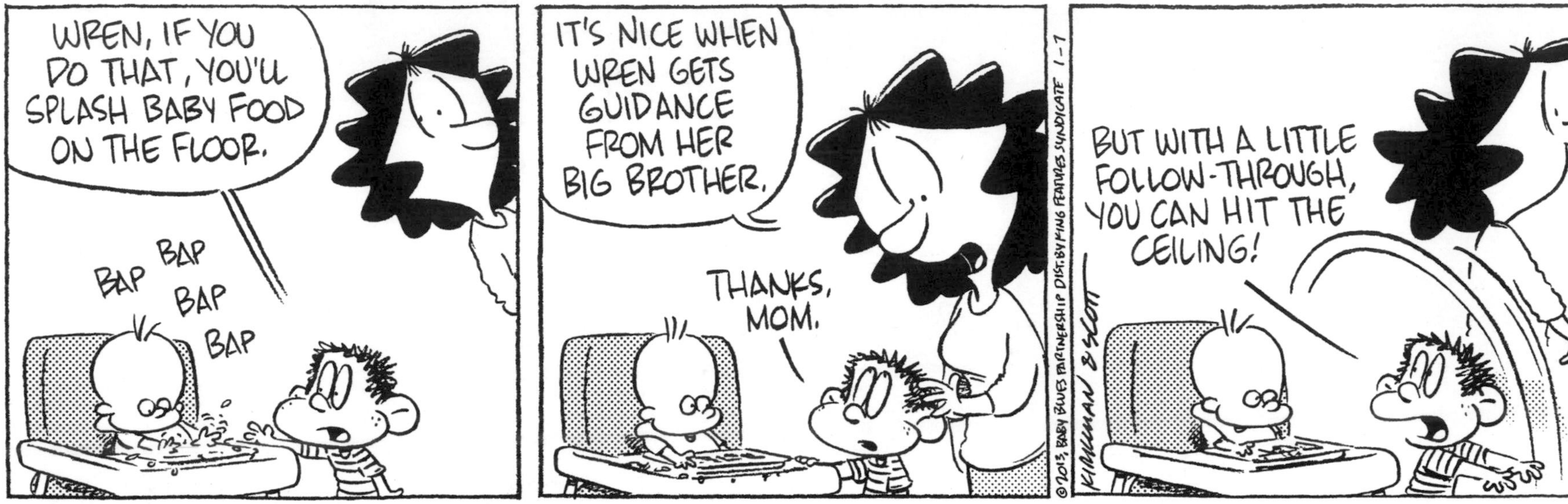

WREN, IF YOU DO THAT, YOU'LL SPLASH BABY FOOD ON THE FLOOR.
BAP BAP BAP BAP
IT'S NICE WHEN WREN GETS GUIDANCE FROM HER BIG BROTHER.
THANKS, MOM.
©2013, BABY BLUES PARTNERSHIP DIST. BY KING FEATURES SYNDICATE 1-7
KIRKMAN & SCOTT
BUT WITH A LITTLE FOLLOW-THROUGH, YOU CAN HIT THE CEILING!

Jerry: This is the kind of brotherly guidance little sisters appreciate so much later in life.

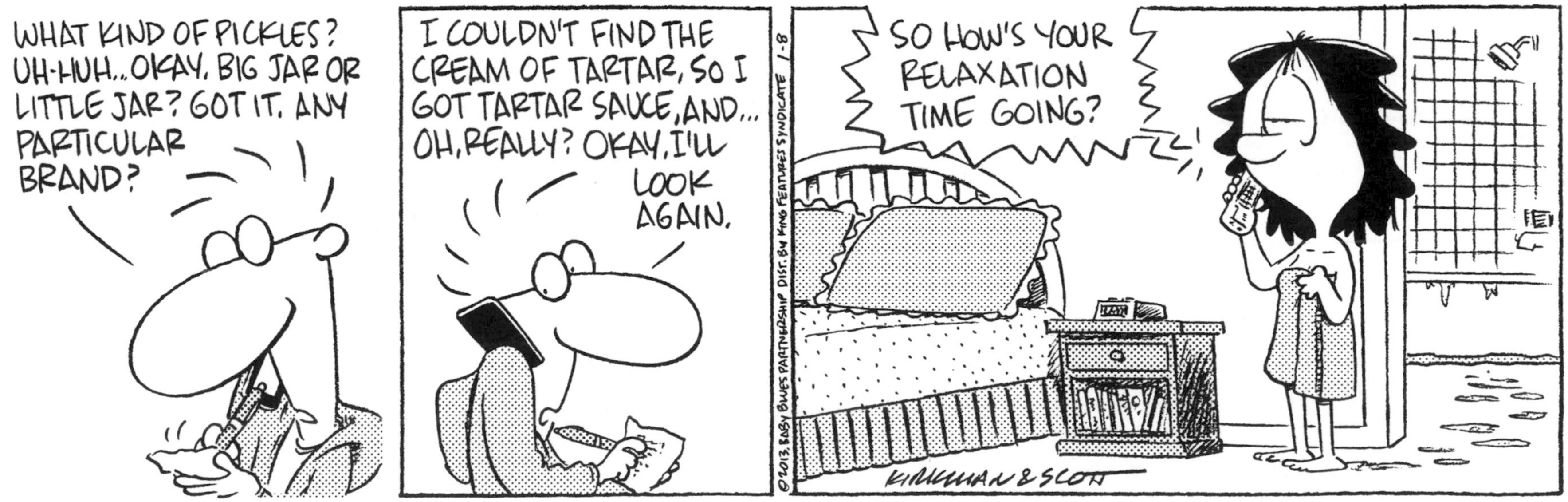

WHAT KIND OF PICKLES? UH-HUH... OKAY. BIG JAR OR LITTLE JAR? GOT IT. ANY PARTICULAR BRAND?
I COULDN'T FIND THE CREAM OF TARTAR, SO I GOT TARTAR SAUCE, AND... OH, REALLY? OKAY. I'LL
LOOK AGAIN.
1-8
©2013, BABY BLUES PARTNERSHIP DIST. BY KING FEATURES SYNDICATE
SO HOW'S YOUR RELAXATION TIME GOING?
KIRKMAN & SCOTT

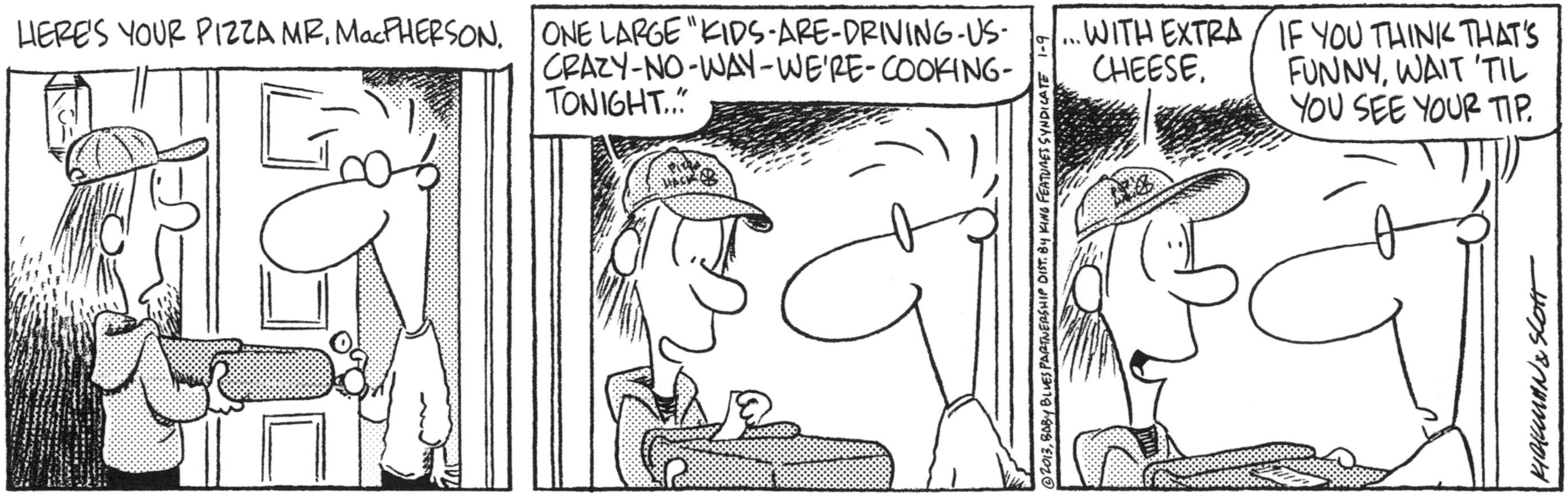
HERE'S YOUR PIZZA MR. MacPHERSON.
ONE LARGE "KIDS-ARE-DRIVING-US-CRAZY-NO-WAY-WE'RE-COOKING-TONIGHT..."
©2013, BABY BLUES PARTNERSHIP DIST. BY KING FEATURES SYNDICATE 1-9
...WITH EXTRA CHEESE.
IF YOU THINK THAT'S FUNNY, WAIT 'TIL YOU SEE YOUR TIP.
KIRKMAN & SCOTT

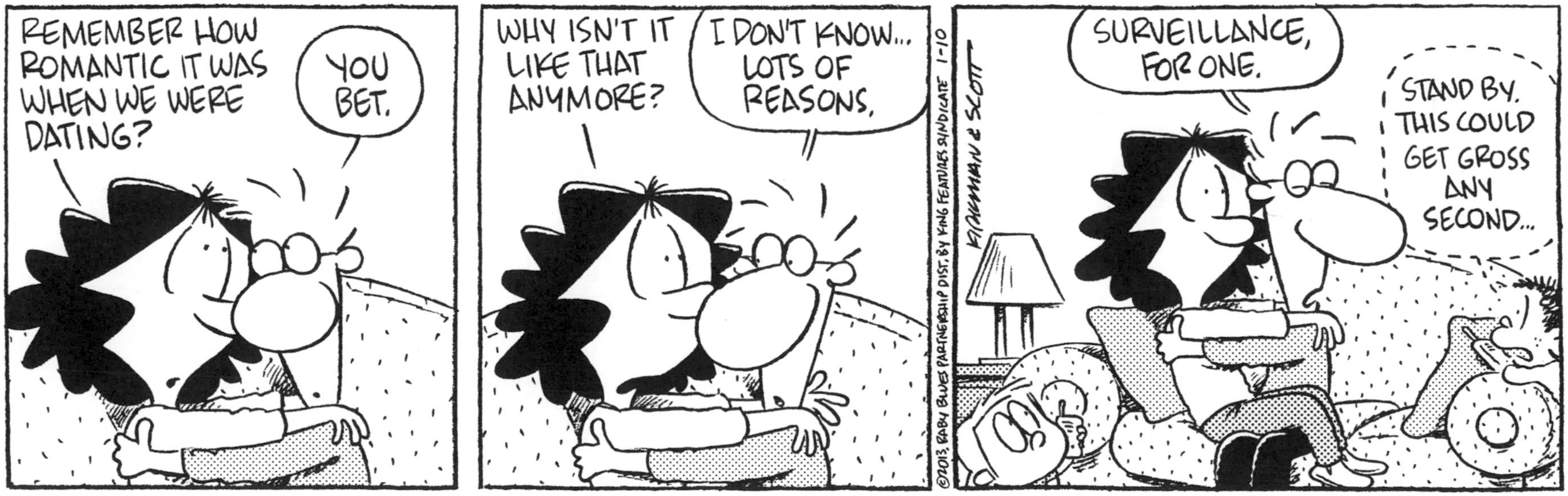
REMEMBER HOW ROMANTIC IT WAS WHEN WE WERE DATING?
YOU BET.
WHY ISN'T IT LIKE THAT ANYMORE?
I DON'T KNOW... LOTS OF REASONS.
©2013, BABY BLUES PARTNERSHIP DIST. BY KING FEATURES SYNDICATE 1-10
KIRKMAN & SCOTT
SURVEILLANCE, FOR ONE.
STAND BY. THIS COULD GET GROSS ANY SECOND...

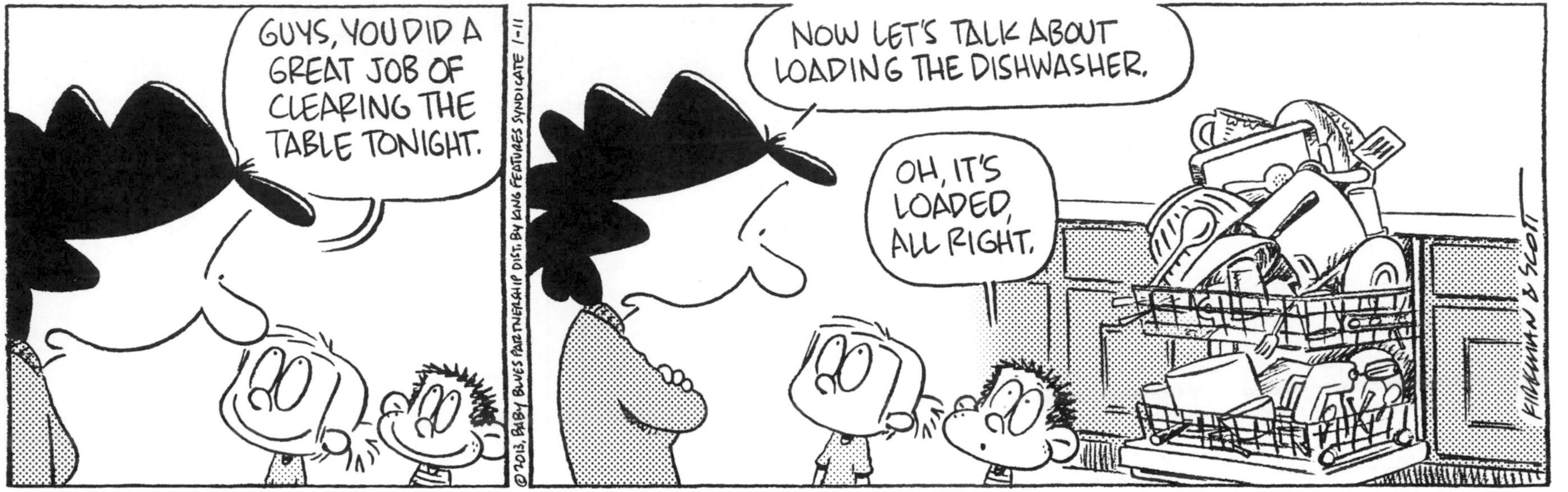
GUYS, YOU DID A GREAT JOB OF CLEARING THE TABLE TONIGHT.
©2013, BABY BLUES PARTNERSHIP DIST. BY KING FEATURES SYNDICATE 1-11
NOW LET'S TALK ABOUT LOADING THE DISHWASHER.
OH, IT'S LOADED, ALL RIGHT.
KIRKMAN & SCOTT

Jerry: Ripped from reality. My younger daughter no longer loads the dishwasher unsupervised.

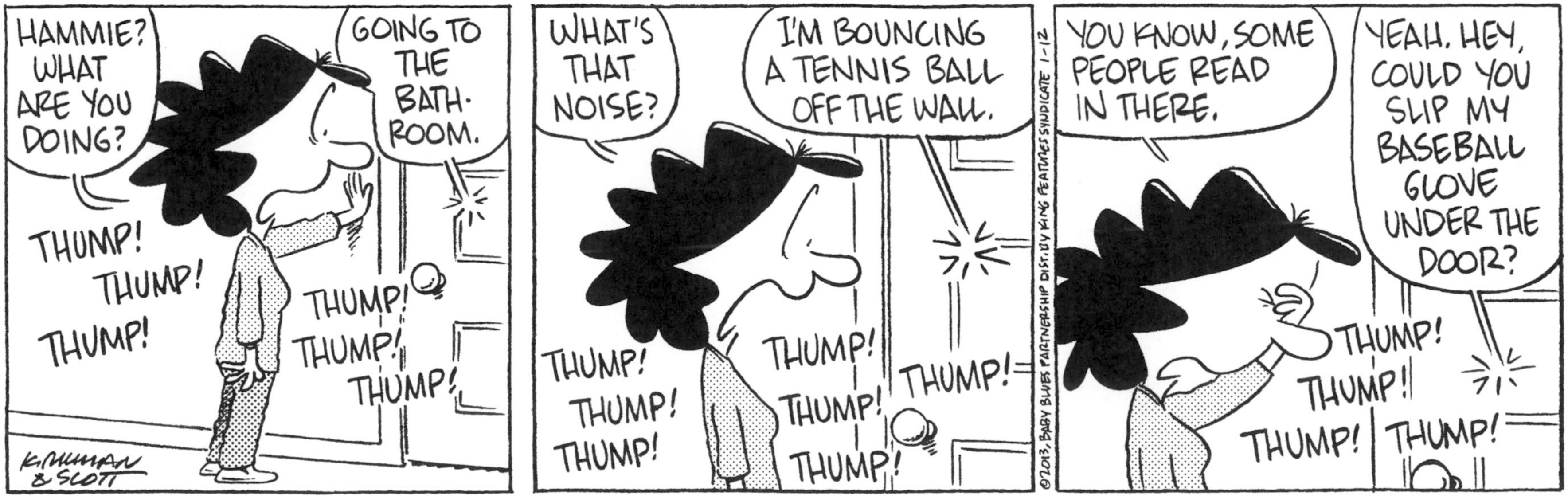
HAMMIE? WHAT ARE YOU DOING?
GOING TO THE BATH-ROOM.
THUMP! THUMP! THUMP!
THUMP! THUMP! THUMP!
KIRKMAN & SCOTT
WHAT'S THAT NOISE?
I'M BOUNCING A TENNIS BALL OFF THE WALL.
THUMP! THUMP! THUMP!
THUMP! THUMP! THUMP!
THUMP!
©2013, BABY BLUES PARTNERSHIP DIST. BY KING FEATURES SYNDICATE 1-12
YOU KNOW, SOME PEOPLE READ IN THERE.
YEAH. HEY, COULD YOU SLIP MY BASEBALL GLOVE UNDER THE DOOR?
THUMP! THUMP! THUMP!
THUMP!

Rick: I like this one so much because it's all left to the imagination. Thank goodness.

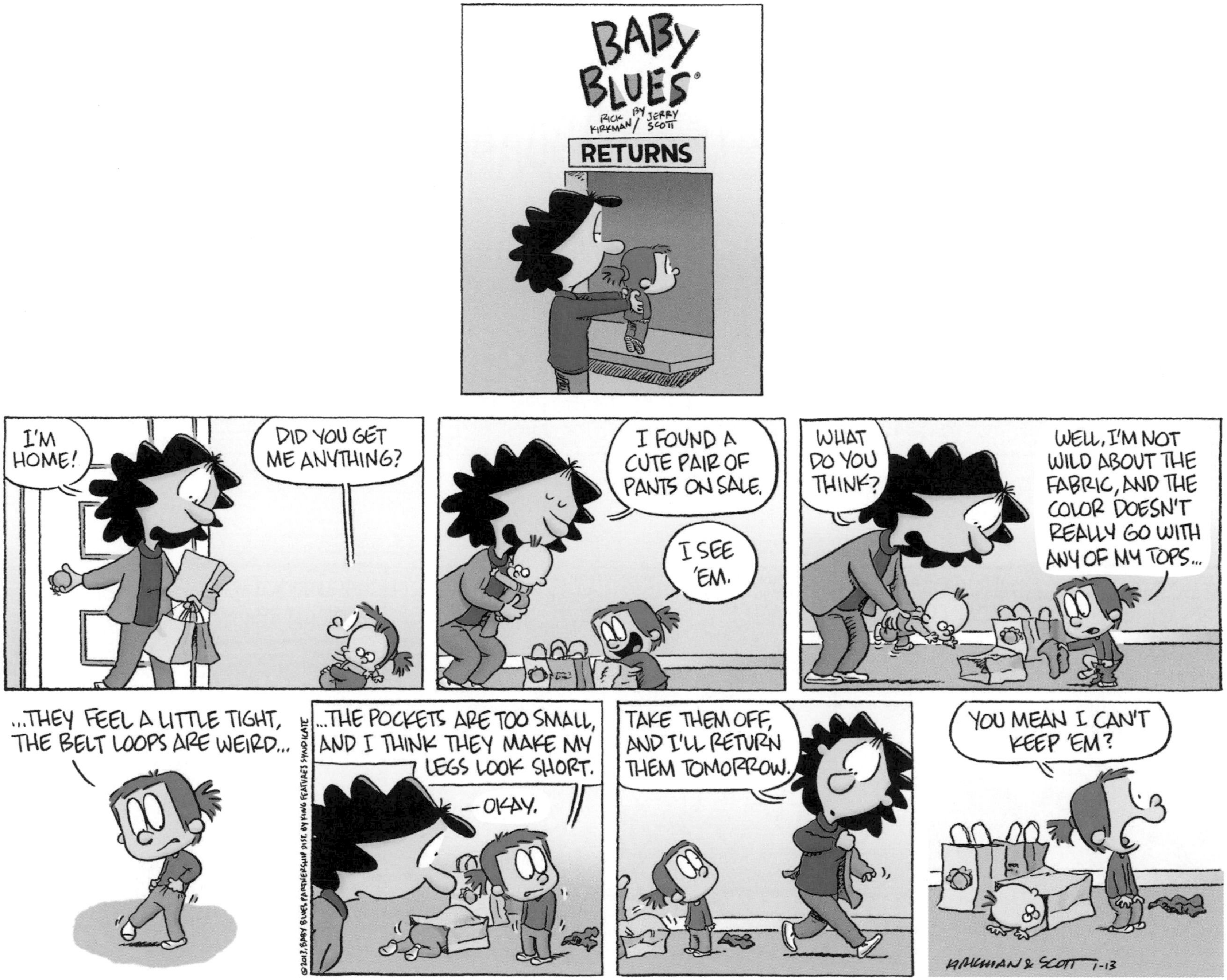
BABY BLUES®
RICK KIRKMAN / BY JERRY SCOTT
RETURNS
I'M HOME!
DID YOU GET ME ANYTHING?
I FOUND A CUTE PAIR OF PANTS ON SALE.
I SEE 'EM.
WHAT DO YOU THINK?
WELL, I'M NOT WILD ABOUT THE FABRIC, AND THE COLOR DOESN'T REALLY GO WITH ANY OF MY TOPS...
...THEY FEEL A LITTLE TIGHT, THE BELT LOOPS ARE WEIRD...
...THE POCKETS ARE TOO SMALL, AND I THINK THEY MAKE MY LEGS LOOK SHORT.
—OKAY.
TAKE THEM OFF, AND I'LL RETURN THEM TOMORROW.
YOU MEAN I CAN'T KEEP 'EM?
©2013, BABY BLUES PARTNERSHIP DIST. BY KING FEATURES SYNDICATE
KIRKMAN & SCOTT 1-13

Rick: I just realized that Wren's actions in the background are surprisingly catlike.

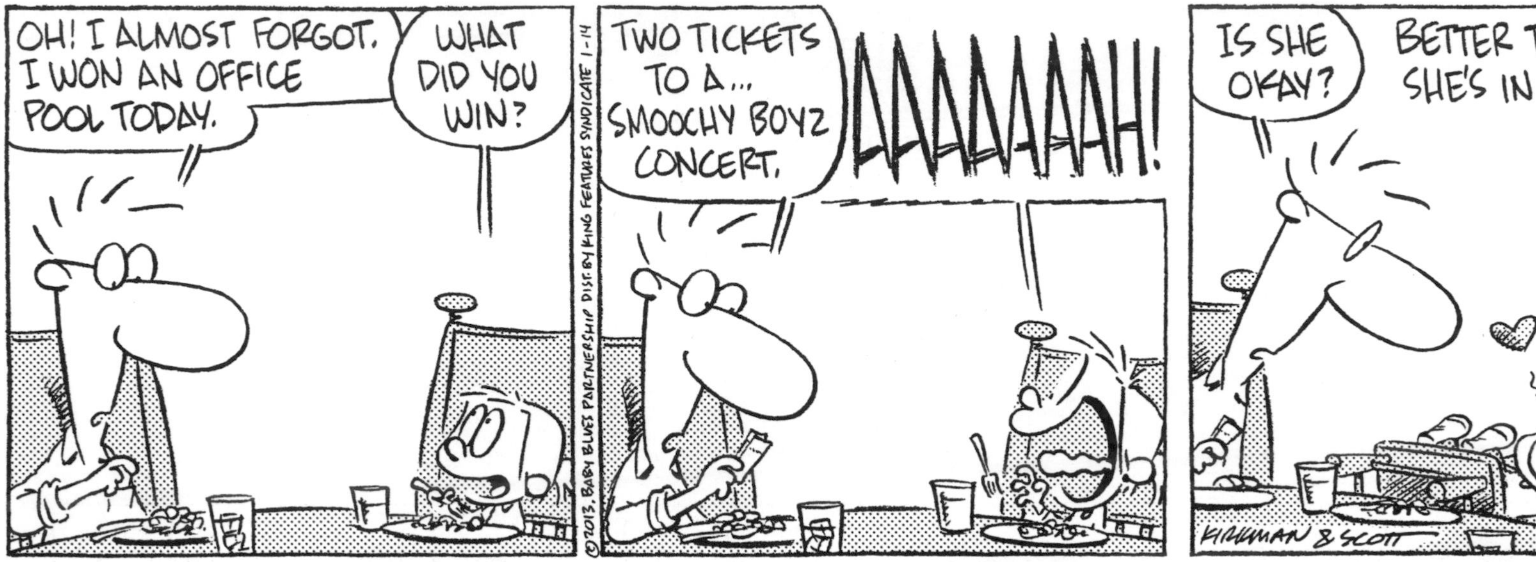
OH! I ALMOST FORGOT. I WON AN OFFICE POOL TODAY.
WHAT DID YOU WIN?
©2013, BABY BLUES PARTNERSHIP DIST. BY KING FEATURES SYNDICATE 1-14
TWO TICKETS TO A... SMOOCHY BOYZ CONCERT.
AAAAAAAAH!
IS SHE OKAY?
BETTER THAN OKAY... SHE'S IN HEAVEN.
KIRKMAN & SCOTT

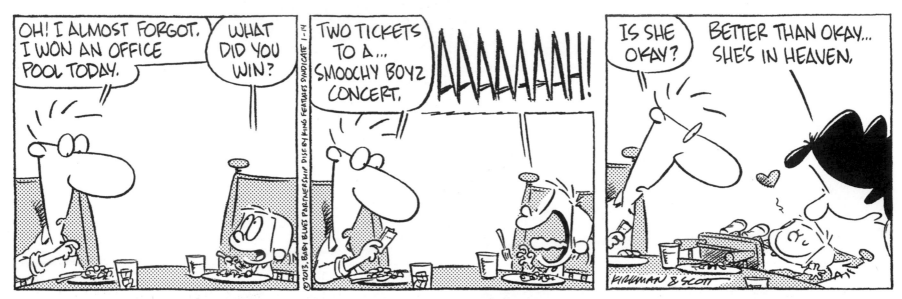

Jerry: I drove three nine-year-old girls to an Avril Lavigne concert in Los Angeles many years ago. There was gummy bear and glitter residue in the minivan carpet afterward that never went away.

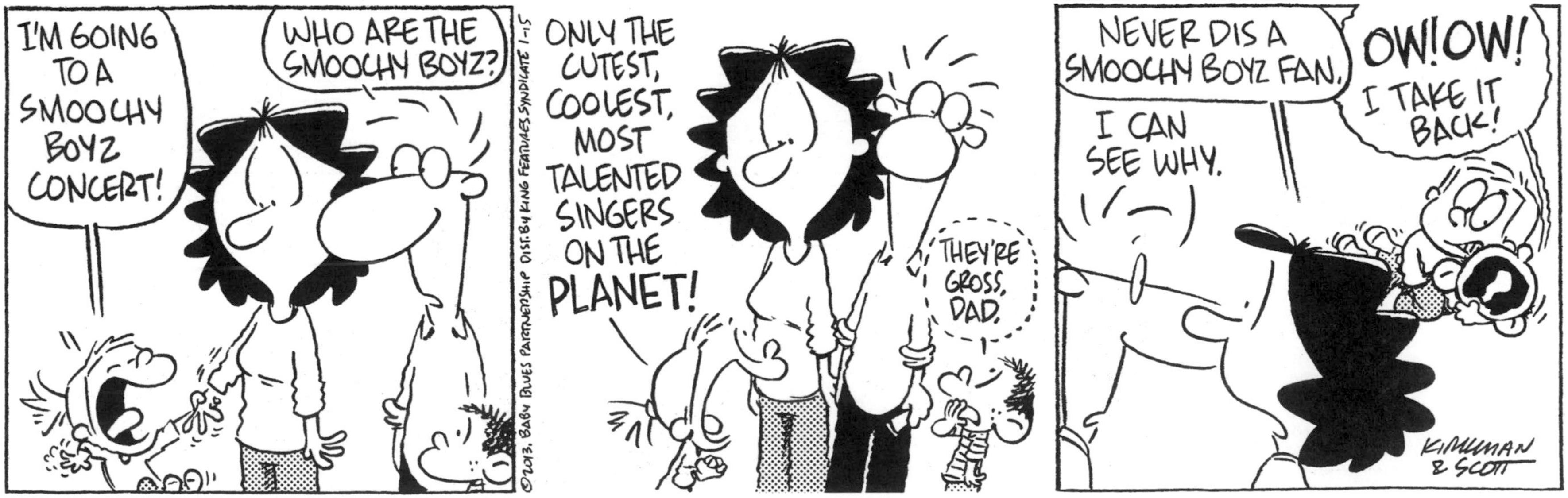
I'M GOING TO A SMOOCHY BOYZ CONCERT!
WHO ARE THE SMOOCHY BOYZ?
©2013, BABY BLUES PARTNERSHIP DIST. BY KING FEATURES SYNDICATE 1-15
ONLY THE CUTEST, COOLEST, MOST TALENTED SINGERS ON THE PLANET!
THEY'RE GROSS, DAD.
NEVER DIS A SMOOCHY BOYZ FAN.
I CAN SEE WHY.
OW! OW! I TAKE IT BACK!
KIRKMAN & SCOTT

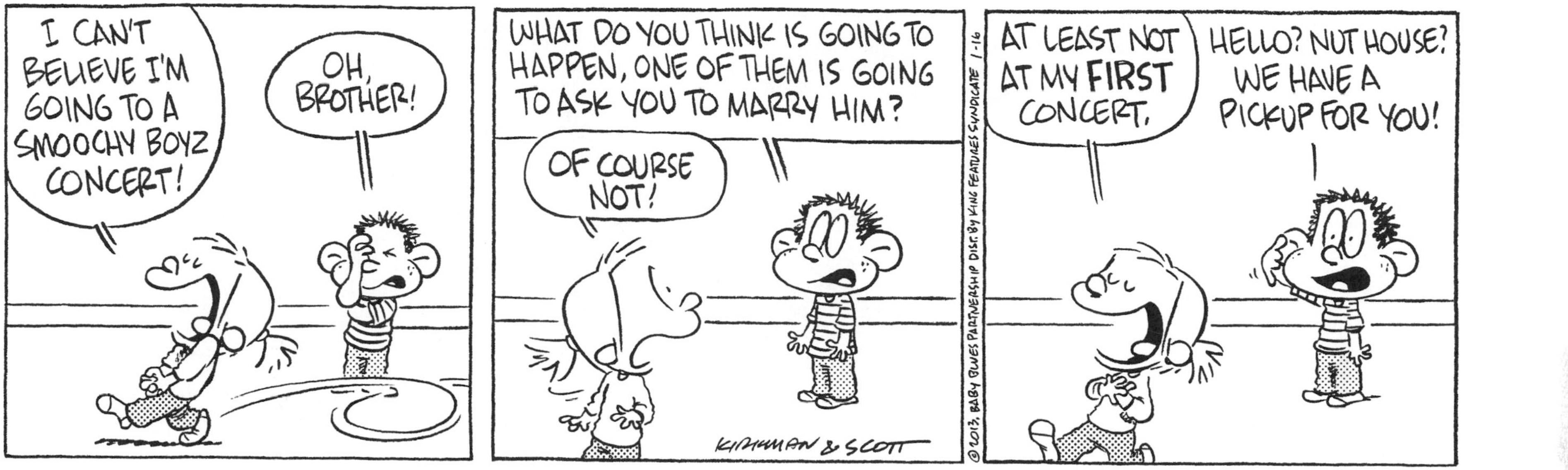

I CAN'T BELIEVE I'M GOING TO A SMOOCHY BOYZ CONCERT!
OH, BROTHER!
WHAT DO YOU THINK IS GOING TO HAPPEN, ONE OF THEM IS GOING TO ASK YOU TO MARRY HIM?
OF COURSE NOT!
KIRKMAN & SCOTT
©2013, BABY BLUES PARTNERSHIP DIST. BY KING FEATURES SYNDICATE 1-16
AT LEAST NOT AT MY **FIRST** CONCERT.
HELLO? NUT HOUSE? WE HAVE A PICKUP FOR YOU!

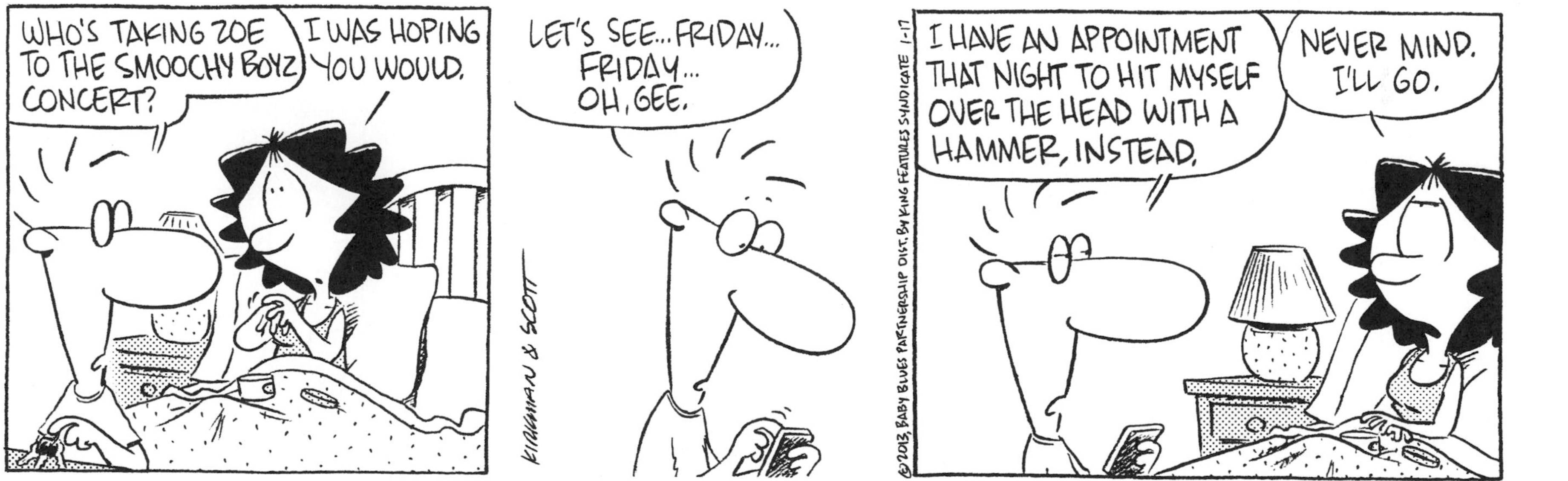

WHO'S TAKING ZOE TO THE SMOOCHY BOYZ CONCERT?
I WAS HOPING YOU WOULD.
KIRKMAN & SCOTT
LET'S SEE... FRIDAY... FRIDAY... OH, GEE.
©2013, BABY BLUES PARTNERSHIP DIST. BY KING FEATURES SYNDICATE 1-17
I HAVE AN APPOINTMENT THAT NIGHT TO HIT MYSELF OVER THE HEAD WITH A HAMMER, INSTEAD.
NEVER MIND. I'LL GO.

Rick: Darryl's last line is exactly how I would feel if the Smoochy Boyz were real. Which they're not. But we expect royalties if anyone decides to form that group.

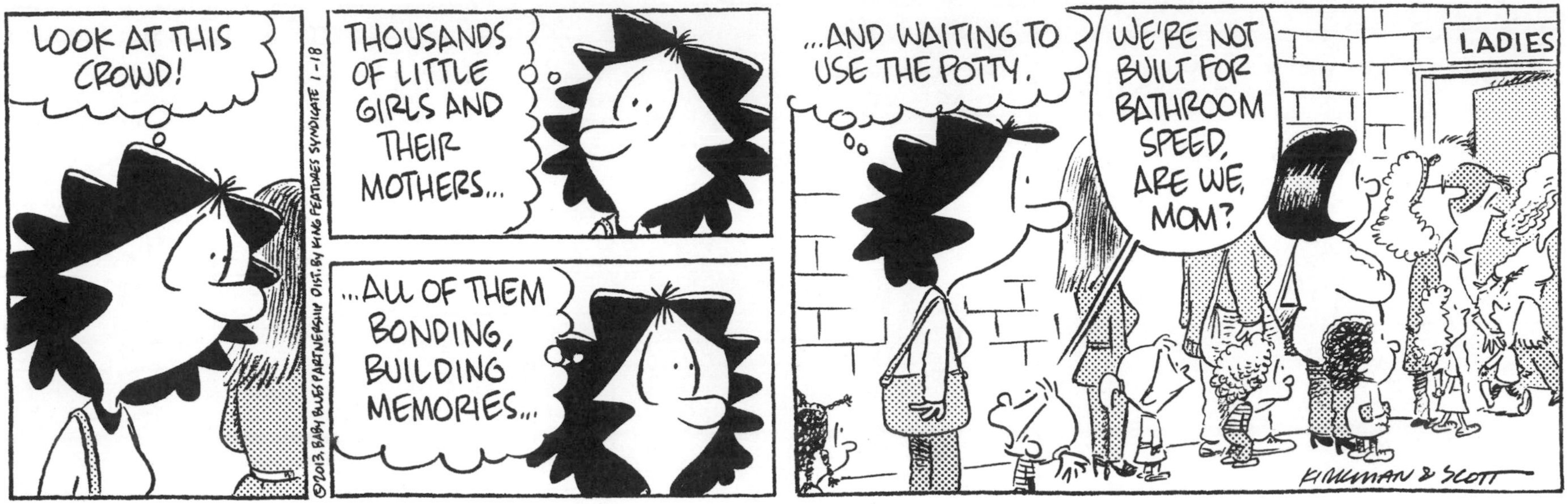
LOOK AT THIS CROWD!
©2013, BABY BLUES PARTNERSHIP DIST. BY KING FEATURES SYNDICATE 1-18
THOUSANDS OF LITTLE GIRLS AND THEIR MOTHERS...
...ALL OF THEM BONDING, BUILDING MEMORIES...
...AND WAITING TO USE THE POTTY.
WE'RE NOT BUILT FOR BATHROOM SPEED, ARE WE, MOM?
LADIES
KIRKMAN & SCOTT

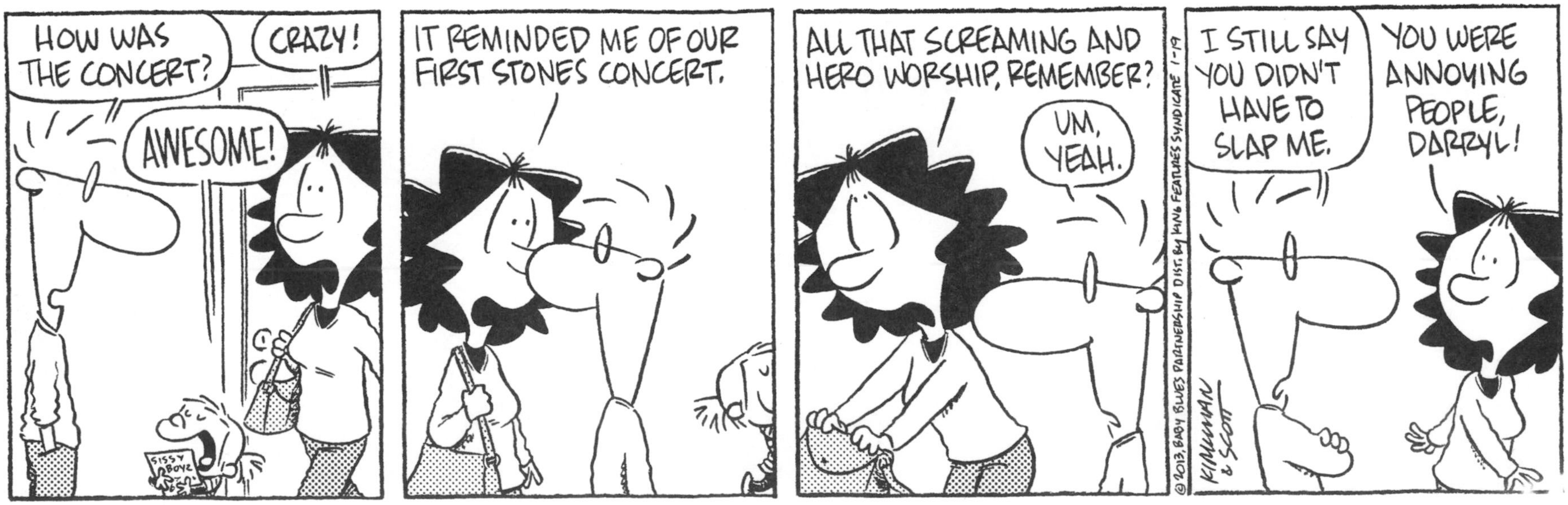
HOW WAS THE CONCERT?
CRAZY!
AWESOME!
SISSY BOYZ
IT REMINDED ME OF OUR FIRST STONES CONCERT.
ALL THAT SCREAMING AND HERO WORSHIP, REMEMBER?
UM, YEAH.
©2013, BABY BLUES PARTNERSHIP DIST. BY KING FEATURES SYNDICATE 1-19
KIRKMAN & SCOTT
I STILL SAY YOU DIDN'T HAVE TO SLAP ME.
YOU WERE ANNOYING PEOPLE, DARRYL!

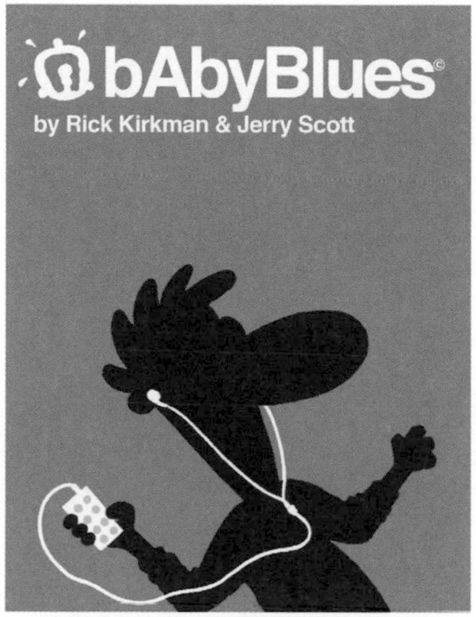
bAbyBlues
by Rick Kirkman & Jerry Scott

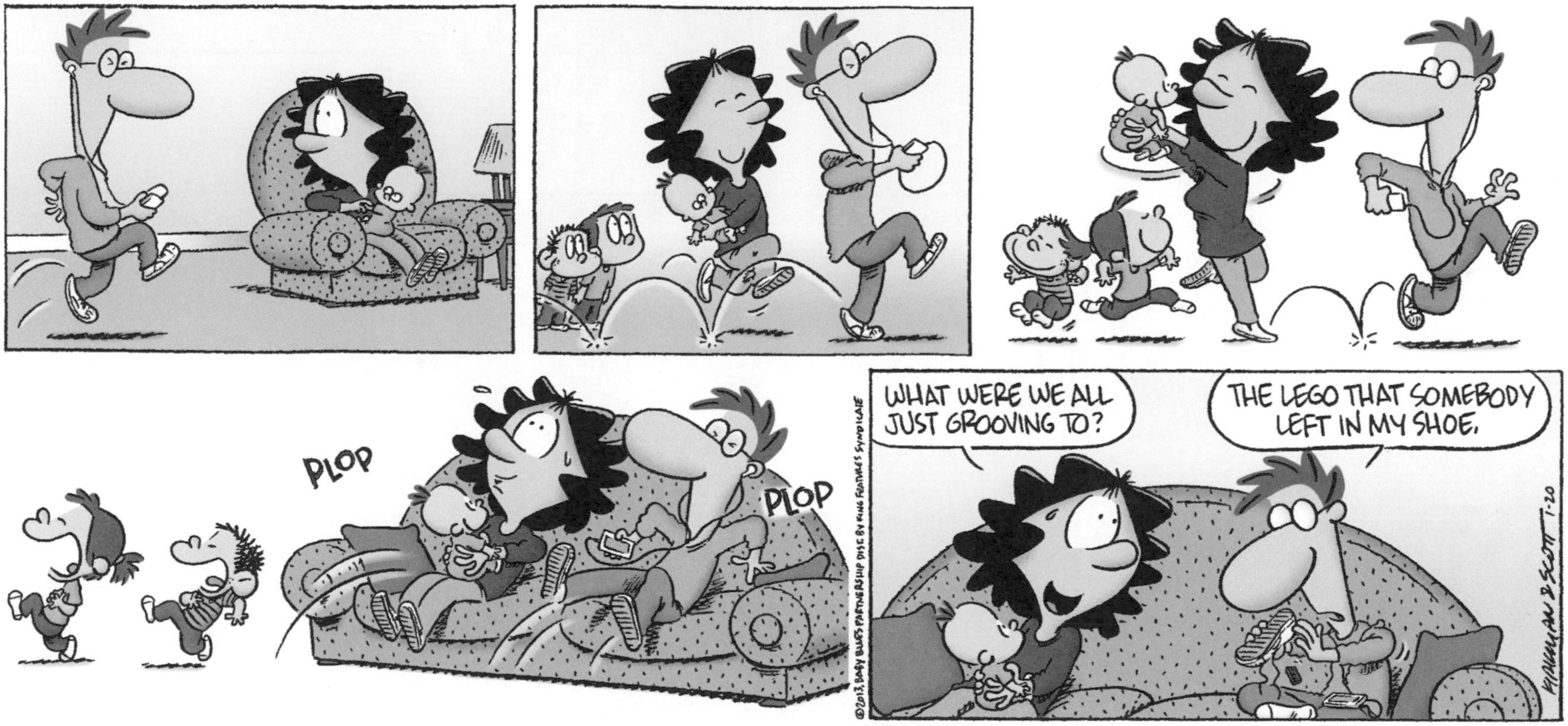
PLOP
PLOP
WHAT WERE WE ALL JUST GROOVING TO?
THE LEGO THAT SOMEBODY LEFT IN MY SHOE.

Rick: Once again, Internet research comes to the rescue for a *Baby Blues* version of the iconic iTunes/iPod ads.

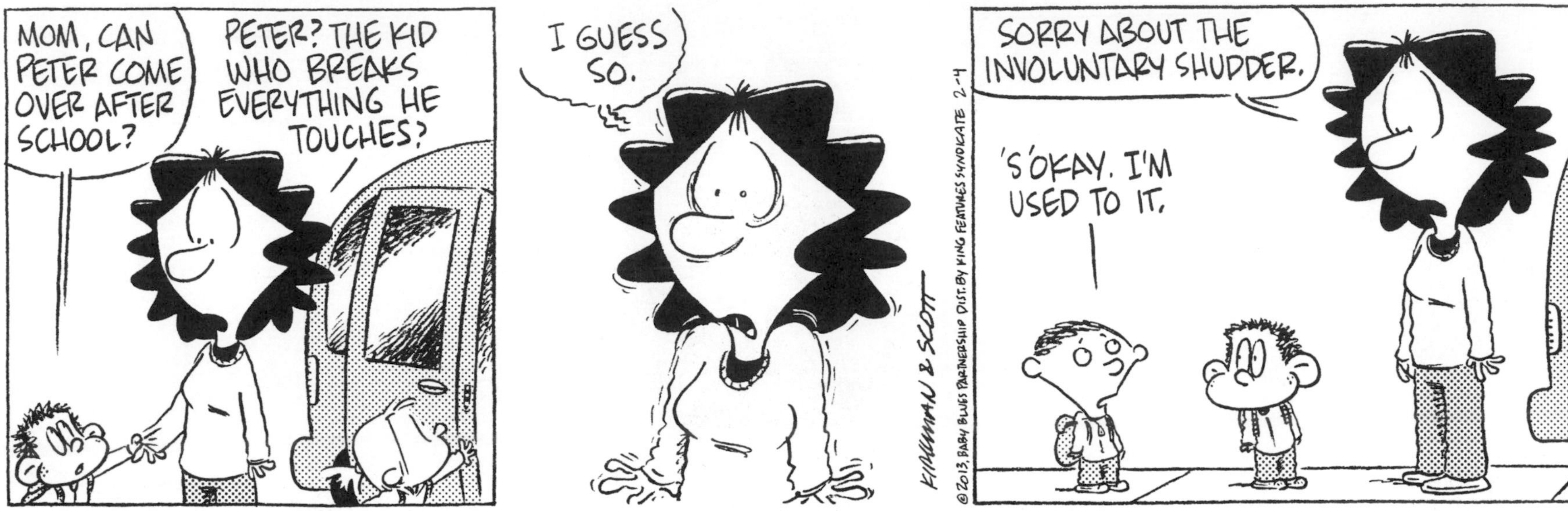
MOM, CAN PETER COME OVER AFTER SCHOOL?
PETER? THE KID WHO BREAKS EVERYTHING HE TOUCHES?
I GUESS SO.
KIRKMAN & SCOTT
©2013, BABY BLUES PARTNERSHIP DIST. BY KING FEATURES SYNDICATE 2-4
SORRY ABOUT THE INVOLUNTARY SHUDDER.
'S'OKAY. I'M USED TO IT.

Rick: Peter was inspired by one of my daughter's friends, who really did break something every time he came over.

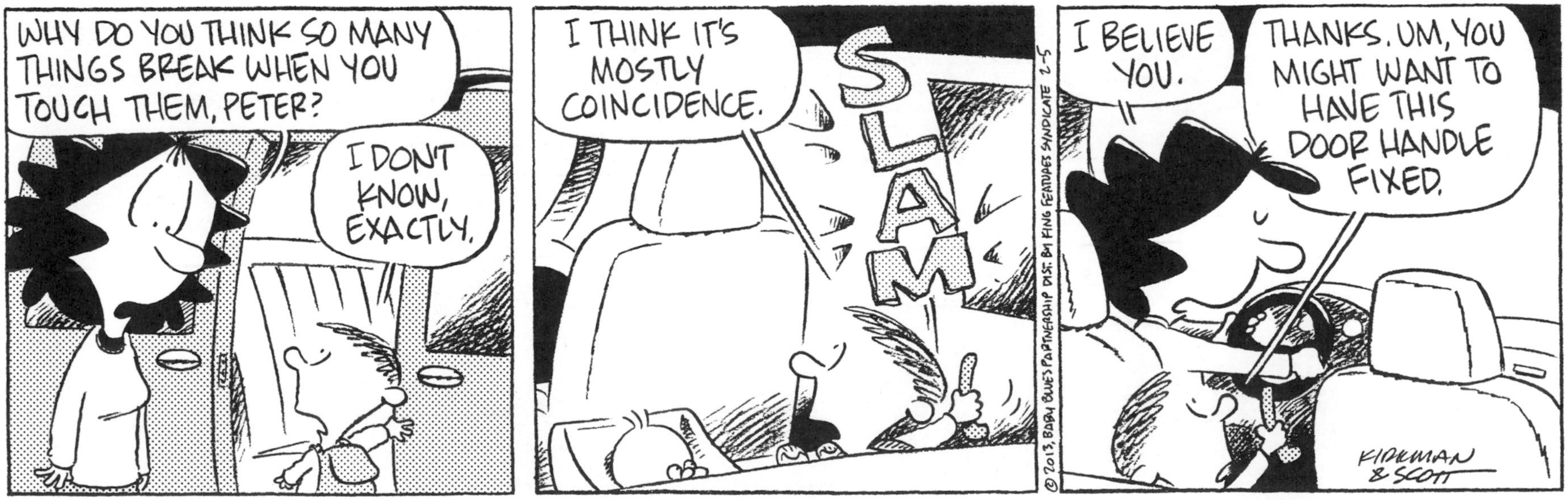
WHY DO YOU THINK SO MANY THINGS BREAK WHEN YOU TOUCH THEM, PETER?
I DON'T KNOW, EXACTLY.
I THINK IT'S MOSTLY COINCIDENCE.
SLAM
©2013, BABY BLUES PARTNERSHIP DIST. BY KING FEATURES SYNDICATE 2-5
I BELIEVE YOU.
THANKS. UM, YOU MIGHT WANT TO HAVE THIS DOOR HANDLE FIXED.
KIRKMAN & SCOTT

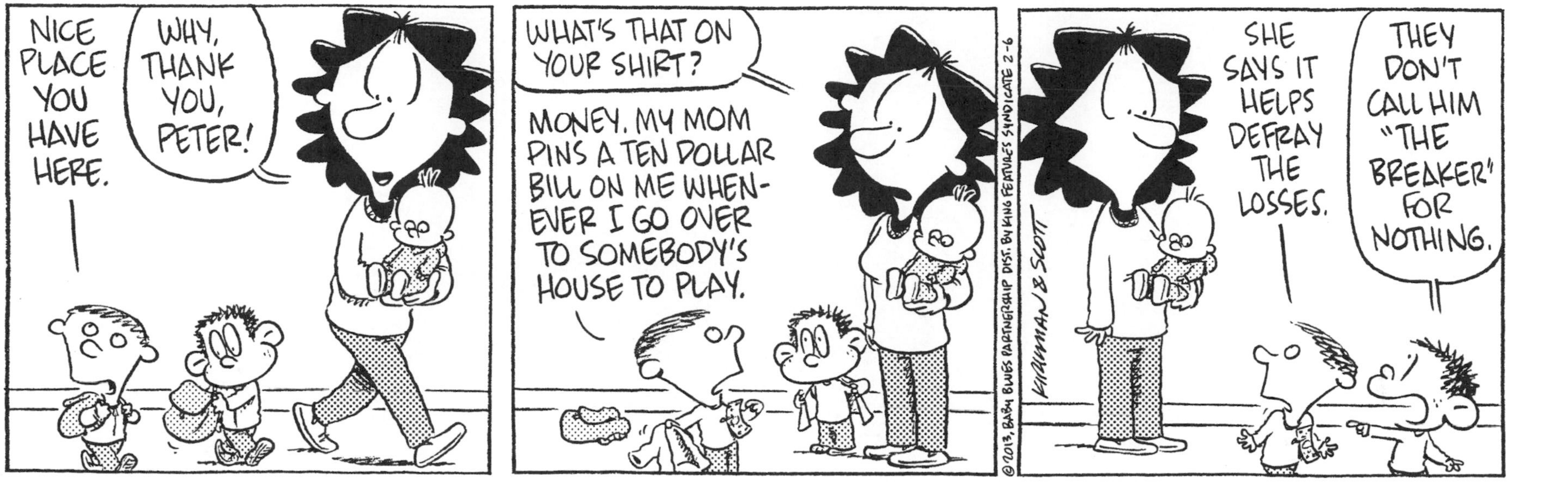
NICE PLACE YOU HAVE HERE.
WHY, THANK YOU, PETER!
WHAT'S THAT ON YOUR SHIRT?
MONEY. MY MOM PINS A TEN DOLLAR BILL ON ME WHENEVER I GO OVER TO SOMEBODY'S HOUSE TO PLAY.
©2013, BABY BLUES PARTNERSHIP DIST. BY KING FEATURES SYNDICATE 2-6
KIRKMAN & SCOTT
SHE SAYS IT HELPS DEFRAY THE LOSSES.
THEY DON'T CALL HIM "THE BREAKER" FOR NOTHING.

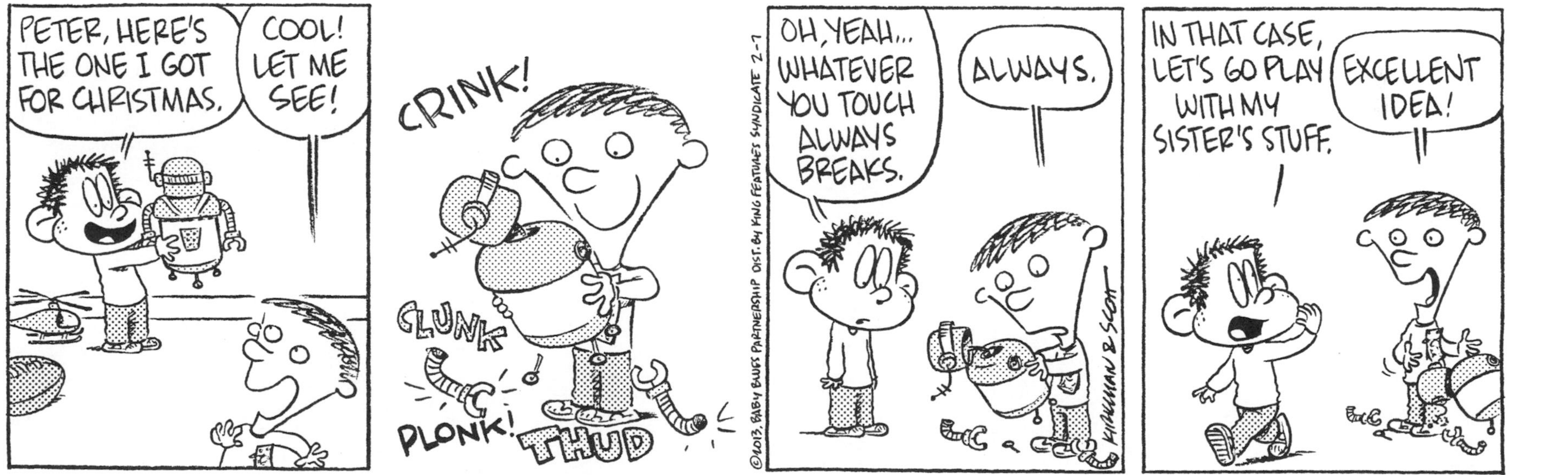
PETER, HERE'S THE ONE I GOT FOR CHRISTMAS.
COOL! LET ME SEE!
CRINK!
CLUNK
PLONK!
THUD
©2013, BABY BLUES PARTNERSHIP DIST. BY KING FEATURES SYNDICATE 2-7
OH, YEAH... WHATEVER YOU TOUCH ALWAYS BREAKS.
ALWAYS.
KIRKMAN & SCOTT
IN THAT CASE, LET'S GO PLAY WITH MY SISTER'S STUFF.
EXCELLENT IDEA!

Rick: Someone told me they did this with their kid: clipped money to their kid's clothes when he went on a playdate, to cover the inevitable damage.

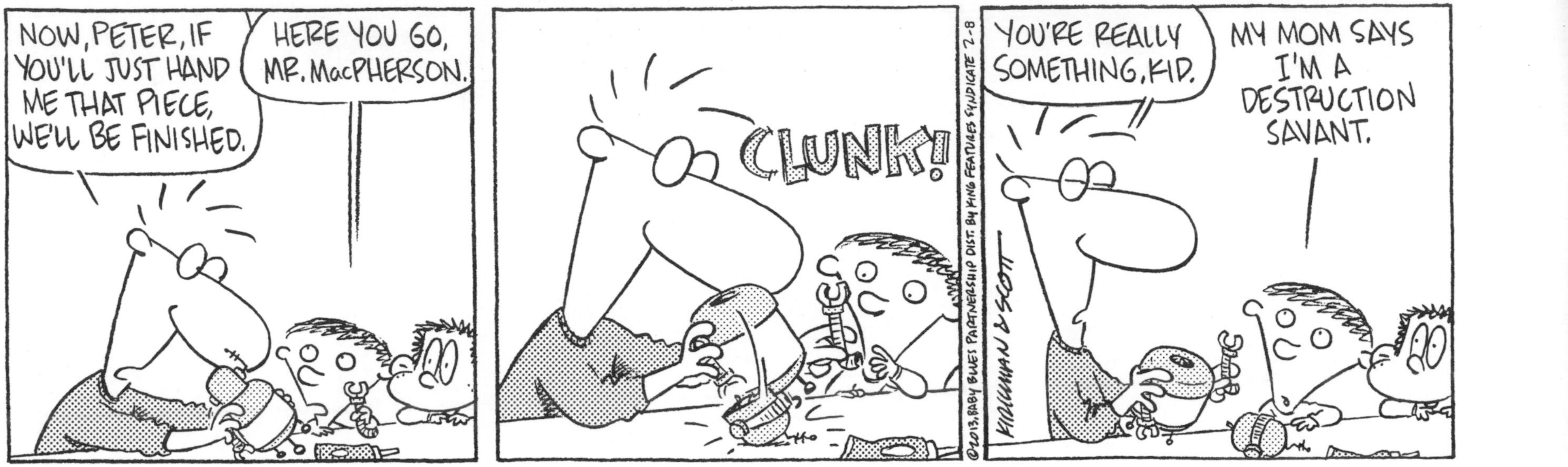
NOW, PETER, IF YOU'LL JUST HAND ME THAT PIECE, WE'LL BE FINISHED.
HERE YOU GO, MR. MacPHERSON.
CLUNK!
©2013, BABY BLUES PARTNERSHIP DIST. BY KING FEATURES SYNDICATE 2-8
KIRKMAN & SCOTT
YOU'RE REALLY SOMETHING, KID.
MY MOM SAYS I'M A DESTRUCTION SAVANT.

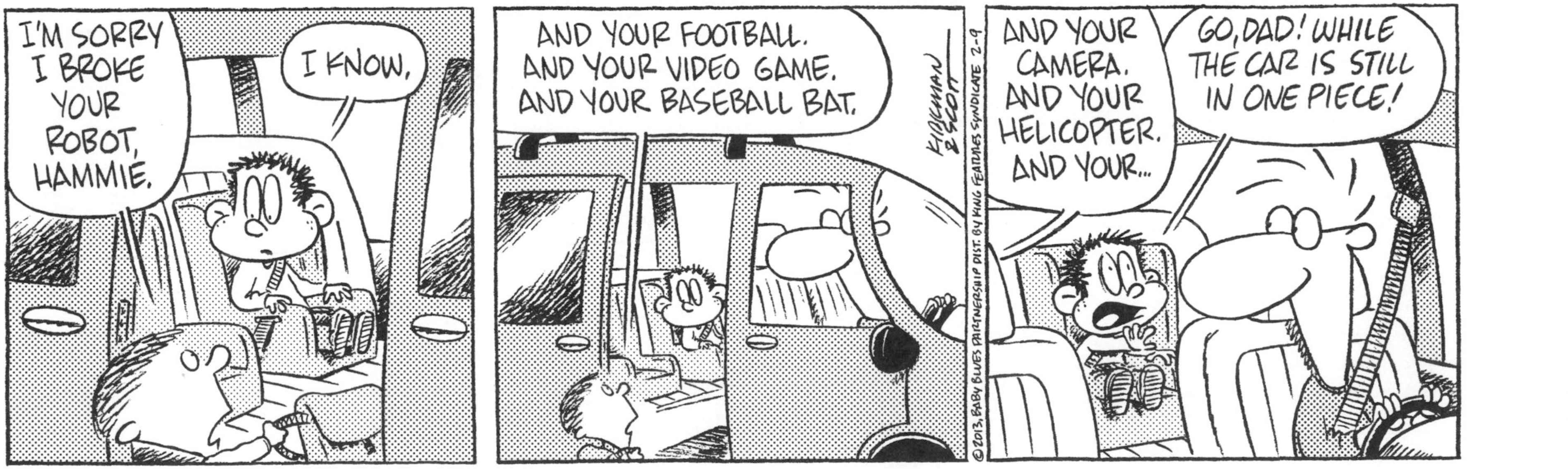
I'M SORRY I BROKE YOUR ROBOT, HAMMIE.
I KNOW.
AND YOUR FOOTBALL. AND YOUR VIDEO GAME. AND YOUR BASEBALL BAT.
KIRKMAN & SCOTT
©2013, BABY BLUES PARTNERSHIP DIST. BY KING FEATURES SYNDICATE 2-9
AND YOUR CAMERA. AND YOUR HELICOPTER. AND YOUR...
GO, DAD! WHILE THE CAR IS STILL IN ONE PIECE!

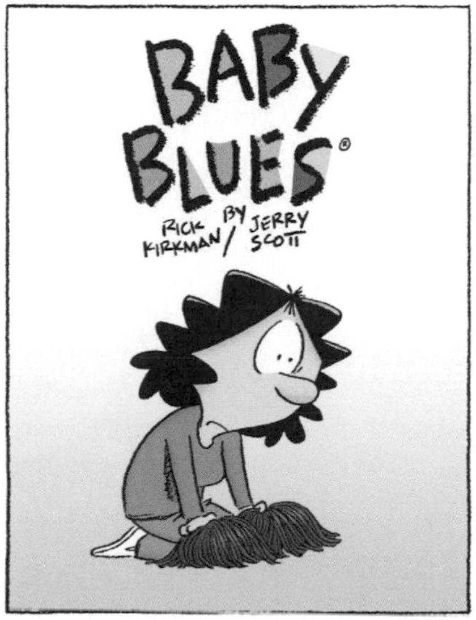
BABY BLUES®
BY RICK KIRKMAN / JERRY SCOTT

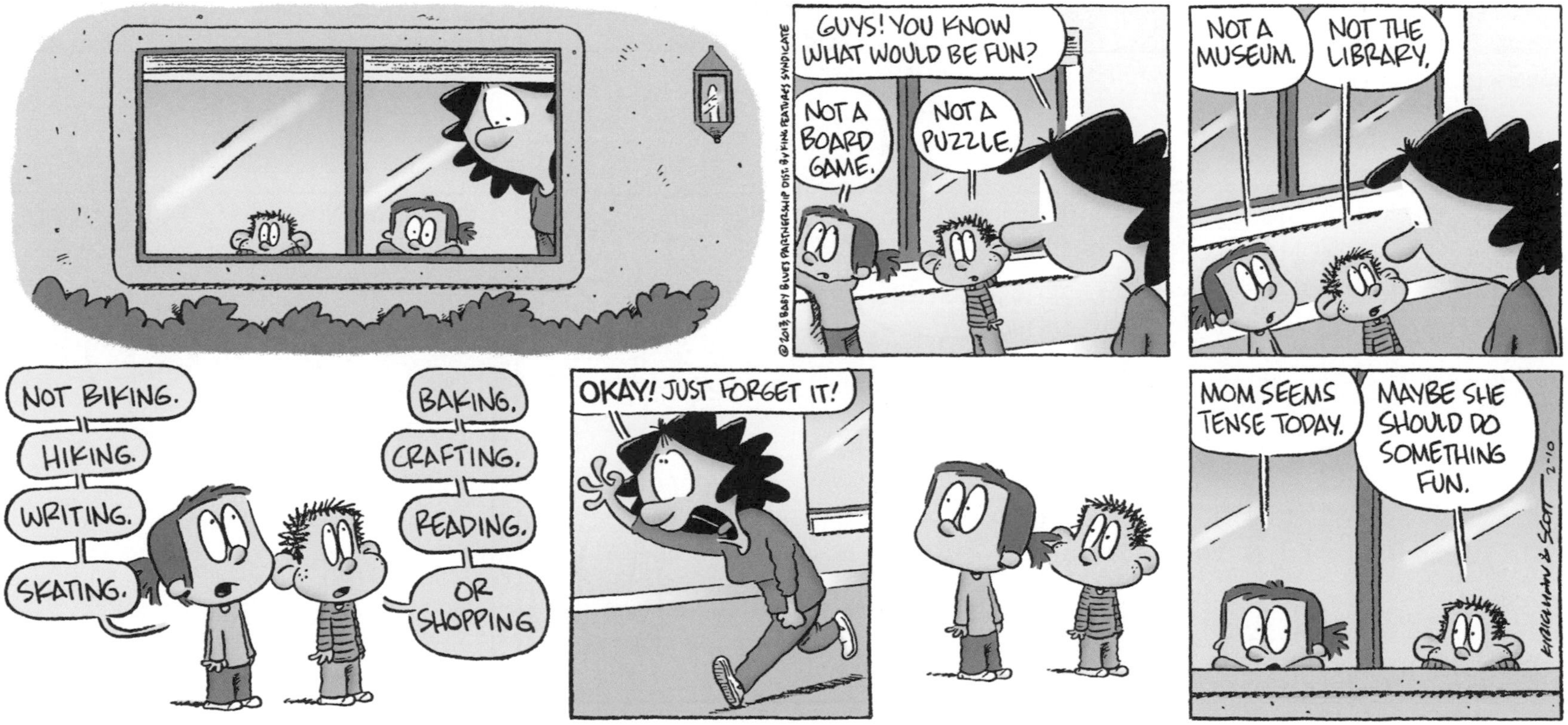
GUYS! YOU KNOW WHAT WOULD BE FUN?
NOT A BOARD GAME.
NOT A PUZZLE.
NOT A MUSEUM.
NOT THE LIBRARY.
NOT BIKING.
HIKING.
WRITING.
SKATING.
BAKING.
CRAFTING.
READING.
OR SHOPPING.
OKAY! JUST FORGET IT!
MOM SEEMS TENSE TODAY.
MAYBE SHE SHOULD DO SOMETHING FUN.
KIRKMAN & SCOTT 2-10
©2013, BABY BLUES PARTNERSHIP DIST. BY KING FEATURES SYNDICATE

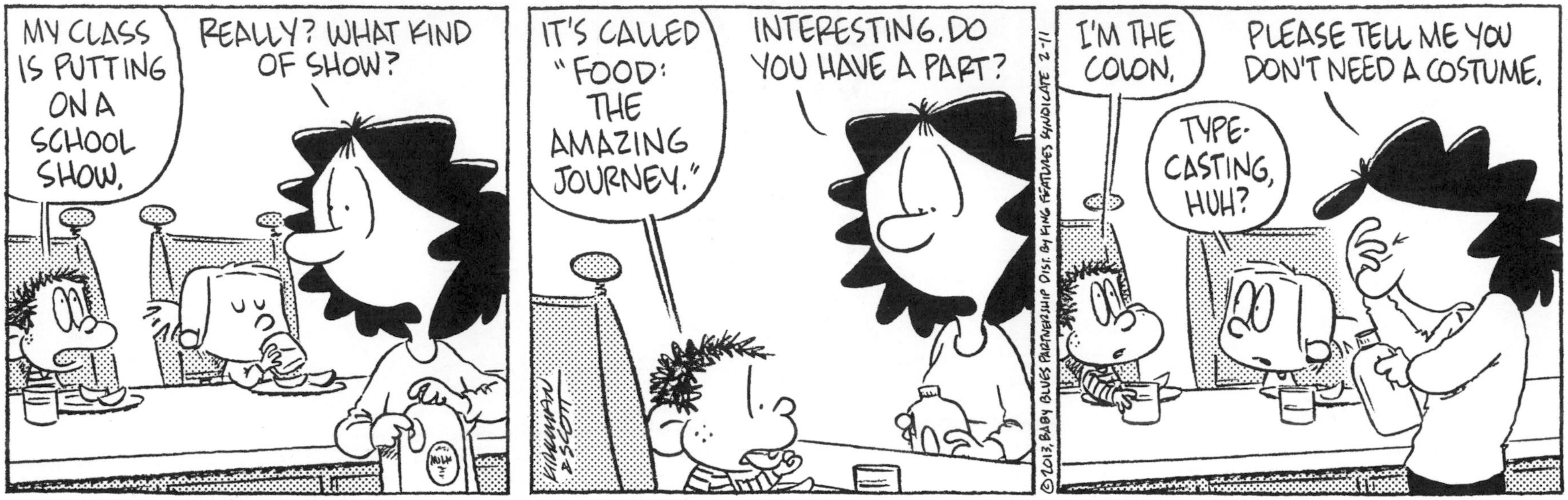
MY CLASS IS PUTTING ON A SCHOOL SHOW.
REALLY? WHAT KIND OF SHOW?
IT'S CALLED "FOOD: THE AMAZING JOURNEY."
INTERESTING. DO YOU HAVE A PART?
I'M THE COLON.
TYPE-CASTING, HUH?
PLEASE TELL ME YOU DON'T NEED A COSTUME.
KIRKMAN & SCOTT
©2013, BABY BLUES PARTNERSHIP DIST. BY KING FEATURES SYNDICATE 2-11

Jerry: This is a school show I'd go see.

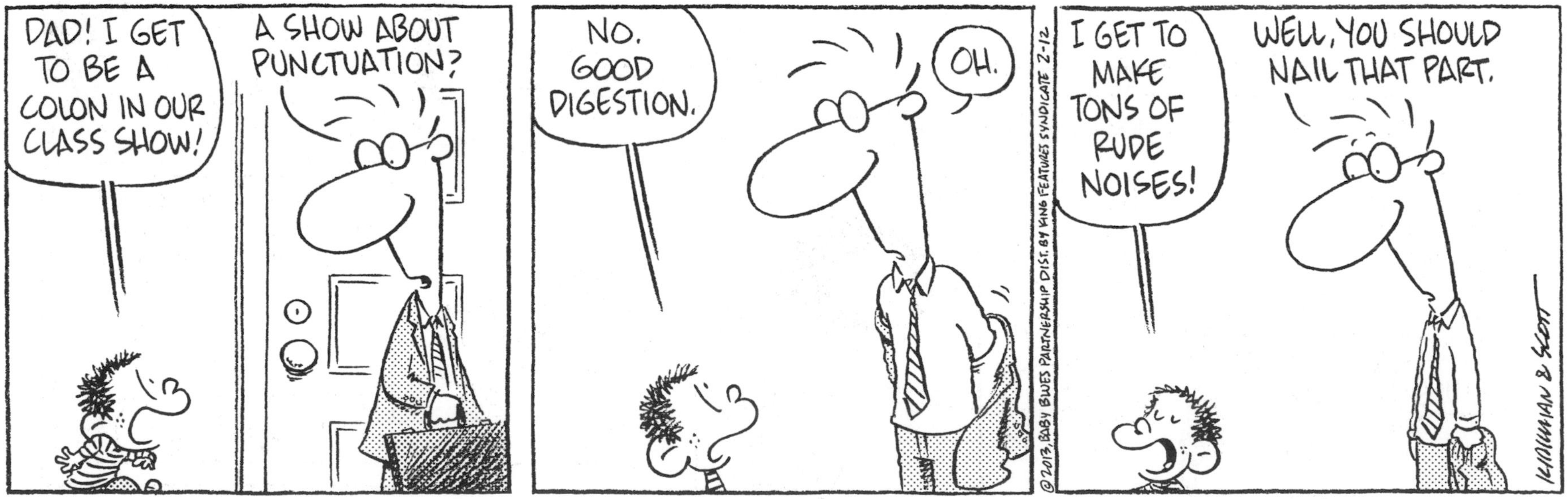
DAD! I GET TO BE A COLON IN OUR CLASS SHOW!
A SHOW ABOUT PUNCTUATION?
NO. GOOD DIGESTION.
OH.
I GET TO MAKE TONS OF RUDE NOISES!
WELL, YOU SHOULD NAIL THAT PART.
©2013, BABY BLUES PARTNERSHIP DIST. BY KING FEATURES SYNDICATE 2-12
KIRKMAN & SCOTT

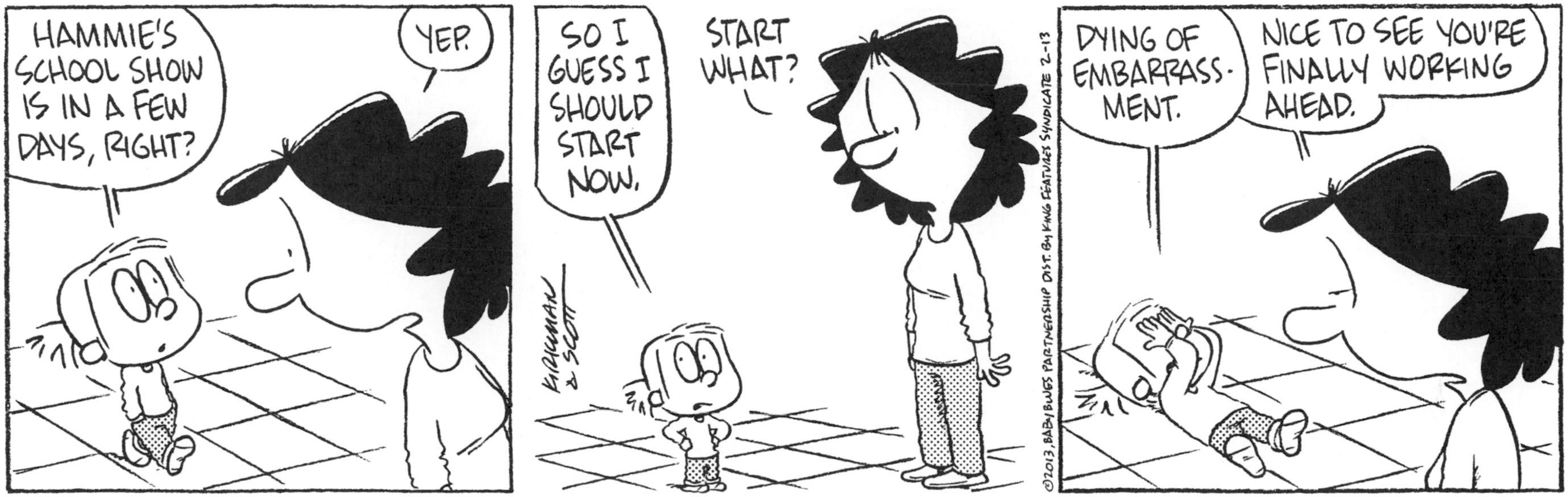
HAMMIE'S SCHOOL SHOW IS IN A FEW DAYS, RIGHT?
YEP.
SO I GUESS I SHOULD START NOW.
START WHAT?
KIRKMAN & SCOTT
©2013, BABY BLUES PARTNERSHIP DIST. BY KING FEATURES SYNDICATE 2-13
DYING OF EMBARRASS-MENT.
NICE TO SEE YOU'RE FINALLY WORKING AHEAD.

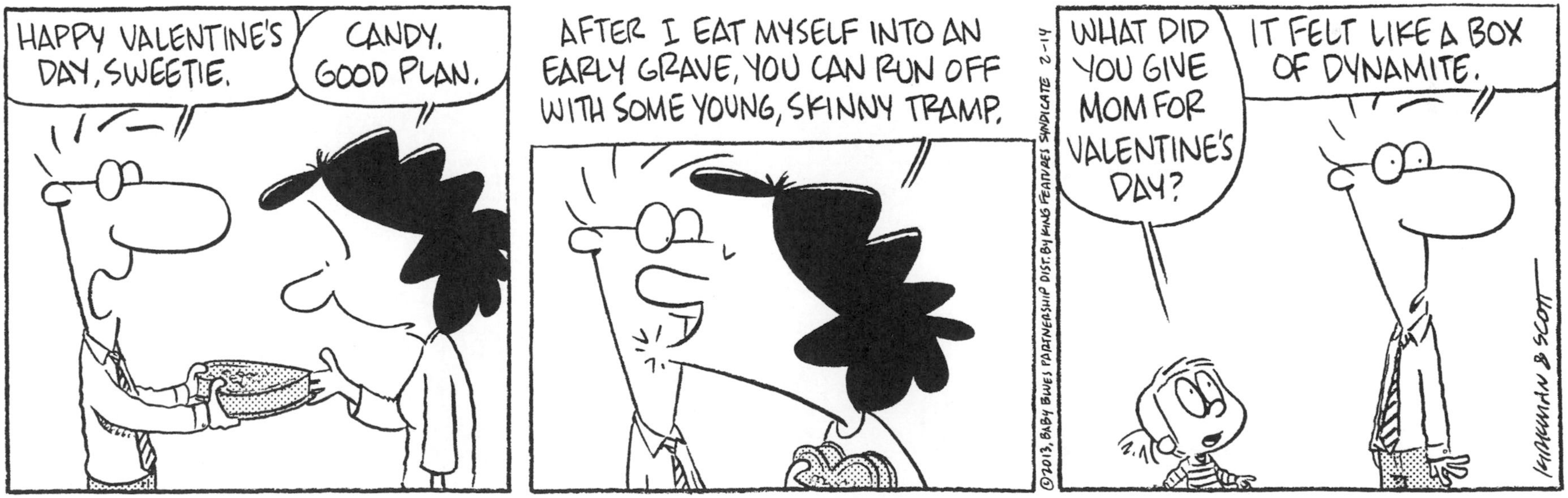
HAPPY VALENTINE'S DAY, SWEETIE.
CANDY. GOOD PLAN.
AFTER I EAT MYSELF INTO AN EARLY GRAVE, YOU CAN RUN OFF WITH SOME YOUNG, SKINNY TRAMP.
©2013, BABY BLUES PARTNERSHIP DIST. BY KING FEATURES SYNDICATE 2-14
WHAT DID YOU GIVE MOM FOR VALENTINE'S DAY?
IT FELT LIKE A BOX OF DYNAMITE.
KIRKMAN & SCOTT

Rick: One of my all-time favorite gags.

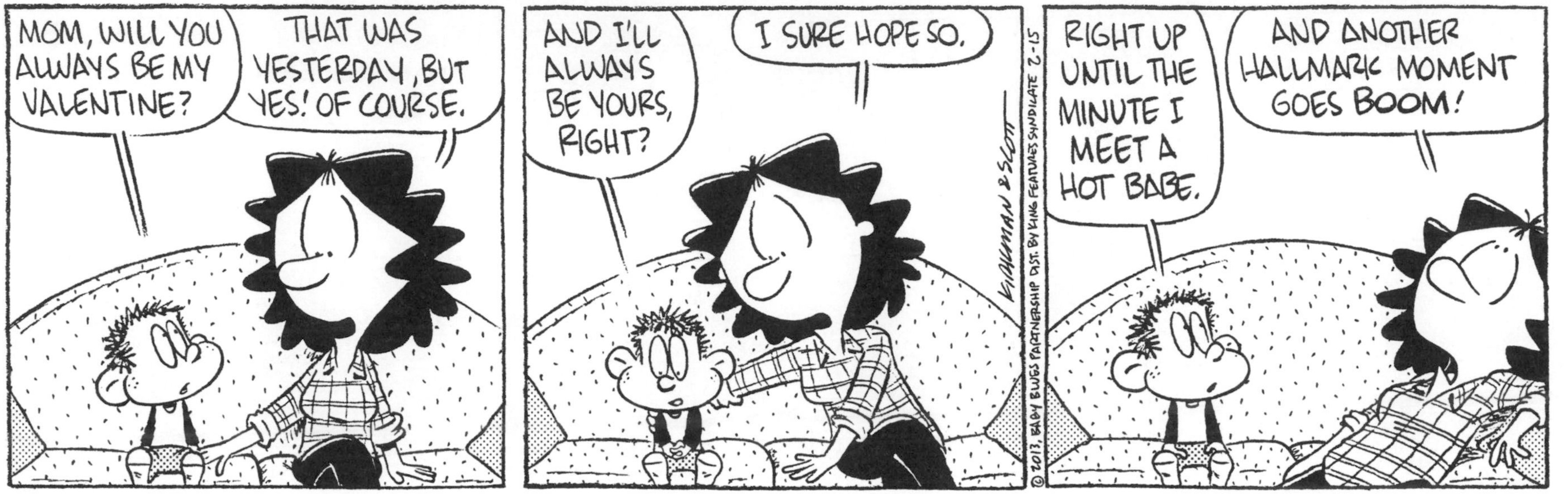
MOM, WILL YOU ALWAYS BE MY VALENTINE?
THAT WAS YESTERDAY, BUT YES! OF COURSE.
AND I'LL ALWAYS BE YOURS, RIGHT?
I SURE HOPE SO.
KIRKMAN & SCOTT
© 2013, BABY BLUES PARTNERSHIP DIST. BY KING FEATURES SYNDICATE 2-15
RIGHT UP UNTIL THE MINUTE I MEET A HOT BABE.
AND ANOTHER HALLMARK MOMENT GOES BOOM!

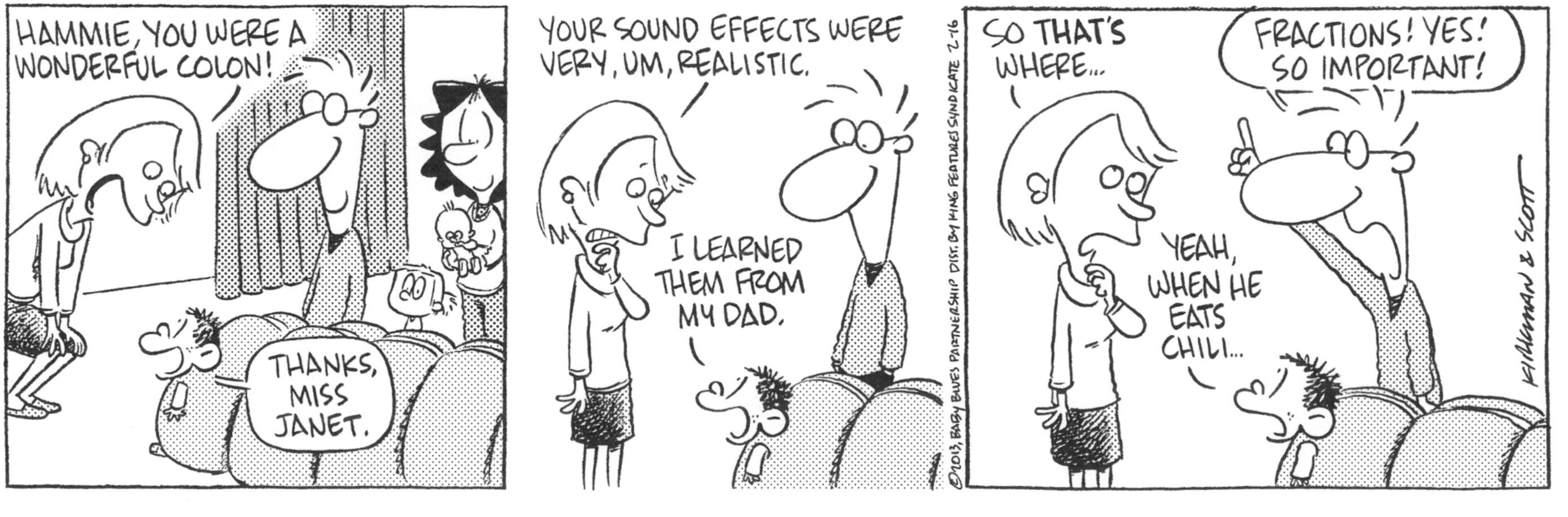
HAMMIE, YOU WERE A WONDERFUL COLON!
THANKS, MISS JANET.
YOUR SOUND EFFECTS WERE VERY, UM, REALISTIC.
I LEARNED THEM FROM MY DAD.
© 2013, BABY BLUES PARTNERSHIP DIST. BY KING FEATURES SYNDICATE 2-16
SO THAT'S WHERE...
FRACTIONS! YES! SO IMPORTANT!
YEAH, WHEN HE EATS CHILI...
KIRKMAN & SCOTT

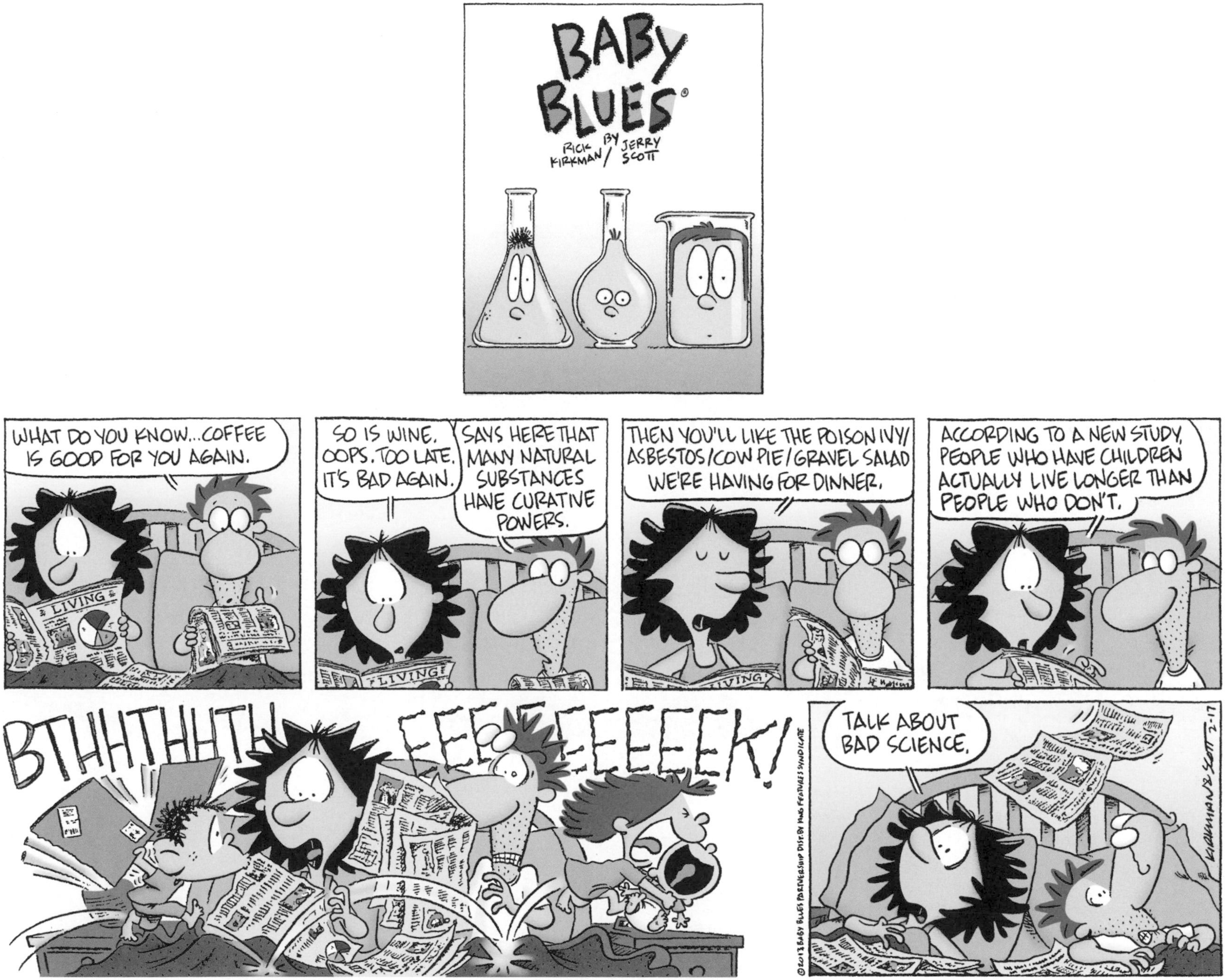
BABY BLUES®
BY RICK KIRKMAN / JERRY SCOTT
WHAT DO YOU KNOW...COFFEE IS GOOD FOR YOU AGAIN.
SO IS WINE. OOPS. TOO LATE. IT'S BAD AGAIN.
SAYS HERE THAT MANY NATURAL SUBSTANCES HAVE CURATIVE POWERS.
THEN YOU'LL LIKE THE POISON IVY/ ASBESTOS/COW PIE/GRAVEL SALAD WE'RE HAVING FOR DINNER.
ACCORDING TO A NEW STUDY, PEOPLE WHO HAVE CHILDREN ACTUALLY LIVE LONGER THAN PEOPLE WHO DON'T.
BTHHTHHTH
EEEEEEEEEK!
©2013 BABY BLUES PARTNERSHIP DIST. BY KING FEATURES SYNDICATE
TALK ABOUT BAD SCIENCE.
KIRKMAN & SCOTT 2-17

Rick: There should be a name for what we get from all these kinds of news reports: Research Whiplash. Fun action to draw here and more weird things I do to the characters' heads in title panels.

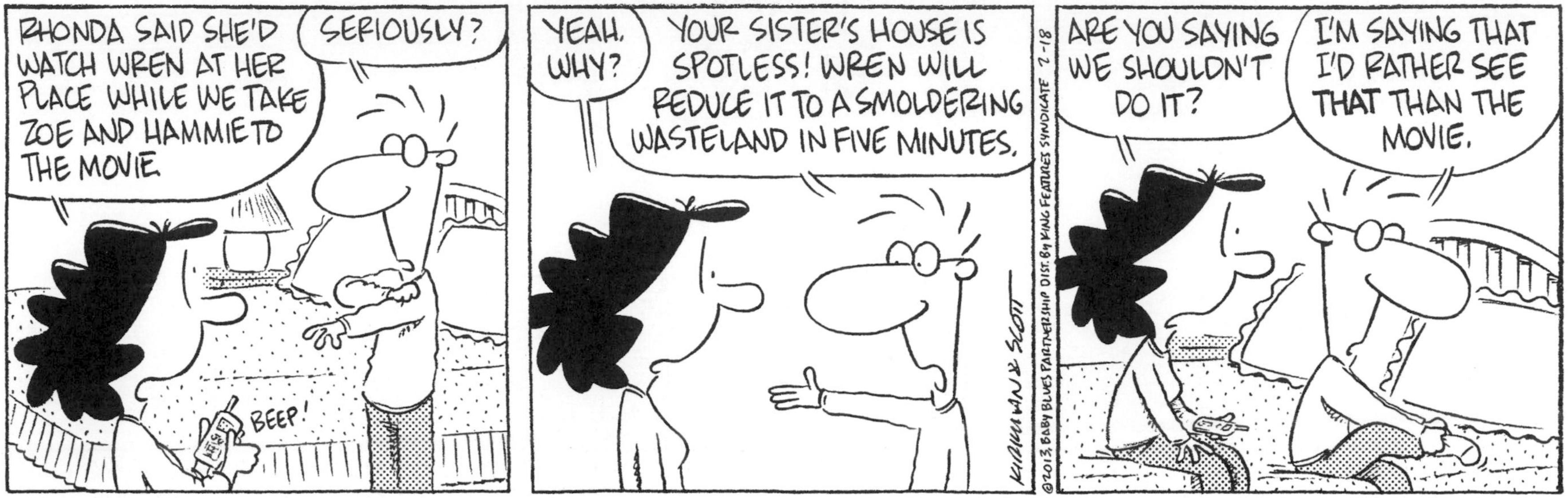
RHONDA SAID SHE'D WATCH WREN AT HER PLACE WHILE WE TAKE ZOE AND HAMMIE TO THE MOVIE.
SERIOUSLY?
BEEP!
YEAH. WHY?
YOUR SISTER'S HOUSE IS SPOTLESS! WREN WILL REDUCE IT TO A SMOLDERING WASTELAND IN FIVE MINUTES.
KIRKMAN & SCOTT
©2013, BABY BLUES PARTNERSHIP DIST. BY KING FEATURES SYNDICATE 2-18
ARE YOU SAYING WE SHOULDN'T DO IT?
I'M SAYING THAT I'D RATHER SEE THAT THAN THE MOVIE.

Rick: This series was inspired by my assistant and her sister.

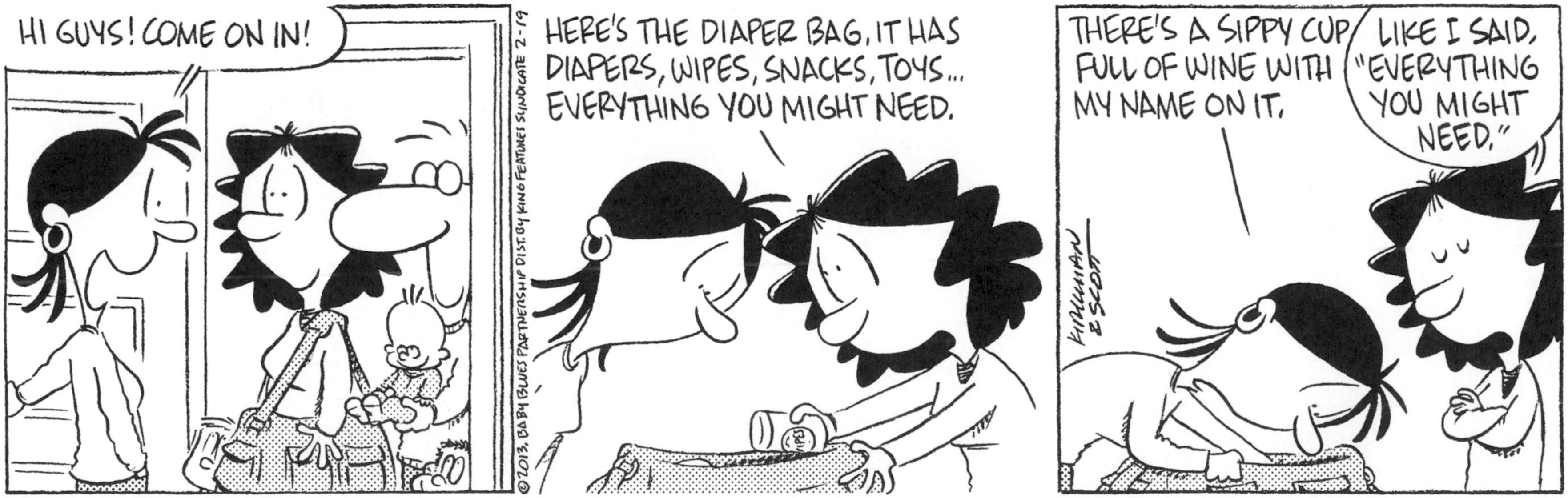
HI GUYS! COME ON IN!
©2013, BABY BLUES PARTNERSHIP DIST. BY KING FEATURES SYNDICATE 2-19
HERE'S THE DIAPER BAG. IT HAS DIAPERS, WIPES, SNACKS, TOYS... EVERYTHING YOU MIGHT NEED.
KIRKMAN & SCOTT
THERE'S A SIPPY CUP FULL OF WINE WITH MY NAME ON IT.
LIKE I SAID, "EVERYTHING YOU MIGHT NEED."

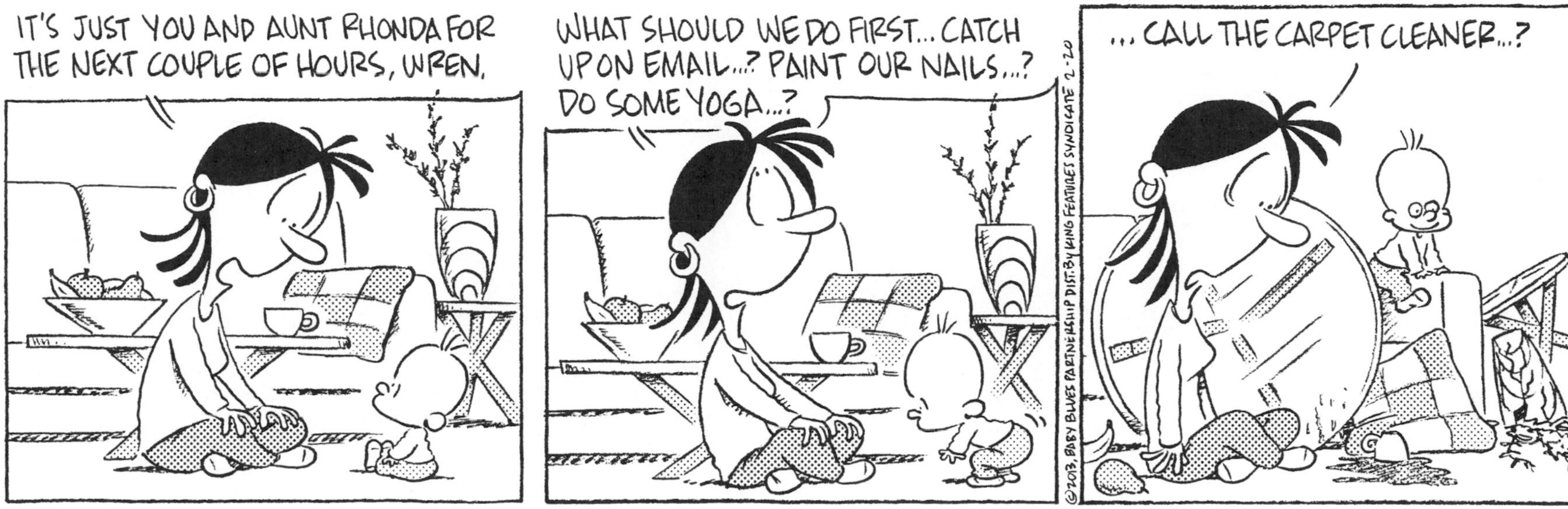
IT'S JUST YOU AND AUNT RHONDA FOR THE NEXT COUPLE OF HOURS, WREN.
WHAT SHOULD WE DO FIRST... CATCH UP ON EMAIL...? PAINT OUR NAILS...? DO SOME YOGA...?
©2013, BABY BLUES PARTNERSHIP DIST. BY KING FEATURES SYNDICATE 2-20
... CALL THE CARPET CLEANER...?
KIRKMAN & SCOTT

Jerry: Welcome to the NFL, Rhonda.

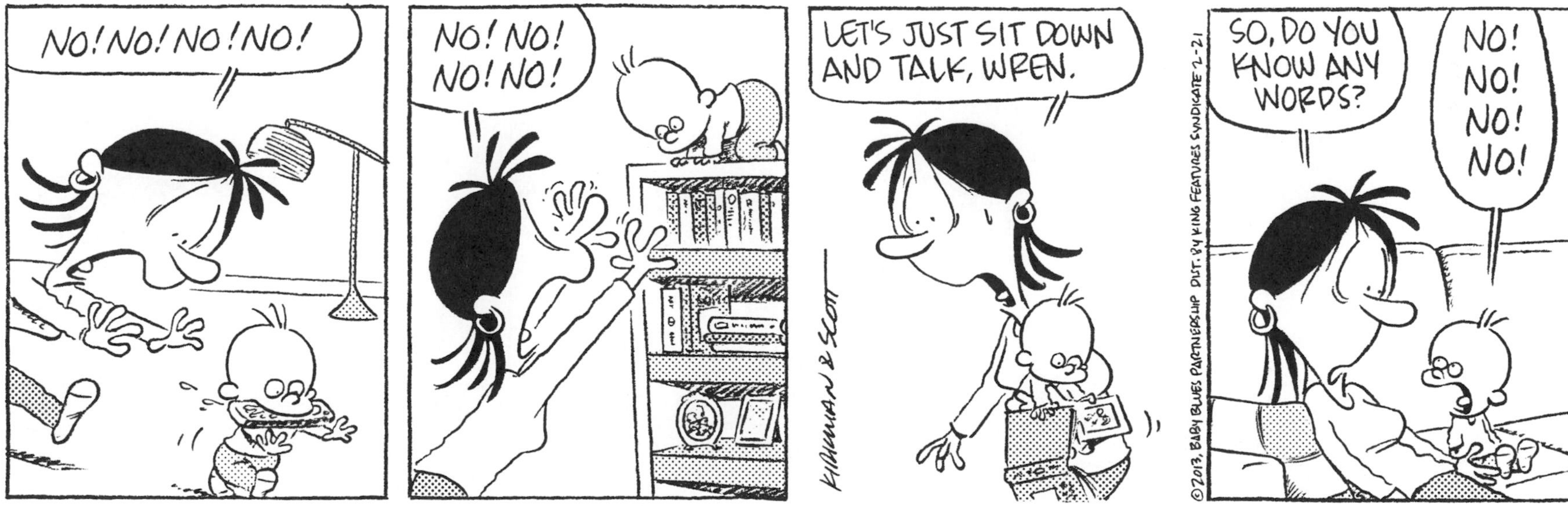
NO! NO! NO! NO!
NO! NO! NO! NO!
KIRKMAN & SCOTT
LET'S JUST SIT DOWN AND TALK, WREN.
©2013, BABY BLUES PARTNERSHIP DIST. BY KING FEATURES SYNDICATE 2-21
SO, DO YOU KNOW ANY WORDS?
NO! NO! NO! NO!

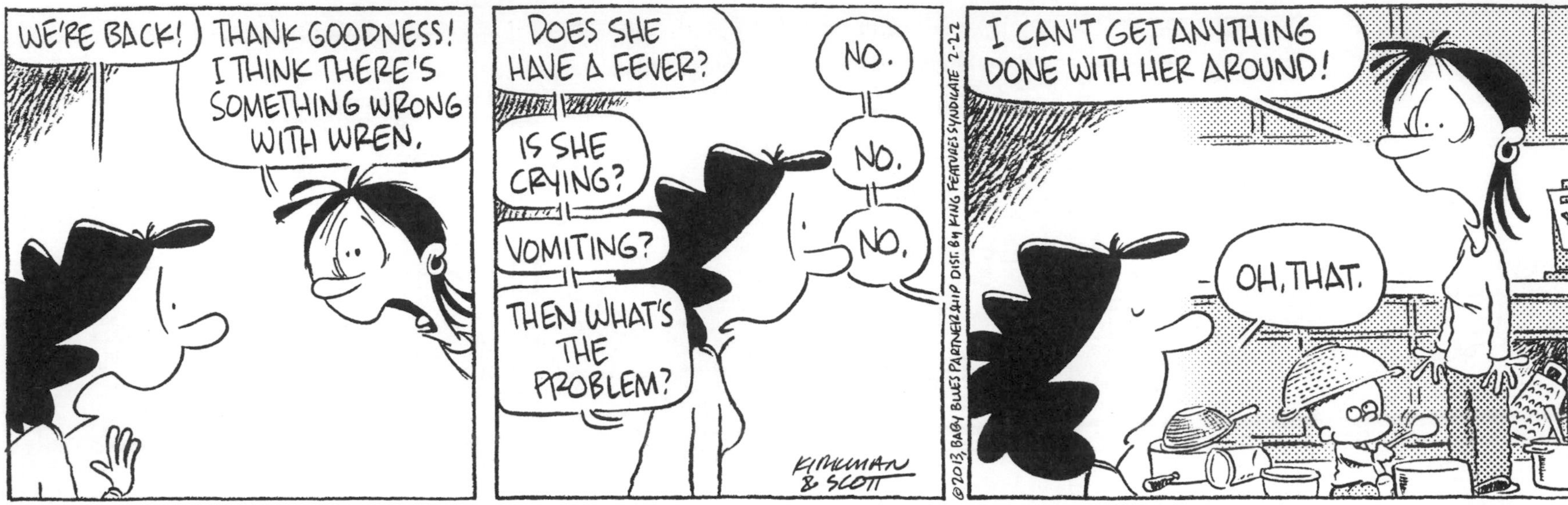
WE'RE BACK!
THANK GOODNESS! I THINK THERE'S SOMETHING WRONG WITH WREN.
DOES SHE HAVE A FEVER?
NO.
IS SHE CRYING?
NO.
VOMITING?
NO.
THEN WHAT'S THE PROBLEM?
KIRKMAN & SCOTT
©2013, BABY BLUES PARTNERSHIP DIST. BY KING FEATURES SYNDICATE 2-22
I CAN'T GET ANYTHING DONE WITH HER AROUND!
OH, THAT.

Rick: These last two strips were pretty much the point of the story. Jerry worked backward from there to create the series, but each gag has to push toward that conclusion and have a self-contained joke in each one. Not easy, but this is a great lesson in how to do it right.

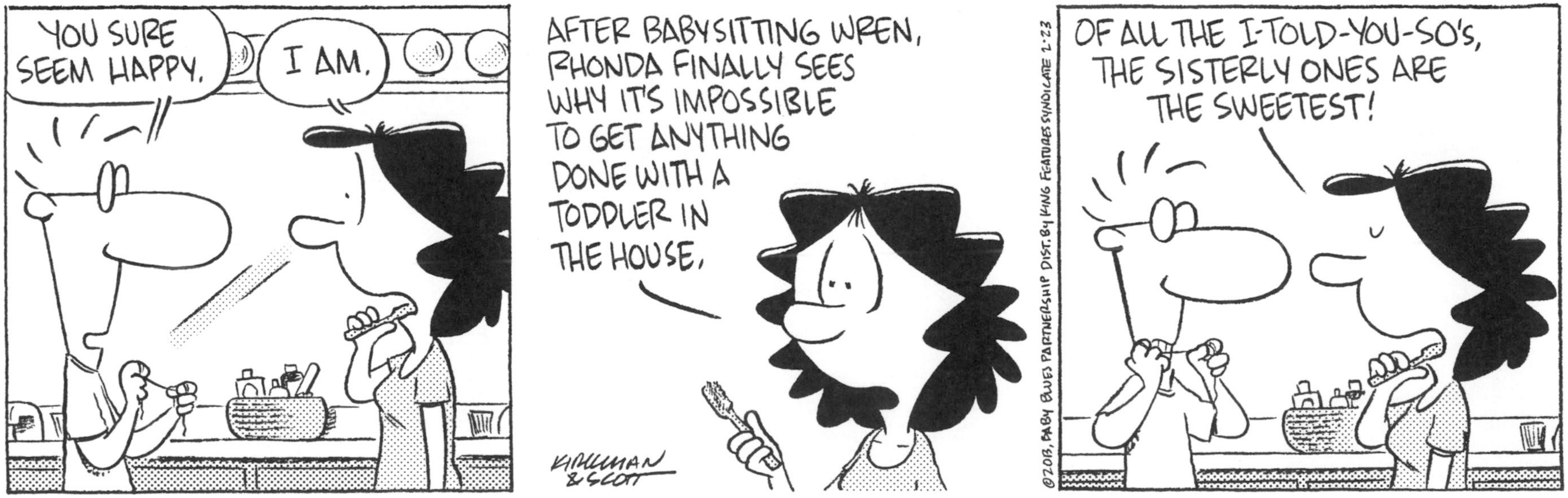
YOU SURE SEEM HAPPY.
I AM.
AFTER BABYSITTING WREN, RHONDA FINALLY SEES WHY IT'S IMPOSSIBLE TO GET ANYTHING DONE WITH A TODDLER IN THE HOUSE.
KIRKMAN & SCOTT
©2013, BABY BLUES PARTNERSHIP DIST. BY KING FEATURES SYNDICATE 2-23
OF ALL THE I-TOLD-YOU-SO'S, THE SISTERLY ONES ARE THE SWEETEST!

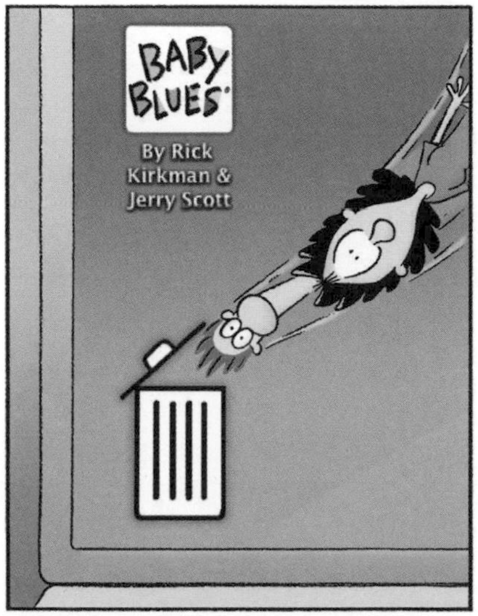

BABY BLUES
By Rick Kirkman & Jerry Scott

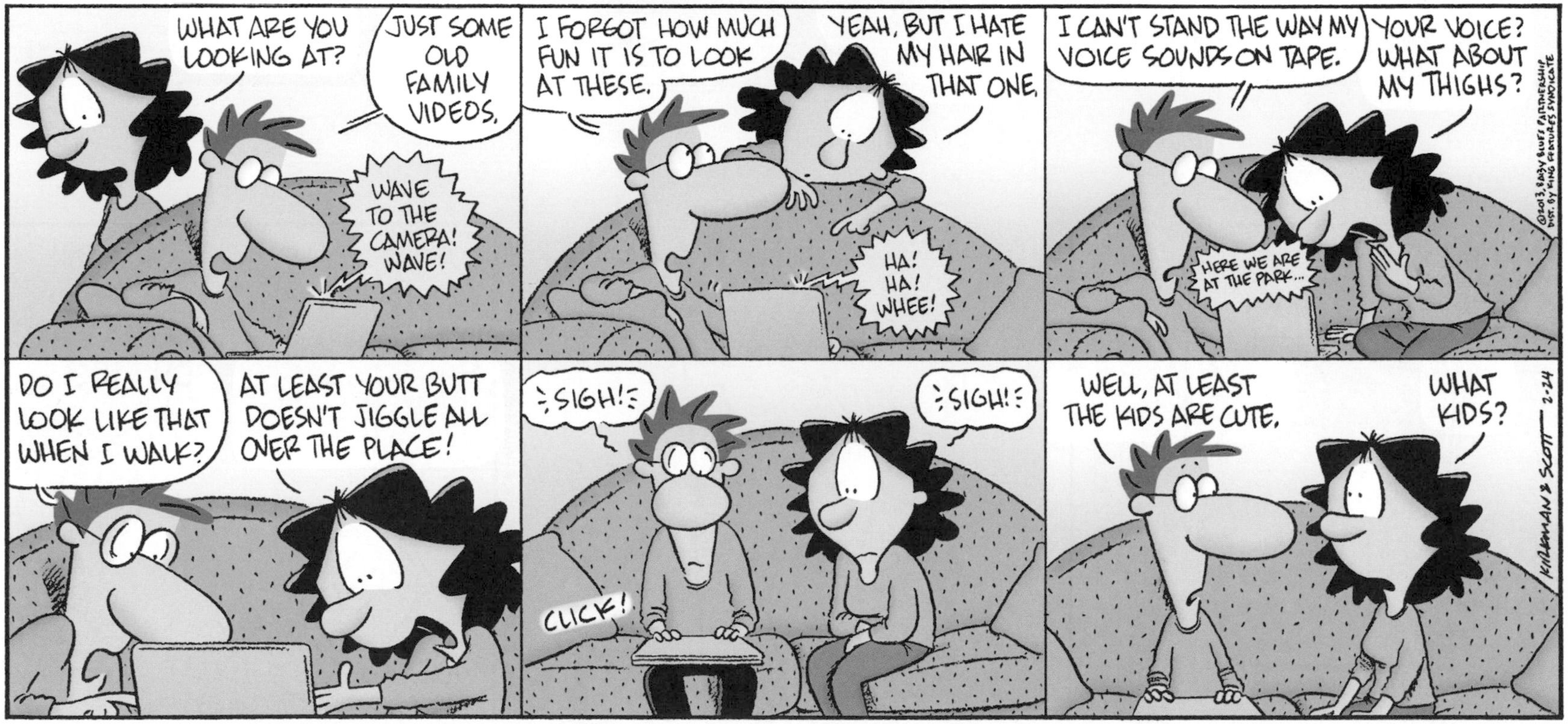

WHAT ARE YOU LOOKING AT?
JUST SOME OLD FAMILY VIDEOS.
WAVE TO THE CAMERA! WAVE!
I FORGOT HOW MUCH FUN IT IS TO LOOK AT THESE.
YEAH, BUT I HATE MY HAIR IN THAT ONE.
HA! HA! WHEE!
I CAN'T STAND THE WAY MY VOICE SOUNDS ON TAPE.
YOUR VOICE? WHAT ABOUT MY THIGHS?
HERE WE ARE AT THE PARK...
©2013, BABY BLUES PARTNERSHIP DIST. BY KING FEATURES SYNDICATE
DO I REALLY LOOK LIKE THAT WHEN I WALK?
AT LEAST YOUR BUTT DOESN'T JIGGLE ALL OVER THE PLACE!
SIGH!
SIGH!
CLICK!
WELL, AT LEAST THE KIDS ARE CUTE.
WHAT KIDS?
KIRKMAN & SCOTT 2-24

Rick: This points out something about the digital era. Old traditional photos looked like they were old—faded, discolored, worn. When you saw your young self in them, there was a real sense of elapsed time. It felt like you earned those pounds and that gray hair or lack of hair. Now, with digital photos, everything looks like it was taken yesterday, even though it was ten years ago. That's what's so depressing: It feels like all that change happened in an instant.

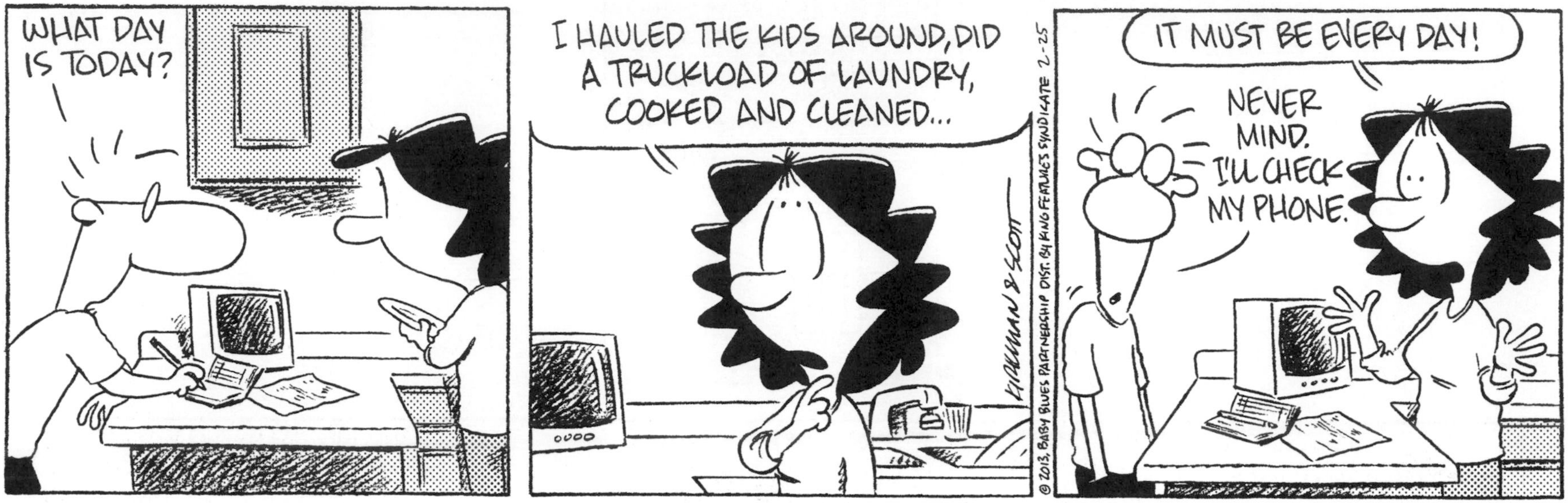
WHAT DAY IS TODAY?
I HAULED THE KIDS AROUND, DID A TRUCKLOAD OF LAUNDRY, COOKED AND CLEANED...
KIRKMAN & SCOTT
© 2013, BABY BLUES PARTNERSHIP DIST. BY KING FEATURES SYNDICATE 2-25
IT MUST BE EVERY DAY!
NEVER MIND. I'LL CHECK MY PHONE.

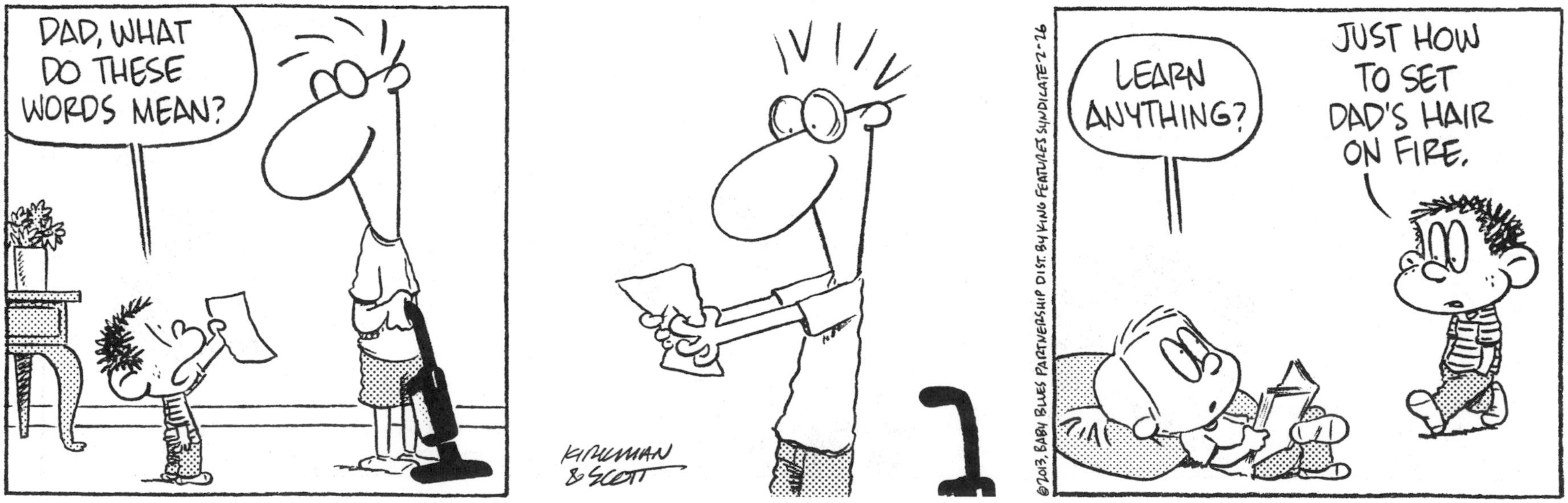
DAD, WHAT DO THESE WORDS MEAN?
KIRKMAN & SCOTT
© 2013, BABY BLUES PARTNERSHIP DIST. BY KING FEATURES SYNDICATE 2-26
LEARN ANYTHING?
JUST HOW TO SET DAD'S HAIR ON FIRE.

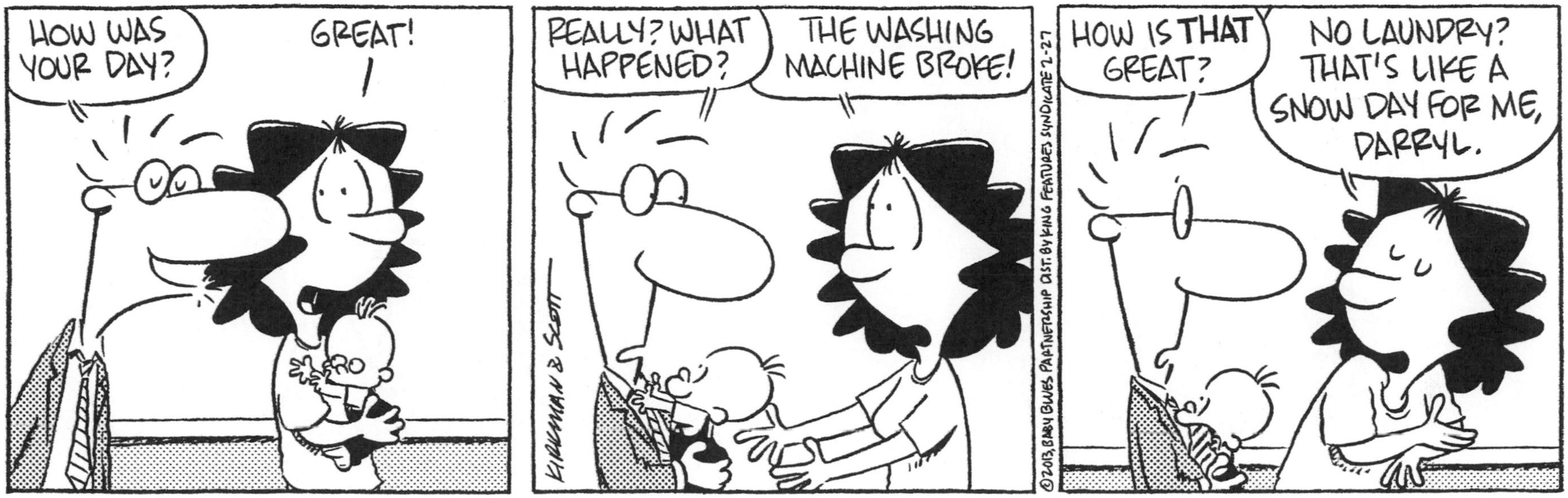
HOW WAS YOUR DAY?
GREAT!
REALLY? WHAT HAPPENED?
THE WASHING MACHINE BROKE!
KIRKMAN & SCOTT
©2013, BABY BLUES PARTNERSHIP DIST. BY KING FEATURES SYNDICATE 2-27
HOW IS **THAT** GREAT?
NO LAUNDRY? THAT'S LIKE A SNOW DAY FOR ME, DARRYL.

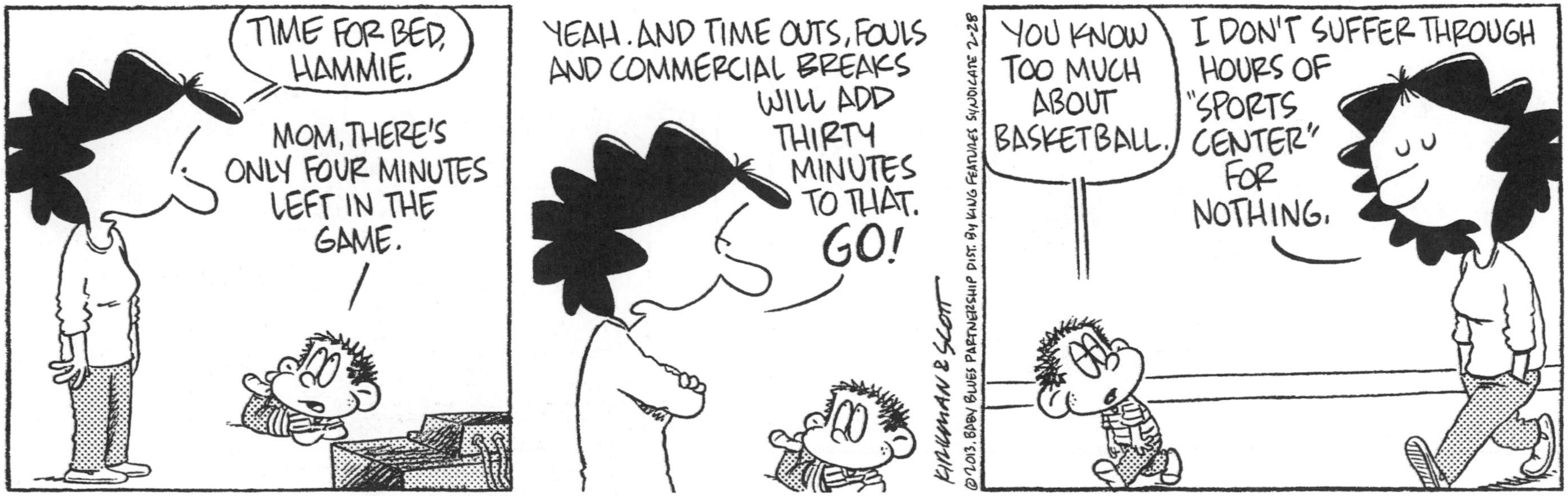
TIME FOR BED, HAMMIE.
MOM, THERE'S ONLY FOUR MINUTES LEFT IN THE GAME.
YEAH. AND TIME OUTS, FOULS AND COMMERCIAL BREAKS WILL ADD THIRTY MINUTES TO THAT. GO!
KIRKMAN & SCOTT
©2013, BABY BLUES PARTNERSHIP DIST. BY KING FEATURES SYNDICATE 2-28
YOU KNOW TOO MUCH ABOUT BASKETBALL.
I DON'T SUFFER THROUGH HOURS OF "SPORTS CENTER" FOR NOTHING.

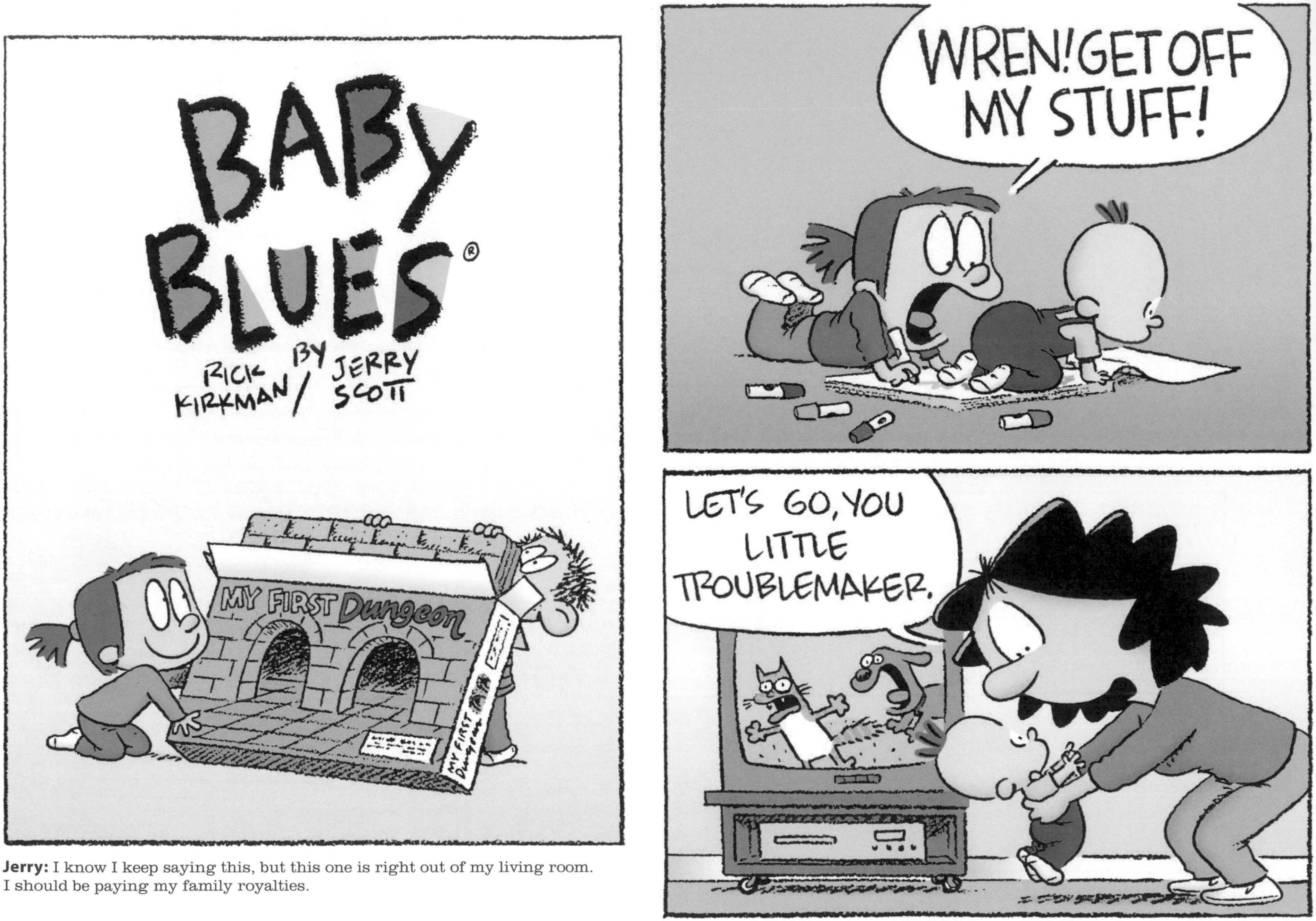
BABY BLUES®
BY RICK KIRKMAN/ JERRY SCOTT
MY FIRST Dungeon
WREN! GET OFF MY STUFF!
LET'S GO, YOU LITTLE TROUBLEMAKER.

Jerry: I know I keep saying this, but this one is right out of my living room. I should be paying my family royalties.

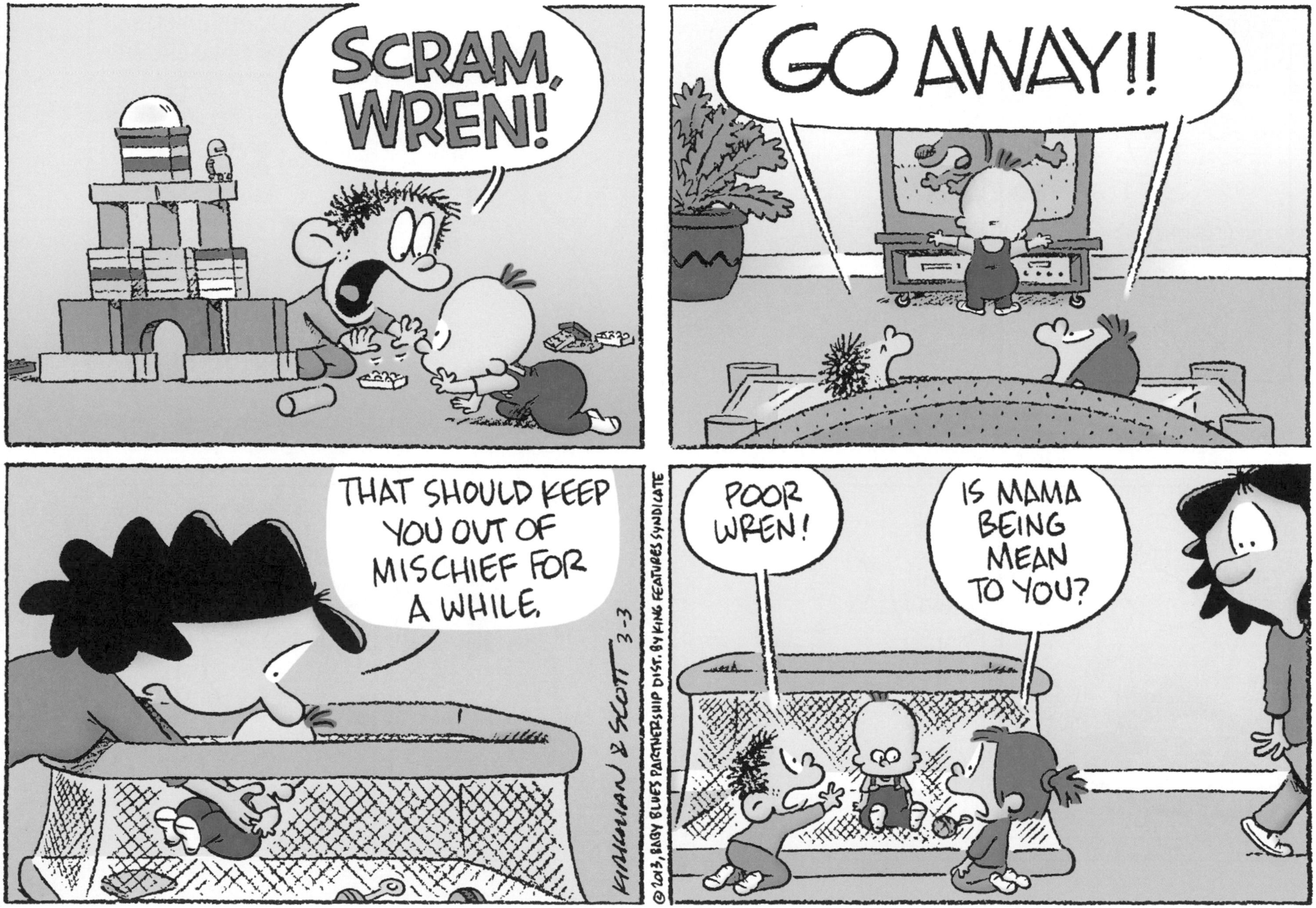
SCRAM, WREN!
GO AWAY!!
THAT SHOULD KEEP YOU OUT OF MISCHIEF FOR A WHILE.
KIRKMAN & SCOTT 3-3
© 2013, BABY BLUES PARTNERSHIP DIST. BY KING FEATURES SYNDICATE
POOR WREN!
IS MAMA BEING MEAN TO YOU?

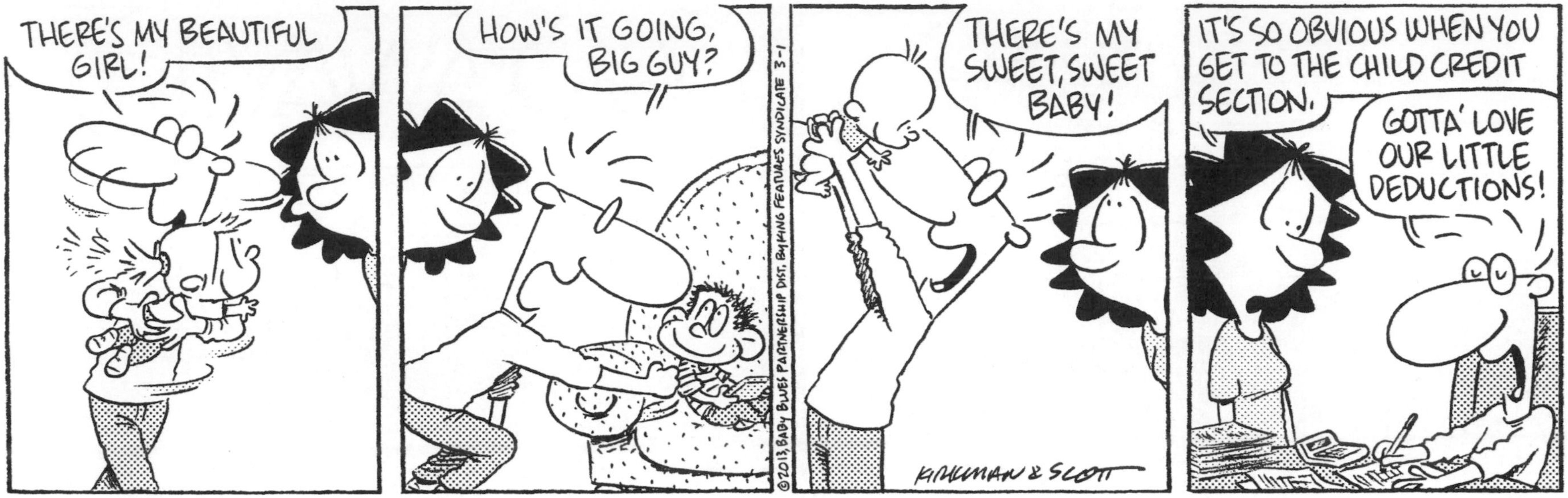
THERE'S MY BEAUTIFUL GIRL!
HOW'S IT GOING, BIG GUY?
©2013, BABY BLUES PARTNERSHIP DIST. BY KING FEATURES SYNDICATE 3-1
THERE'S MY SWEET, SWEET BABY!
KIRKMAN & SCOTT
IT'S SO OBVIOUS WHEN YOU GET TO THE CHILD CREDIT SECTION.
GOTTA' LOVE OUR LITTLE DEDUCTIONS!

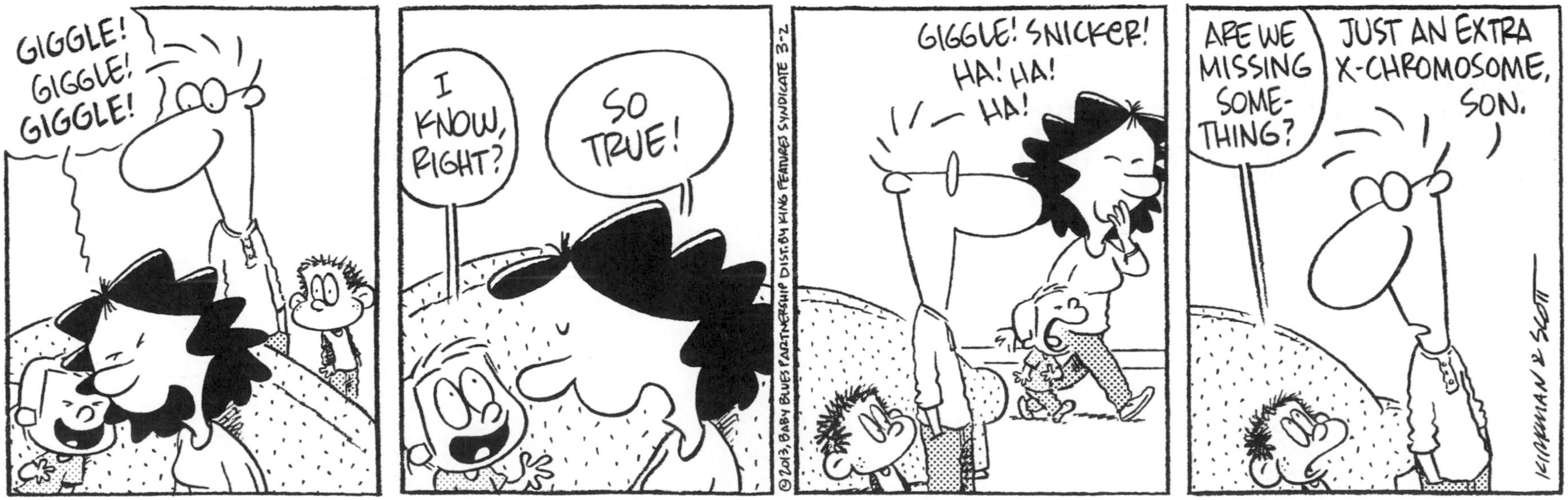
GIGGLE! GIGGLE! GIGGLE!
I KNOW, RIGHT?
SO TRUE!
©2013, BABY BLUES PARTNERSHIP DIST. BY KING FEATURES SYNDICATE 3-2
GIGGLE! SNICKER! HA! HA! HA!
ARE WE MISSING SOME-THING?
JUST AN EXTRA X-CHROMOSOME, SON.
KIRKMAN & SCOTT

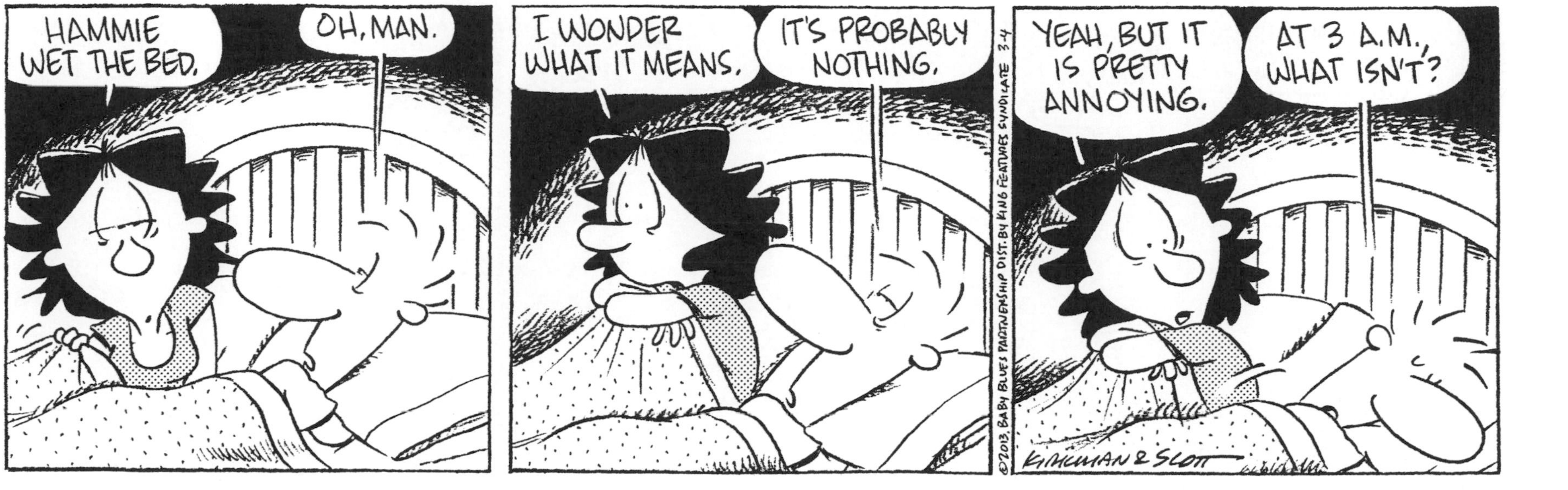
HAMMIE WET THE BED.
OH, MAN.
I WONDER WHAT IT MEANS.
IT'S PROBABLY NOTHING.
YEAH, BUT IT IS PRETTY ANNOYING.
AT 3 A.M., WHAT ISN'T?
©2013, BABY BLUES PARTNERSHIP DIST. BY KING FEATURES SYNDICATE 3-4
KIRKMAN & SCOTT

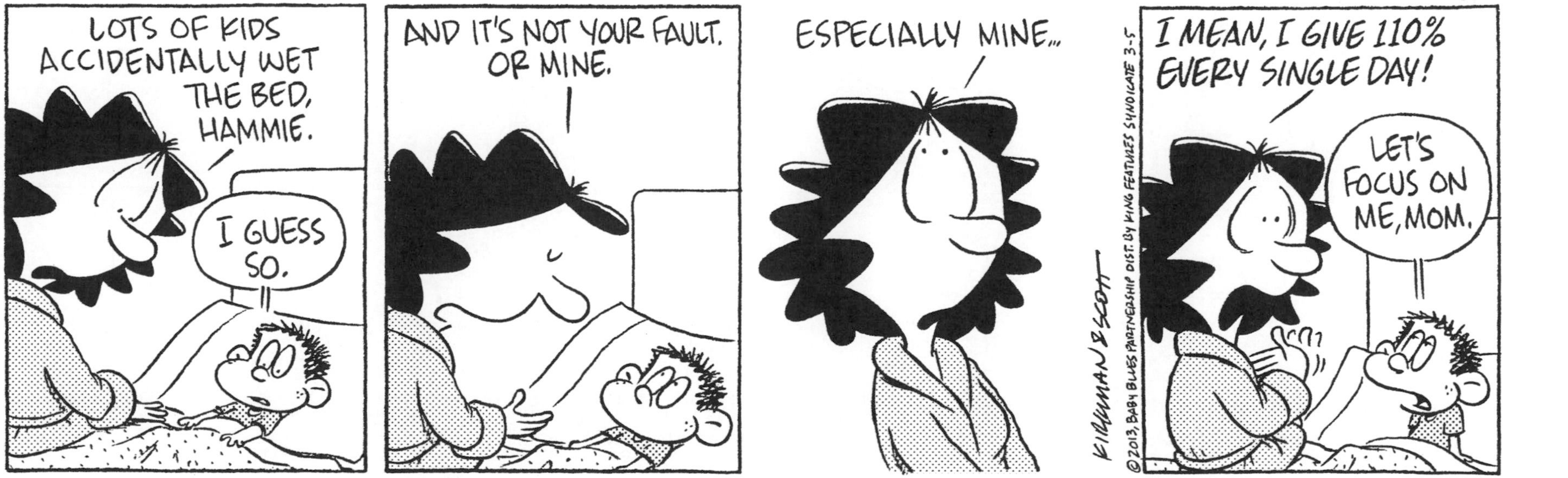
LOTS OF KIDS ACCIDENTALLY WET THE BED, HAMMIE.
I GUESS SO.
AND IT'S NOT YOUR FAULT. OR MINE.
ESPECIALLY MINE...
I MEAN, I GIVE 110% EVERY SINGLE DAY!
LET'S FOCUS ON ME, MOM.
KIRKMAN & SCOTT
©2013, BABY BLUES PARTNERSHIP DIST. BY KING FEATURES SYNDICATE 3-5

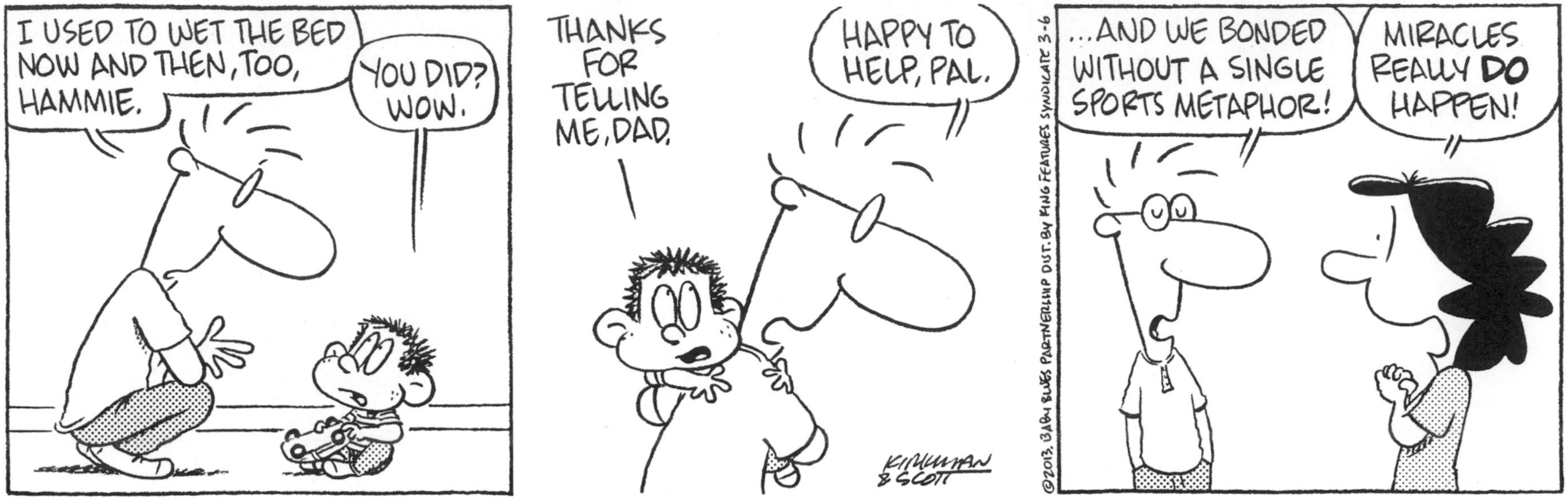
I USED TO WET THE BED NOW AND THEN, TOO, HAMMIE.
YOU DID? WOW.
THANKS FOR TELLING ME, DAD.
HAPPY TO HELP, PAL.
KIRKMAN & SCOTT
©2013, BABY BLUES PARTNERSHIP DIST. BY KING FEATURES SYNDICATE 3-6
...AND WE BONDED WITHOUT A SINGLE SPORTS METAPHOR!
MIRACLES REALLY **DO** HAPPEN!

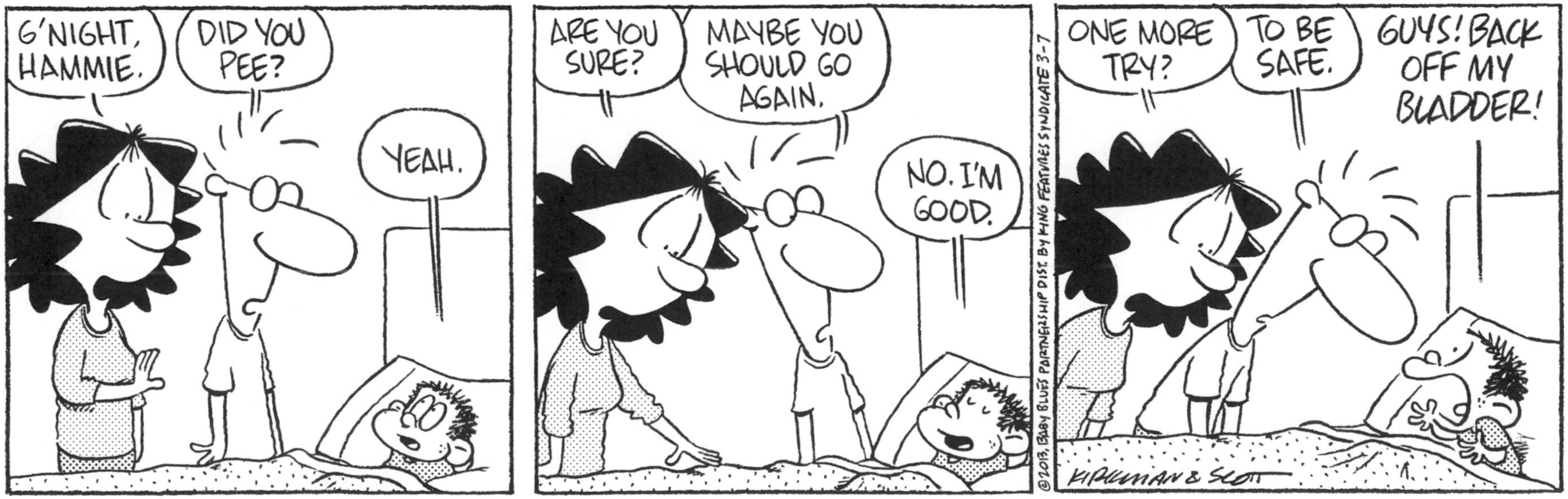
G'NIGHT, HAMMIE.
DID YOU PEE?
YEAH.
ARE YOU SURE?
MAYBE YOU SHOULD GO AGAIN.
NO. I'M GOOD.
©2013, BABY BLUES PARTNERSHIP DIST. BY KING FEATURES SYNDICATE 3-7
ONE MORE TRY?
TO BE SAFE.
GUYS! BACK OFF MY BLADDER!
KIRKMAN & SCOTT

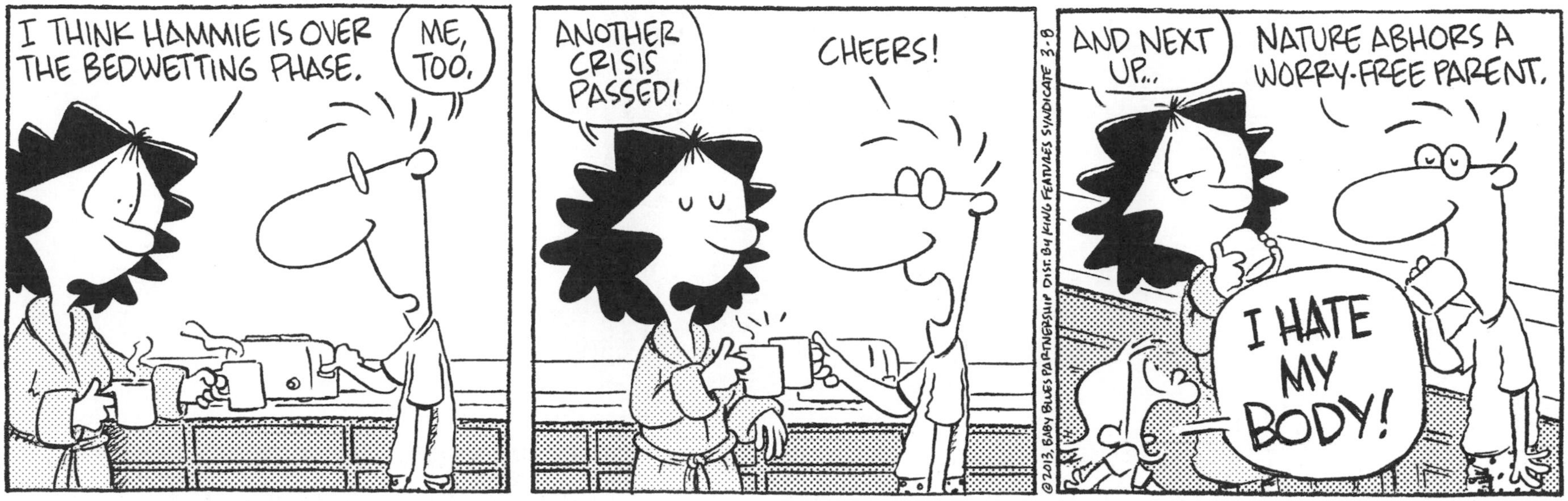
I THINK HAMMIE IS OVER THE BEDWETTING PHASE.
ME, TOO.
ANOTHER CRISIS PASSED!
CHEERS!
©2013, BABY BLUES PARTNERSHIP DIST. BY KING FEATURES SYNDICATE 3-8
AND NEXT UP...
NATURE ABHORS A WORRY-FREE PARENT.
I HATE MY BODY!

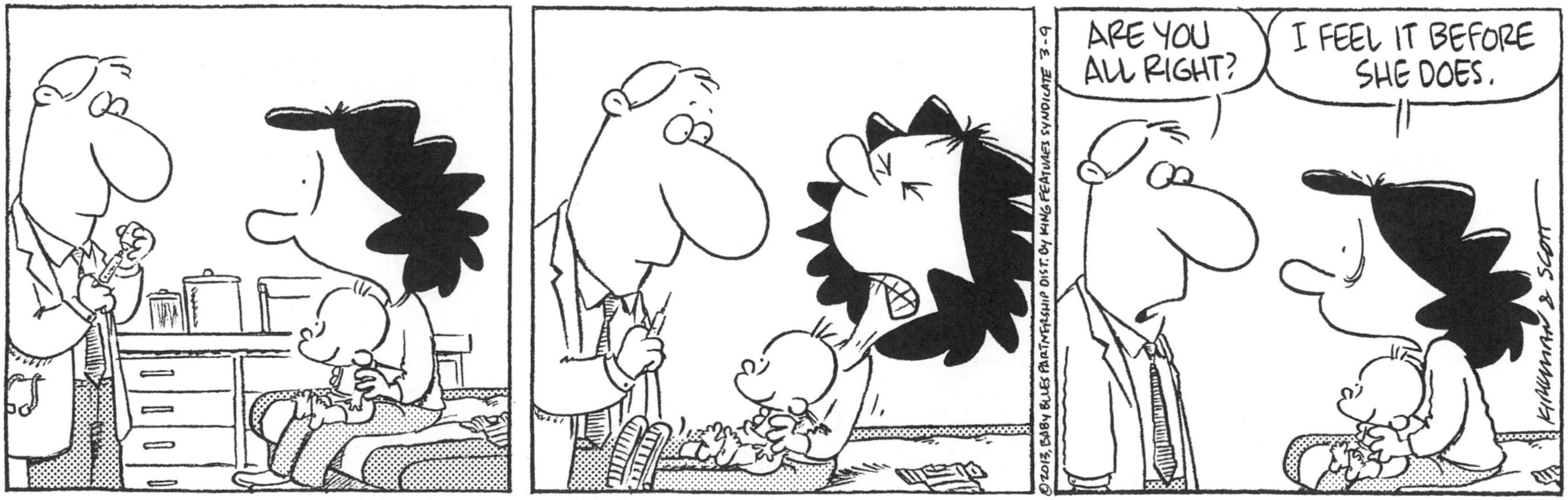
©2013, BABY BLUES PARTNERSHIP DIST. BY KING FEATURES SYNDICATE 3-9
ARE YOU ALL RIGHT?
I FEEL IT BEFORE SHE DOES.
KIRKMAN & SCOTT

Rick: I only have to turn to my wife for reference.

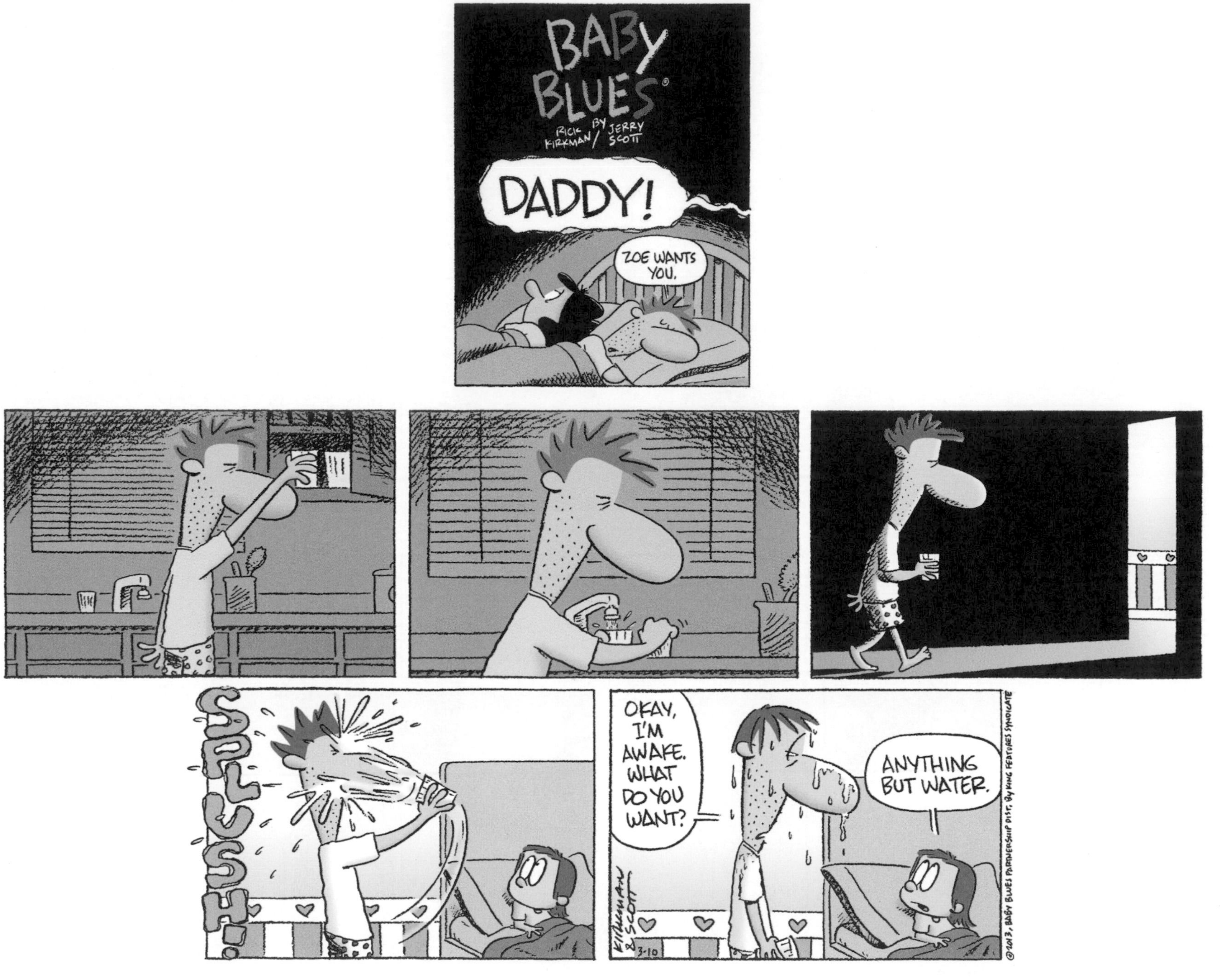
BABY BLUES®
BY RICK KIRKMAN / JERRY SCOTT
DADDY!
ZOE WANTS YOU.
SPLUSH!
OKAY, I'M AWAKE. WHAT DO YOU WANT?
ANYTHING BUT WATER.
©2013, BABY BLUES PARTNERSHIP DIST. BY KING FEATURES SYNDICATE

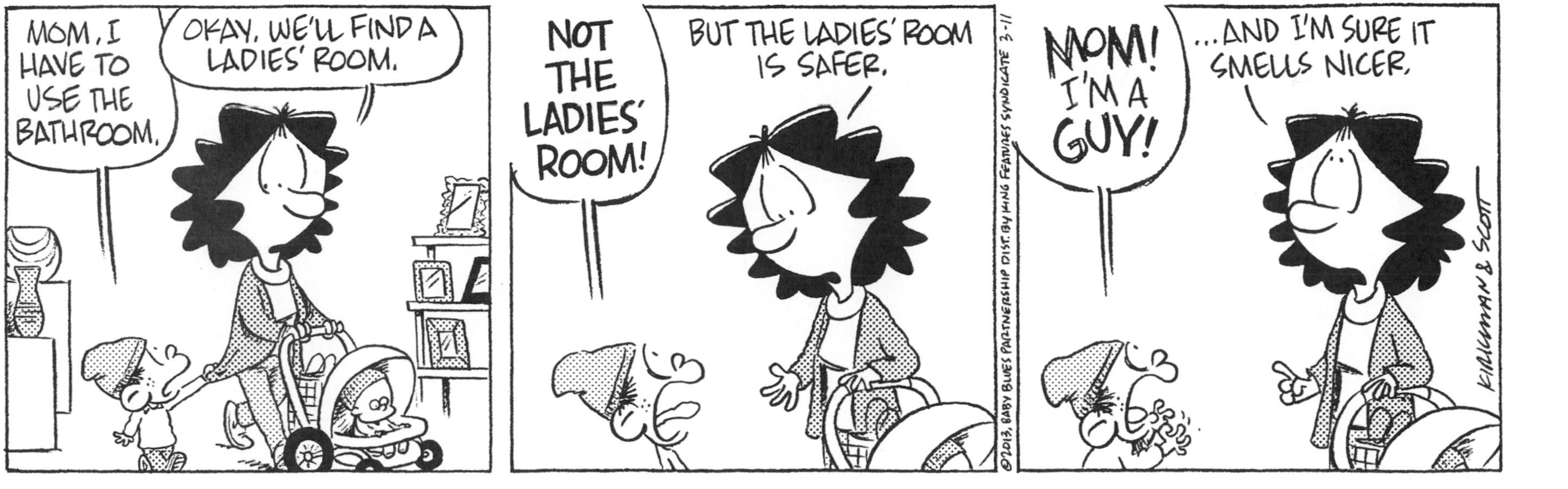
MOM, I HAVE TO USE THE BATHROOM.
OKAY. WE'LL FIND A LADIES' ROOM.
NOT THE LADIES' ROOM!
BUT THE LADIES' ROOM IS SAFER.
©2013, BABY BLUES PARTNERSHIP DIST. BY KING FEATURES SYNDICATE 3-11
MOM! I'M A GUY!
...AND I'M SURE IT SMELLS NICER.
KIRKMAN & SCOTT

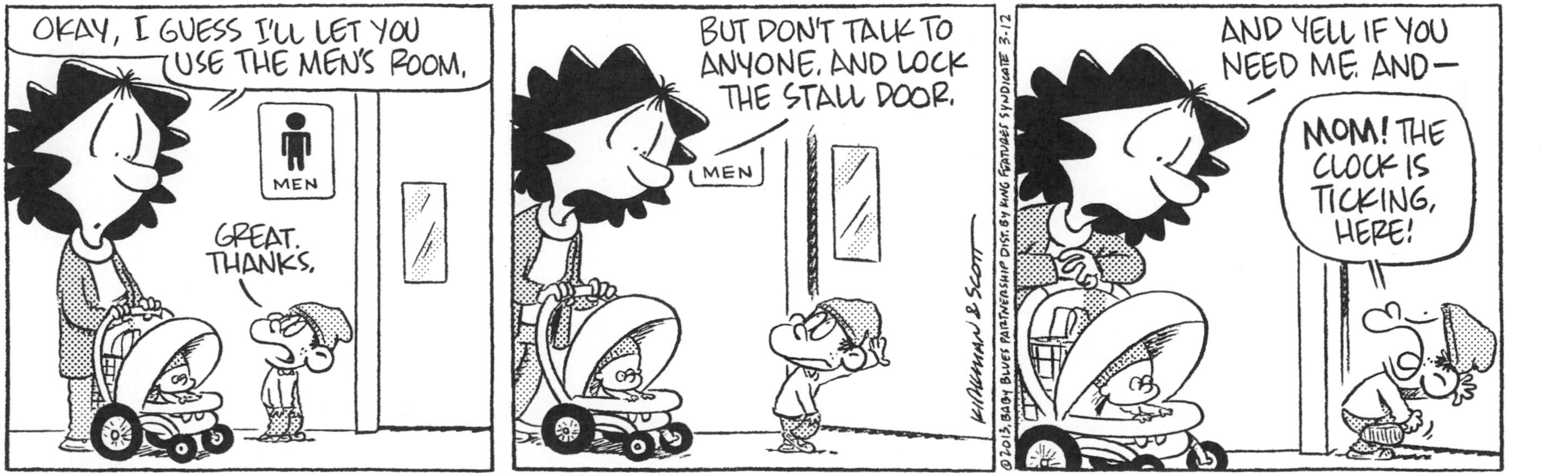
OKAY, I GUESS I'LL LET YOU USE THE MEN'S ROOM.
MEN
GREAT. THANKS.
BUT DON'T TALK TO ANYONE. AND LOCK THE STALL DOOR.
MEN
KIRKMAN & SCOTT
©2013, BABY BLUES PARTNERSHIP DIST. BY KING FEATURES SYNDICATE 3-12
AND YELL IF YOU NEED ME. AND—
MOM! THE CLOCK IS TICKING, HERE!

Jerry: Those first few times standing outside a public restroom waiting for your son can be nerve-racking for moms. But for us dads with daughters, there's the extra work of trying not to look like some kind of pervert while you hover around the ladies' room door.

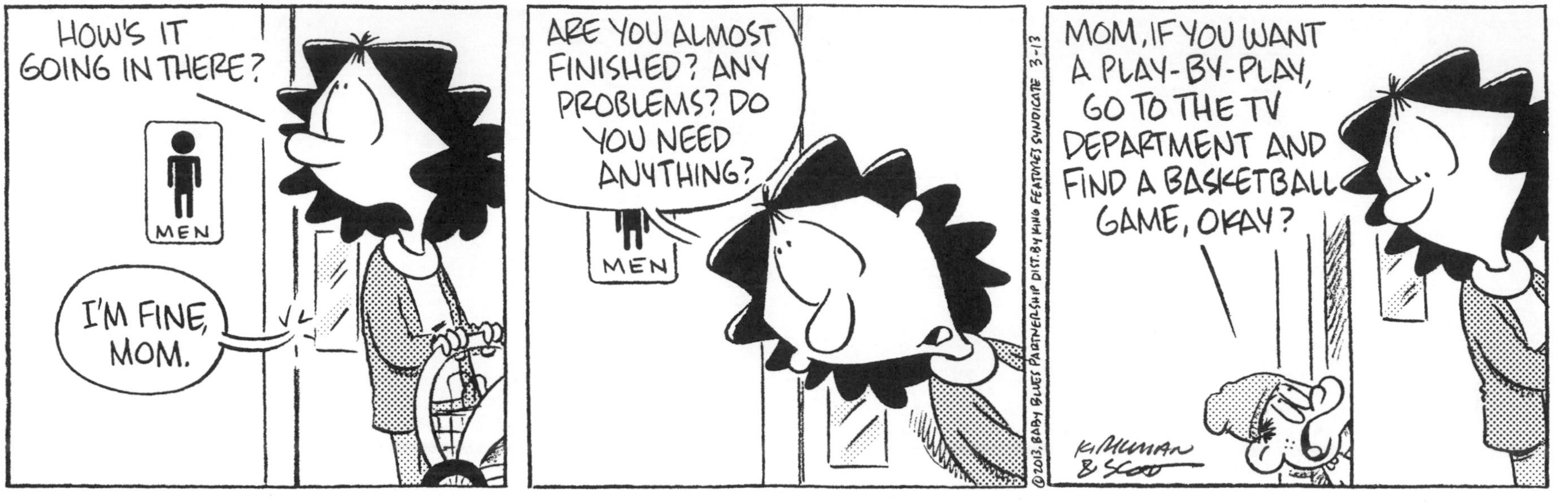
HOW'S IT GOING IN THERE?
I'M FINE, MOM.
ARE YOU ALMOST FINISHED? ANY PROBLEMS? DO YOU NEED ANYTHING?
MEN
MOM, IF YOU WANT A PLAY-BY-PLAY, GO TO THE TV DEPARTMENT AND FIND A BASKETBALL GAME, OKAY?
©2013, BABY BLUES PARTNERSHIP DIST. BY KING FEATURES SYNDICATE 3-13
KIRKMAN & SCOTT

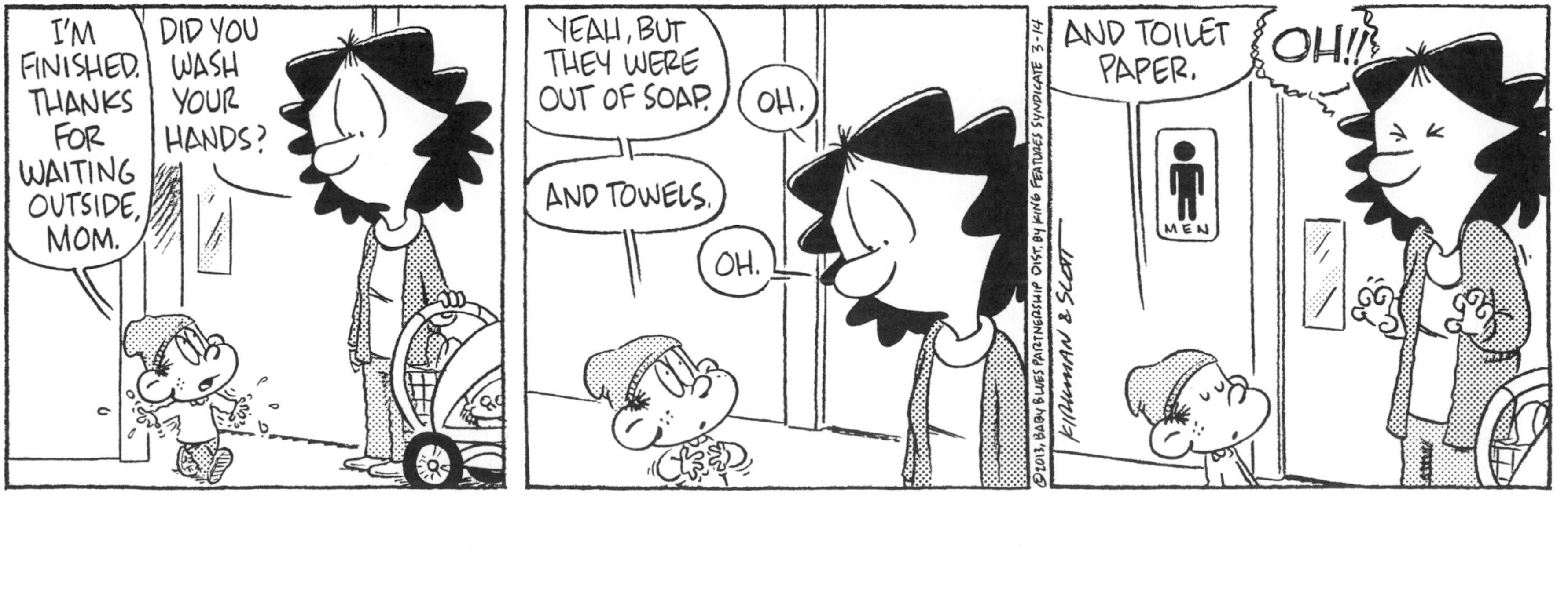
I'M FINISHED. THANKS FOR WAITING OUTSIDE, MOM.
DID YOU WASH YOUR HANDS?
YEAH, BUT THEY WERE OUT OF SOAP.
OH.
AND TOWELS.
OH.
AND TOILET PAPER.
OH!!
MEN
©2013, BABY BLUES PARTNERSHIP DIST. BY KING FEATURES SYNDICATE 3-14
KIRKMAN & SCOTT

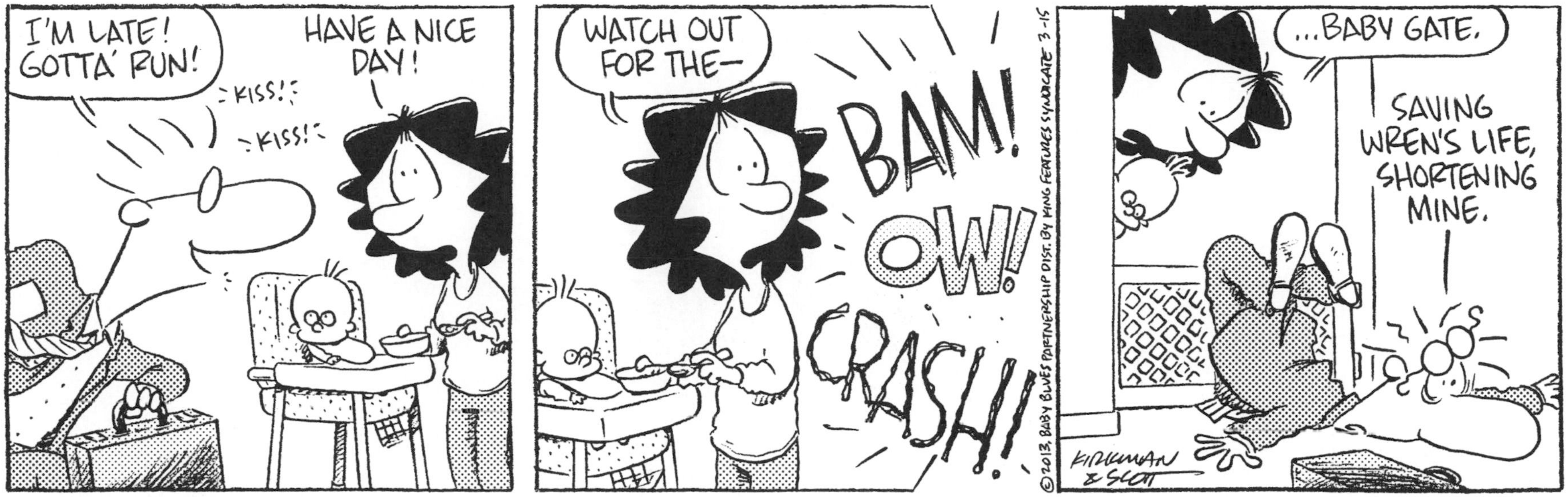
I'M LATE! GOTTA' RUN!
KISS!
KISS!
HAVE A NICE DAY!
WATCH OUT FOR THE—
BAM!
OW!
CRASH!!
©2013, BABY BLUES PARTNERSHIP DIST. BY KING FEATURES SYNDICATE 3-15
...BABY GATE.
SAVING WREN'S LIFE, SHORTENING MINE.
KIRKMAN & SCOTT

Rick: Hmm. Maybe this explains some of the aches and pains I have now.

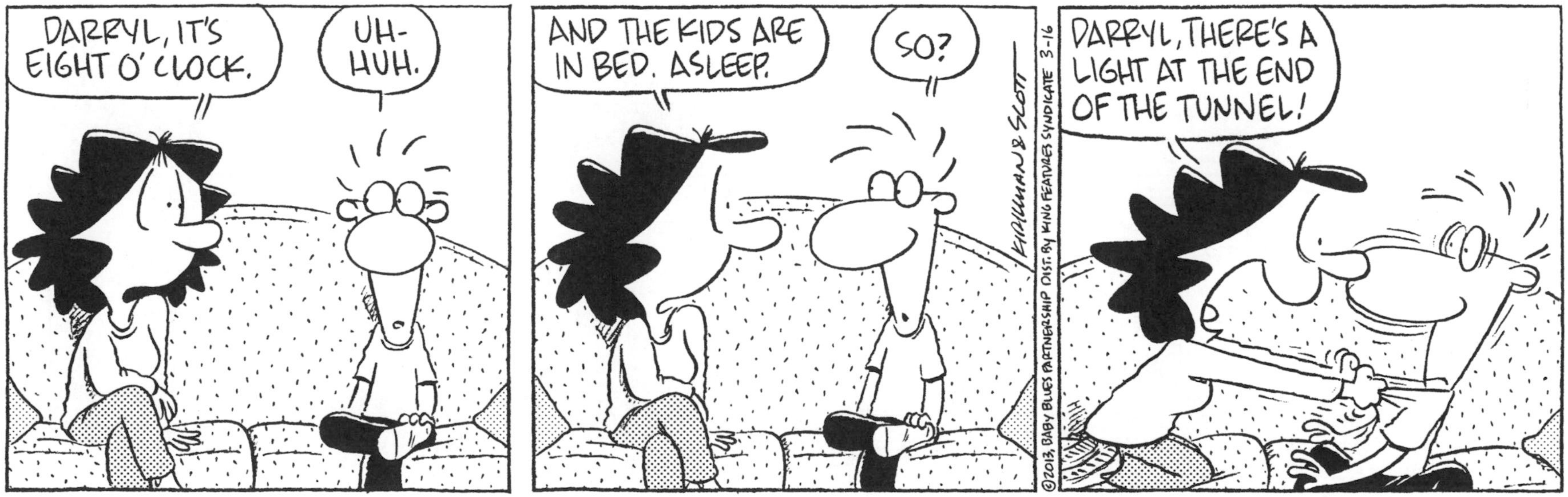
DARRYL, IT'S EIGHT O' CLOCK.
UH-HUH.
AND THE KIDS ARE IN BED. ASLEEP.
SO?
KIRKMAN & SCOTT
©2013, BABY BLUES PARTNERSHIP DIST. BY KING FEATURES SYNDICATE 3-16
DARRYL, THERE'S A LIGHT AT THE END OF THE TUNNEL!

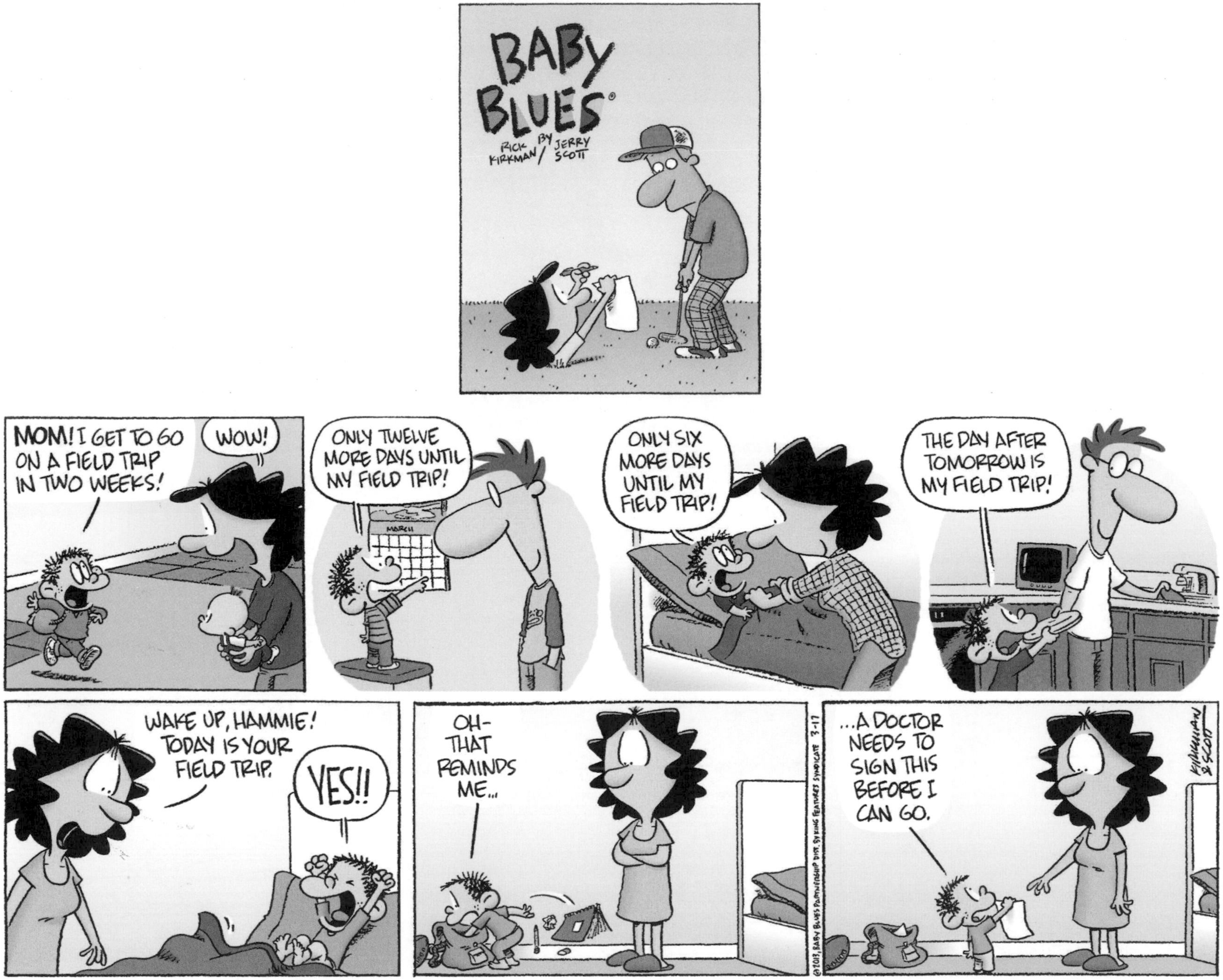
BABY BLUES®
RICK KIRKMAN / BY JERRY SCOTT
MOM! I GET TO GO ON A FIELD TRIP IN TWO WEEKS!
WOW!
ONLY TWELVE MORE DAYS UNTIL MY FIELD TRIP!
MARCH
ONLY SIX MORE DAYS UNTIL MY FIELD TRIP!
THE DAY AFTER TOMORROW IS MY FIELD TRIP!
WAKE UP, HAMMIE! TODAY IS YOUR FIELD TRIP.
YES!!
OH- THAT REMINDS ME...
...A DOCTOR NEEDS TO SIGN THIS BEFORE I CAN GO.
KIRKMAN & SCOTT

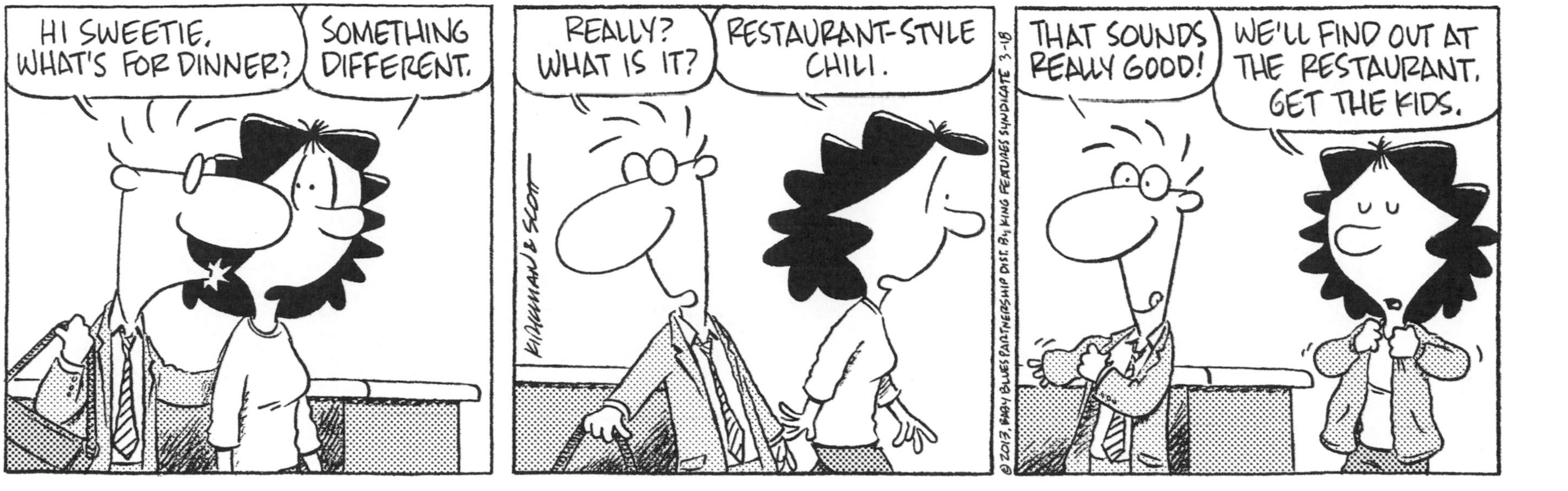
HI SWEETIE. WHAT'S FOR DINNER?
SOMETHING DIFFERENT.
REALLY? WHAT IS IT?
RESTAURANT-STYLE CHILI.
KIRKMAN & SCOTT
©2013, BABY BLUES PARTNERSHIP DIST. BY KING FEATURES SYNDICATE 3-18
THAT SOUNDS REALLY GOOD!
WE'LL FIND OUT AT THE RESTAURANT. GET THE KIDS.

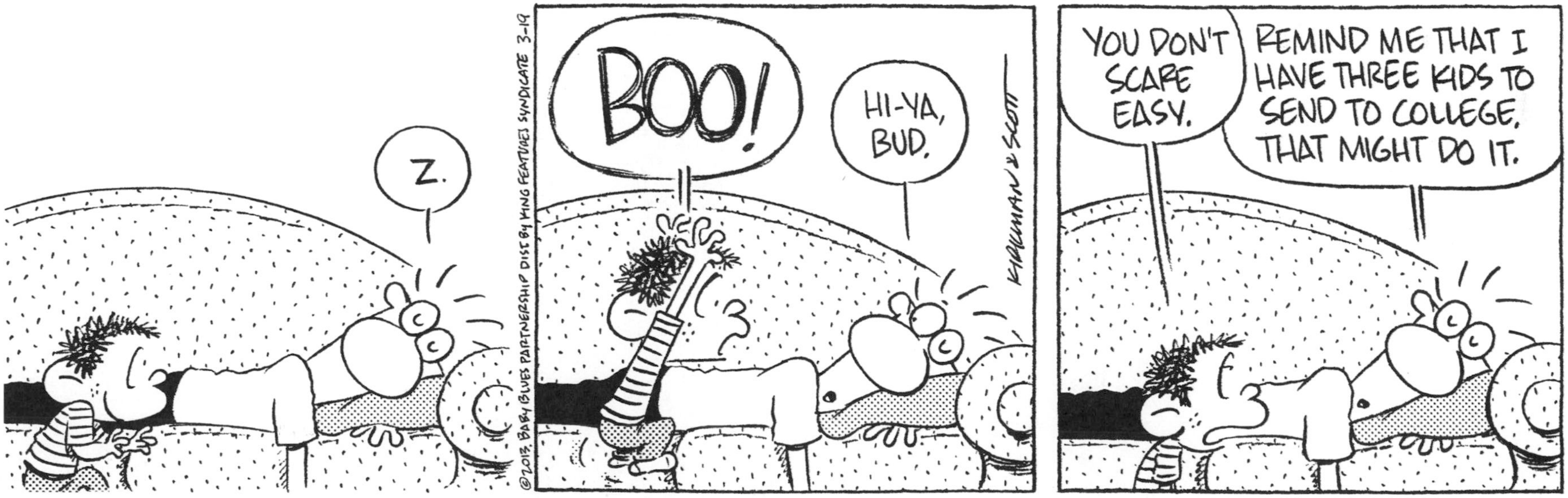
Z.
©2013, BABY BLUES PARTNERSHIP DIST BY KING FEATURES SYNDICATE 3-19
BOO!
HI-YA, BUD.
KIRKMAN & SCOTT
YOU DON'T SCARE EASY.
REMIND ME THAT I HAVE THREE KIDS TO SEND TO COLLEGE. THAT MIGHT DO IT.

Jerry: "Night of the Out-of-State Tuition." Now THAT would be a horror movie.

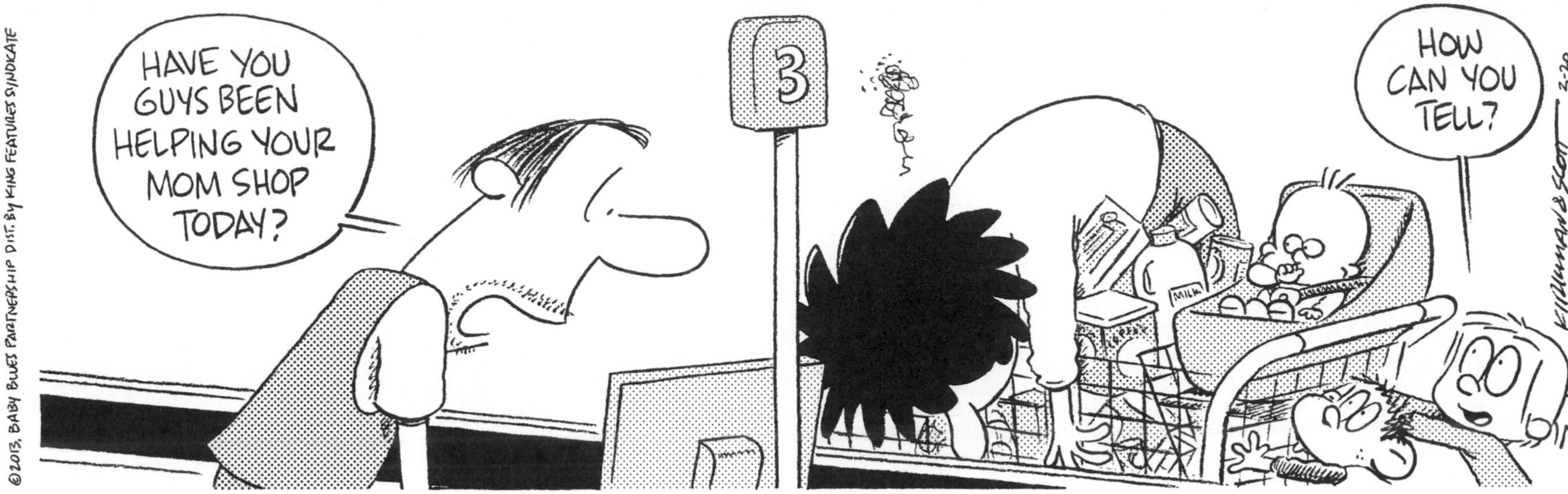
HAVE YOU GUYS BEEN HELPING YOUR MOM SHOP TODAY?
3
MILK
HOW CAN YOU TELL?
KIRKMAN & SCOTT
3-20
©2013, BABY BLUES PARTNERSHIP DIST. BY KING FEATURES SYNDICATE

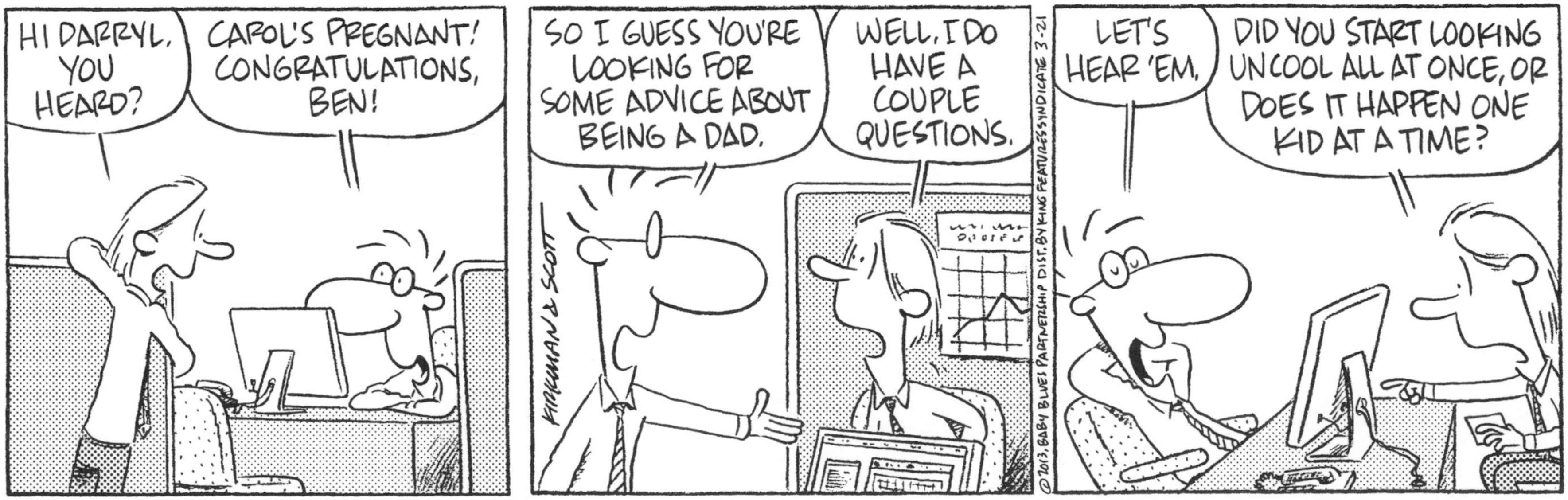
HI DARRYL. YOU HEARD?
CAROL'S PREGNANT! CONGRATULATIONS, BEN!
SO I GUESS YOU'RE LOOKING FOR SOME ADVICE ABOUT BEING A DAD.
WELL, I DO HAVE A COUPLE QUESTIONS.
LET'S HEAR 'EM.
DID YOU START LOOKING UNCOOL ALL AT ONCE, OR DOES IT HAPPEN ONE KID AT A TIME?
KIRKMAN & SCOTT
©2013, BABY BLUES PARTNERSHIP DIST. BY KING FEATURES SYNDICATE 3-21

Jerry: I've been known to give advice to new fathers. Many of them have forgiven me.

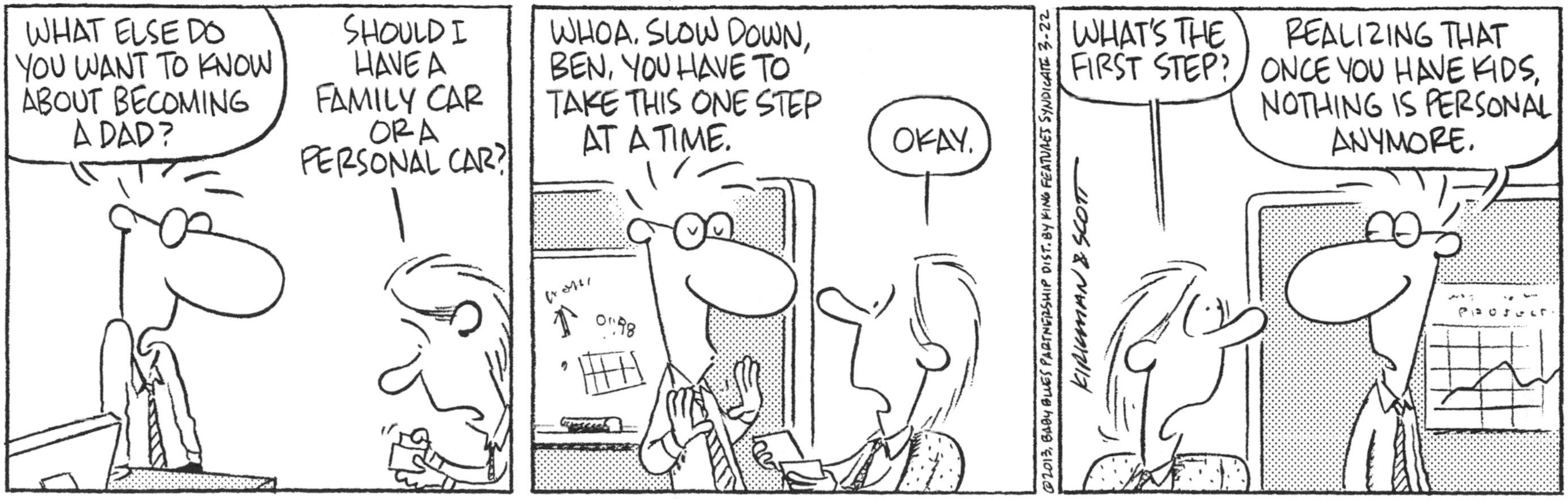
WHAT ELSE DO YOU WANT TO KNOW ABOUT BECOMING A DAD?
SHOULD I HAVE A FAMILY CAR OR A PERSONAL CAR?
WHOA. SLOW DOWN, BEN. YOU HAVE TO TAKE THIS ONE STEP AT A TIME.
OKAY.
©2013, BABY BLUES PARTNERSHIP DIST. BY KING FEATURES SYNDICATE 3-22
KIRKMAN & SCOTT
WHAT'S THE FIRST STEP?
REALIZING THAT ONCE YOU HAVE KIDS, NOTHING IS PERSONAL ANYMORE.

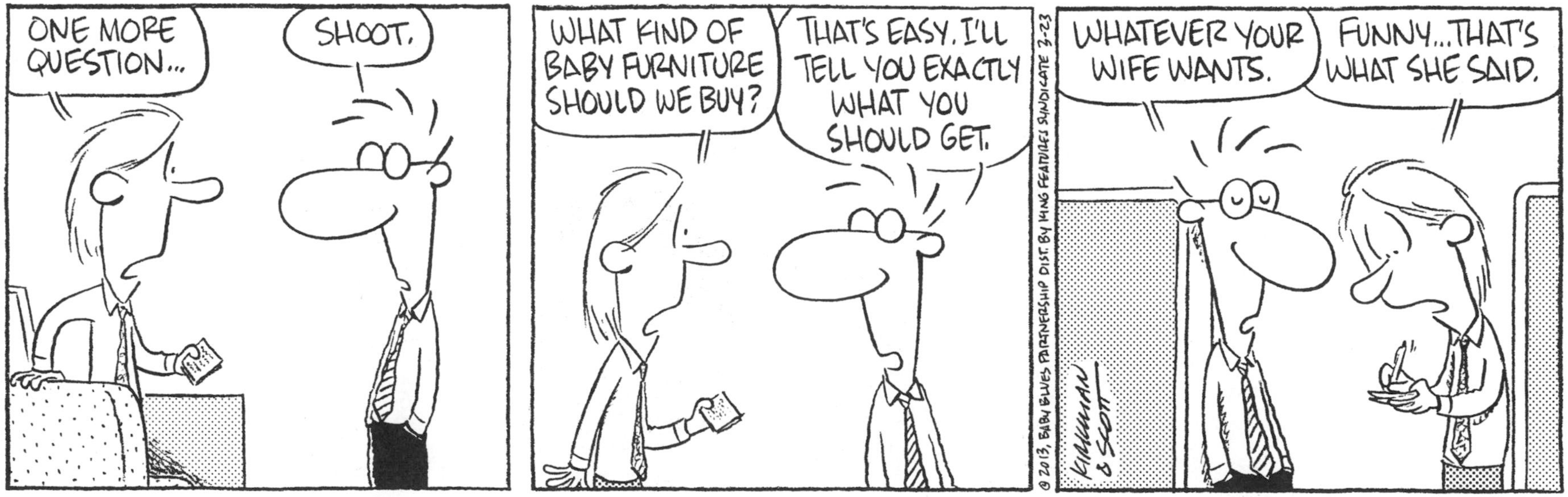
ONE MORE QUESTION...
SHOOT.
WHAT KIND OF BABY FURNITURE SHOULD WE BUY?
THAT'S EASY. I'LL TELL YOU EXACTLY WHAT YOU SHOULD GET.
©2013, BABY BLUES PARTNERSHIP DIST BY KING FEATURES SYNDICATE 3-23
KIRKMAN & SCOTT
WHATEVER YOUR WIFE WANTS.
FUNNY...THAT'S WHAT SHE SAID.

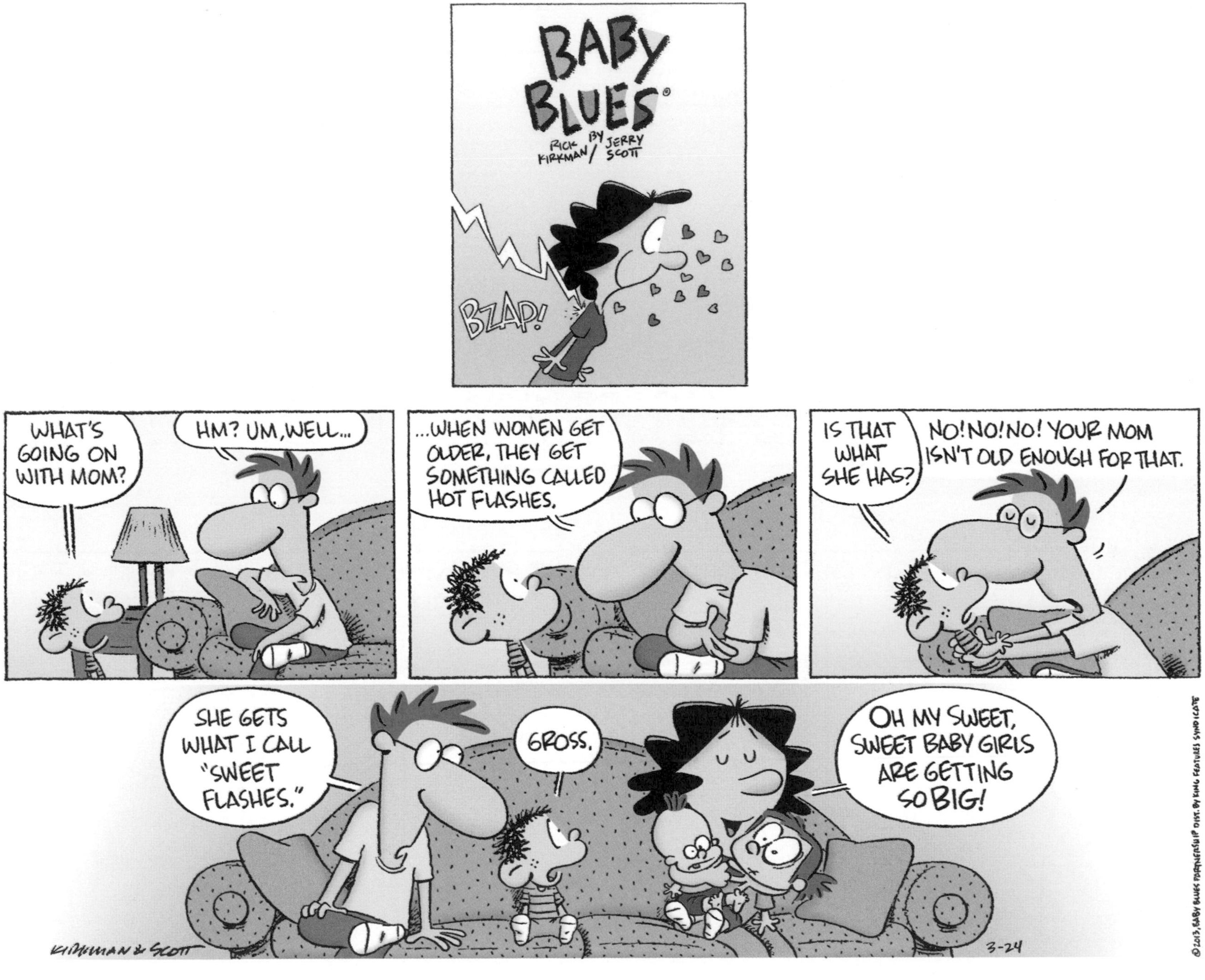
BABY BLUES®
RICK KIRKMAN / BY / JERRY SCOTT
BZAP!
WHAT'S GOING ON WITH MOM?
HM? UM, WELL...
...WHEN WOMEN GET OLDER, THEY GET SOMETHING CALLED HOT FLASHES.
IS THAT WHAT SHE HAS?
NO! NO! NO! YOUR MOM ISN'T OLD ENOUGH FOR THAT.
SHE GETS WHAT I CALL "SWEET FLASHES."
GROSS.
OH MY SWEET, SWEET BABY GIRLS ARE GETTING SO BIG!
KIRKMAN & SCOTT
3-24
©2013, BABY BLUES PARTNERSHIP DIST. BY KING FEATURES SYNDICATE

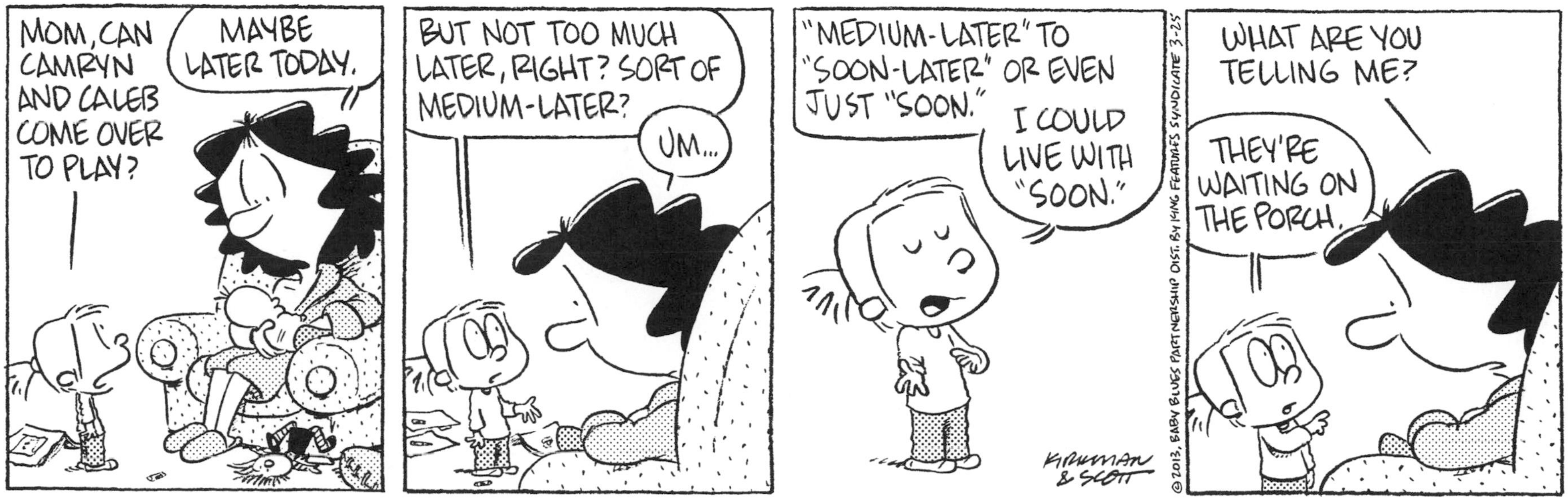
MOM, CAN CAMRYN AND CALEB COME OVER TO PLAY?
MAYBE LATER TODAY.
BUT NOT TOO MUCH LATER, RIGHT? SORT OF MEDIUM-LATER?
UM...
"MEDIUM-LATER" TO "SOON-LATER" OR EVEN JUST "SOON."
I COULD LIVE WITH "SOON."
KIRKMAN & SCOTT
© 2013, BABY BLUES PARTNERSHIP DIST. BY KING FEATURES SYNDICATE 3-25
WHAT ARE YOU TELLING ME?
THEY'RE WAITING ON THE PORCH.

Rick: Here we had auctioned off putting your kids' names in the strip to benefit the Wyakin Warrior Foundation to help injured vets find a new career path.

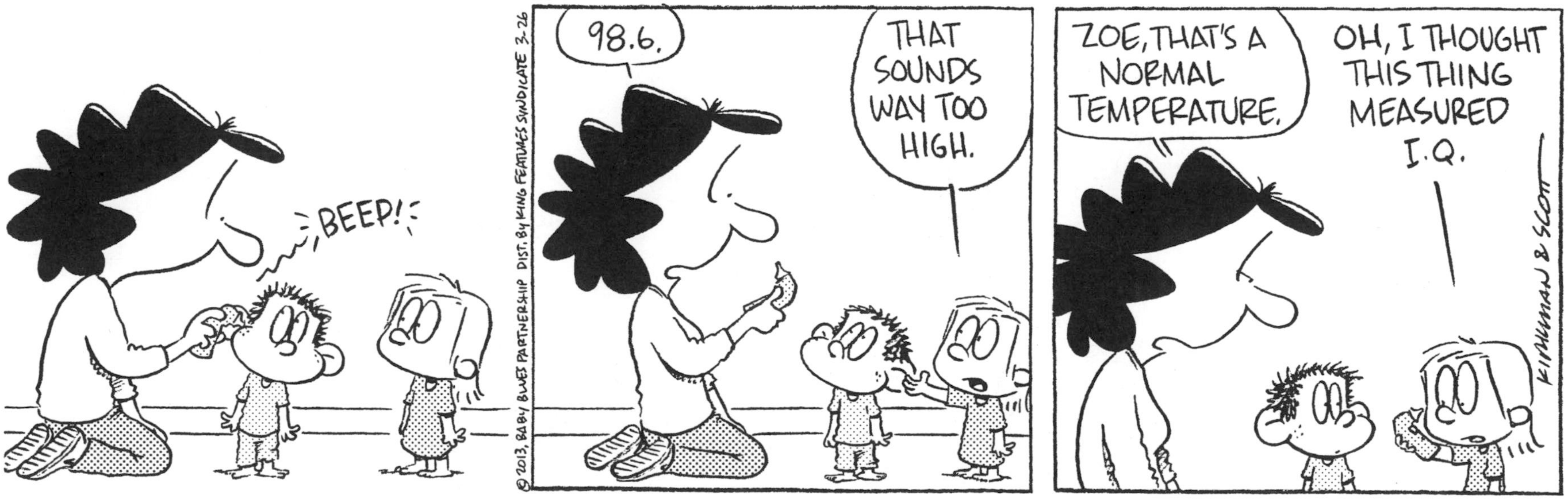
BEEP!
© 2013, BABY BLUES PARTNERSHIP DIST. BY KING FEATURES SYNDICATE 3-26
98.6.
THAT SOUNDS WAY TOO HIGH.
ZOE, THAT'S A NORMAL TEMPERATURE.
OH, I THOUGHT THIS THING MEASURED I.Q.
KIRKMAN & SCOTT

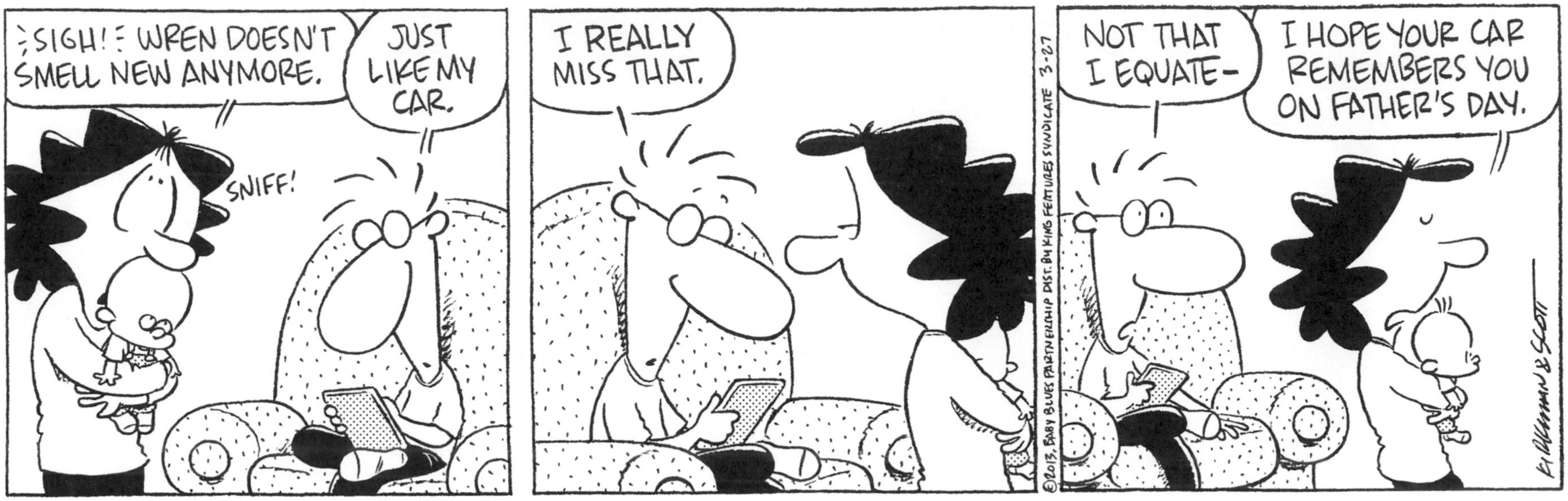
;SIGH!; WREN DOESN'T SMELL NEW ANYMORE.
SNIFF!
JUST LIKE MY CAR.
I REALLY MISS THAT.
NOT THAT I EQUATE-
I HOPE YOUR CAR REMEMBERS YOU ON FATHER'S DAY.
©2013, BABY BLUES PARTNERSHIP DIST. BY KING FEATURES SYNDICATE 3-27
KIRKMAN & SCOTT

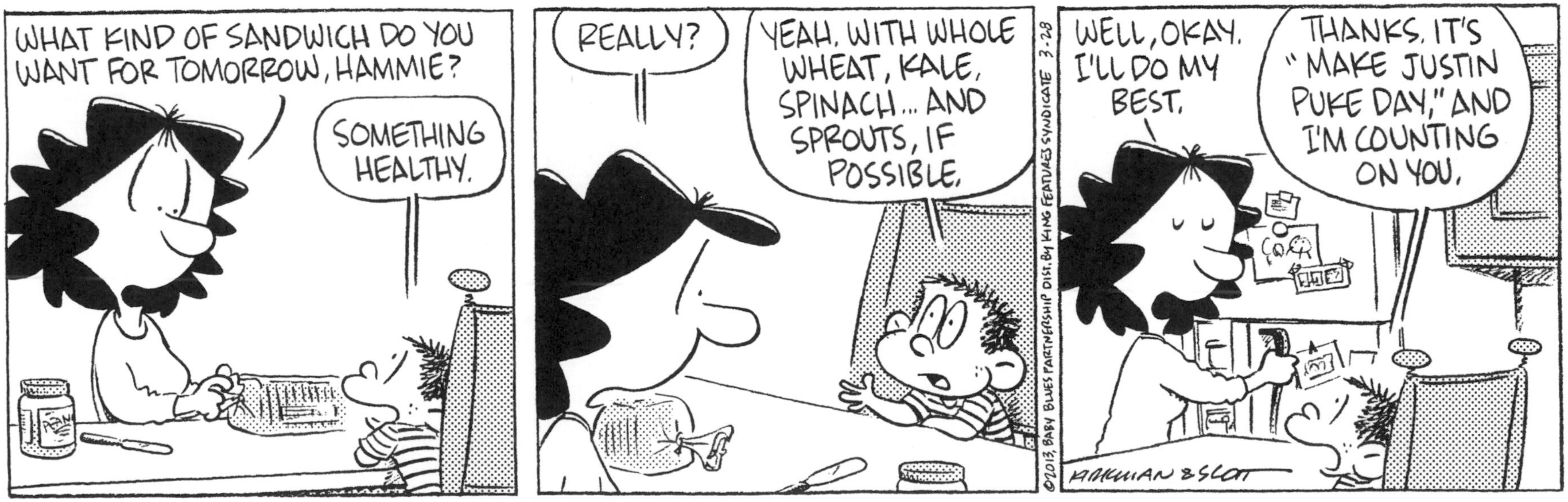
WHAT KIND OF SANDWICH DO YOU WANT FOR TOMORROW, HAMMIE?
SOMETHING HEALTHY.
REALLY?
YEAH, WITH WHOLE WHEAT, KALE, SPINACH... AND SPROUTS, IF POSSIBLE.
WELL, OKAY. I'LL DO MY BEST.
THANKS. IT'S "MAKE JUSTIN PUKE DAY," AND I'M COUNTING ON YOU.
©2013, BABY BLUES PARTNERSHIP DIST. BY KING FEATURES SYNDICATE 3-28
KIRKMAN & SCOTT

Jerry: Some vegetarian readers were less amused with us than usual the day this ran.

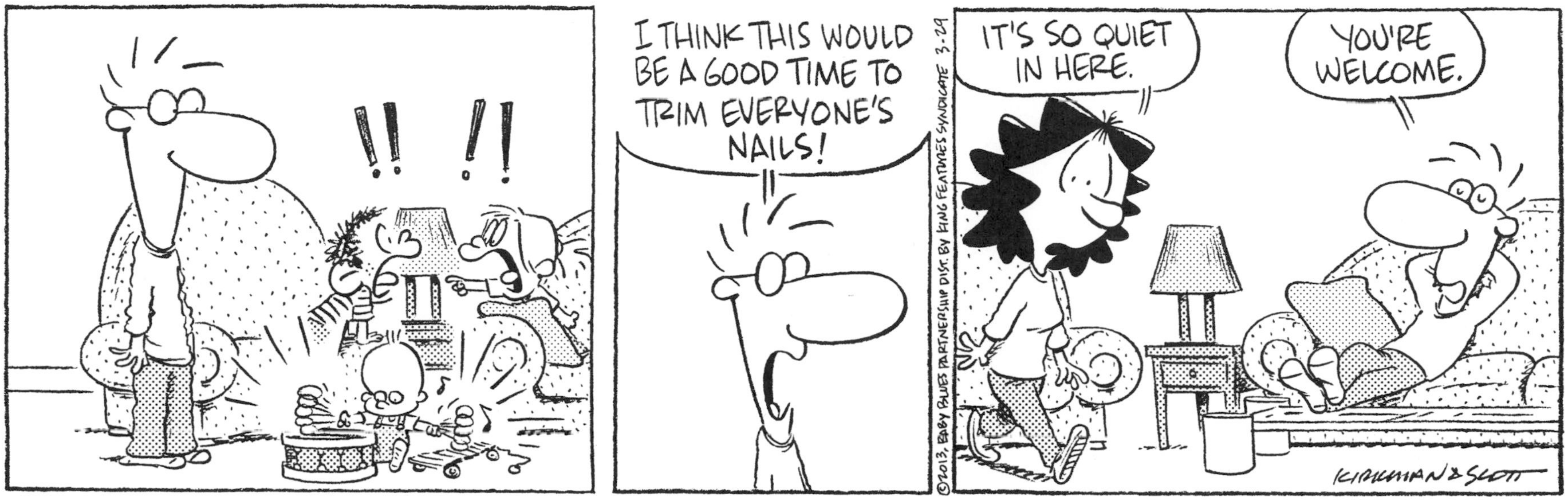
!! !!
I THINK THIS WOULD BE A GOOD TIME TO TRIM EVERYONE'S NAILS!
©2013, BABY BLUES PARTNERSHIP DIST. BY KING FEATURES SYNDICATE 3-29
IT'S SO QUIET IN HERE.
YOU'RE WELCOME.
KIRKMAN & SCOTT

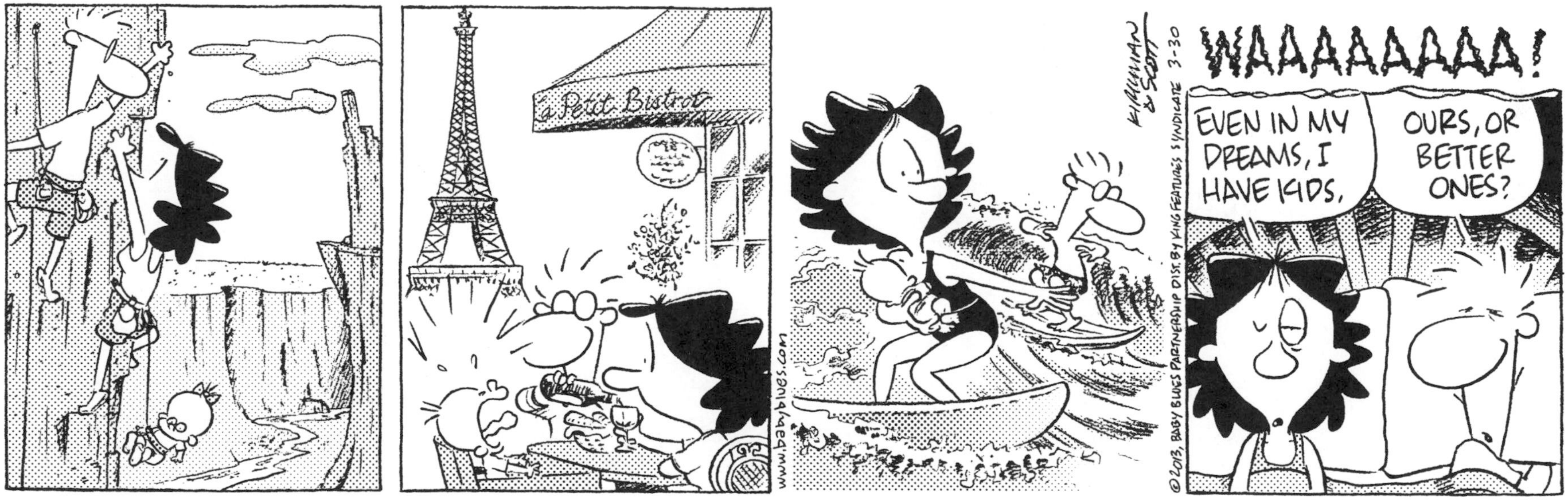
www.babyblues.com
KIRKMAN & SCOTT
©2013, BABY BLUES PARTNERSHIP DIST. BY KING FEATURES SYNDICATE 3-30
WAAAAAAA!
EVEN IN MY DREAMS, I HAVE KIDS.
OURS, OR BETTER ONES?

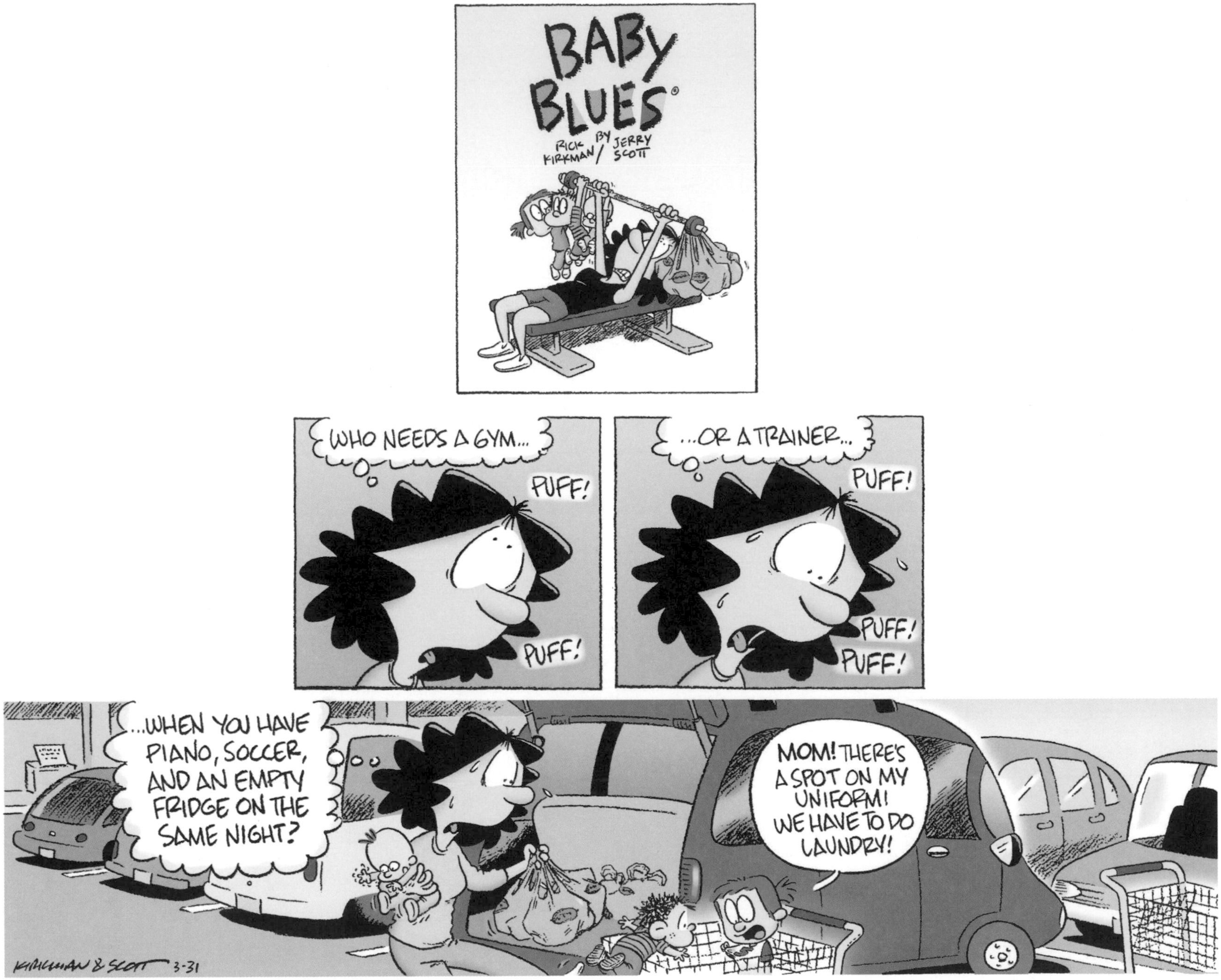
BABY BLUES®
BY RICK KIRKMAN / JERRY SCOTT
WHO NEEDS A GYM...
PUFF!
PUFF!
...OR A TRAINER...
PUFF!
PUFF!
PUFF!
...WHEN YOU HAVE PIANO, SOCCER, AND AN EMPTY FRIDGE ON THE SAME NIGHT?
MOM! THERE'S A SPOT ON MY UNIFORM! WE HAVE TO DO LAUNDRY!
KIRKMAN & SCOTT 3-31

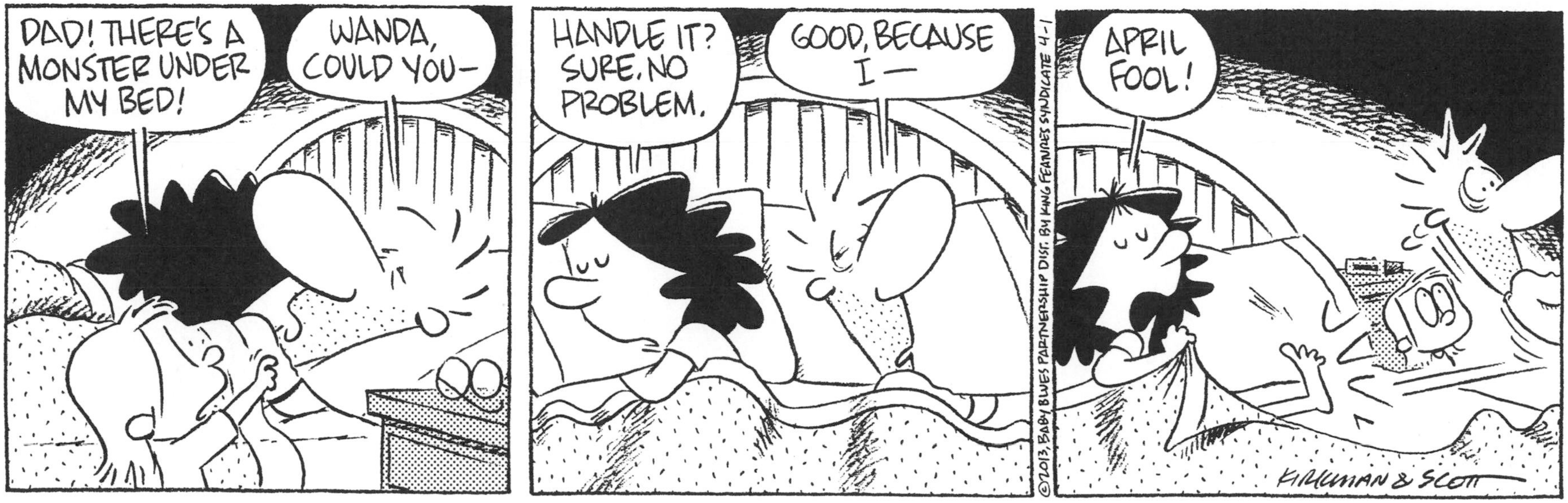
DAD! THERE'S A MONSTER UNDER MY BED!
WANDA, COULD YOU—
HANDLE IT? SURE. NO PROBLEM.
GOOD, BECAUSE I—
©2013, BABY BLUES PARTNERSHIP DIST. BY KING FEATURES SYNDICATE 4-1
APRIL FOOL!
KIRKMAN & SCOTT

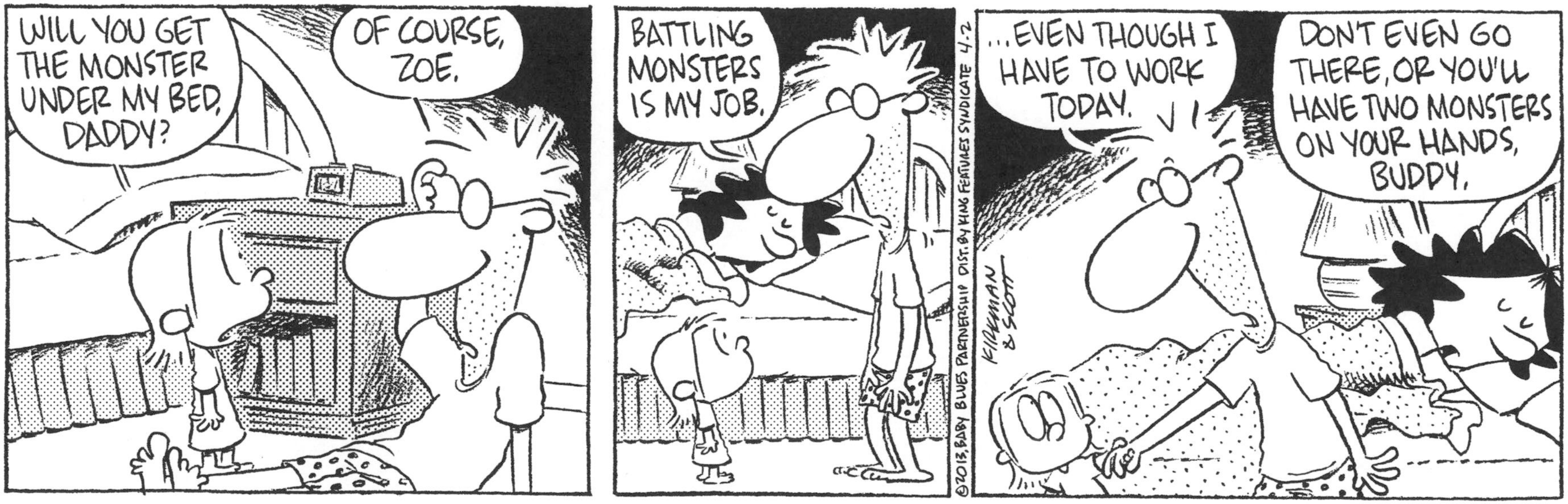
WILL YOU GET THE MONSTER UNDER MY BED, DADDY?
OF COURSE, ZOE.
BATTLING MONSTERS IS MY JOB.
©2013, BABY BLUES PARTNERSHIP DIST. BY KING FEATURES SYNDICATE 4-2
KIRKMAN & SCOTT
...EVEN THOUGH I HAVE TO WORK TODAY.
DON'T EVEN GO THERE, OR YOU'LL HAVE TWO MONSTERS ON YOUR HANDS, BUDDY.

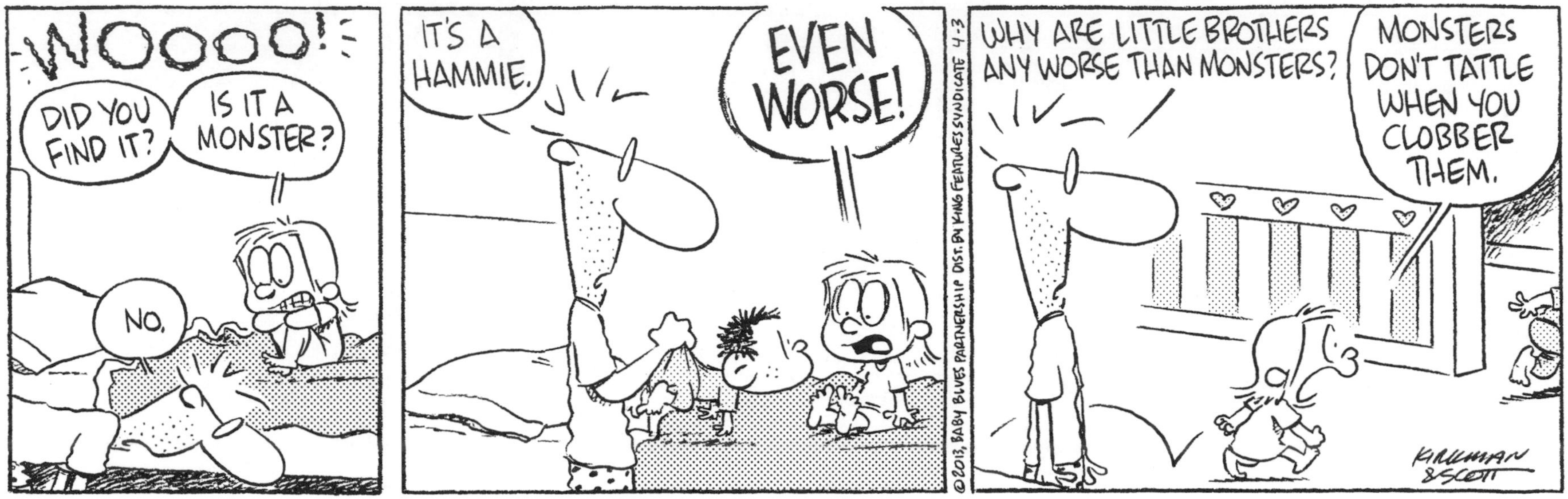
WOOOO!
DID YOU FIND IT?
IS IT A MONSTER?
NO.
IT'S A HAMMIE.
EVEN WORSE!
©2013, BABY BLUES PARTNERSHIP DIST. BY KING FEATURES SYNDICATE 4-3
WHY ARE LITTLE BROTHERS ANY WORSE THAN MONSTERS?
MONSTERS DON'T TATTLE WHEN YOU CLOBBER THEM.
KIRKMAN & SCOTT

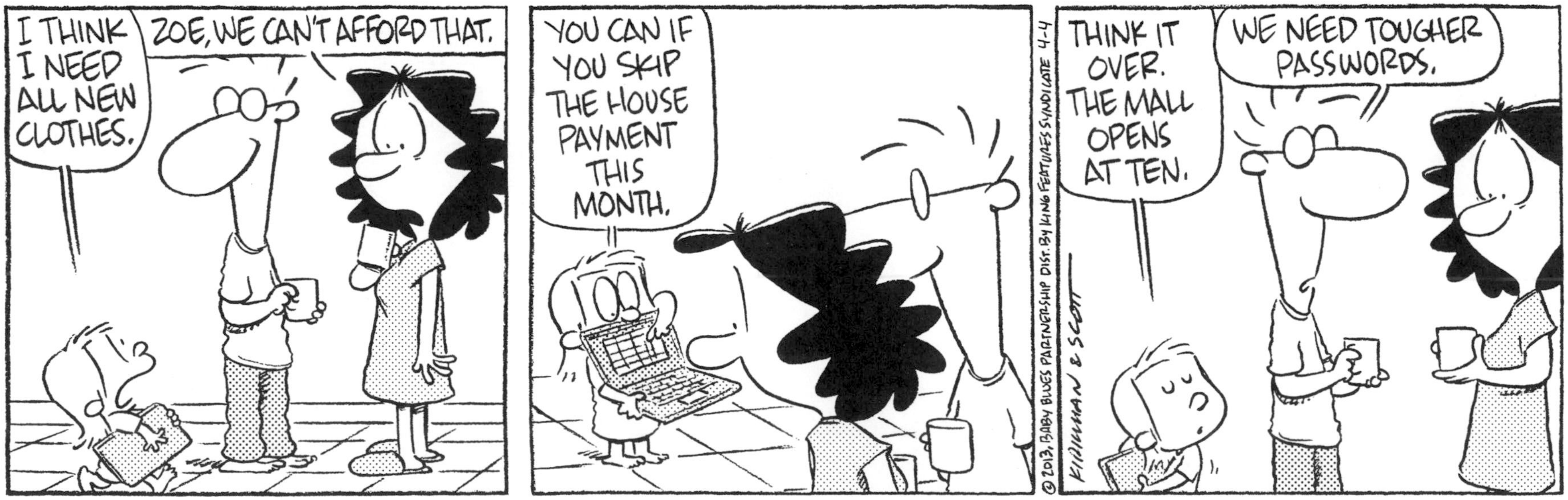
I THINK I NEED ALL NEW CLOTHES.
ZOE, WE CAN'T AFFORD THAT.
YOU CAN IF YOU SKIP THE HOUSE PAYMENT THIS MONTH.
©2013, BABY BLUES PARTNERSHIP DIST. BY KING FEATURES SYNDICATE 4-4
KIRKMAN & SCOTT
THINK IT OVER. THE MALL OPENS AT TEN.
WE NEED TOUGHER PASSWORDS.

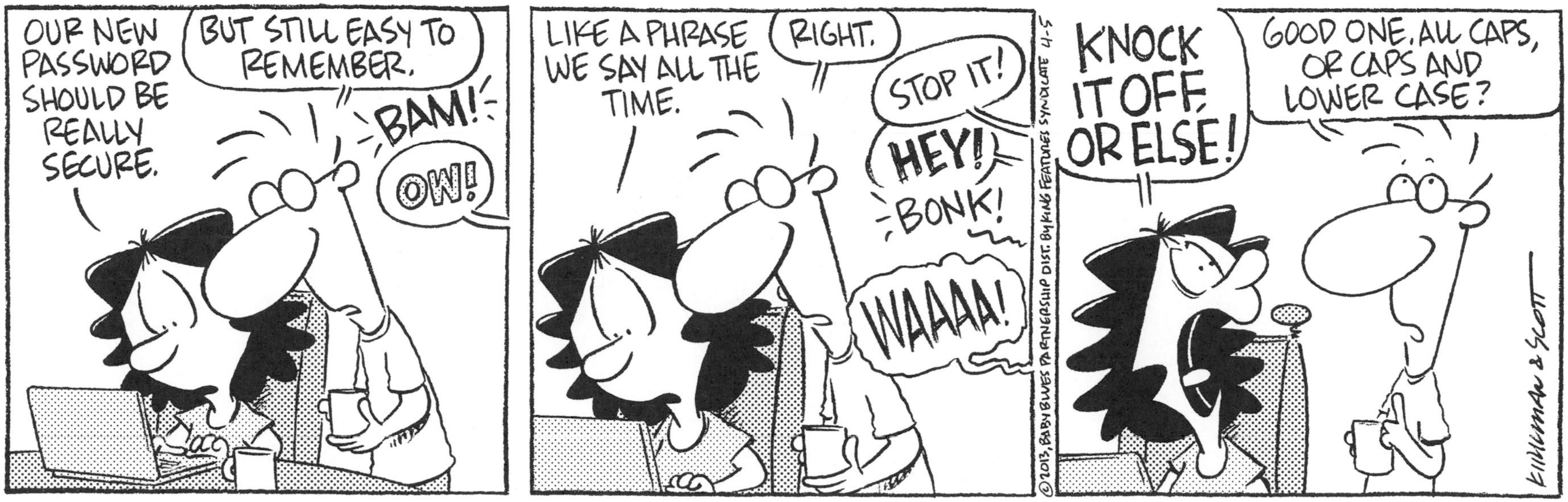
OUR NEW PASSWORD SHOULD BE REALLY SECURE.
BUT STILL EASY TO REMEMBER.
BAM!
OW!
LIKE A PHRASE WE SAY ALL THE TIME.
RIGHT.
STOP IT!
HEY!
BONK!
WAAAA!
KNOCK IT OFF, OR ELSE!
GOOD ONE. ALL CAPS, OR CAPS AND LOWER CASE?
© 2013, BABY BLUES PARTNERSHIP DIST. BY KING FEATURES SYNDICATE 4-5
KIRKMAN & SCOTT

Jerry: If this is anyone's real password, I apologize for ruining it for you.

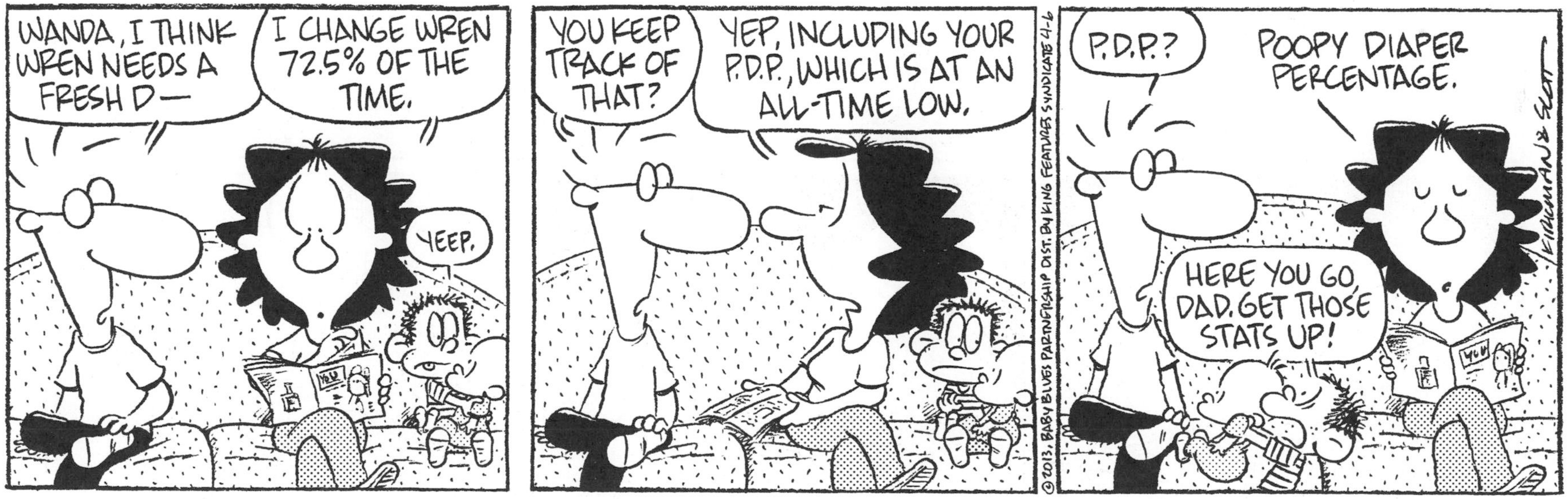
WANDA, I THINK WREN NEEDS A FRESH D—
I CHANGE WREN 72.5% OF THE TIME.
YEEP.
YOU KEEP TRACK OF THAT?
YEP, INCLUDING YOUR P.D.P., WHICH IS AT AN ALL-TIME LOW.
P.D.P.?
POOPY DIAPER PERCENTAGE.
HERE YOU GO, DAD. GET THOSE STATS UP!
© 2013, BABY BLUES PARTNERSHIP DIST. BY KING FEATURES SYNDICATE 4-6
KIRKMAN & SCOTT

BABY BLUES®
BY RICK KIRKMAN / JERRY SCOTT
BZZZ BZZZ
?
BZZZ BZZZ
THAT'S MY CELL PHONE!
BZZZ BZZZ
HEY!
OOPS!
BZZZ BZZZ
OW!
FUMP!
DAD, ARE WE OUT OF CEREAL?
HELLO? HELLO?
KIRKMAN & SCOTT
4-7
© 2013, BABY BLUES PARTNERSHIP DIST. BY KING FEATURES SYNDICATE
BOY! HE SURE WOKE UP CRANKY!
#@
BETTER CALL MOM TO WARN HER.

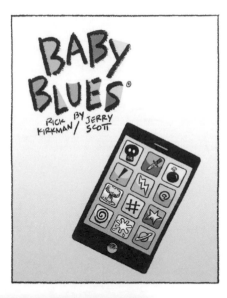

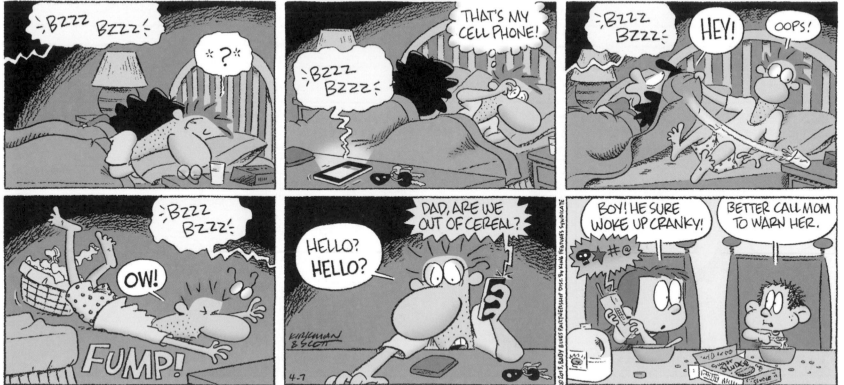

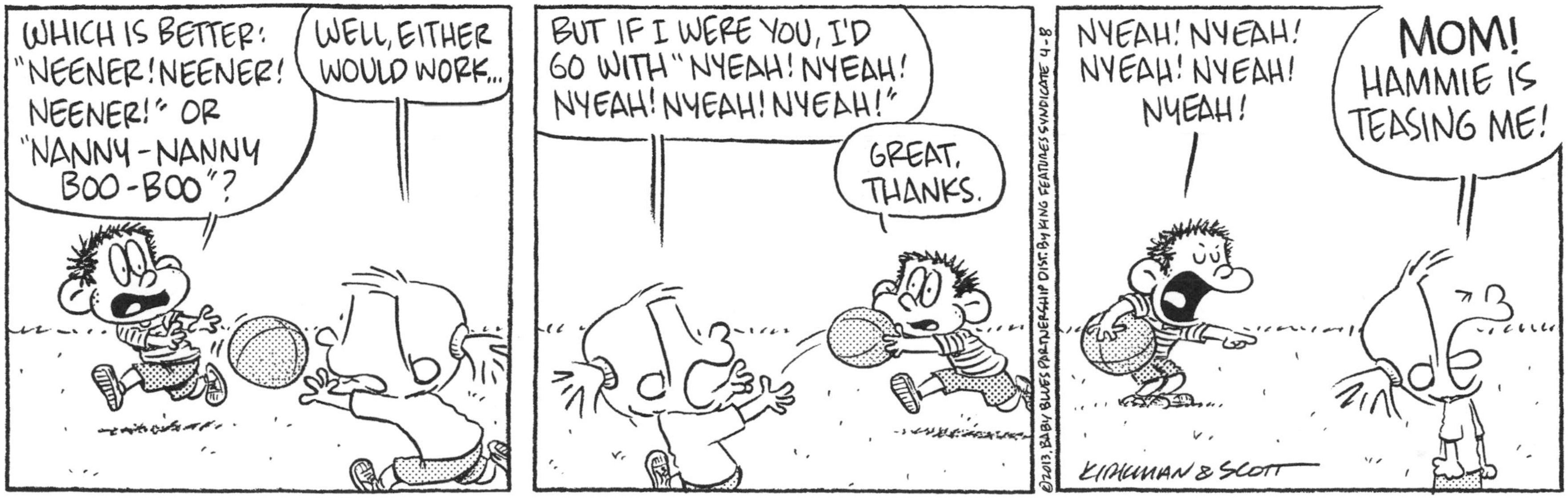
WHICH IS BETTER: "NEENER! NEENER! NEENER!" OR "NANNY-NANNY BOO-BOO"?
WELL, EITHER WOULD WORK...
BUT IF I WERE YOU, I'D GO WITH "NYEAH! NYEAH! NYEAH! NYEAH! NYEAH!"
GREAT. THANKS.
NYEAH! NYEAH! NYEAH! NYEAH! NYEAH!
MOM! HAMMIE IS TEASING ME!
©2013, BABY BLUES PARTNERSHIP DIST. BY KING FEATURES SYNDICATE 4-8
KIRKMAN & SCOTT

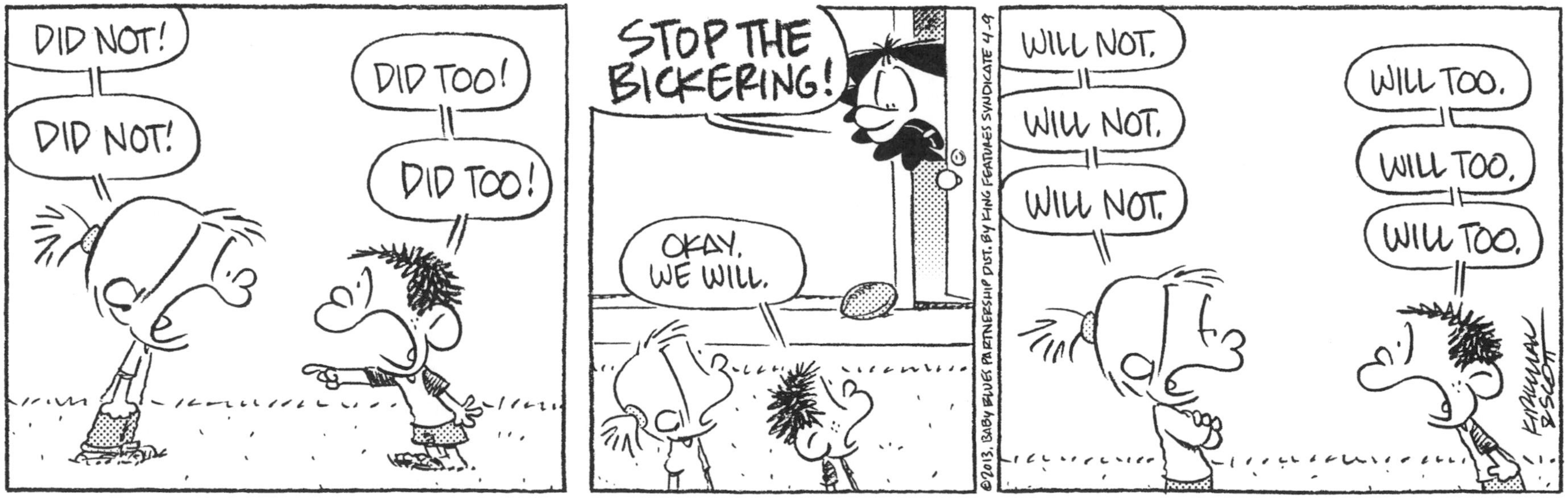
DID NOT!
DID NOT!
DID TOO!
DID TOO!
STOP THE BICKERING!
OKAY. WE WILL.
WILL NOT.
WILL NOT.
WILL NOT.
WILL TOO.
WILL TOO.
WILL TOO.
©2013, BABY BLUES PARTNERSHIP DIST. BY KING FEATURES SYNDICATE 4-9
KIRKMAN & SCOTT

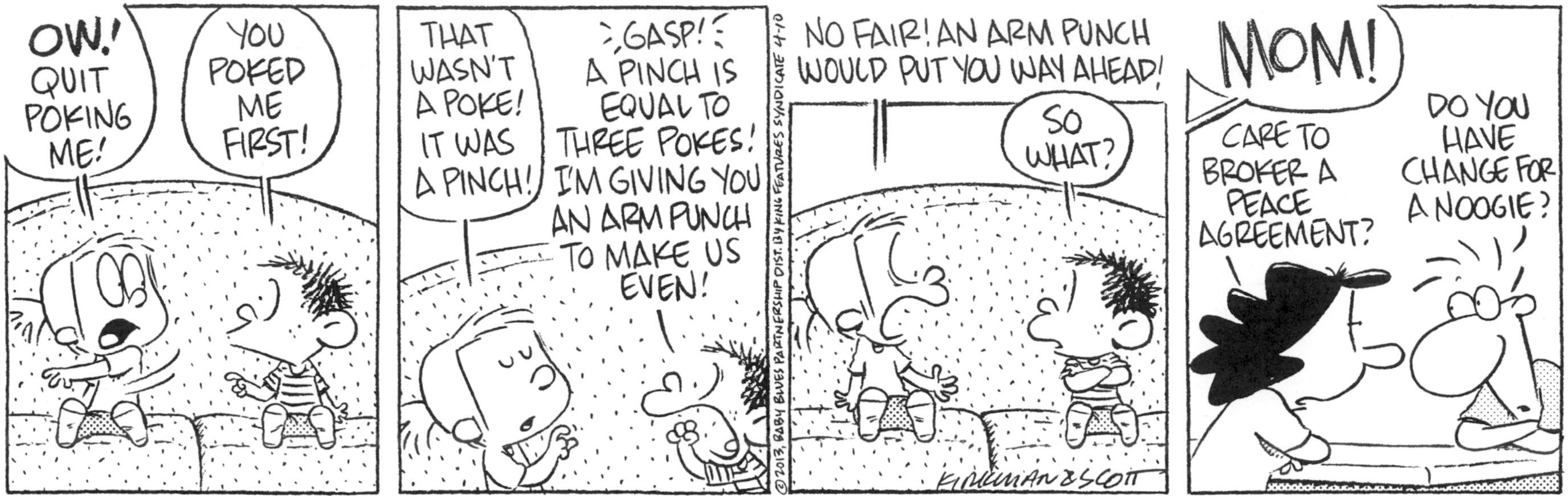
OW! QUIT POKING ME!
YOU POKED ME FIRST!
THAT WASN'T A POKE! IT WAS A PINCH!
GASP! A PINCH IS EQUAL TO THREE POKES! I'M GIVING YOU AN ARM PUNCH TO MAKE US EVEN!
©2013, BABY BLUES PARTNERSHIP DIST. BY KING FEATURES SYNDICATE 4-10
NO FAIR! AN ARM PUNCH WOULD PUT YOU WAY AHEAD!
SO WHAT?
KIRKMAN & SCOTT
MOM!
CARE TO BROKER A PEACE AGREEMENT?
DO YOU HAVE CHANGE FOR A NOOGIE?

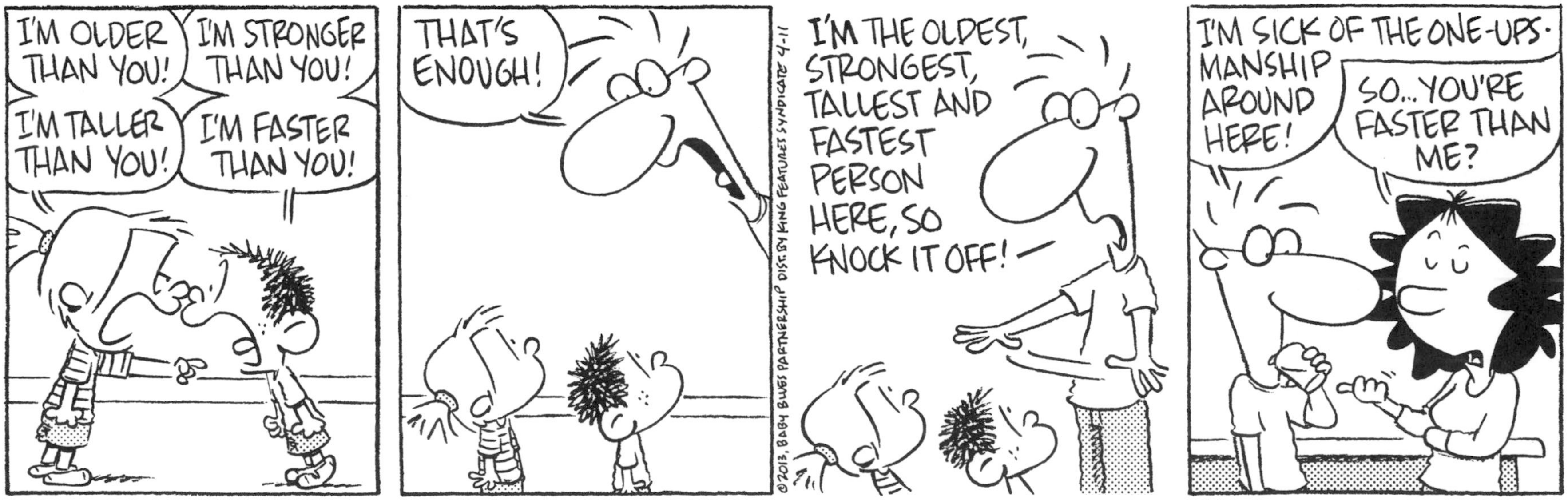
I'M OLDER THAN YOU!
I'M STRONGER THAN YOU!
I'M TALLER THAN YOU!
I'M FASTER THAN YOU!
THAT'S ENOUGH!
©2013, BABY BLUES PARTNERSHIP DIST. BY KING FEATURES SYNDICATE 4-11
I'M THE OLDEST, STRONGEST, TALLEST AND FASTEST PERSON HERE, SO KNOCK IT OFF!
I'M SICK OF THE ONE-UPS-MANSHIP AROUND HERE!
SO... YOU'RE FASTER THAN ME?

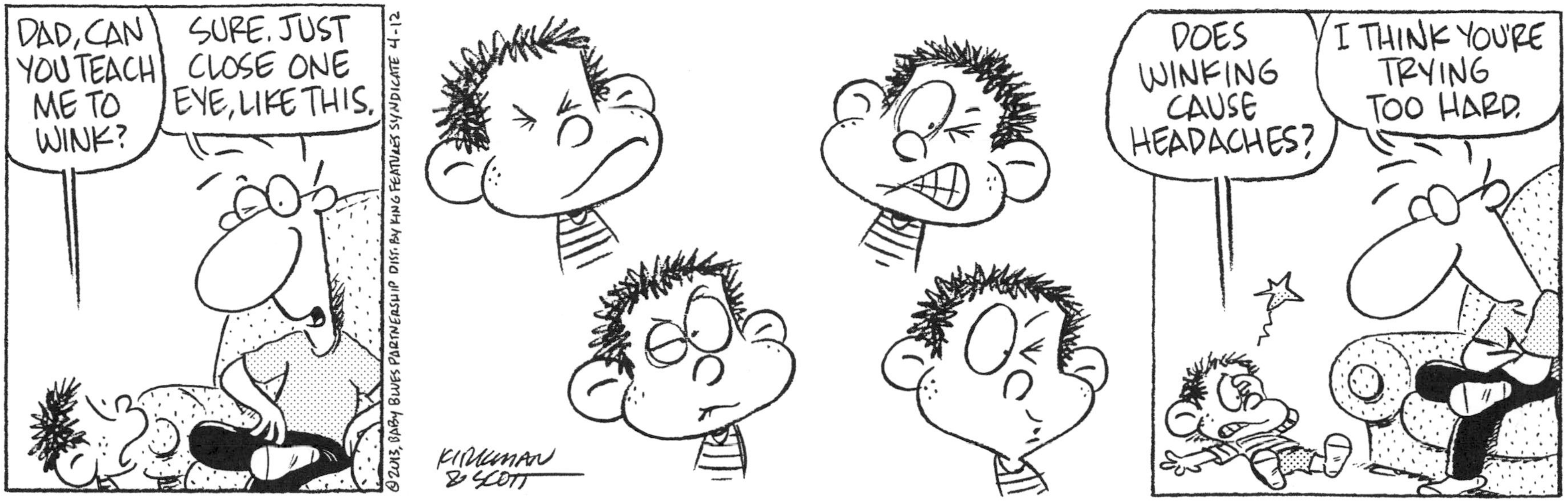
DAD, CAN YOU TEACH ME TO WINK?
SURE. JUST CLOSE ONE EYE, LIKE THIS.
©2013, BABY BLUES PARTNERSHIP DIST. BY KING FEATURES SYNDICATE 4-12
KIRKMAN & SCOTT
DOES WINKING CAUSE HEADACHES?
I THINK YOU'RE TRYING TOO HARD.

Rick: Always fun to draw extreme faces.

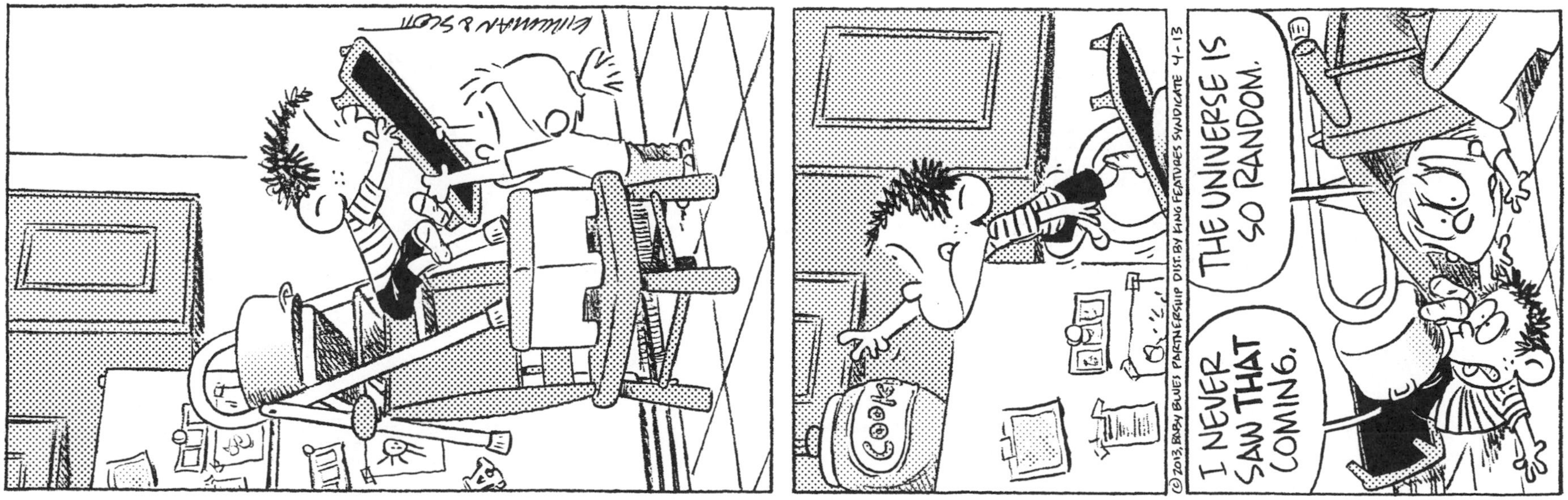
KIRKMAN & SCOTT
©2013, BABY BLUES PARTNERSHIP DIST. BY KING FEATURES SYNDICATE 4-13
THE UNIVERSE IS SO RANDOM.
I NEVER SAW **THAT** COMING.

Rick: One of those gags where you just have to do it sideways to fit everything in.

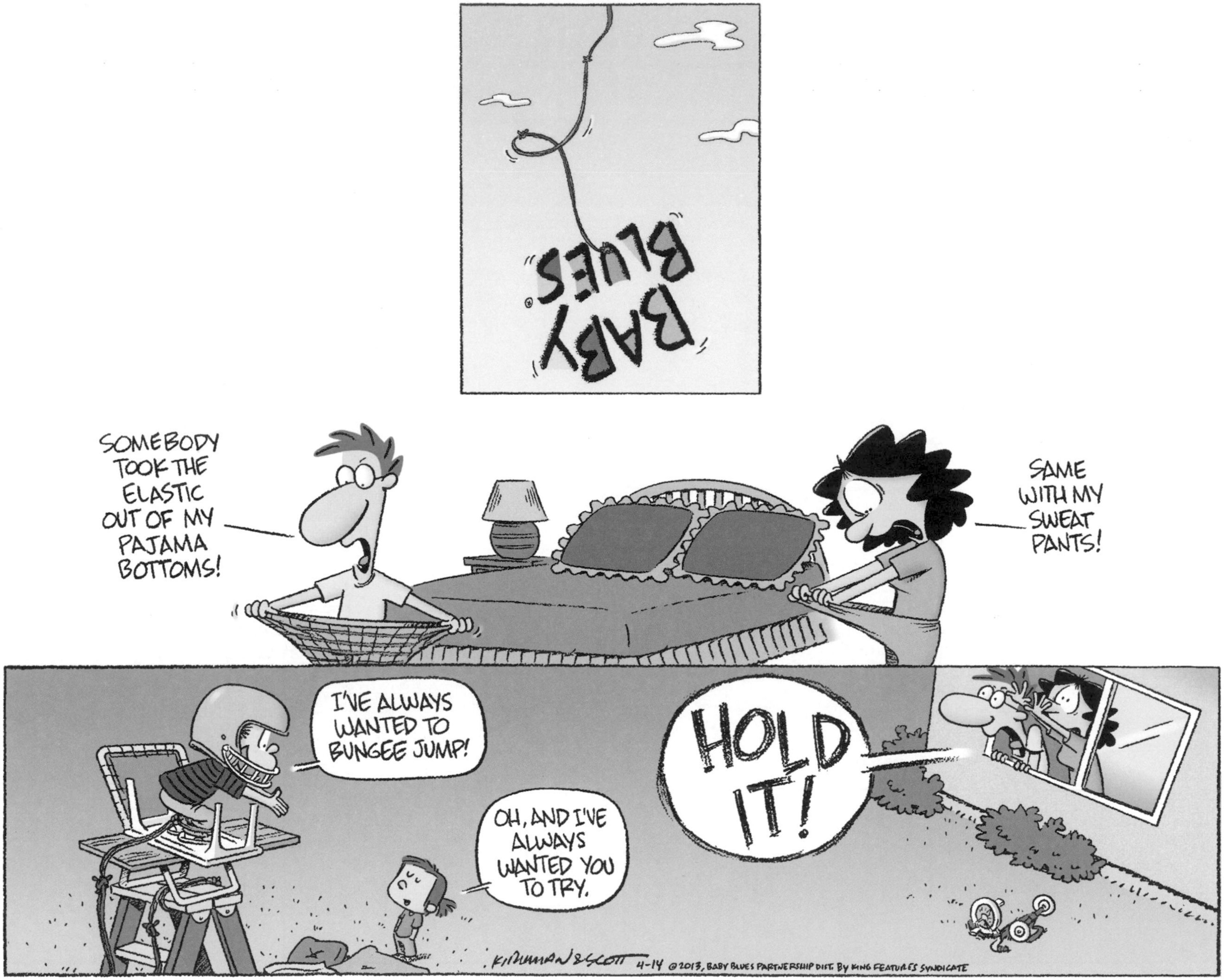
BABY BLUES®
SOMEBODY TOOK THE ELASTIC OUT OF MY PAJAMA BOTTOMS!
SAME WITH MY SWEAT PANTS!
I'VE ALWAYS WANTED TO BUNGEE JUMP!
OH, AND I'VE ALWAYS WANTED YOU TO TRY.
HOLD IT!
KIRKMAN & SCOTT 4-14 ©2013, BABY BLUES PARTNERSHIP DIST. BY KING FEATURES SYNDICATE

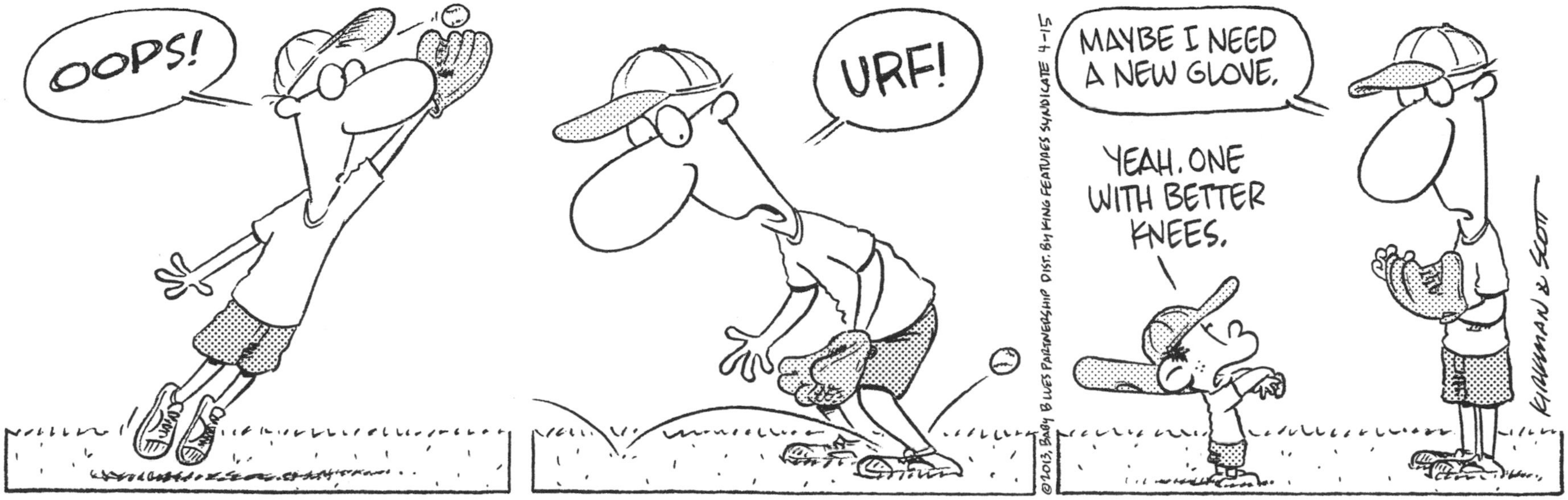
OOPS!
URF!
©2013, BABY BLUES PARTNERSHIP DIST. BY KING FEATURES SYNDICATE 4-15
MAYBE I NEED A NEW GLOVE.
YEAH. ONE WITH BETTER KNEES.
KIRKMAN & SCOTT

Jerry: I had shoulder surgery a while back, so I passed my fading baseball skills on to Darryl so I wouldn't feel so alone.

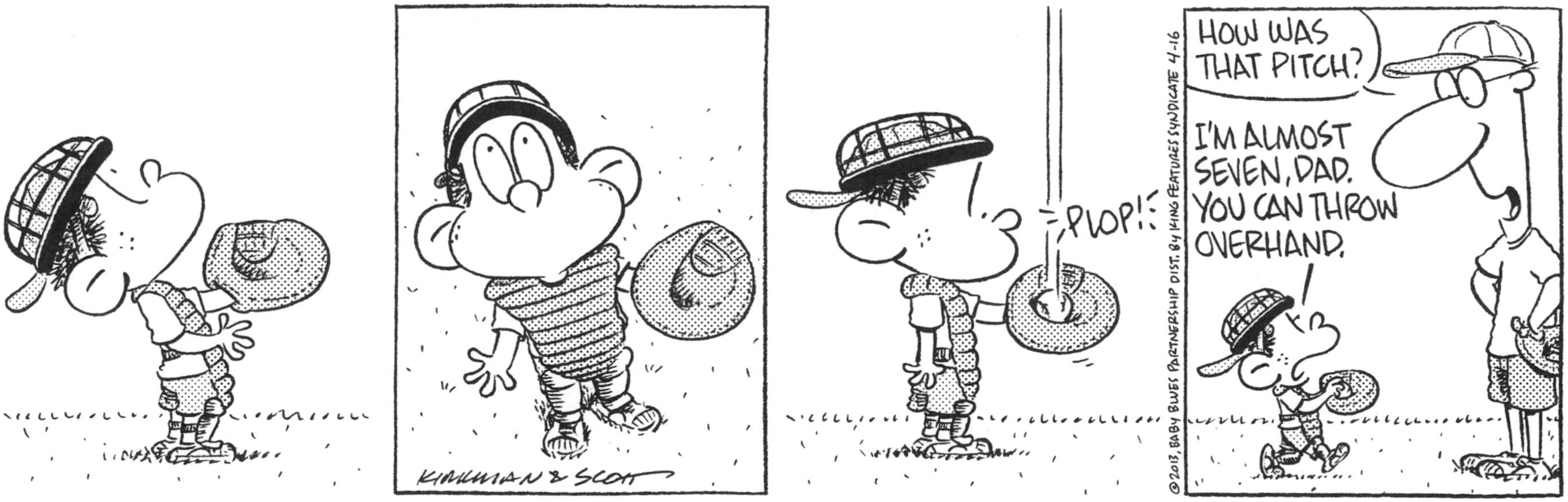
KIRKMAN & SCOTT
PLOP!
©2013, BABY BLUES PARTNERSHIP DIST. BY KING FEATURES SYNDICATE 4-16
HOW WAS THAT PITCH?
I'M ALMOST SEVEN, DAD. YOU CAN THROW OVERHAND.

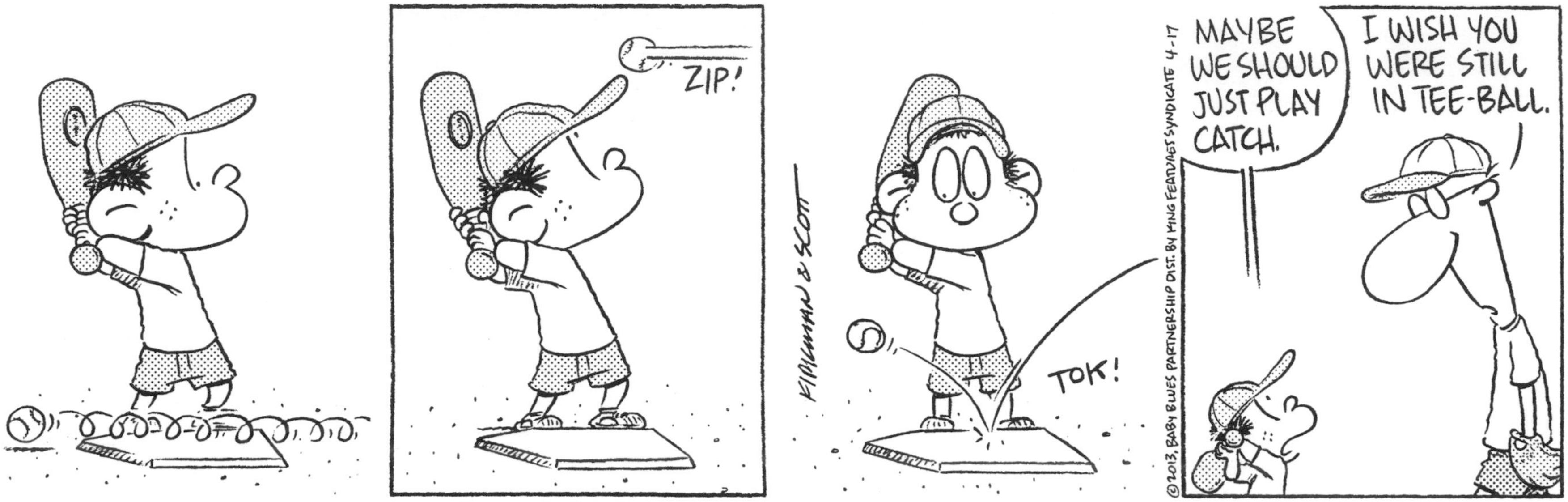
ZIP!
KIRKMAN & SCOTT
TOK!
©2013, BABY BLUES PARTNERSHIP DIST. BY KING FEATURES SYNDICATE 4-17
MAYBE WE SHOULD JUST PLAY CATCH.
I WISH YOU WERE STILL IN TEE-BALL.

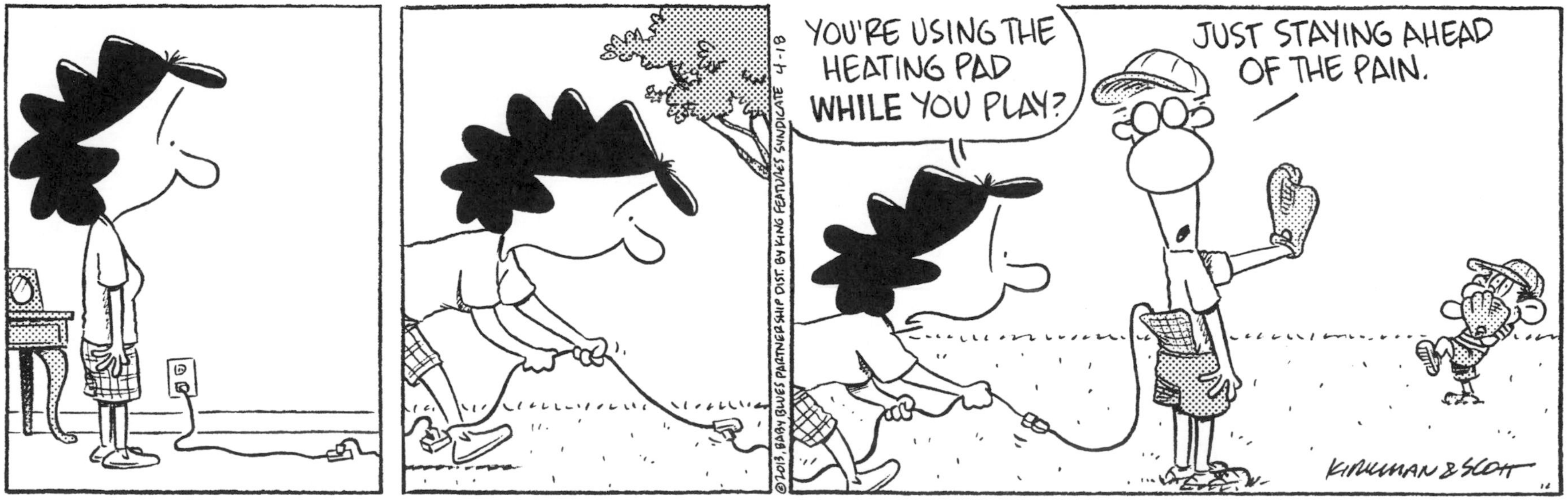
©2013, BABY BLUES PARTNERSHIP DIST. BY KING FEATURES SYNDICATE 4-18
YOU'RE USING THE HEATING PAD WHILE YOU PLAY?
JUST STAYING AHEAD OF THE PAIN.
KIRKMAN & SCOTT

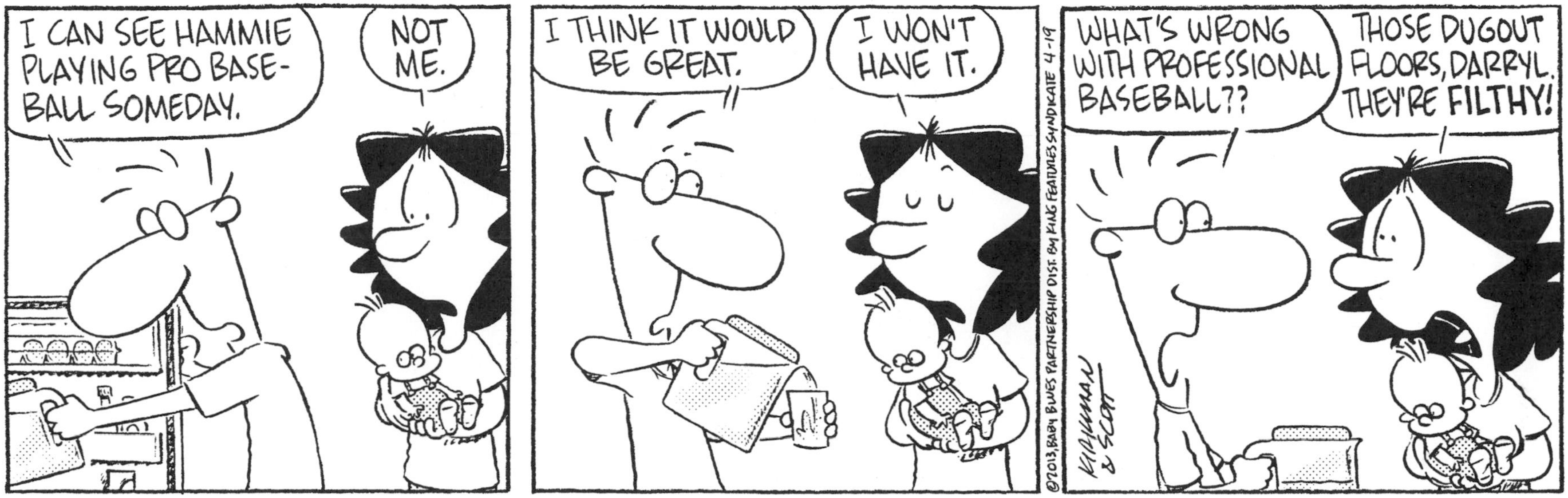
I CAN SEE HAMMIE PLAYING PRO BASE-BALL SOMEDAY.
NOT ME.
I THINK IT WOULD BE GREAT.
I WON'T HAVE IT.
©2013, BABY BLUES PARTNERSHIP DIST. BY KING FEATURES SYNDICATE 4-19
WHAT'S WRONG WITH PROFESSIONAL BASEBALL??
THOSE DUGOUT FLOORS, DARRYL. THEY'RE **FILTHY**!
KIRKMAN & SCOTT

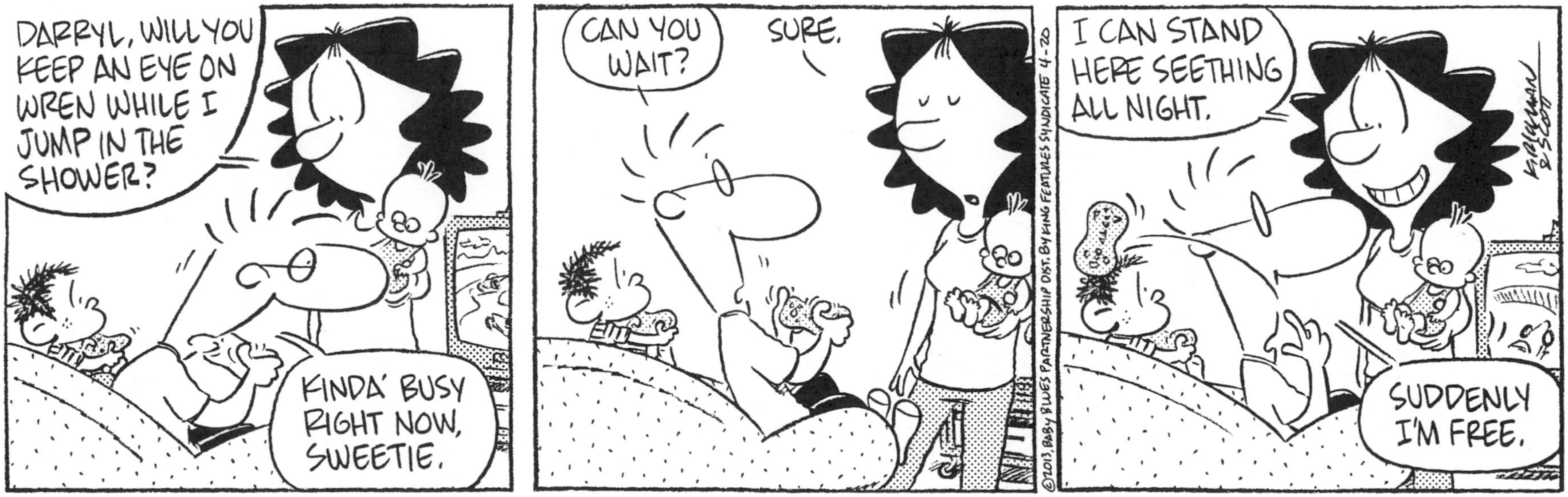
DARRYL, WILL YOU KEEP AN EYE ON WREN WHILE I JUMP IN THE SHOWER?
KINDA' BUSY RIGHT NOW, SWEETIE.
CAN YOU WAIT?
SURE.
©2013 BABY BLUES PARTNERSHIP DIST. BY KING FEATURES SYNDICATE 4-20
I CAN STAND HERE SEETHING ALL NIGHT.
SUDDENLY I'M FREE.
KIRKMAN & SCOTT

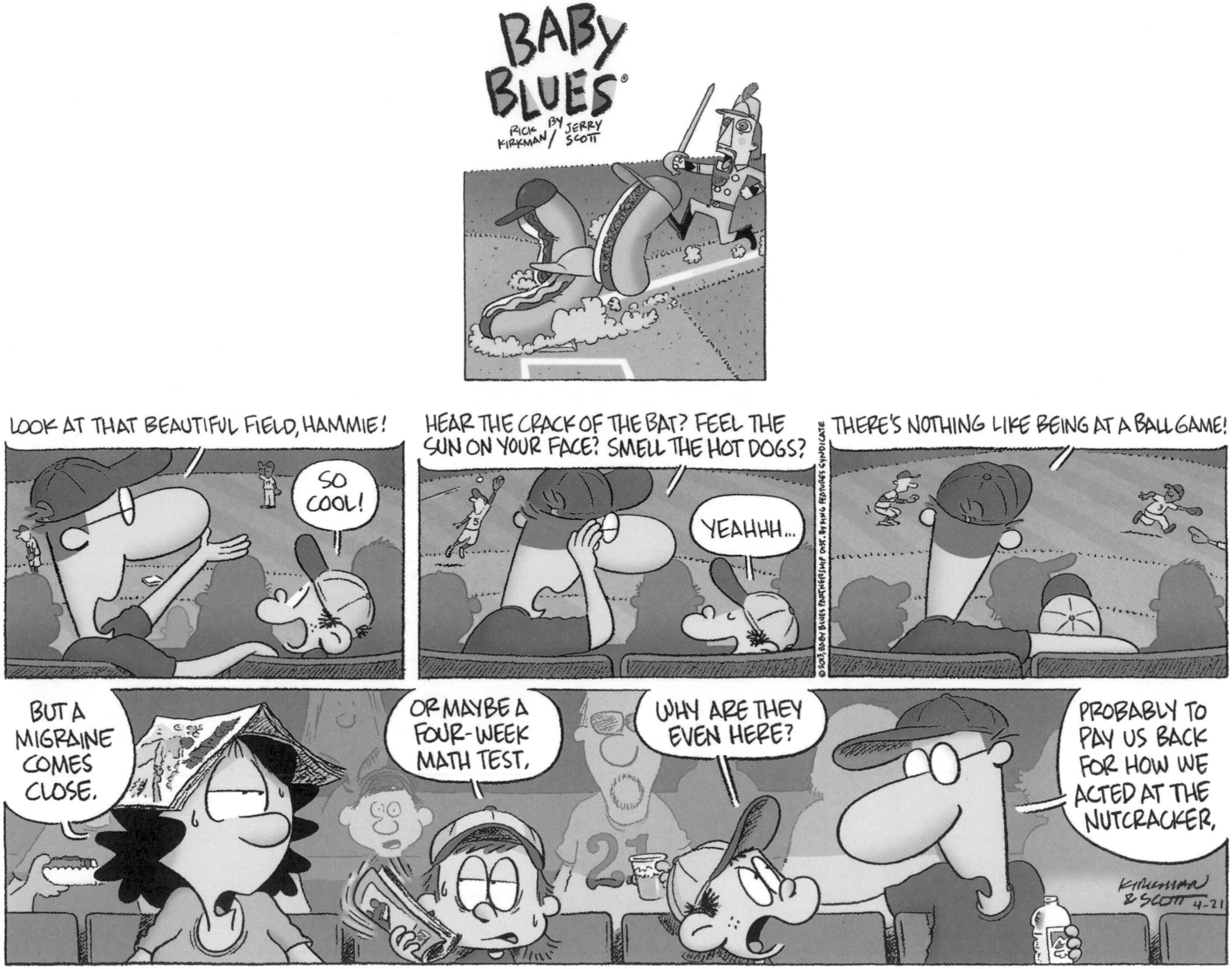
BABY BLUES®
BY RICK KIRKMAN / JERRY SCOTT
LOOK AT THAT BEAUTIFUL FIELD, HAMMIE!
SO COOL!
HEAR THE CRACK OF THE BAT? FEEL THE SUN ON YOUR FACE? SMELL THE HOT DOGS?
YEAHHH...
©2013, BABY BLUES PARTNERSHIP DIST. BY KING FEATURES SYNDICATE
THERE'S NOTHING LIKE BEING AT A BALL GAME!
BUT A MIGRAINE COMES CLOSE.
OR MAYBE A FOUR-WEEK MATH TEST.
WHY ARE THEY EVEN HERE?
PROBABLY TO PAY US BACK FOR HOW WE ACTED AT THE NUTCRACKER.
KIRKMAN & SCOTT 4-21

Jerry: I have seen enough performances of *The Nutcracker* to know the story. And snoring is considered a compliment in some countries. I think I read that someplace.

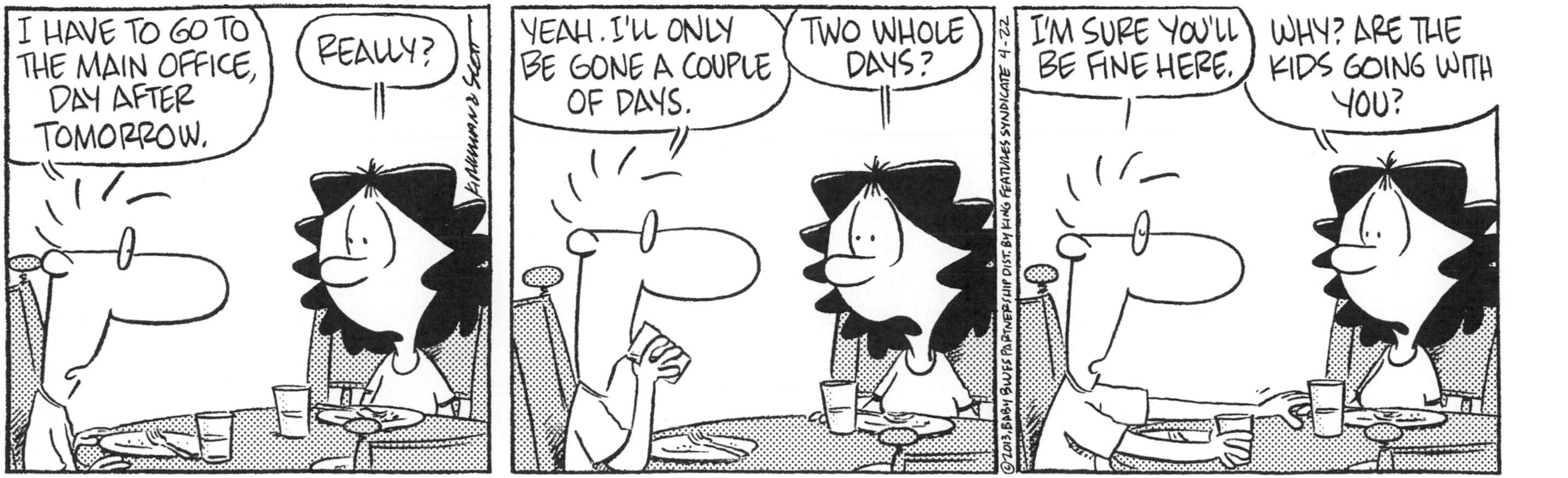
I HAVE TO GO TO THE MAIN OFFICE, DAY AFTER TOMORROW.
REALLY?
YEAH. I'LL ONLY BE GONE A COUPLE OF DAYS.
TWO WHOLE DAYS?
I'M SURE YOU'LL BE FINE HERE.
WHY? ARE THE KIDS GOING WITH YOU?
©2013, BABY BLUES PARTNERSHIP DIST. BY KING FEATURES SYNDICATE 4-22

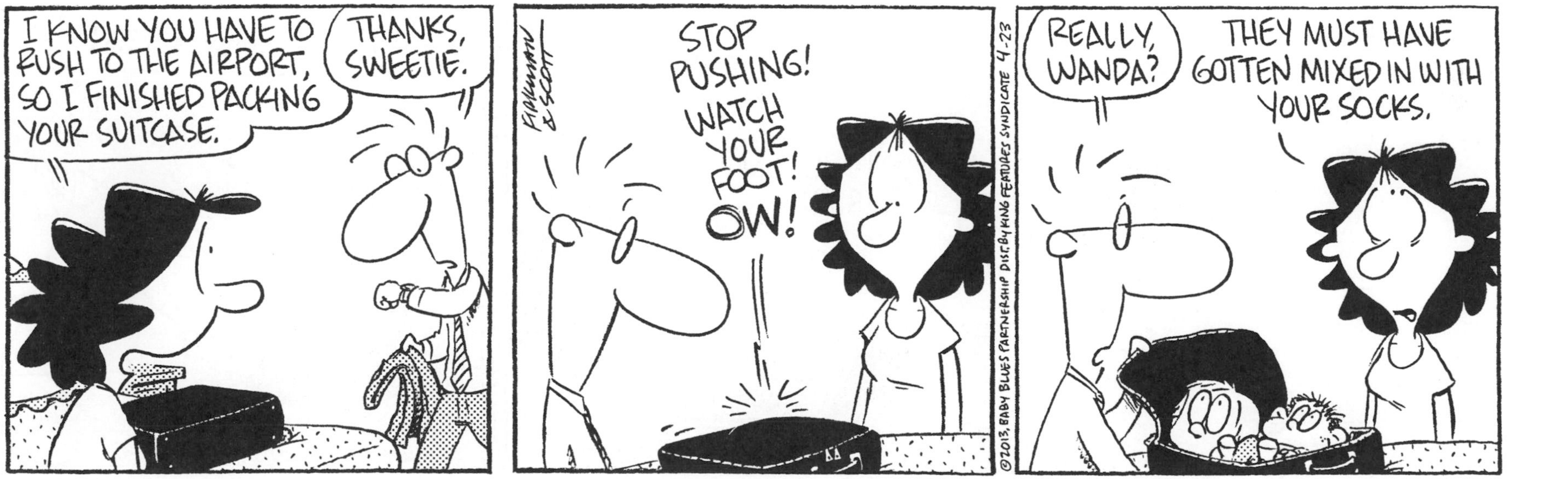
I KNOW YOU HAVE TO RUSH TO THE AIRPORT, SO I FINISHED PACKING YOUR SUITCASE.
THANKS, SWEETIE.
STOP PUSHING!
WATCH YOUR FOOT!
OW!
REALLY, WANDA?
THEY MUST HAVE GOTTEN MIXED IN WITH YOUR SOCKS.
©2013, BABY BLUES PARTNERSHIP DIST. BY KING FEATURES SYNDICATE 4-23

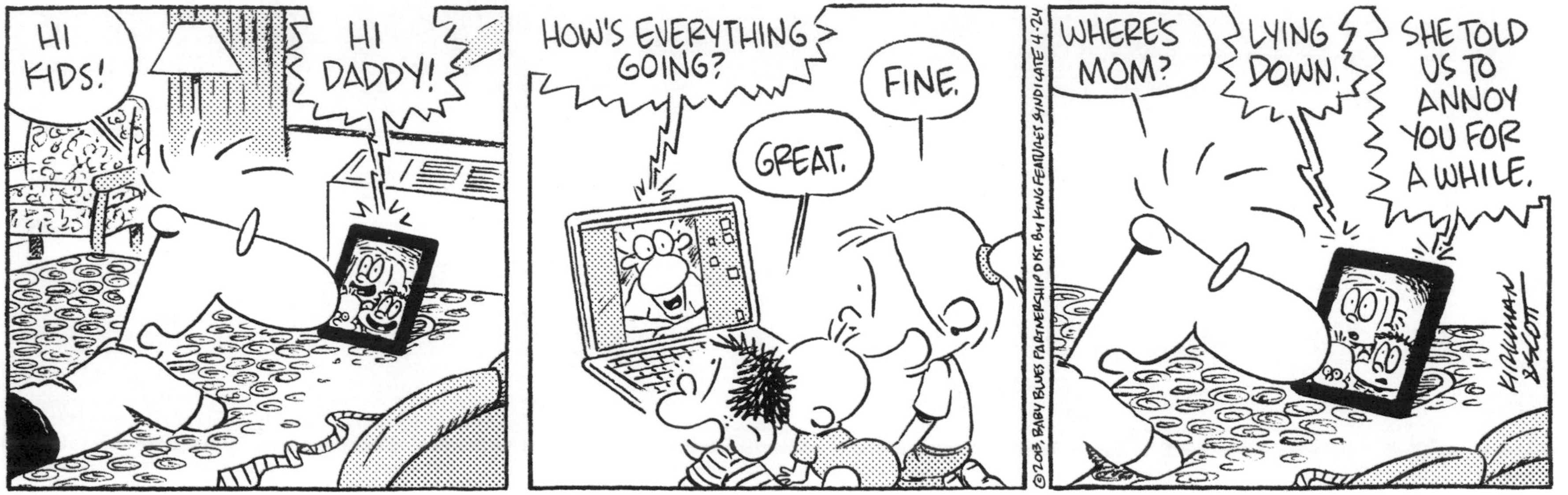
HI KIDS!
HI DADDY!
HOW'S EVERYTHING GOING?
GREAT.
FINE.
©2013, BABY BLUES PARTNERSHIP DIST. BY KING FEATURES SYNDICATE 4-24
WHERE'S MOM?
LYING DOWN.
SHE TOLD US TO ANNOY YOU FOR A WHILE.
KIRKMAN & SCOTT

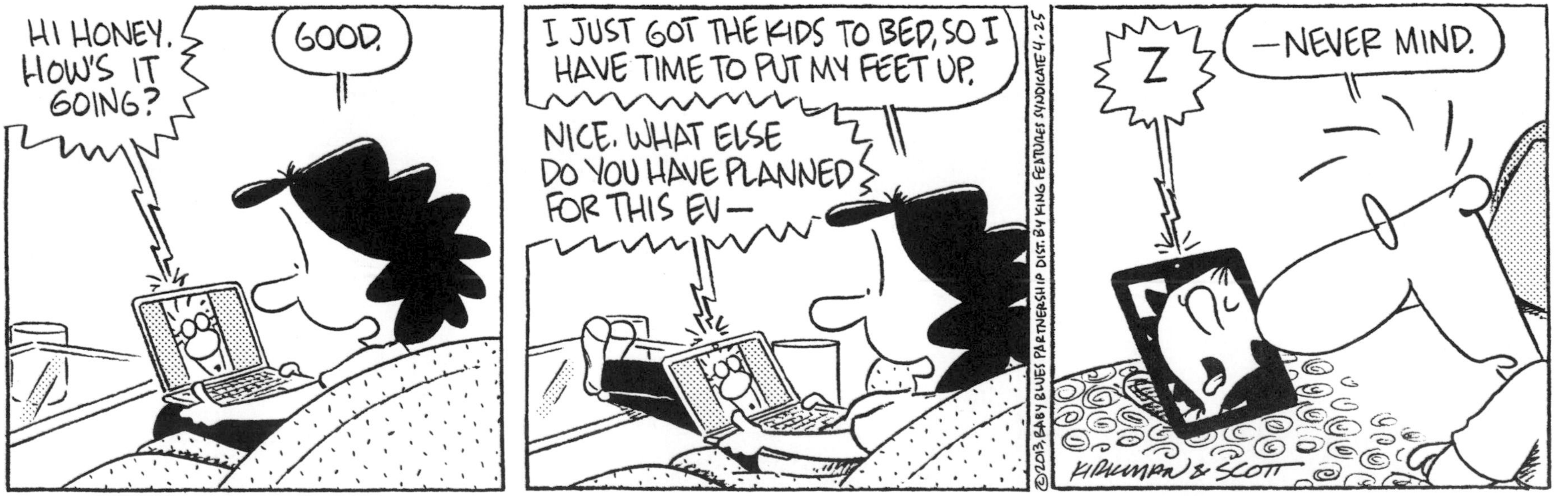
HI HONEY. HOW'S IT GOING?
GOOD.
I JUST GOT THE KIDS TO BED, SO I HAVE TIME TO PUT MY FEET UP.
NICE. WHAT ELSE DO YOU HAVE PLANNED FOR THIS EV—
©2013, BABY BLUES PARTNERSHIP DIST. BY KING FEATURES SYNDICATE 4-25
Z
—NEVER MIND.
KIRKMAN & SCOTT

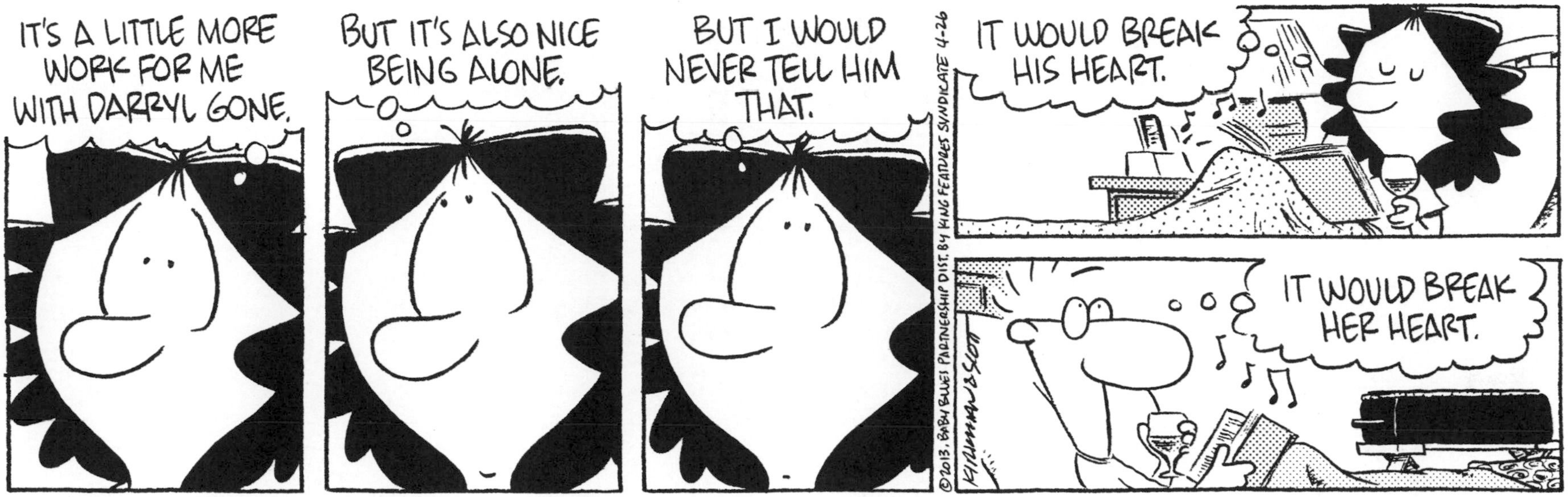
IT'S A LITTLE MORE WORK FOR ME WITH DARRYL GONE.
BUT IT'S ALSO NICE BEING ALONE.
BUT I WOULD NEVER TELL HIM THAT.
IT WOULD BREAK HIS HEART.
IT WOULD BREAK HER HEART.
©2013, BABY BLUES PARTNERSHIP DIST. BY KING FEATURES SYNDICATE 4-26
KIRKMAN & SCOTT

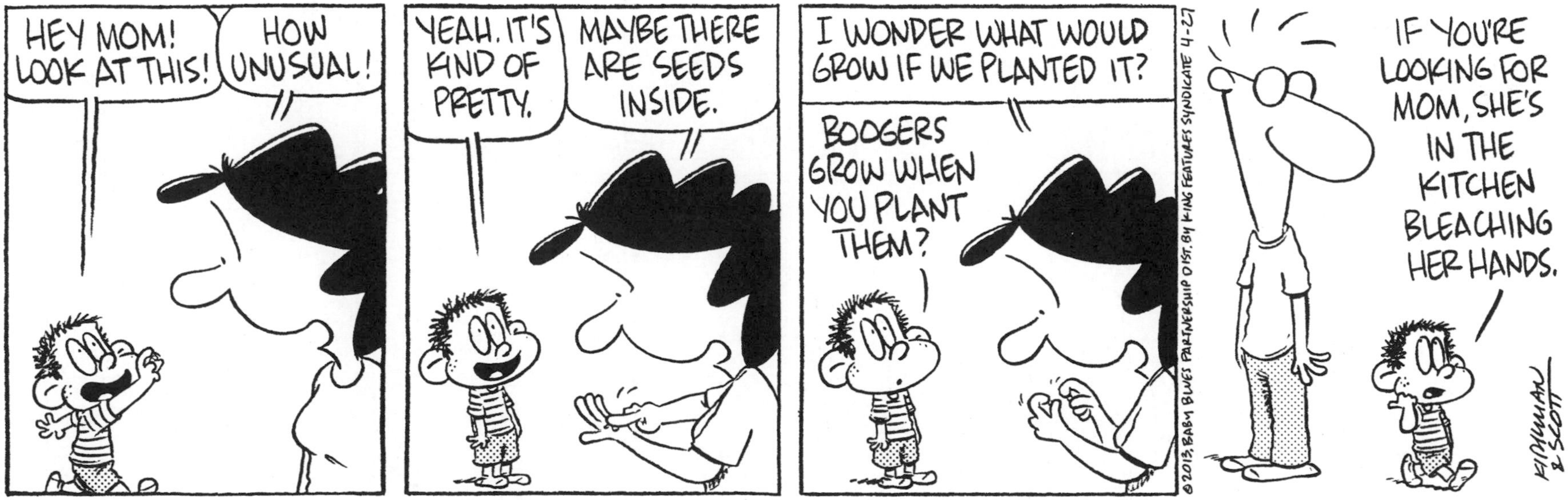
HEY MOM! LOOK AT THIS!
HOW UNUSUAL!
YEAH. IT'S KIND OF PRETTY.
MAYBE THERE ARE SEEDS INSIDE.
I WONDER WHAT WOULD GROW IF WE PLANTED IT?
BOOGERS GROW WHEN YOU PLANT THEM?
IF YOU'RE LOOKING FOR MOM, SHE'S IN THE KITCHEN BLEACHING HER HANDS.
©2013, BABY BLUES PARTNERSHIP DIST. BY KING FEATURES SYNDICATE 4-27
KIRKMAN & SCOTT

Jerry: Collecting is good. But not all collections are equally good.

BABY BLUES®
HOLD
I GET TO PUSH THE BUTTONS WHEN WE GET IN!
NO! IT'S MY TURN!
WHY DON'T WE JUST SHARE?
YEAH! THERE'S TONS OF BUTTONS IN THERE!
I'LL DO THE FIRST ROW.
AND I'LL PUSH THE SECOND ROW.
AND I'LL PUSH THE THIRD ROW.
AND I'LL PUSH THE FOURTH ROW.
AND I'LL PUSH THE FIFTH ROW.
AND I'LL PUSH THE SIXTH ROW.
KIRKMAN & SCOTT 4-28
G
LO
DING!
©2013, BABY BLUES PARTNERSHIP DIST. BY KING FEATURES SYNDICATE
HAVE YOU EVER NOTICED HOW WE'RE ALWAYS ALONE IN ELEVATORS?
7
ONLY ELEVEN MORE STOPS!

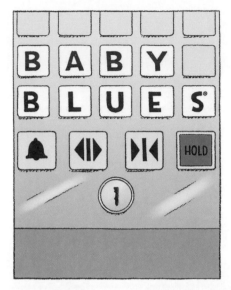

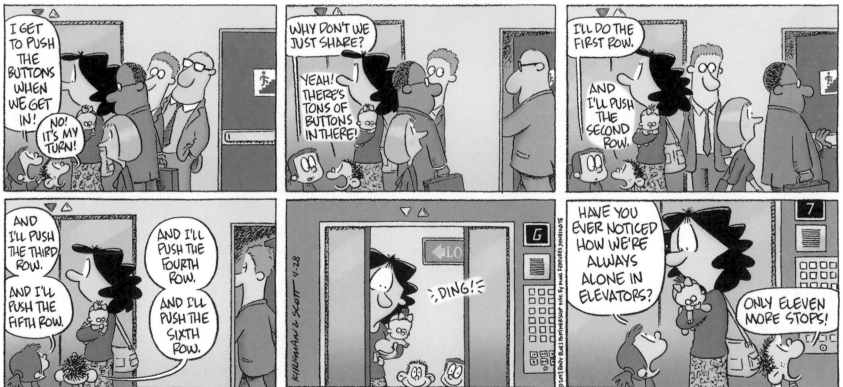

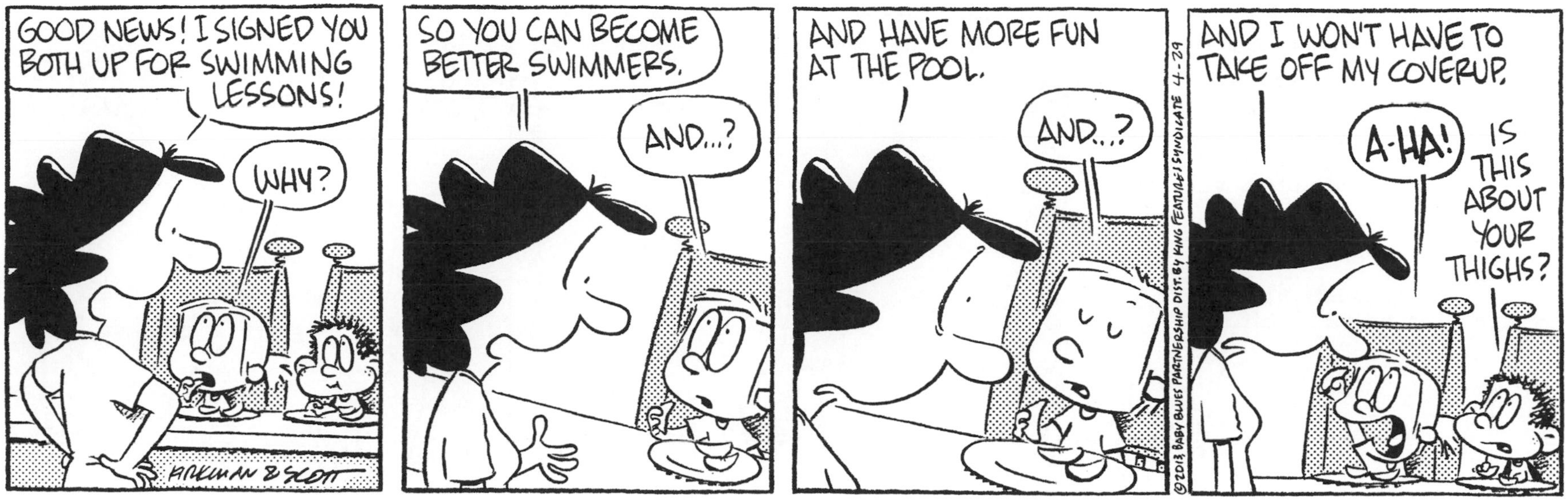
GOOD NEWS! I SIGNED YOU BOTH UP FOR SWIMMING LESSONS!
WHY?
KIRKMAN & SCOTT
SO YOU CAN BECOME BETTER SWIMMERS.
AND...?
AND HAVE MORE FUN AT THE POOL.
AND...?
©2013 BABY BLUES PARTNERSHIP DIST. BY KING FEATURES SYNDICATE 4-29
AND I WON'T HAVE TO TAKE OFF MY COVERUP.
A-HA!
IS THIS ABOUT YOUR THIGHS?

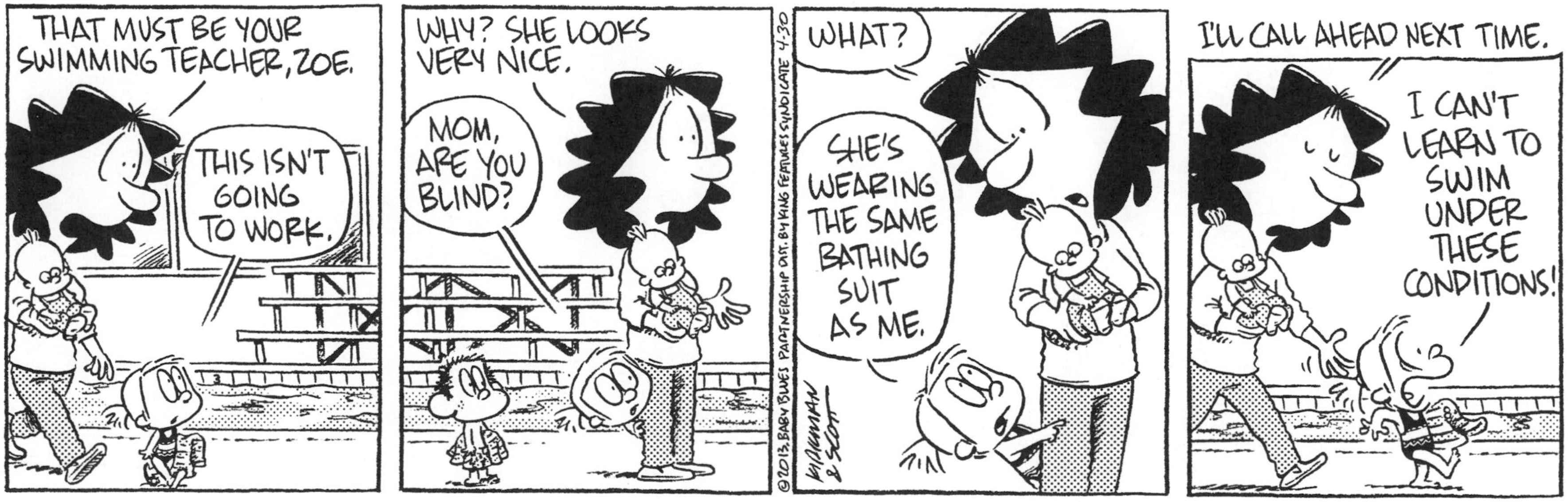
THAT MUST BE YOUR SWIMMING TEACHER, ZOE.
THIS ISN'T GOING TO WORK.
WHY? SHE LOOKS VERY NICE.
MOM, ARE YOU BLIND?
©2013, BABY BLUES PARTNERSHIP DIST. BY KING FEATURES SYNDICATE 4-30
WHAT?
SHE'S WEARING THE SAME BATHING SUIT AS ME.
KIRKMAN & SCOTT
I'LL CALL AHEAD NEXT TIME.
I CAN'T LEARN TO SWIM UNDER THESE CONDITIONS!

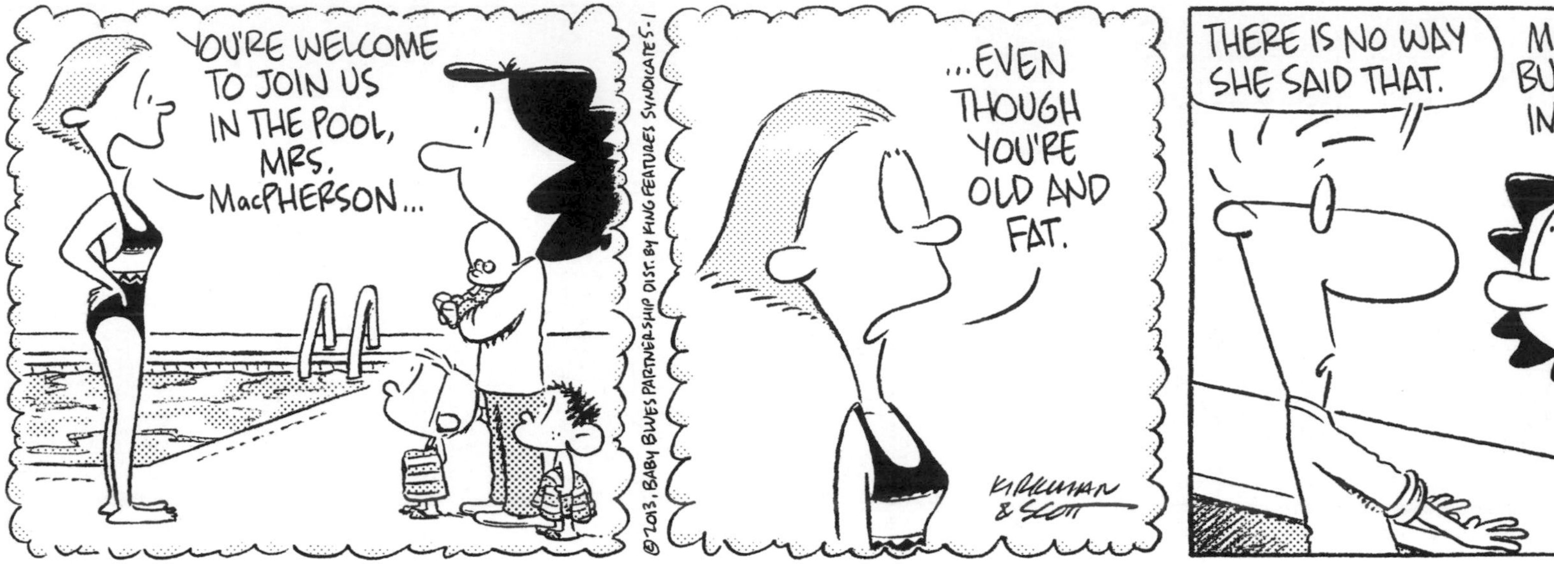
YOU'RE WELCOME TO JOIN US IN THE POOL, MRS. MacPHERSON...
©2013, BABY BLUES PARTNERSHIP DIST. BY KING FEATURES SYNDICATE 5-1
...EVEN THOUGH YOU'RE OLD AND FAT.
KIRKMAN & SCOTT
THERE IS NO WAY SHE SAID THAT.
MAYBE NOT, BUT HER BODY IMPLIED IT.

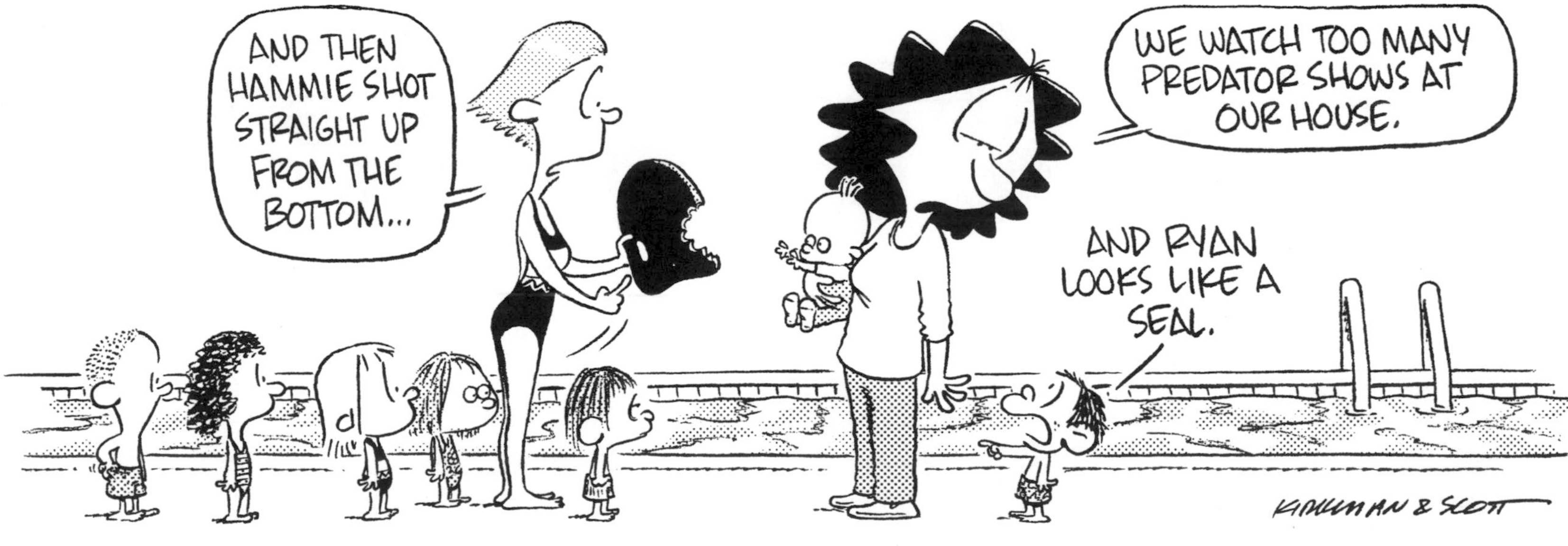
AND THEN HAMMIE SHOT STRAIGHT UP FROM THE BOTTOM...
WE WATCH TOO MANY PREDATOR SHOWS AT OUR HOUSE.
AND RYAN LOOKS LIKE A SEAL.
KIRKMAN & SCOTT
©2013, BABY BLUES PARTNERSHIP DIST. BY KING FEATURES SYNDICATE 5-2

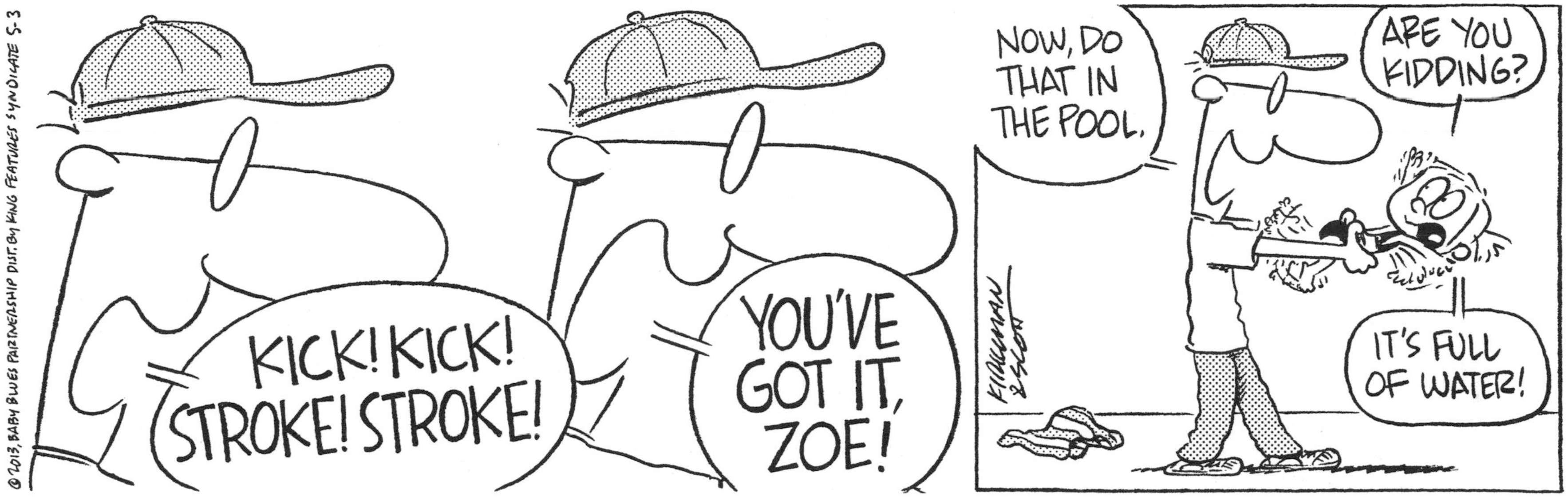
KICK! KICK! STROKE! STROKE!
YOU'VE GOT IT, ZOE!
NOW, DO THAT IN THE POOL.
ARE YOU KIDDING?
IT'S FULL OF WATER!
© 2013, BABY BLUES PARTNERSHIP DIST. BY KING FEATURES SYNDICATE 5-3
KIRKMAN & SCOTT

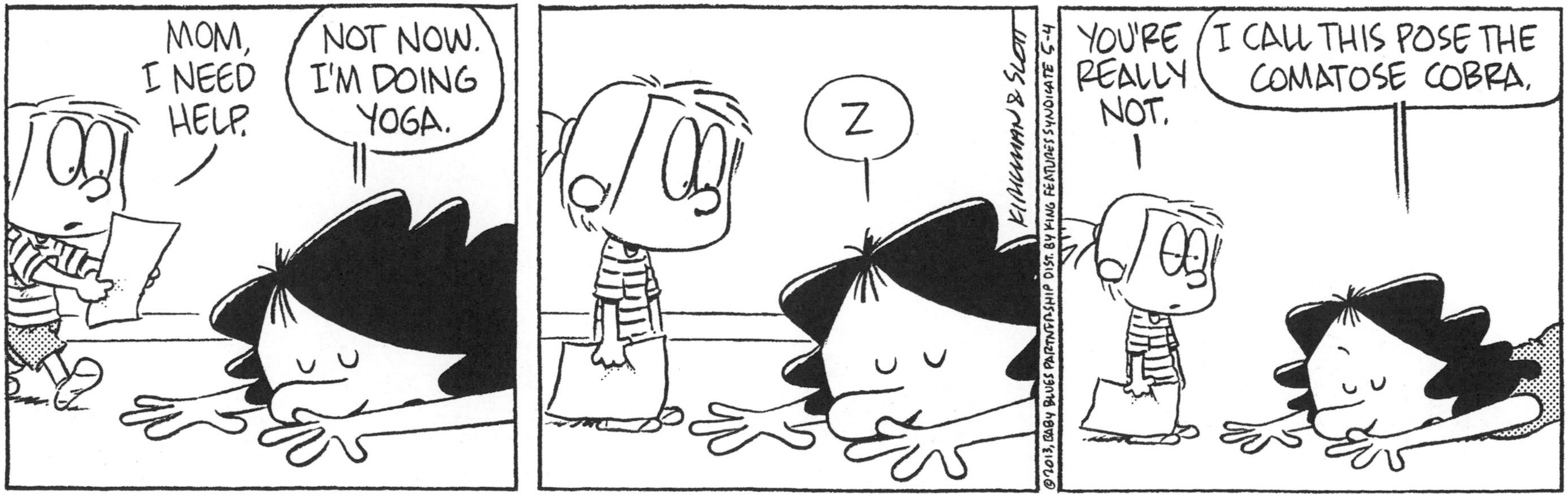
MOM, I NEED HELP.
NOT NOW. I'M DOING YOGA.
Z
YOU'RE REALLY NOT.
I CALL THIS POSE THE COMATOSE COBRA.
KIRKMAN & SCOTT
© 2013, BABY BLUES PARTNERSHIP DIST. BY KING FEATURES SYNDICATE 5-4

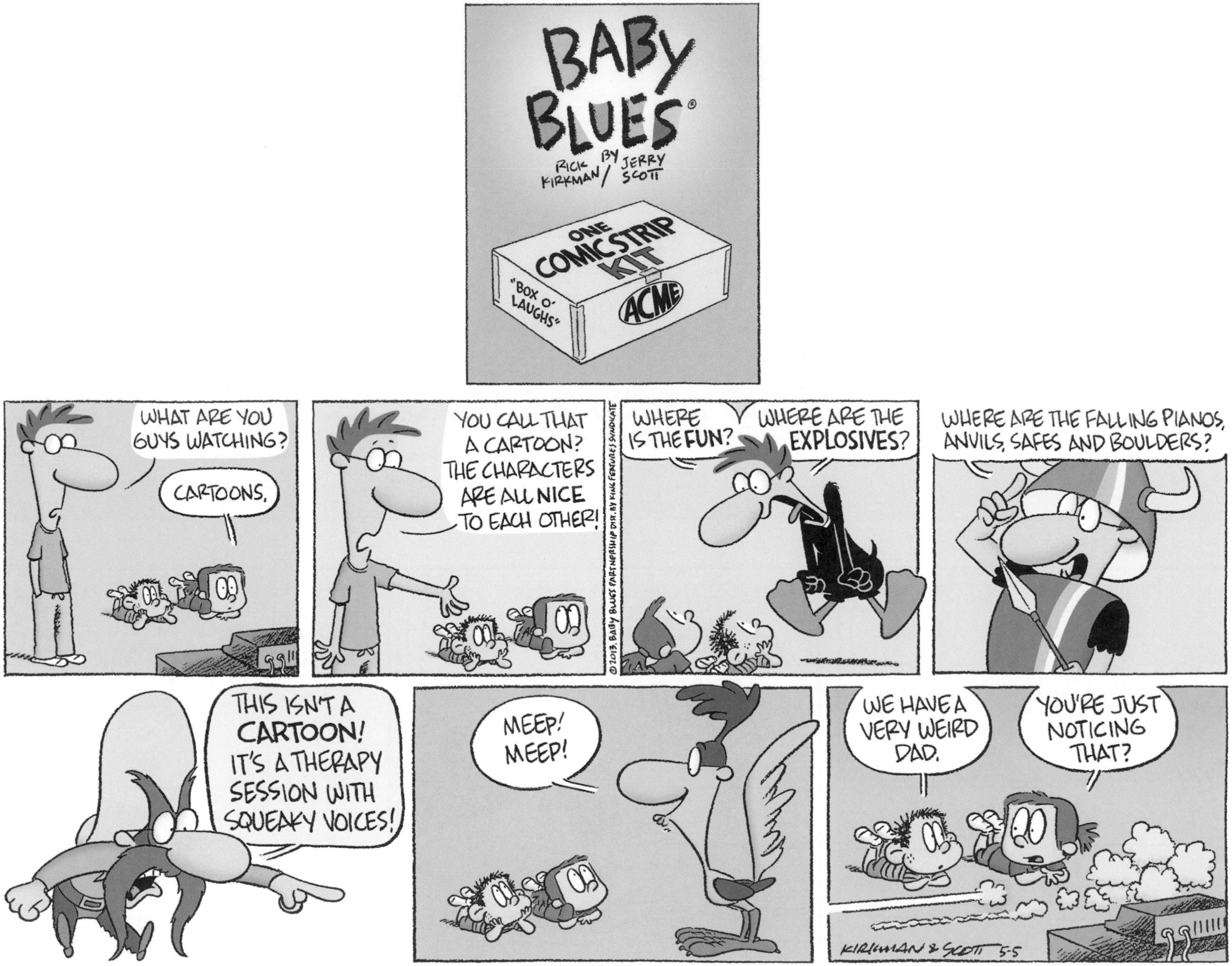
BABY BLUES®
BY RICK KIRKMAN / JERRY SCOTT
ONE COMICSTRIP KIT
"BOX O' LAUGHS"
ACME
WHAT ARE YOU GUYS WATCHING?
CARTOONS.
YOU CALL THAT A CARTOON? THE CHARACTERS ARE ALL NICE TO EACH OTHER!
© 2013, BABY BLUES PARTNERSHIP DIST. BY KING FEATURES SYNDICATE
WHERE IS THE FUN?
WHERE ARE THE EXPLOSIVES?
WHERE ARE THE FALLING PIANOS, ANVILS, SAFES AND BOULDERS?
THIS ISN'T A CARTOON! IT'S A THERAPY SESSION WITH SQUEAKY VOICES!
MEEP! MEEP!
WE HAVE A VERY WEIRD DAD.
YOU'RE JUST NOTICING THAT?
KIRKMAN & SCOTT 5-5

Rick: This was one of my favorite Sundays to draw, once again leaning on Google for reference, transforming Darryl into some of my childhood favorites: Daffy Duck, Elmer Fudd (from "What's Opera, Doc?"), Yosemite Sam, and the Road Runner. And of course, the title panel subject? Acme, official supplier to *Looney Tunes*.

Jerry: Big respect to Rick for the artwork on these *Looney Tunes* characters. Spot on!

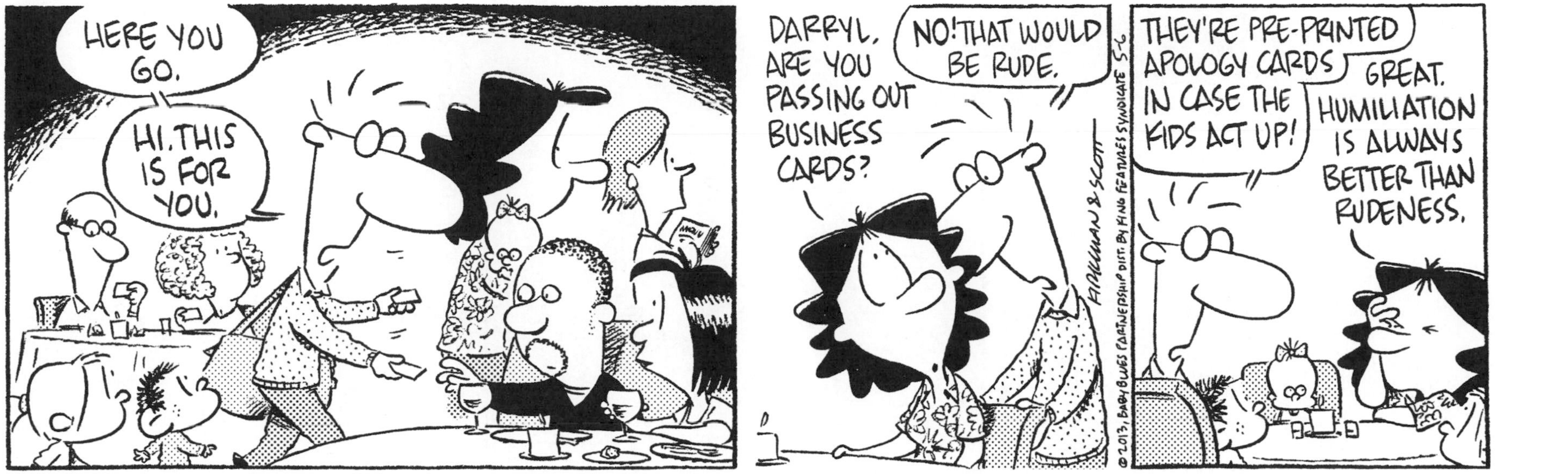
HERE YOU GO.
HI. THIS IS FOR YOU.
DARRYL, ARE YOU PASSING OUT BUSINESS CARDS?
NO! THAT WOULD BE RUDE.
THEY'RE PRE-PRINTED APOLOGY CARDS IN CASE THE KIDS ACT UP!
GREAT. HUMILIATION IS ALWAYS BETTER THAN RUDENESS.
KIRKMAN & SCOTT
© 2013, BABY BLUES PARTNERSHIP DIST. BY KING FEATURES SYNDICATE 5-6

Rick: This is such a good idea, it should be an actual thing.

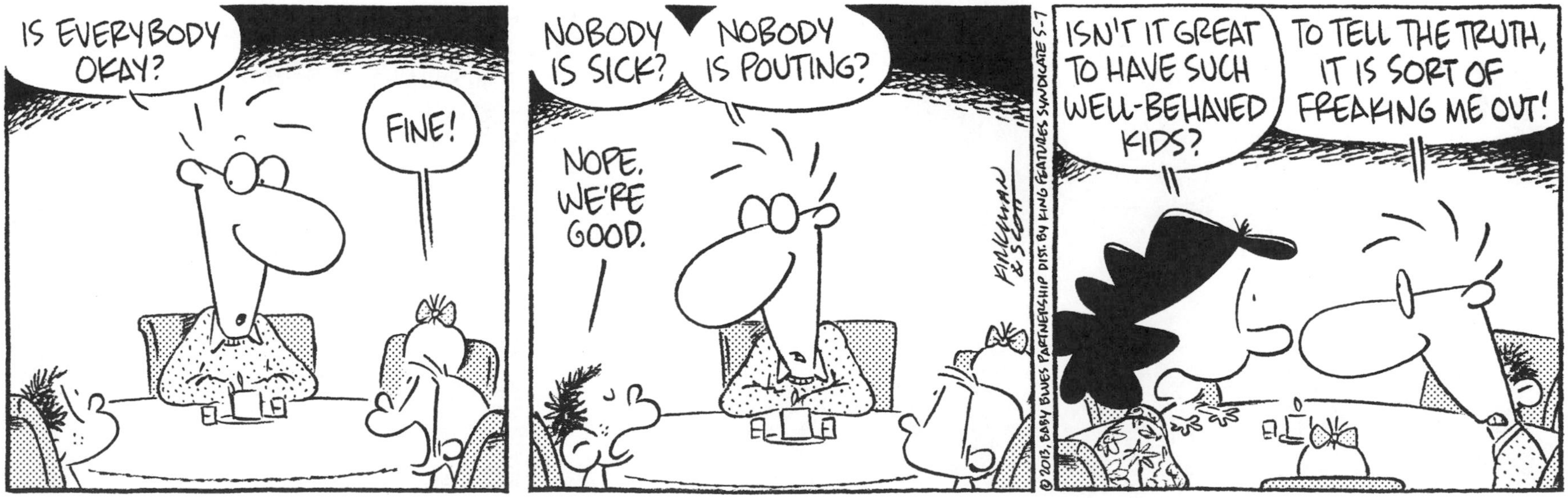
IS EVERYBODY OKAY?
FINE!
NOBODY IS SICK?
NOBODY IS POUTING?
NOPE. WE'RE GOOD.
KIRKMAN & SCOTT
© 2013, BABY BLUES PARTNERSHIP DIST. BY KING FEATURES SYNDICATE 5-7
ISN'T IT GREAT TO HAVE SUCH WELL-BEHAVED KIDS?
TO TELL THE TRUTH, IT IS SORT OF FREAKING ME OUT!

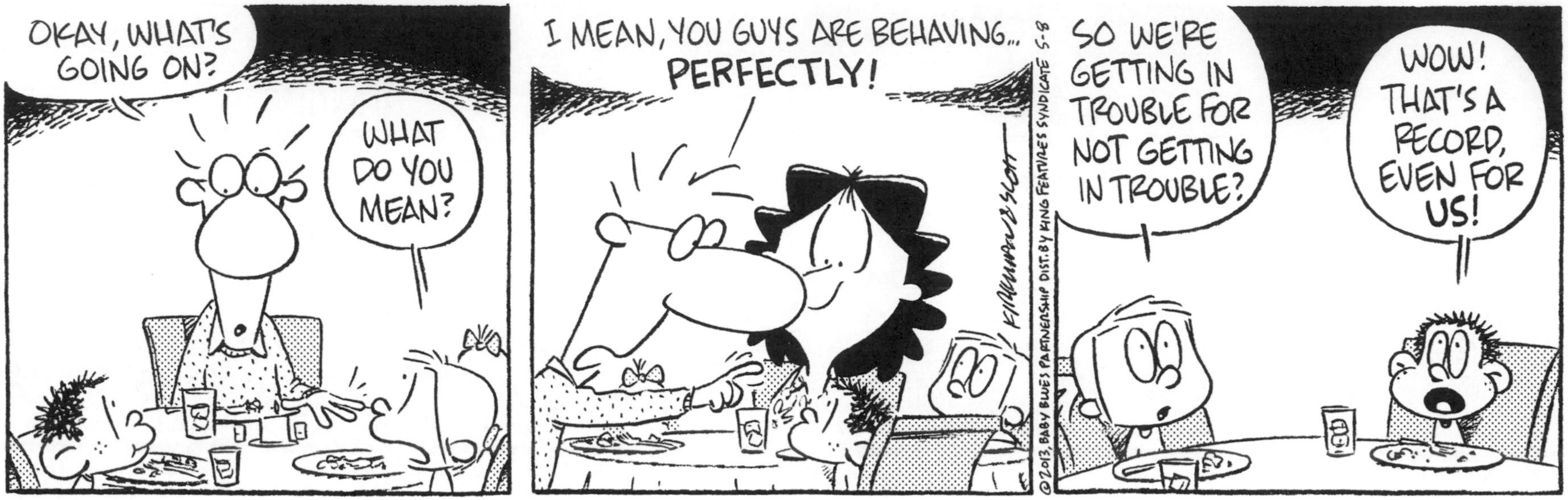

OKAY, WHAT'S GOING ON?
WHAT DO YOU MEAN?
I MEAN, YOU GUYS ARE BEHAVING... **PERFECTLY!**
SO WE'RE GETTING IN TROUBLE FOR NOT GETTING IN TROUBLE?
WOW! THAT'S A RECORD, EVEN FOR **US!**
©2013, BABY BLUES PARTNERSHIP DIST. BY KING FEATURES SYNDICATE 5-8

Jerry: Kids do this just to keep us off balance. Works, too.

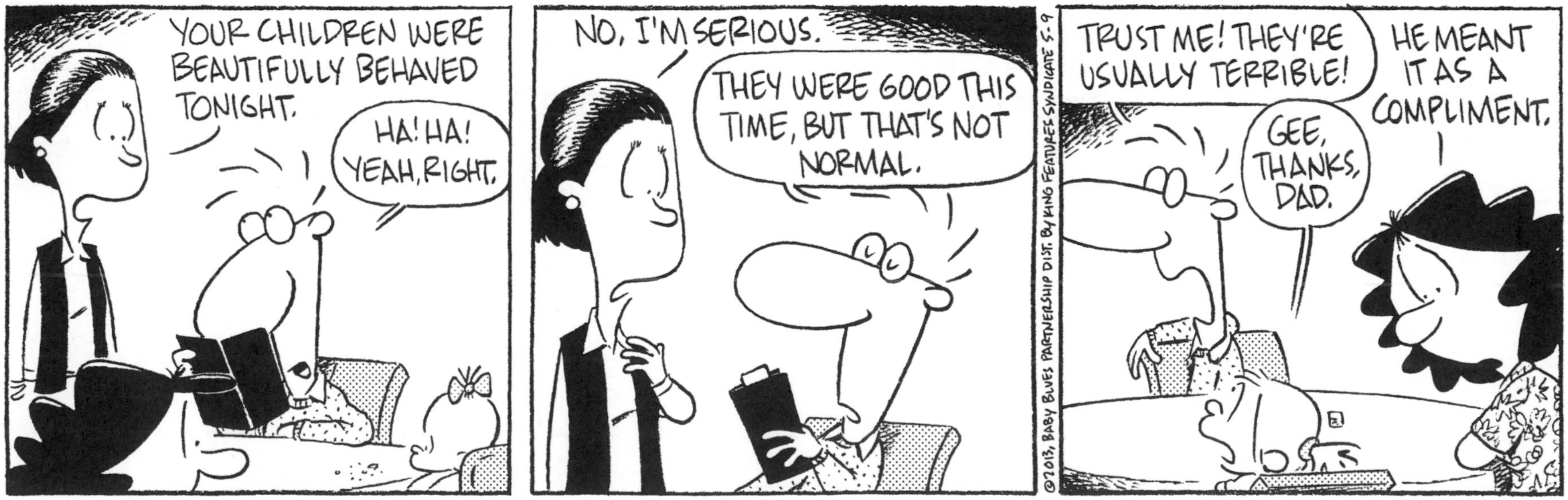

YOUR CHILDREN WERE BEAUTIFULLY BEHAVED TONIGHT.
HA! HA! YEAH, RIGHT.
NO, I'M SERIOUS.
THEY WERE GOOD THIS TIME, BUT THAT'S NOT NORMAL.
©2013, BABY BLUES PARTNERSHIP DIST. BY KING FEATURES SYNDICATE 5-9
TRUST ME! THEY'RE USUALLY TERRIBLE!
GEE, THANKS, DAD.
HE MEANT IT AS A COMPLIMENT.

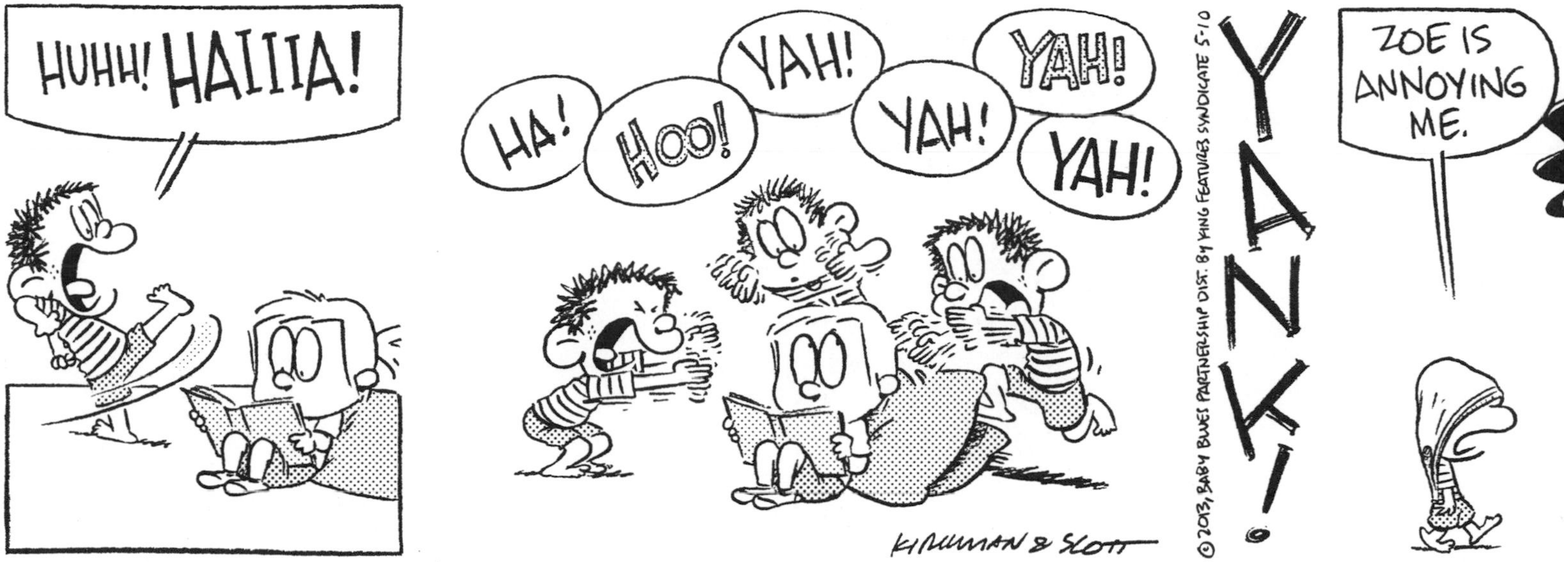
HUHH! HAIIIA!
HA!
HOO!
YAH!
YAH!
YAH!
YAH!
©2013, BABY BLUES PARTNERSHIP DIST. BY KING FEATURES SYNDICATE 5-10
YANK!
ZOE IS ANNOYING ME.
KIRKMAN & SCOTT

Rick: Another great opportunity to draw Hammie in action.

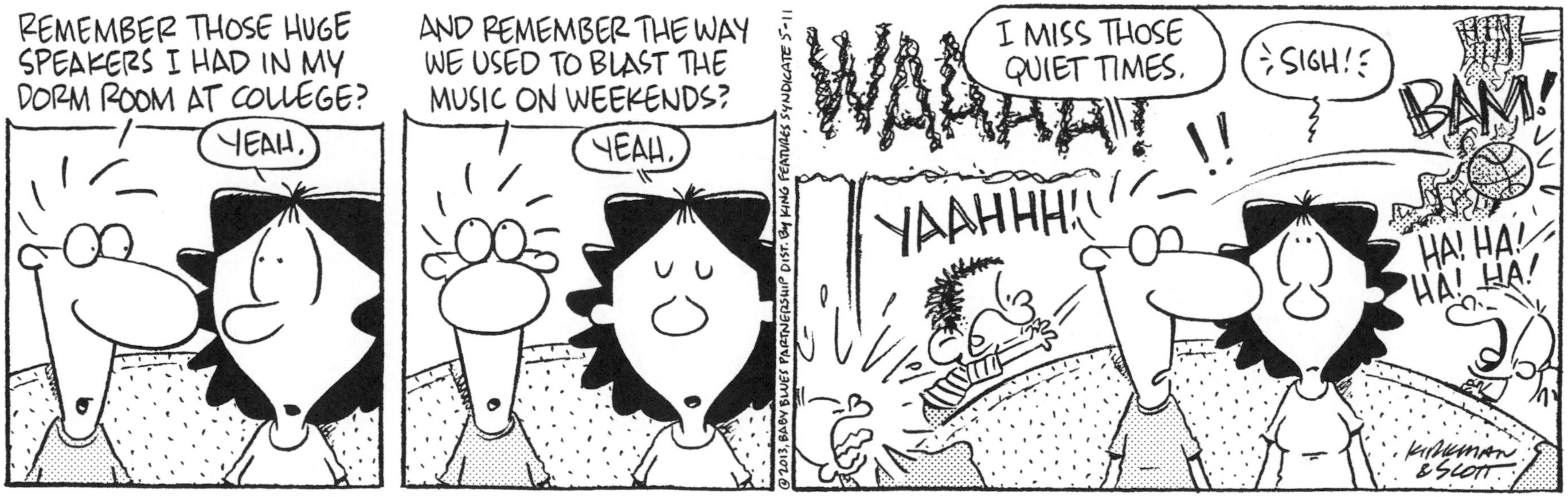
REMEMBER THOSE HUGE SPEAKERS I HAD IN MY DORM ROOM AT COLLEGE?
YEAH.
AND REMEMBER THE WAY WE USED TO BLAST THE MUSIC ON WEEKENDS?
YEAH.
©2013, BABY BLUES PARTNERSHIP DIST. BY KING FEATURES SYNDICATE 5-11
WAAAA!
I MISS THOSE QUIET TIMES.
SIGH!
BAM!
!!
YAAHHH!
HA! HA! HA! HA!
KIRKMAN & SCOTT

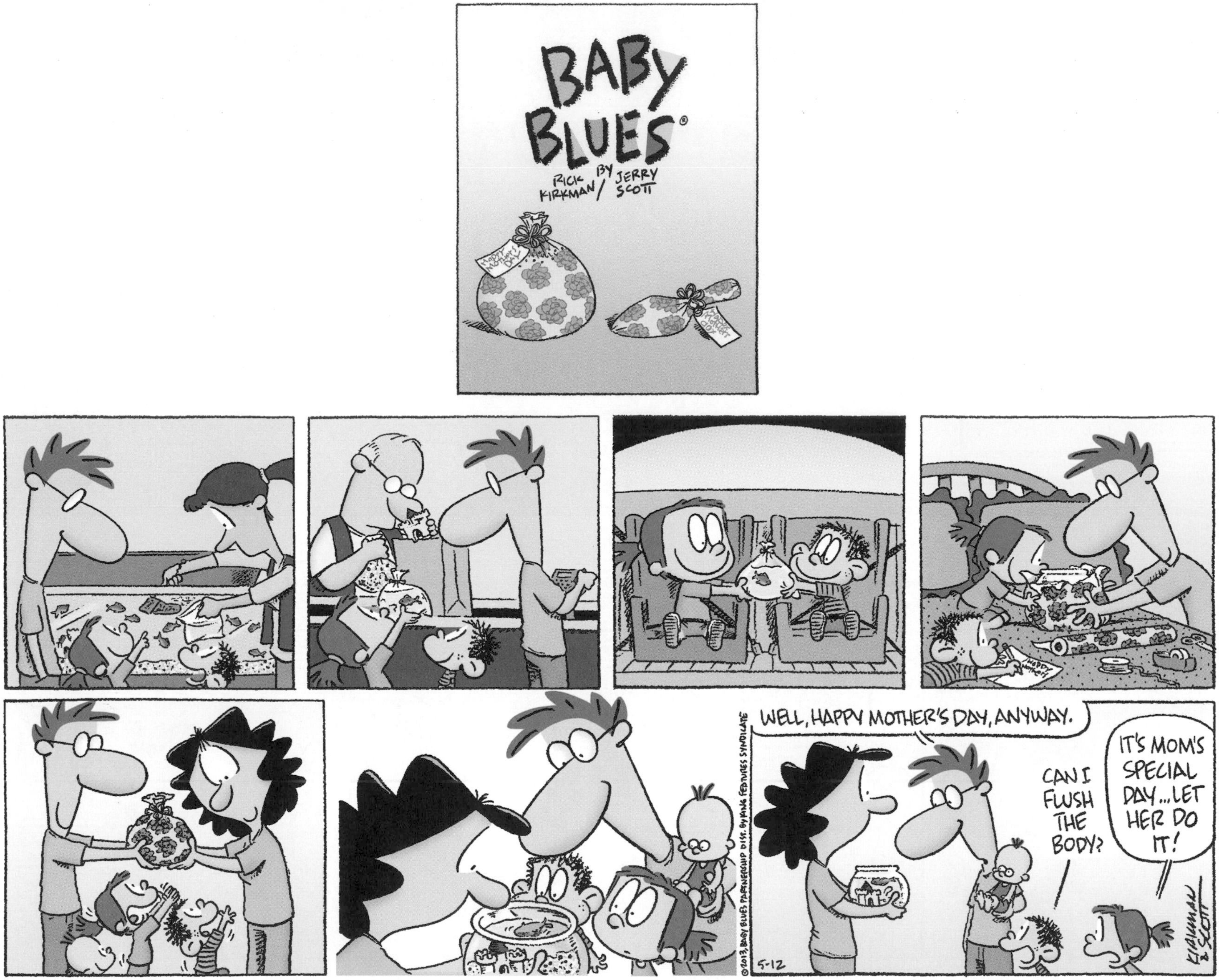
BABY BLUES®
BY RICK KIRKMAN / JERRY SCOTT
©2013, BABY BLUES PARTNERSHIP DIST. BY KING FEATURES SYNDICATE
5-12
WELL, HAPPY MOTHER'S DAY, ANYWAY.
CAN I FLUSH THE BODY?
IT'S MOM'S SPECIAL DAY... LET HER DO IT!
KIRKMAN & SCOTT

Jerry: The MacPhersons extend their record of unfortunate luck with small pets.

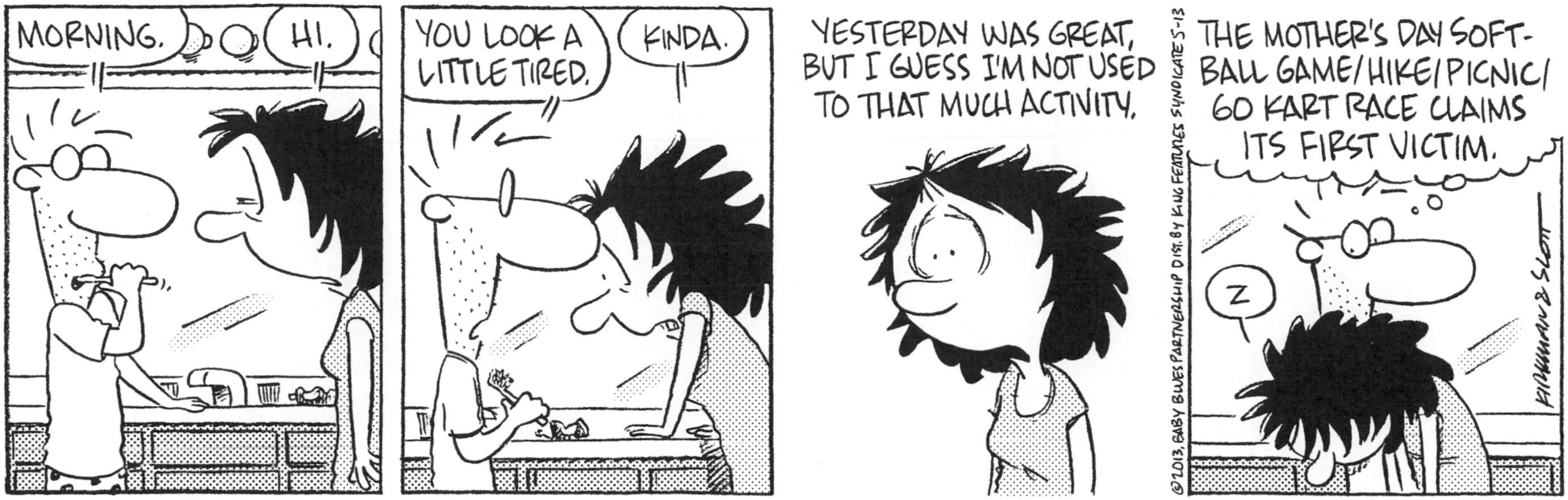
MORNING.
HI.
YOU LOOK A LITTLE TIRED.
KINDA.
YESTERDAY WAS GREAT, BUT I GUESS I'M NOT USED TO THAT MUCH ACTIVITY.
THE MOTHER'S DAY SOFT-BALL GAME/HIKE/PICNIC/GO KART RACE CLAIMS ITS FIRST VICTIM.
Z
©2013, BABY BLUES PARTNERSHIP DIST. BY KING FEATURES SYNDICATE 5-13
KIRKMAN & SCOTT

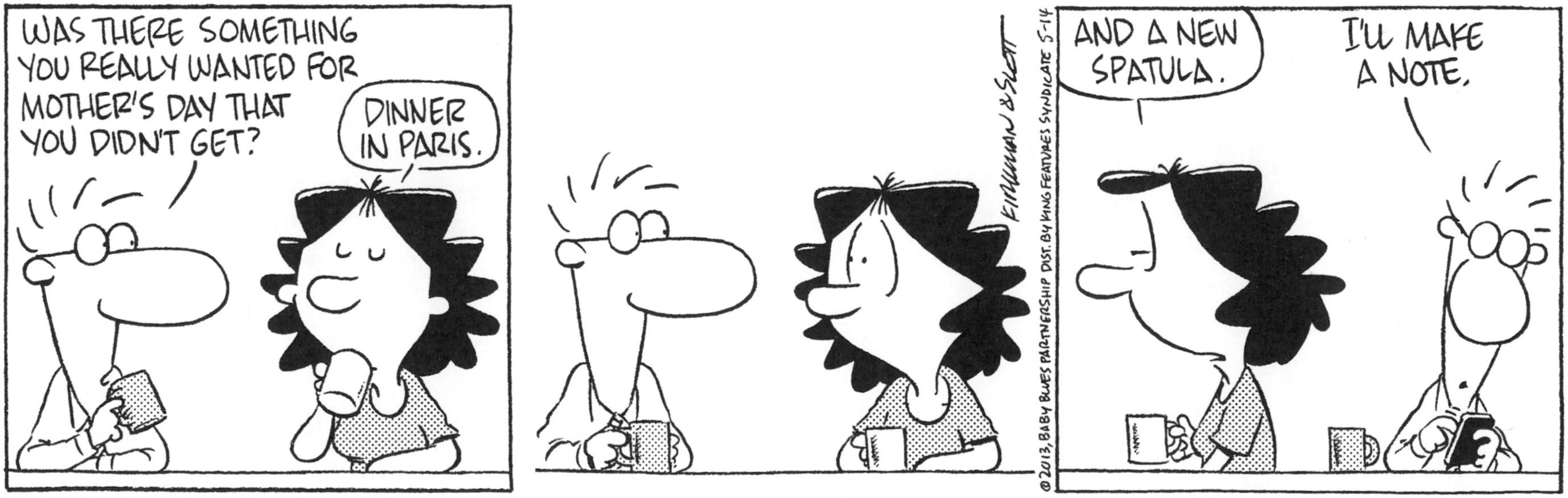
WAS THERE SOMETHING YOU REALLY WANTED FOR MOTHER'S DAY THAT YOU DIDN'T GET?
DINNER IN PARIS.
KIRKMAN & SCOTT
©2013, BABY BLUES PARTNERSHIP DIST. BY KING FEATURES SYNDICATE 5-14
AND A NEW SPATULA.
I'LL MAKE A NOTE.

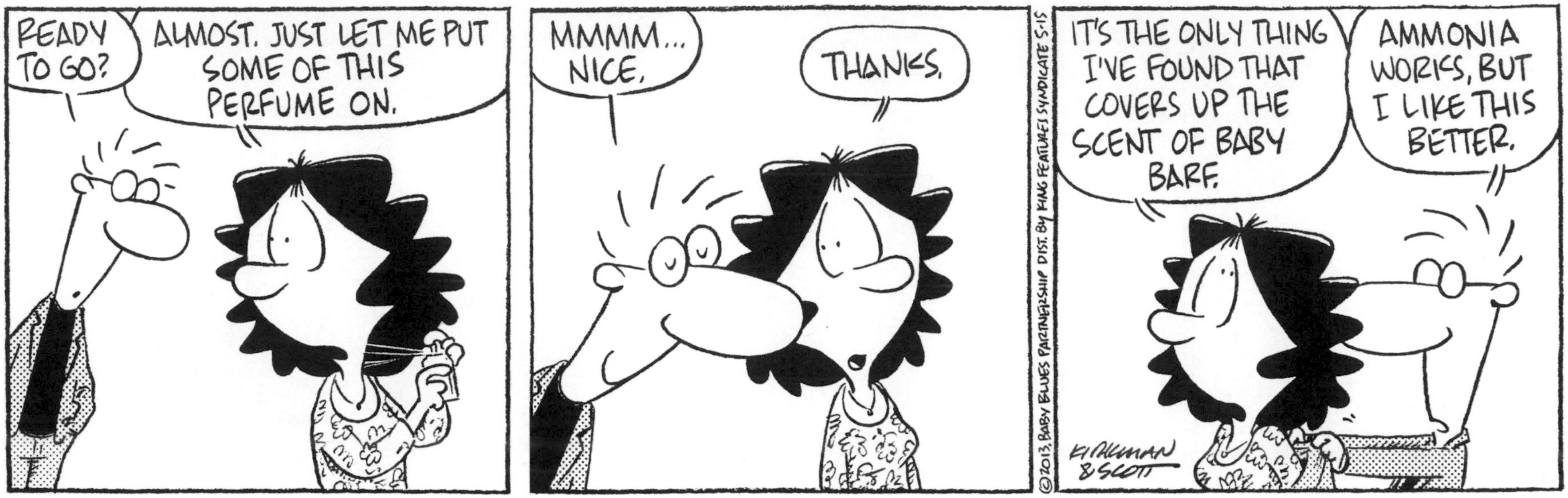
READY TO GO?
ALMOST. JUST LET ME PUT SOME OF THIS PERFUME ON.
MMMM... NICE.
THANKS.
©2013, BABY BLUES PARTNERSHIP DIST. BY KING FEATURES SYNDICATE 5-15
IT'S THE ONLY THING I'VE FOUND THAT COVERS UP THE SCENT OF BABY BARF.
AMMONIA WORKS, BUT I LIKE THIS BETTER.
KIRKMAN & SCOTT

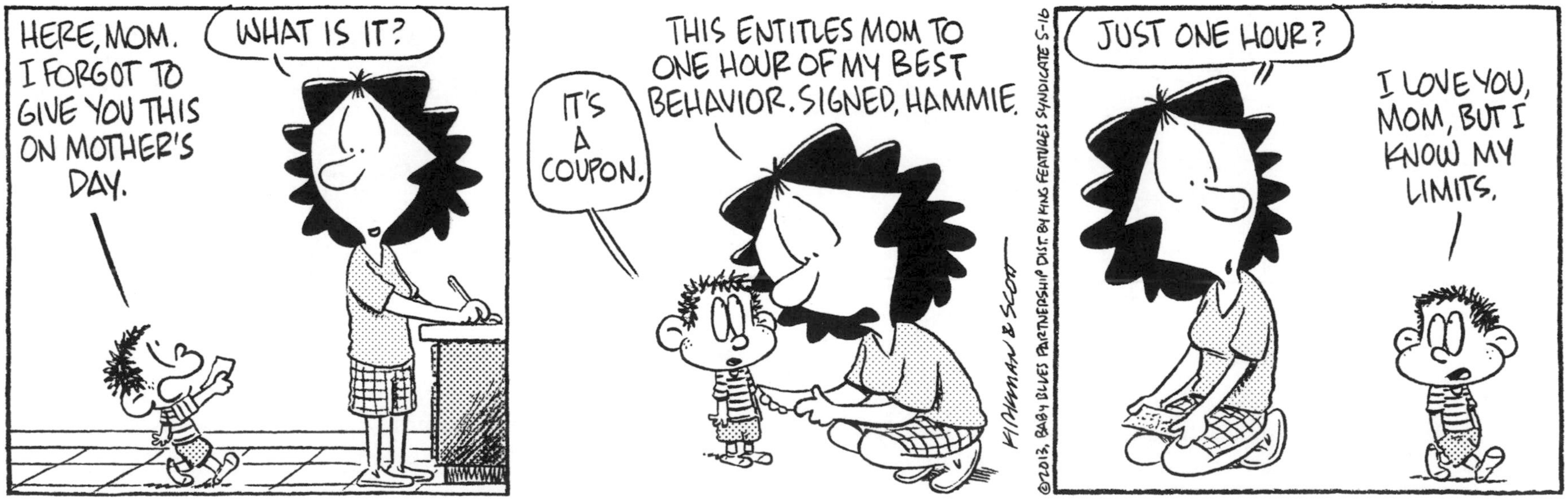
HERE, MOM. I FORGOT TO GIVE YOU THIS ON MOTHER'S DAY.
WHAT IS IT?
IT'S A COUPON.
THIS ENTITLES MOM TO ONE HOUR OF MY BEST BEHAVIOR. SIGNED, HAMMIE.
KIRKMAN & SCOTT
©2013, BABY BLUES PARTNERSHIP DIST. BY KING FEATURES SYNDICATE 5-16
JUST ONE HOUR?
I LOVE YOU, MOM, BUT I KNOW MY LIMITS.

MOM, WREN'S SANDBOX NEEDS MORE SAND.
I JUST ADDED SOME!
I KNOW, BUT IT'S ALMOST GONE.
I'LL TELL YOUR DAD TO PICK UP SOME ON HIS WAY HOME.
WHERE DOES IT ALL GO?
I MIGHT HAVE A GUESS.
©2013, BABY BLUES PARTNERSHIP DIST. BY KING FEATURES SYNDICATE 5-17
KIRKMAN & SCOTT

EAT, SLEEP, POOP.
THAT'S YOUR LIFE, WREN.
YOUR LIFE AND DAD'S WEEKENDS.
I ALSO SCRATCH.
©2013, BABY BLUES PARTNERSHIP DIST. BY KING FEATURES SYNDICATE 5-18
KIRKMAN & SCOTT

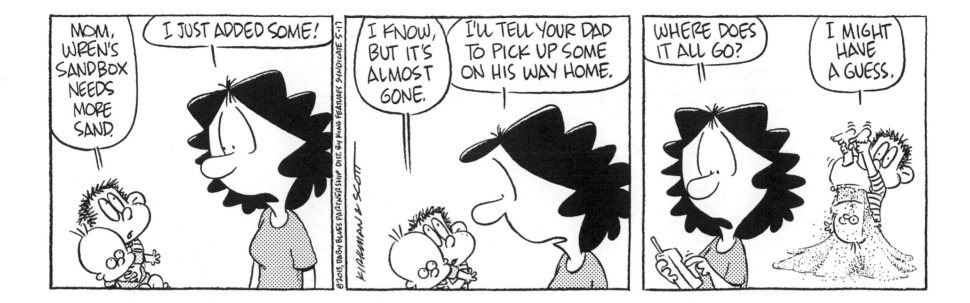

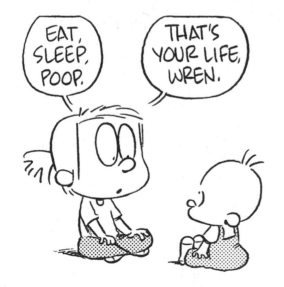

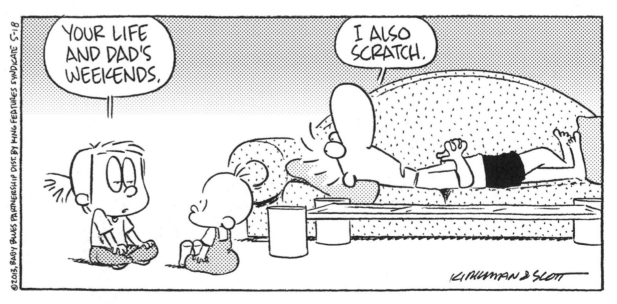

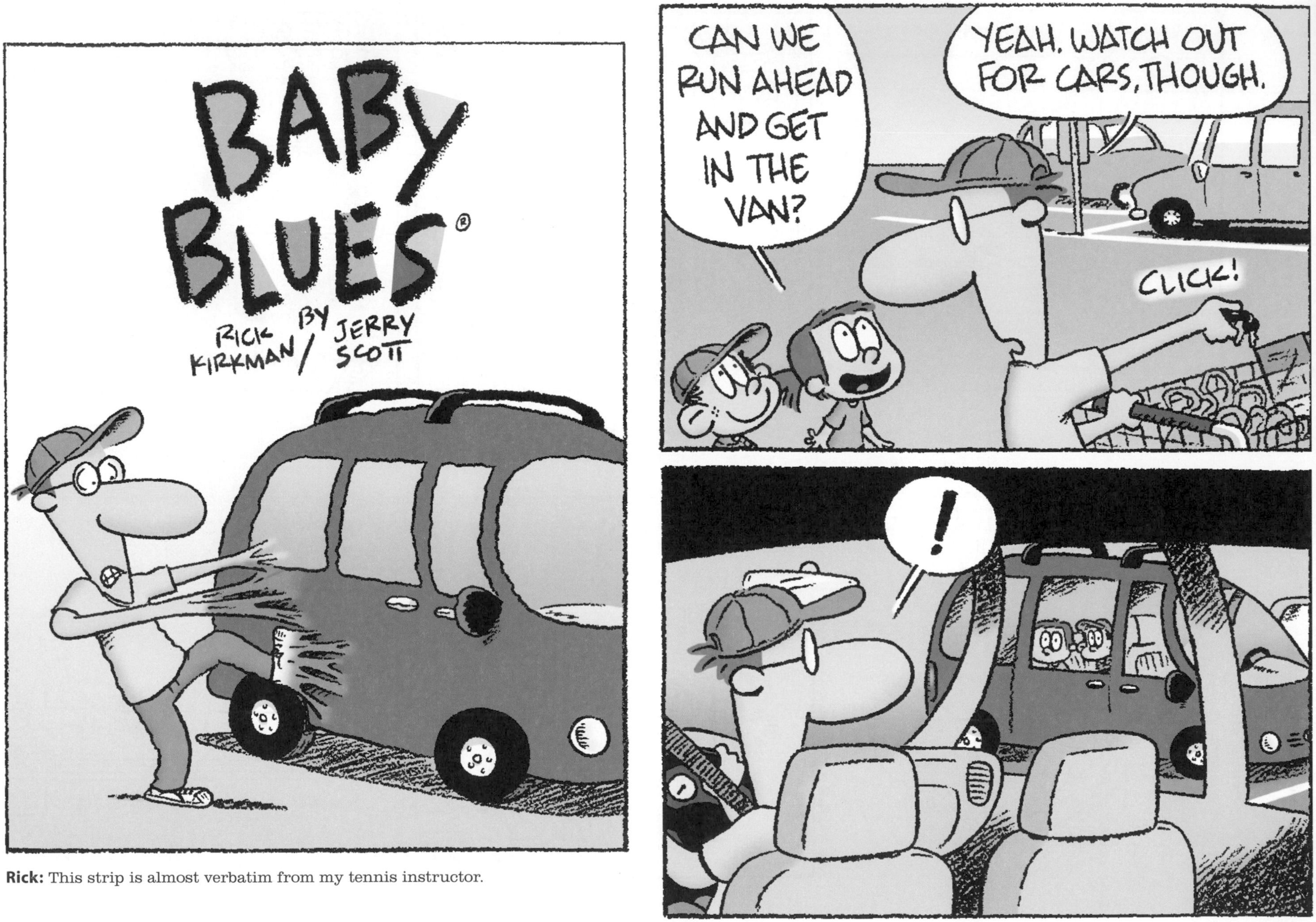
BABY BLUES®
BY RICK KIRKMAN / JERRY SCOTT
CAN WE RUN AHEAD AND GET IN THE VAN?
YEAH. WATCH OUT FOR CARS, THOUGH.
CLICK!
!

Rick: This strip is almost verbatim from my tennis instructor.

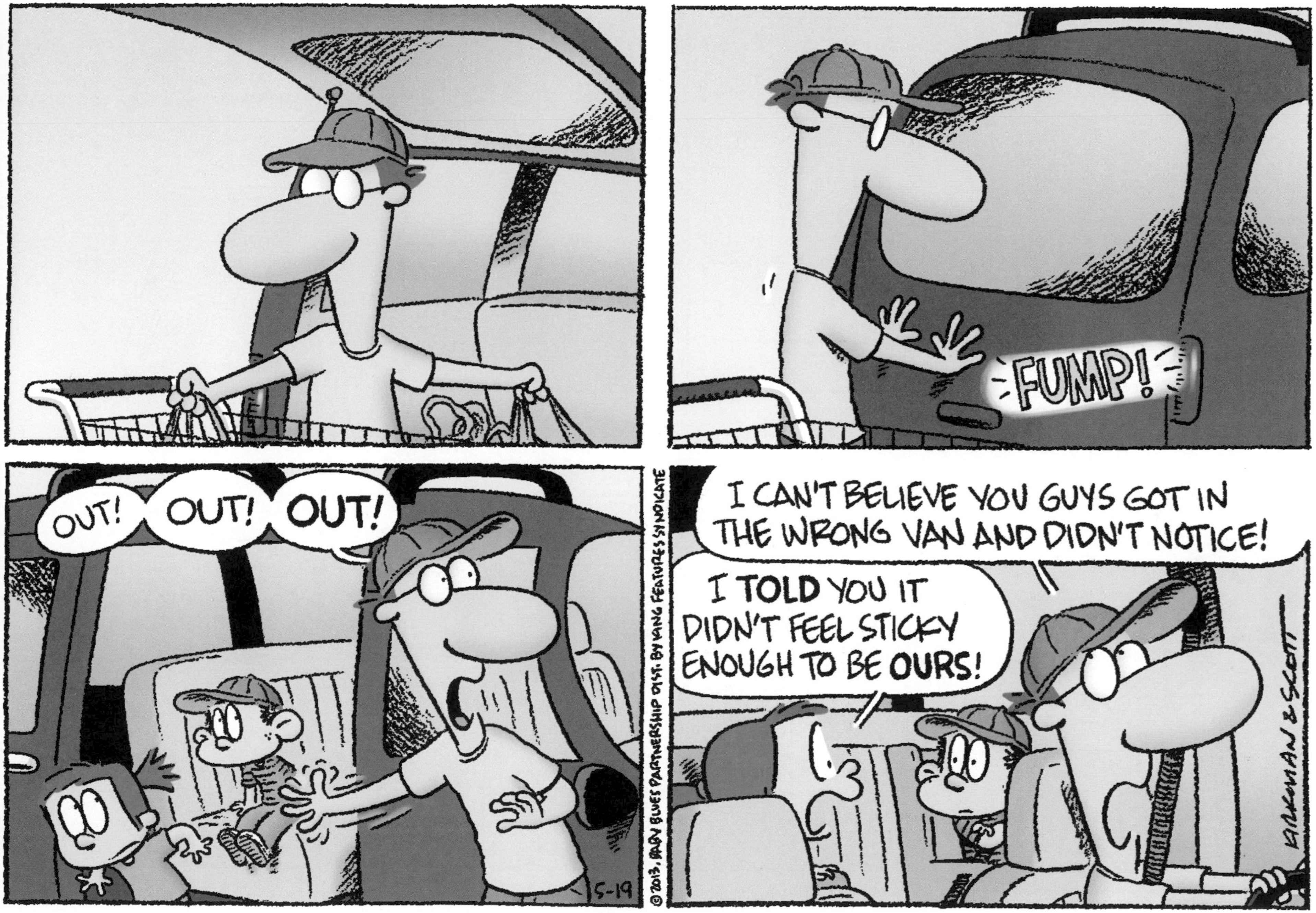
FUMP!
OUT! OUT! OUT!
5-19
©2013, BABY BLUES PARTNERSHIP DIST. BY KING FEATURES SYNDICATE
I CAN'T BELIEVE YOU GUYS GOT IN THE WRONG VAN AND DIDN'T NOTICE!
I TOLD YOU IT DIDN'T FEEL STICKY ENOUGH TO BE OURS!
KIRKMAN & SCOTT

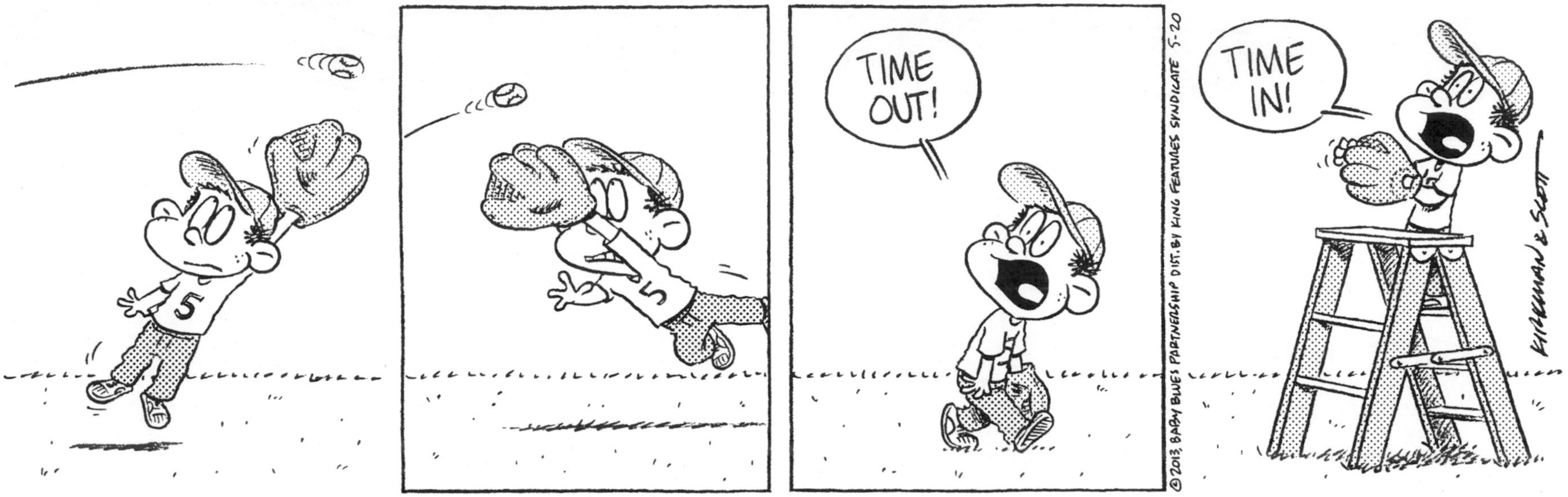

TIME OUT!
©2013, BABY BLUES PARTNERSHIP DIST. BY KING FEATURES SYNDICATE 5-20
TIME IN!
KIRKMAN & SCOTT

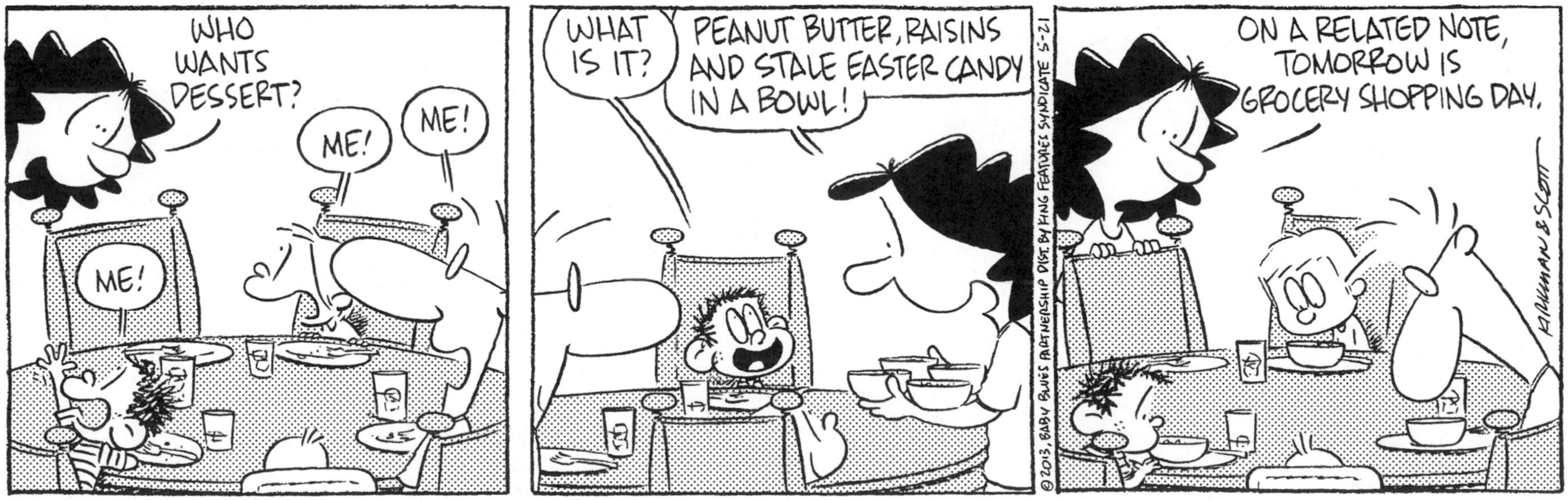

WHO WANTS DESSERT?
ME!
ME!
ME!
WHAT IS IT?
PEANUT BUTTER, RAISINS AND STALE EASTER CANDY IN A BOWL!
©2013, BABY BLUES PARTNERSHIP DIST. BY KING FEATURES SYNDICATE 5-21
ON A RELATED NOTE, TOMORROW IS GROCERY SHOPPING DAY.
KIRKMAN & SCOTT

Jerry: I actually made this dessert once. It's better than it sounds and even uglier than you think.

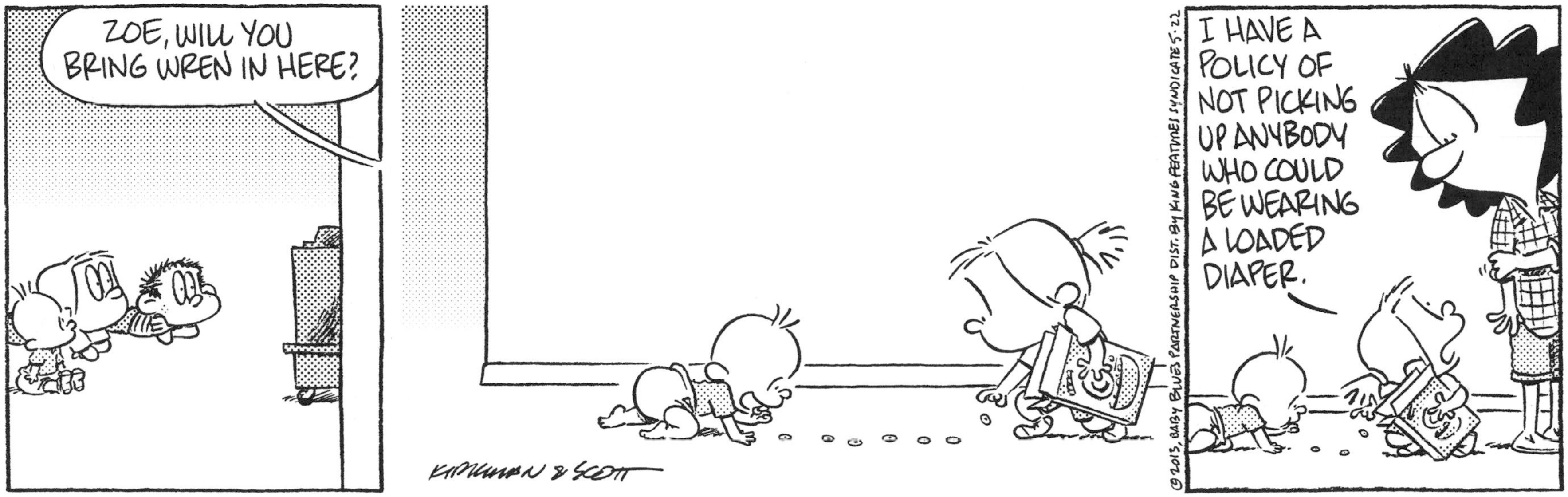
ZOE, WILL YOU BRING WREN IN HERE?
KIRKMAN & SCOTT
© 2013, BABY BLUES PARTNERSHIP DIST. BY KING FEATURES SYNDICATE 5-22
I HAVE A POLICY OF NOT PICKING UP ANYBODY WHO COULD BE WEARING A LOADED DIAPER.

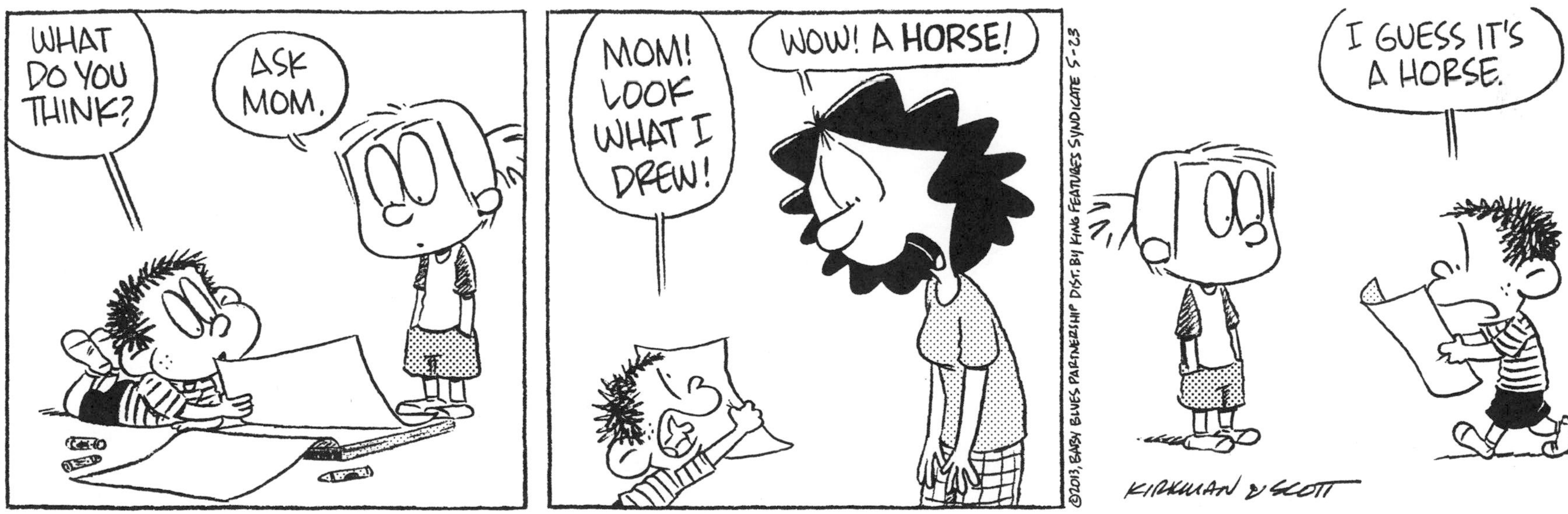
WHAT DO YOU THINK?
ASK MOM.
MOM! LOOK WHAT I DREW!
WOW! A **HORSE**!
© 2013, BABY BLUES PARTNERSHIP DIST. BY KING FEATURES SYNDICATE 5-23
I GUESS IT'S A HORSE.
KIRKMAN & SCOTT

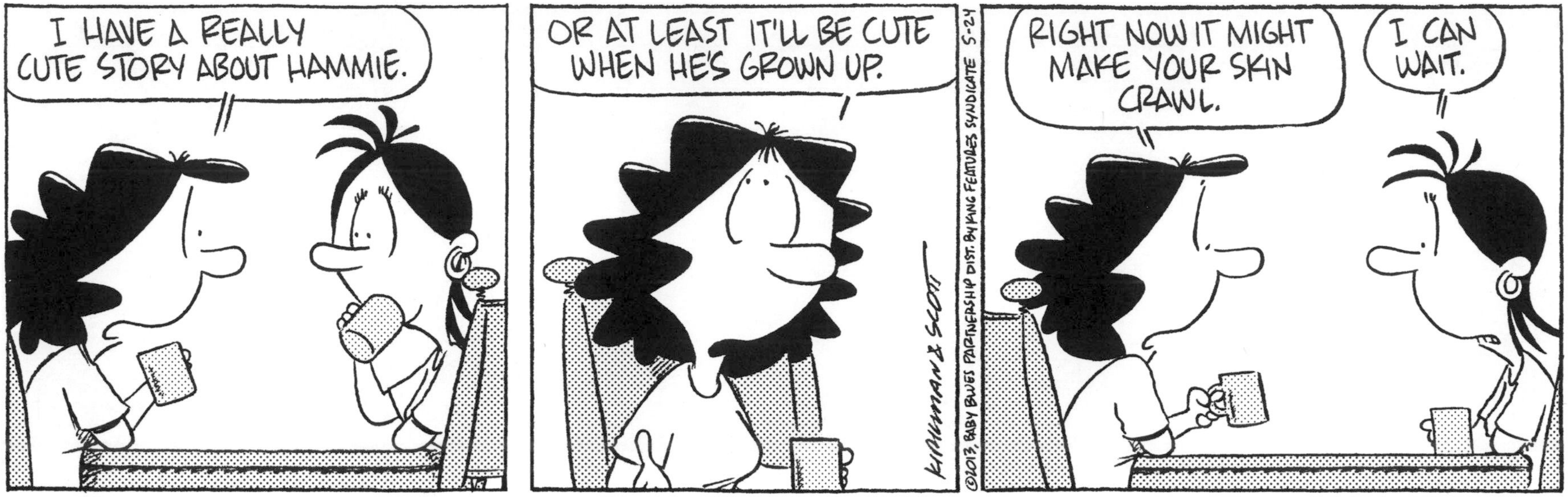
I HAVE A REALLY CUTE STORY ABOUT HAMMIE.
OR AT LEAST IT'LL BE CUTE WHEN HE'S GROWN UP.
RIGHT NOW IT MIGHT MAKE YOUR SKIN CRAWL.
I CAN WAIT.
KIRKMAN & SCOTT
©2013, BABY BLUES PARTNERSHIP DIST. BY KING FEATURES SYNDICATE 5-24

Jerry: A lot of kid stories are better left unshared outside the immediate family.

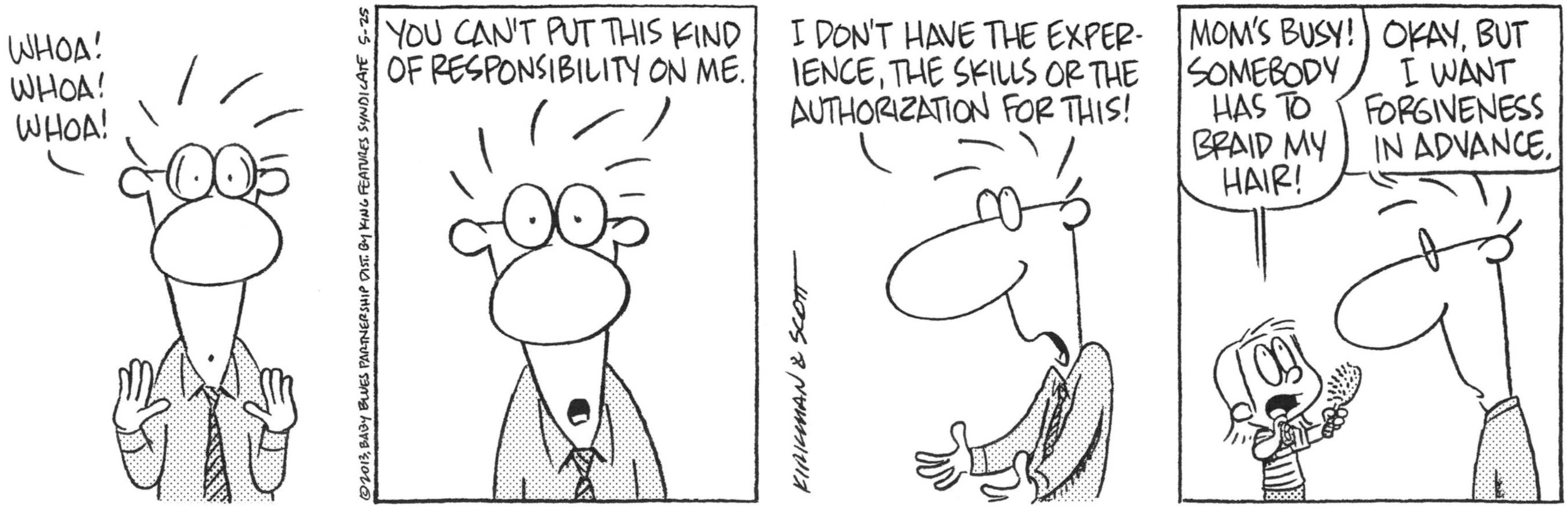
WHOA! WHOA! WHOA!
YOU CAN'T PUT THIS KIND OF RESPONSIBILITY ON ME.
I DON'T HAVE THE EXPERIENCE, THE SKILLS OR THE AUTHORIZATION FOR THIS!
MOM'S BUSY! SOMEBODY HAS TO BRAID MY HAIR!
OKAY, BUT I WANT FORGIVENESS IN ADVANCE.
KIRKMAN & SCOTT
©2013, BABY BLUES PARTNERSHIP DIST. BY KING FEATURES SYNDICATE 5-25

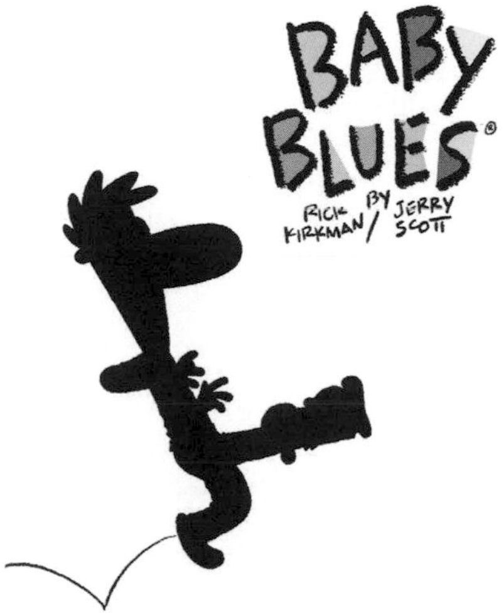
BABY BLUES®
BY RICK KIRKMAN / JERRY SCOTT

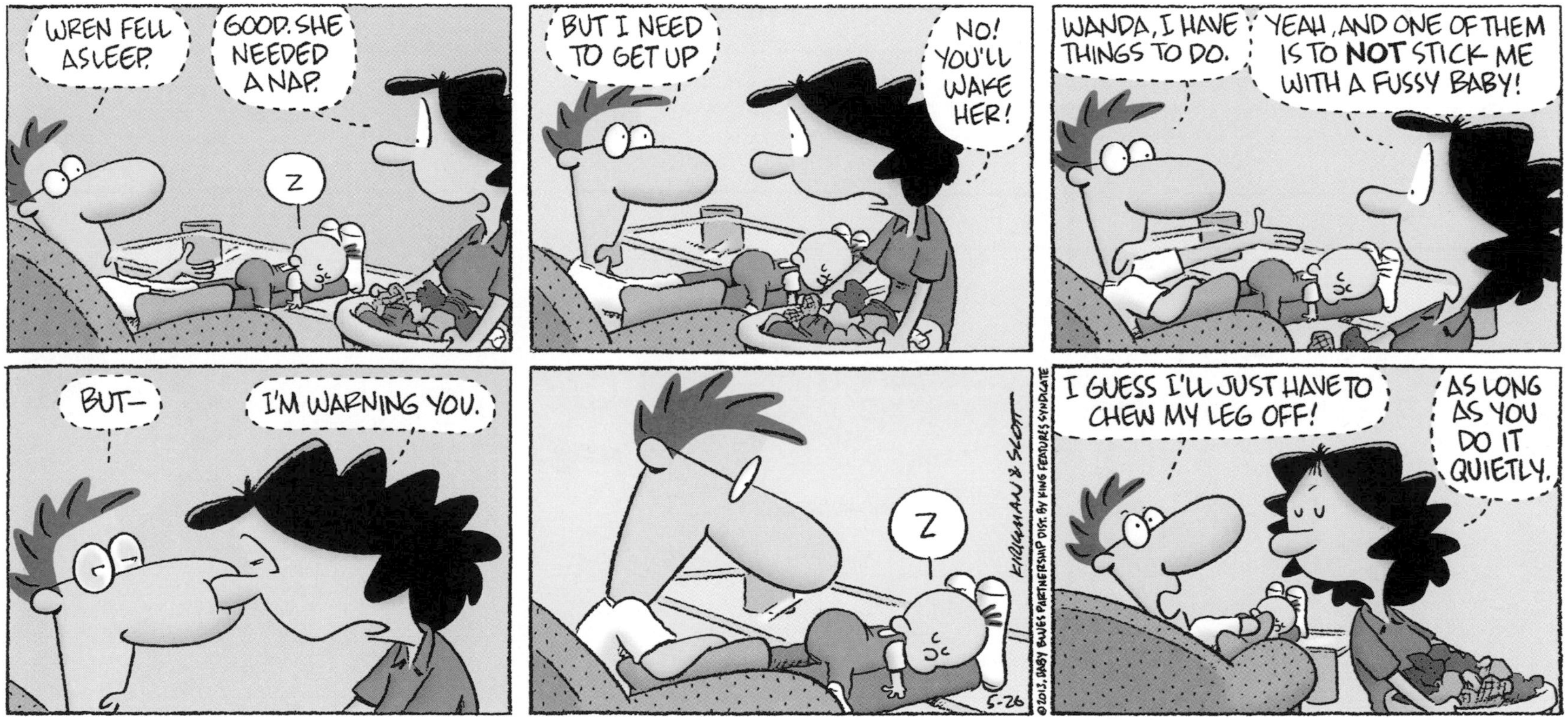
WREN FELL ASLEEP.
GOOD. SHE NEEDED A NAP.
Z
BUT I NEED TO GET UP
NO! YOU'LL WAKE HER!
WANDA, I HAVE THINGS TO DO.
YEAH, AND ONE OF THEM IS TO **NOT** STICK ME WITH A FUSSY BABY!
BUT–
I'M WARNING YOU.
Z
KIRKMAN & SCOTT
5-26
©2013, BABY BLUES PARTNERSHIP DIST. BY KING FEATURES SYNDICATE
I GUESS I'LL JUST HAVE TO CHEW MY LEG OFF!
AS LONG AS YOU DO IT QUIETLY.

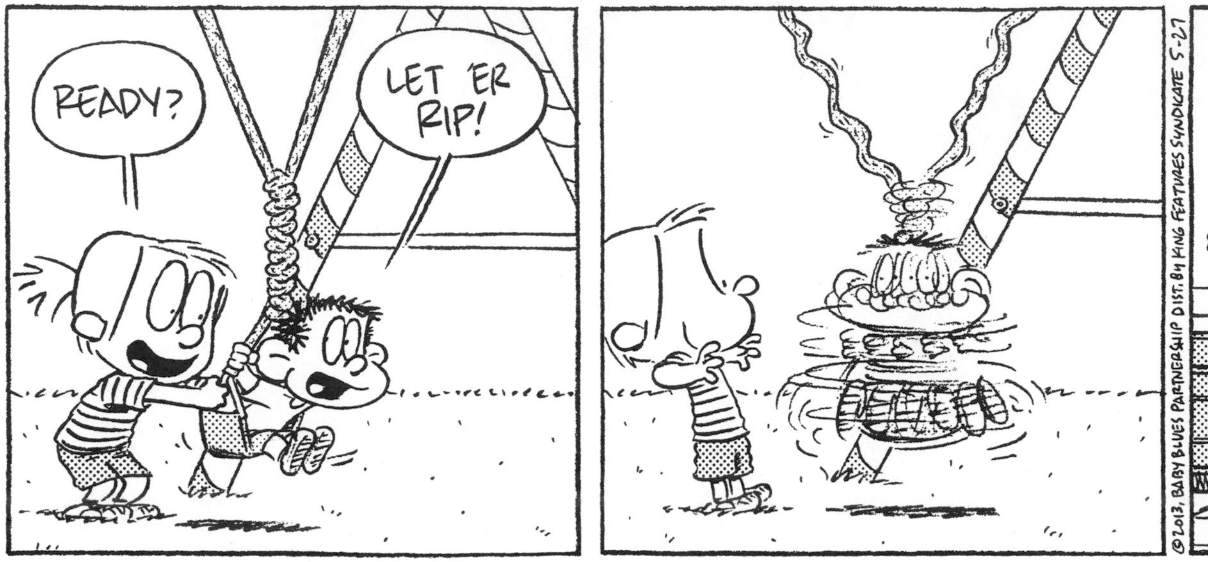
READY?
LET 'ER RIP!
HOW DO YOU UNSCREW SOMEBODY OUT OF THE GROUND?
© 2013, BABY BLUES PARTNERSHIP DIST. BY KING FEATURES SYNDICATE 5-27
KIRKMAN & SCOTT

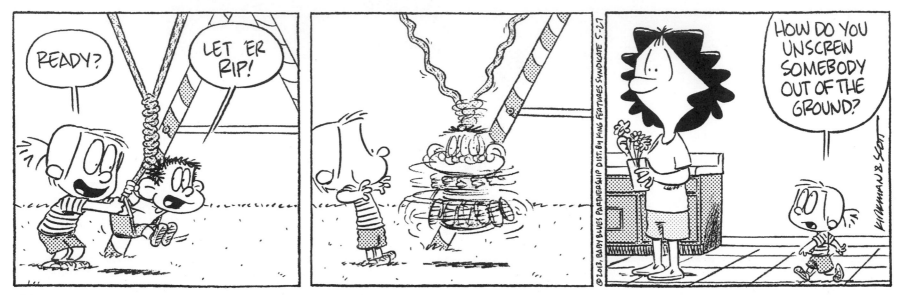

Rick: The middle panel is one of my favorite drawings I've done. Secret: In the original, Hammie was a little too small, but I was so happy with how the drawing came out, I didn't think I could do it as well again. So I made him larger in Photoshop afterward.

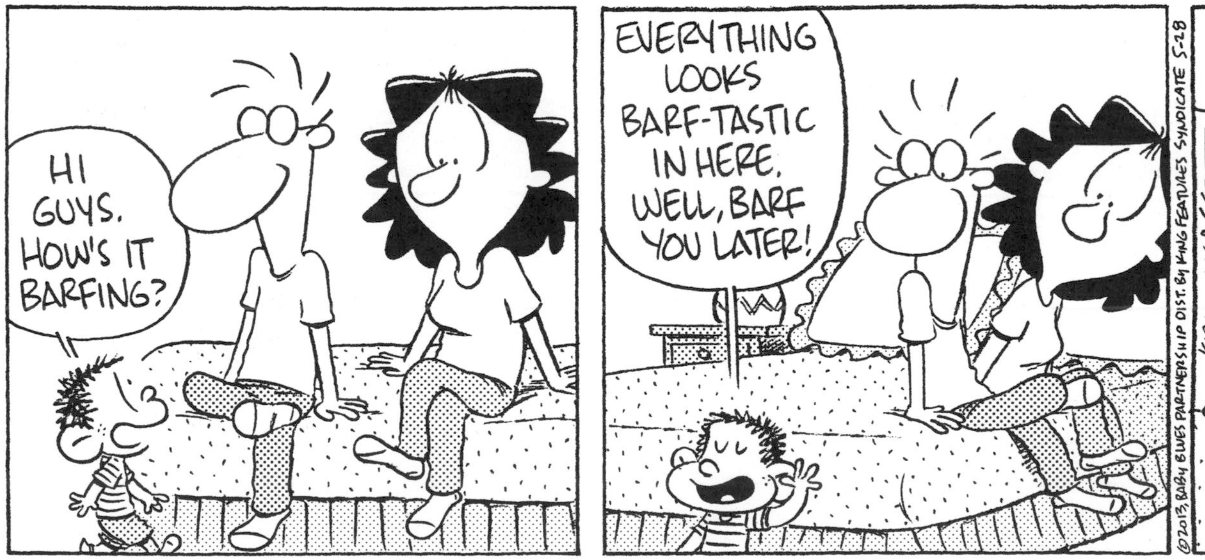
HI GUYS. HOW'S IT BARFING?
EVERYTHING LOOKS BARF-TASTIC IN HERE. WELL, BARF YOU LATER!
© 2013, BABY BLUES PARTNERSHIP DIST. BY KING FEATURES SYNDICATE 5-28
KIRKMAN & SCOTT
SHOULD I PUT A STOP TO THAT?
ONLY IF YOU VALUE YOUR SANITY.

Jerry: Hammie's sense of humor is modeled on my own when I was his age. And maybe currently.

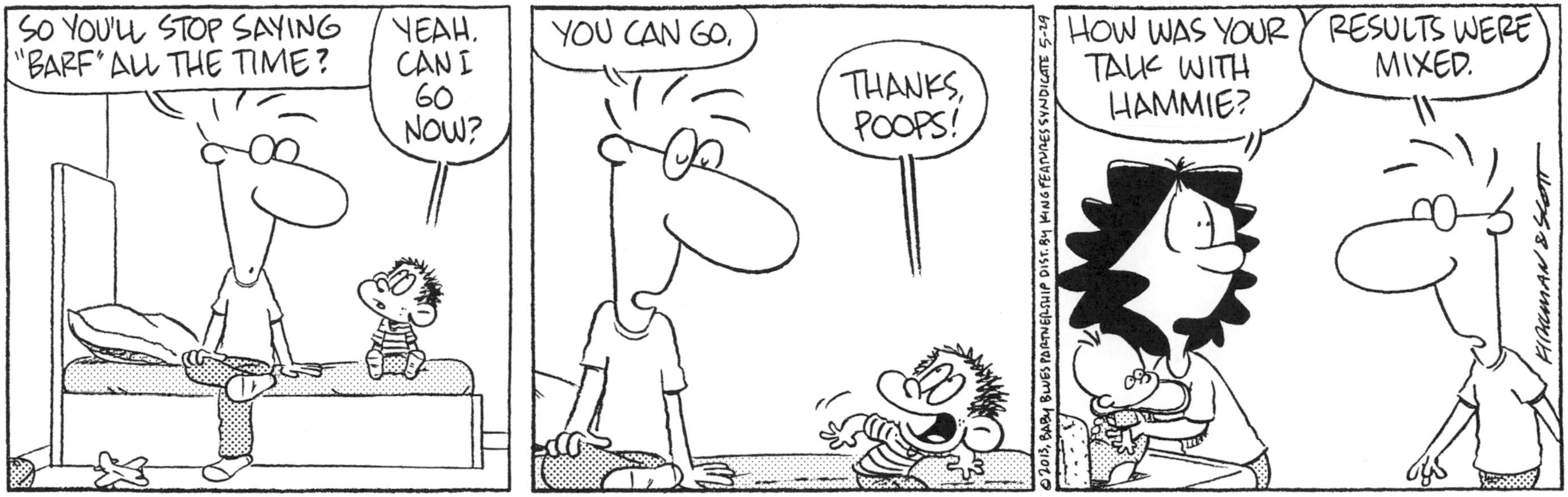
SO YOU'LL STOP SAYING "BARF" ALL THE TIME?
YEAH. CAN I GO NOW?
YOU CAN GO.
THANKS, POOPS!
©2013, BABY BLUES PARTNERSHIP DIST. BY KING FEATURES SYNDICATE 5-29
HOW WAS YOUR TALK WITH HAMMIE?
RESULTS WERE MIXED.
KIRKMAN & SCOTT

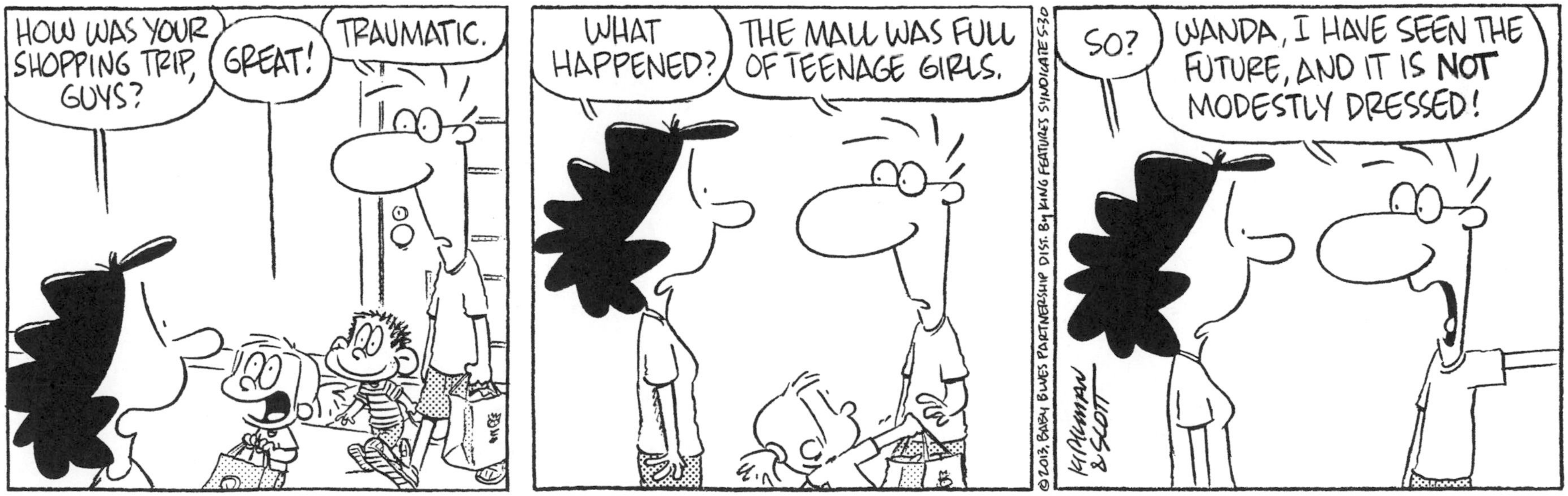
HOW WAS YOUR SHOPPING TRIP, GUYS?
GREAT!
TRAUMATIC.
WHAT HAPPENED?
THE MALL WAS FULL OF TEENAGE GIRLS.
©2013, BABY BLUES PARTNERSHIP DIST. BY KING FEATURES SYNDICATE 5-30
KIRKMAN & SCOTT
SO?
WANDA, I HAVE SEEN THE FUTURE, AND IT IS **NOT** MODESTLY DRESSED!

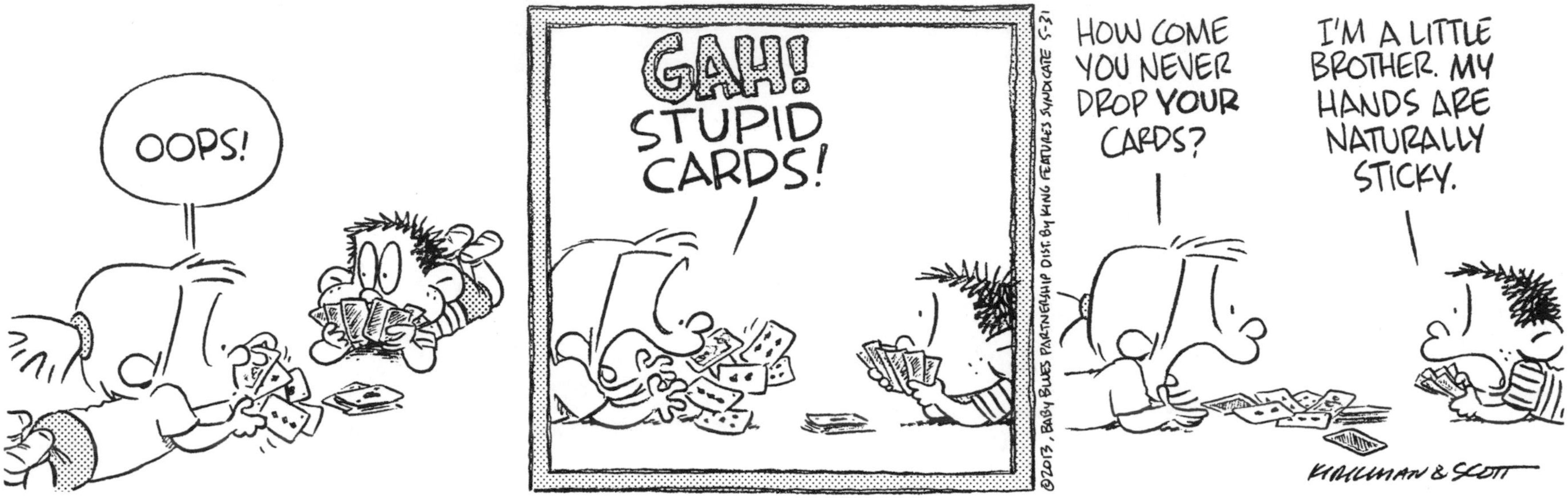
OOPS!
GAH! STUPID CARDS!
©2013, BABY BLUES PARTNERSHIP DIST. BY KING FEATURES SYNDICATE 5-31
HOW COME YOU NEVER DROP **YOUR** CARDS?
I'M A LITTLE BROTHER. **MY** HANDS ARE NATURALLY STICKY.
KIRKMAN & SCOTT

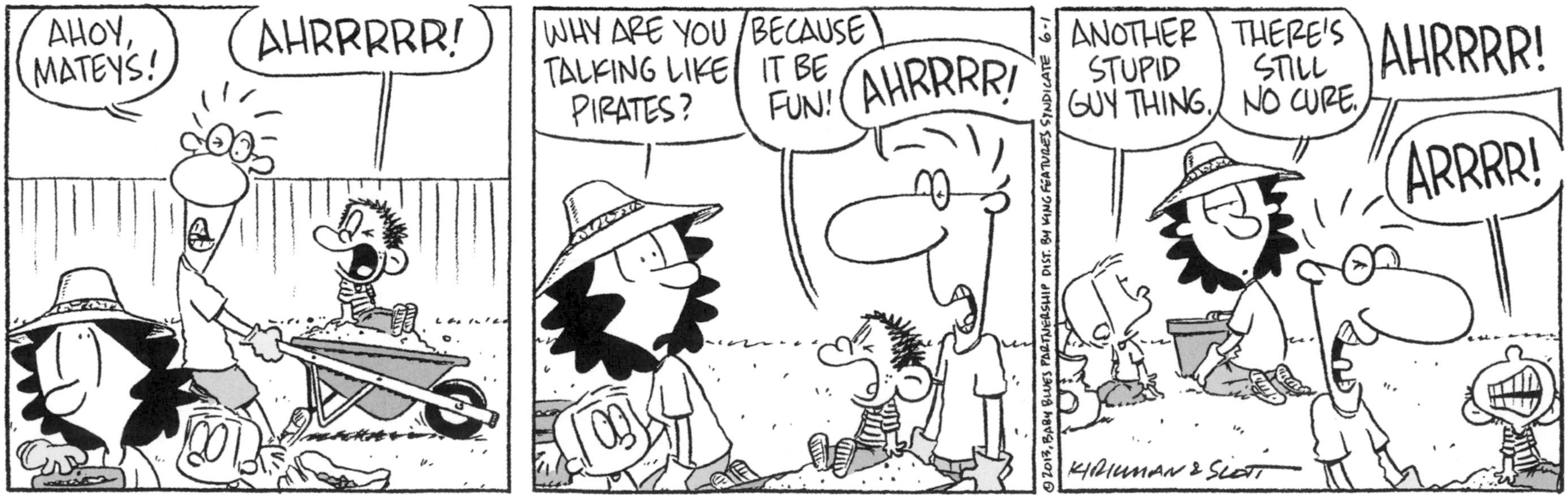
AHOY, MATEYS!
AHRRRRRR!
WHY ARE YOU TALKING LIKE PIRATES?
BECAUSE IT BE FUN!
AHRRRR!
©2013, BABY BLUES PARTNERSHIP DIST. BY KING FEATURES SYNDICATE 6-1
ANOTHER STUPID GUY THING.
THERE'S STILL NO CURE.
AHRRRR!
ARRRR!
KIRKMAN & SCOTT

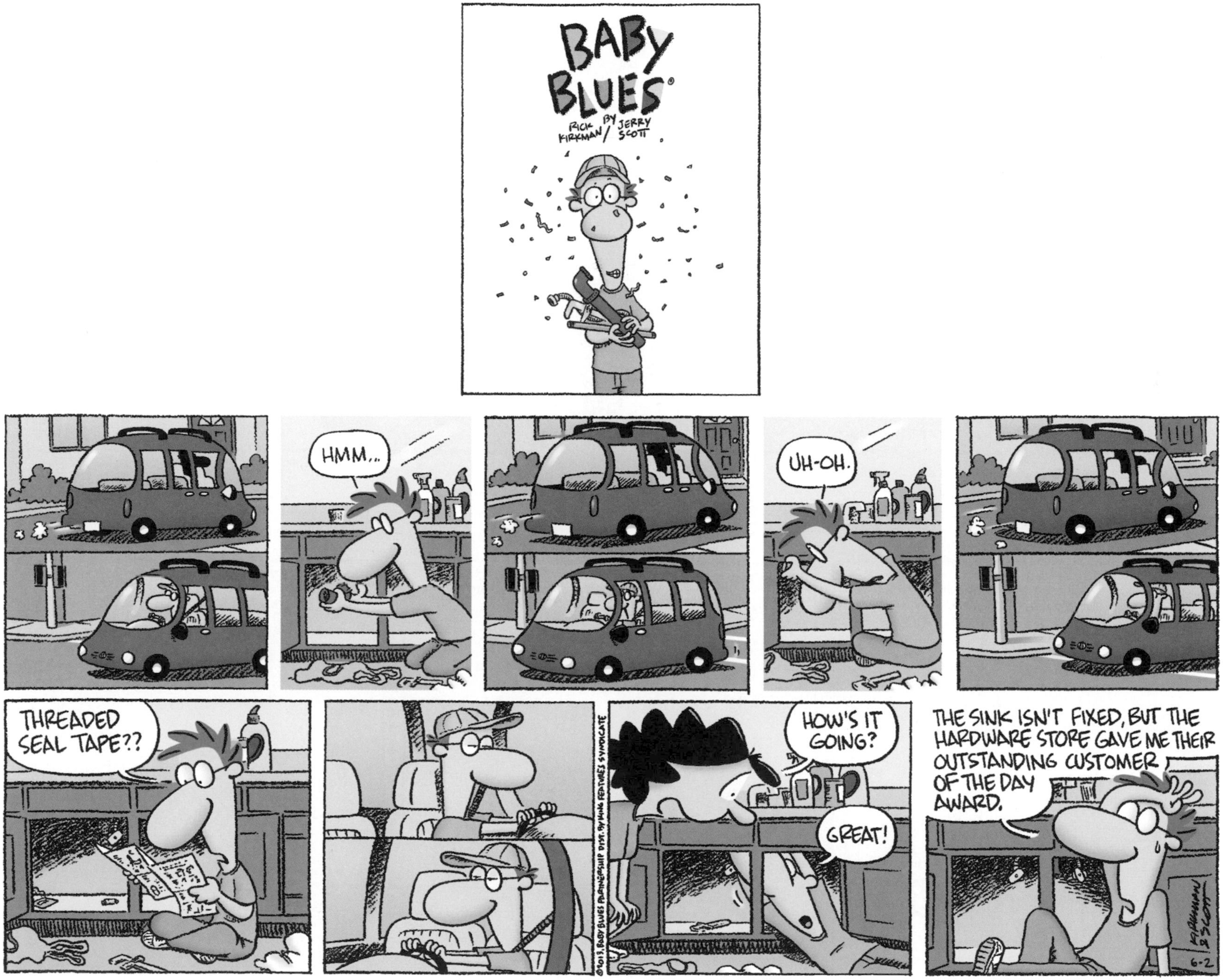
BABY BLUES®
RICK KIRKMAN / BY JERRY SCOTT
HMM...
UH-OH.
THREADED SEAL TAPE??
HOW'S IT GOING?
GREAT!
THE SINK ISN'T FIXED, BUT THE HARDWARE STORE GAVE ME THEIR OUTSTANDING CUSTOMER OF THE DAY AWARD.

Rick: Unfortunately, this is lifted directly from my attempt to fix a faucet. I should definitely stick to cartooning. The award is cool, though.

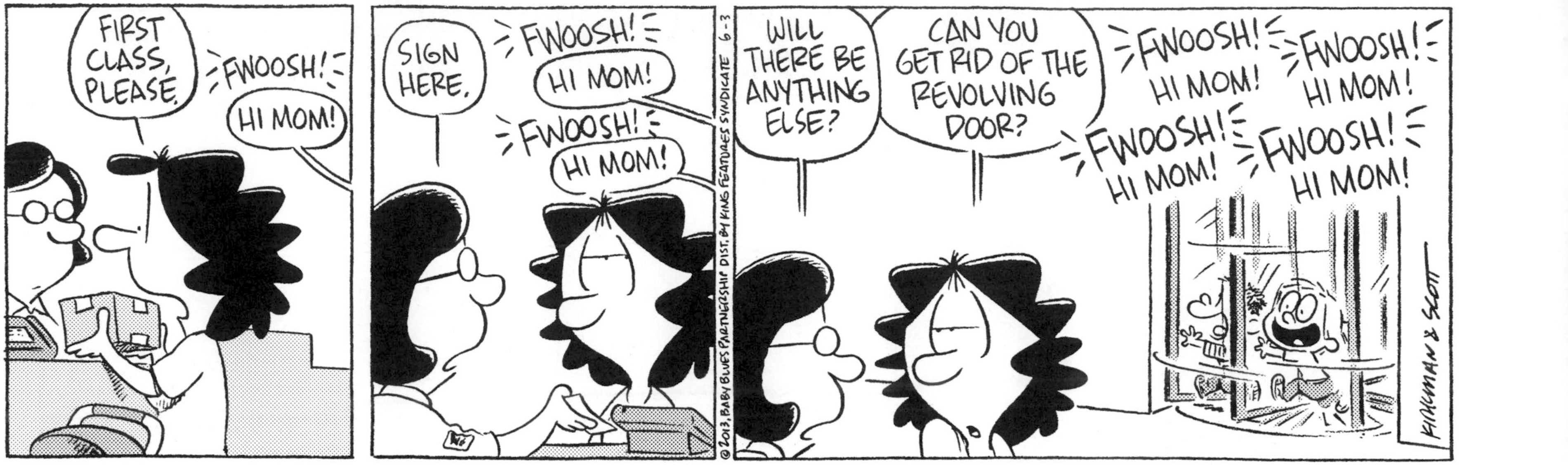
FIRST CLASS, PLEASE.
FWOOSH!
HI MOM!
SIGN HERE.
FWOOSH!
HI MOM!
FWOOSH!
HI MOM!
©2013, BABY BLUES PARTNERSHIP DIST. BY KING FEATURES SYNDICATE 6-3
WILL THERE BE ANYTHING ELSE?
CAN YOU GET RID OF THE REVOLVING DOOR?
FWOOSH! HI MOM!
FWOOSH! HI MOM!
FWOOSH! HI MOM!
FWOOSH! HI MOM!
KIRKMAN & SCOTT

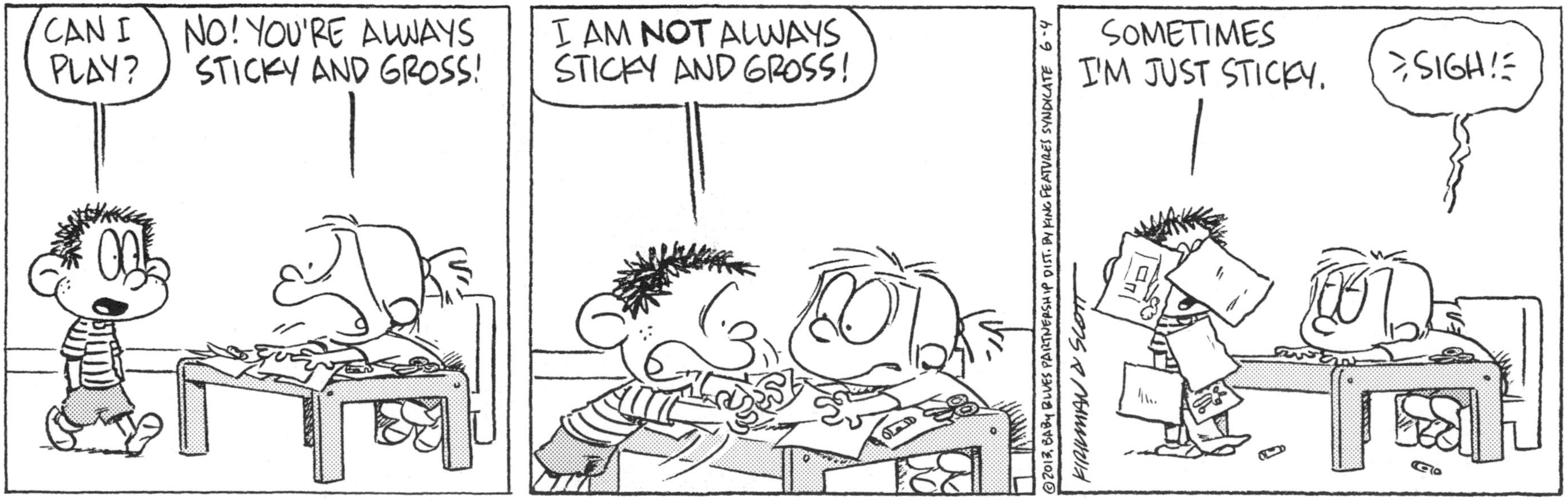
CAN I PLAY?
NO! YOU'RE ALWAYS STICKY AND GROSS!
I AM **NOT** ALWAYS STICKY AND GROSS!
©2013, BABY BLUES PARTNERSHIP DIST. BY KING FEATURES SYNDICATE 6-4
KIRKMAN & SCOTT
SOMETIMES I'M JUST STICKY.
SIGH!

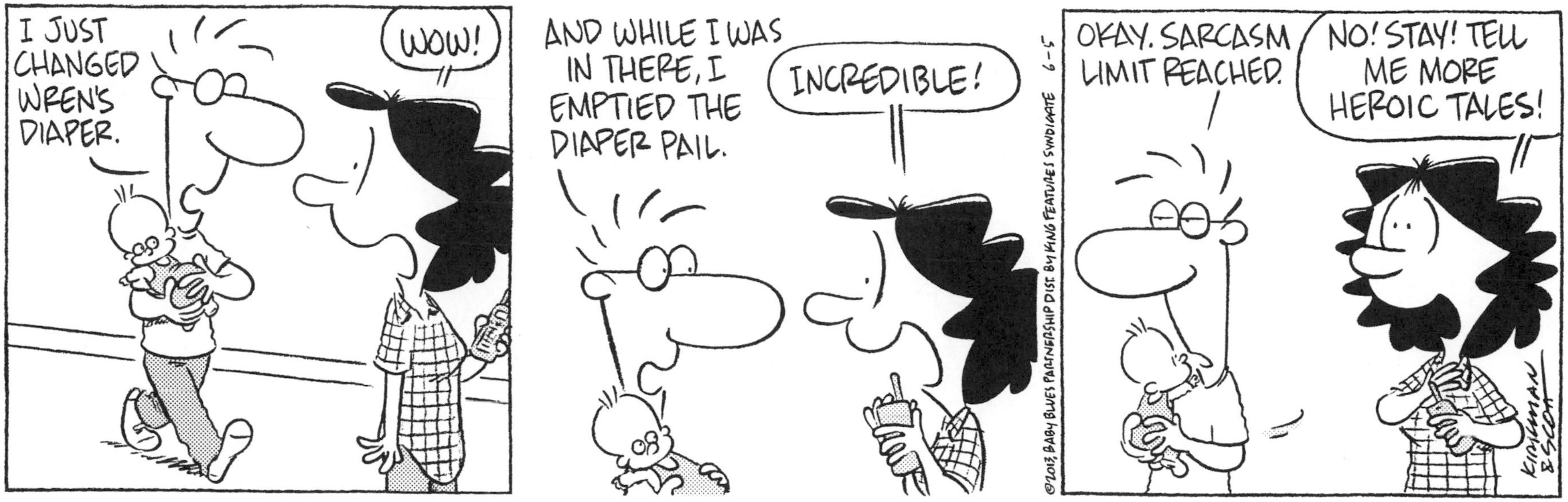
I JUST CHANGED WREN'S DIAPER.
WOW!
AND WHILE I WAS IN THERE, I EMPTIED THE DIAPER PAIL.
INCREDIBLE!
OKAY. SARCASM LIMIT REACHED.
NO! STAY! TELL ME MORE HEROIC TALES!
6-5
©2013 BABY BLUES PARTNERSHIP DIST. BY KING FEATURES SYNDICATE
KIRKMAN & SCOTT

Jerry: For some reason, this one cracks me up. I think it's the expression on Wanda's face in the last panel.

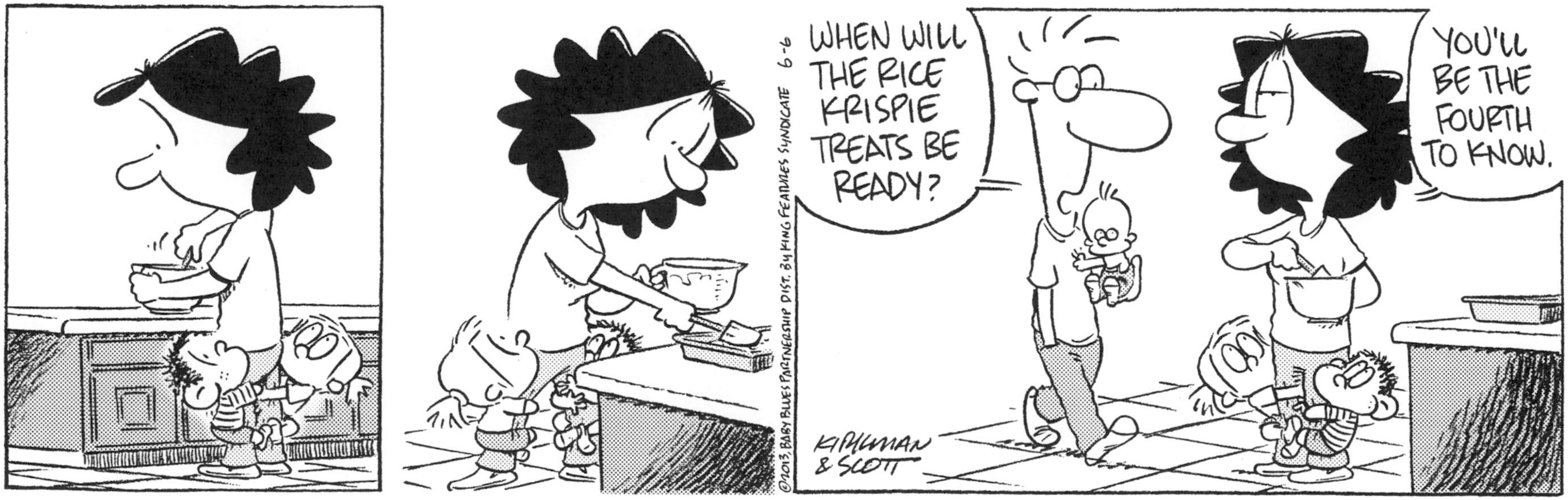
WHEN WILL THE RICE KRISPIE TREATS BE READY?
YOU'LL BE THE FOURTH TO KNOW.
6-6
©2013 BABY BLUES PARTNERSHIP DIST. BY KING FEATURES SYNDICATE
KIRKMAN & SCOTT

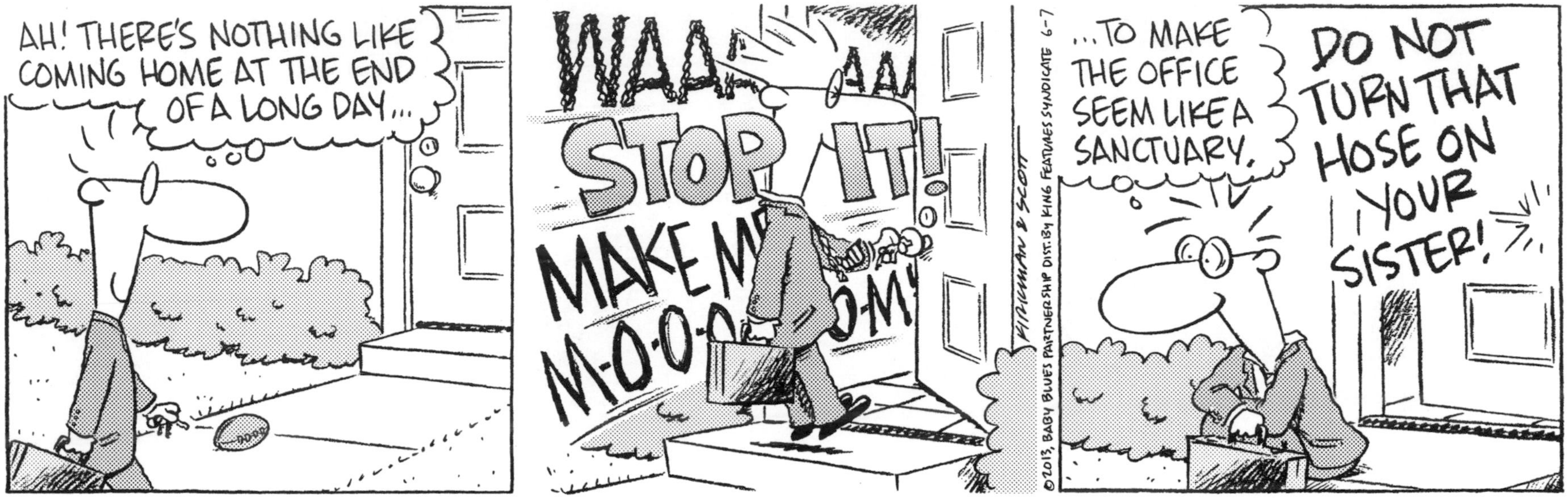
AH! THERE'S NOTHING LIKE COMING HOME AT THE END OF A LONG DAY...
WAA
AAA
STOP
IT!
MAKE M
M-O-O-O
O-M!
KIRKMAN & SCOTT
© 2013, BABY BLUES PARTNERSHIP DIST. BY KING FEATURES SYNDICATE 6-7
...TO MAKE THE OFFICE SEEM LIKE A SANCTUARY.
DO NOT TURN THAT HOSE ON YOUR SISTER!

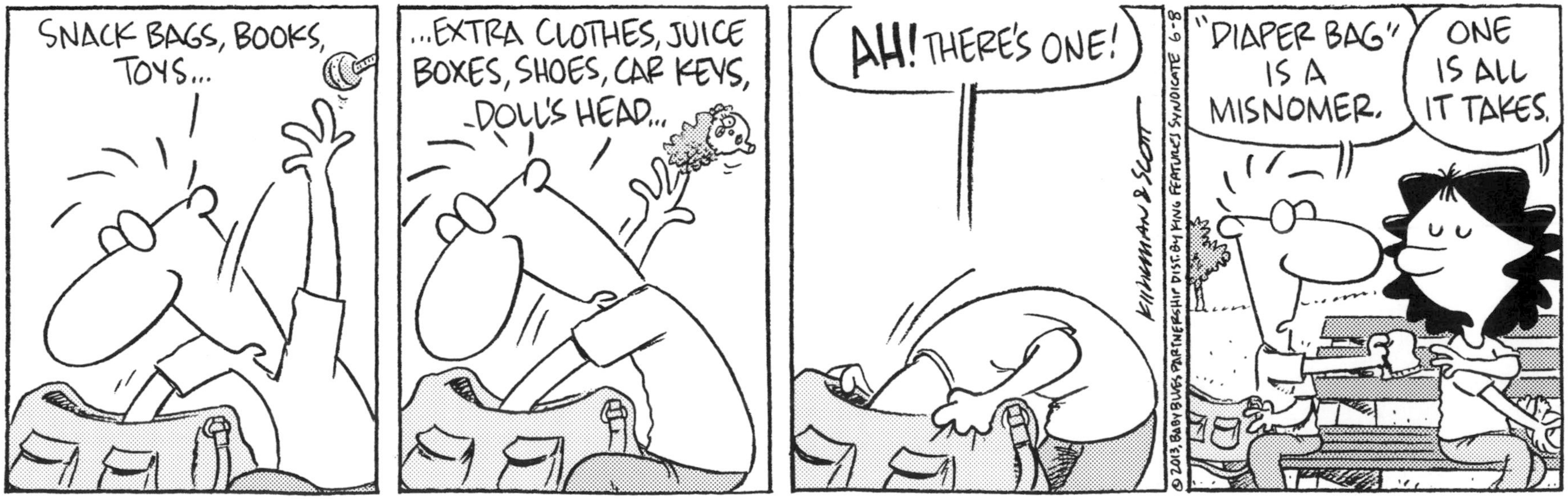
SNACK BAGS, BOOKS, TOYS...
...EXTRA CLOTHES, JUICE BOXES, SHOES, CAR KEYS, DOLL'S HEAD...
AH! THERE'S ONE!
KIRKMAN & SCOTT
© 2013, BABY BLUES PARTNERSHIP DIST. BY KING FEATURES SYNDICATE 6-8
"DIAPER BAG" IS A MISNOMER.
ONE IS ALL IT TAKES.

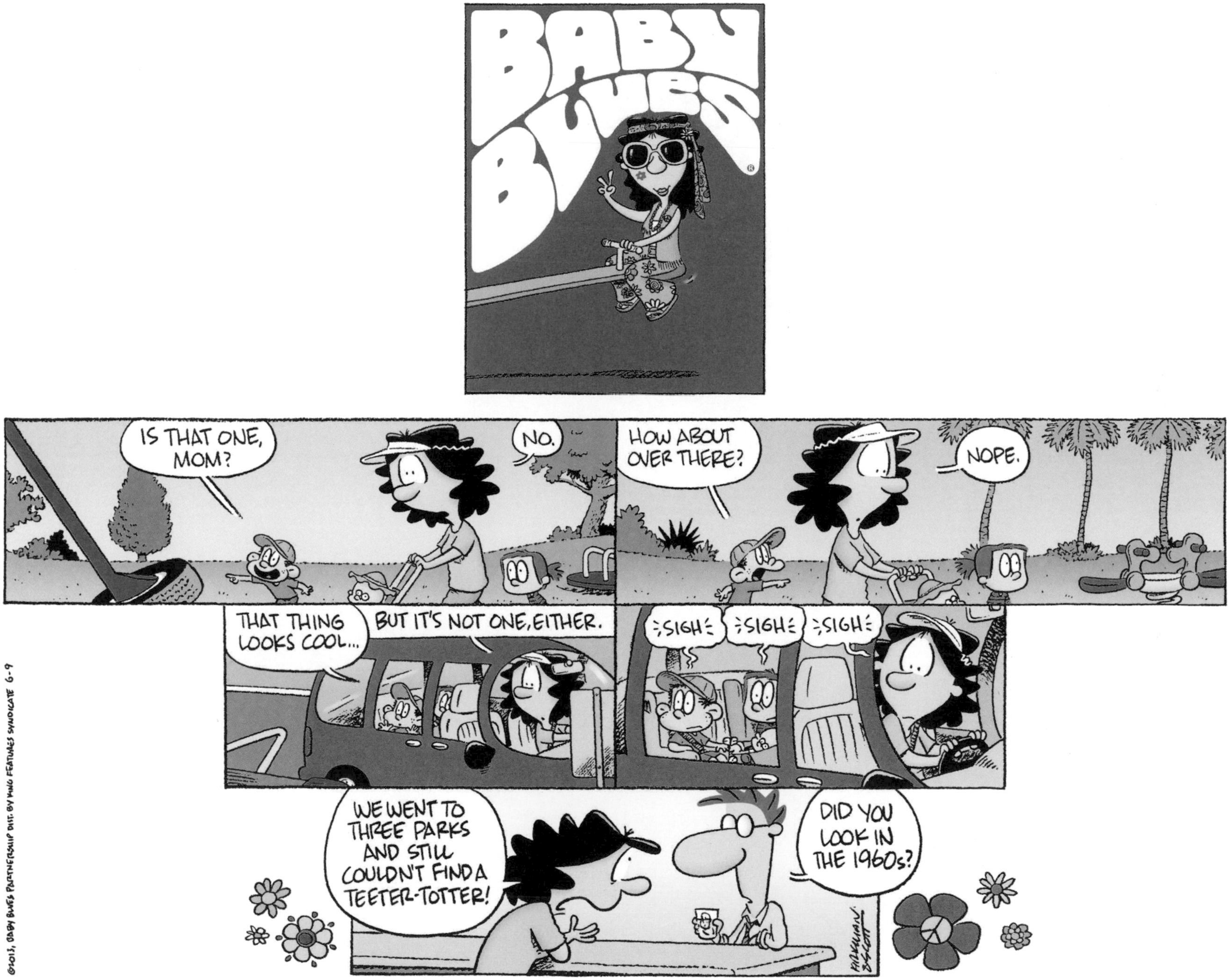
BABY BLUES
IS THAT ONE, MOM?
NO.
HOW ABOUT OVER THERE?
NOPE.
THAT THING LOOKS COOL...
BUT IT'S NOT ONE, EITHER.
SIGH
SIGH
SIGH
WE WENT TO THREE PARKS AND STILL COULDN'T FIND A TEETER-TOTTER!
DID YOU LOOK IN THE 1960s?
KIRKMAN SCOTT

Rick: This title panel took me pretty far in the Wayback Machine. I used to love doing lettering like that in the '60s.

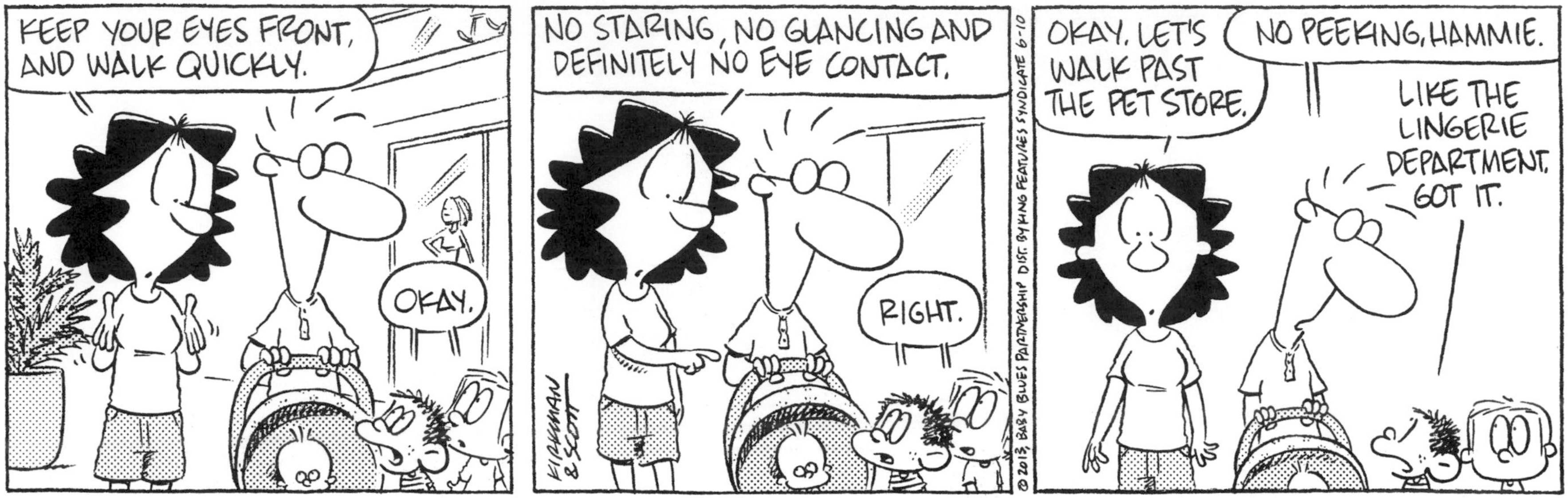
KEEP YOUR EYES FRONT, AND WALK QUICKLY.
OKAY.
NO STARING, NO GLANCING AND DEFINITELY NO EYE CONTACT.
RIGHT.
KIRKMAN & SCOTT
© 2013, BABY BLUES PARTNERSHIP DIST. BY KING FEATURES SYNDICATE 6-10
OKAY. LET'S WALK PAST THE PET STORE.
NO PEEKING, HAMMIE.
LIKE THE LINGERIE DEPARTMENT. GOT IT.

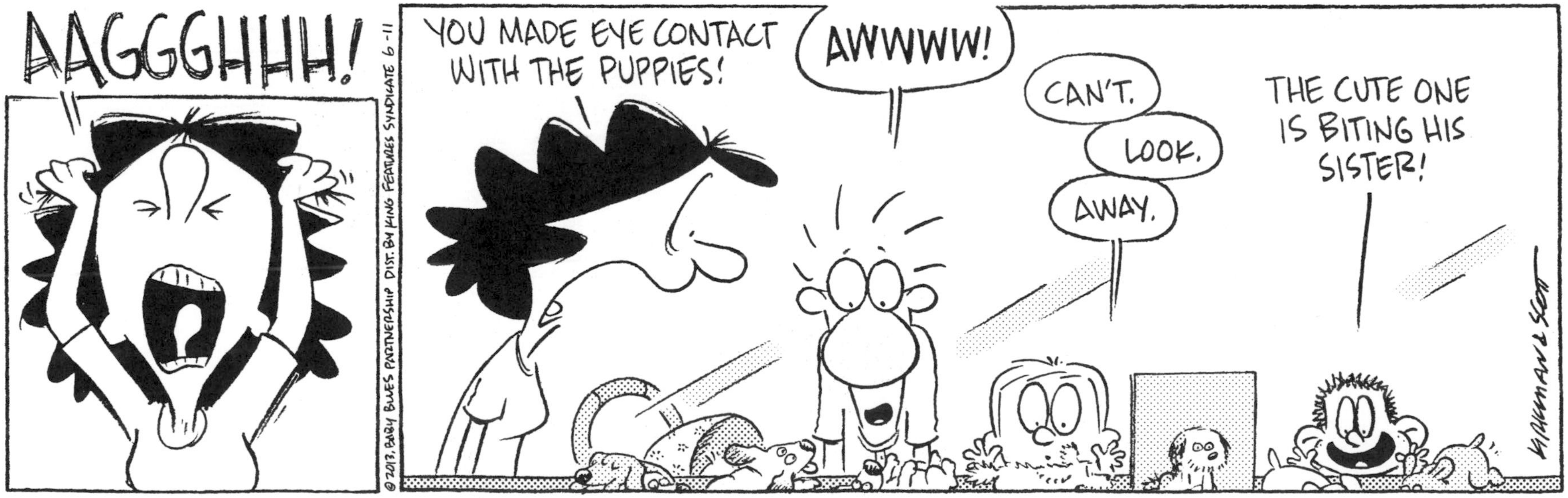
AAGGGHHH!
© 2013, BABY BLUES PARTNERSHIP DIST. BY KING FEATURES SYNDICATE 6-11
YOU MADE EYE CONTACT WITH THE PUPPIES!
AWWWW!
CAN'T.
LOOK.
AWAY.
THE CUTE ONE IS BITING HIS SISTER!
KIRKMAN & SCOTT

Rick: From the instant this strip came out we were bombarded with complaint e-mails warning us not to let the kids get a puppy from a pet store, or they'd never read the strip again. Never mind that the strips were done weeks ahead of time. Or that they didn't even wait to see the outcome of the series before they complained. And haven't any of them ever seen Charlie Brown and the football strips?

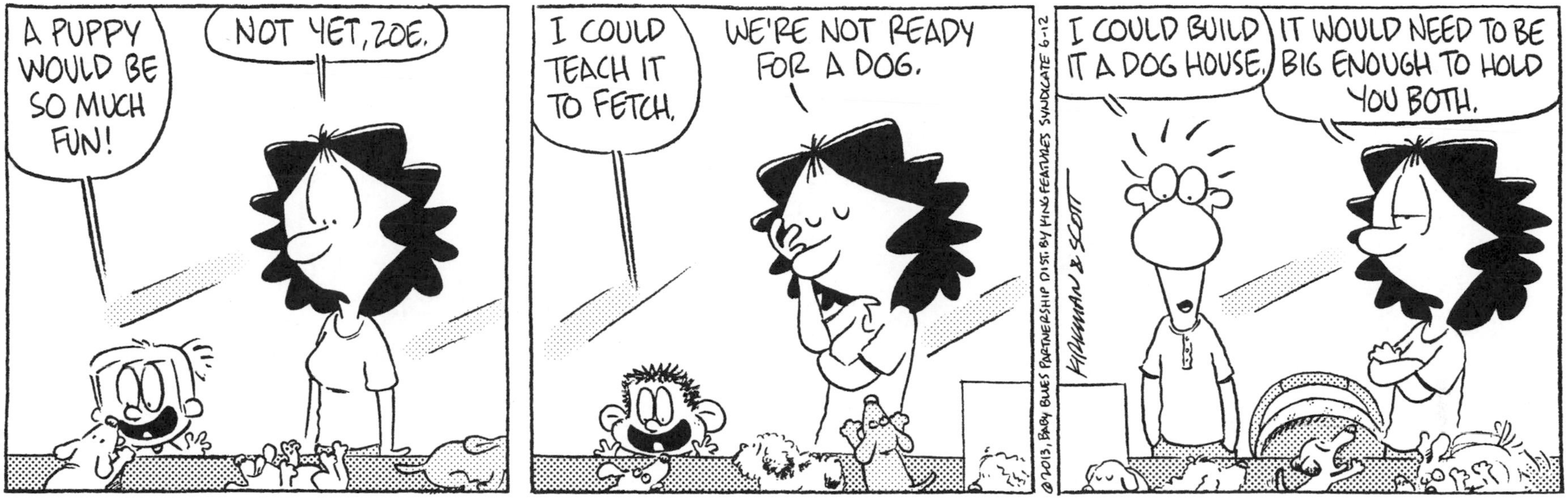
A PUPPY WOULD BE SO MUCH FUN!
NOT YET, ZOE.
I COULD TEACH IT TO FETCH.
WE'RE NOT READY FOR A DOG.
©2013, BABY BLUES PARTNERSHIP DIST. BY KING FEATURES SYNDICATE 6-12
KIRKMAN & SCOTT
I COULD BUILD IT A DOG HOUSE.
IT WOULD NEED TO BE BIG ENOUGH TO HOLD YOU BOTH.

Jerry: We had no intention of letting the MacPhersons get a puppy. Remember what happened to the Mother's Day goldfish?

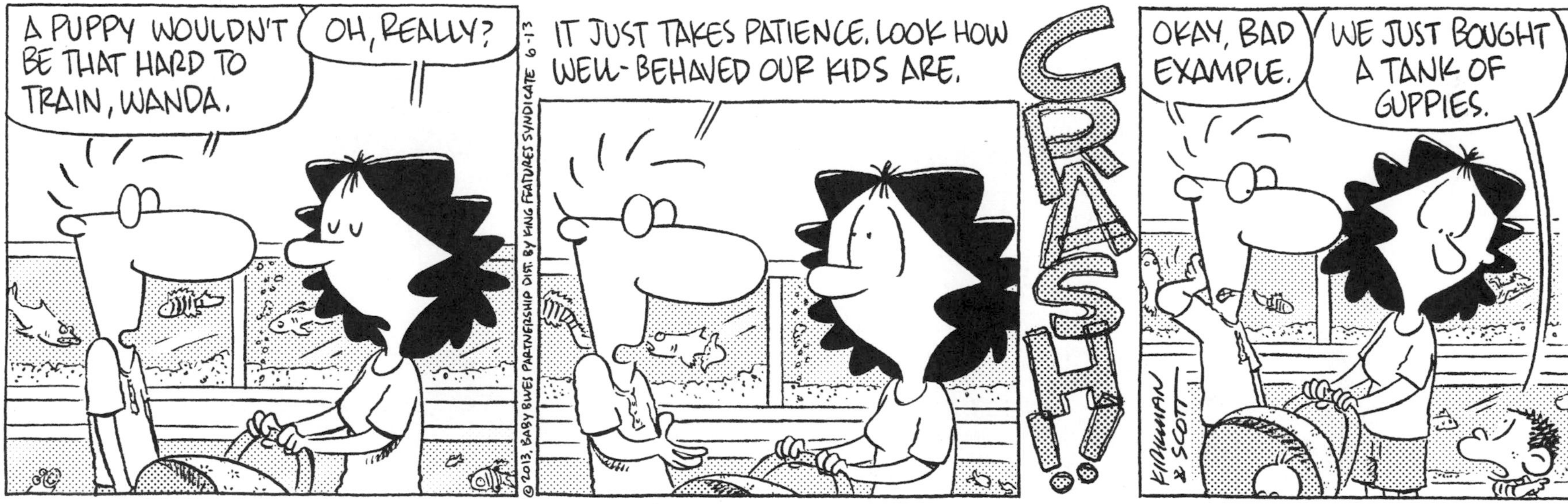
A PUPPY WOULDN'T BE THAT HARD TO TRAIN, WANDA.
OH, REALLY?
©2013, BABY BLUES PARTNERSHIP DIST. BY KING FEATURES SYNDICATE 6-13
IT JUST TAKES PATIENCE. LOOK HOW WELL-BEHAVED OUR KIDS ARE.
CRASH!!
OKAY, BAD EXAMPLE.
WE JUST BOUGHT A TANK OF GUPPIES.
KIRKMAN & SCOTT

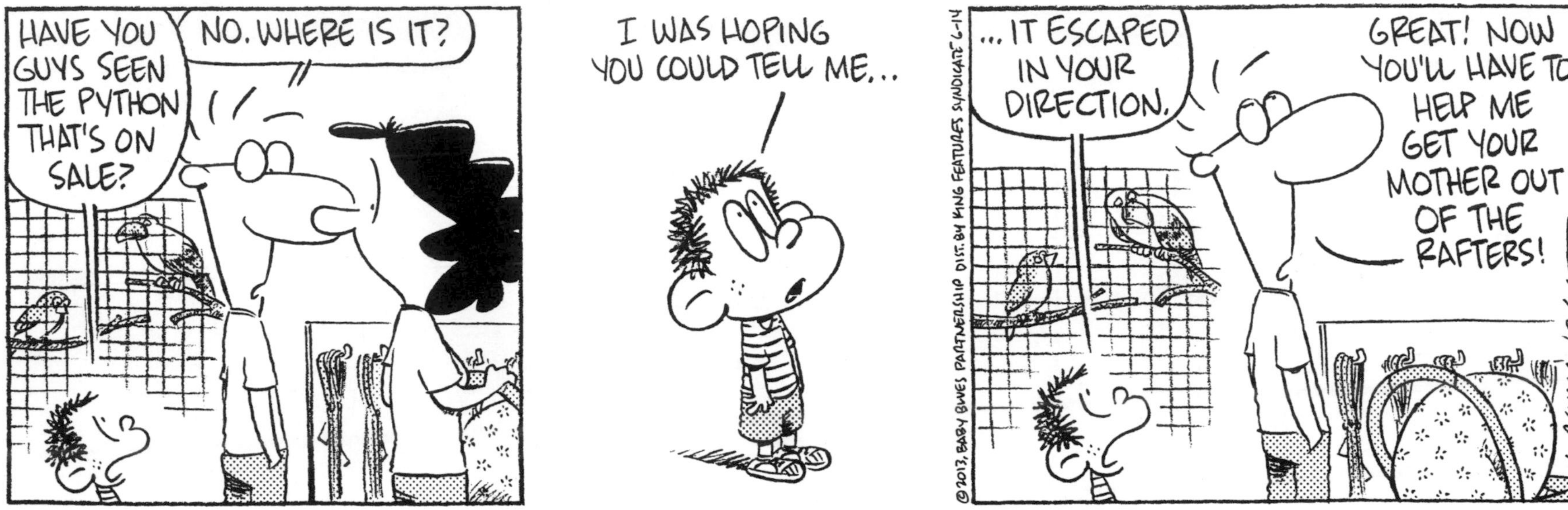
HAVE YOU GUYS SEEN THE PYTHON THAT'S ON SALE?
NO. WHERE IS IT?
I WAS HOPING YOU COULD TELL ME...
...IT ESCAPED IN YOUR DIRECTION.
GREAT! NOW YOU'LL HAVE TO HELP ME GET YOUR MOTHER OUT OF THE RAFTERS!
© 2013, BABY BLUES PARTNERSHIP DIST. BY KING FEATURES SYNDICATE 6-14
KIRKMAN & SCOTT

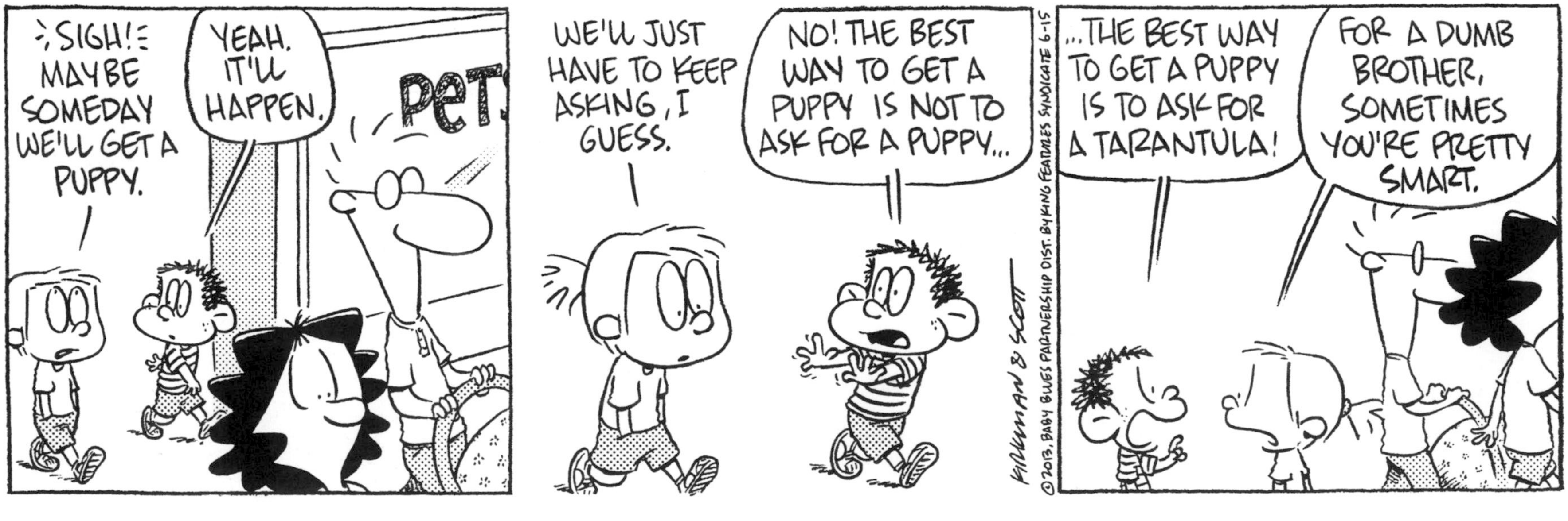
SIGH! MAYBE SOMEDAY WE'LL GET A PUPPY.
YEAH. IT'LL HAPPEN.
PETS
WE'LL JUST HAVE TO KEEP ASKING, I GUESS.
NO! THE BEST WAY TO GET A PUPPY IS NOT TO ASK FOR A PUPPY...
...THE BEST WAY TO GET A PUPPY IS TO ASK FOR A TARANTULA!
FOR A DUMB BROTHER, SOMETIMES YOU'RE PRETTY SMART.
KIRKMAN & SCOTT
© 2013, BABY BLUES PARTNERSHIP DIST. BY KING FEATURES SYNDICATE 6-15

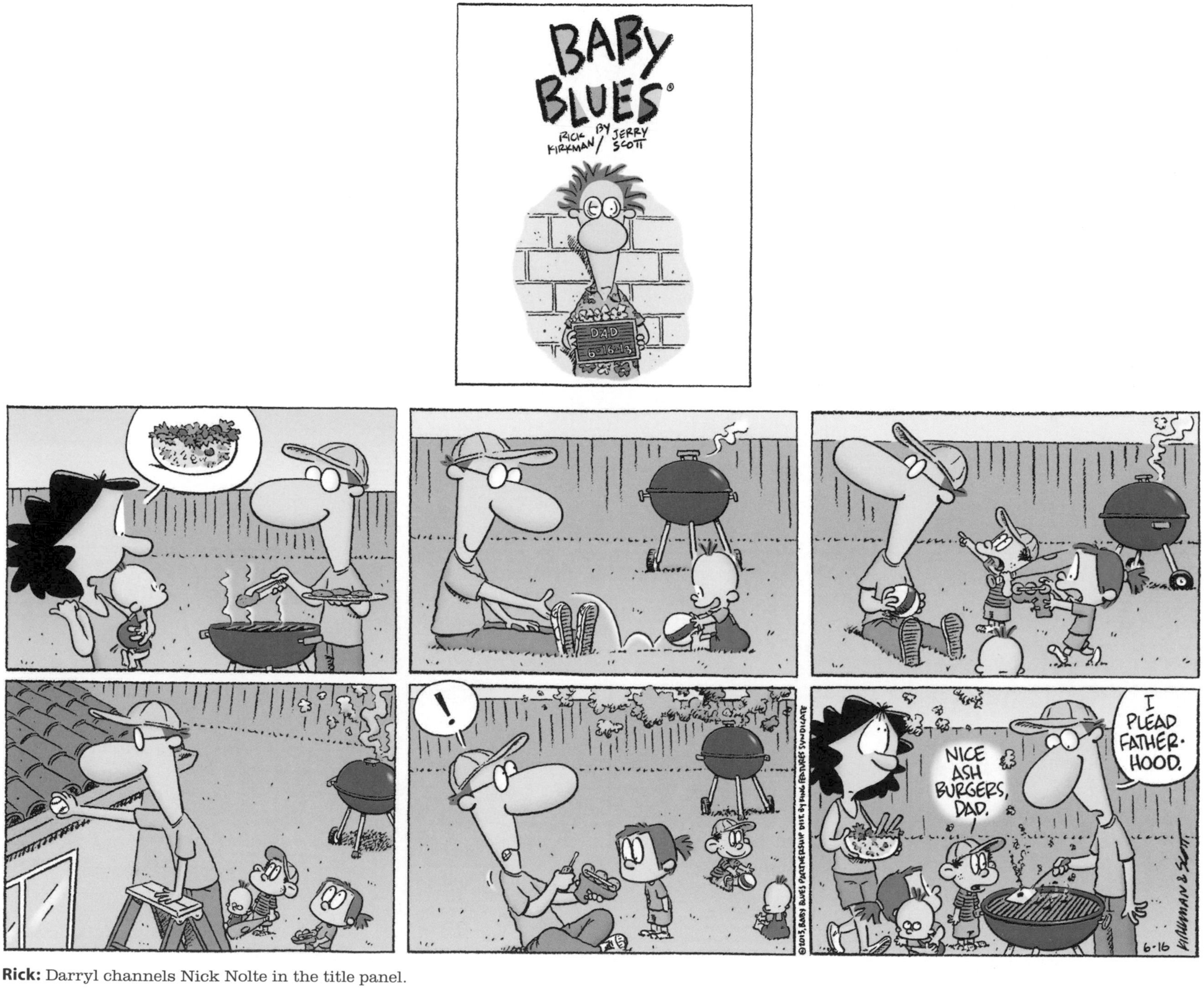
BABY BLUES®
BY RICK KIRKMAN / JERRY SCOTT
DAD 6-16-13
!
©2013, BABY BLUES PARTNERSHIP DIST. BY KING FEATURES SYNDICATE
NICE ASH BURGERS, DAD.
I PLEAD FATHER-HOOD.
KIRKMAN & SCOTT
6-16

Rick: Darryl channels Nick Nolte in the title panel.

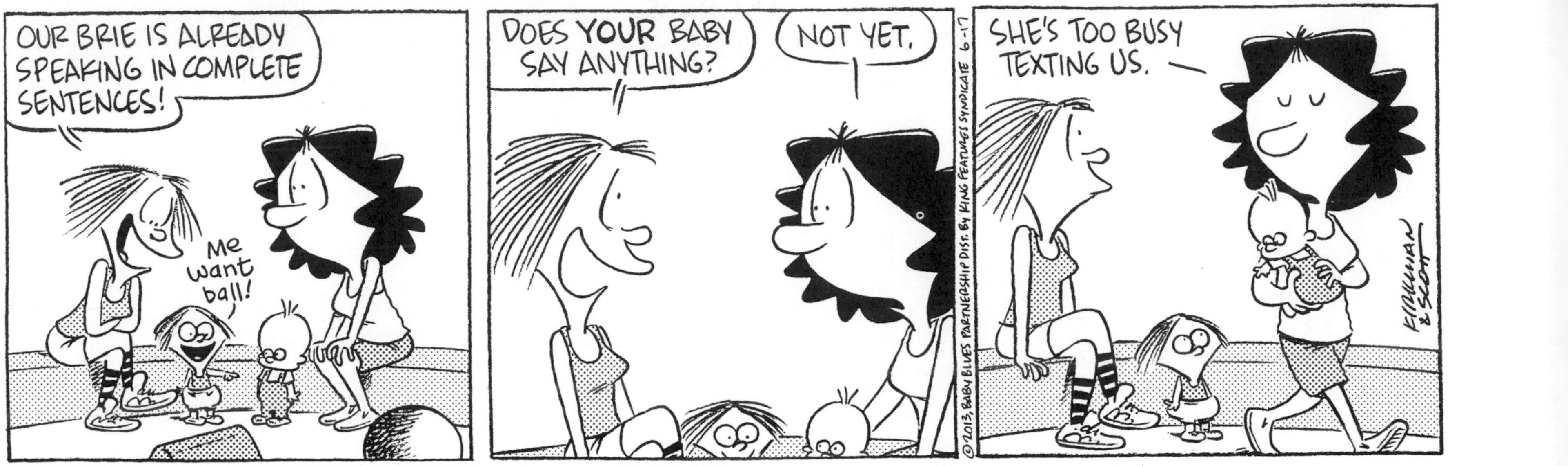
OUR BRIE IS ALREADY SPEAKING IN COMPLETE SENTENCES!
Me want ball!
DOES YOUR BABY SAY ANYTHING?
NOT YET.
SHE'S TOO BUSY TEXTING US.
©2013, BABY BLUES PARTNERSHIP DIST. BY KING FEATURES SYNDICATE 6-17
KIRKMAN & SCOTT

Rick: My assistant's pediatrician actually asked her whether her toddler was texting yet. What?

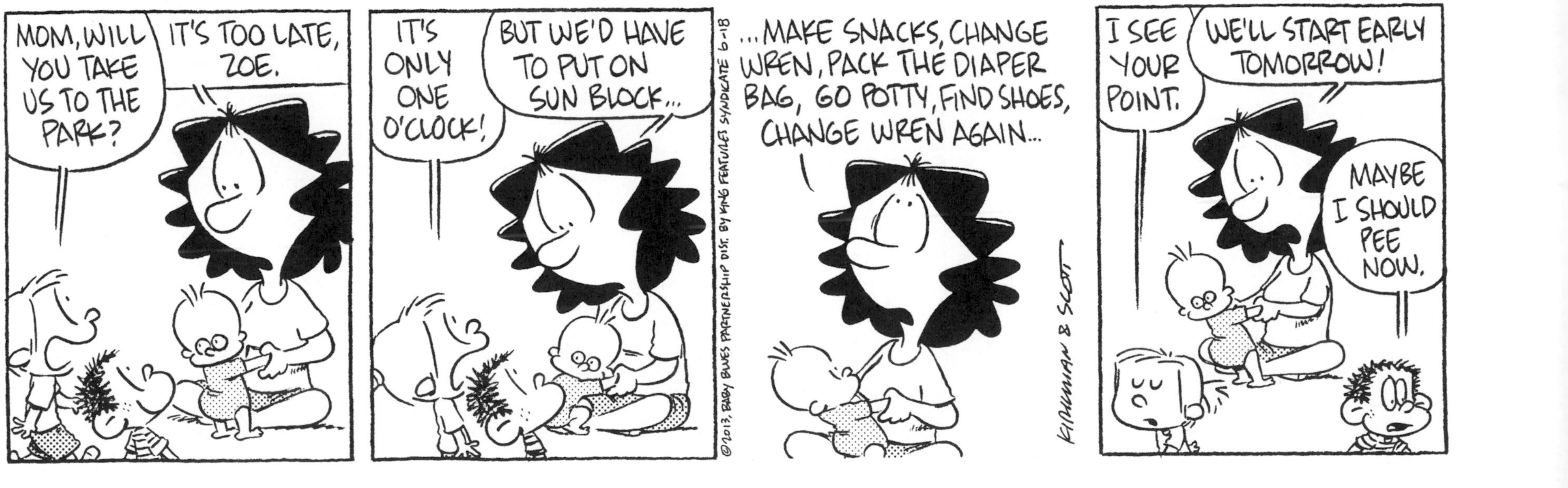
MOM, WILL YOU TAKE US TO THE PARK?
IT'S TOO LATE, ZOE.
IT'S ONLY ONE O'CLOCK!
BUT WE'D HAVE TO PUT ON SUN BLOCK...
...MAKE SNACKS, CHANGE WREN, PACK THE DIAPER BAG, GO POTTY, FIND SHOES, CHANGE WREN AGAIN...
I SEE YOUR POINT.
WE'LL START EARLY TOMORROW!
MAYBE I SHOULD PEE NOW.
©2013, BABY BLUES PARTNERSHIP DIST. BY KING FEATURES SYNDICATE 6-18
KIRKMAN & SCOTT

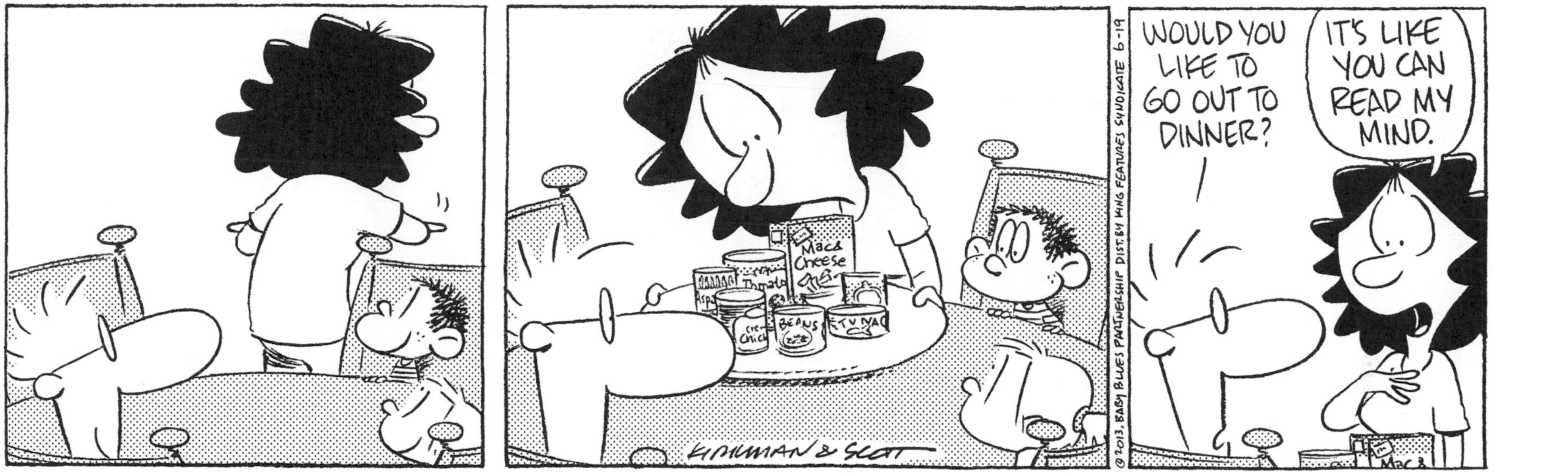
WOULD YOU LIKE TO GO OUT TO DINNER?
IT'S LIKE YOU CAN READ MY MIND.

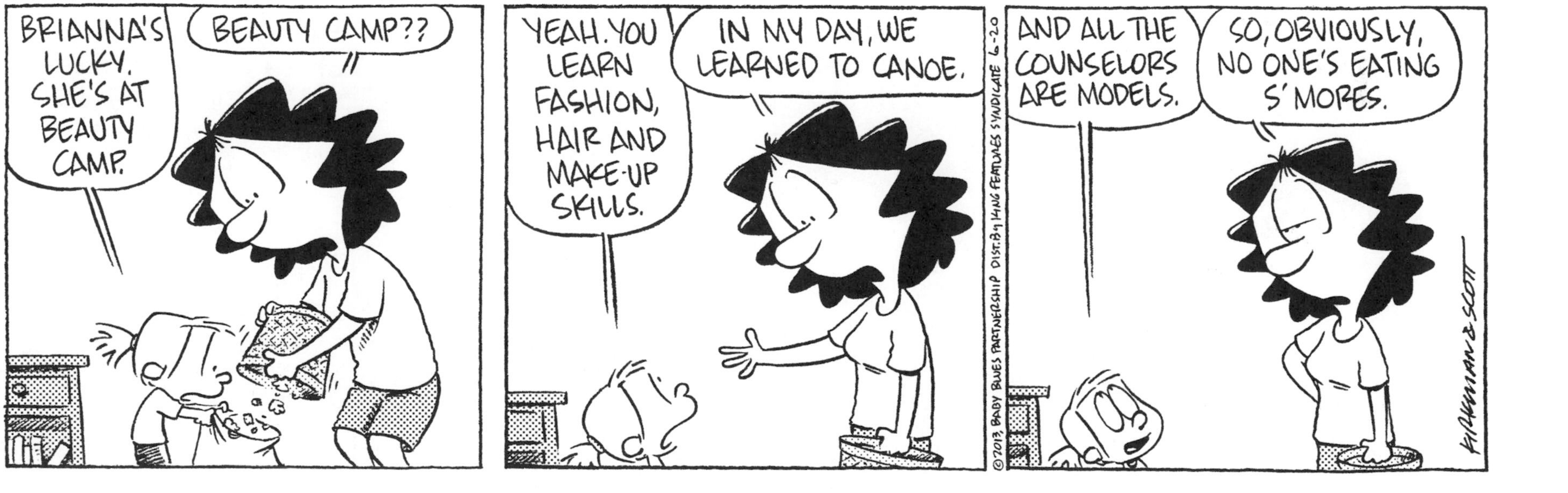
BRIANNA'S LUCKY. SHE'S AT BEAUTY CAMP.
BEAUTY CAMP??
YEAH. YOU LEARN FASHION, HAIR AND MAKE-UP SKILLS.
IN MY DAY, WE LEARNED TO CANOE.
AND ALL THE COUNSELORS ARE MODELS.
SO, OBVIOUSLY, NO ONE'S EATING S'MORES.

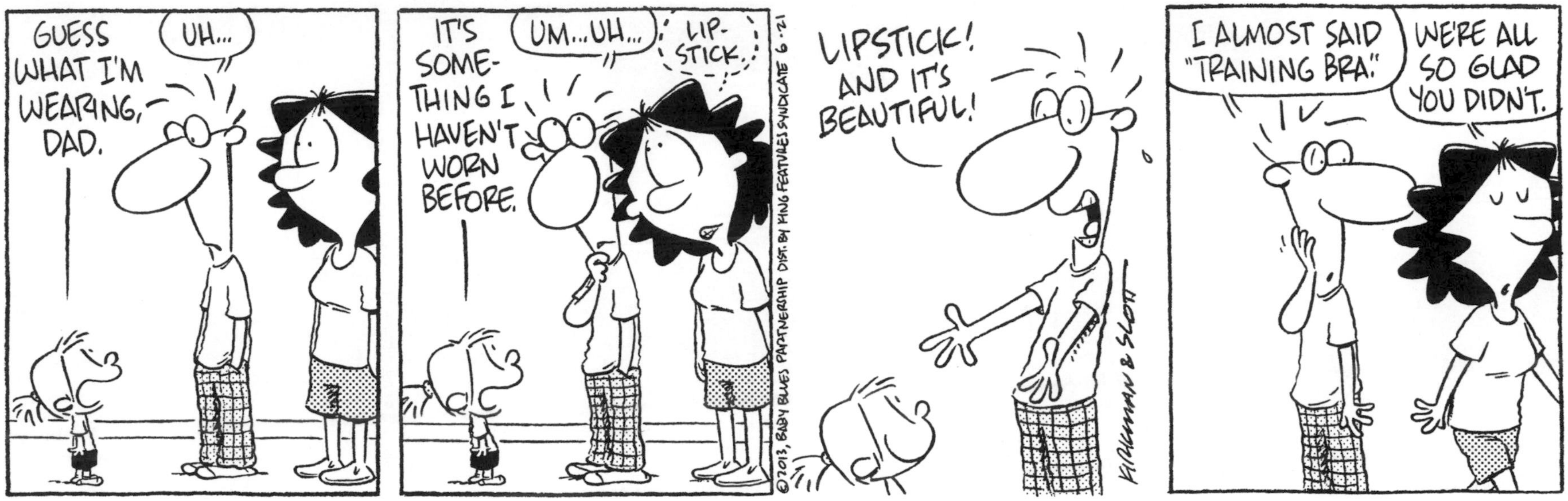
GUESS WHAT I'M WEARING, DAD.
UH...
IT'S SOMETHING I HAVEN'T WORN BEFORE.
UM...UH...
LIP-STICK.
©2013, BABY BLUES PARTNERSHIP DIST. BY KING FEATURES SYNDICATE 6-21
LIPSTICK! AND IT'S BEAUTIFUL!
KIRKMAN & SCOTT
I ALMOST SAID "TRAINING BRA."
WE'RE ALL SO GLAD YOU DIDN'T.

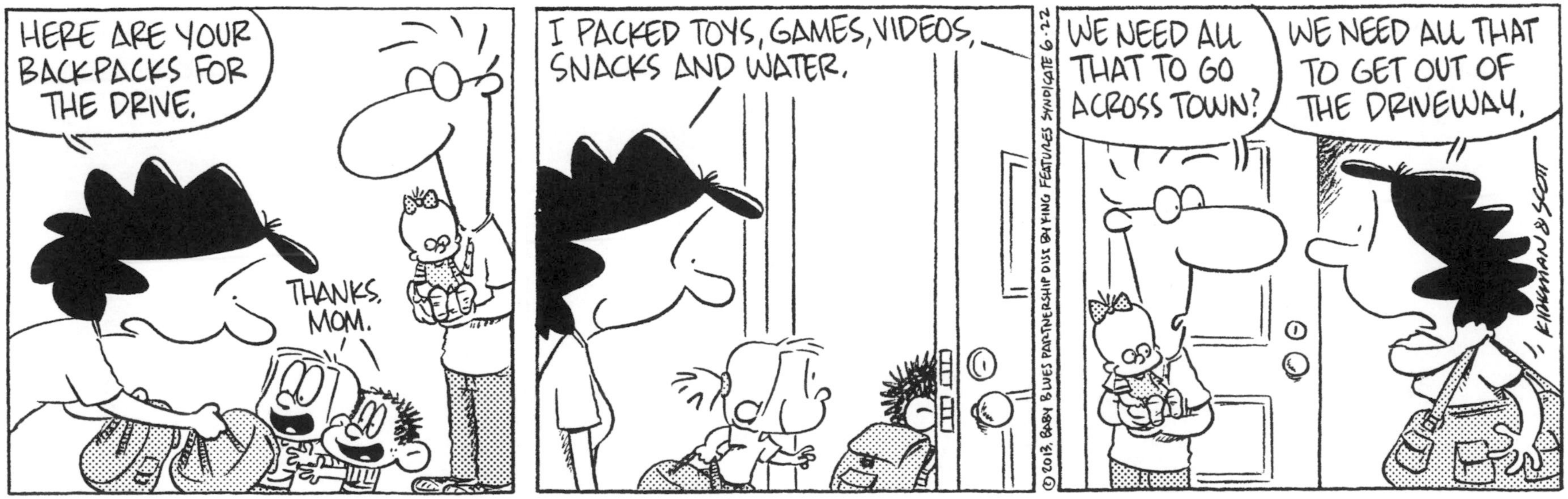
HERE ARE YOUR BACKPACKS FOR THE DRIVE.
THANKS, MOM.
I PACKED TOYS, GAMES, VIDEOS, SNACKS AND WATER.
©2013, BABY BLUES PARTNERSHIP DIST BY KING FEATURES SYNDICATE 6-22
WE NEED ALL THAT TO GO ACROSS TOWN?
WE NEED ALL THAT TO GET OUT OF THE DRIVEWAY.
KIRKMAN & SCOTT

Jerry: We could survive for weeks in our car just on the stuff my wife keeps in the trunk and probably feed another family with the cracker crumbs wedged under the backseat.

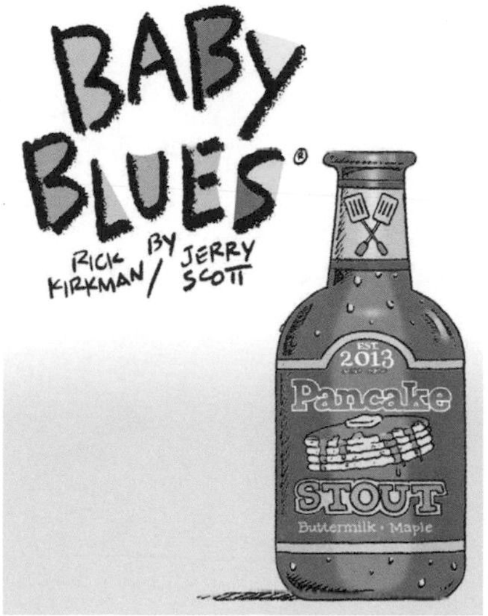
BABY BLUES®
BY
RICK KIRKMAN / JERRY SCOTT
EST 2013
Pancake
STOUT
Buttermilk · Maple

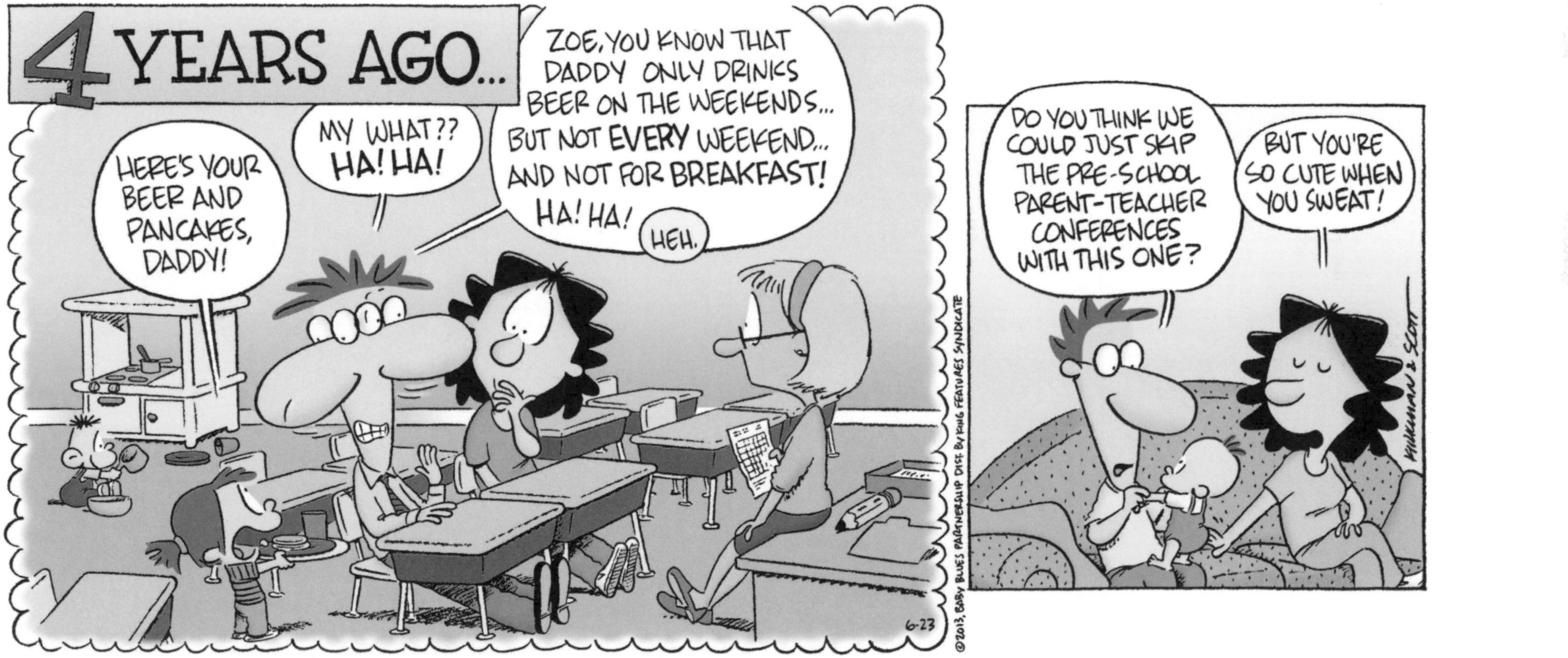
4 YEARS AGO...
HERE'S YOUR BEER AND PANCAKES, DADDY!
MY WHAT?? HA! HA!
ZOE, YOU KNOW THAT DADDY ONLY DRINKS BEER ON THE WEEKENDS... BUT NOT EVERY WEEKEND... AND NOT FOR BREAKFAST! HA! HA!
HEH.
6-23
©2013, BABY BLUES PARTNERSHIP DIST. BY KING FEATURES SYNDICATE
DO YOU THINK WE COULD JUST SKIP THE PRE-SCHOOL PARENT-TEACHER CONFERENCES WITH THIS ONE?
BUT YOU'RE SO CUTE WHEN YOU SWEAT!
KIRKMAN & SCOTT

Rick: Another strip inspired by the life of my tennis instructor. He's got a million of 'em, all embarrassing.

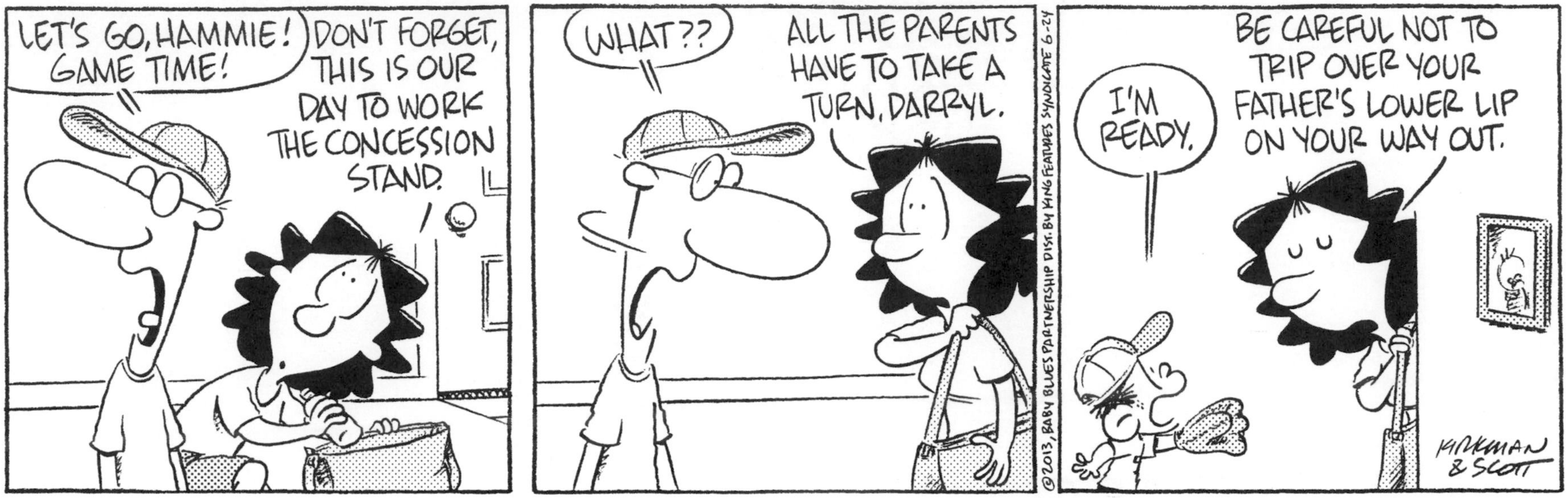
LET'S GO, HAMMIE! GAME TIME!
DON'T FORGET, THIS IS OUR DAY TO WORK THE CONCESSION STAND.
WHAT??
ALL THE PARENTS HAVE TO TAKE A TURN, DARRYL.
©2013, BABY BLUES PARTNERSHIP DIST. BY KING FEATURES SYNDICATE 6-24
I'M READY.
BE CAREFUL NOT TO TRIP OVER YOUR FATHER'S LOWER LIP ON YOUR WAY OUT.
KIRKMAN & SCOTT

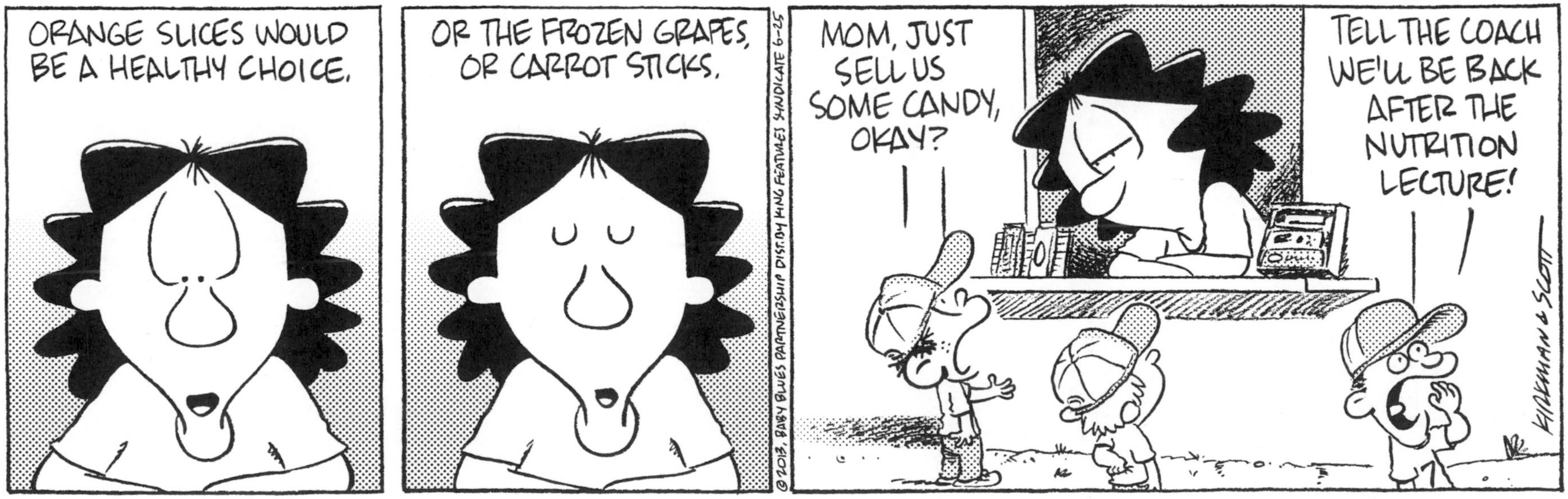
ORANGE SLICES WOULD BE A HEALTHY CHOICE.
OR THE FROZEN GRAPES, OR CARROT STICKS.
©2013, BABY BLUES PARTNERSHIP DIST. BY KING FEATURES SYNDICATE 6-25
MOM, JUST SELL US SOME CANDY, OKAY?
TELL THE COACH WE'LL BE BACK AFTER THE NUTRITION LECTURE!
KIRKMAN & SCOTT

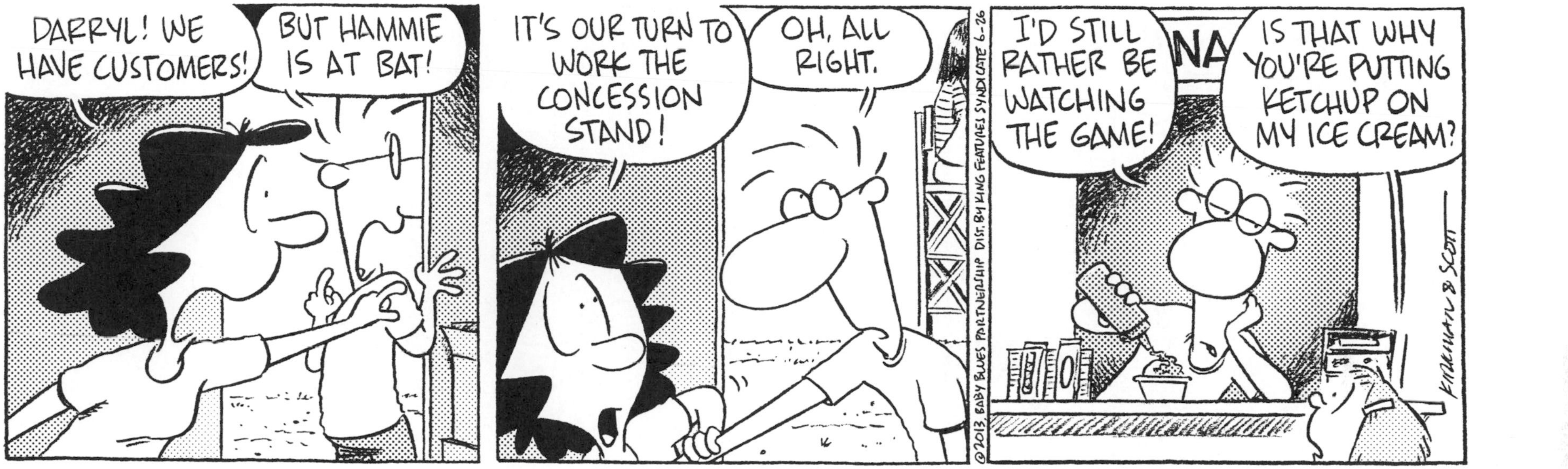
DARRYL! WE HAVE CUSTOMERS!
BUT HAMMIE IS AT BAT!
IT'S OUR TURN TO WORK THE CONCESSION STAND!
OH, ALL RIGHT.
©2013, BABY BLUES PARTNERSHIP DIST. BY KING FEATURES SYNDICATE 6-26
I'D STILL RATHER BE WATCHING THE GAME!
IS THAT WHY YOU'RE PUTTING KETCHUP ON MY ICE CREAM?
KIRKMAN & SCOTT

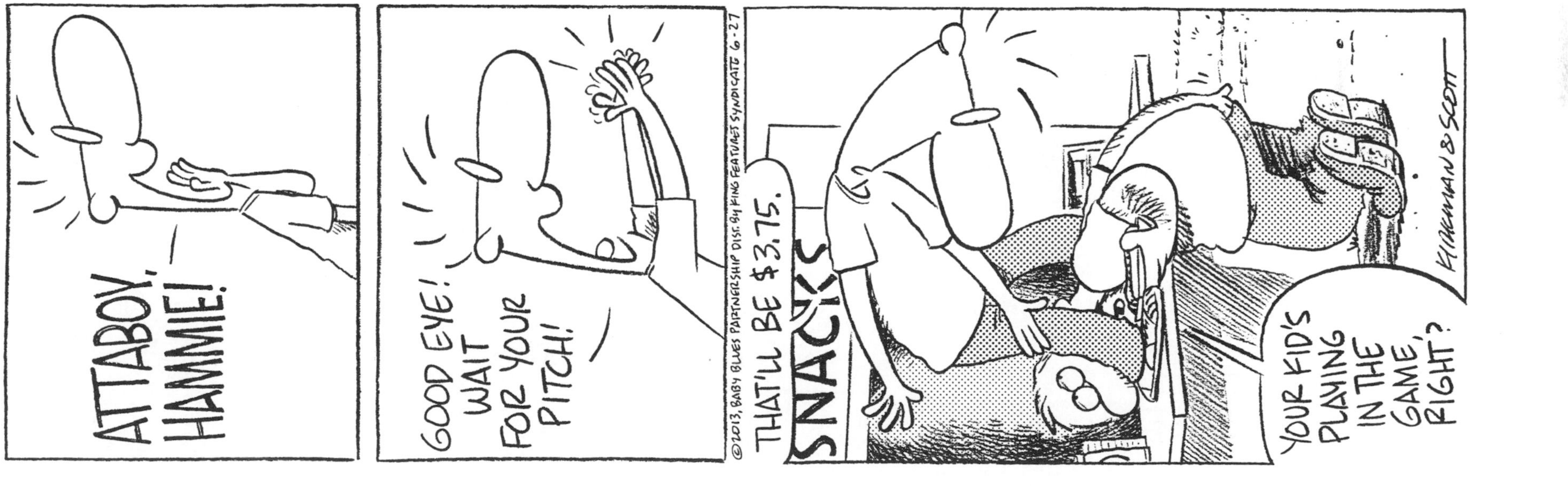
YOUR KID'S PLAYING IN THE GAME, RIGHT?
SNACKS
THAT'LL BE $3.75.
KIRKMAN & SCOTT
©2013, BABY BLUES PARTNERSHIP DIST. BY KING FEATURES SYNDICATE 6-27
GOOD EYE! WAIT FOR YOUR PITCH!
ATTABOY, HAMMIE!

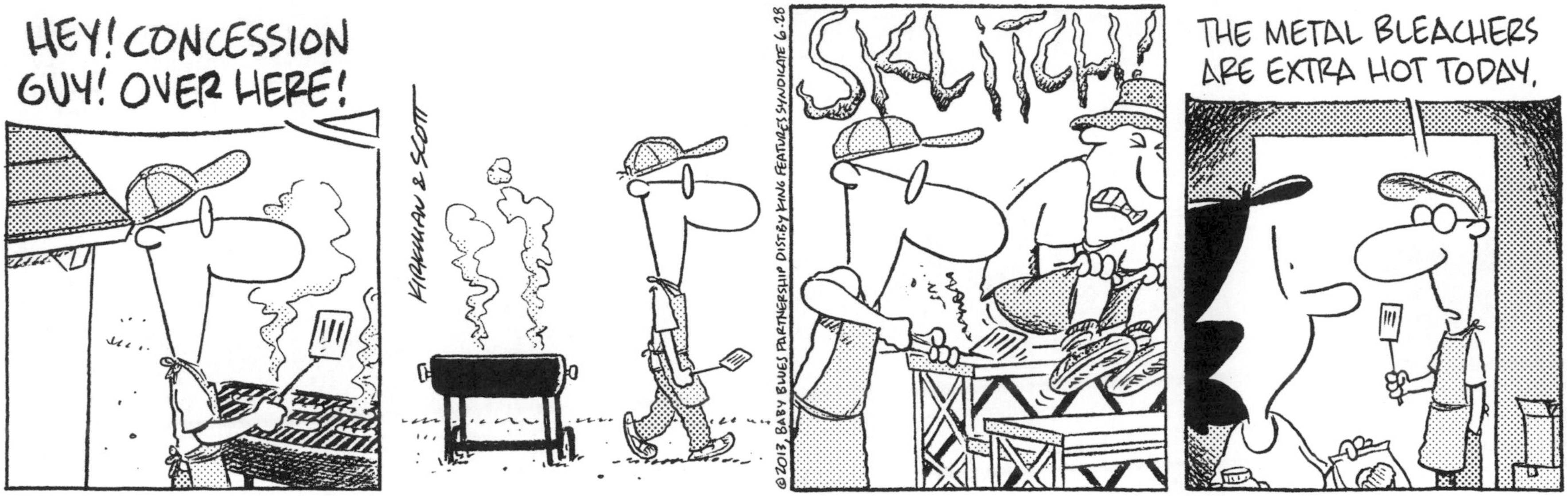
HEY! CONCESSION GUY! OVER HERE!
KIRKMAN & SCOTT
SKLITCH!
©2013, BABY BLUES PARTNERSHIP DIST. BY KING FEATURES SYNDICATE 6-28
THE METAL BLEACHERS ARE EXTRA HOT TODAY.

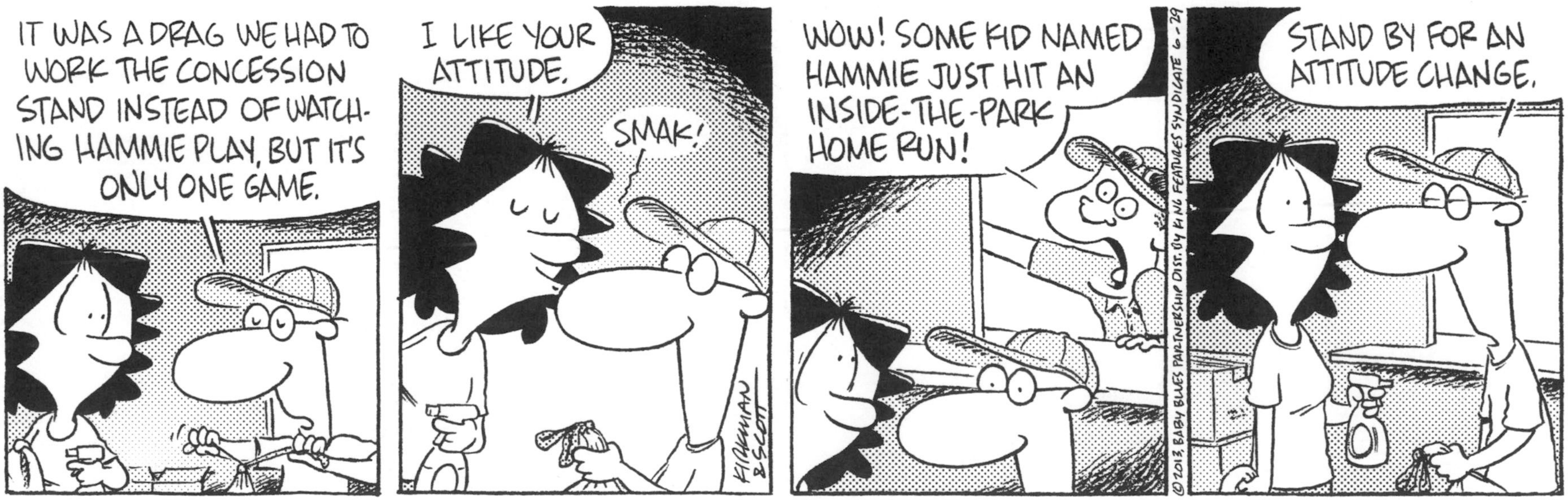
IT WAS A DRAG WE HAD TO WORK THE CONCESSION STAND INSTEAD OF WATCHING HAMMIE PLAY, BUT IT'S ONLY ONE GAME.
I LIKE YOUR ATTITUDE.
SMAK!
KIRKMAN & SCOTT
WOW! SOME KID NAMED HAMMIE JUST HIT AN INSIDE-THE-PARK HOME RUN!
©2013, BABY BLUES PARTNERSHIP DIST. BY KING FEATURES SYNDICATE 6-29
STAND BY FOR AN ATTITUDE CHANGE.

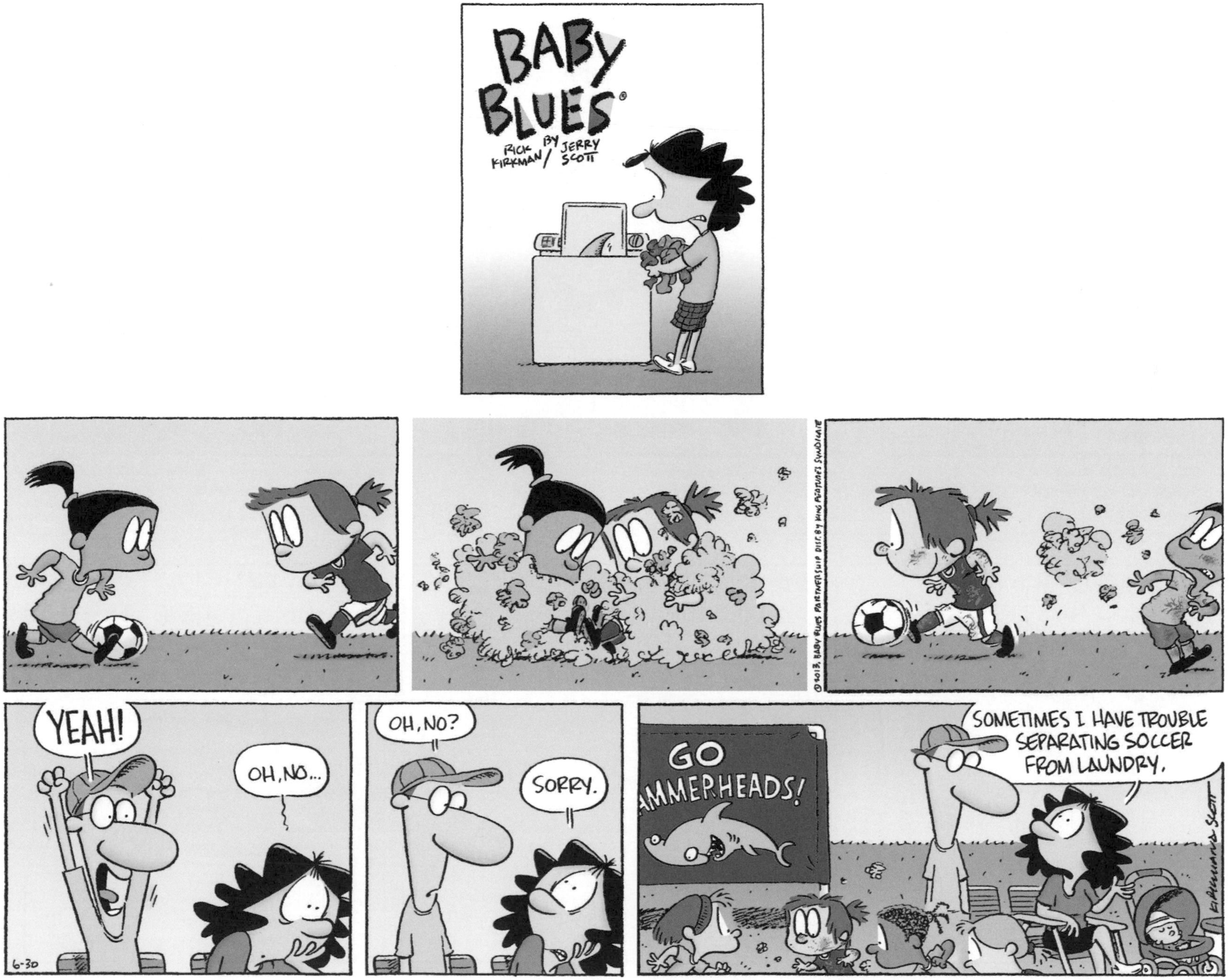
BABY BLUES®
RICK KIRKMAN / BY / JERRY SCOTT
6-30
YEAH!
OH, NO...
OH, NO?
SORRY.
GO
AMMERHEADS!
SOMETIMES I HAVE TROUBLE SEPARATING SOCCER FROM LAUNDRY.

Rick: That was my daughter's soccer team's name, and I did make a banner with that shark.

Jerry: My daughter played for The Killer Ladybugs. All the designs I made for their banner were rejected for unsuitable content.

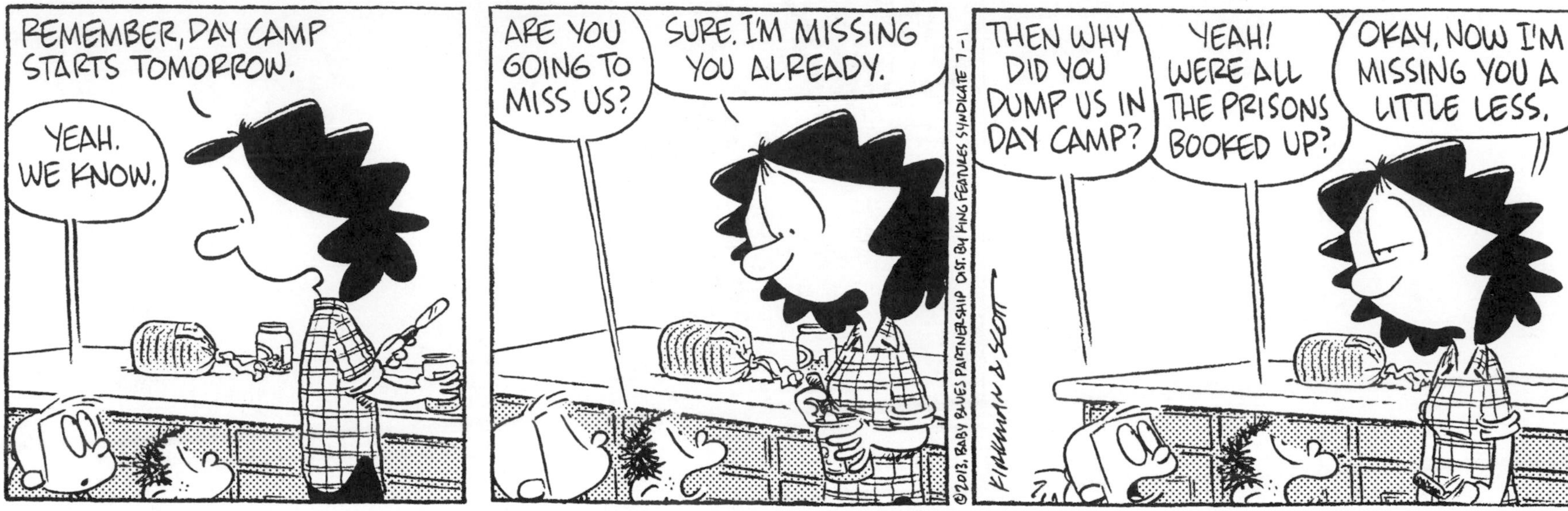
REMEMBER, DAY CAMP STARTS TOMORROW.
YEAH. WE KNOW.
ARE YOU GOING TO MISS US?
SURE. I'M MISSING YOU ALREADY.
©2013, BABY BLUES PARTNERSHIP DIST. BY KING FEATURES SYNDICATE 7-1
KIRKMAN & SCOTT
THEN WHY DID YOU DUMP US IN DAY CAMP?
YEAH! WERE ALL THE PRISONS BOOKED UP?
OKAY, NOW I'M MISSING YOU A LITTLE LESS.

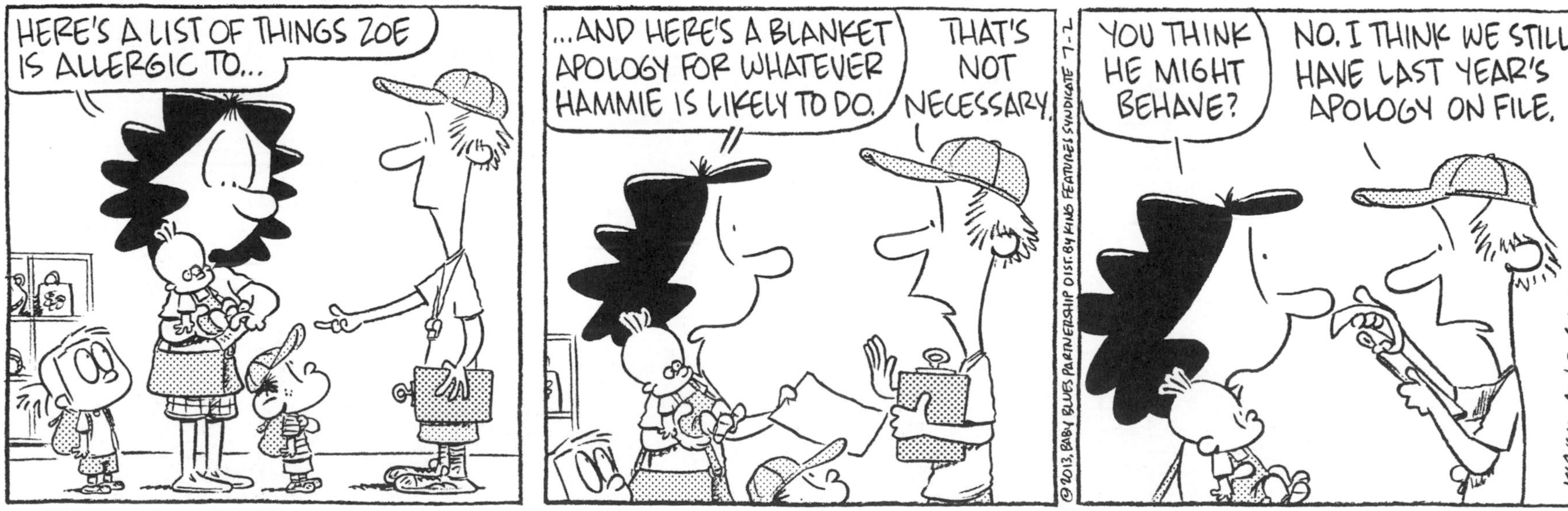
HERE'S A LIST OF THINGS ZOE IS ALLERGIC TO...
...AND HERE'S A BLANKET APOLOGY FOR WHATEVER HAMMIE IS LIKELY TO DO.
THAT'S NOT NECESSARY.
©2013, BABY BLUES PARTNERSHIP DIST. BY KING FEATURES SYNDICATE 7-2
YOU THINK HE MIGHT BEHAVE?
NO. I THINK WE STILL HAVE LAST YEAR'S APOLOGY ON FILE.
KIRKMAN & SCOTT

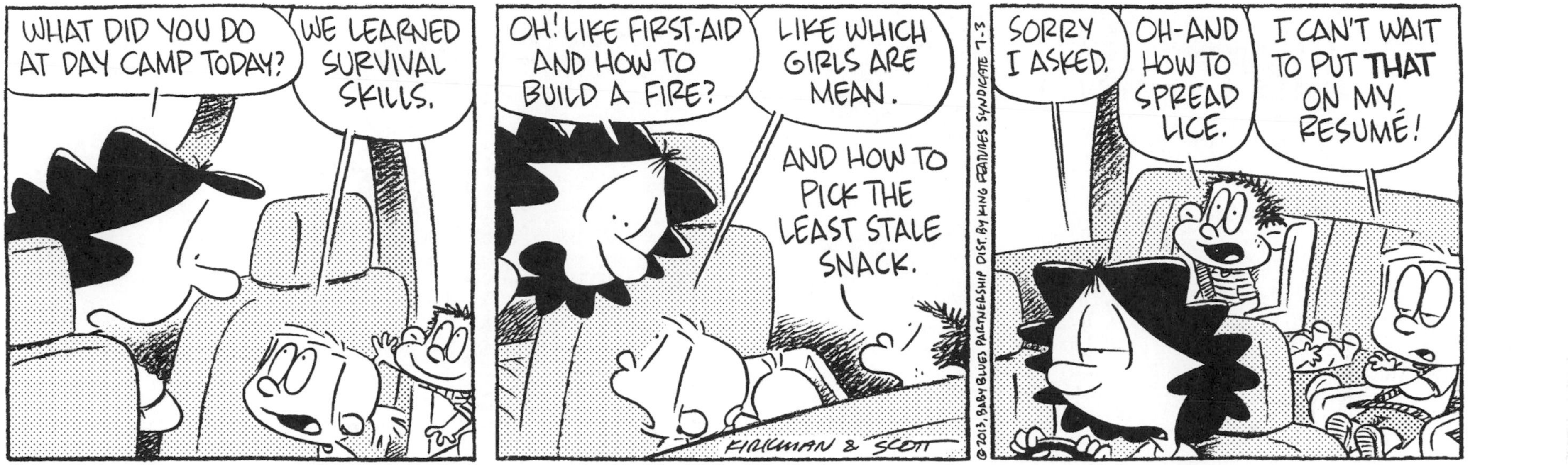
WHAT DID YOU DO AT DAY CAMP TODAY?
WE LEARNED SURVIVAL SKILLS.
OH! LIKE FIRST-AID AND HOW TO BUILD A FIRE?
LIKE WHICH GIRLS ARE MEAN.
AND HOW TO PICK THE LEAST STALE SNACK.
KIRKMAN & SCOTT
©2013, BABY BLUES PARTNERSHIP DIST. BY KING FEATURES SYNDICATE 7-3
SORRY I ASKED.
OH-AND HOW TO SPREAD LICE.
I CAN'T WAIT TO PUT **THAT** ON MY RESUMÉ!

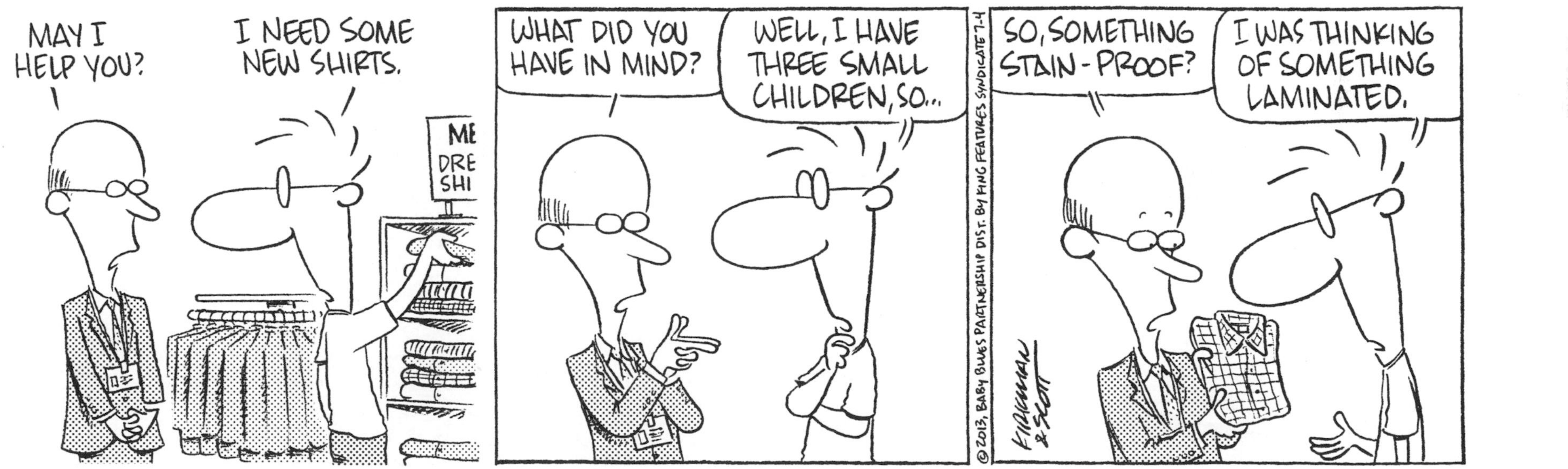
MAY I HELP YOU?
I NEED SOME NEW SHIRTS.
ME DRE SHI
WHAT DID YOU HAVE IN MIND?
WELL, I HAVE THREE SMALL CHILDREN, SO...
©2013, BABY BLUES PARTNERSHIP DIST. BY KING FEATURES SYNDICATE 7-4
KIRKMAN & SCOTT
SO, SOMETHING STAIN-PROOF?
I WAS THINKING OF SOMETHING LAMINATED.

Rick: I think this is such a great idea, it should be real: laminated clothes for parents. We should have a business of creating actual products from comic strip ideas.

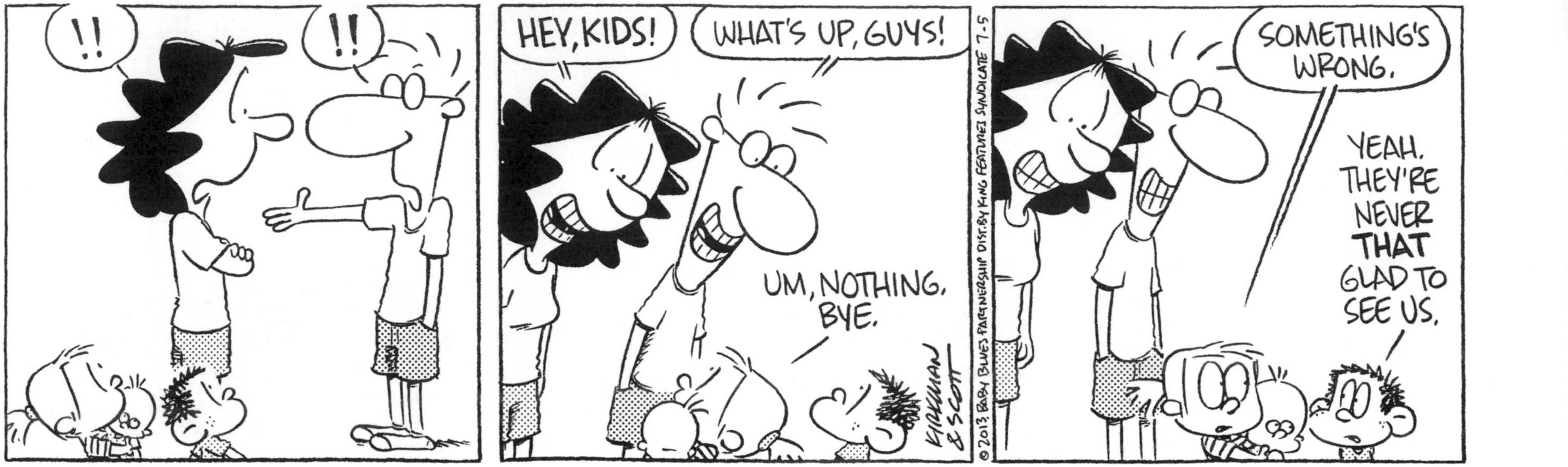
!!
!!
HEY, KIDS!
WHAT'S UP, GUYS!
UM, NOTHING. BYE.
KIRKMAN & SCOTT
© 2013 BABY BLUES PARTNERSHIP DIST. BY KING FEATURES SYNDICATE 7-5
SOMETHING'S WRONG.
YEAH. THEY'RE NEVER **THAT** GLAD TO SEE US.

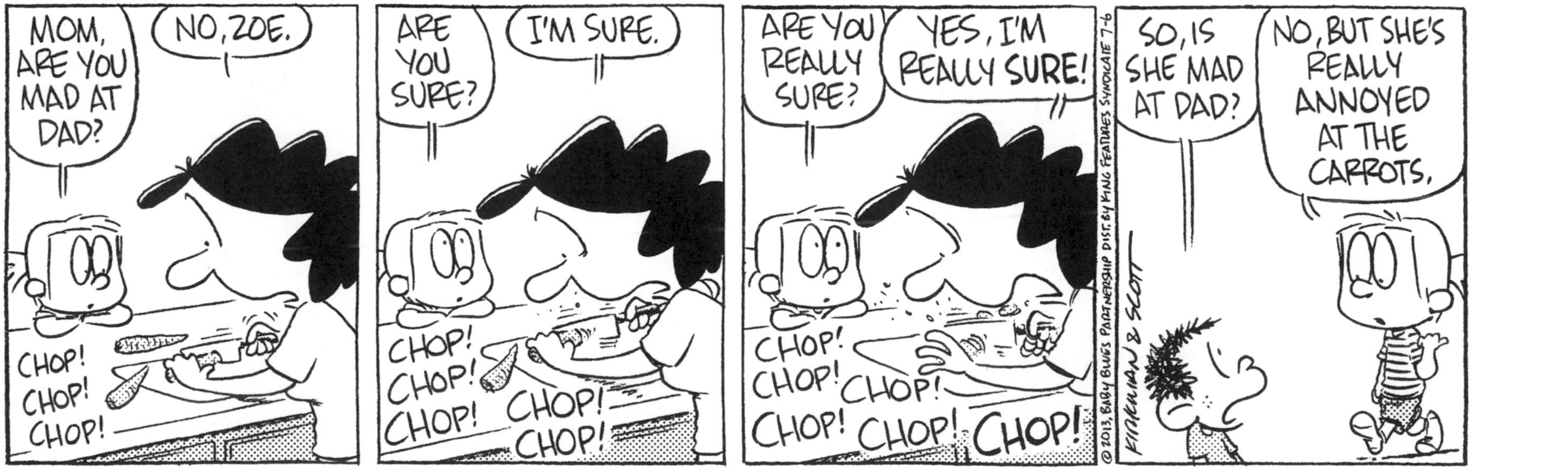
MOM, ARE YOU MAD AT DAD?
NO, ZOE.
CHOP! CHOP! CHOP!
ARE YOU SURE?
I'M SURE.
CHOP! CHOP! CHOP! CHOP! CHOP!
ARE YOU REALLY SURE?
YES, I'M REALLY **SURE!**
CHOP! CHOP! CHOP! CHOP! CHOP! CHOP!
© 2013, BABY BLUES PARTNERSHIP DIST. BY KING FEATURES SYNDICATE 7-6
KIRKMAN & SCOTT
SO, IS SHE MAD AT DAD?
NO, BUT SHE'S REALLY ANNOYED AT THE CARROTS.

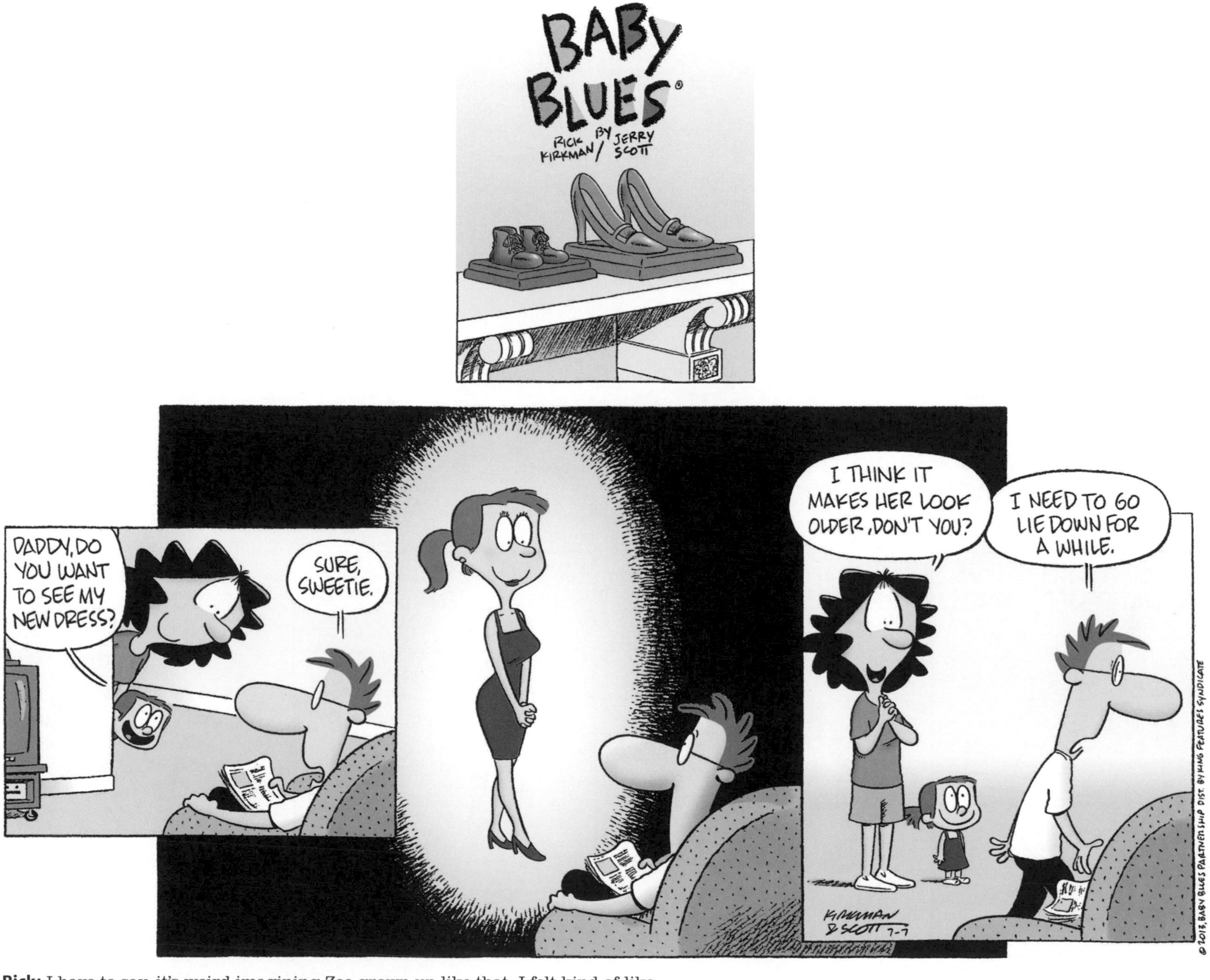
BABY BLUES®
RICK KIRKMAN / BY JERRY SCOTT
DADDY, DO YOU WANT TO SEE MY NEW DRESS?
SURE, SWEETIE.
I THINK IT MAKES HER LOOK OLDER, DON'T YOU?
I NEED TO GO LIE DOWN FOR A WHILE.
KIRKMAN & SCOTT 7-7
©2013, BABY BLUES PARTNERSHIP DIST. BY KING FEATURES SYNDICATE

Rick: I have to say, it's weird imagining Zoe grown up like that. I felt kind of like Darryl after drawing it.

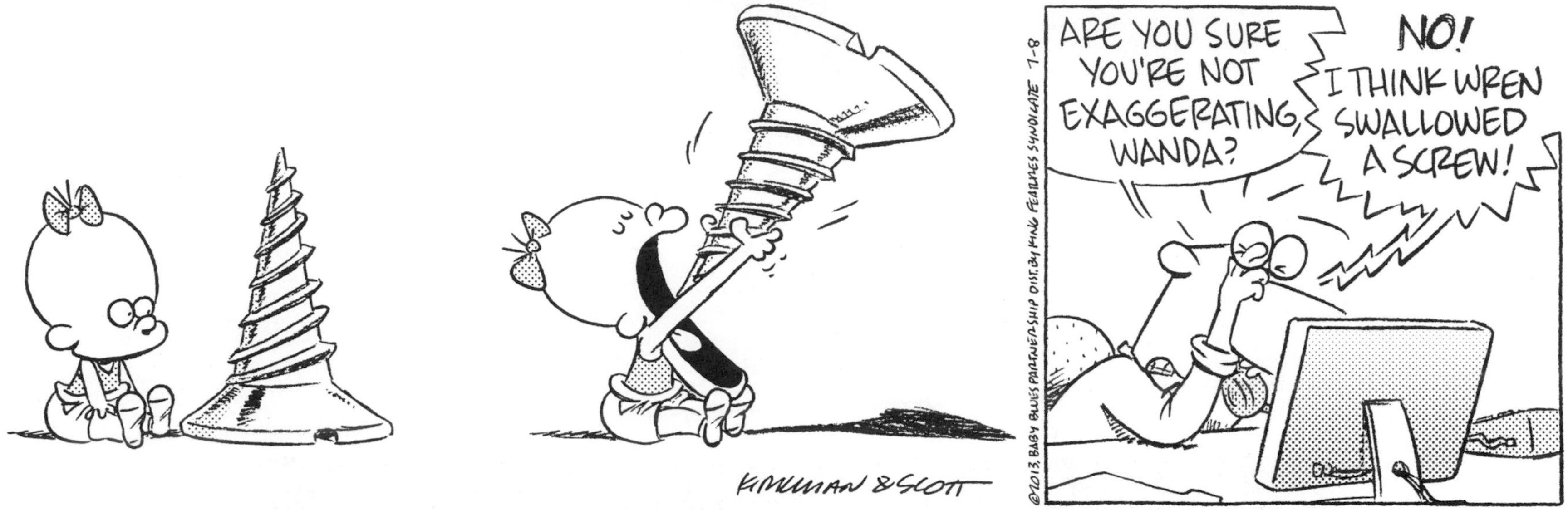
ARE YOU SURE YOU'RE NOT EXAGGERATING, WANDA?
NO! I THINK WREN SWALLOWED A SCREW!
KIRKMAN & SCOTT
©2013, BABY BLUES PARTNERSHIP DIST. BY KING FEATURES SYNDICATE 1-8

Jerry: When I write something like, "Wren tries to swallow an impossibly large, dangerous-looking screw," Rick doesn't disappoint when he draws it.

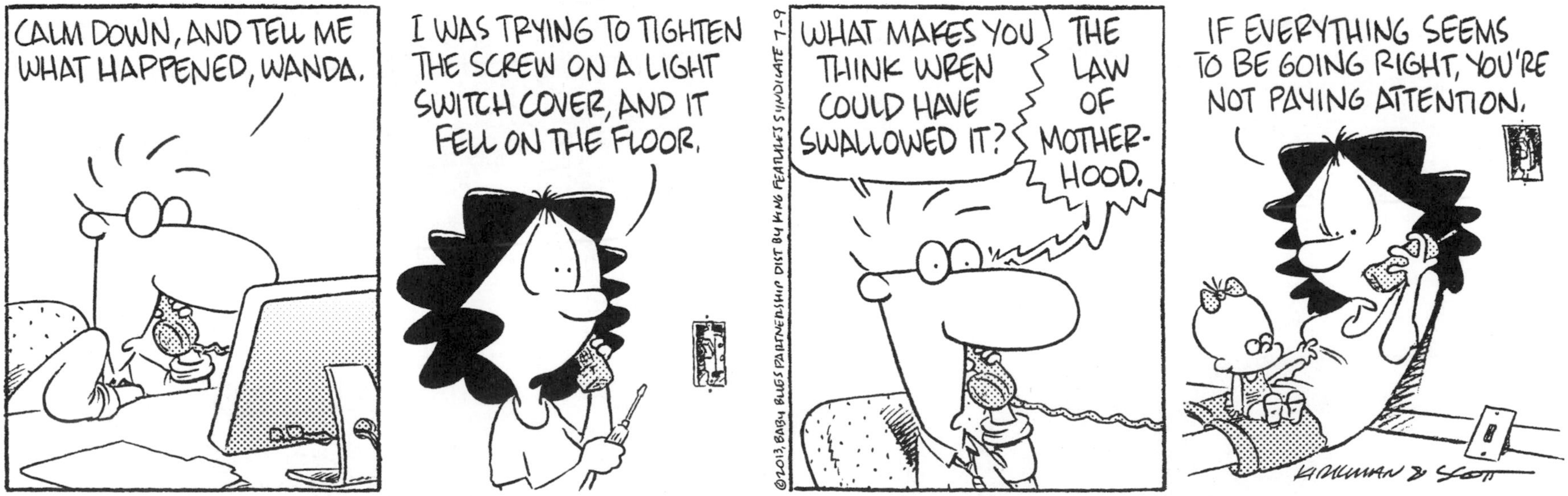
CALM DOWN, AND TELL ME WHAT HAPPENED, WANDA.
I WAS TRYING TO TIGHTEN THE SCREW ON A LIGHT SWITCH COVER, AND IT FELL ON THE FLOOR.
WHAT MAKES YOU THINK WREN COULD HAVE SWALLOWED IT?
THE LAW OF MOTHERHOOD.
IF EVERYTHING SEEMS TO BE GOING RIGHT, YOU'RE NOT PAYING ATTENTION.
KIRKMAN & SCOTT
©2013, BABY BLUES PARTNERSHIP DIST BY KING FEATURES SYNDICATE 1-9

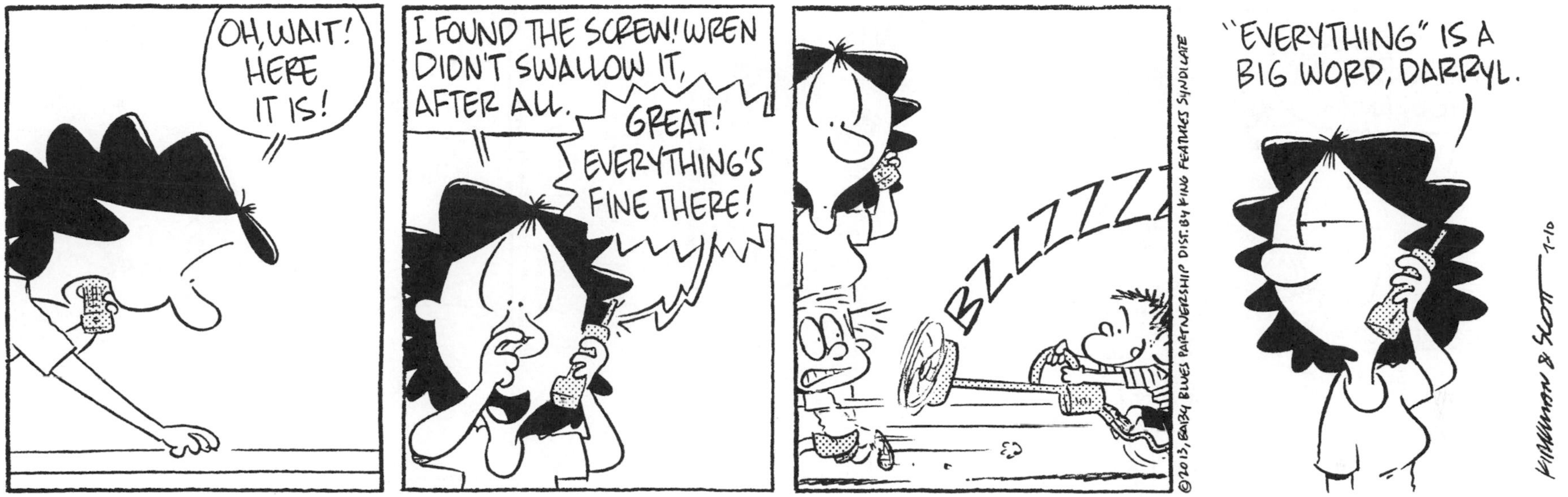
OH, WAIT! HERE IT IS!
I FOUND THE SCREW! WREN DIDN'T SWALLOW IT, AFTER ALL.
GREAT! EVERYTHING'S FINE THERE!
BZZZZZZ
©2013, BABY BLUES PARTNERSHIP DIST. BY KING FEATURES SYNDICATE
"EVERYTHING" IS A BIG WORD, DARRYL.
KIRKMAN & SCOTT 7-10

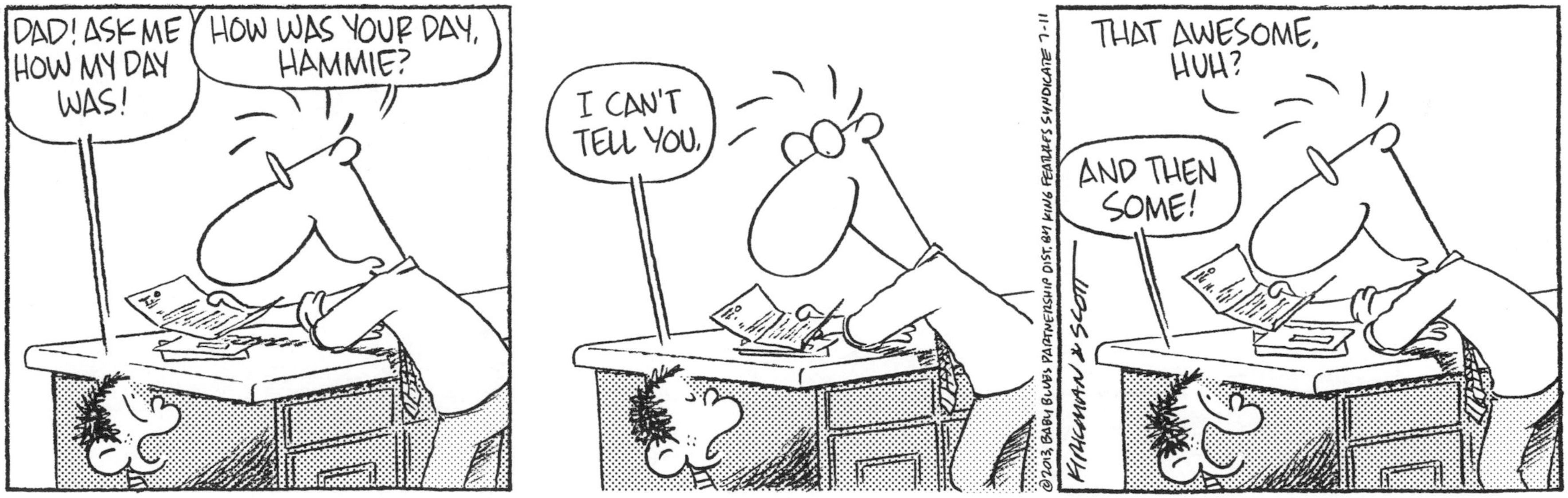
DAD! ASK ME HOW MY DAY WAS!
HOW WAS YOUR DAY, HAMMIE?
I CAN'T TELL YOU.
©2013, BABY BLUES PARTNERSHIP DIST. BY KING FEATURES SYNDICATE 7-11
KIRKMAN & SCOTT
THAT AWESOME, HUH?
AND THEN SOME!

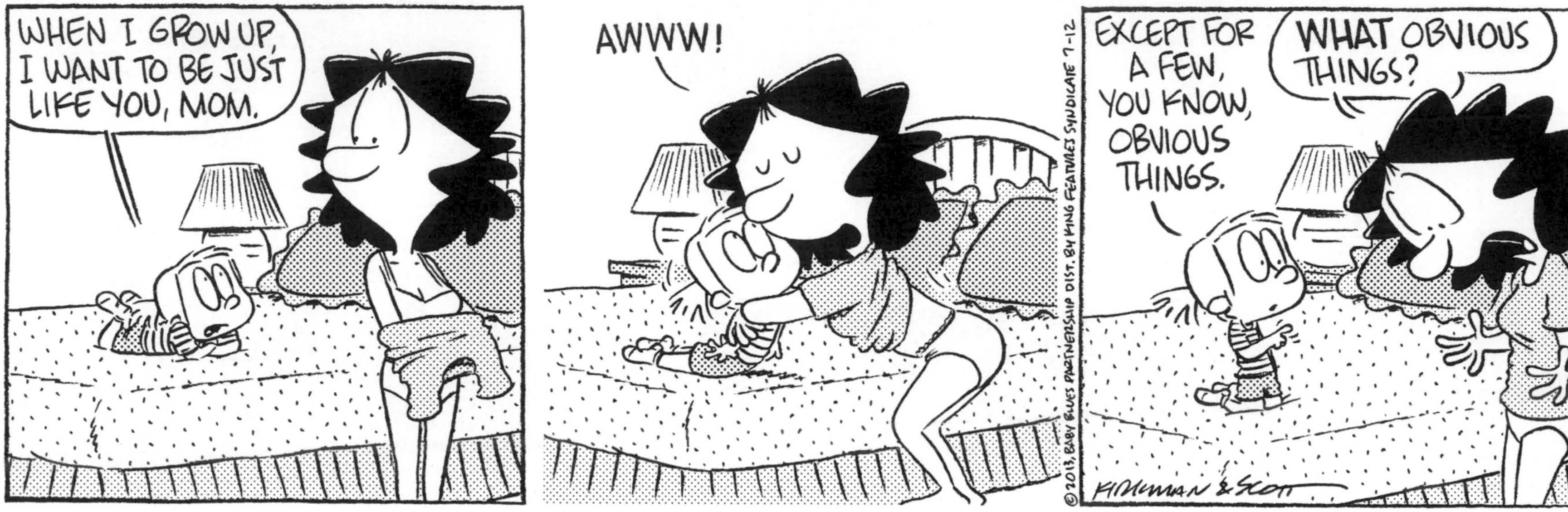
WHEN I GROW UP, I WANT TO BE JUST LIKE YOU, MOM.
AWWW!
©2013, BABY BLUES PARTNERSHIP DIST. BY KING FEATURES SYNDICATE 7-12
EXCEPT FOR A FEW, YOU KNOW, OBVIOUS THINGS.
WHAT OBVIOUS THINGS?
KIRKMAN & SCOTT

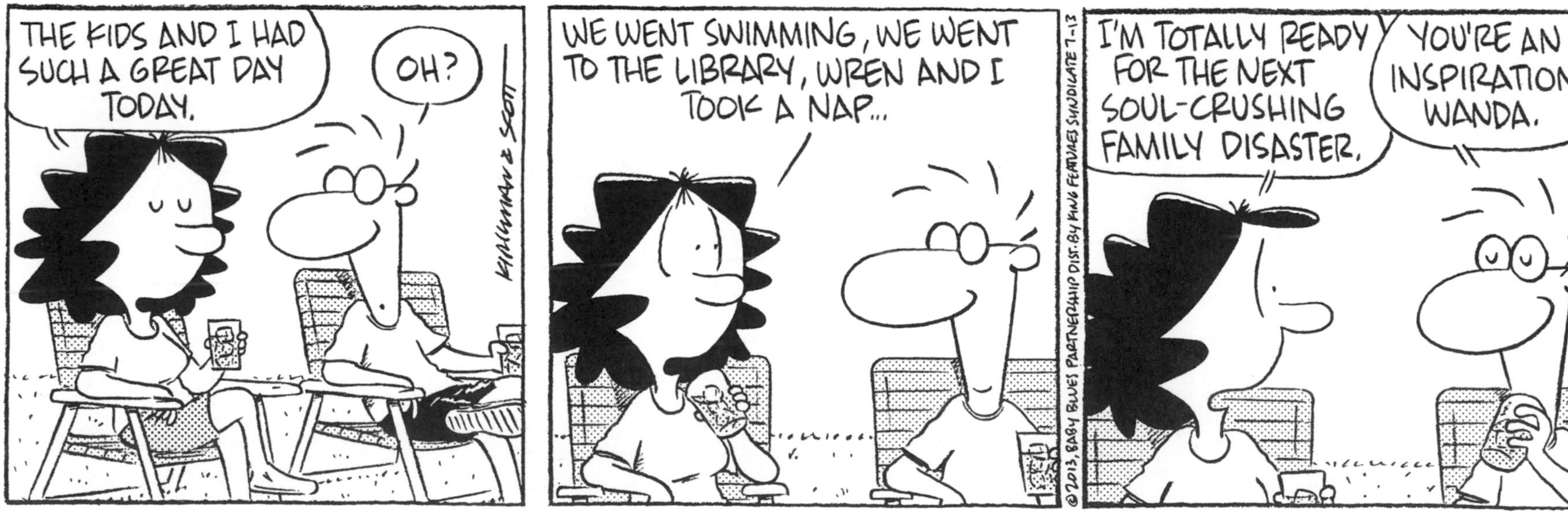
THE KIDS AND I HAD SUCH A GREAT DAY TODAY.
OH?
KIRKMAN & SCOTT
WE WENT SWIMMING, WE WENT TO THE LIBRARY, WREN AND I TOOK A NAP...
©2013, BABY BLUES PARTNERSHIP DIST. BY KING FEATURES SYNDICATE 7-13
I'M TOTALLY READY FOR THE NEXT SOUL-CRUSHING FAMILY DISASTER.
YOU'RE AN INSPIRATION, WANDA.

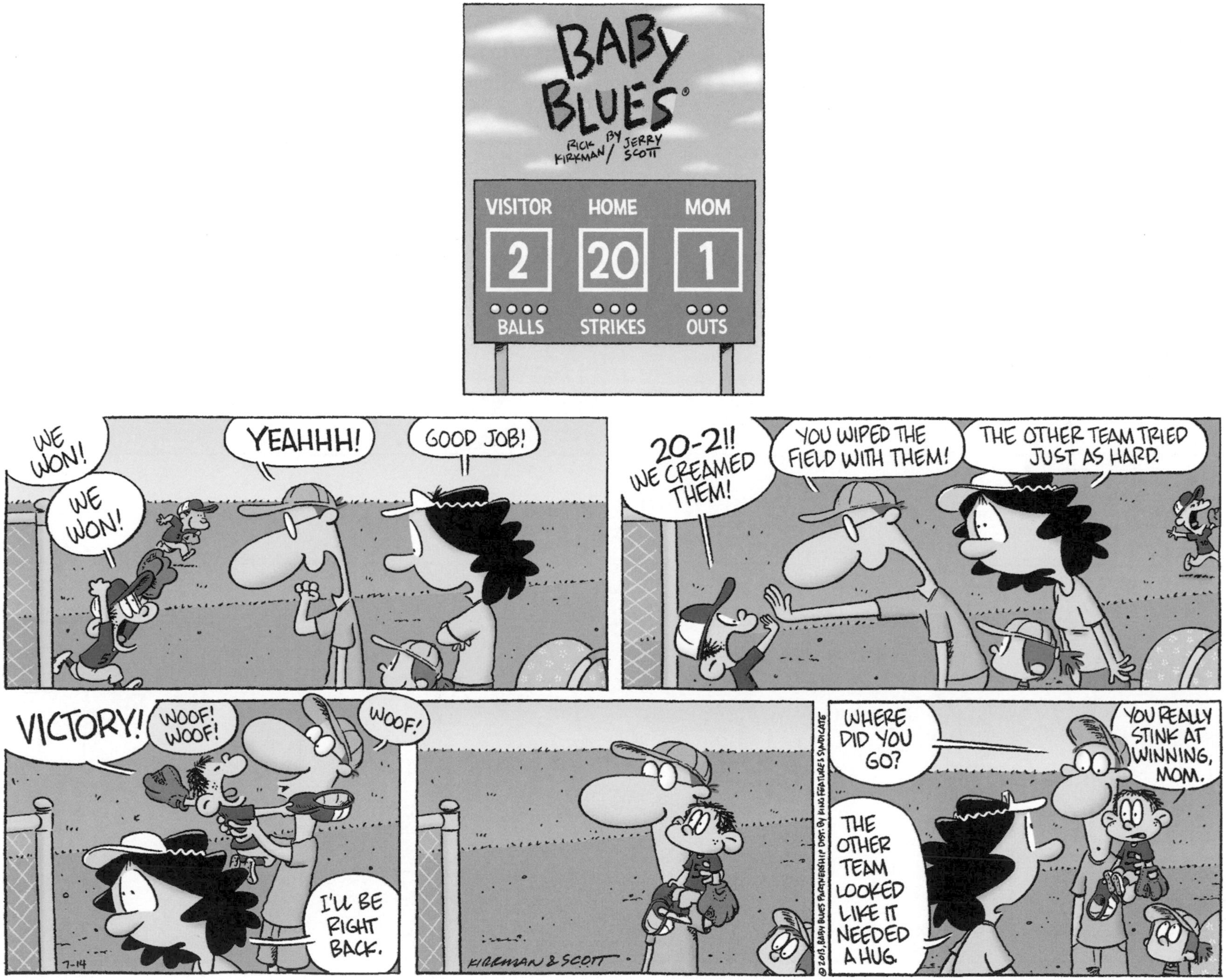
BABY BLUES®
BY RICK KIRKMAN / JERRY SCOTT
VISITOR HOME MOM
2 20 1
BALLS STRIKES OUTS
WE WON!
WE WON!
YEAHHH!
GOOD JOB!
20-2!! WE CREAMED THEM!
YOU WIPED THE FIELD WITH THEM!
THE OTHER TEAM TRIED JUST AS HARD.
VICTORY!
WOOF! WOOF!
WOOF!
I'LL BE RIGHT BACK.
7-14
KIRKMAN & SCOTT
© 2013, BABY BLUES PARTNERSHIP DIST. BY KING FEATURES SYNDICATE
WHERE DID YOU GO?
YOU REALLY STINK AT WINNING, MOM.
THE OTHER TEAM LOOKED LIKE IT NEEDED A HUG.

Jerry: Moms!

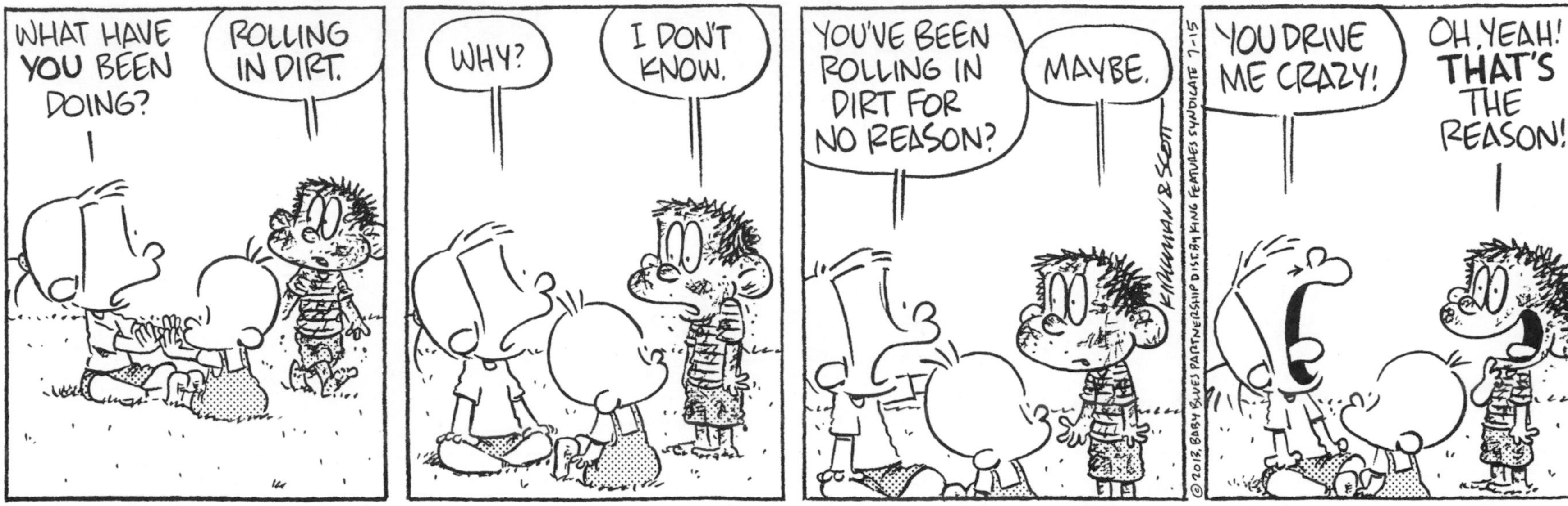
WHAT HAVE **YOU** BEEN DOING?
ROLLING IN DIRT.
WHY?
I DON'T KNOW.
YOU'VE BEEN ROLLING IN DIRT FOR NO REASON?
MAYBE.
YOU DRIVE ME CRAZY!
OH, YEAH! **THAT'S** THE REASON!
KIRKMAN & SCOTT
© 2013, BABY BLUES PARTNERSHIP DIST. BY KING FEATURES SYNDICATE 7-15

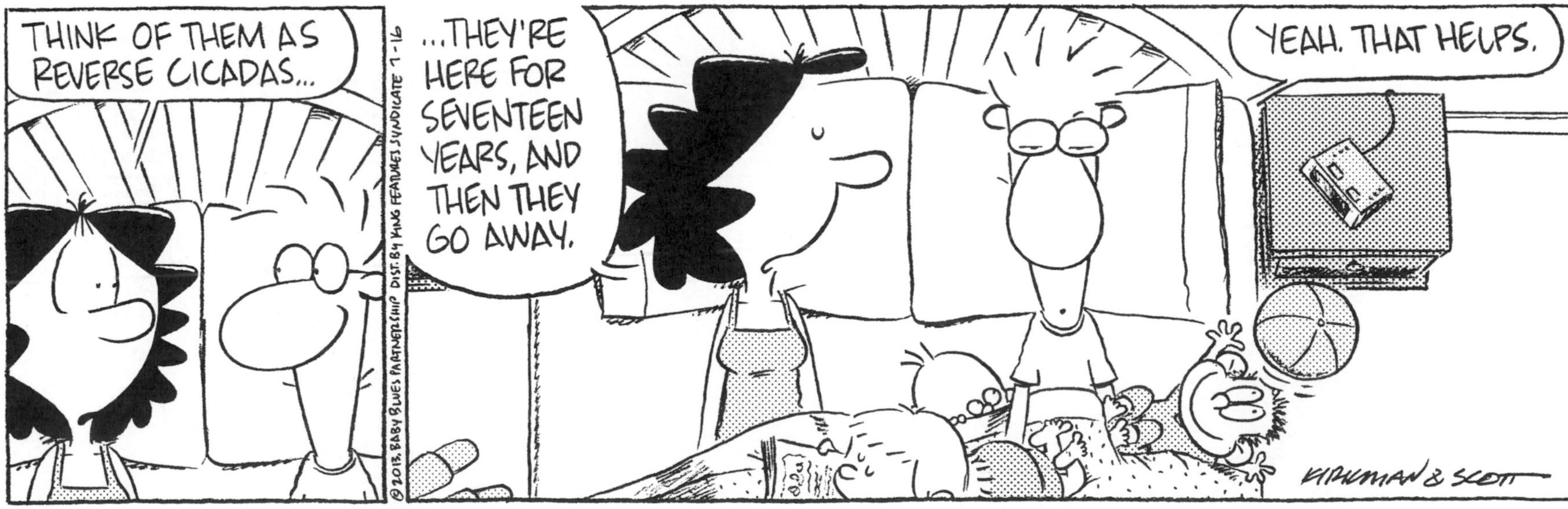
THINK OF THEM AS REVERSE CICADAS...
...THEY'RE HERE FOR SEVENTEEN YEARS, AND THEN THEY GO AWAY.
YEAH. THAT HELPS.
© 2013, BABY BLUES PARTNERSHIP DIST. BY KING FEATURES SYNDICATE 7-16
KIRKMAN & SCOTT

Rick: This is such a great comparison. Kudos, Jerry.

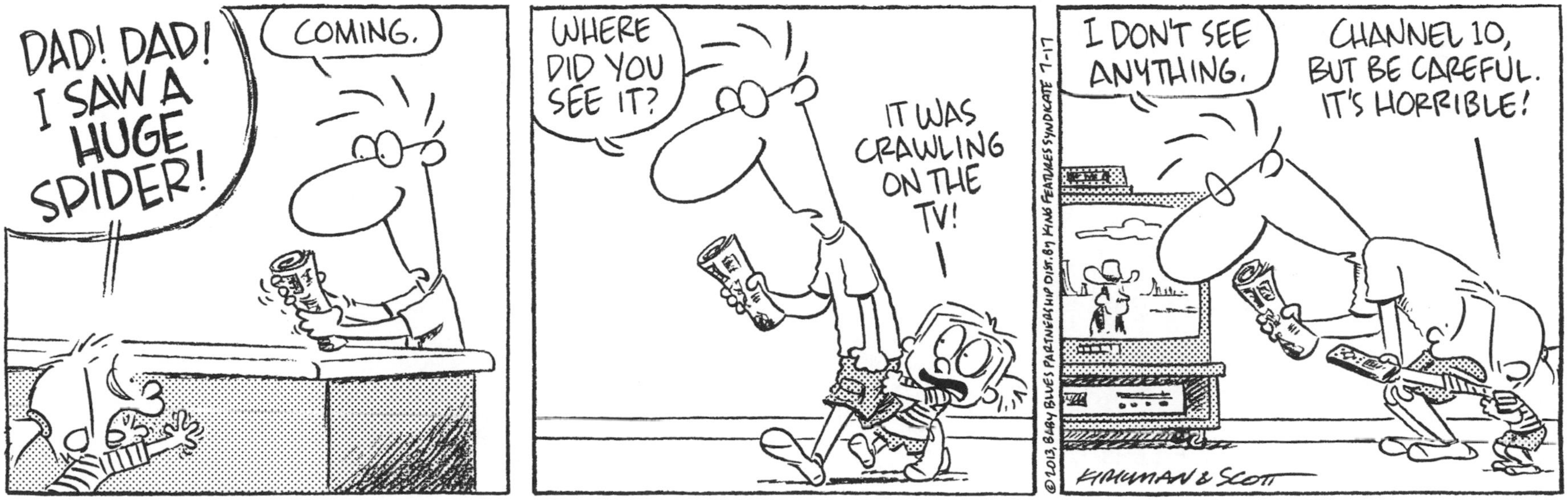
DAD! DAD! I SAW A HUGE SPIDER!
COMING.
WHERE DID YOU SEE IT?
IT WAS CRAWLING ON THE TV!
I DON'T SEE ANYTHING.
CHANNEL 10, BUT BE CAREFUL. IT'S HORRIBLE!
KIRKMAN & SCOTT

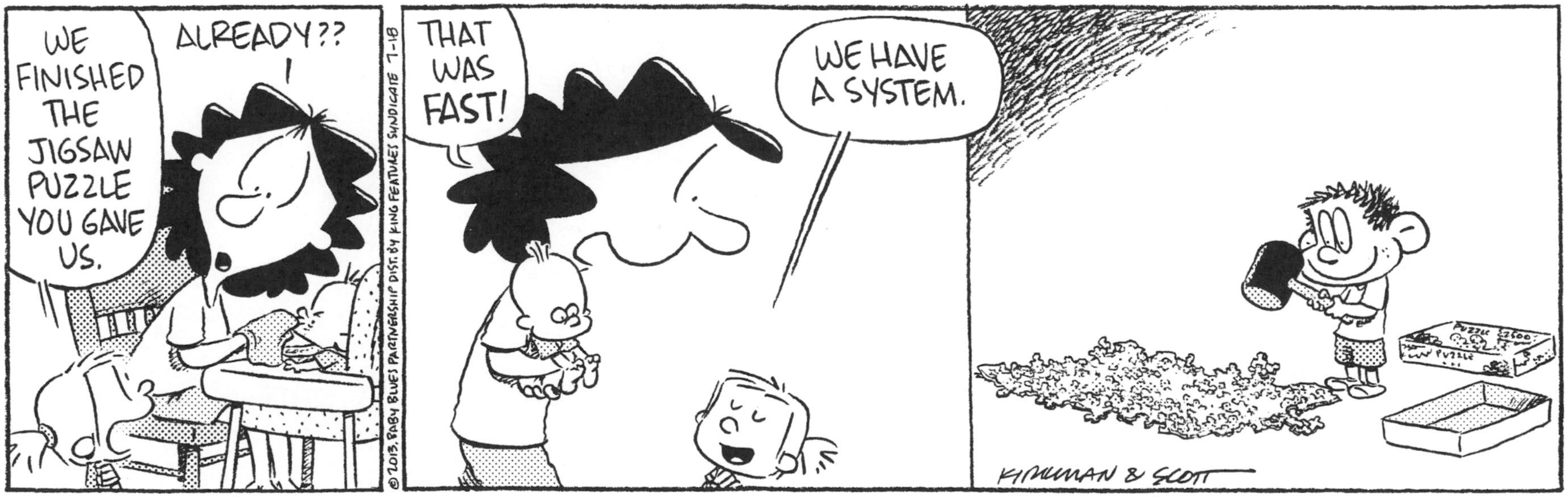
WE FINISHED THE JIGSAW PUZZLE YOU GAVE US.
ALREADY??
THAT WAS FAST!
WE HAVE A SYSTEM.
KIRKMAN & SCOTT

Rick: I'm adding another thing to the list of "Things I Hate to Draw": jigsaw puzzles.

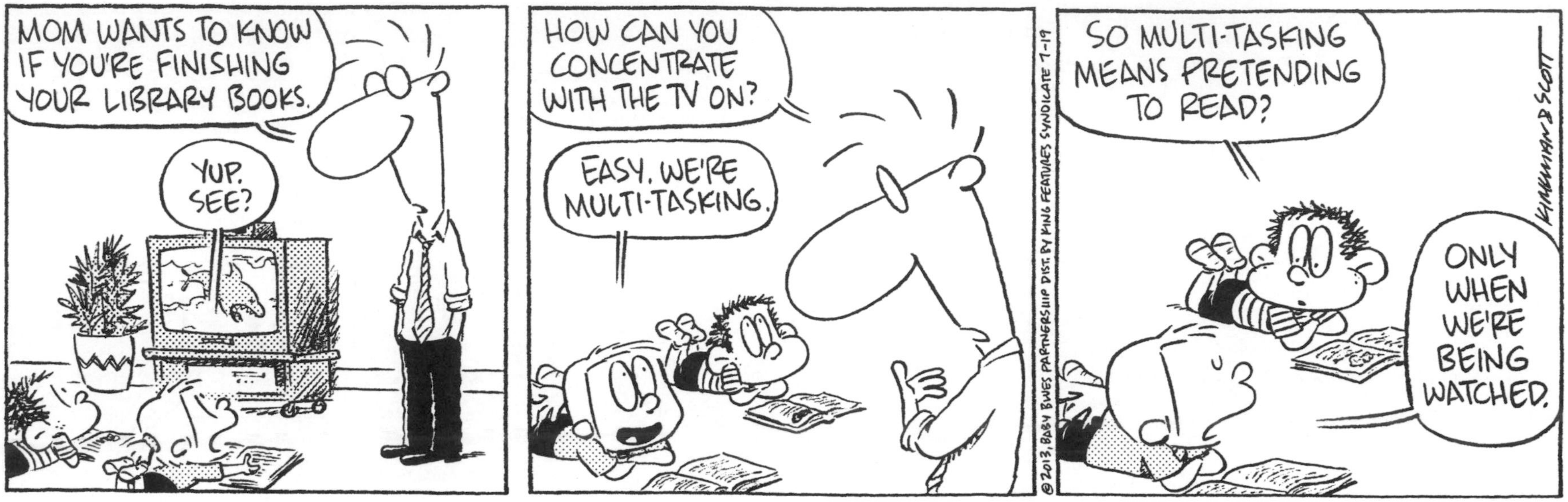
MOM WANTS TO KNOW IF YOU'RE FINISHING YOUR LIBRARY BOOKS.
YUP. SEE?
HOW CAN YOU CONCENTRATE WITH THE TV ON?
EASY. WE'RE MULTI-TASKING.
© 2013, BABY BLUES PARTNERSHIP DIST. BY KING FEATURES SYNDICATE 7-19
SO MULTI-TASKING MEANS PRETENDING TO READ?
ONLY WHEN WE'RE BEING WATCHED.
KIRKMAN & SCOTT

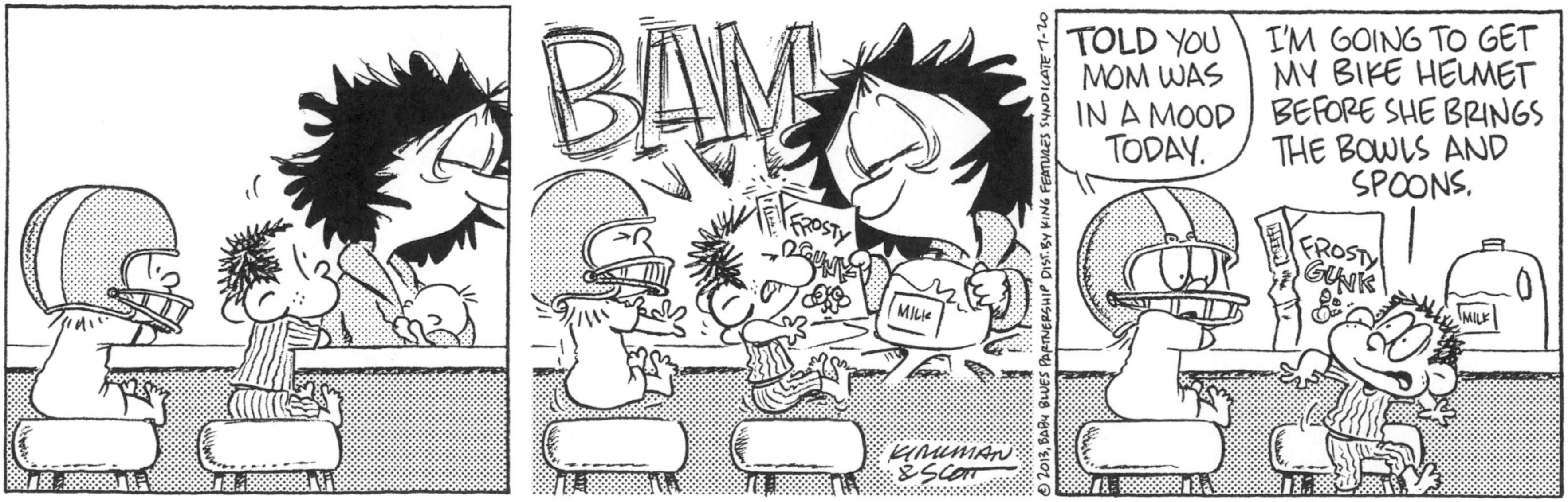
BAM
FROSTY GUNK
MILK
KIRKMAN & SCOTT
© 2013, BABY BLUES PARTNERSHIP DIST. BY KING FEATURES SYNDICATE 7-20
TOLD YOU MOM WAS IN A MOOD TODAY.
I'M GOING TO GET MY BIKE HELMET BEFORE SHE BRINGS THE BOWLS AND SPOONS.
FROSTY GUNK
MILK

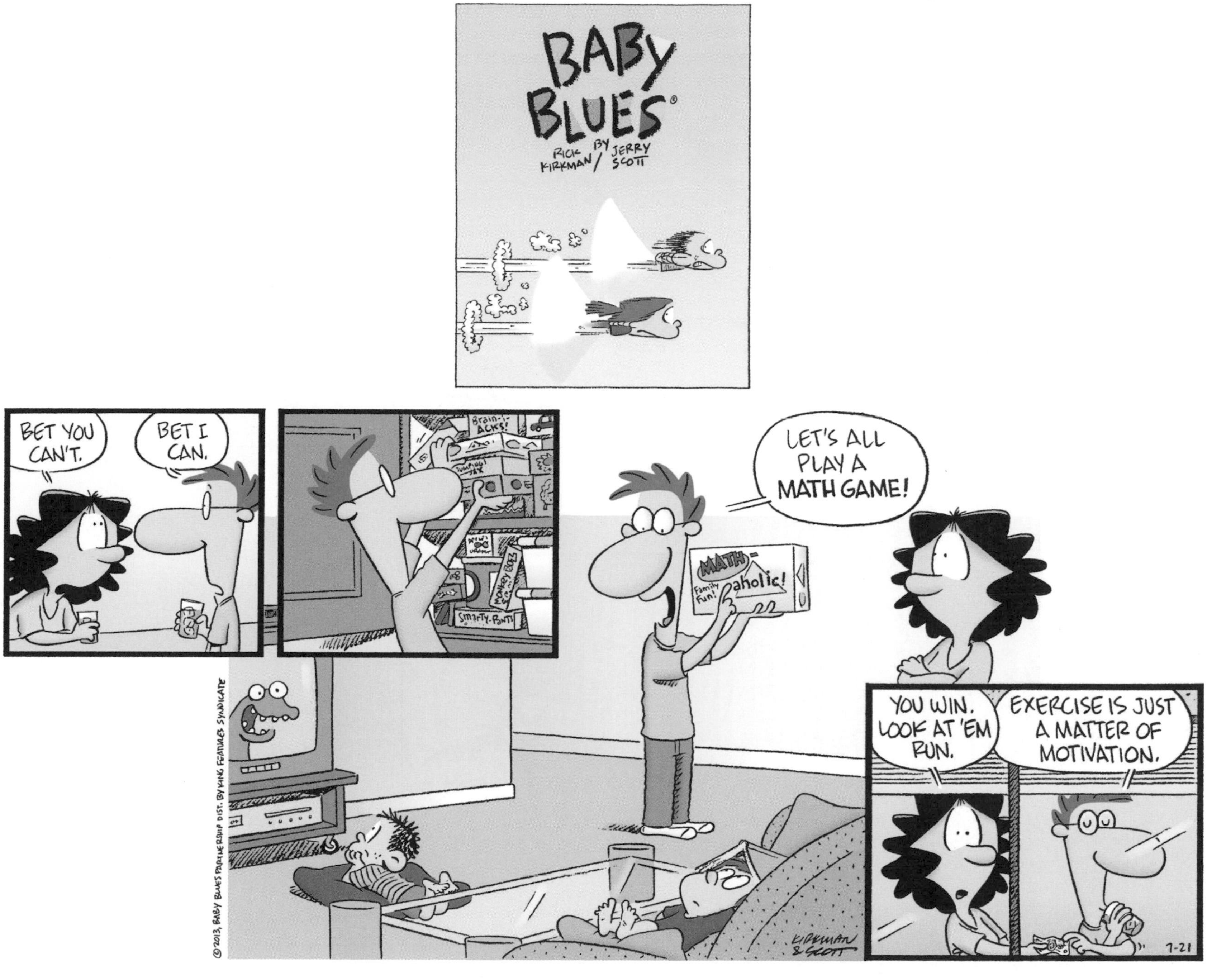
BABY BLUES®
BY RICK KIRKMAN / JERRY SCOTT
BET YOU CAN'T.
BET I CAN.
Brain-ACKS!
SMARTY-PANTS
LET'S ALL PLAY A MATH GAME!
MATH-aholic! Family Fun!
YOU WIN. LOOK AT 'EM RUN.
EXERCISE IS JUST A MATTER OF MOTIVATION.
KIRKMAN & SCOTT
7-21
© 2013, BABY BLUES PARTNERSHIP DIST. BY KING FEATURES SYNDICATE

IF YOU KEEP MAKING THAT FACE, IT'LL STICK THAT WAY.
©2013, BABY BLUES PARTNERSHIP DIST. BY KING FEATURES SYNDICATE 7-22
ANOTHER PROMISE BROKEN...
KIRKMAN & SCOTT

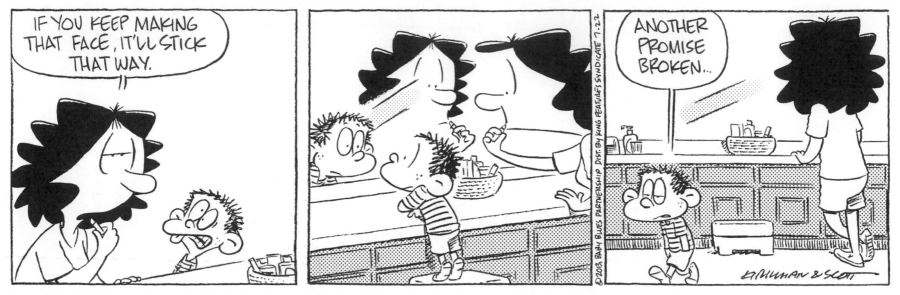

Jerry: I tested this warning a whole lot when I was a kid. Absolutely not true, unless male pattern baldness is a side effect.

©2013, BABY BLUES PARTNERSHIP DIST. BY KING FEATURES SYNDICATE 7-23
KIRKMAN & SCOTT

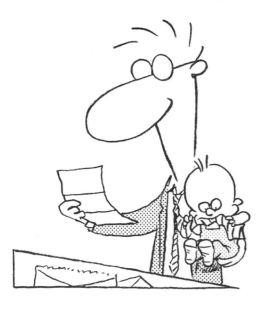

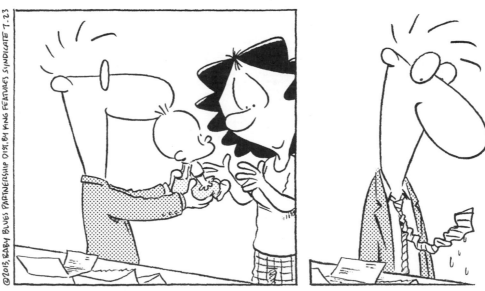

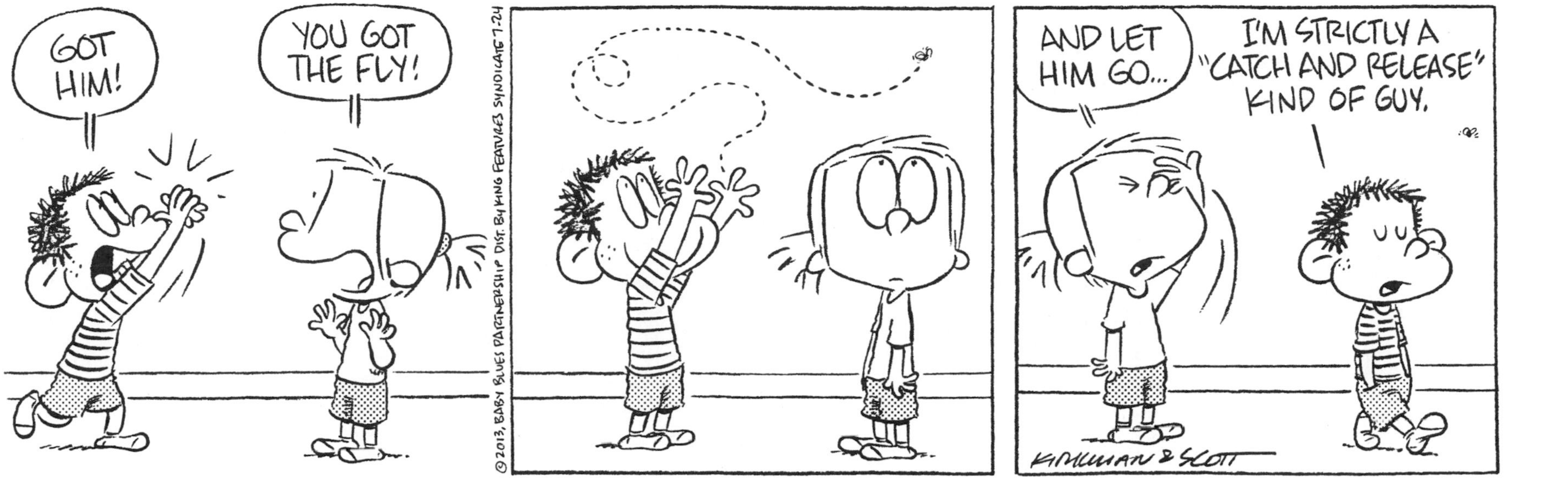
GOT HIM!
YOU GOT THE FLY!
©2013, BABY BLUES PARTNERSHIP DIST. BY KING FEATURES SYNDICATE 7-24
AND LET HIM GO...
I'M STRICTLY A "CATCH AND RELEASE" KIND OF GUY.
KIRKMAN & SCOTT

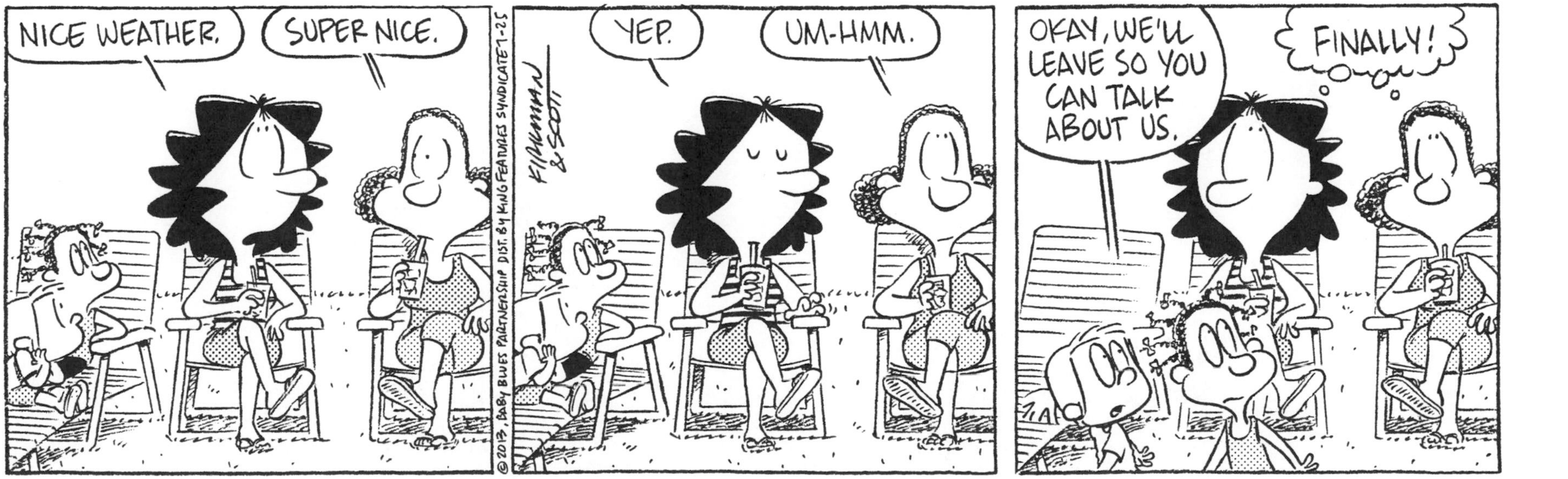
NICE WEATHER.
SUPER NICE.
©2013, BABY BLUES PARTNERSHIP DIST. BY KING FEATURES SYNDICATE 7-25
KIRKMAN & SCOTT
YEP.
UM-HMM.
OKAY, WE'LL LEAVE SO YOU CAN TALK ABOUT US.
FINALLY!

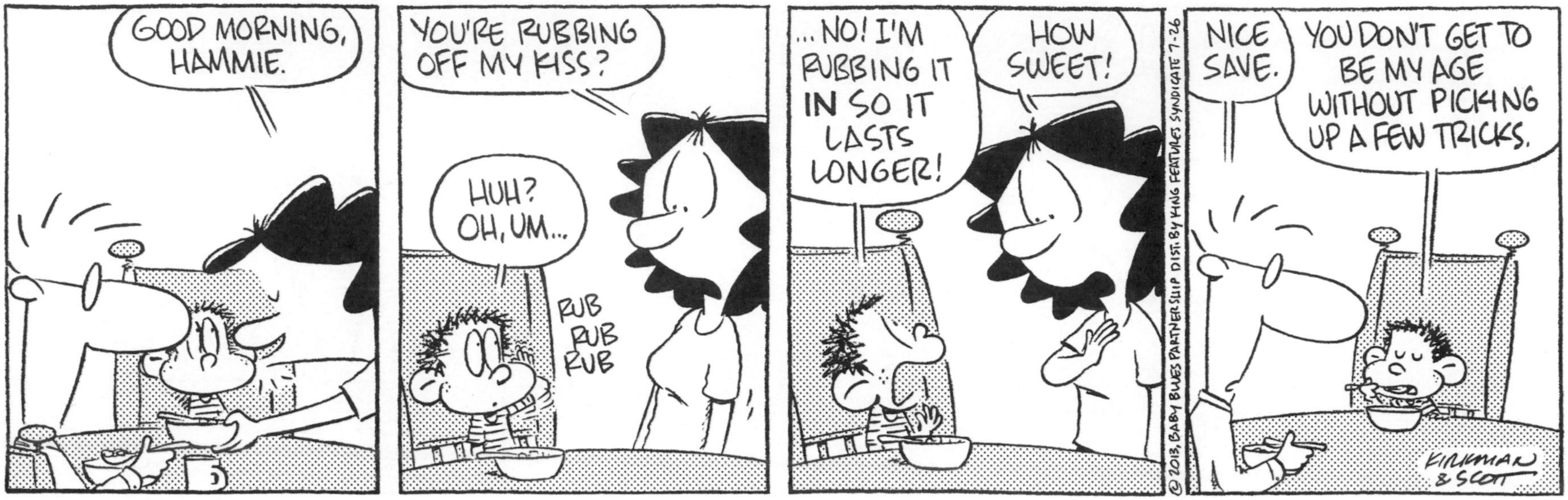
GOOD MORNING, HAMMIE.
YOU'RE RUBBING OFF MY KISS?
HUH? OH, UM...
RUB RUB RUB
...NO! I'M RUBBING IT **IN** SO IT LASTS LONGER!
HOW SWEET!
© 2013, BABY BLUES PARTNERSHIP DIST. BY KING FEATURES SYNDICATE 7-26
NICE SAVE.
YOU DON'T GET TO BE MY AGE WITHOUT PICKING UP A FEW TRICKS.
KIRKMAN & SCOTT

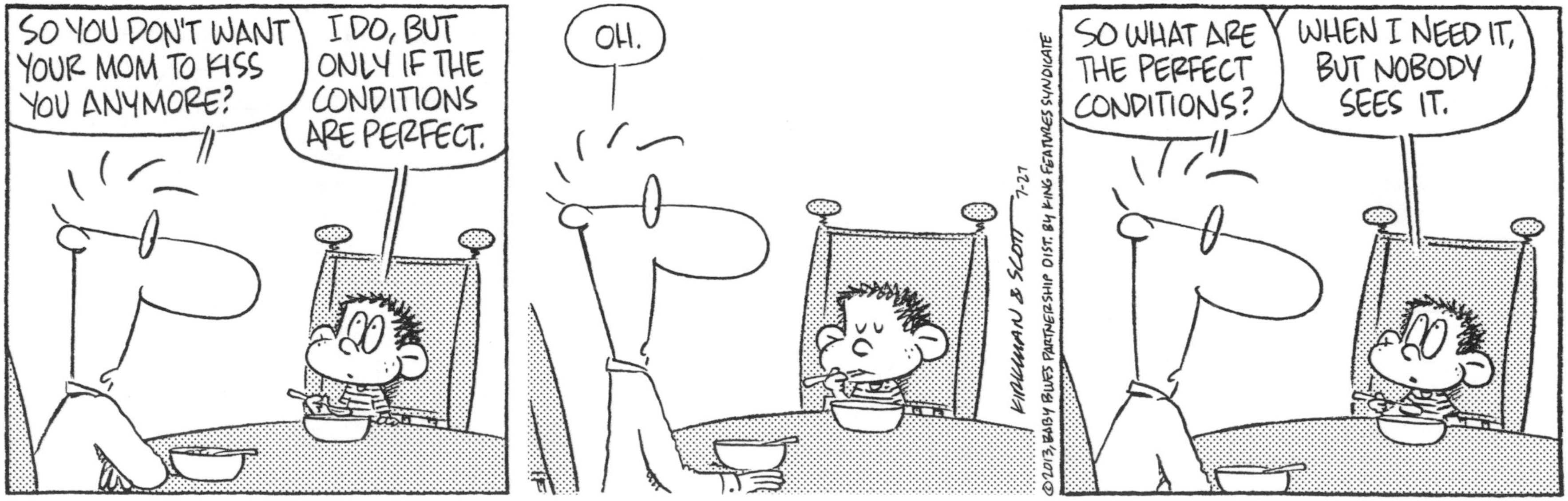
SO YOU DON'T WANT YOUR MOM TO KISS YOU ANYMORE?
I DO, BUT ONLY IF THE CONDITIONS ARE PERFECT.
OH.
KIRKMAN & SCOTT 7-27
©2013, BABY BLUES PARTNERSHIP DIST. BY KING FEATURES SYNDICATE
SO WHAT ARE THE PERFECT CONDITIONS?
WHEN I NEED IT, BUT NOBODY SEES IT.

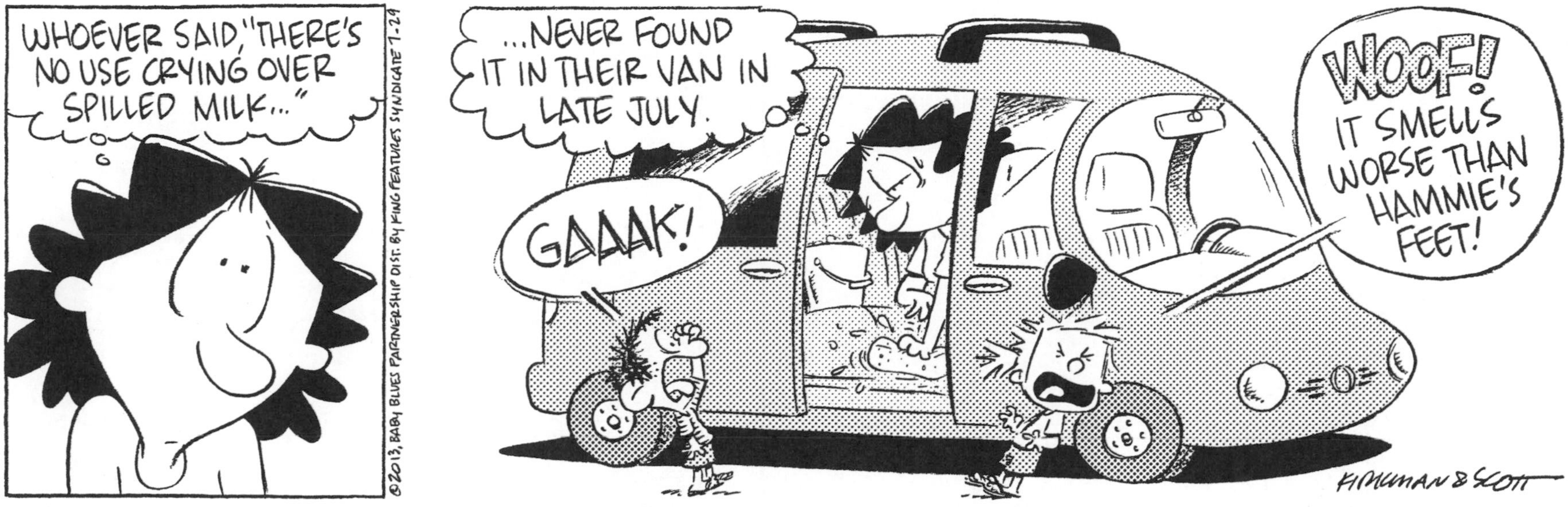
WHOEVER SAID, "THERE'S NO USE CRYING OVER SPILLED MILK..."
©2013, BABY BLUES PARTNERSHIP DIST. BY KING FEATURES SYNDICATE 7-29
...NEVER FOUND IT IN THEIR VAN IN LATE JULY.
GAAAK!
WOOF! IT SMELLS WORSE THAN HAMMIE'S FEET!
KIRKMAN & SCOTT

Rick: I suppose every family van has its own unique smell, kind of like how we all have our own unique gut bacteria. Eww.

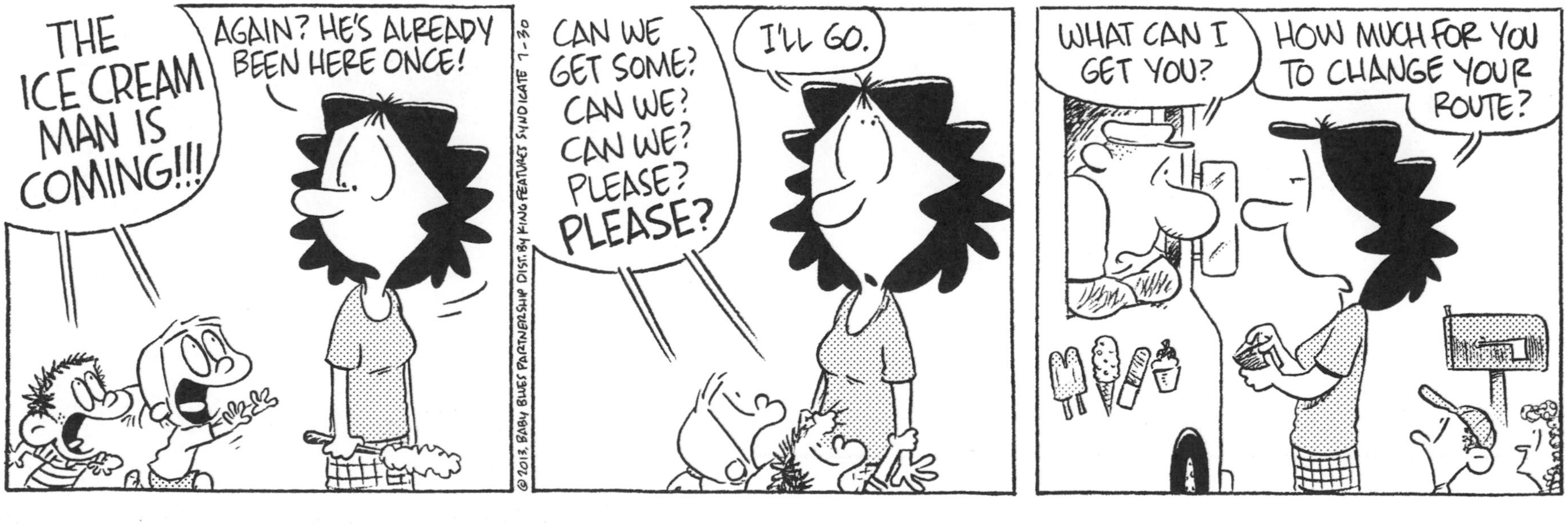
THE ICE CREAM MAN IS COMING!!!
AGAIN? HE'S ALREADY BEEN HERE ONCE!
©2013, BABY BLUES PARTNERSHIP DIST. BY KING FEATURES SYNDICATE 7-30
CAN WE GET SOME? CAN WE? CAN WE? PLEASE? PLEASE?
I'LL GO.
WHAT CAN I GET YOU?
HOW MUCH FOR YOU TO CHANGE YOUR ROUTE?

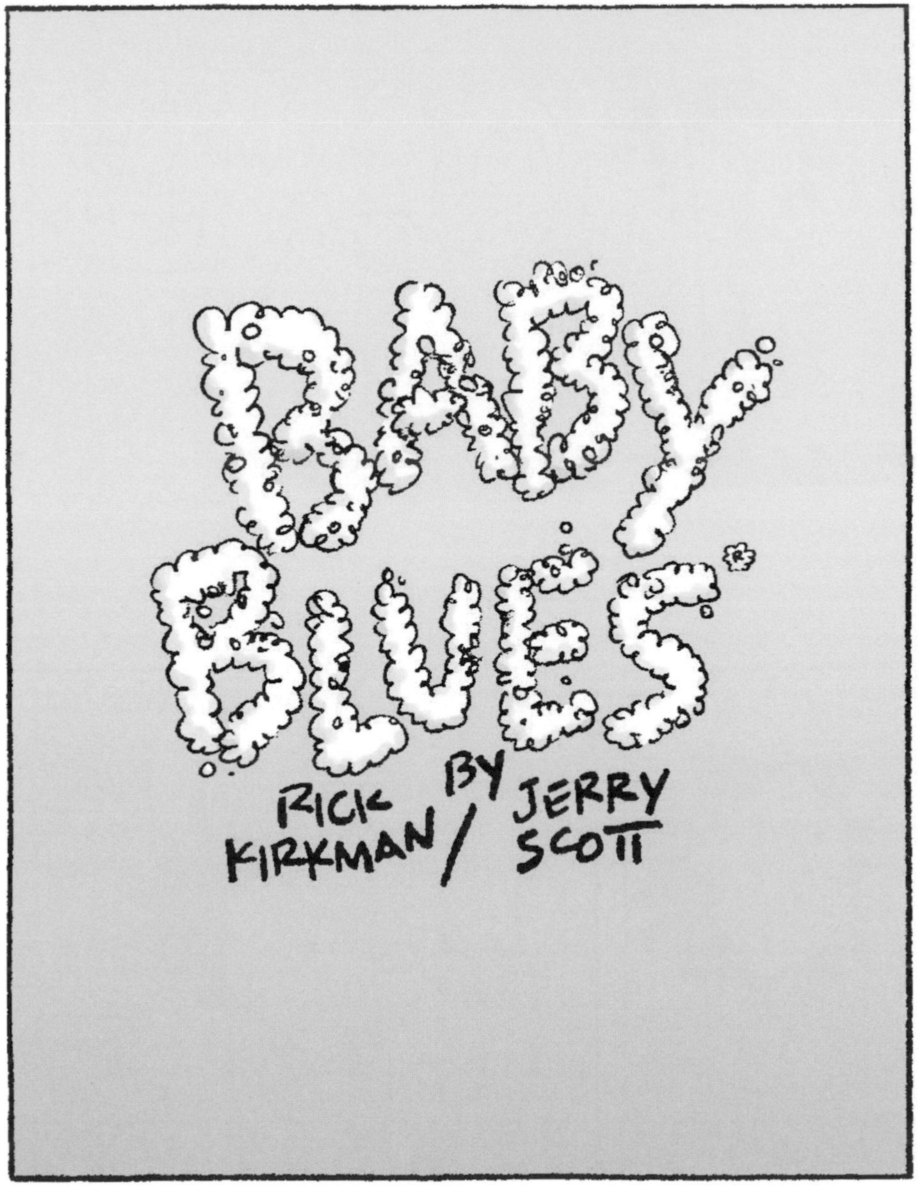
BABY BLUES®
BY
RICK KIRKMAN / JERRY SCOTT

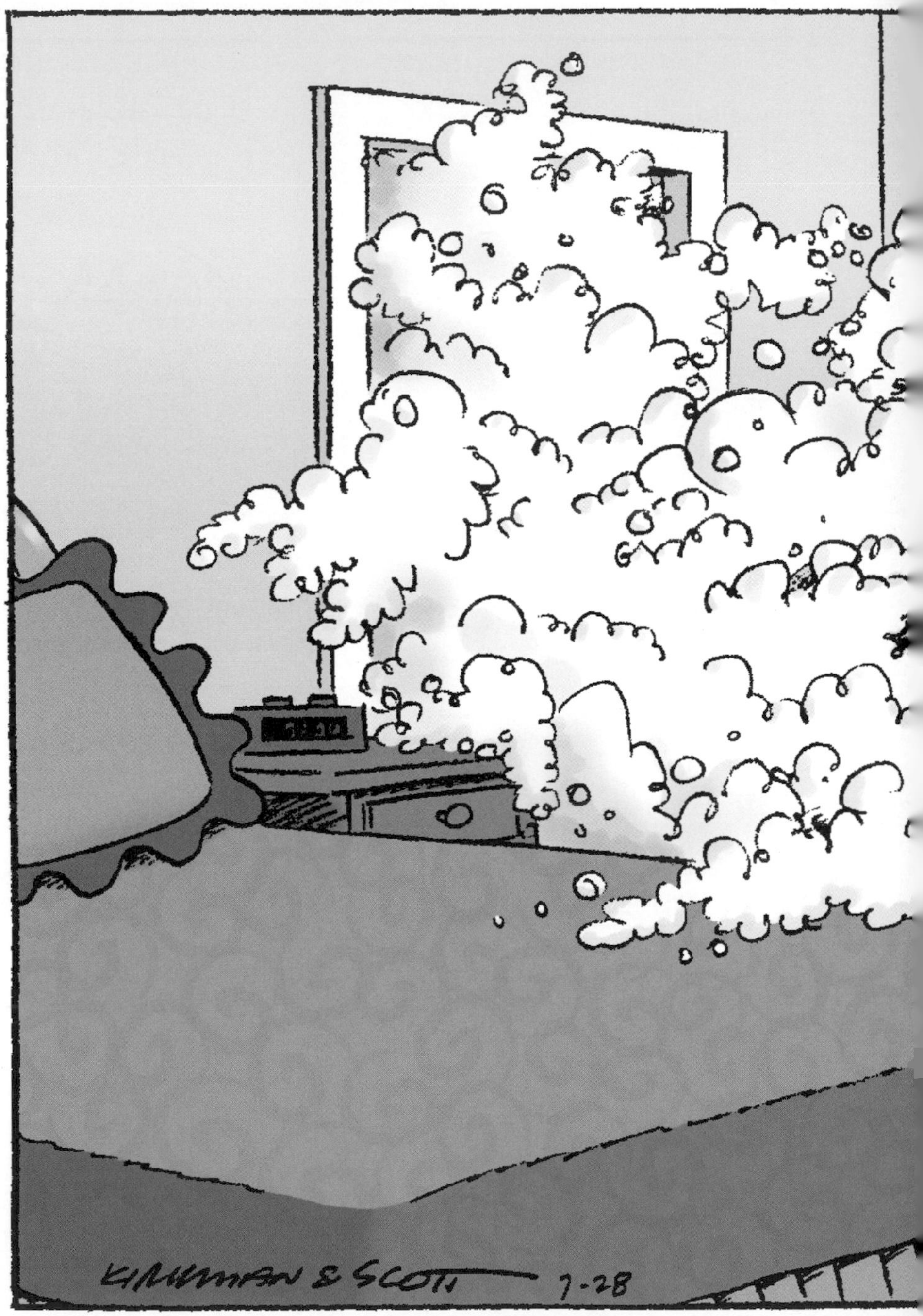
KIRKMAN & SCOTT 7-28

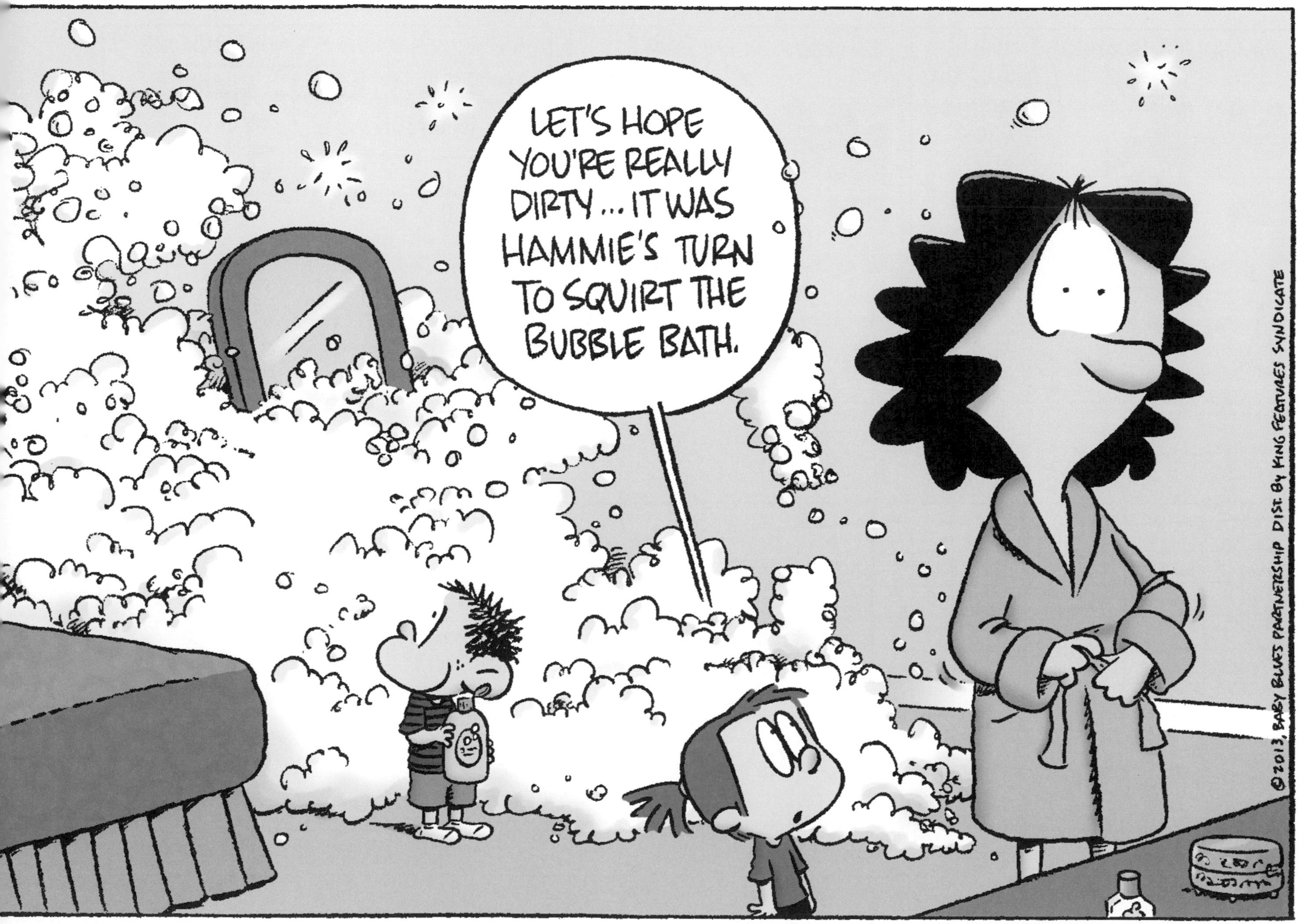
LET'S HOPE YOU'RE REALLY DIRTY... IT WAS HAMMIE'S TURN TO SQUIRT THE BUBBLE BATH.
©2013, BABY BLUES PARTNERSHIP DIST. BY KING FEATURES SYNDICATE

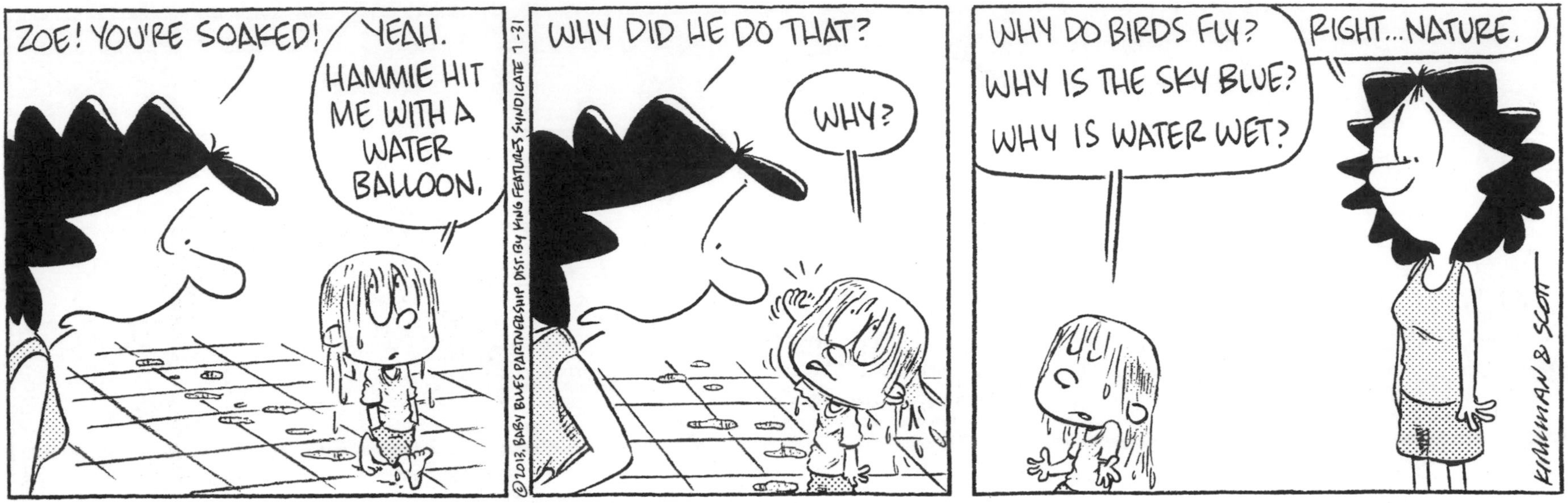
ZOE! YOU'RE SOAKED!
YEAH. HAMMIE HIT ME WITH A WATER BALLOON.
WHY DID HE DO THAT?
WHY?
WHY DO BIRDS FLY? WHY IS THE SKY BLUE? WHY IS WATER WET?
RIGHT...NATURE.
KIRKMAN & SCOTT
©2013, BABY BLUES PARTNERSHIP DIST. BY KING FEATURES SYNDICATE 7-31

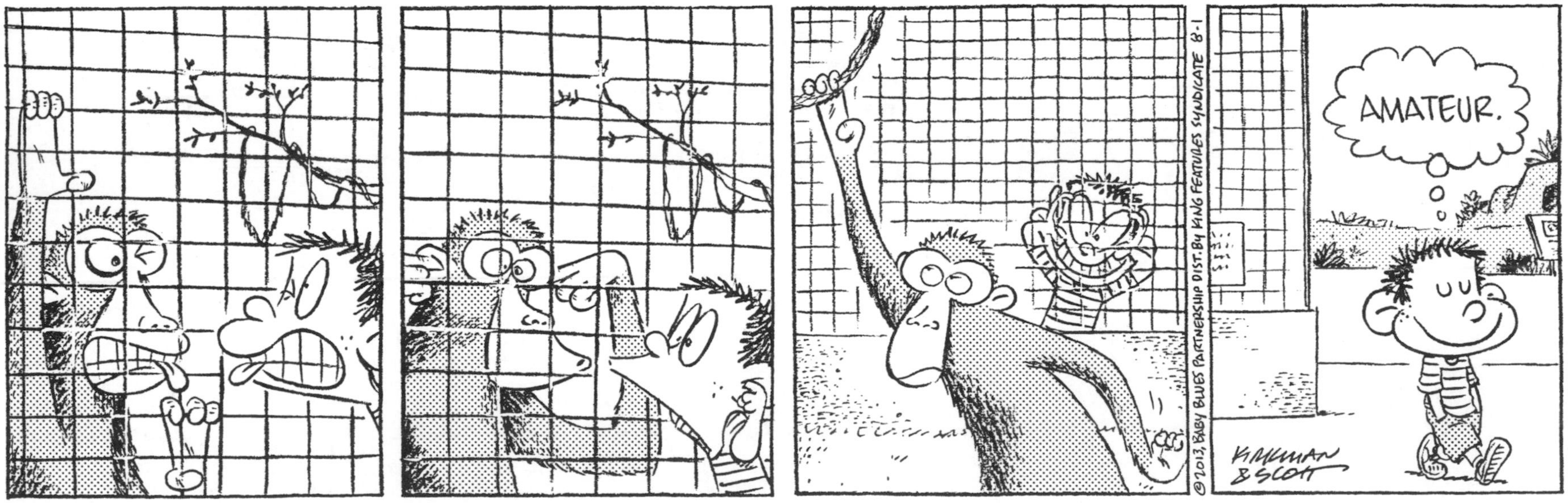
AMATEUR.
KIRKMAN & SCOTT
©2013, BABY BLUES PARTNERSHIP DIST. BY KING FEATURES SYNDICATE 8-1

Rick: This was fun fooling around with monkey faces.

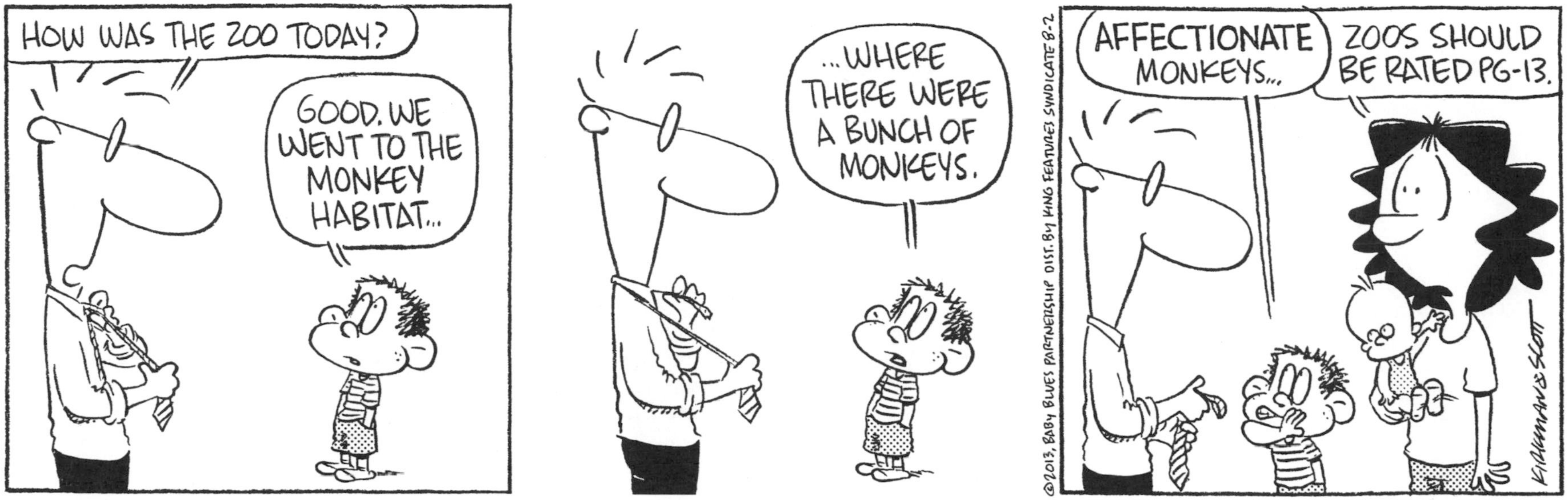
HOW WAS THE ZOO TODAY?
GOOD. WE WENT TO THE MONKEY HABITAT...
...WHERE THERE WERE A BUNCH OF MONKEYS.
AFFECTIONATE MONKEYS...
ZOOS SHOULD BE RATED PG-13.
©2013, BABY BLUES PARTNERSHIP DIST. BY KING FEATURES SYNDICATE 8-2
KIRKMAN & SCOTT

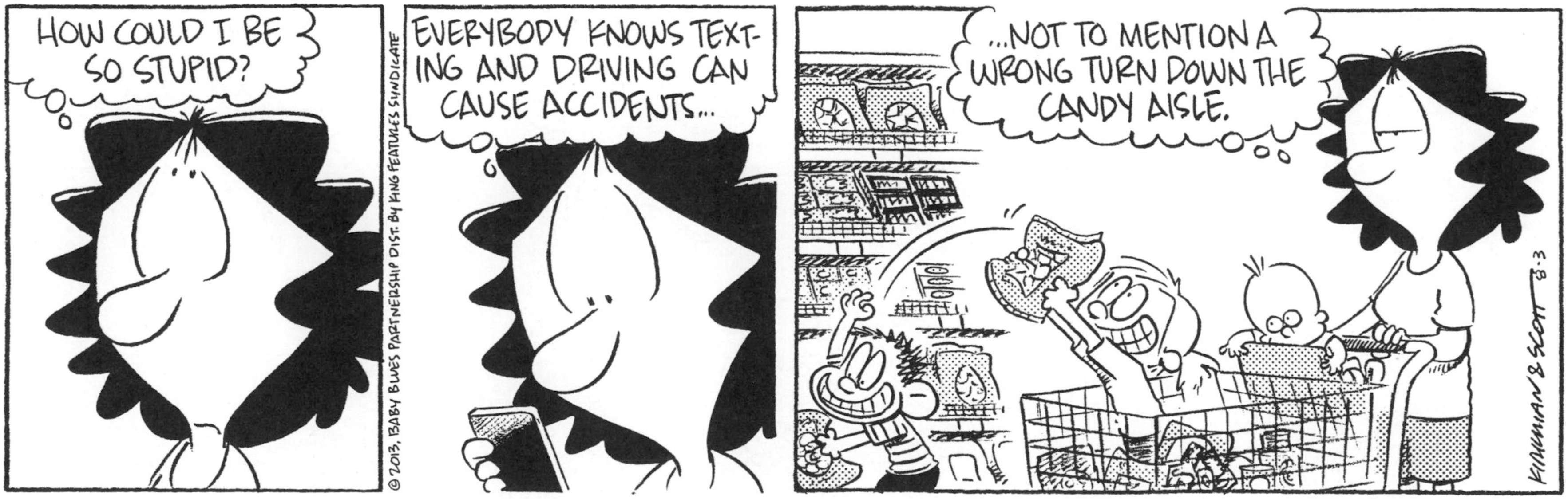
HOW COULD I BE SO STUPID?
©2013, BABY BLUES PARTNERSHIP DIST. BY KING FEATURES SYNDICATE
EVERYBODY KNOWS TEXTING AND DRIVING CAN CAUSE ACCIDENTS...
...NOT TO MENTION A WRONG TURN DOWN THE CANDY AISLE.
KIRKMAN & SCOTT 8-3

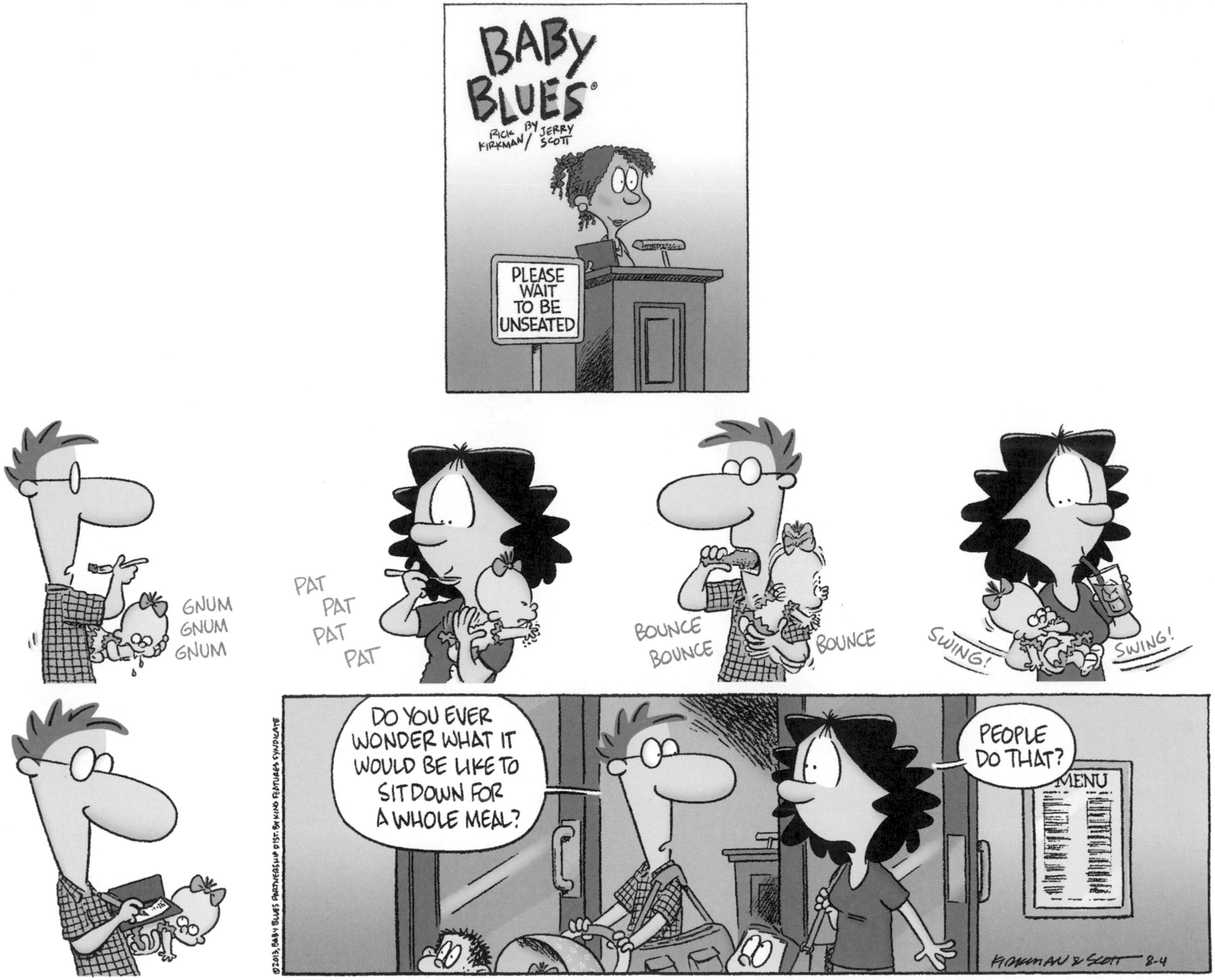

BABY BLUES®
BY RICK KIRKMAN / JERRY SCOTT
PLEASE WAIT TO BE UNSEATED
GNUM GNUM GNUM
PAT PAT PAT PAT
BOUNCE BOUNCE BOUNCE
SWING! SWING!
DO YOU EVER WONDER WHAT IT WOULD BE LIKE TO SIT DOWN FOR A WHOLE MEAL?
PEOPLE DO THAT?
MENU
©2013, BABY BLUES PARTNERSHIP DIST. BY KING FEATURES SYNDICATE
KIRKMAN & SCOTT 8-4

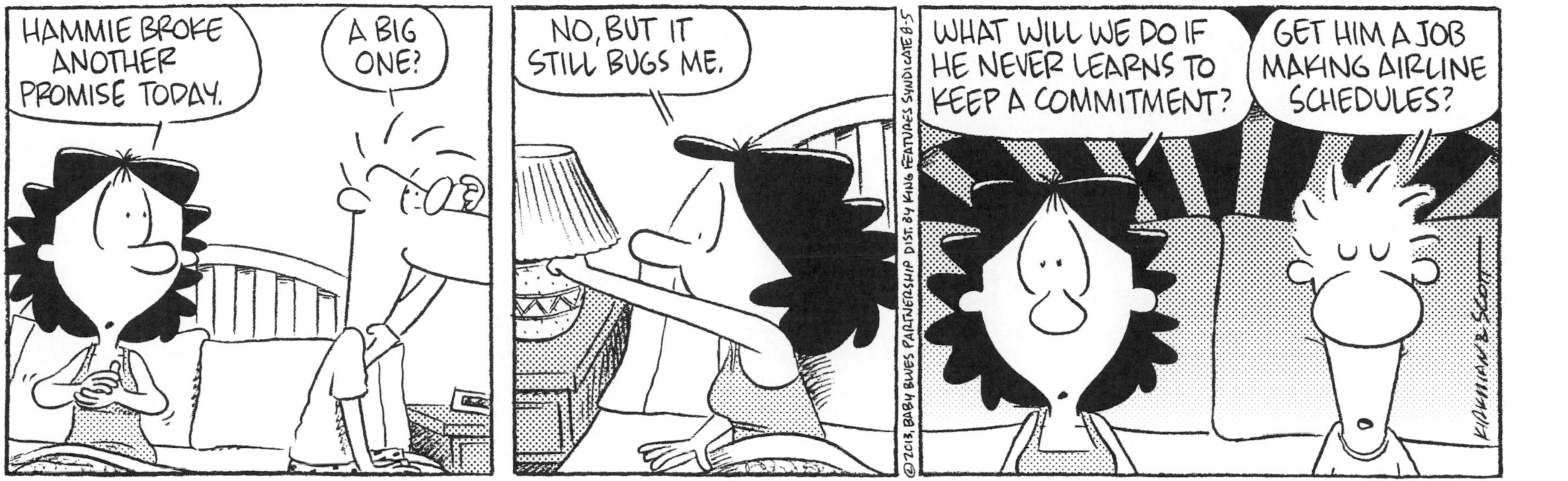
HAMMIE BROKE ANOTHER PROMISE TODAY.
A BIG ONE?
NO, BUT IT STILL BUGS ME.
©2013, BABY BLUES PARTNERSHIP DIST. BY KING FEATURES SYNDICATE 8-5
WHAT WILL WE DO IF HE NEVER LEARNS TO KEEP A COMMITMENT?
GET HIM A JOB MAKING AIRLINE SCHEDULES?
KIRKMAN & SCOTT

Jerry: I don't travel a lot, but when I do it's usually, um, eventful.

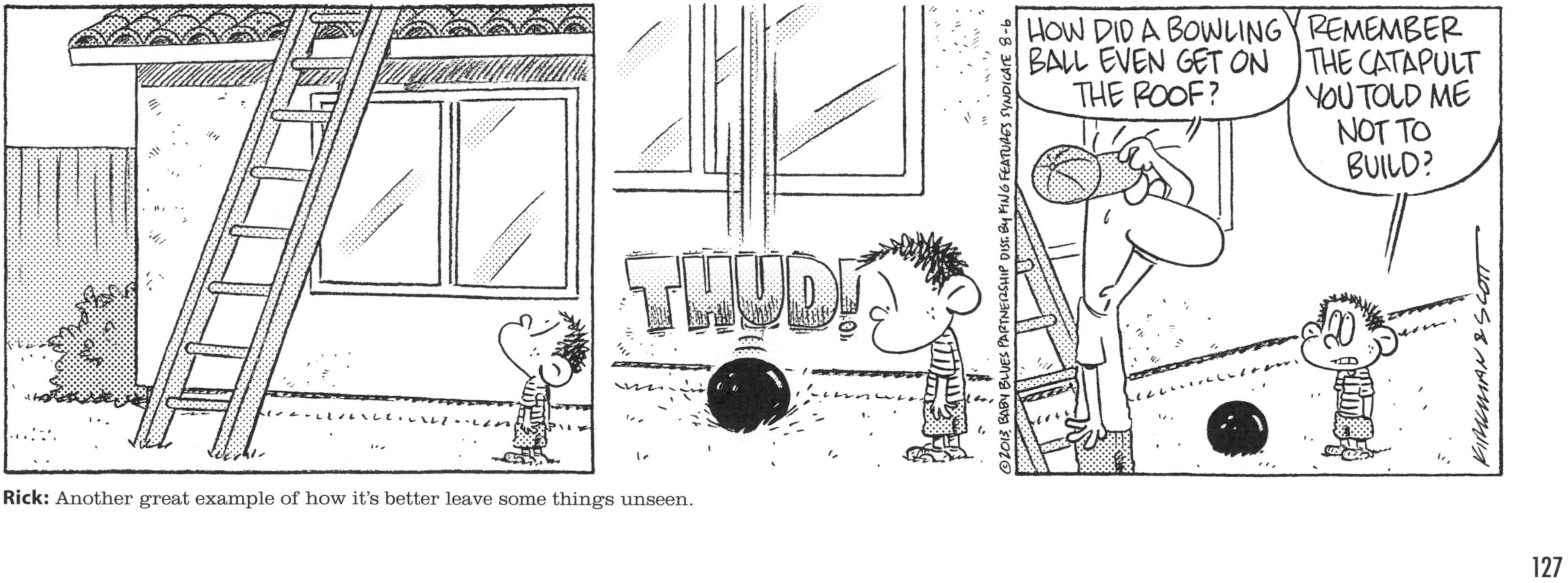
THUD!
©2013, BABY BLUES PARTNERSHIP DIST. BY KING FEATURES SYNDICATE 8-6
HOW DID A BOWLING BALL EVEN GET ON THE ROOF?
REMEMBER THE CATAPULT YOU TOLD ME NOT TO BUILD?
KIRKMAN & SCOTT

Rick: Another great example of how it's better leave some things unseen.

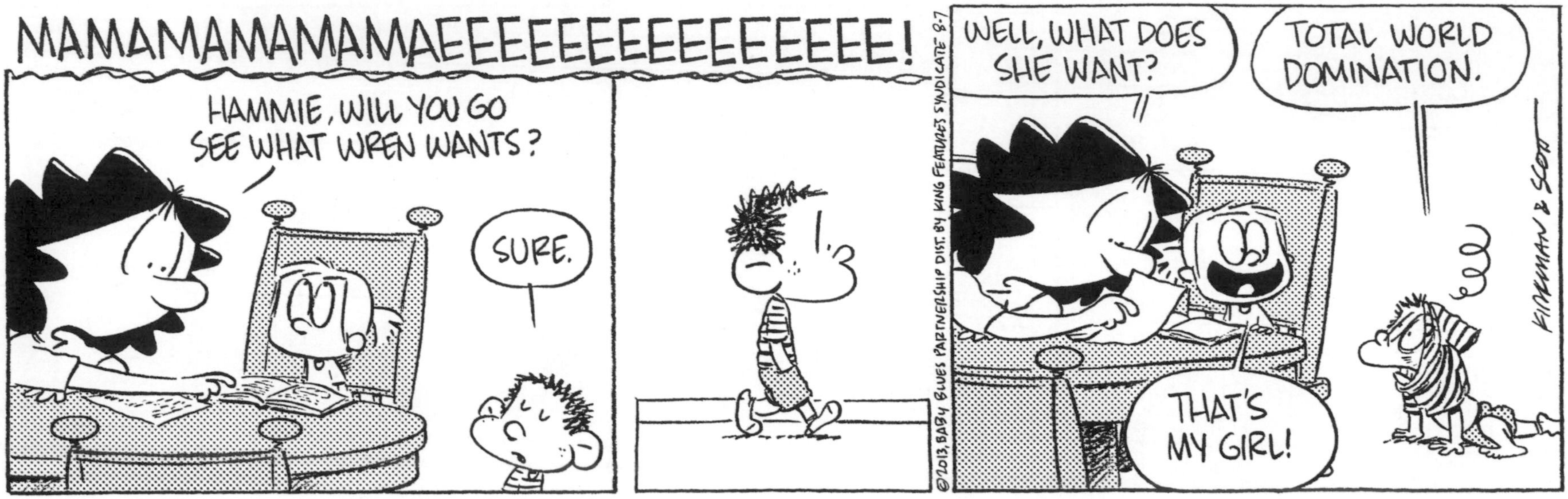
MAMAMAMAMAMAEEEEEEEEEEEEEEEE!
HAMMIE, WILL YOU GO SEE WHAT WREN WANTS?
SURE.
©2013, BABY BLUES PARTNERSHIP DIST. BY KING FEATURES SYNDICATE 8-7
WELL, WHAT DOES SHE WANT?
TOTAL WORLD DOMINATION.
THAT'S MY GIRL!
KIRKMAN & SCOTT

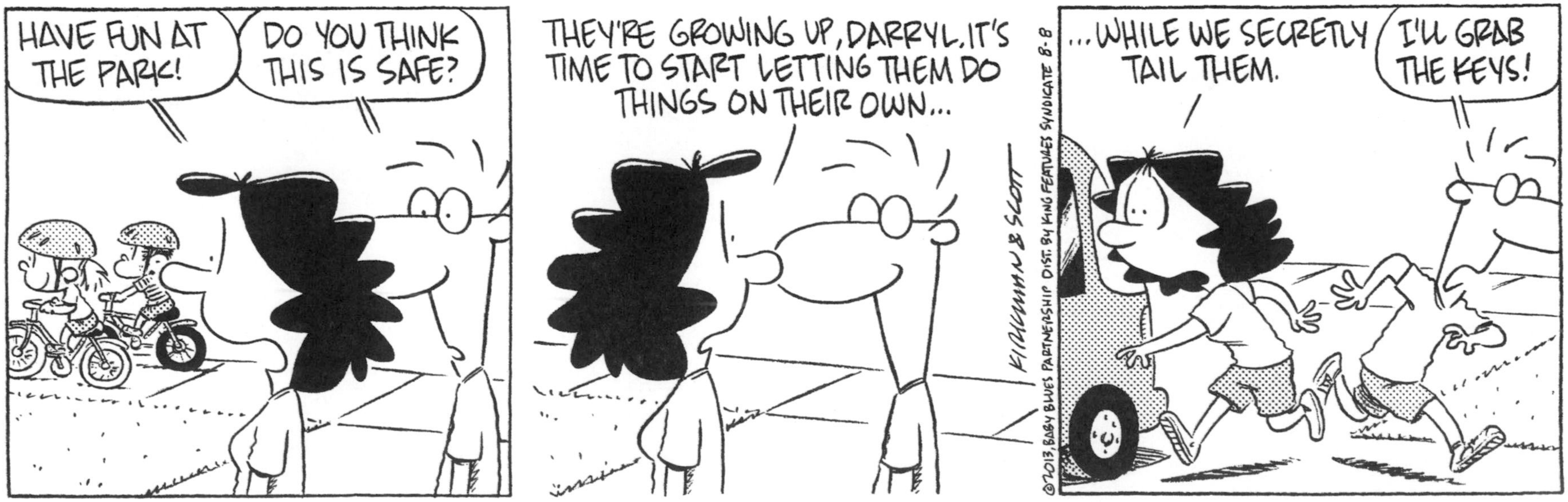
HAVE FUN AT THE PARK!
DO YOU THINK THIS IS SAFE?
THEY'RE GROWING UP, DARRYL. IT'S TIME TO START LETTING THEM DO THINGS ON THEIR OWN...
KIRKMAN & SCOTT
©2013, BABY BLUES PARTNERSHIP DIST. BY KING FEATURES SYNDICATE 8-8
...WHILE WE SECRETLY TAIL THEM.
I'LL GRAB THE KEYS!

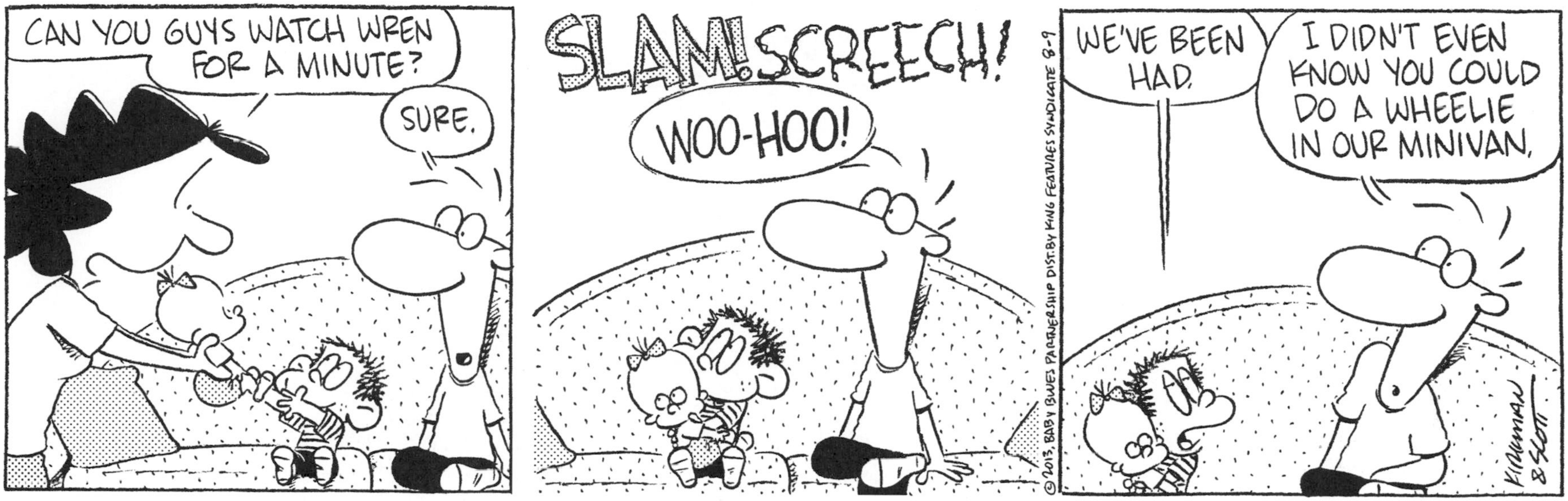
CAN YOU GUYS WATCH WREN FOR A MINUTE?
SURE.
SLAM! SCREECH!
WOO-HOO!
© 2013, BABY BLUES PARTNERSHIP DIST. BY KING FEATURES SYNDICATE 8-9
WE'VE BEEN HAD.
I DIDN'T EVEN KNOW YOU COULD DO A WHEELIE IN OUR MINIVAN.
KIRKMAN & SCOTT

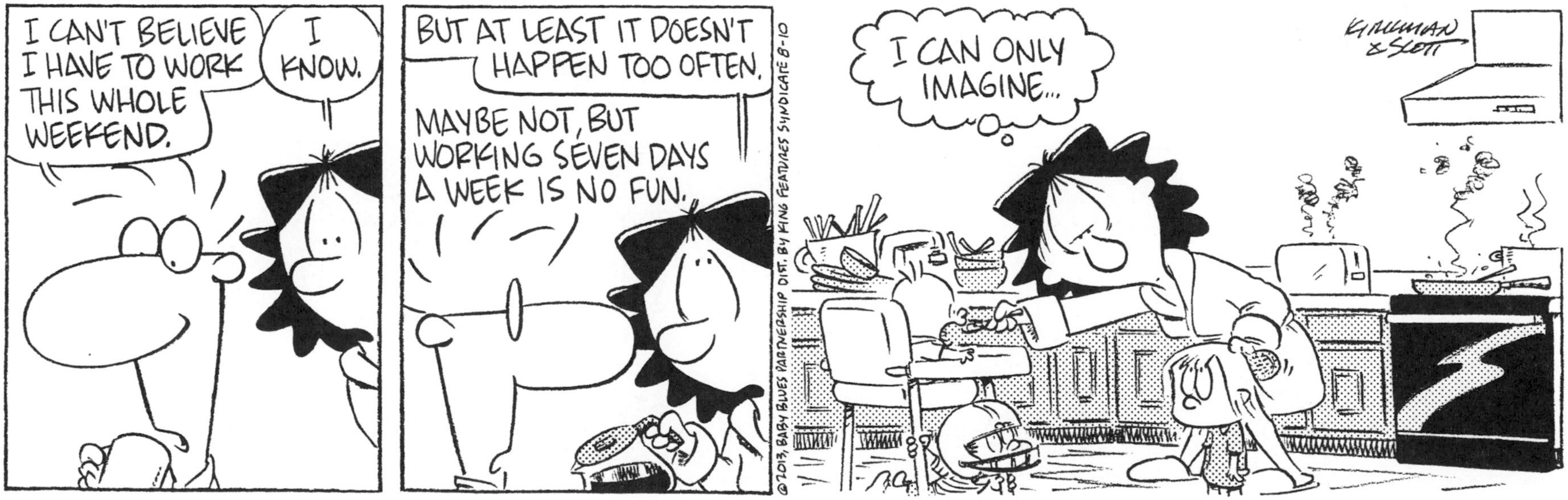
I CAN'T BELIEVE I HAVE TO WORK THIS WHOLE WEEKEND.
I KNOW.
BUT AT LEAST IT DOESN'T HAPPEN TOO OFTEN.
MAYBE NOT, BUT WORKING SEVEN DAYS A WEEK IS NO FUN.
© 2013, BABY BLUES PARTNERSHIP DIST. BY KING FEATURES SYNDICATE 8-10
KIRKMAN & SCOTT
I CAN ONLY IMAGINE...

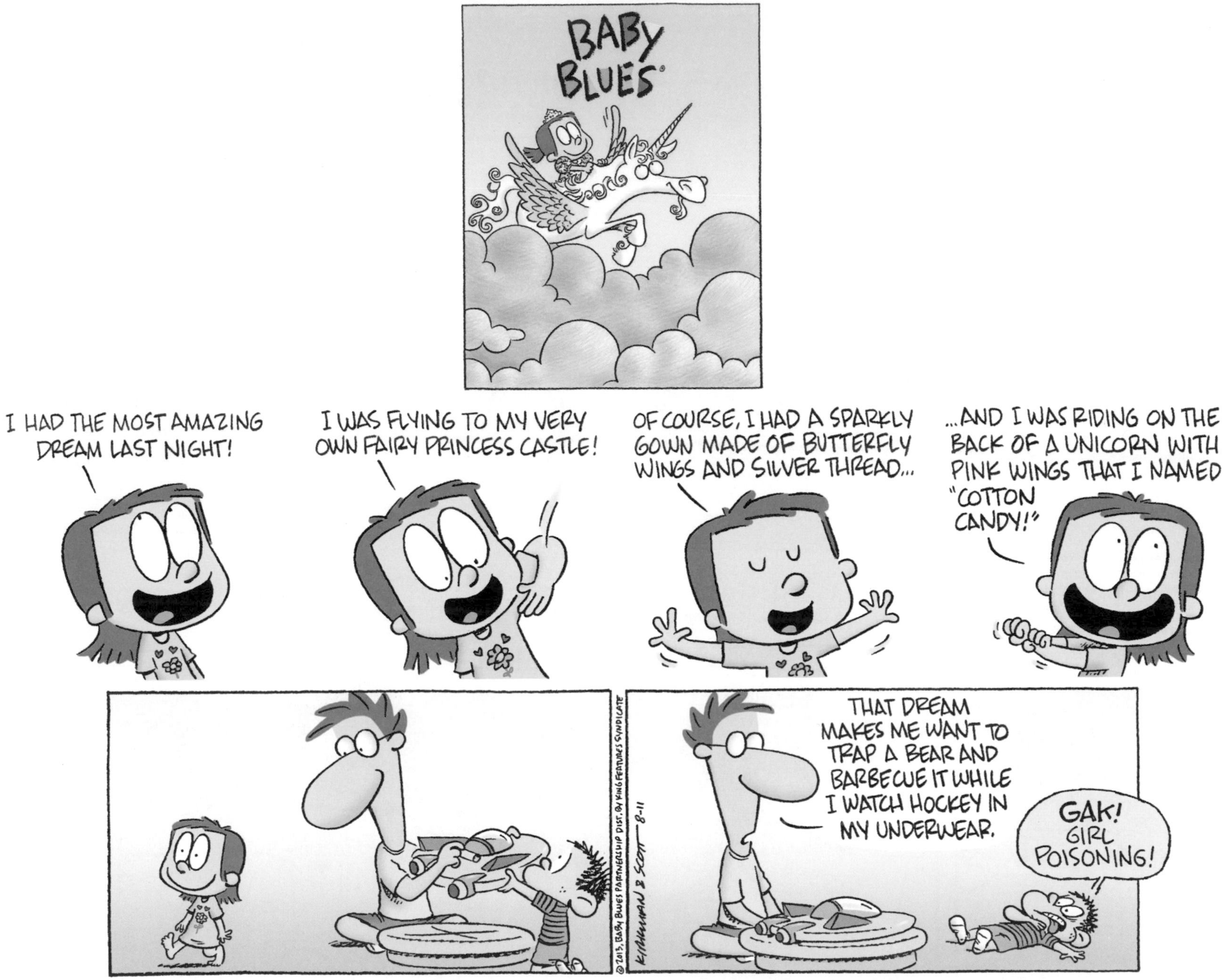
BABY BLUES
I HAD THE MOST AMAZING DREAM LAST NIGHT!
I WAS FLYING TO MY VERY OWN FAIRY PRINCESS CASTLE!
OF COURSE, I HAD A SPARKLY GOWN MADE OF BUTTERFLY WINGS AND SILVER THREAD...
...AND I WAS RIDING ON THE BACK OF A UNICORN WITH PINK WINGS THAT I NAMED "COTTON CANDY!"
©2013, BABY BLUES PARTNERSHIP DIST. BY KING FEATURES SYNDICATE
KIRKMAN & SCOTT 8-11
THAT DREAM MAKES ME WANT TO TRAP A BEAR AND BARBECUE IT WHILE I WATCH HOCKEY IN MY UNDERWEAR.
GAK! GIRL POISONING!

Rick: Subheading under "Things I Hate to Draw: Horses." Add unicorns. By the way, this strip drew a vitriolic rant on Facebook accusing us of being "Male Chauvinist Pigs" who had "set the female population back a couple hundred years."

Jerry: I'm the Male Chauvinist Pig who wrote it, based on one of my daughter's equally saccharine dreams. I don't make this stuff up. I'm just an embedded reporter.

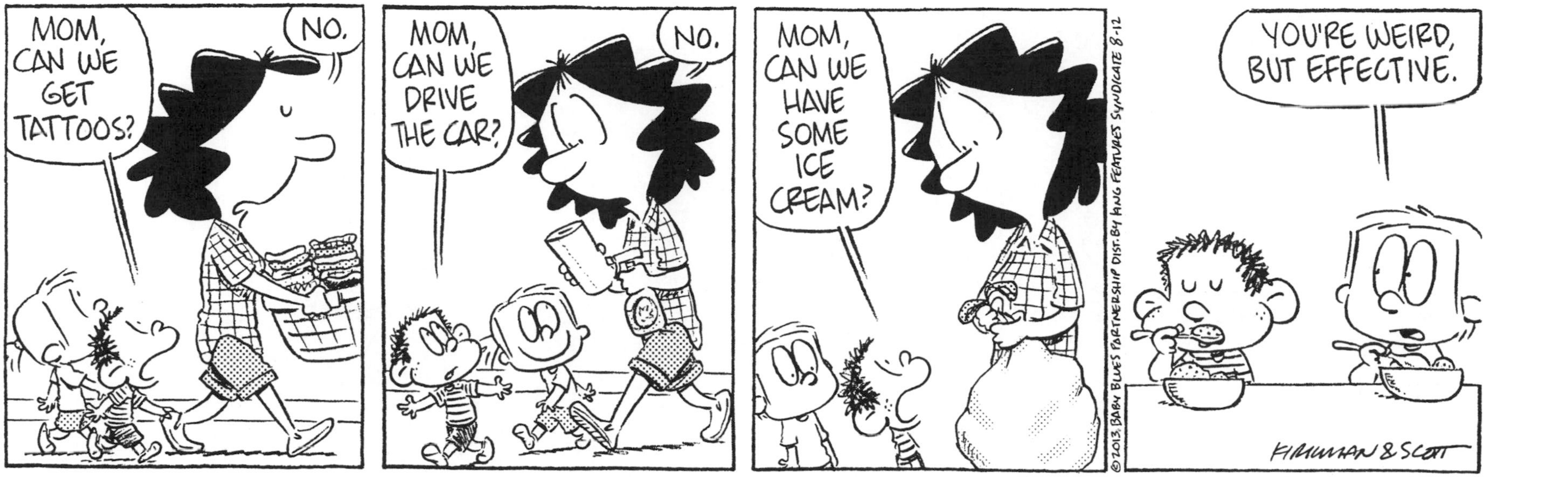
MOM, CAN WE GET TATTOOS?
NO.
MOM, CAN WE DRIVE THE CAR?
NO.
MOM, CAN WE HAVE SOME ICE CREAM?
©2013, BABY BLUES PARTNERSHIP DIST. BY KING FEATURES SYNDICATE 8-12
YOU'RE WEIRD, BUT EFFECTIVE.
KIRKMAN & SCOTT

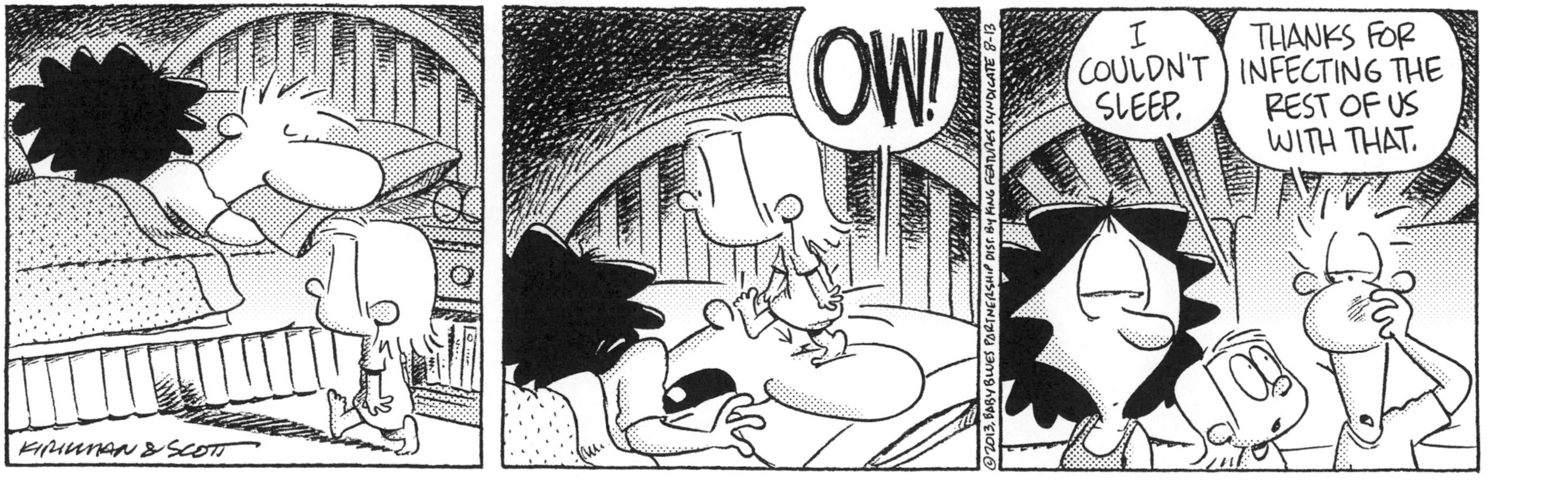
KIRKMAN & SCOTT
OW!
©2013, BABY BLUES PARTNERSHIP DIST. BY KING FEATURES SYNDICATE 8-13
I COULDN'T SLEEP.
THANKS FOR INFECTING THE REST OF US WITH THAT.

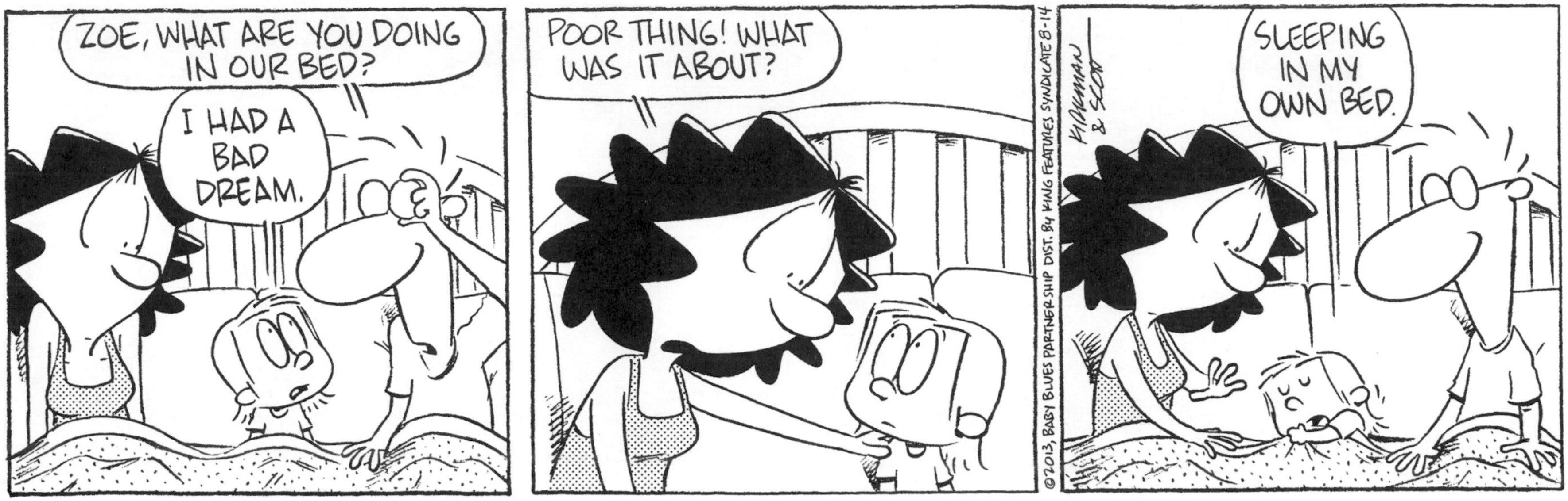
ZOE, WHAT ARE YOU DOING IN OUR BED?
I HAD A BAD DREAM.
POOR THING! WHAT WAS IT ABOUT?
©2013, BABY BLUES PARTNERSHIP DIST. BY KING FEATURES SYNDICATE 8-14
KIRKMAN & SCOTT
SLEEPING IN MY OWN BED.

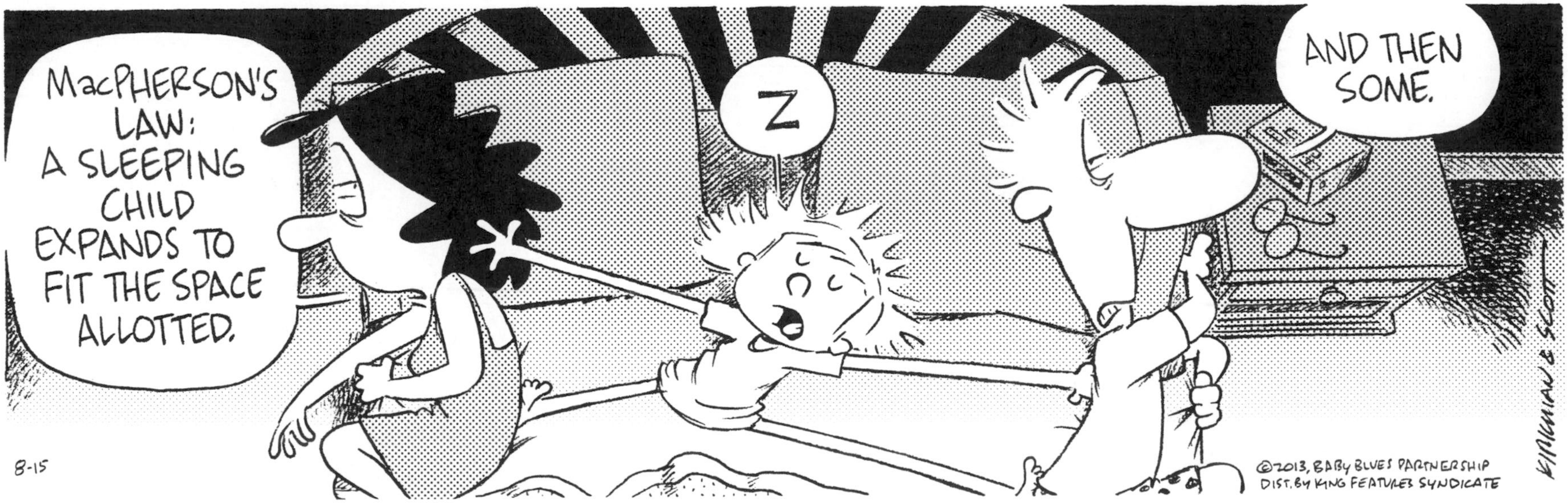
MacPHERSON'S LAW: A SLEEPING CHILD EXPANDS TO FIT THE SPACE ALLOTTED.
Z
AND THEN SOME.
8-15
©2013, BABY BLUES PARTNERSHIP DIST. BY KING FEATURES SYNDICATE
KIRKMAN & SCOTT

Rick: I could draw this from memory of what it was like to sleep with one of our daughters.

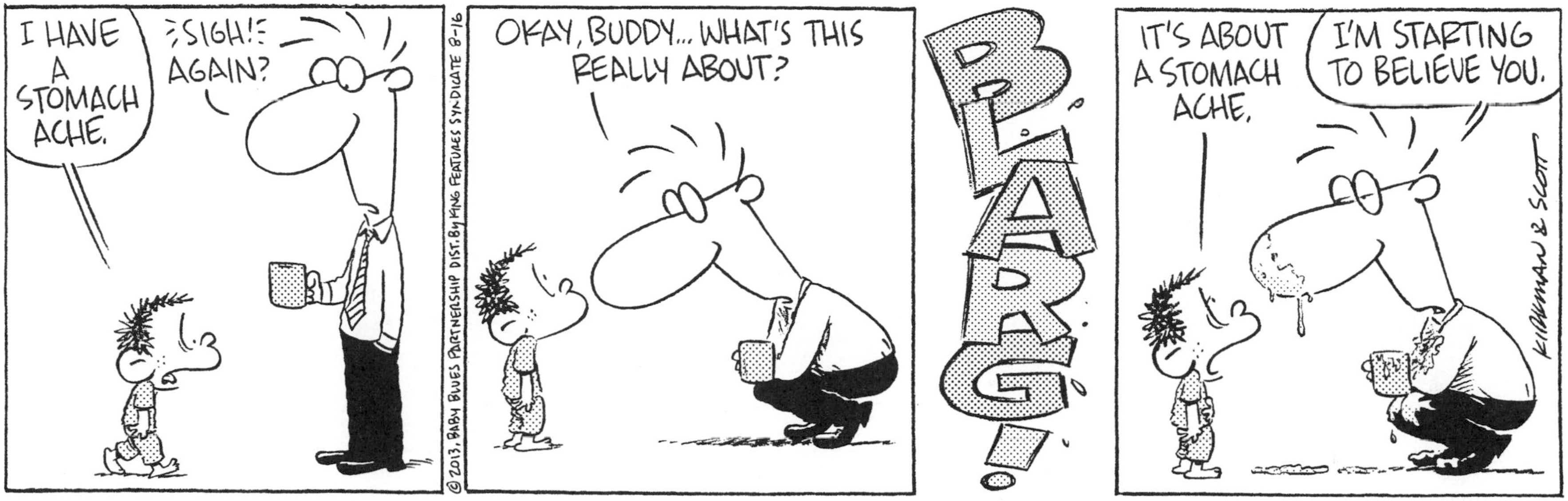
I HAVE A STOMACH ACHE.
SIGH! AGAIN?
© 2013, BABY BLUES PARTNERSHIP DIST. BY KING FEATURES SYNDICATE 8-16
OKAY, BUDDY... WHAT'S THIS REALLY ABOUT?
BLAARG!
IT'S ABOUT A STOMACH ACHE.
I'M STARTING TO BELIEVE YOU.
KIRKMAN & SCOTT

Jerry: Sometimes a cigar is just a cigar.

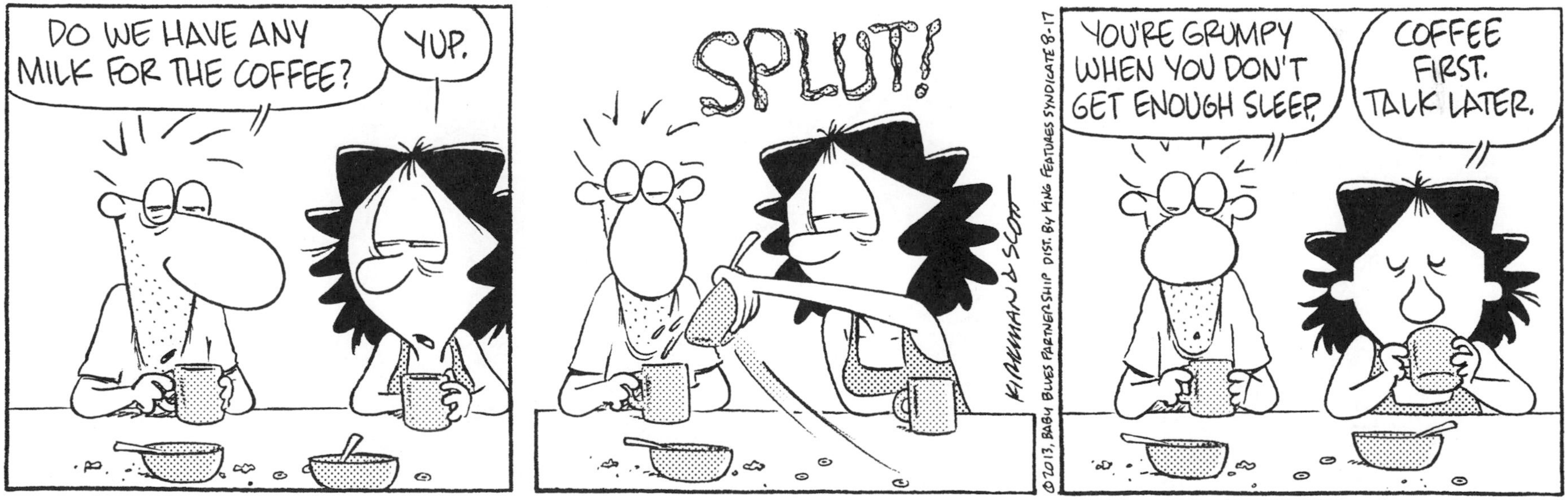
DO WE HAVE ANY MILK FOR THE COFFEE?
YUP.
SPLUT!
KIRKMAN & SCOTT
© 2013, BABY BLUES PARTNERSHIP DIST. BY KING FEATURES SYNDICATE 8-17
YOU'RE GRUMPY WHEN YOU DON'T GET ENOUGH SLEEP.
COFFEE FIRST. TALK LATER.

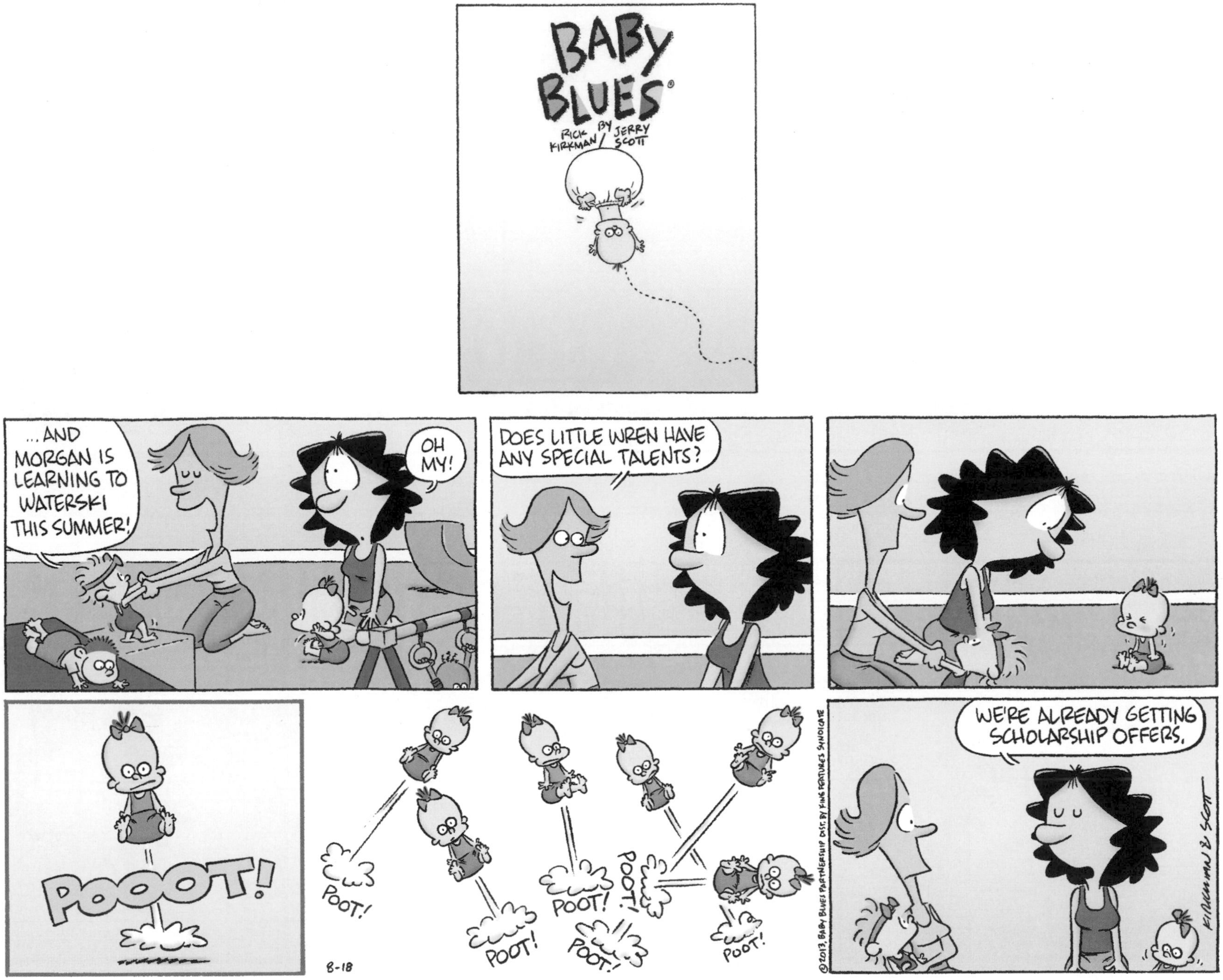
BABY BLUES®
RICK KIRKMAN / BY JERRY SCOTT
...AND MORGAN IS LEARNING TO WATERSKI THIS SUMMER!
OH MY!
DOES LITTLE WREN HAVE ANY SPECIAL TALENTS?
POOOT!
POOT!
POOT!
POOT!
POOT!
POOT!
POOT!
8-18
©2013, BABY BLUES PARTNERSHIP DIST. BY KING FEATURES SYNDICATE
WE'RE ALREADY GETTING SCHOLARSHIP OFFERS.
KIRKMAN & SCOTT

Jerry: We have the original strip hanging in our daughter's room. She doesn't want me to tell you why.

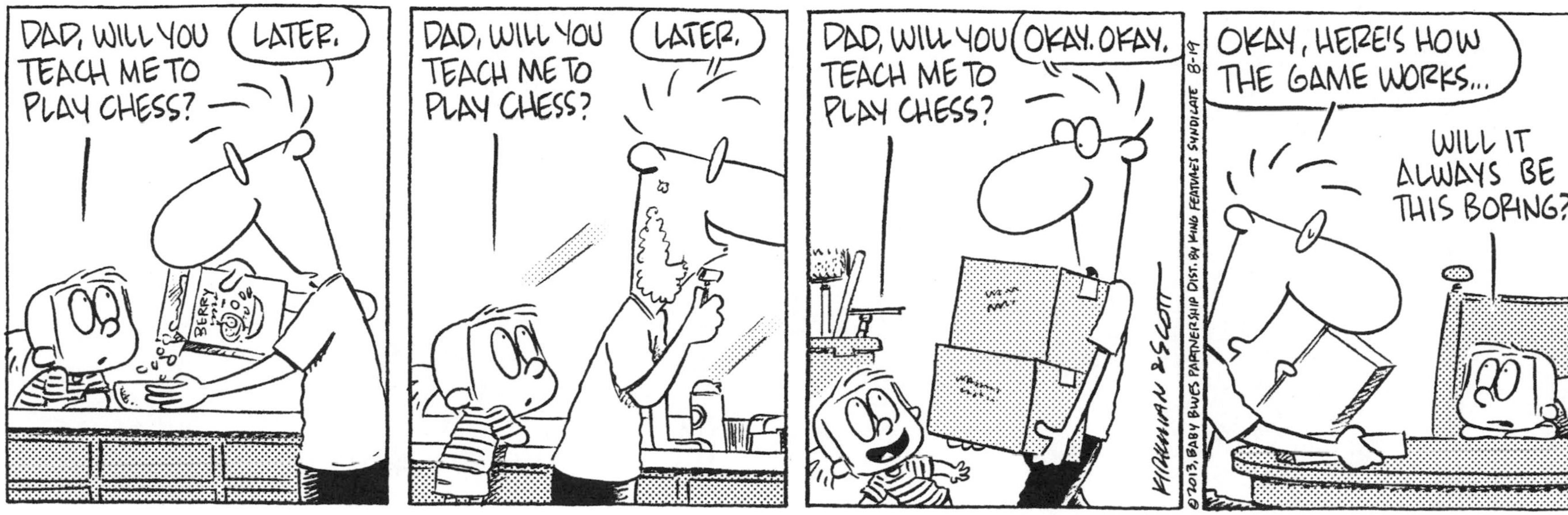
DAD, WILL YOU TEACH ME TO PLAY CHESS?
LATER.
DAD, WILL YOU TEACH ME TO PLAY CHESS?
LATER.
DAD, WILL YOU TEACH ME TO PLAY CHESS?
OKAY. OKAY.
KIRKMAN & SCOTT
©2013, BABY BLUES PARTNERSHIP DIST. BY KING FEATURES SYNDICATE 8-19
OKAY, HERE'S HOW THE GAME WORKS...
WILL IT ALWAYS BE THIS BORING?

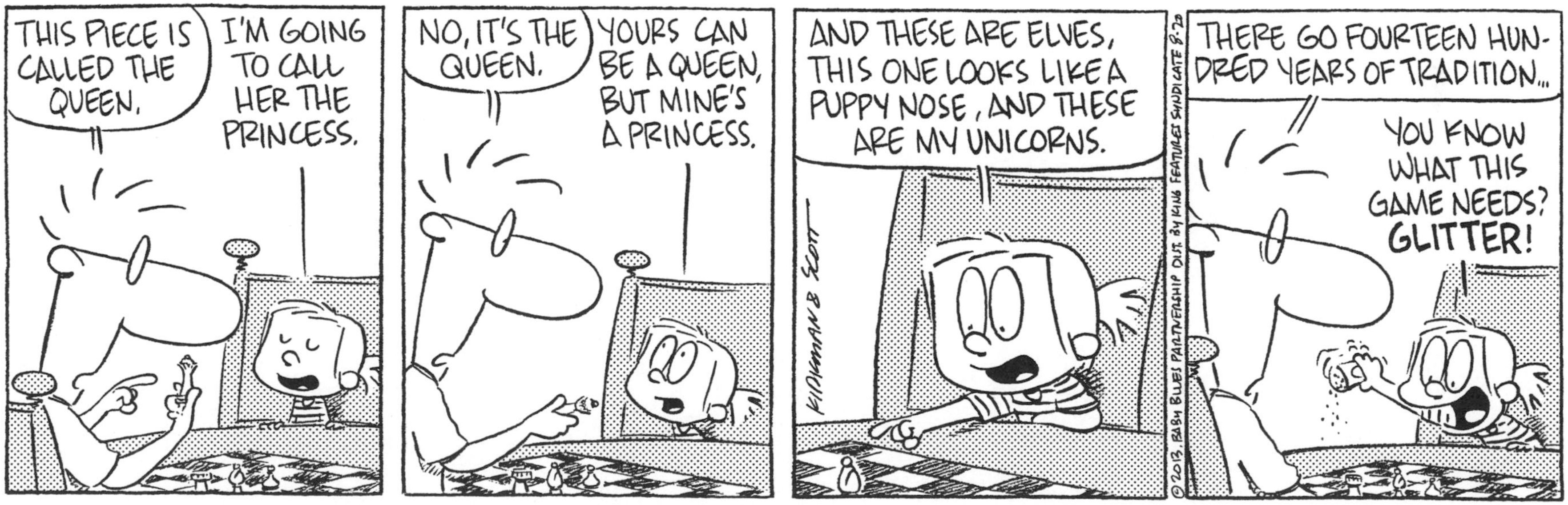
THIS PIECE IS CALLED THE QUEEN.
I'M GOING TO CALL HER THE PRINCESS.
NO, IT'S THE QUEEN.
YOURS CAN BE A QUEEN, BUT MINE'S A PRINCESS.
KIRKMAN & SCOTT
AND THESE ARE ELVES, THIS ONE LOOKS LIKE A PUPPY NOSE, AND THESE ARE MY UNICORNS.
©2013, BABY BLUES PARTNERSHIP DIST. BY KING FEATURES SYNDICATE 8-20
THERE GO FOURTEEN HUNDRED YEARS OF TRADITION...
YOU KNOW WHAT THIS GAME NEEDS? GLITTER!

Rick: A theme is developing. Add to "Things I Hate to Draw": chess and checker boards.

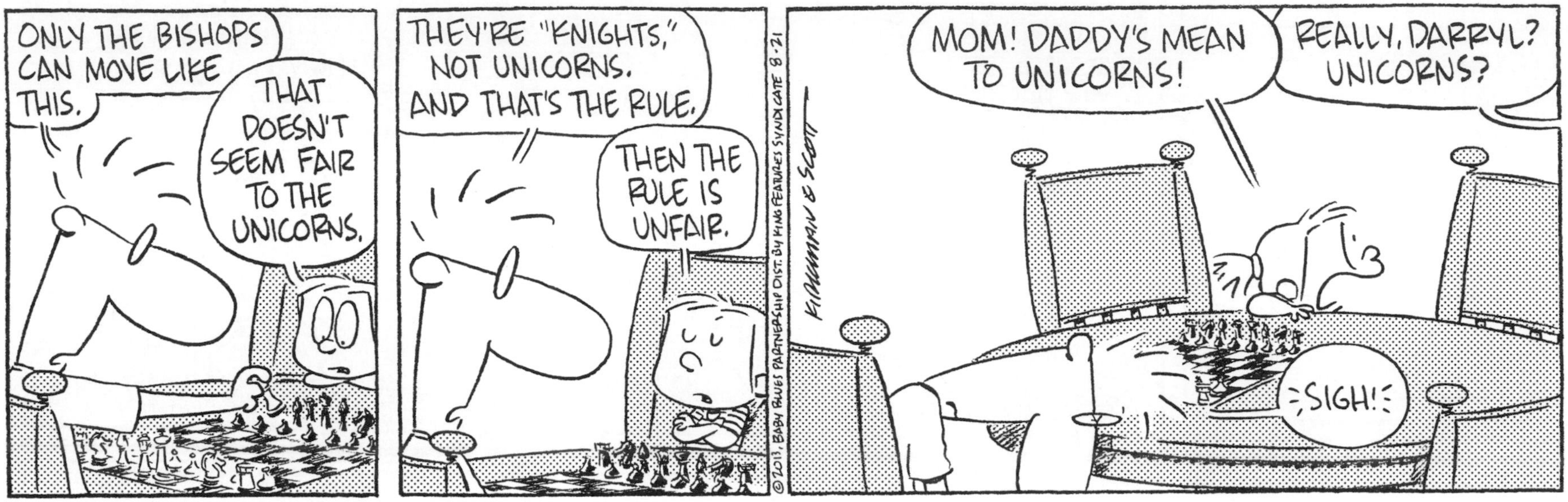
ONLY THE BISHOPS CAN MOVE LIKE THIS.
THAT DOESN'T SEEM FAIR TO THE UNICORNS.
THEY'RE "KNIGHTS," NOT UNICORNS. AND THAT'S THE RULE.
THEN THE RULE IS UNFAIR.
MOM! DADDY'S MEAN TO UNICORNS!
REALLY, DARRYL? UNICORNS?
SIGH!
©2013, BABY BLUES PARTNERSHIP DIST. BY KING FEATURES SYNDICATE 8·21
KIRKMAN & SCOTT

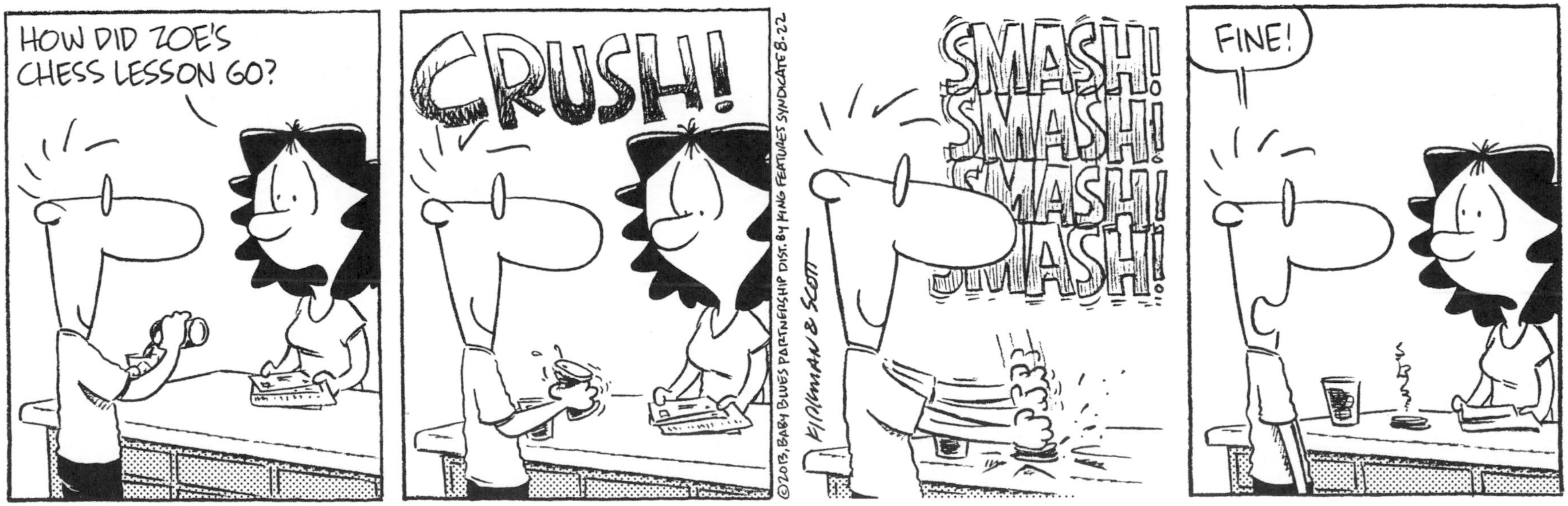
HOW DID ZOE'S CHESS LESSON GO?
CRUSH!
SMASH! SMASH! SMASH! SMASH!
FINE!
©2013, BABY BLUES PARTNERSHIP DIST. BY KING FEATURES SYNDICATE 8·22
KIRKMAN & SCOTT

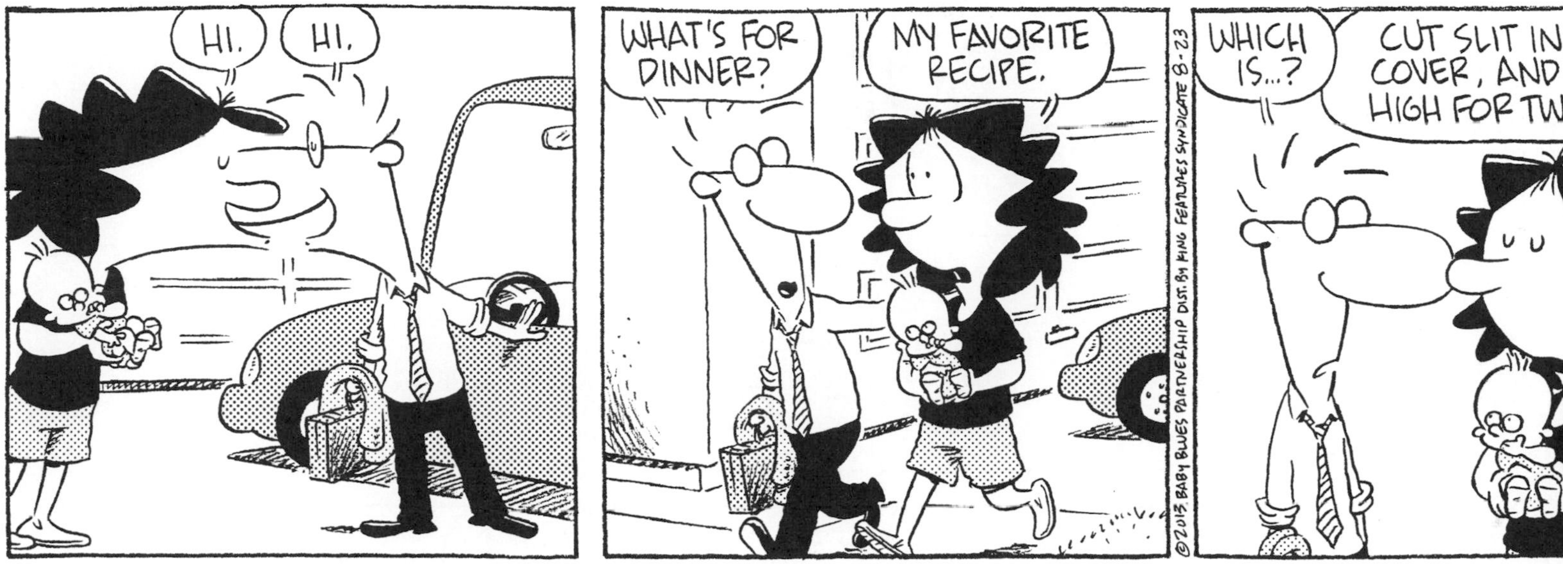
HI.
HI.
WHAT'S FOR DINNER?
MY FAVORITE RECIPE.
©2013 BABY BLUES PARTNERSHIP DIST. BY KING FEATURES SYNDICATE 8-23
WHICH IS...?
CUT SLIT IN PLASTIC COVER, AND HEAT ON HIGH FOR TWO MINUTES.
KIRKMAN & SCOTT

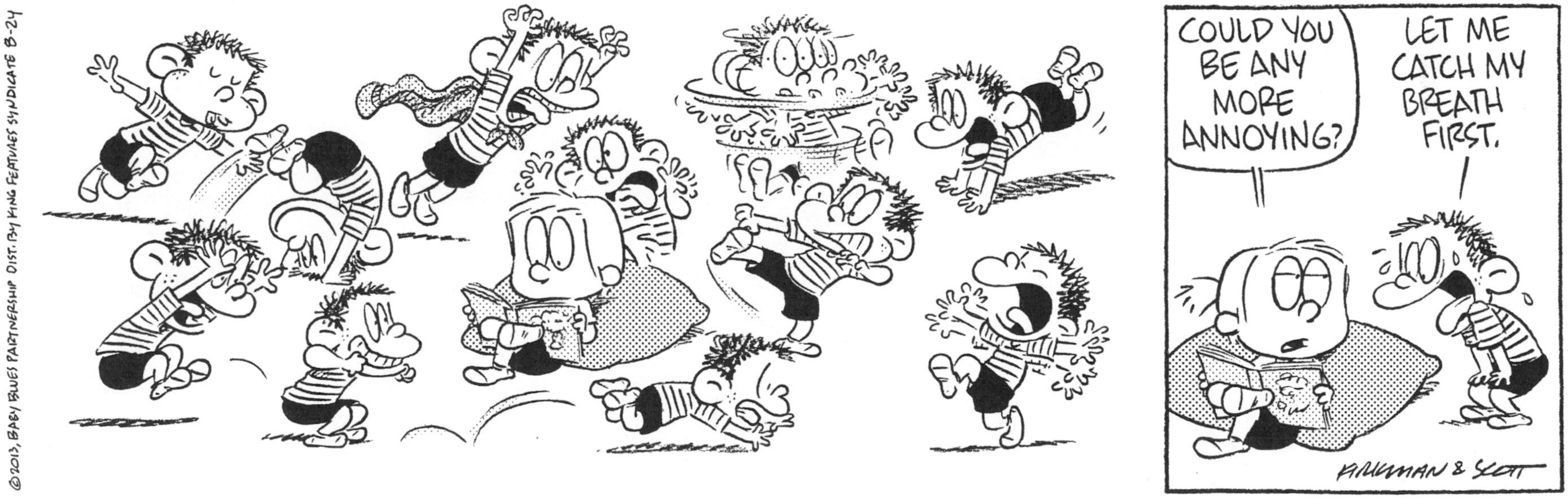
©2013, BABY BLUES PARTNERSHIP DIST. BY KING FEATURES SYNDICATE 8-24
COULD YOU BE ANY MORE ANNOYING?
LET ME CATCH MY BREATH FIRST.
KIRKMAN & SCOTT

Rick: One of my favorite action-filled Hammie drawings.

Jerry: This gives you a pretty good idea of what I was like as a little brother.

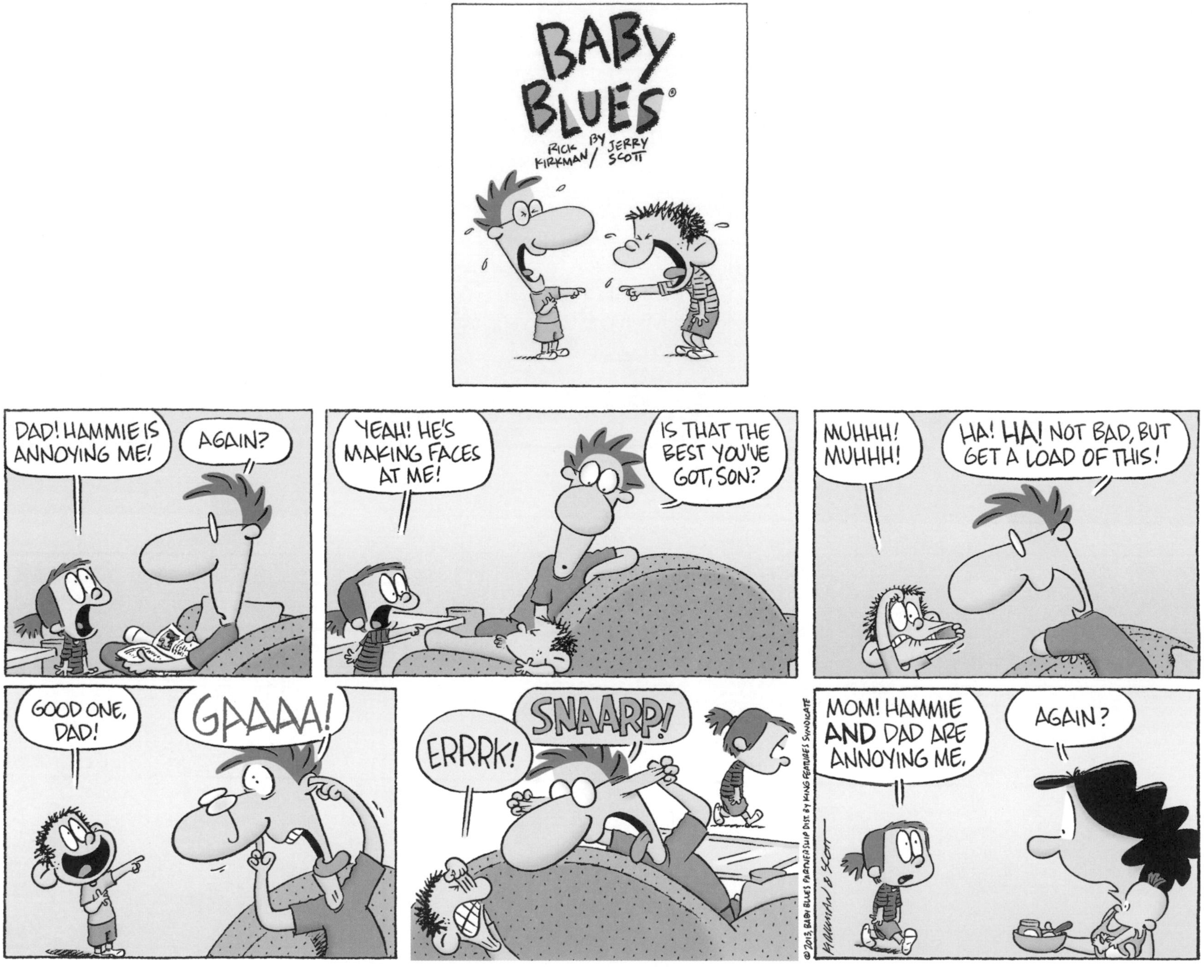
BABY BLUES®
BY RICK KIRKMAN / JERRY SCOTT
DAD! HAMMIE IS ANNOYING ME!
AGAIN?
YEAH! HE'S MAKING FACES AT ME!
IS THAT THE BEST YOU'VE GOT, SON?
MUHHH! MUHHH!
HA! HA! NOT BAD, BUT GET A LOAD OF THIS!
GOOD ONE, DAD!
GAAAA!
ERRRK!
SNAARP!
©2013, BABY BLUES PARTNERSHIP DIST. BY KING FEATURES SYNDICATE
KIRKMAN & SCOTT
MOM! HAMMIE AND DAD ARE ANNOYING ME.
AGAIN?

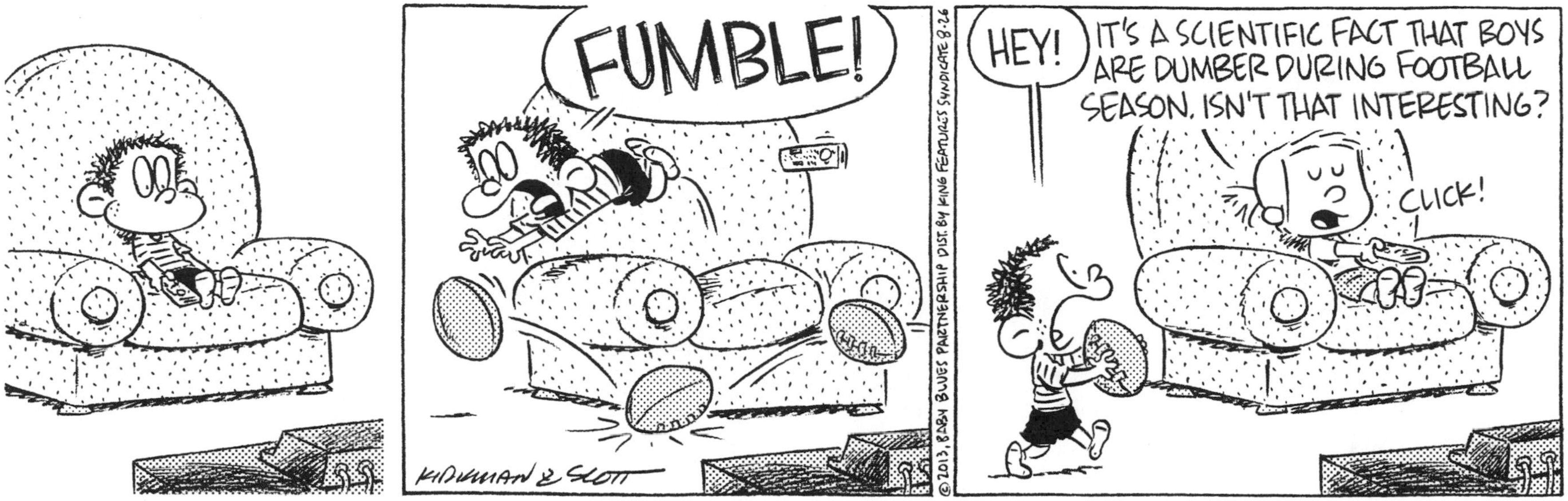
FUMBLE!
KIRKMAN & SCOTT
© 2013, BABY BLUES PARTNERSHIP DIST. BY KING FEATURES SYNDICATE 8-26
HEY!
IT'S A SCIENTIFIC FACT THAT BOYS ARE DUMBER DURING FOOTBALL SEASON. ISN'T THAT INTERESTING?
CLICK!

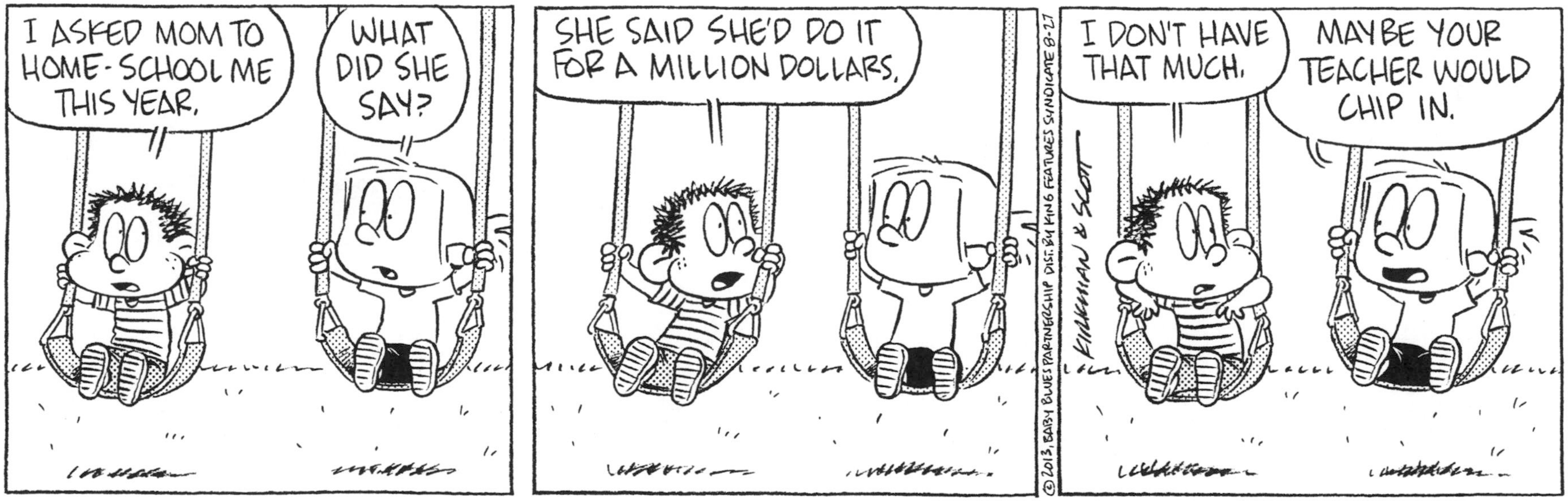
I ASKED MOM TO HOME-SCHOOL ME THIS YEAR.
WHAT DID SHE SAY?
SHE SAID SHE'D DO IT FOR A MILLION DOLLARS.
© 2013, BABY BLUES PARTNERSHIP DIST. BY KING FEATURES SYNDICATE 8-27
KIRKMAN & SCOTT
I DON'T HAVE THAT MUCH.
MAYBE YOUR TEACHER WOULD CHIP IN.

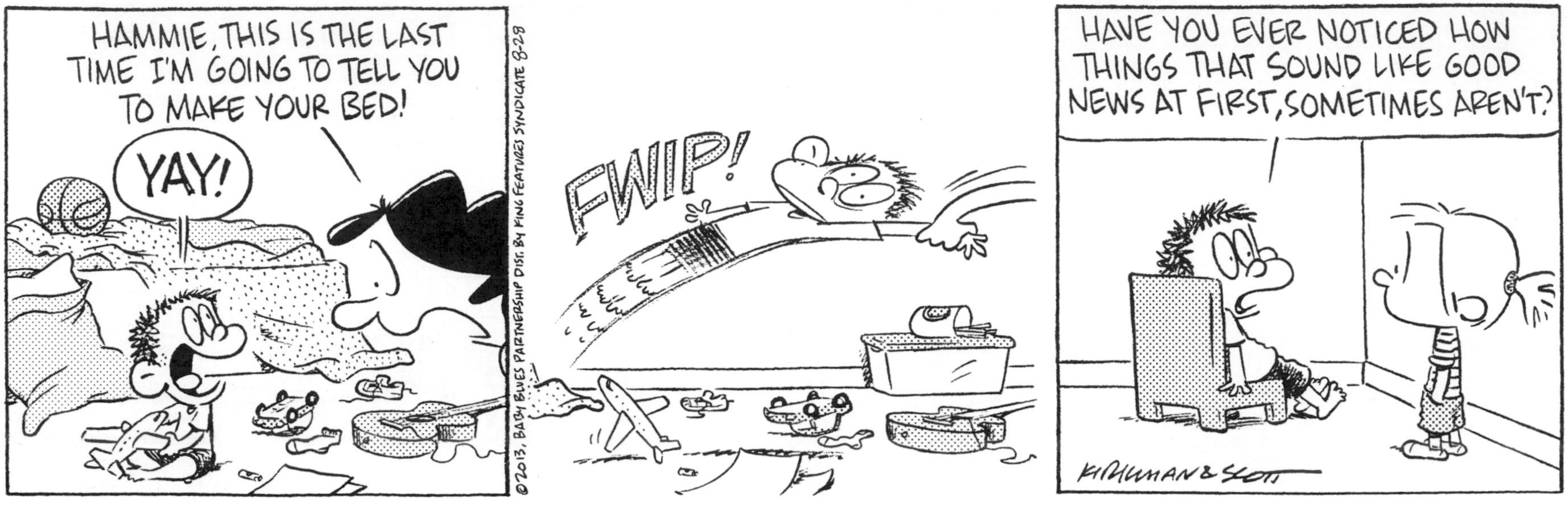
HAMMIE, THIS IS THE LAST TIME I'M GOING TO TELL YOU TO MAKE YOUR BED!
YAY!
©2013, BABY BLUES PARTNERSHIP DIST. BY KING FEATURES SYNDICATE 8-28
FWIP!
HAVE YOU EVER NOTICED HOW THINGS THAT SOUND LIKE GOOD NEWS AT FIRST, SOMETIMES AREN'T?
KIRKMAN & SCOTT

Jerry: You can't take a mom too literally.

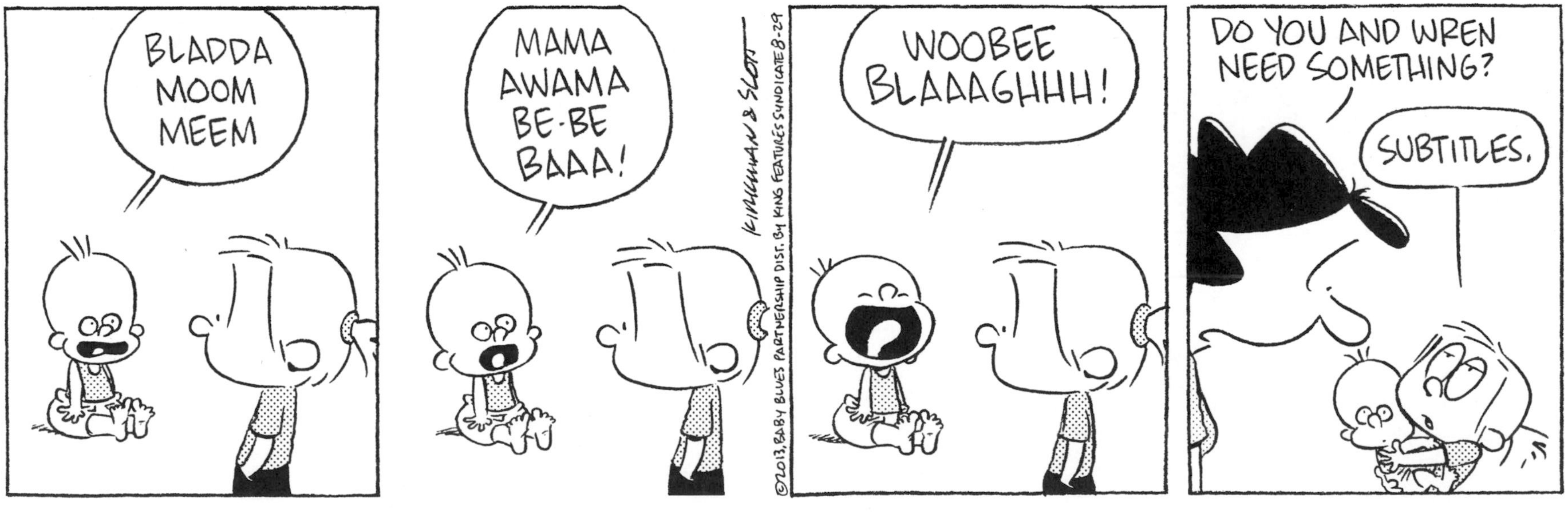
BLADDA MOOM MEEM
MAMA AWAMA BE-BE BAAA!
KIRKMAN & SCOTT
©2013, BABY BLUES PARTNERSHIP DIST. BY KING FEATURES SYNDICATE 8-29
WOOBEE BLAAAGHHH!
DO YOU AND WREN NEED SOMETHING?
SUBTITLES.

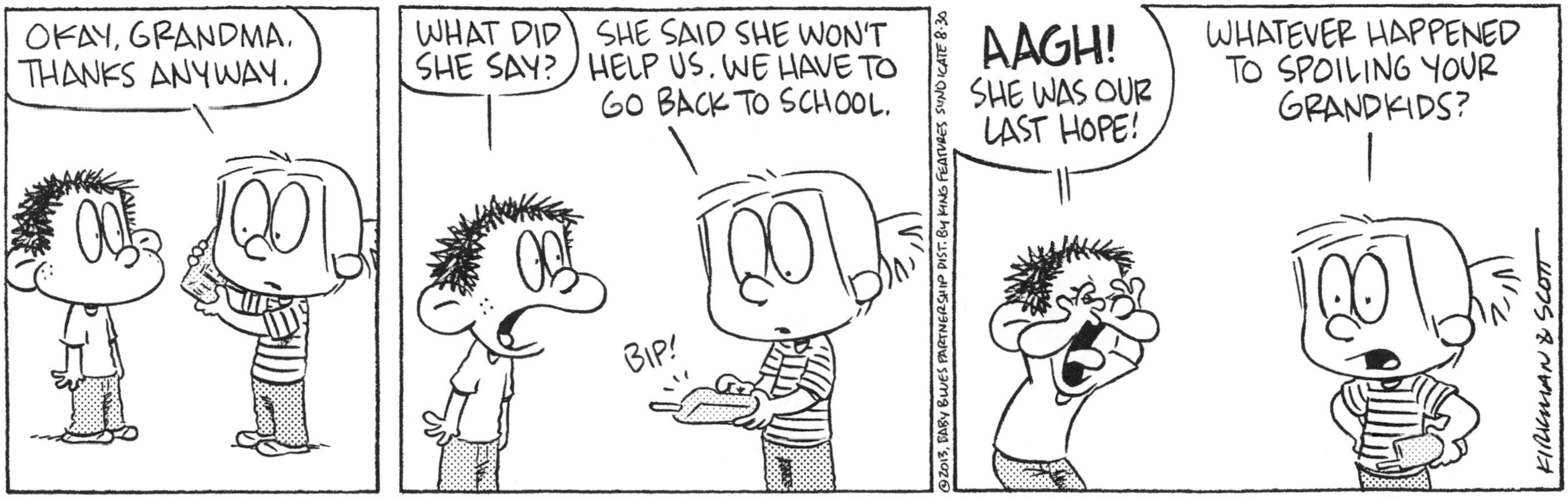
OKAY, GRANDMA. THANKS ANYWAY.
WHAT DID SHE SAY?
SHE SAID SHE WON'T HELP US. WE HAVE TO GO BACK TO SCHOOL.
BIP!
©2013, BABY BLUES PARTNERSHIP DIST. BY KING FEATURES SYNDICATE 8-30
AAGH! SHE WAS OUR LAST HOPE!
WHATEVER HAPPENED TO SPOILING YOUR GRANDKIDS?
KIRKMAN & SCOTT

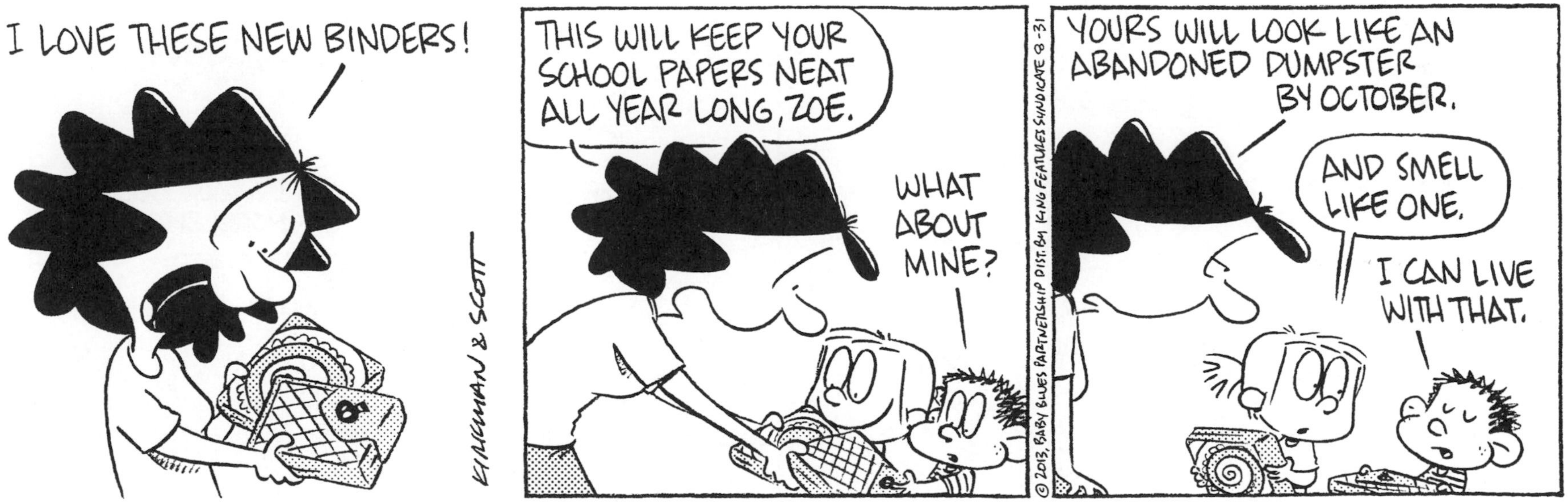
I LOVE THESE NEW BINDERS!
KIRKMAN & SCOTT
THIS WILL KEEP YOUR SCHOOL PAPERS NEAT ALL YEAR LONG, ZOE.
WHAT ABOUT MINE?
©2013, BABY BLUES PARTNERSHIP DIST. BY KING FEATURES SYNDICATE 8-31
YOURS WILL LOOK LIKE AN ABANDONED DUMPSTER BY OCTOBER.
AND SMELL LIKE ONE.
I CAN LIVE WITH THAT.

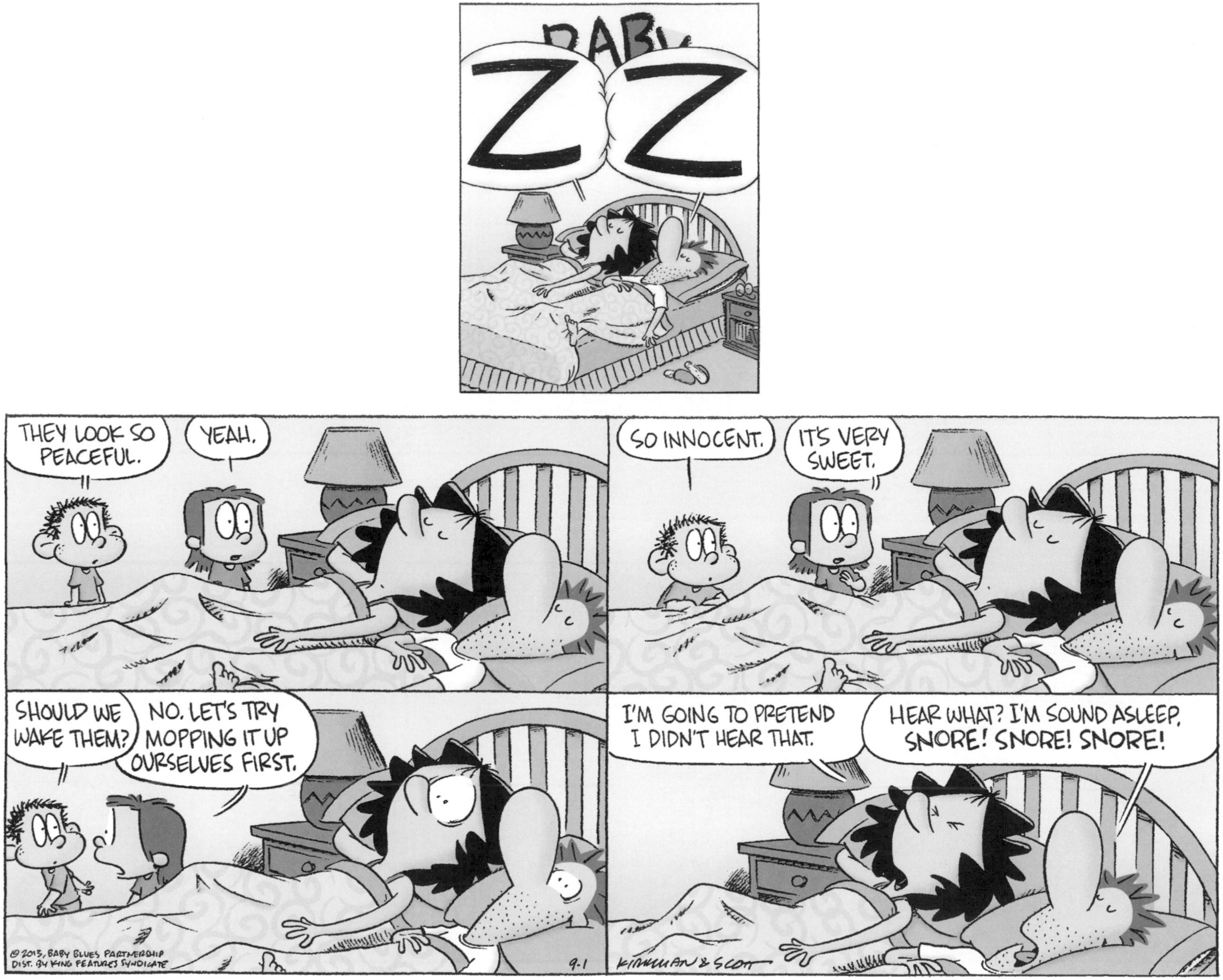
BABY
Z
Z
THEY LOOK SO PEACEFUL.
YEAH.
SO INNOCENT.
IT'S VERY SWEET.
SHOULD WE WAKE THEM?
NO. LET'S TRY MOPPING IT UP OURSELVES FIRST.
I'M GOING TO PRETEND I DIDN'T HEAR THAT.
HEAR WHAT? I'M SOUND ASLEEP. SNORE! SNORE! SNORE!
© 2013, BABY BLUES PARTNERSHIP DIST. BY KING FEATURES SYNDICATE
9-1
KIRKMAN & SCOTT

Rick: Just a sublimely written gag.

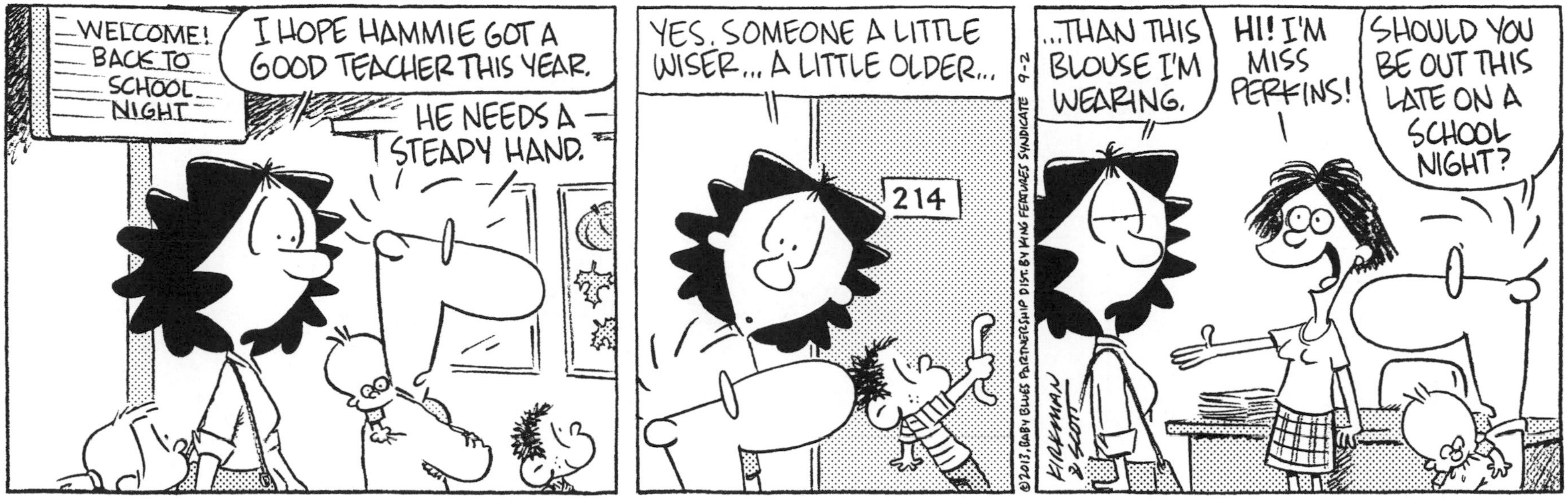
WELCOME! BACK TO SCHOOL NIGHT
I HOPE HAMMIE GOT A GOOD TEACHER THIS YEAR.
HE NEEDS A STEADY HAND.
YES. SOMEONE A LITTLE WISER... A LITTLE OLDER...
214
...THAN THIS BLOUSE I'M WEARING.
HI! I'M MISS PERKINS!
SHOULD YOU BE OUT THIS LATE ON A SCHOOL NIGHT?
©2013, BABY BLUES PARTNERSHIP DIST. BY KING FEATURES SYNDICATE 9-2
KIRKMAN & SCOTT

Rick: This strip drew an angry e-mail from a reader who thought we were targeting young teachers for derision and being responsible for discouraging young people from going into teaching. Not so.

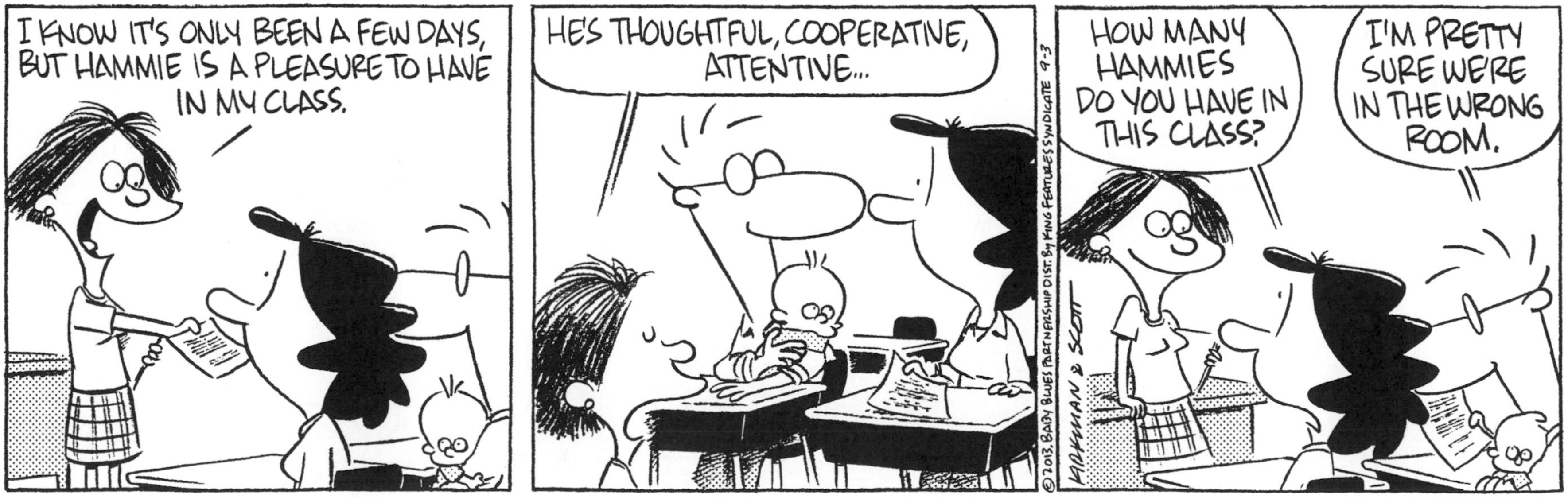
I KNOW IT'S ONLY BEEN A FEW DAYS, BUT HAMMIE IS A PLEASURE TO HAVE IN MY CLASS.
HE'S THOUGHTFUL, COOPERATIVE, ATTENTIVE...
HOW MANY HAMMIES DO YOU HAVE IN THIS CLASS?
I'M PRETTY SURE WE'RE IN THE WRONG ROOM.
©2013, BABY BLUES PARTNERSHIP DIST. BY KING FEATURES SYNDICATE 9-3
KIRKMAN & SCOTT

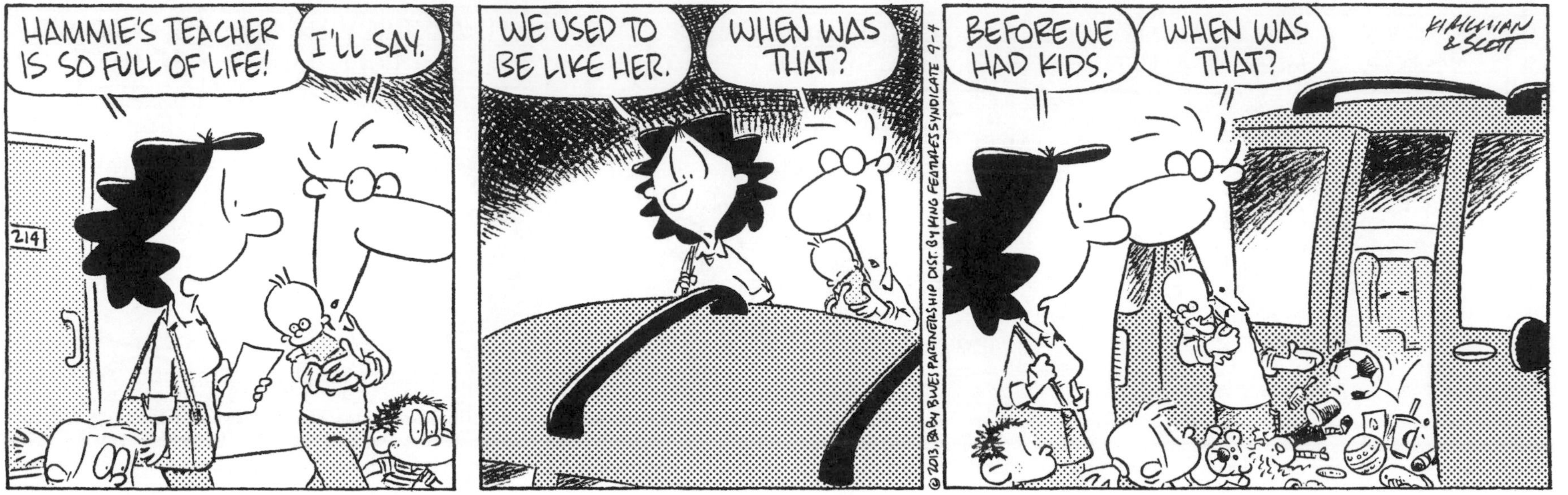
HAMMIE'S TEACHER IS SO FULL OF LIFE!
I'LL SAY.
214
WE USED TO BE LIKE HER.
WHEN WAS THAT?
© 2013, BABY BLUES PARTNERSHIP DIST. BY KING FEATURES SYNDICATE 9-4
BEFORE WE HAD KIDS.
WHEN WAS THAT?
KIRKMAN & SCOTT

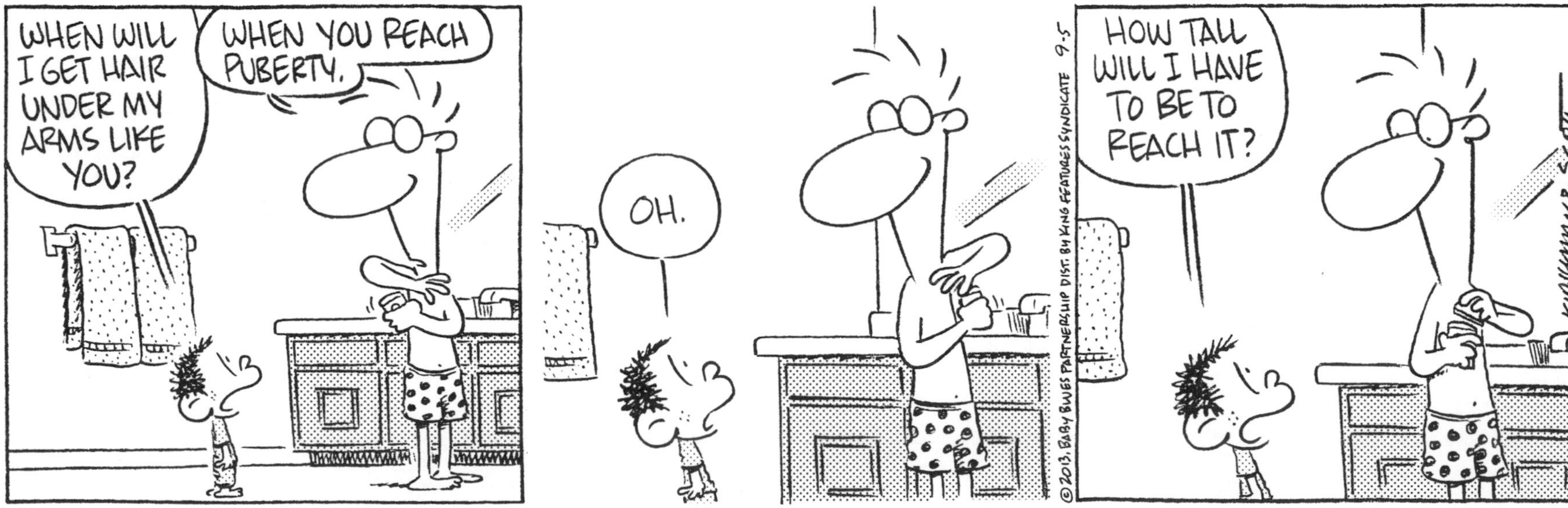
WHEN WILL I GET HAIR UNDER MY ARMS LIKE YOU?
WHEN YOU REACH PUBERTY.
OH.
© 2013, BABY BLUES PARTNERSHIP DIST. BY KING FEATURES SYNDICATE 9-5
HOW TALL WILL I HAVE TO BE TO REACH IT?
KIRKMAN & SCOTT

Jerry: I like the way Rick stages these man-to-man moments with Hammie and Darryl.

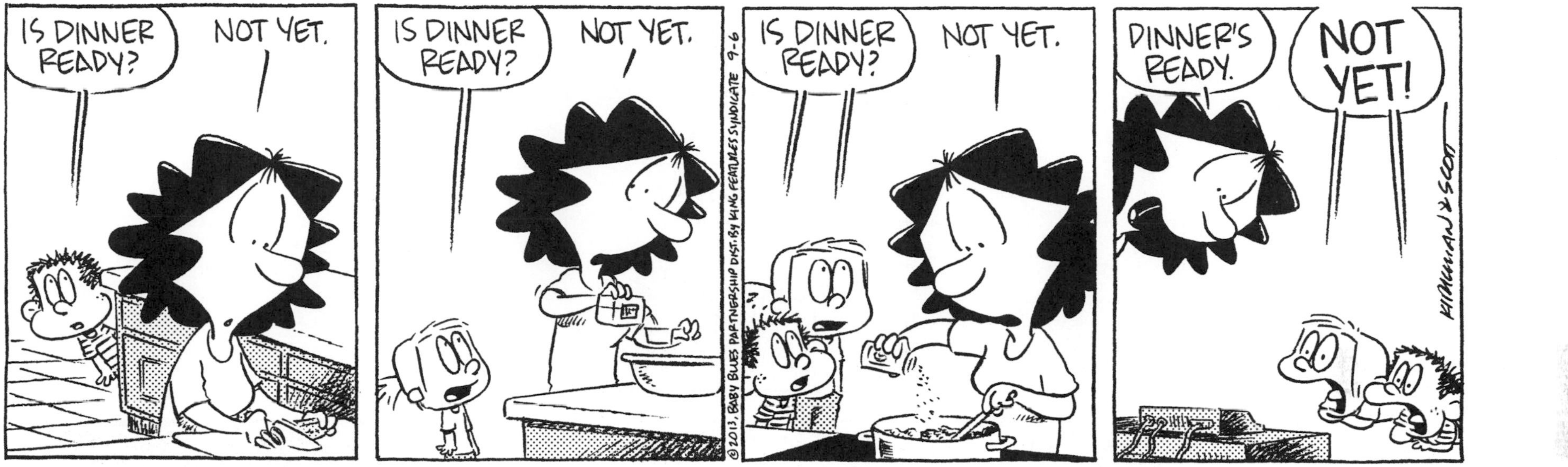
IS DINNER READY?
NOT YET.
IS DINNER READY?
NOT YET.
©2013, BABY BLUES PARTNERSHIP DIST. BY KING FEATURES SYNDICATE 9-6
IS DINNER READY?
NOT YET.
DINNER'S READY.
NOT YET!
KIRKMAN & SCOTT

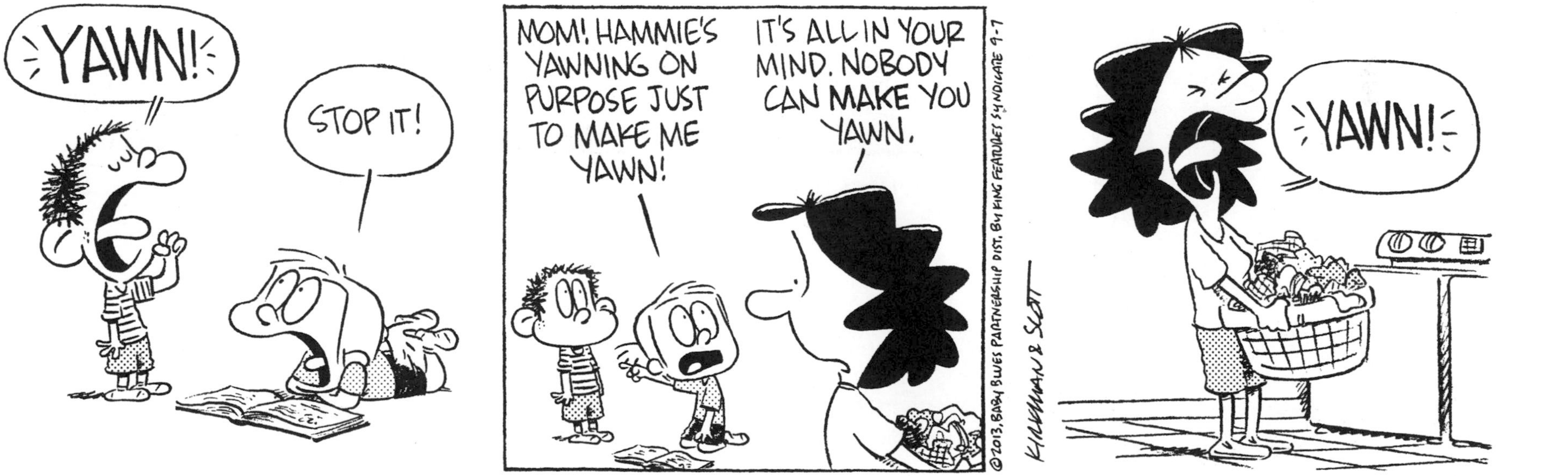
YAWN!
STOP IT!
MOM! HAMMIE'S YAWNING ON PURPOSE JUST TO MAKE ME YAWN!
IT'S ALL IN YOUR MIND. NOBODY CAN **MAKE** YOU YAWN.
©2013, BABY BLUES PARTNERSHIP DIST. BY KING FEATURES SYNDICATE 9-7
KIRKMAN & SCOTT
YAWN!

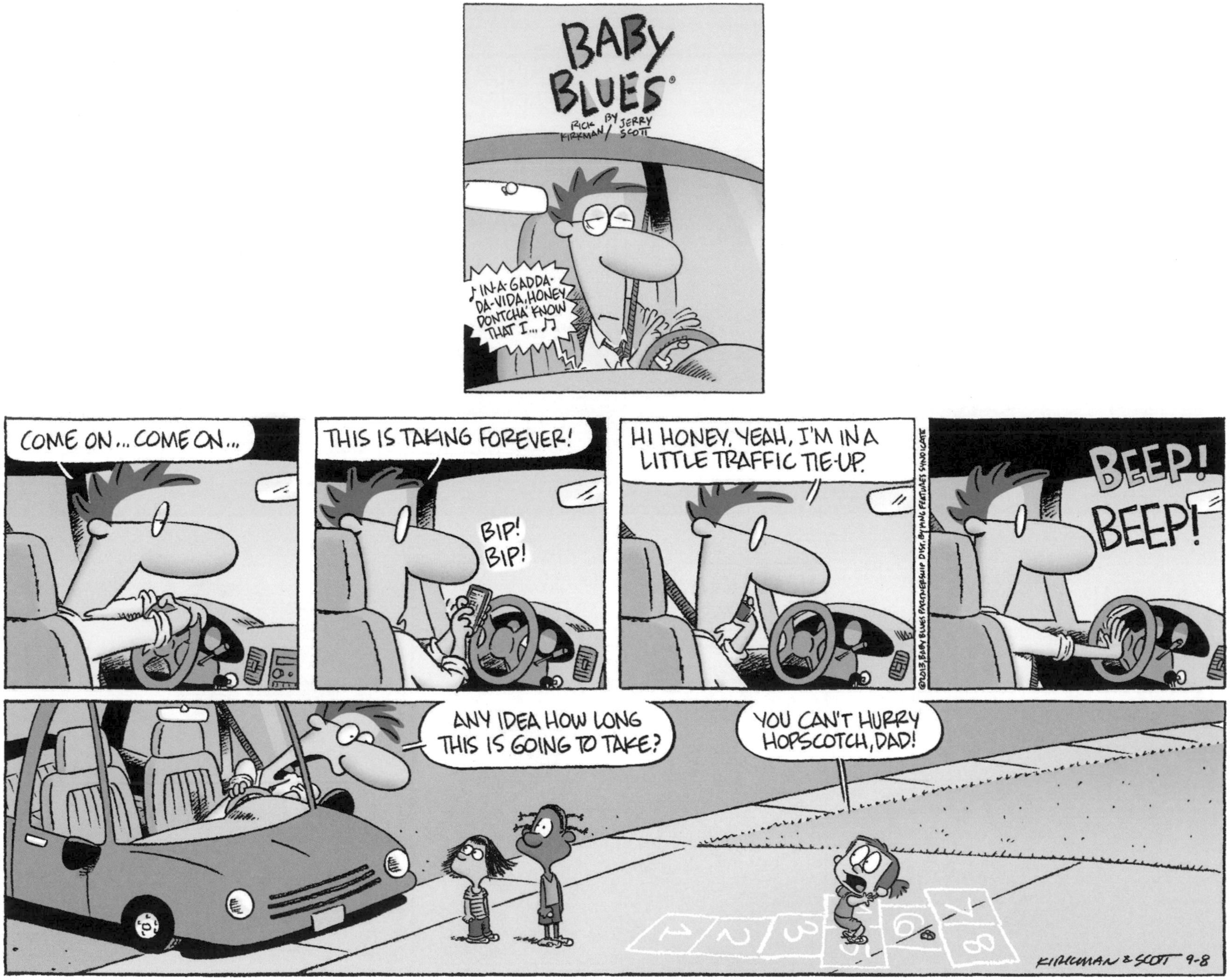
BABY BLUES®
RICK KIRKMAN / BY JERRY SCOTT
♪ IN-A-GADDA-DA-VIDA, HONEY, DONTCHA' KNOW THAT I... ♫
COME ON... COME ON...
THIS IS TAKING FOREVER!
BIP! BIP!
HI HONEY. YEAH, I'M IN A LITTLE TRAFFIC TIE-UP.
©2013, BABY BLUES PARTNERSHIP DIST. BY KING FEATURES SYNDICATE
BEEP! BEEP!
ANY IDEA HOW LONG THIS IS GOING TO TAKE?
YOU CAN'T HURRY HOPSCOTCH, DAD!
KIRKMAN & SCOTT 9-8

Rick: Probably only people from our generation—growing up in the '60s—got this title panel.

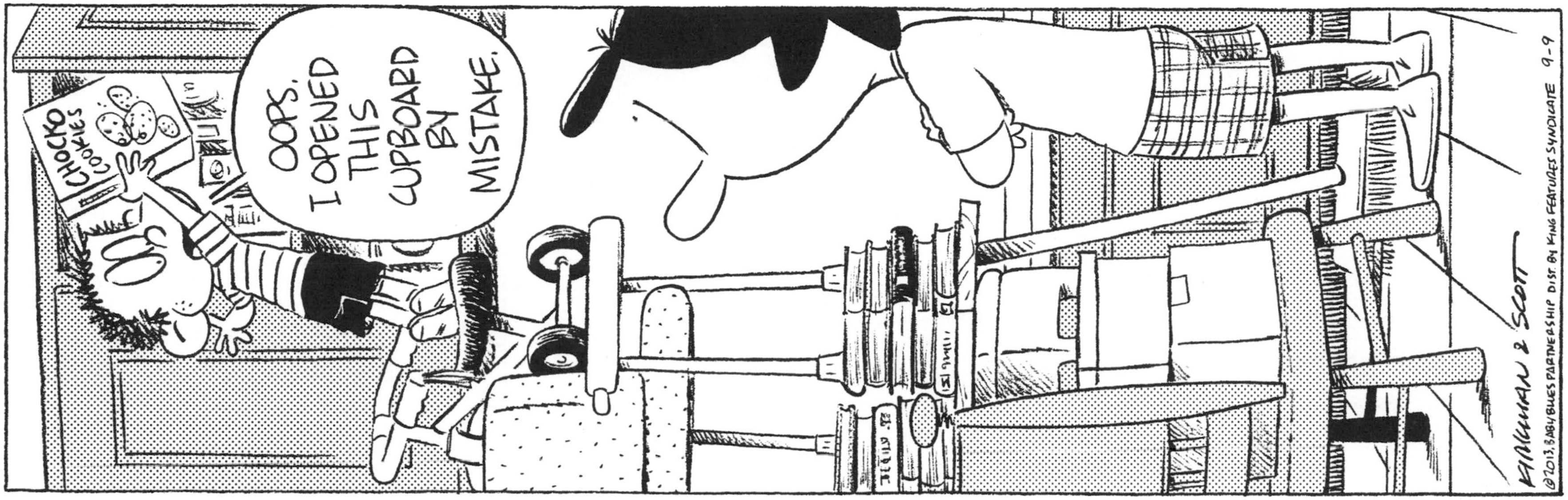
CHOCKO COOKIES
OOPS, I OPENED THIS CUPBOARD BY MISTAKE.
KIRKMAN & SCOTT
©2013, BABY BLUES PARTNERSHIP DIST. BY KING FEATURES SYNDICATE 9-9

Rick: Hey, you try fitting that drawing into a strip going the usual direction.

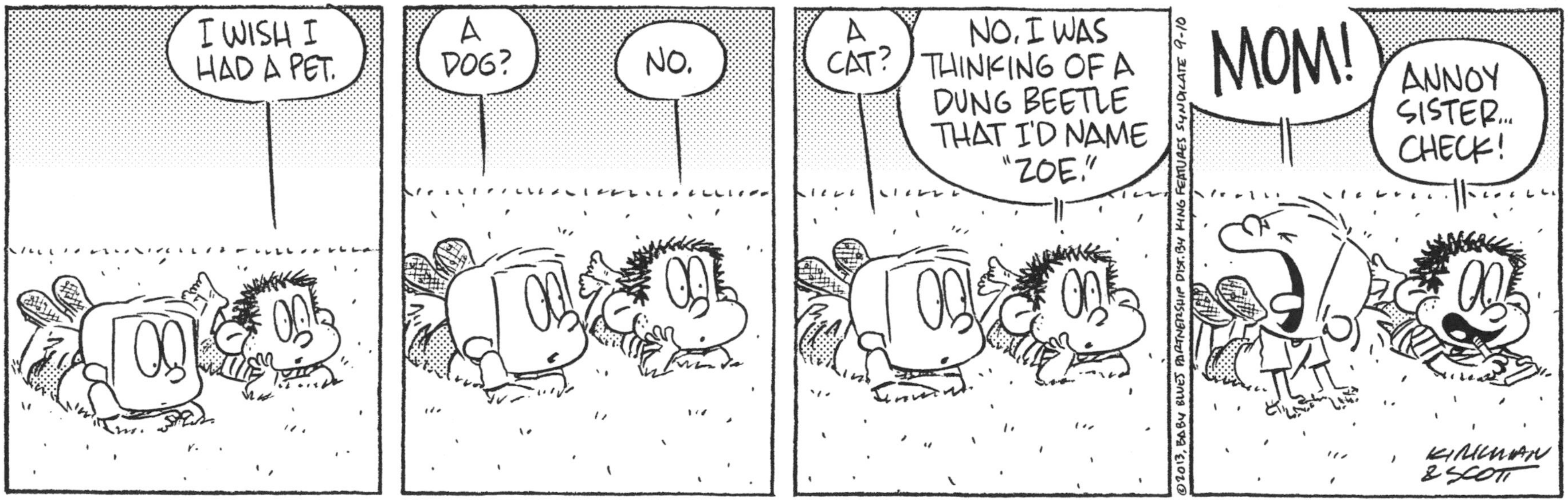
I WISH I HAD A PET.
A DOG?
NO.
A CAT?
NO. I WAS THINKING OF A DUNG BEETLE THAT I'D NAME "ZOE."
©2013, BABY BLUES PARTNERSHIP DIST. BY KING FEATURES SYNDICATE 9-10
MOM!
ANNOY SISTER... CHECK!
KIRKMAN & SCOTT

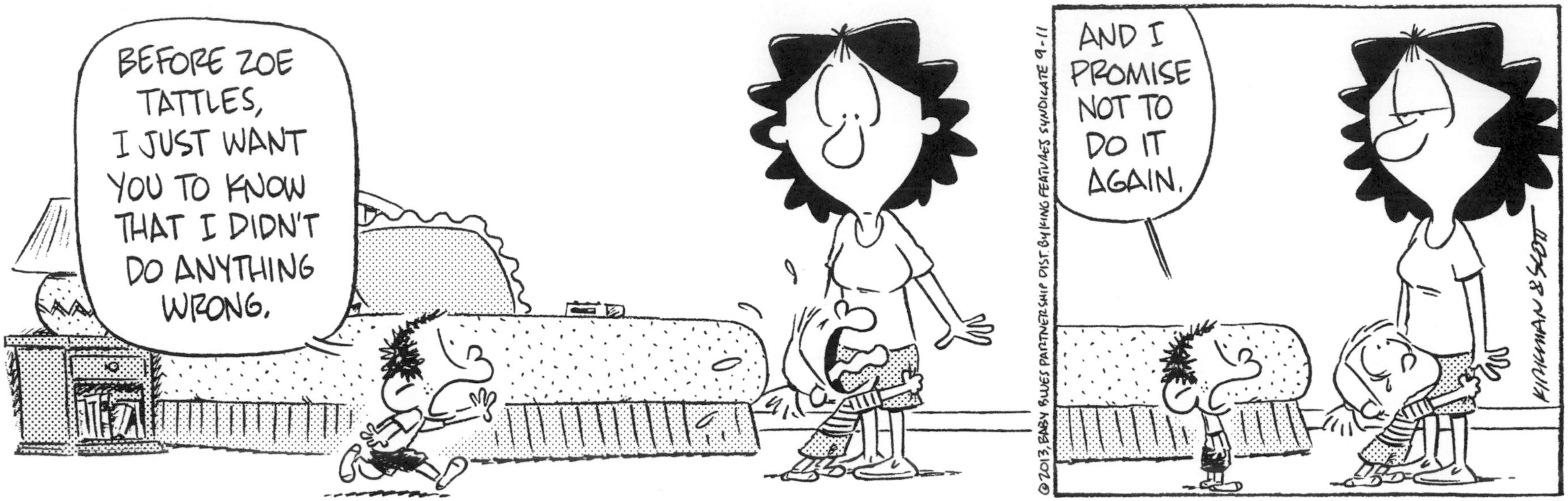
BEFORE ZOE TATTLES, I JUST WANT YOU TO KNOW THAT I DIDN'T DO ANYTHING WRONG.
AND I PROMISE NOT TO DO IT AGAIN.
© 2013, BABY BLUES PARTNERSHIP DIST. BY KING FEATURES SYNDICATE 9-11
KIRKMAN & SCOTT

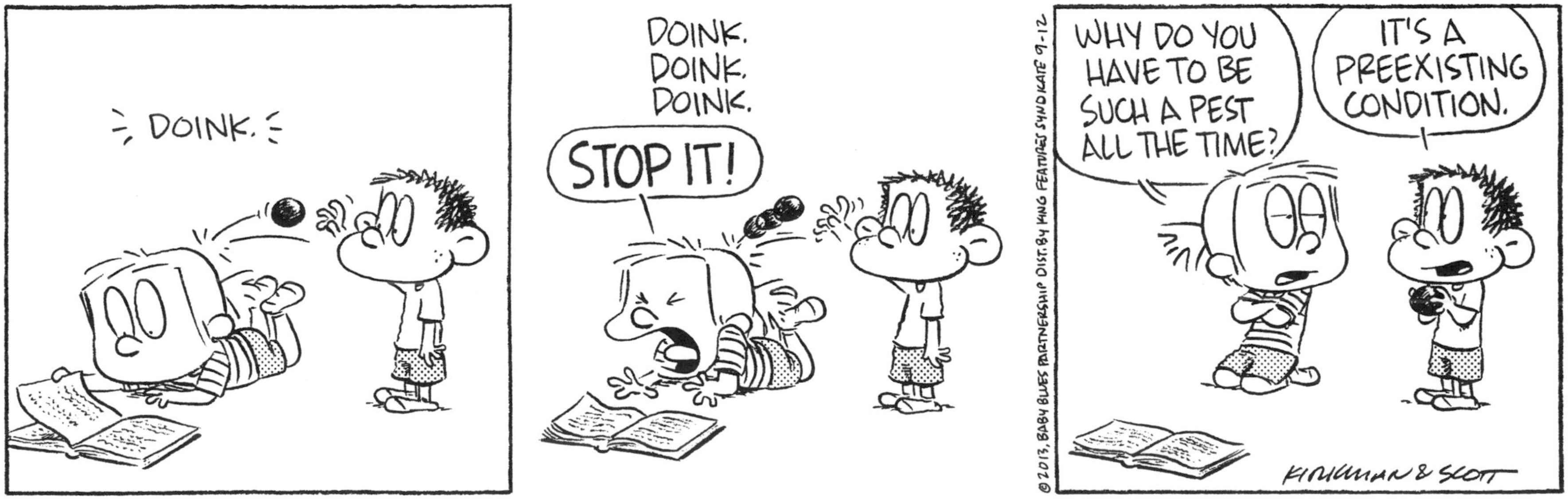
DOINK.
DOINK. DOINK. DOINK.
STOP IT!
WHY DO YOU HAVE TO BE SUCH A PEST ALL THE TIME?
IT'S A PREEXISTING CONDITION.
© 2013, BABY BLUES PARTNERSHIP DIST. BY KING FEATURES SYNDICATE 9-12
KIRKMAN & SCOTT

Jerry: The only one, unfortunately, not covered by health insurance.

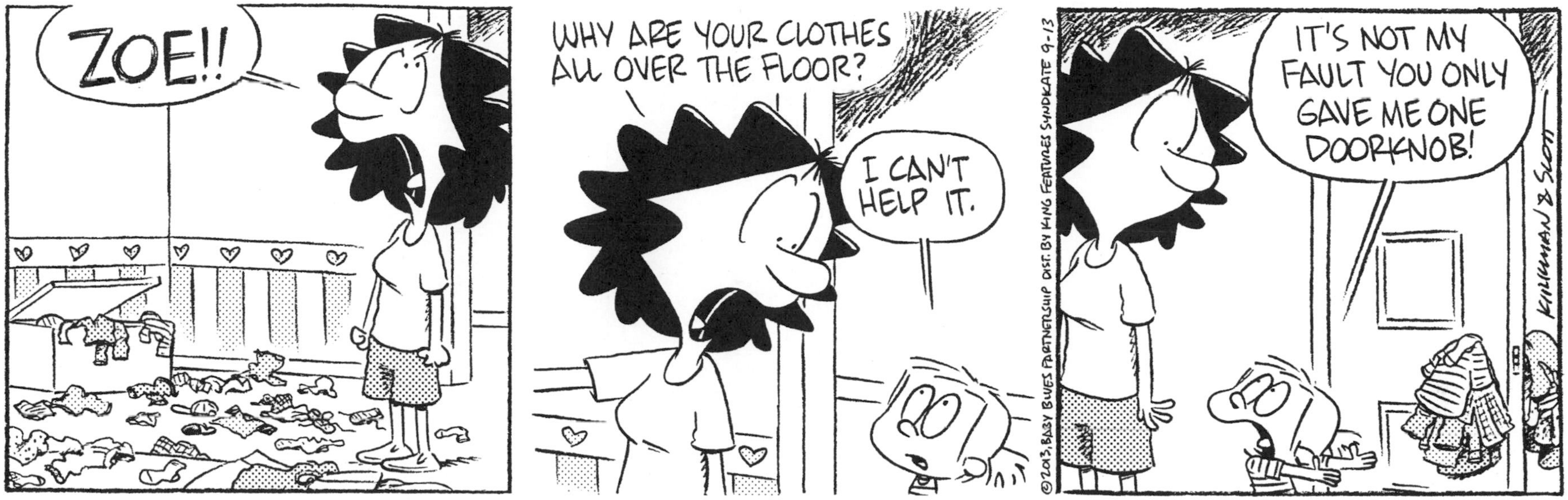
ZOE!!
WHY ARE YOUR CLOTHES ALL OVER THE FLOOR?
I CAN'T HELP IT.
©2013, BABY BLUES PARTNERSHIP DIST. BY KING FEATURES SYNDICATE 9-13
IT'S NOT MY FAULT YOU ONLY GAVE ME ONE DOORKNOB!
KIRKMAN & SCOTT

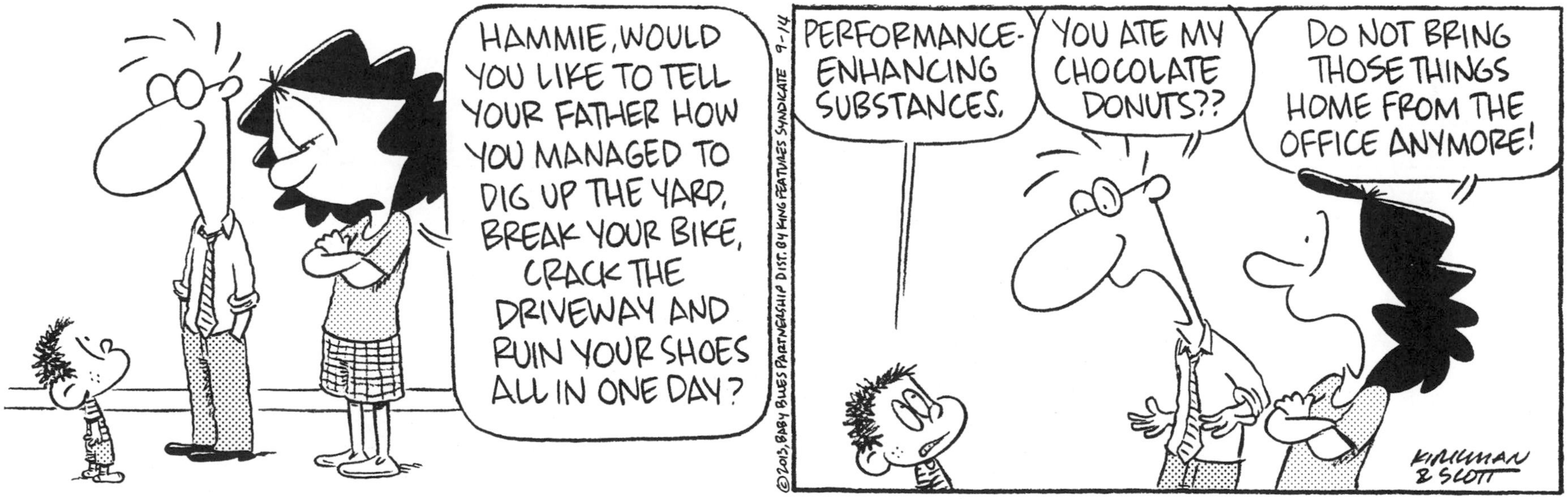
HAMMIE, WOULD YOU LIKE TO TELL YOUR FATHER HOW YOU MANAGED TO DIG UP THE YARD, BREAK YOUR BIKE, CRACK THE DRIVEWAY AND RUIN YOUR SHOES ALL IN ONE DAY?
©2013, BABY BLUES PARTNERSHIP DIST. BY KING FEATURES SYNDICATE 9-14
PERFORMANCE-ENHANCING SUBSTANCES.
YOU ATE MY CHOCOLATE DONUTS??
DO NOT BRING THOSE THINGS HOME FROM THE OFFICE ANYMORE!
KIRKMAN & SCOTT

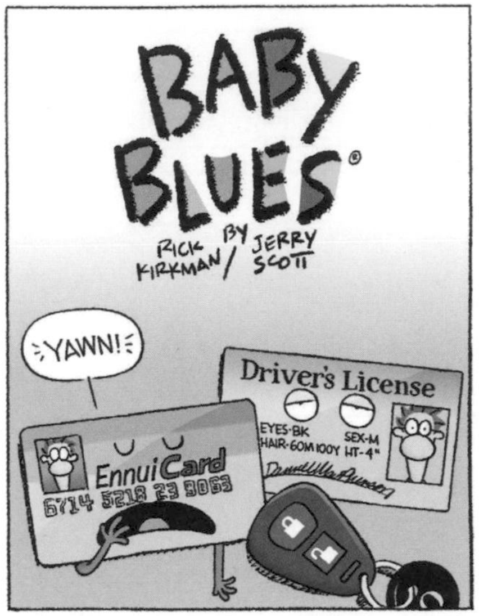
BABY BLUES®
BY RICK KIRKMAN / JERRY SCOTT
YAWN!
Driver's License
EnnuiCard

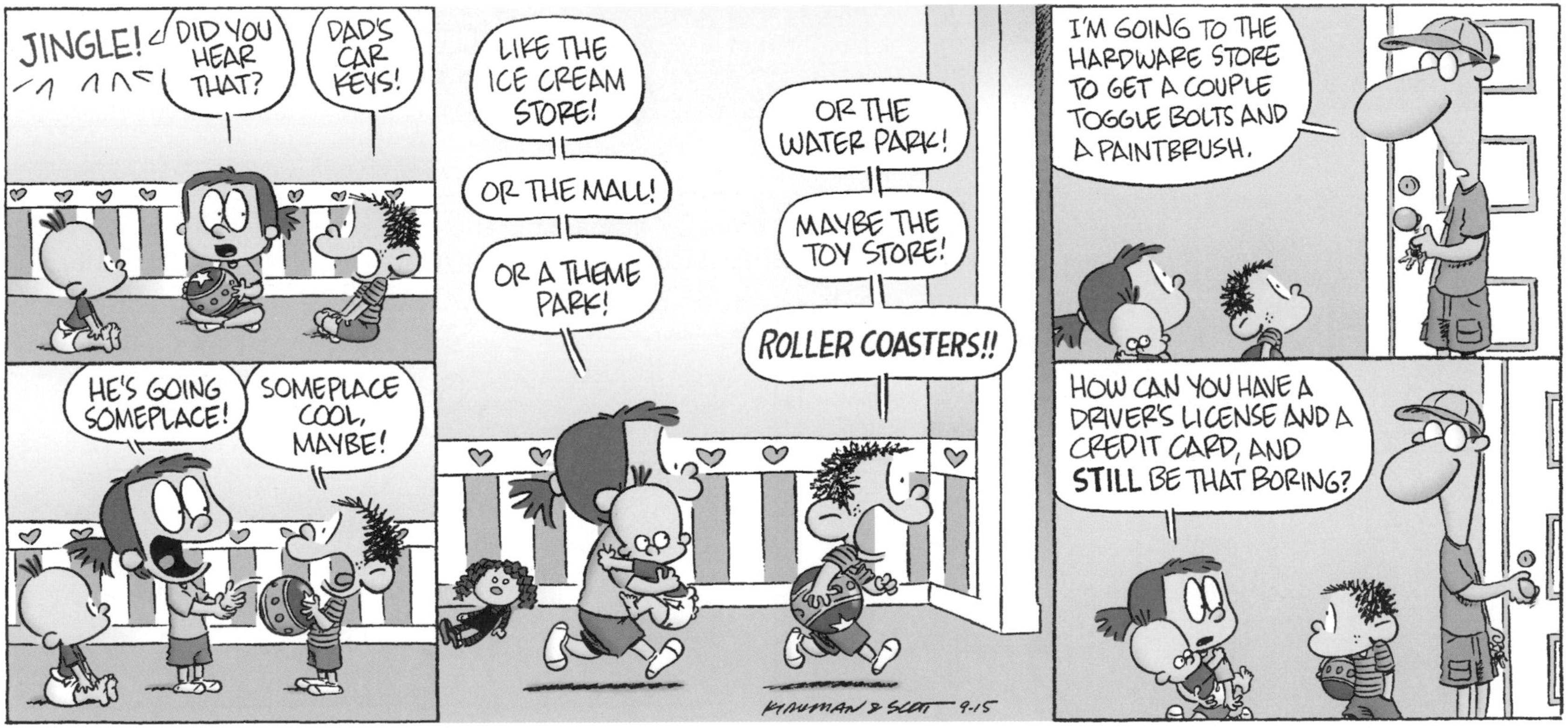
JINGLE!
DID YOU HEAR THAT?
DAD'S CAR KEYS!
HE'S GOING SOMEPLACE!
SOMEPLACE COOL, MAYBE!
LIKE THE ICE CREAM STORE!
OR THE MALL!
OR A THEME PARK!
OR THE WATER PARK!
MAYBE THE TOY STORE!
ROLLER COASTERS!!
KIRKMAN & SCOTT 9-15
I'M GOING TO THE HARDWARE STORE TO GET A COUPLE TOGGLE BOLTS AND A PAINTBRUSH.
HOW CAN YOU HAVE A DRIVER'S LICENSE AND A CREDIT CARD, AND STILL BE THAT BORING?

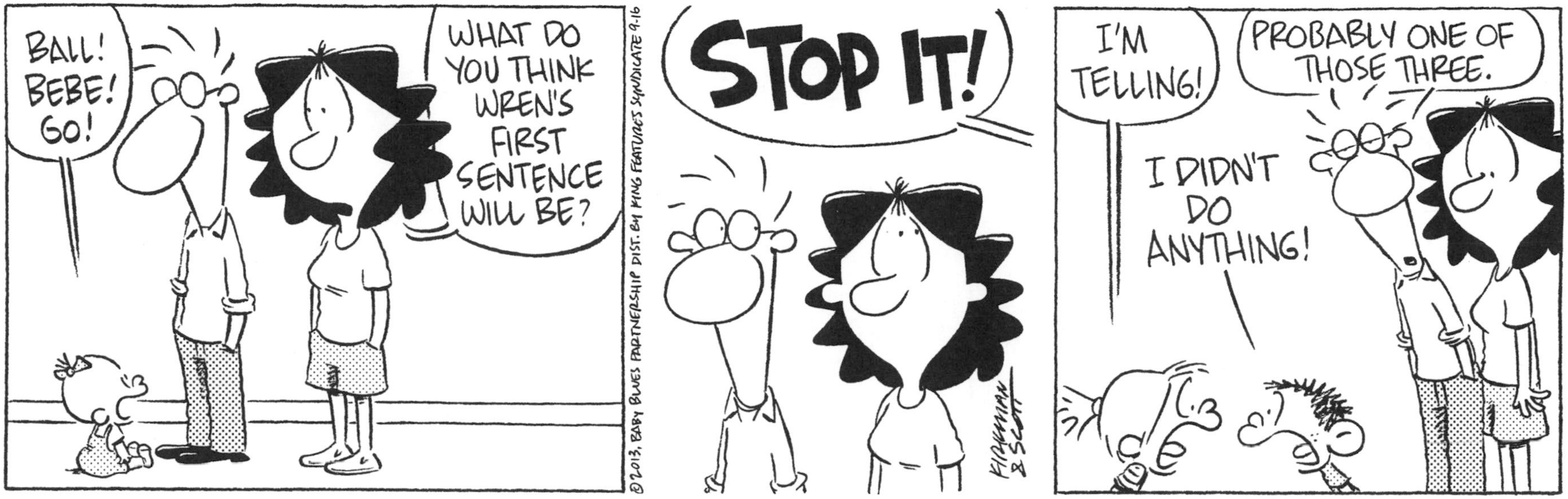
BALL! BEBE! GO!
WHAT DO YOU THINK WREN'S FIRST SENTENCE WILL BE?
©2013, BABY BLUES PARTNERSHIP DIST. BY KING FEATURES SYNDICATE 9-16
STOP IT!
KIRKMAN & SCOTT
I'M TELLING!
I DIDN'T DO ANYTHING!
PROBABLY ONE OF THOSE THREE.

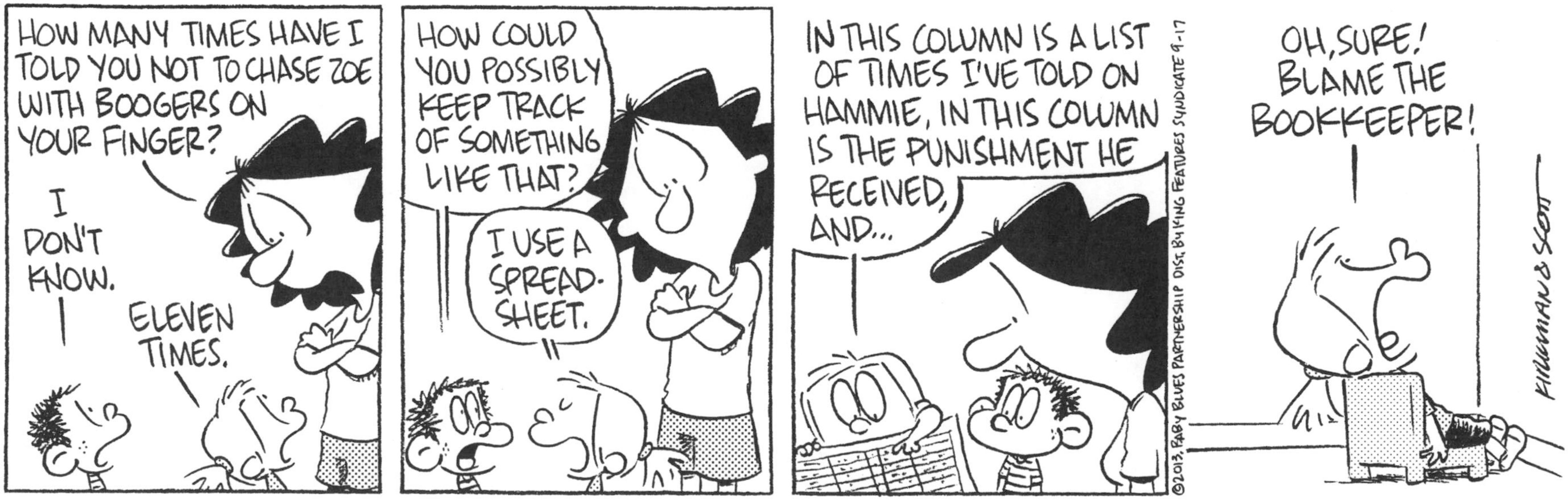
HOW MANY TIMES HAVE I TOLD YOU NOT TO CHASE ZOE WITH BOOGERS ON YOUR FINGER?
I DON'T KNOW.
ELEVEN TIMES.
HOW COULD YOU POSSIBLY KEEP TRACK OF SOMETHING LIKE THAT?
I USE A SPREAD-SHEET.
IN THIS COLUMN IS A LIST OF TIMES I'VE TOLD ON HAMMIE, IN THIS COLUMN IS THE PUNISHMENT HE RECEIVED, AND...
©2013, BABY BLUES PARTNERSHIP DIST. BY KING FEATURES SYNDICATE 9-17
OH, SURE! BLAME THE BOOKKEEPER!
KIRKMAN & SCOTT

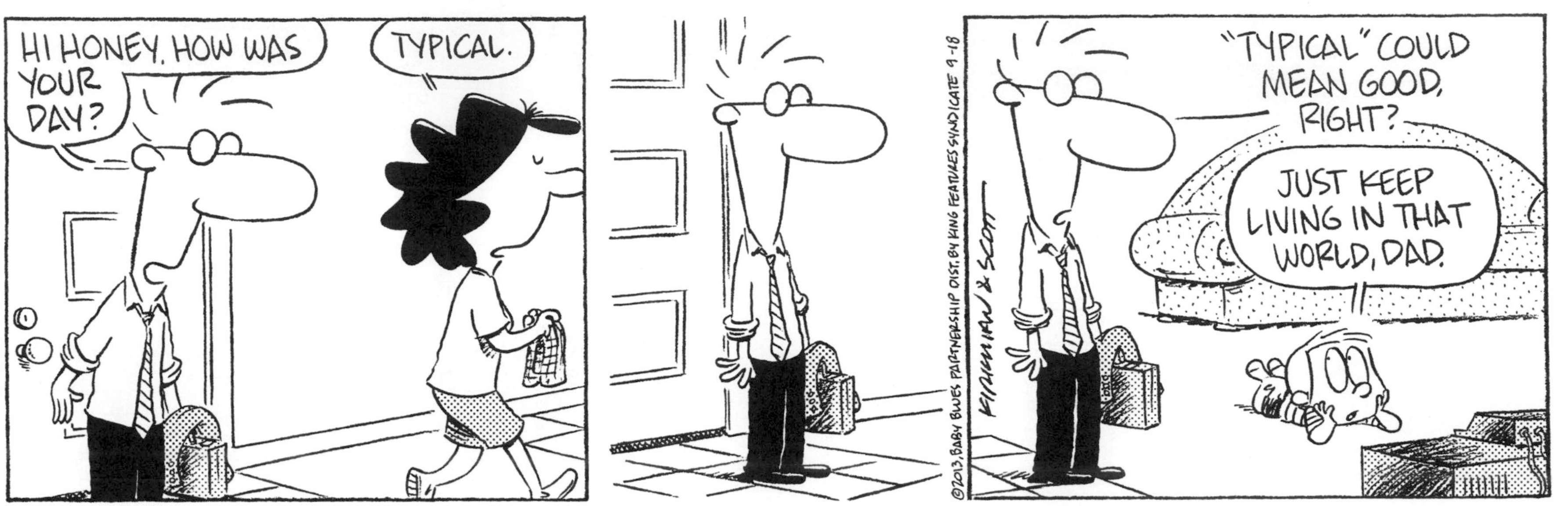
HI HONEY. HOW WAS YOUR DAY?
TYPICAL.
"TYPICAL" COULD MEAN GOOD, RIGHT?
JUST KEEP LIVING IN THAT WORLD, DAD.
©2013, BABY BLUES PARTNERSHIP DIST. BY KING FEATURES SYNDICATE 9-18
KIRKMAN & SCOTT

Jerry: I like it when Zoe is worldly beyond her years.

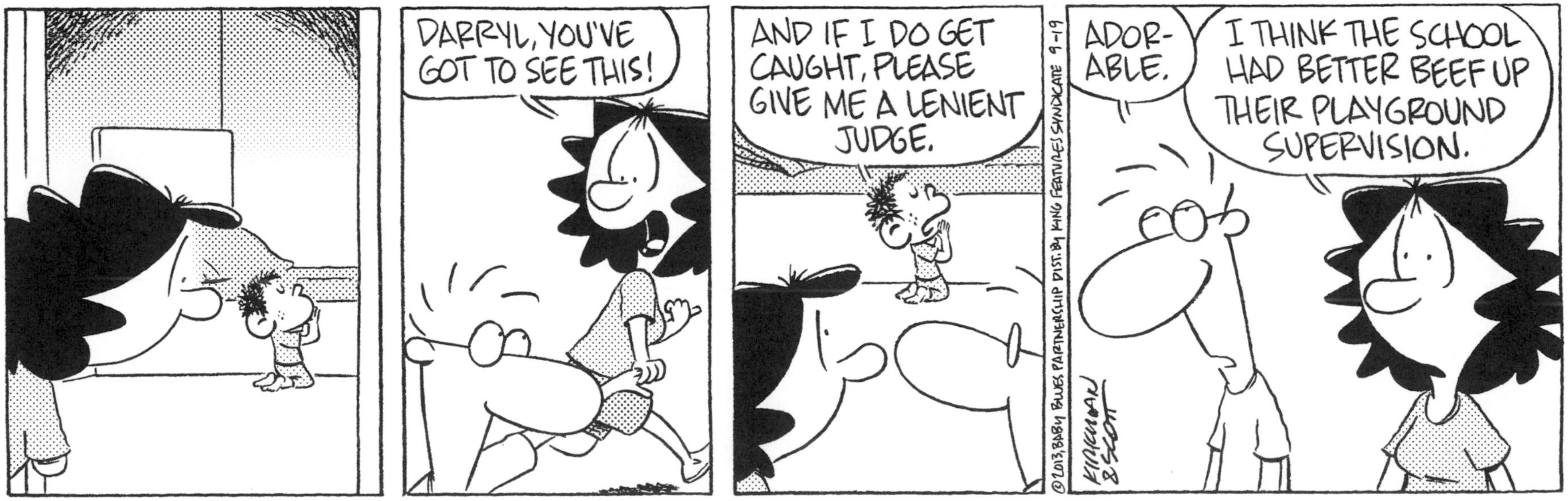
DARRYL, YOU'VE GOT TO SEE THIS!
AND IF I DO GET CAUGHT, PLEASE GIVE ME A LENIENT JUDGE.
©2013, BABY BLUES PARTNERSHIP DIST. BY KING FEATURES SYNDICATE 9-19
KIRKMAN & SCOTT
ADOR-ABLE.
I THINK THE SCHOOL HAD BETTER BEEF UP THEIR PLAYGROUND SUPERVISION.

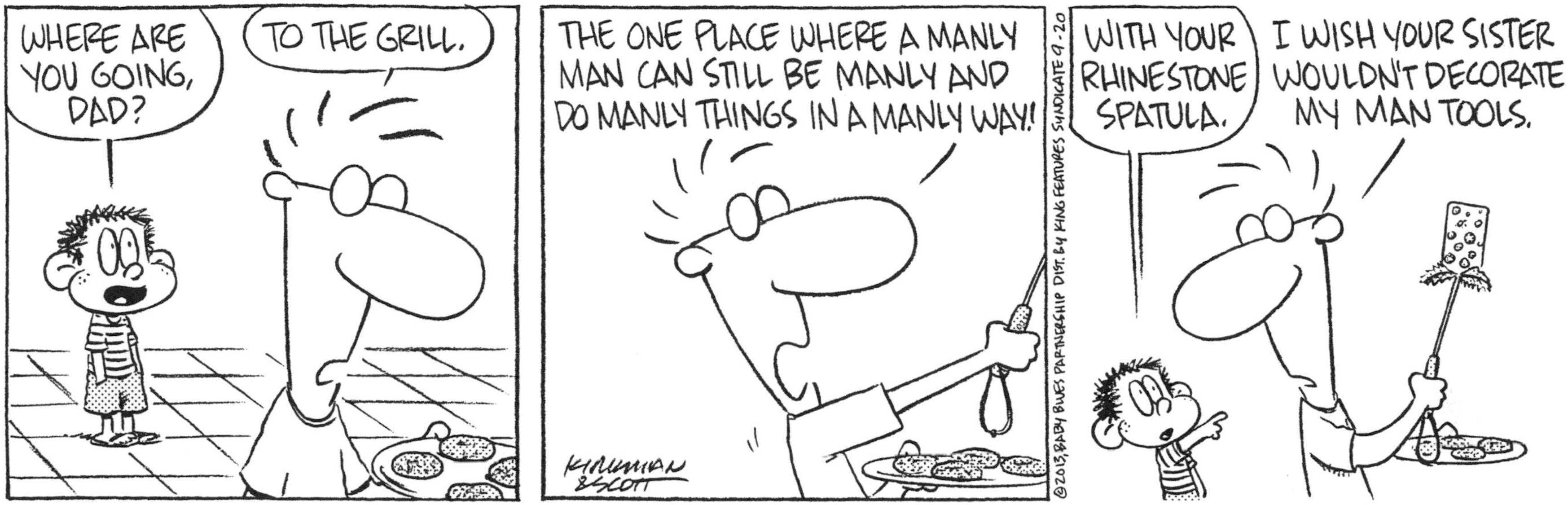
WHERE ARE YOU GOING, DAD?
TO THE GRILL.
THE ONE PLACE WHERE A MANLY MAN CAN STILL BE MANLY AND DO MANLY THINGS IN A MANLY WAY!
KIRKMAN & SCOTT
© 2013, BABY BLUES PARTNERSHIP DIST. BY KING FEATURES SYNDICATE 9-20
WITH YOUR RHINESTONE SPATULA.
I WISH YOUR SISTER WOULDN'T DECORATE MY MAN TOOLS.

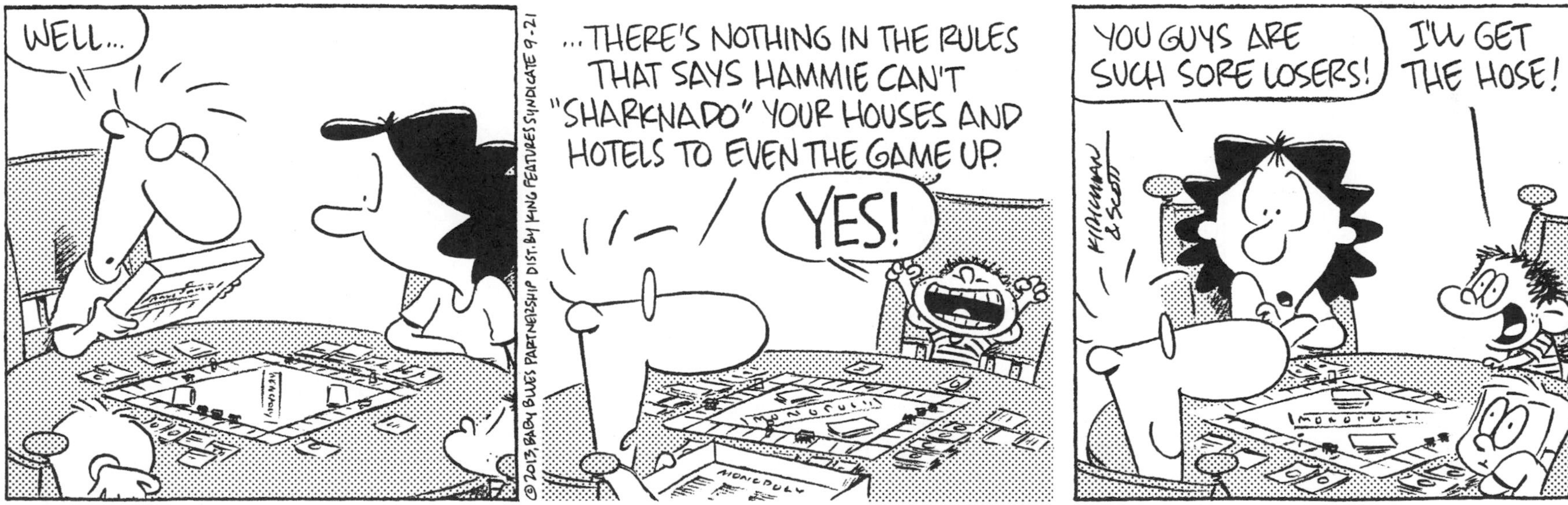
WELL...
© 2013, BABY BLUES PARTNERSHIP DIST. BY KING FEATURES SYNDICATE 9-21
...THERE'S NOTHING IN THE RULES THAT SAYS HAMMIE CAN'T "SHARKNADO" YOUR HOUSES AND HOTELS TO EVEN THE GAME UP.
YES!
YOU GUYS ARE SUCH SORE LOSERS!
I'LL GET THE HOSE!
KIRKMAN & SCOTT

Jerry: I doubt the *Sharknado* reference will stand the test of time, but it was irresistible.

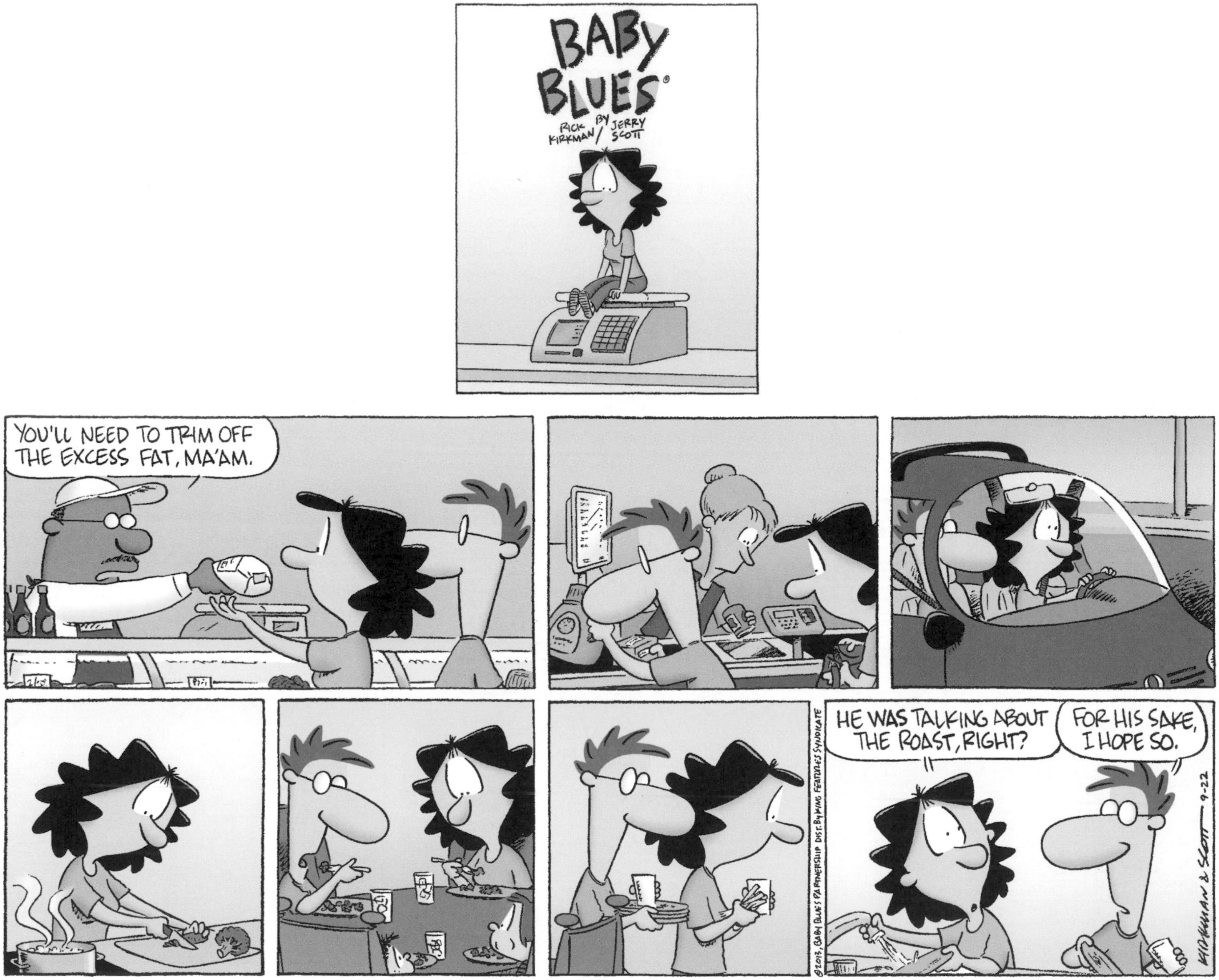
BABY BLUES®
BY RICK KIRKMAN / JERRY SCOTT
YOU'LL NEED TO TRIM OFF THE EXCESS FAT, MA'AM.
HE WAS TALKING ABOUT THE ROAST, RIGHT?
FOR HIS SAKE, I HOPE SO.

Jerry: This strip cracks me up because I often have delayed reactions like Wanda's.

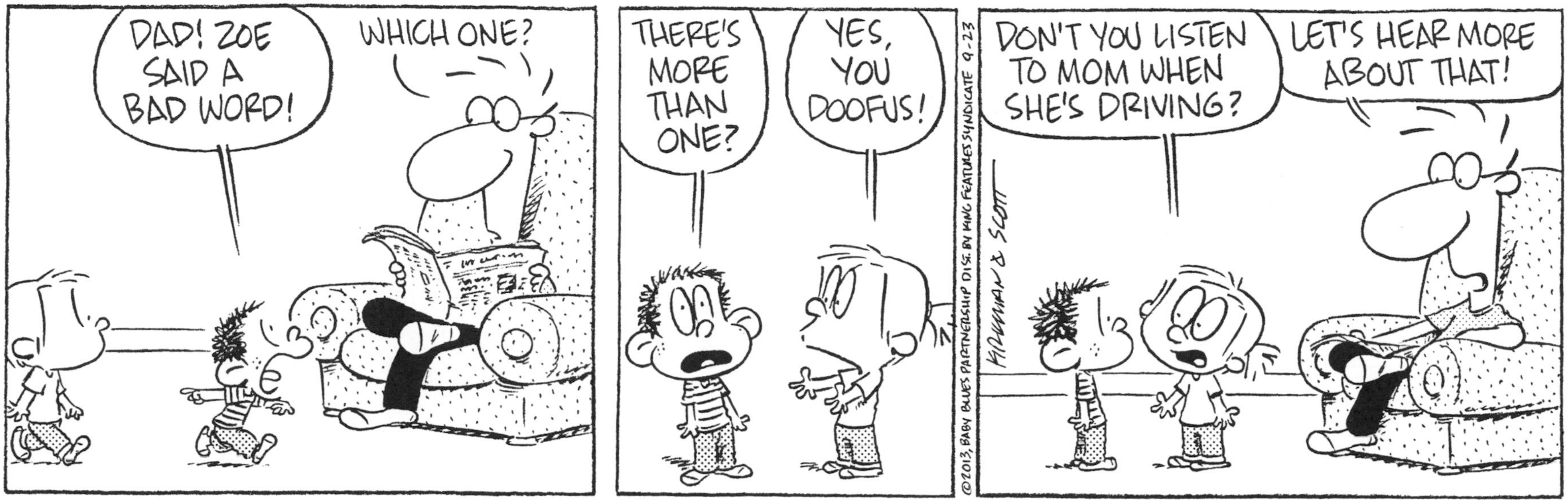
DAD! ZOE SAID A BAD WORD!
WHICH ONE?
THERE'S MORE THAN ONE?
YES, YOU DOOFUS!
©2013, BABY BLUES PARTNERSHIP DIST. BY KING FEATURES SYNDICATE 9-23
KIRKMAN & SCOTT
DON'T YOU LISTEN TO MOM WHEN SHE'S DRIVING?
LET'S HEAR MORE ABOUT THAT!

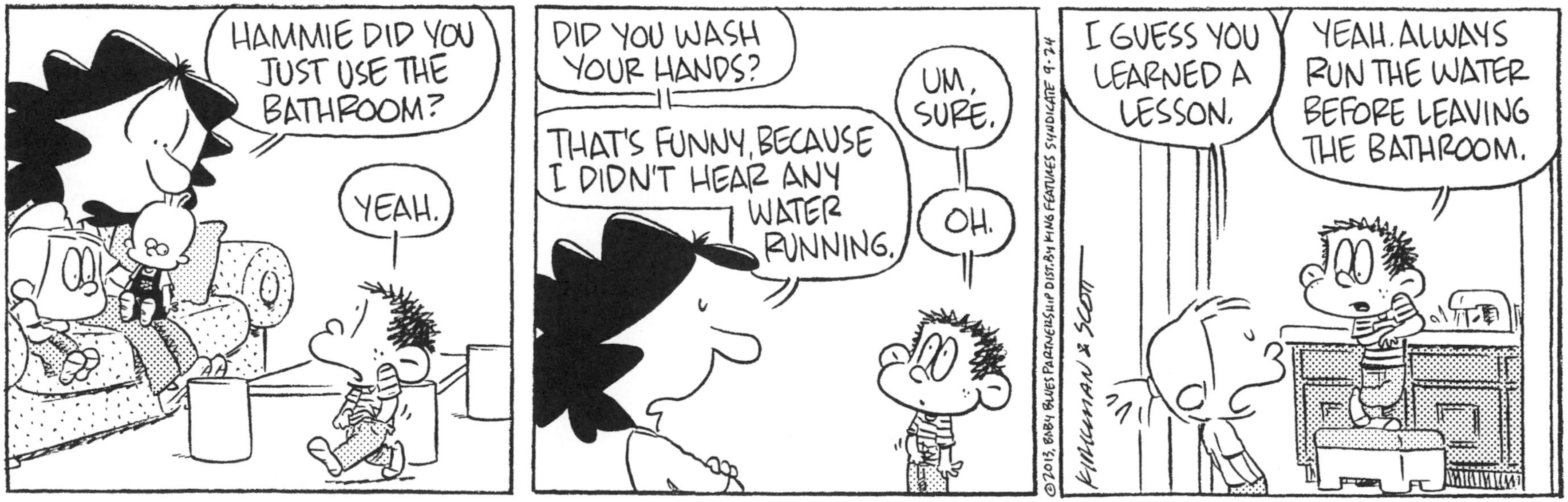
HAMMIE DID YOU JUST USE THE BATHROOM?
YEAH.
DID YOU WASH YOUR HANDS?
UM, SURE.
THAT'S FUNNY, BECAUSE I DIDN'T HEAR ANY WATER RUNNING.
OH.
©2013, BABY BLUES PARTNERSHIP DIST. BY KING FEATURES SYNDICATE 9-24
KIRKMAN & SCOTT
I GUESS YOU LEARNED A LESSON.
YEAH. ALWAYS RUN THE WATER BEFORE LEAVING THE BATHROOM.

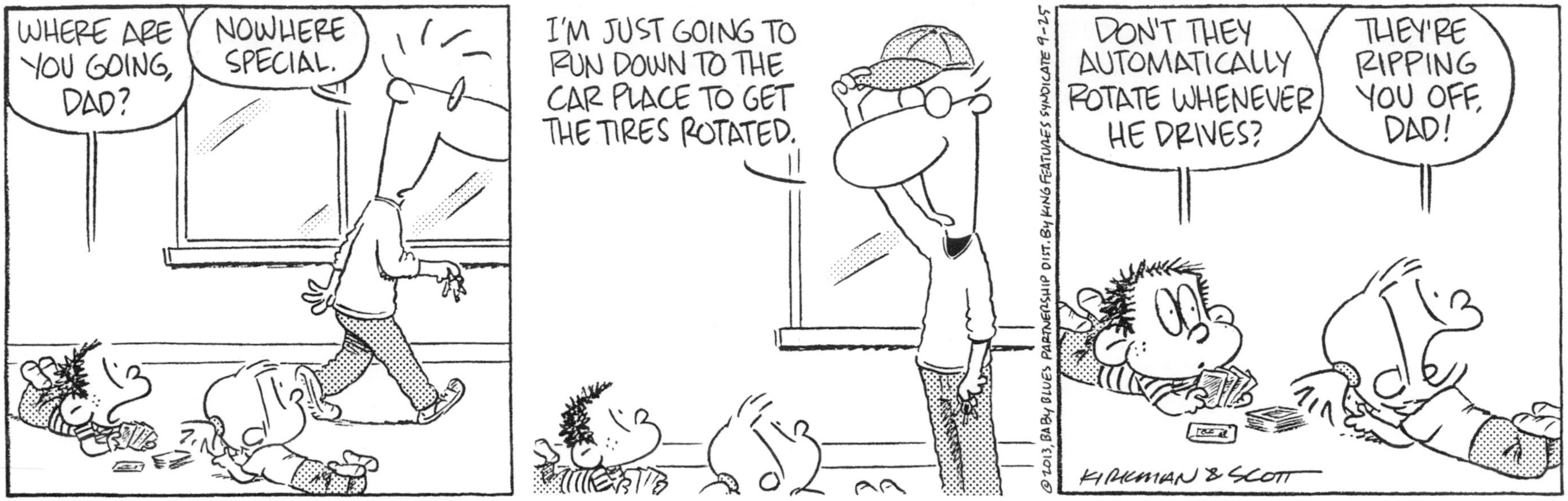
WHERE ARE YOU GOING, DAD?
NOWHERE SPECIAL.
I'M JUST GOING TO RUN DOWN TO THE CAR PLACE TO GET THE TIRES ROTATED.
©2013, BABY BLUES PARTNERSHIP DIST. BY KING FEATURES SYNDICATE 9-25
DON'T THEY AUTOMATICALLY ROTATE WHENEVER HE DRIVES?
THEY'RE RIPPING YOU OFF, DAD!
KIRKMAN & SCOTT

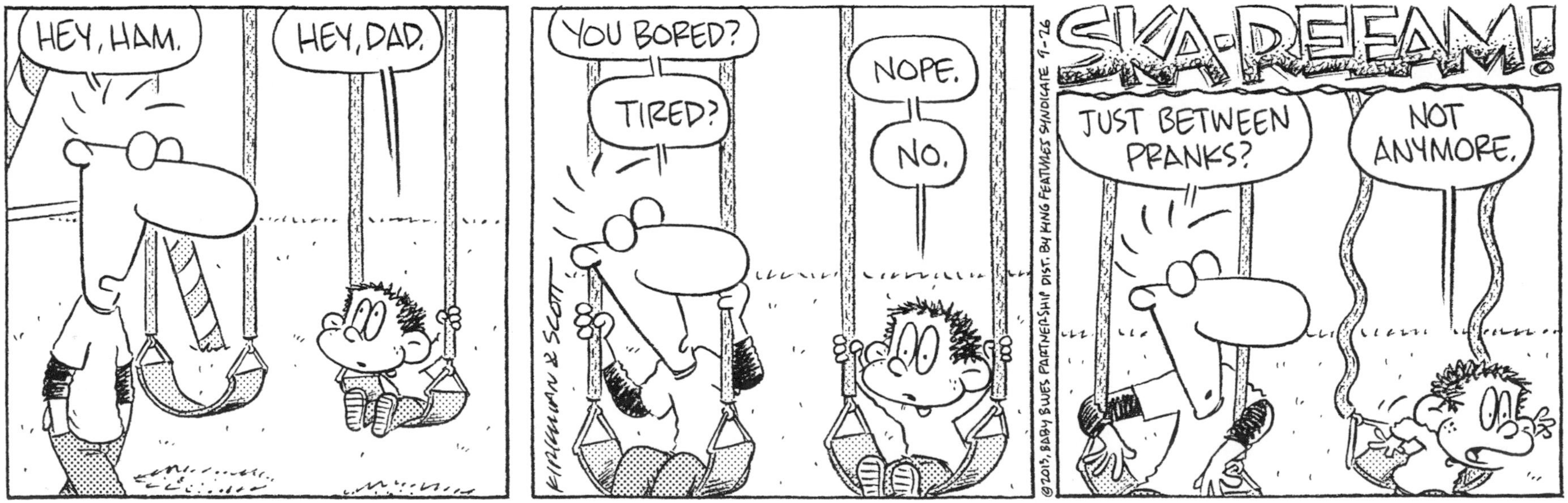
HEY, HAM.
HEY, DAD.
YOU BORED?
TIRED?
NOPE.
NO.
KIRKMAN & SCOTT
©2013, BABY BLUES PARTNERSHIP DIST. BY KING FEATURES SYNDICATE 9-26
SKA-REEAM!
JUST BETWEEN PRANKS?
NOT ANYMORE.

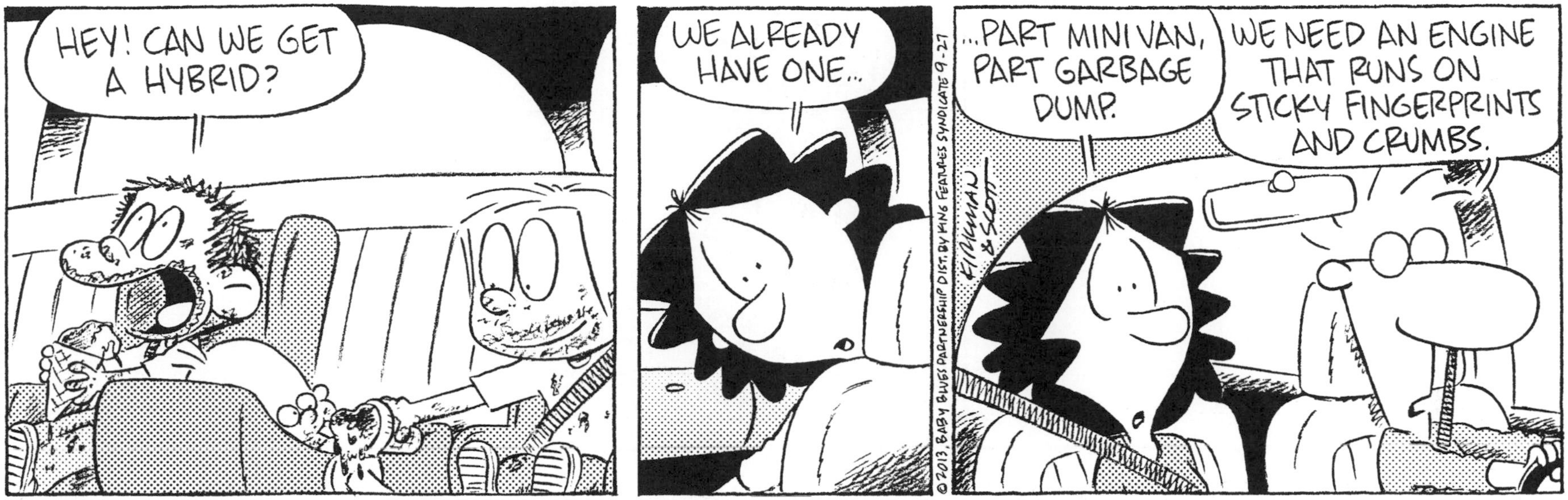
HEY! CAN WE GET A HYBRID?
WE ALREADY HAVE ONE...
© 2013, BABY BLUES PARTNERSHIP DIST. BY KING FEATURES SYNDICATE 9-27
KIRKMAN & SCOTT
...PART MINI VAN, PART GARBAGE DUMP.
WE NEED AN ENGINE THAT RUNS ON STICKY FINGERPRINTS AND CRUMBS.

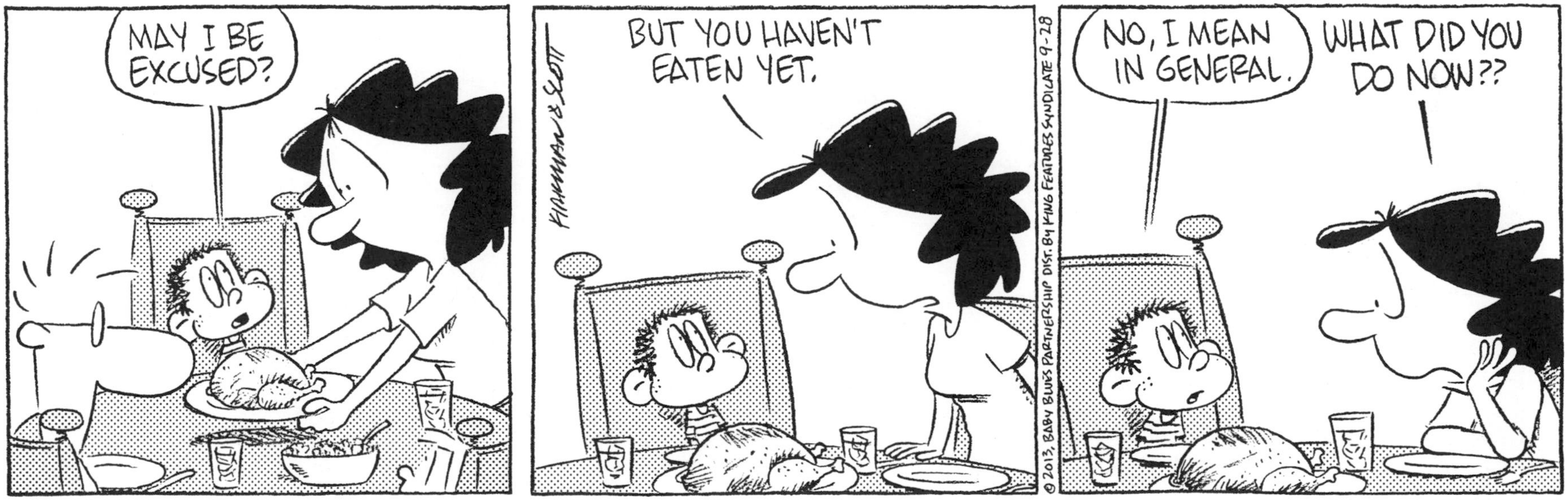
MAY I BE EXCUSED?
KIRKMAN & SCOTT
BUT YOU HAVEN'T EATEN YET.
© 2013, BABY BLUES PARTNERSHIP DIST. BY KING FEATURES SYNDICATE 9-28
NO, I MEAN IN GENERAL.
WHAT DID YOU DO NOW??

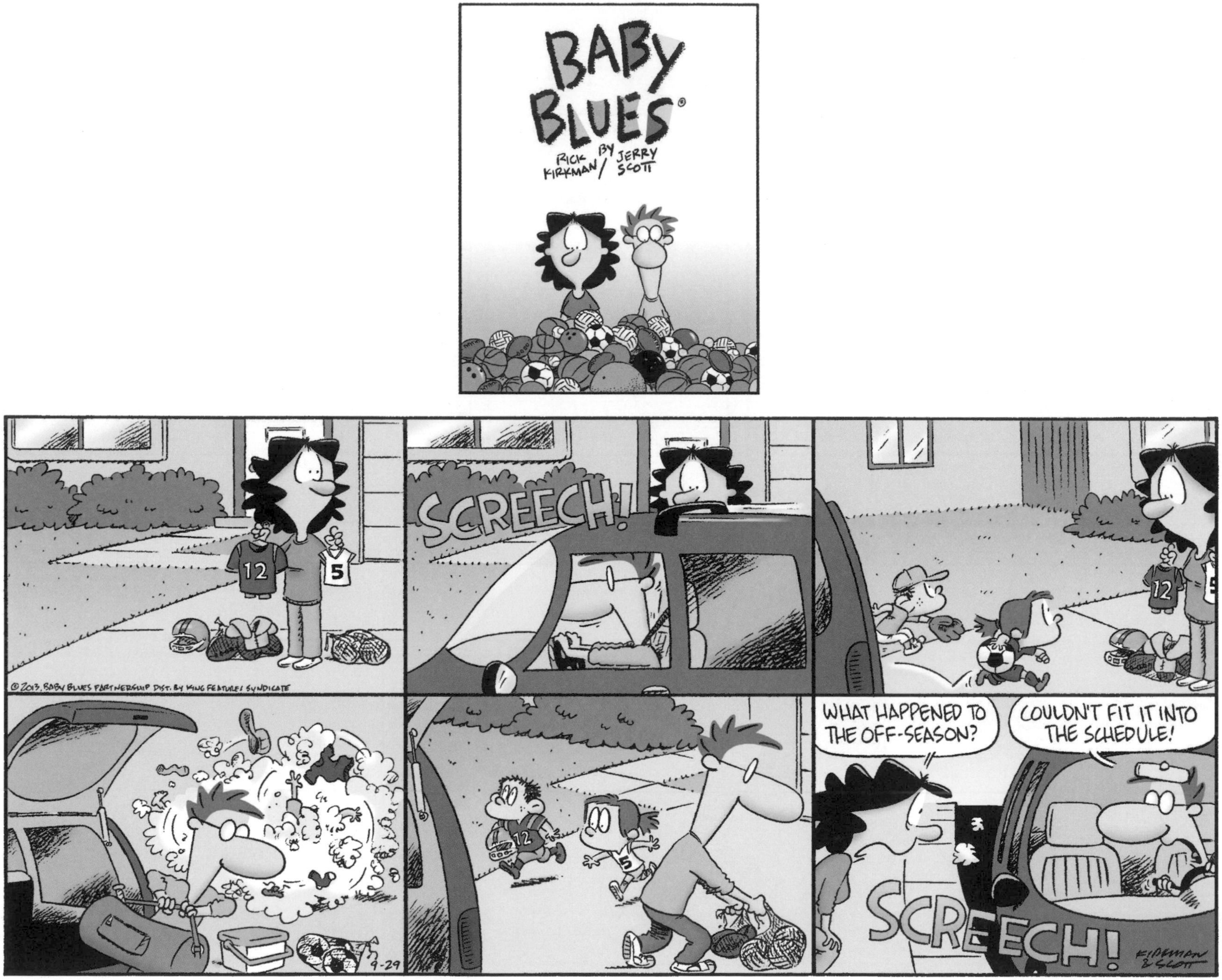
BABY BLUES®
BY RICK KIRKMAN / JERRY SCOTT
© 2013, BABY BLUES PARTNERSHIP DIST. BY KING FEATURES SYNDICATE
12
5
SCREECH!
WHAT HAPPENED TO THE OFF-SEASON?
COULDN'T FIT IT INTO THE SCHEDULE!
SCREECH!
KIRKMAN & SCOTT
9-29

Jerry: God bless you parents of two or more kids in three or more sports.

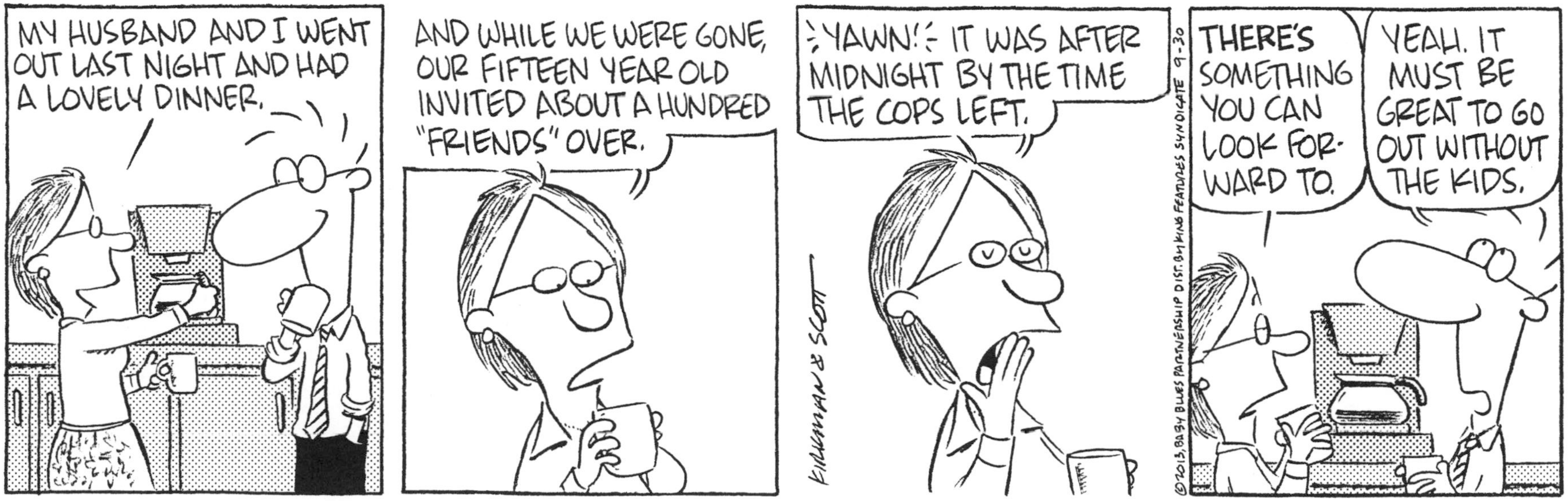
MY HUSBAND AND I WENT OUT LAST NIGHT AND HAD A LOVELY DINNER.
AND WHILE WE WERE GONE, OUR FIFTEEN YEAR OLD INVITED ABOUT A HUNDRED "FRIENDS" OVER.
KIRKMAN & SCOTT
-YAWN!- IT WAS AFTER MIDNIGHT BY THE TIME THE COPS LEFT.
©2013, BABY BLUES PARTNERSHIP DIST. BY KING FEATURES SYNDICATE 9-30
THERE'S SOMETHING YOU CAN LOOK FORWARD TO.
YEAH. IT MUST BE GREAT TO GO OUT WITHOUT THE KIDS.

Rick: Love the twist at the end of this one.

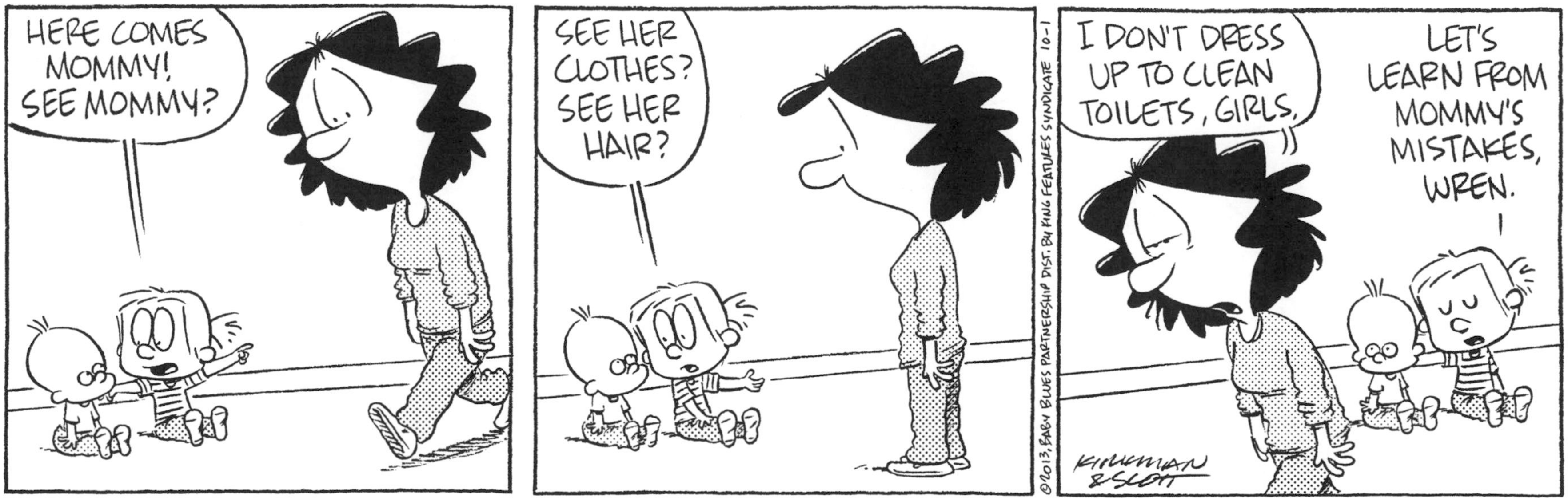
HERE COMES MOMMY! SEE MOMMY?
SEE HER CLOTHES? SEE HER HAIR?
©2013, BABY BLUES PARTNERSHIP DIST. BY KING FEATURES SYNDICATE 10-1
I DON'T DRESS UP TO CLEAN TOILETS, GIRLS.
LET'S LEARN FROM MOMMY'S MISTAKES, WREN.
KIRKMAN & SCOTT

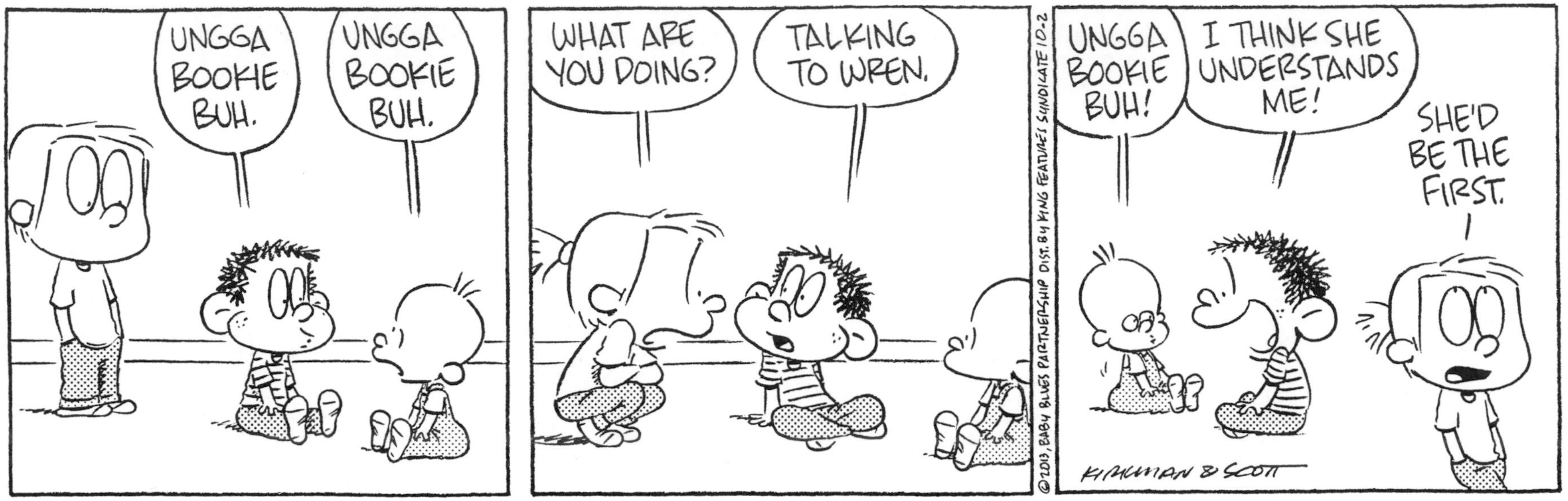
UNGGA BOOKIE BUH.
UNGGA BOOKIE BUH.
WHAT ARE YOU DOING?
TALKING TO WREN.
©2013, BABY BLUES PARTNERSHIP DIST. BY KING FEATURES SYNDICATE 10-2
UNGGA BOOKIE BUH!
I THINK SHE UNDERSTANDS ME!
SHE'D BE THE FIRST.
KIRKMAN & SCOTT

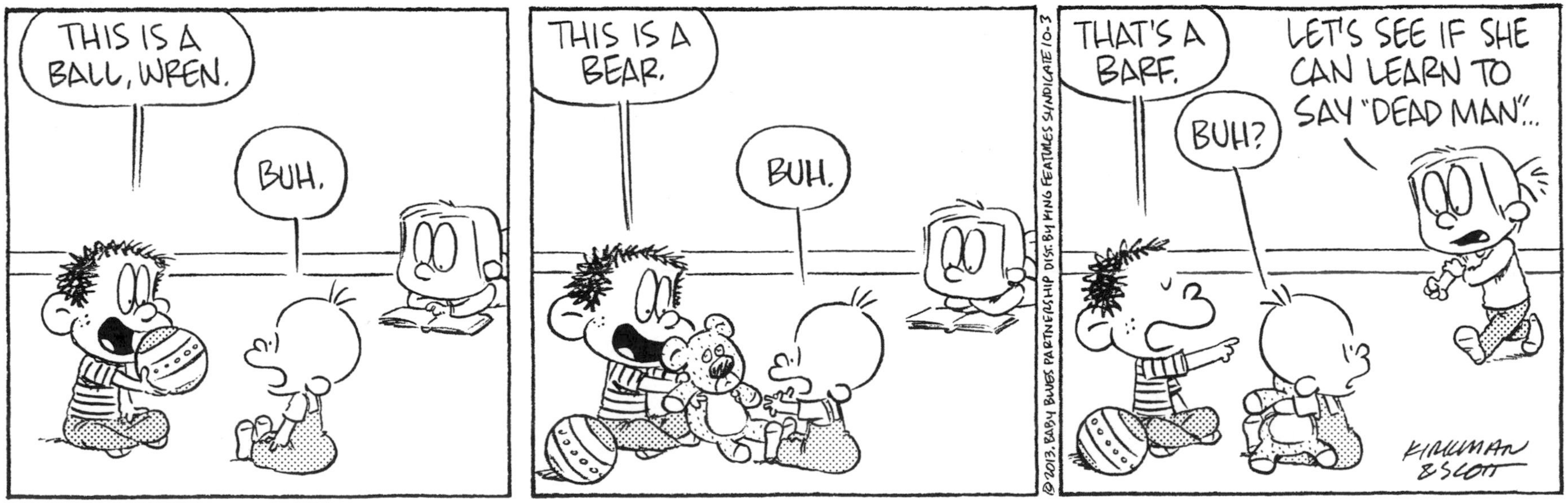
THIS IS A BALL, WREN.
BUH.
THIS IS A BEAR.
BUH.
©2013, BABY BLUES PARTNERSHIP DIST. BY KING FEATURES SYNDICATE 10-3
THAT'S A BARF.
BUH?
LET'S SEE IF SHE CAN LEARN TO SAY "DEAD MAN"...
KIRKMAN & SCOTT

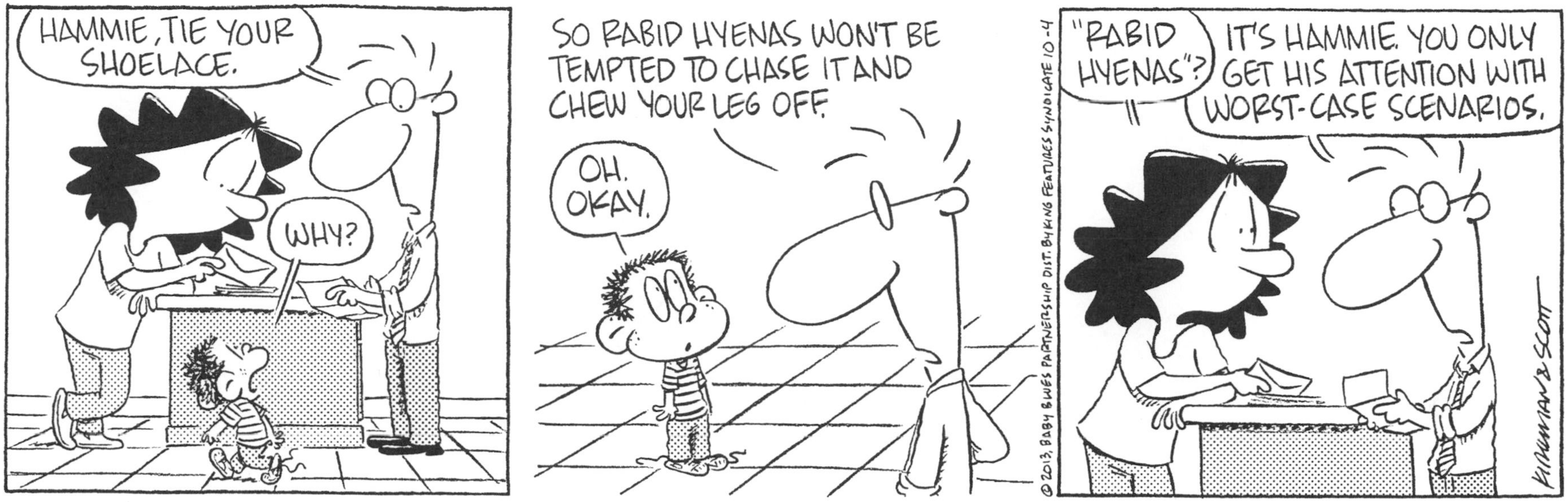
HAMMIE, TIE YOUR SHOELACE.
WHY?
SO RABID HYENAS WON'T BE TEMPTED TO CHASE IT AND CHEW YOUR LEG OFF.
OH. OKAY.
"RABID HYENAS"?
IT'S HAMMIE. YOU ONLY GET HIS ATTENTION WITH WORST-CASE SCENARIOS.
© 2013, BABY BLUES PARTNERSHIP DIST. BY KING FEATURES SYNDICATE 10-4
KIRKMAN & SCOTT

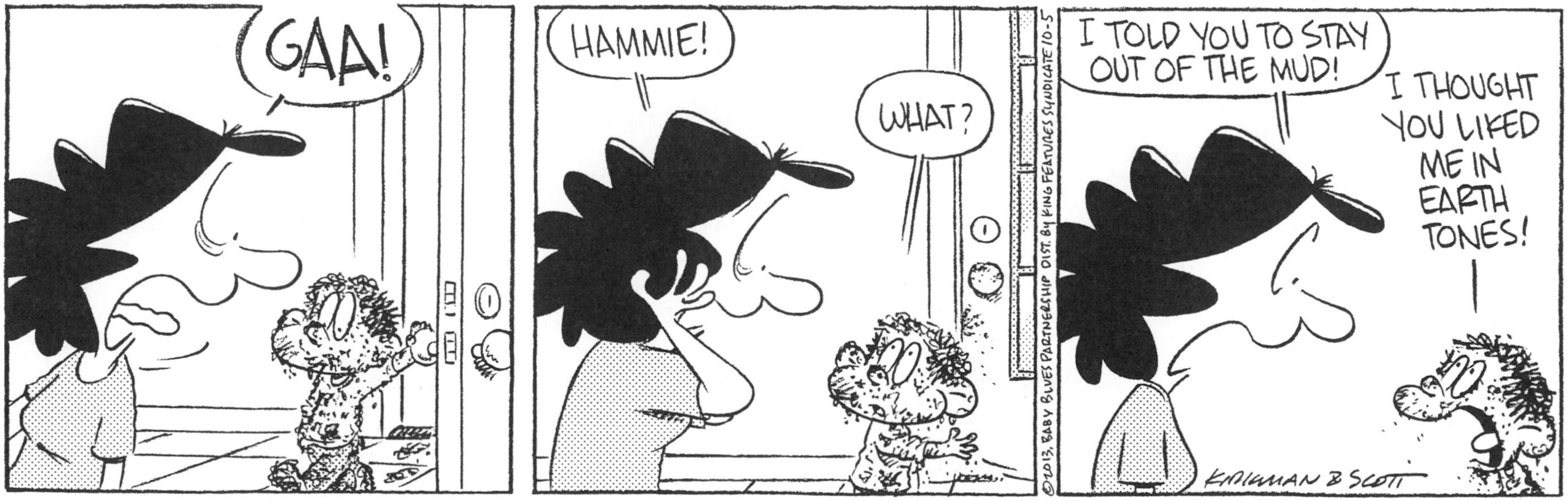
GAA!
HAMMIE!
WHAT?
I TOLD YOU TO STAY OUT OF THE MUD!
I THOUGHT YOU LIKED ME IN EARTH TONES!
© 2013, BABY BLUES PARTNERSHIP DIST. BY KING FEATURES SYNDICATE 10-5
KIRKMAN & SCOTT

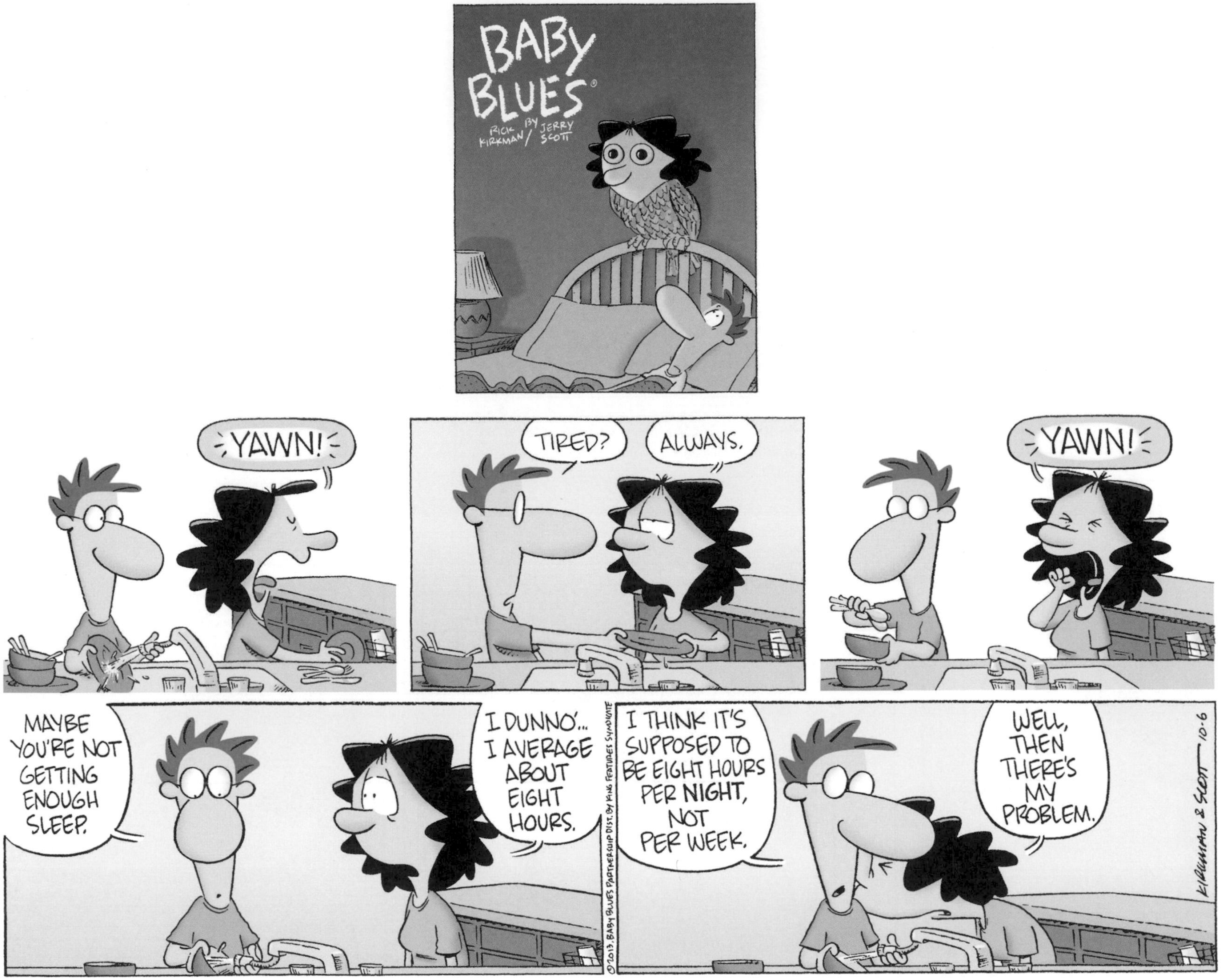
BABY BLUES®
BY RICK KIRKMAN / JERRY SCOTT
YAWN!
TIRED?
ALWAYS.
YAWN!
MAYBE YOU'RE NOT GETTING ENOUGH SLEEP.
I DUNNO'... I AVERAGE ABOUT EIGHT HOURS.
©2013, BABY BLUES PARTNERSHIP DIST. BY KING FEATURES SYNDICATE
I THINK IT'S SUPPOSED TO BE EIGHT HOURS PER NIGHT, NOT PER WEEK.
WELL, THEN THERE'S MY PROBLEM.
KIRKMAN & SCOTT
10-6

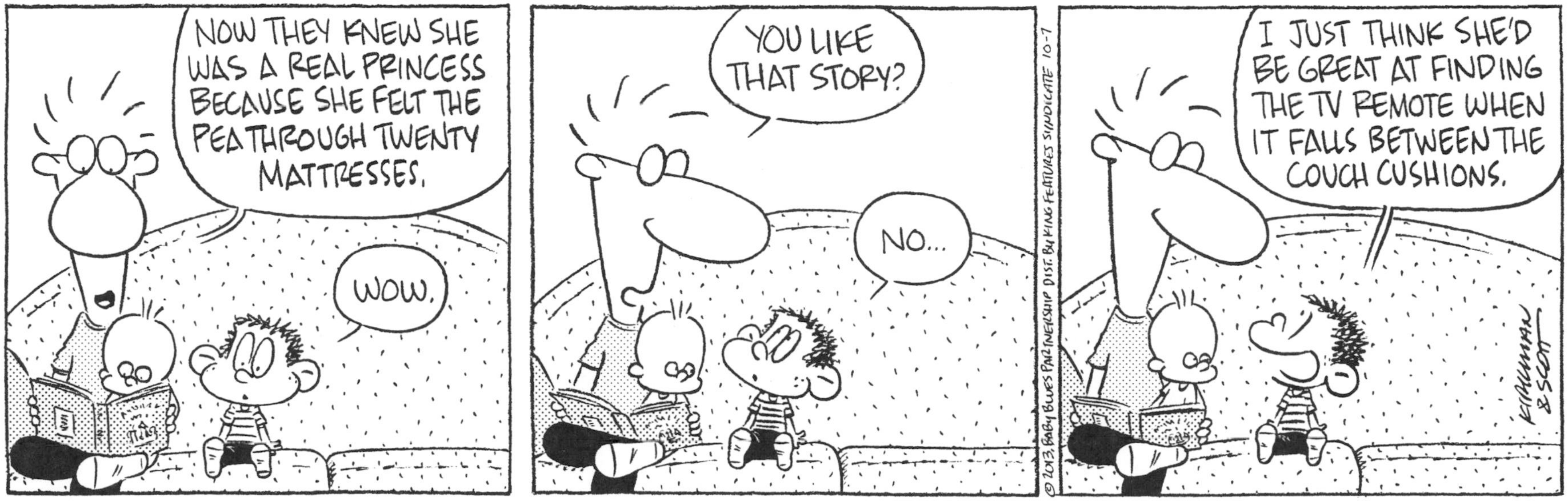
NOW THEY KNEW SHE WAS A REAL PRINCESS BECAUSE SHE FELT THE PEA THROUGH TWENTY MATTRESSES.
WOW.
YOU LIKE THAT STORY?
NO...
© 2013, BABY BLUES PARTNERSHIP DIST. BY KING FEATURES SYNDICATE 10-7
I JUST THINK SHE'D BE GREAT AT FINDING THE TV REMOTE WHEN IT FALLS BETWEEN THE COUCH CUSHIONS.
KIRKMAN & SCOTT

Jerry: Fairy tales can have really practical applications if you look at them in the right way.

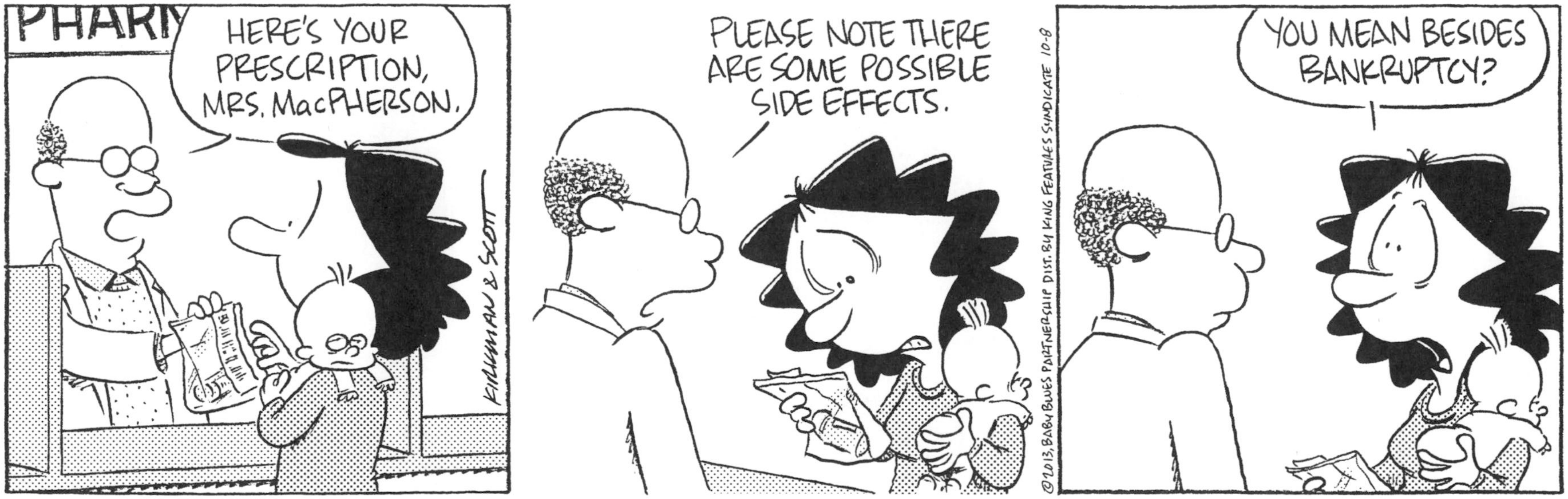
PHARM
HERE'S YOUR PRESCRIPTION, MRS. MacPHERSON.
KIRKMAN & SCOTT
PLEASE NOTE THERE ARE SOME POSSIBLE SIDE EFFECTS.
© 2013, BABY BLUES PARTNERSHIP DIST. BY KING FEATURES SYNDICATE 10-8
YOU MEAN BESIDES BANKRUPTCY?

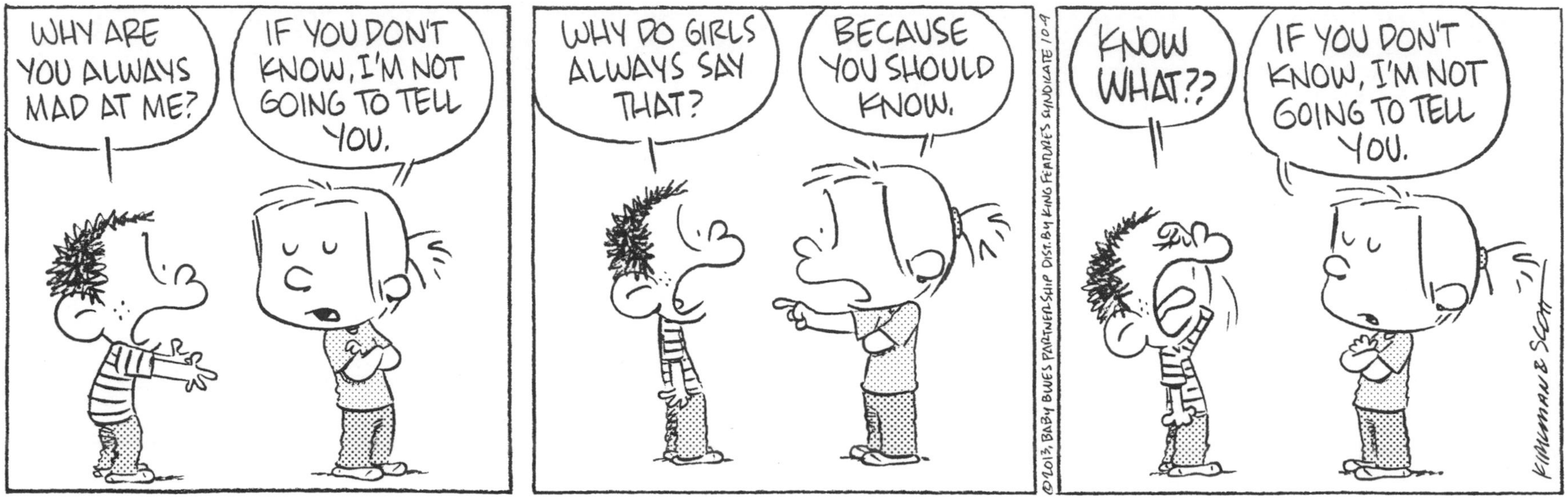
WHY ARE YOU ALWAYS MAD AT ME?
IF YOU DON'T KNOW, I'M NOT GOING TO TELL YOU.
WHY DO GIRLS ALWAYS SAY THAT?
BECAUSE YOU SHOULD KNOW.
KNOW WHAT??
IF YOU DON'T KNOW, I'M NOT GOING TO TELL YOU.
©2013, BABY BLUES PARTNERSHIP DIST. BY KING FEATURES SYNDICATE 10-9
KIRKMAN & SCOTT

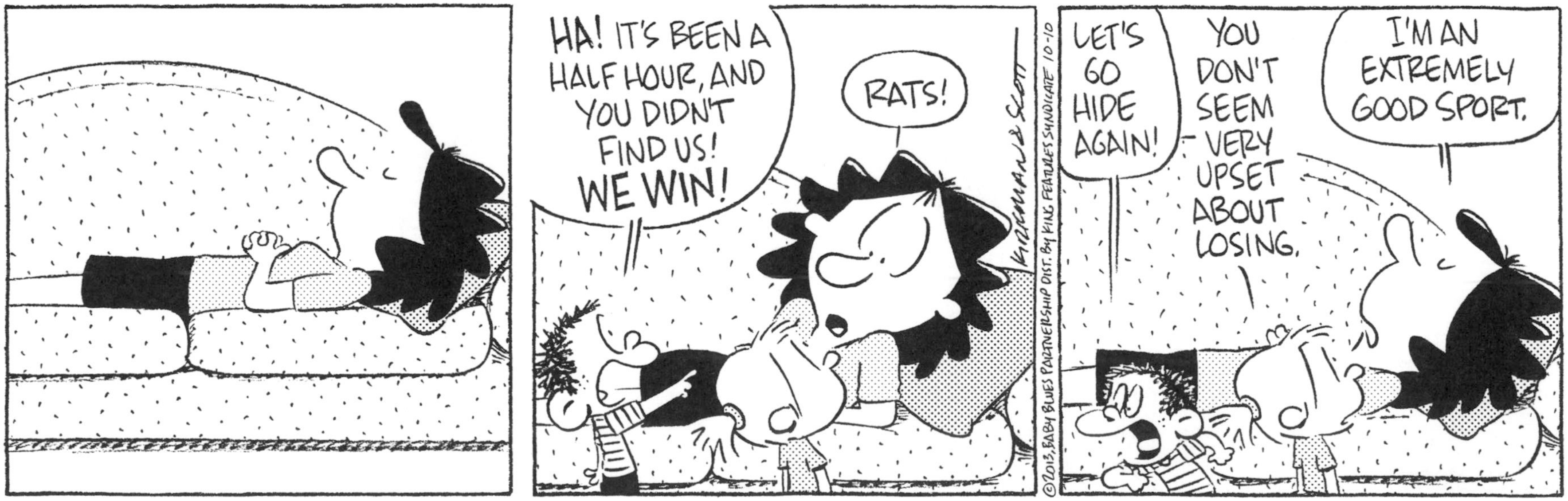
HA! IT'S BEEN A HALF HOUR, AND YOU DIDN'T FIND US! WE WIN!
RATS!
KIRKMAN & SCOTT
©2013, BABY BLUES PARTNERSHIP DIST. BY KING FEATURES SYNDICATE 10-10
LET'S GO HIDE AGAIN!
YOU DON'T SEEM VERY UPSET ABOUT LOSING.
I'M AN EXTREMELY GOOD SPORT.

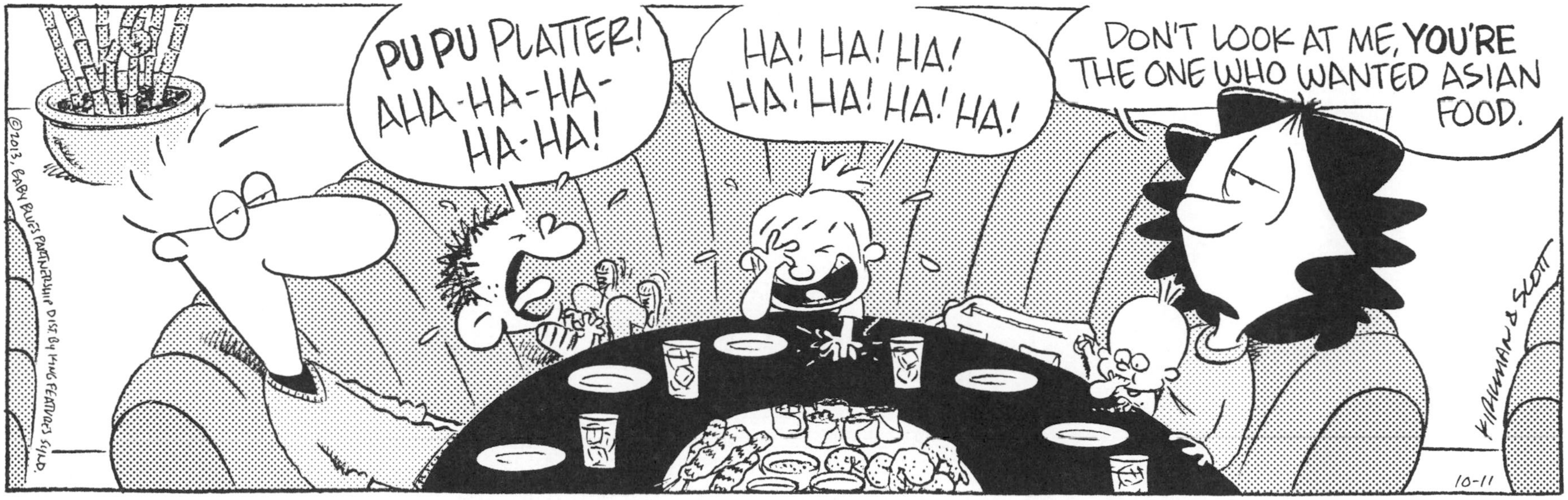
PU PU PLATTER! AHA-HA-HA-HA-HA!
HA! HA! HA! HA! HA! HA! HA!
DON'T LOOK AT ME, YOU'RE THE ONE WHO WANTED ASIAN FOOD.
©2013, BABY BLUES PARTNERSHIP DIST. BY KING FEATURES SYND.
KIRKMAN & SCOTT
10-11

Rick: Secretly, inside, I still giggle when I see that menu item.

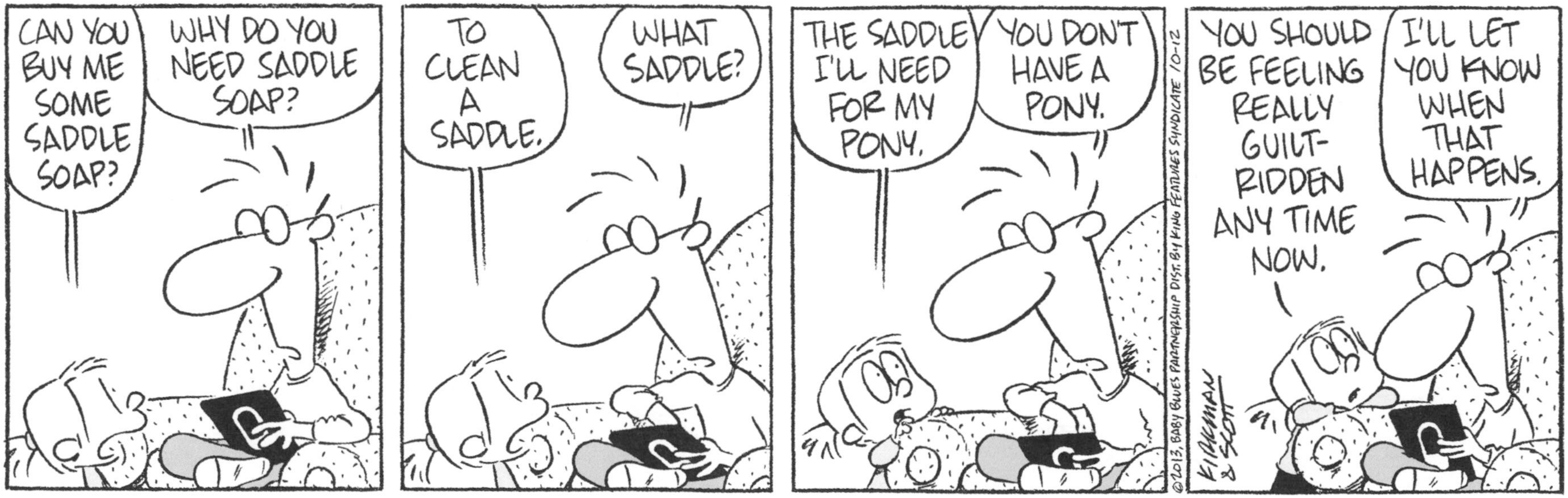
CAN YOU BUY ME SOME SADDLE SOAP?
WHY DO YOU NEED SADDLE SOAP?
TO CLEAN A SADDLE.
WHAT SADDLE?
THE SADDLE I'LL NEED FOR MY PONY.
YOU DON'T HAVE A PONY.
©2013, BABY BLUES PARTNERSHIP DIST. BY KING FEATURES SYNDICATE 10-12
KIRKMAN & SCOTT
YOU SHOULD BE FEELING REALLY GUILT-RIDDEN ANY TIME NOW.
I'LL LET YOU KNOW WHEN THAT HAPPENS.

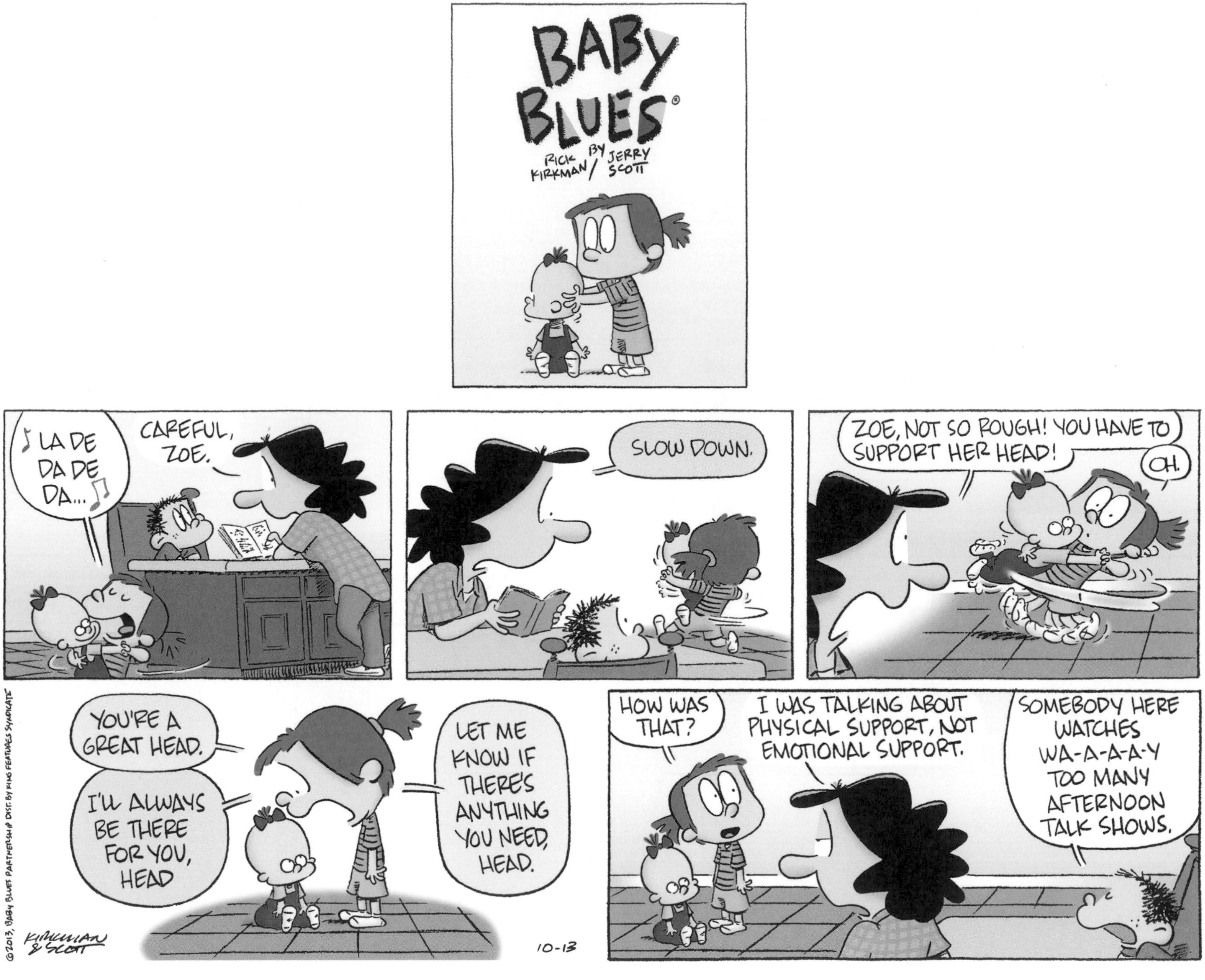
BABY BLUES®
BY RICK KIRKMAN / JERRY SCOTT
♪ LA DE DA DE DA... ♫
CAREFUL, ZOE.
SLOW DOWN.
ZOE, NOT SO ROUGH! YOU HAVE TO SUPPORT HER HEAD!
OH.
YOU'RE A GREAT HEAD.
I'LL ALWAYS BE THERE FOR YOU, HEAD
LET ME KNOW IF THERE'S ANYTHING YOU NEED, HEAD.
©2013, BABY BLUES PARTNERSHIP DIST. BY KING FEATURES SYNDICATE
KIRKMAN & SCOTT
10-13
HOW WAS THAT?
I WAS TALKING ABOUT PHYSICAL SUPPORT, NOT EMOTIONAL SUPPORT.
SOMEBODY HERE WATCHES WA-A-A-A-Y TOO MANY AFTERNOON TALK SHOWS.

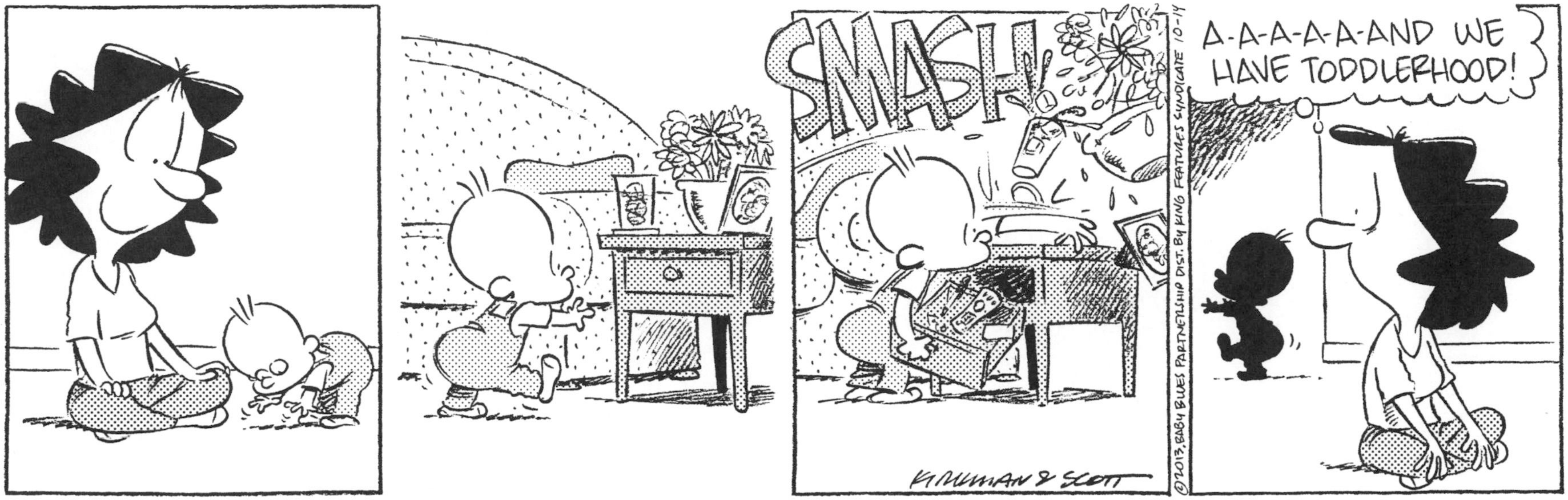
SMASH!
KIRKMAN & SCOTT
©2013, BABY BLUES PARTNERSHIP DIST. BY KING FEATURES SYNDICATE 10-14
A-A-A-A-A-AND WE HAVE TODDLERHOOD!

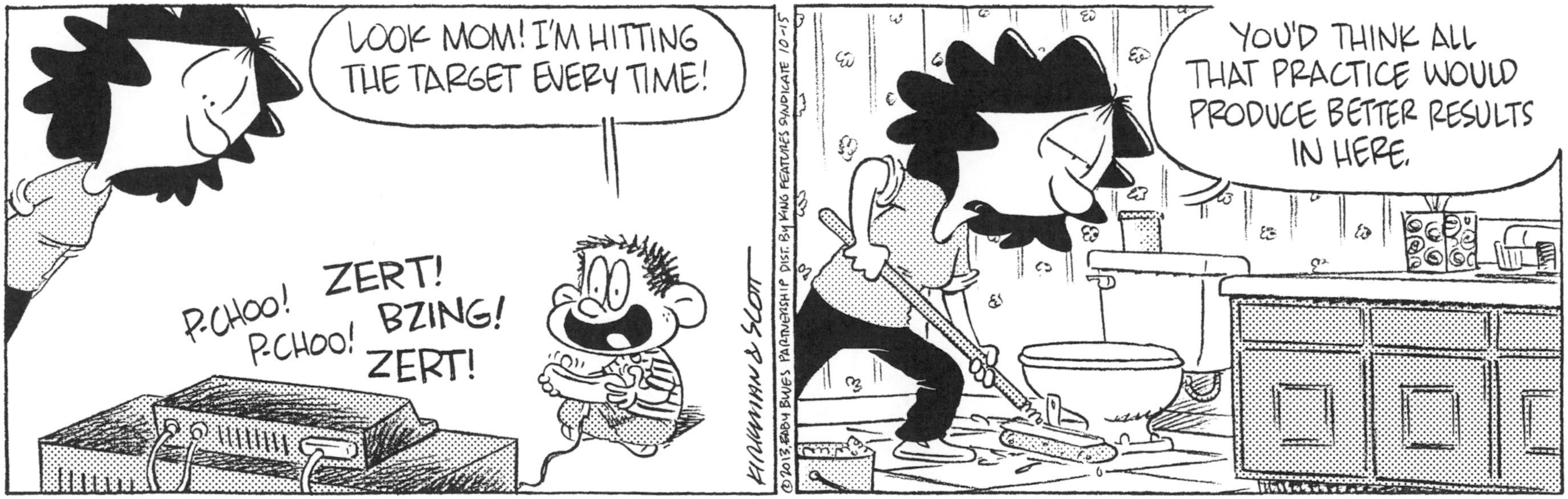
LOOK MOM! I'M HITTING THE TARGET EVERY TIME!
P-CHOO! P-CHOO!
ZERT! BZING! ZERT!
KIRKMAN & SCOTT
©2013, BABY BLUES PARTNERSHIP DIST. BY KING FEATURES SYNDICATE 10-15
YOU'D THINK ALL THAT PRACTICE WOULD PRODUCE BETTER RESULTS IN HERE.

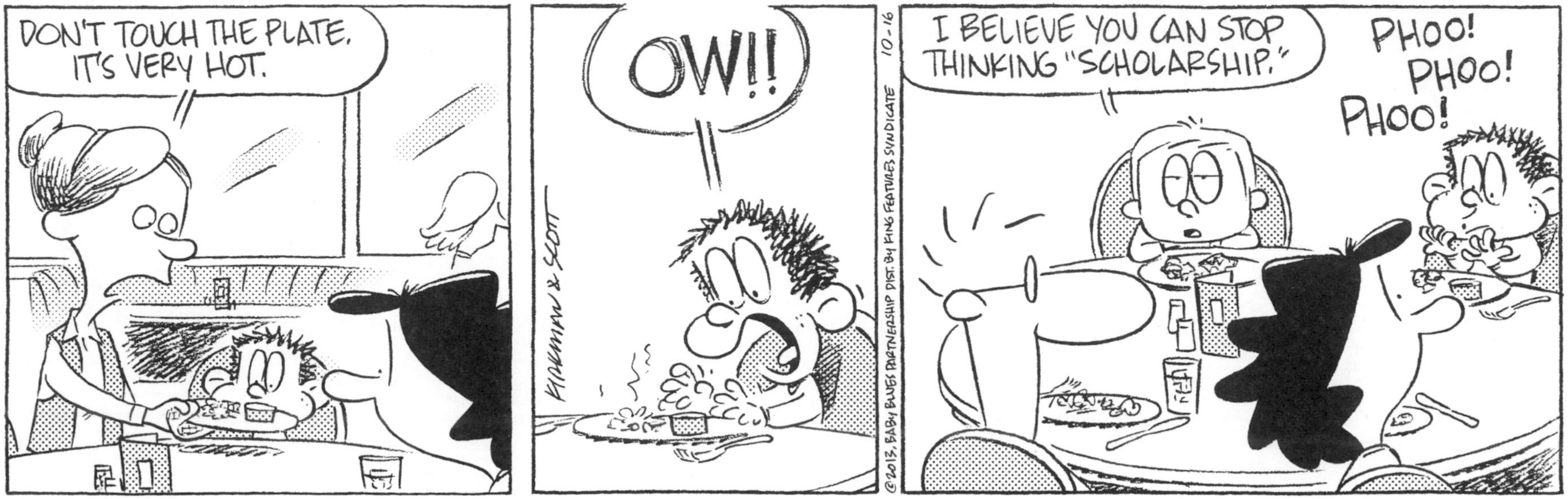
DON'T TOUCH THE PLATE. IT'S VERY HOT.
OW!!
KIRKMAN & SCOTT
10-16
©2013, BABY BLUES PARTNERSHIP DIST. BY KING FEATURES SYNDICATE
I BELIEVE YOU CAN STOP THINKING "SCHOLARSHIP."
PHOO! PHOO! PHOO!

Jerry: Show of hands: How many of you also touch the plate just to see if it's true? I thought so.

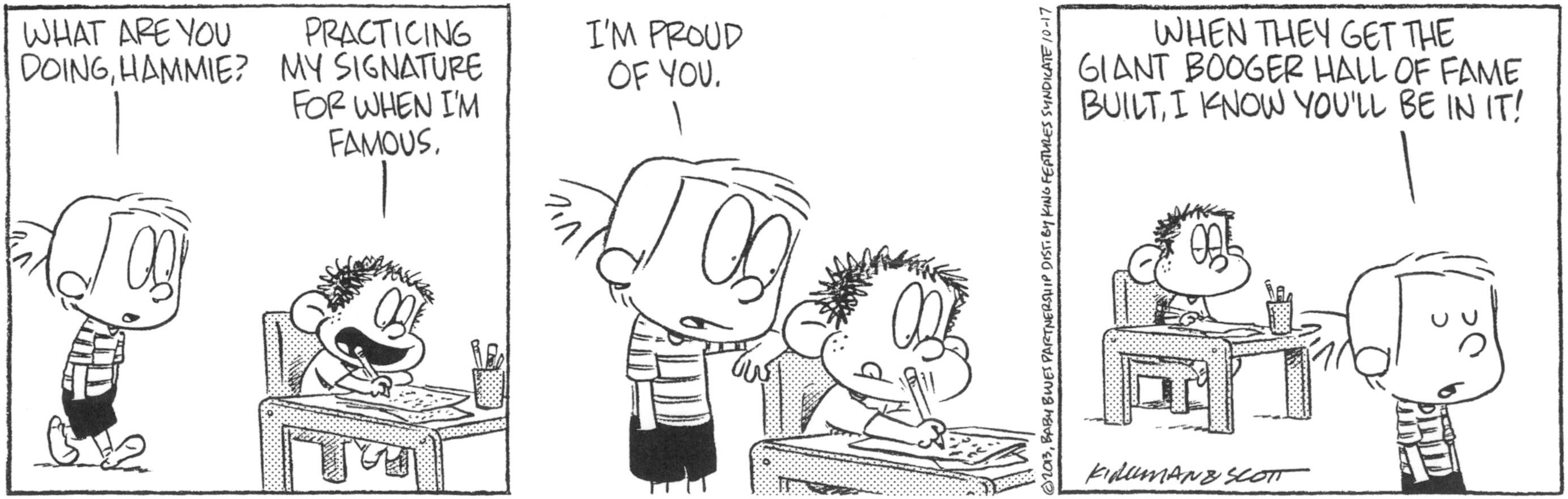
WHAT ARE YOU DOING, HAMMIE?
PRACTICING MY SIGNATURE FOR WHEN I'M FAMOUS.
I'M PROUD OF YOU.
©2013, BABY BLUES PARTNERSHIP DIST. BY KING FEATURES SYNDICATE 10-17
WHEN THEY GET THE GIANT BOOGER HALL OF FAME BUILT, I KNOW YOU'LL BE IN IT!
KIRKMAN & SCOTT

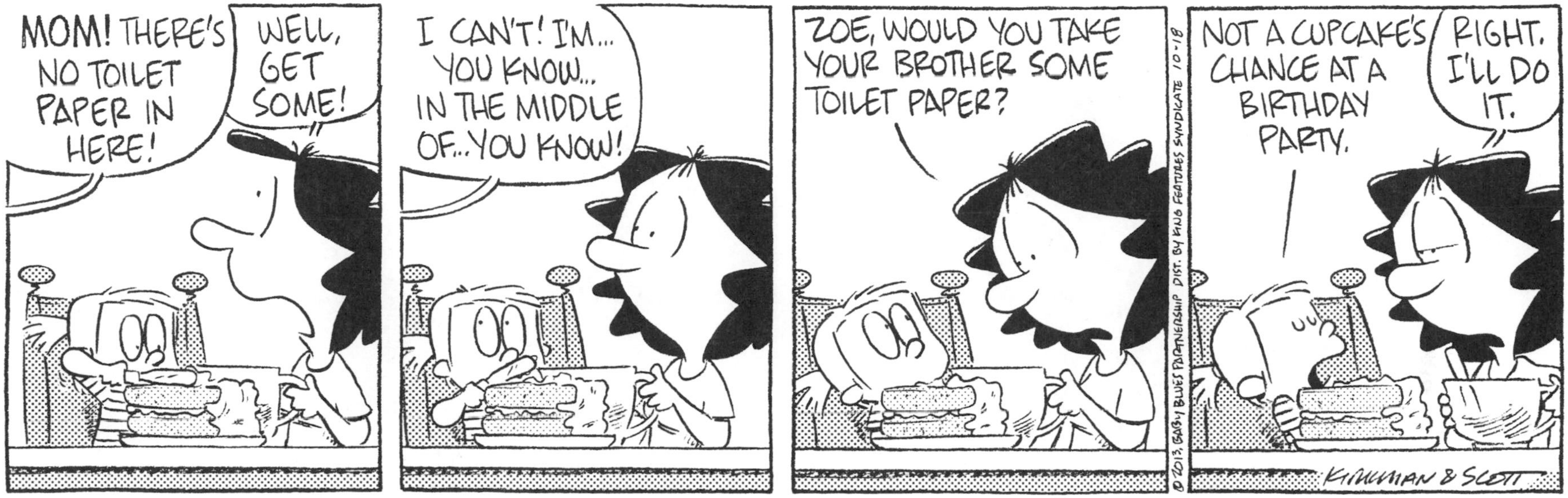
MOM! THERE'S NO TOILET PAPER IN HERE!
WELL, GET SOME!
I CAN'T! I'M... YOU KNOW... IN THE MIDDLE OF... YOU KNOW!
ZOE, WOULD YOU TAKE YOUR BROTHER SOME TOILET PAPER?
© 2013, BABY BLUES PARTNERSHIP DIST. BY KING FEATURES SYNDICATE 10-18
NOT A CUPCAKE'S CHANCE AT A BIRTHDAY PARTY.
RIGHT. I'LL DO IT.
KIRKMAN & SCOTT

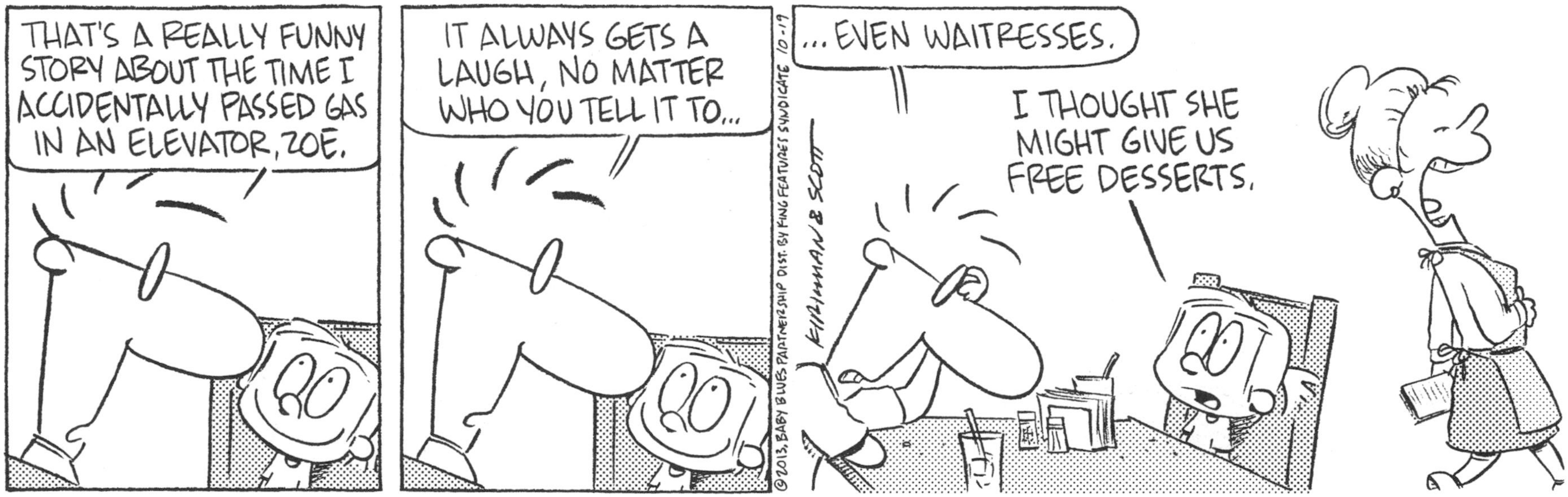
THAT'S A REALLY FUNNY STORY ABOUT THE TIME I ACCIDENTALLY PASSED GAS IN AN ELEVATOR, ZOE.
IT ALWAYS GETS A LAUGH, NO MATTER WHO YOU TELL IT TO...
© 2013, BABY BLUES PARTNERSHIP DIST. BY KING FEATURES SYNDICATE 10-19
KIRKMAN & SCOTT
... EVEN WAITRESSES.
I THOUGHT SHE MIGHT GIVE US FREE DESSERTS.

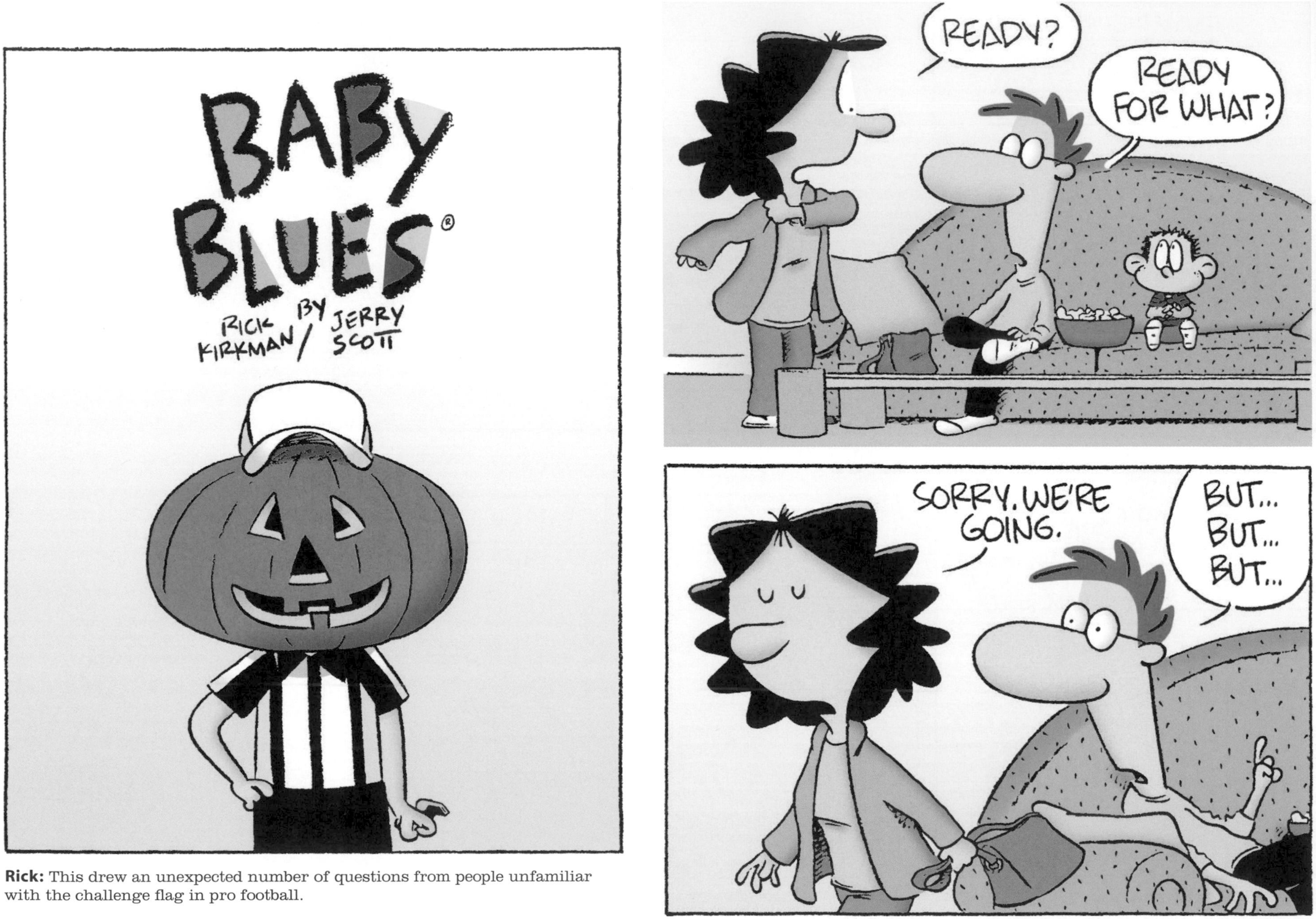
BABY BLUES®
BY RICK KIRKMAN / JERRY SCOTT
READY?
READY FOR WHAT?
SORRY. WE'RE GOING.
BUT... BUT... BUT...

Rick: This drew an unexpected number of questions from people unfamiliar with the challenge flag in pro football.

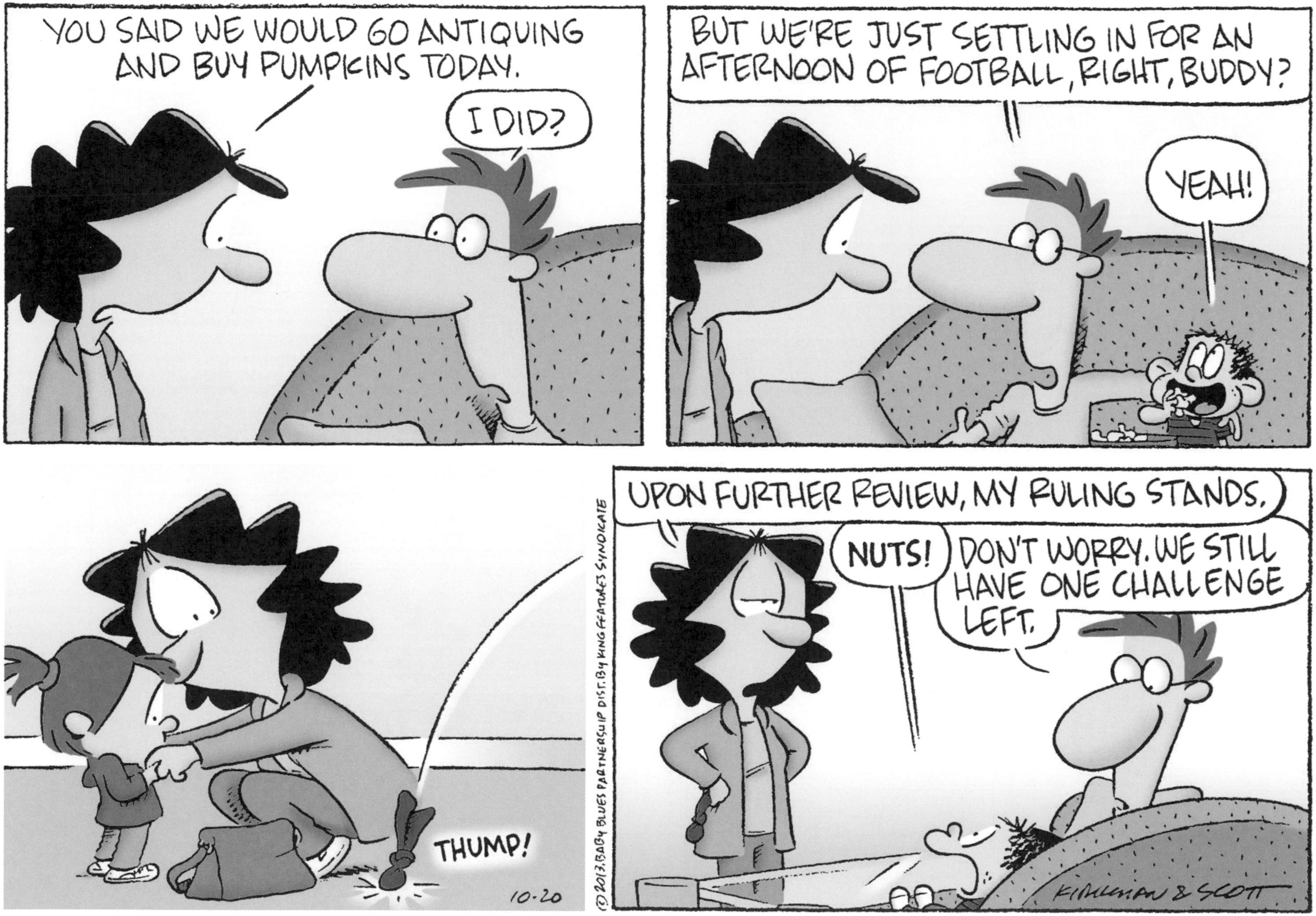
YOU SAID WE WOULD GO ANTIQUING AND BUY PUMPKINS TODAY.
I DID?
BUT WE'RE JUST SETTLING IN FOR AN AFTERNOON OF FOOTBALL, RIGHT, BUDDY?
YEAH!
THUMP!
10-20
© 2013, BABY BLUES PARTNERSHIP DIST. BY KING FEATURES SYNDICATE
UPON FURTHER REVIEW, MY RULING STANDS.
NUTS!
DON'T WORRY. WE STILL HAVE ONE CHALLENGE LEFT.
KIRKMAN & SCOTT

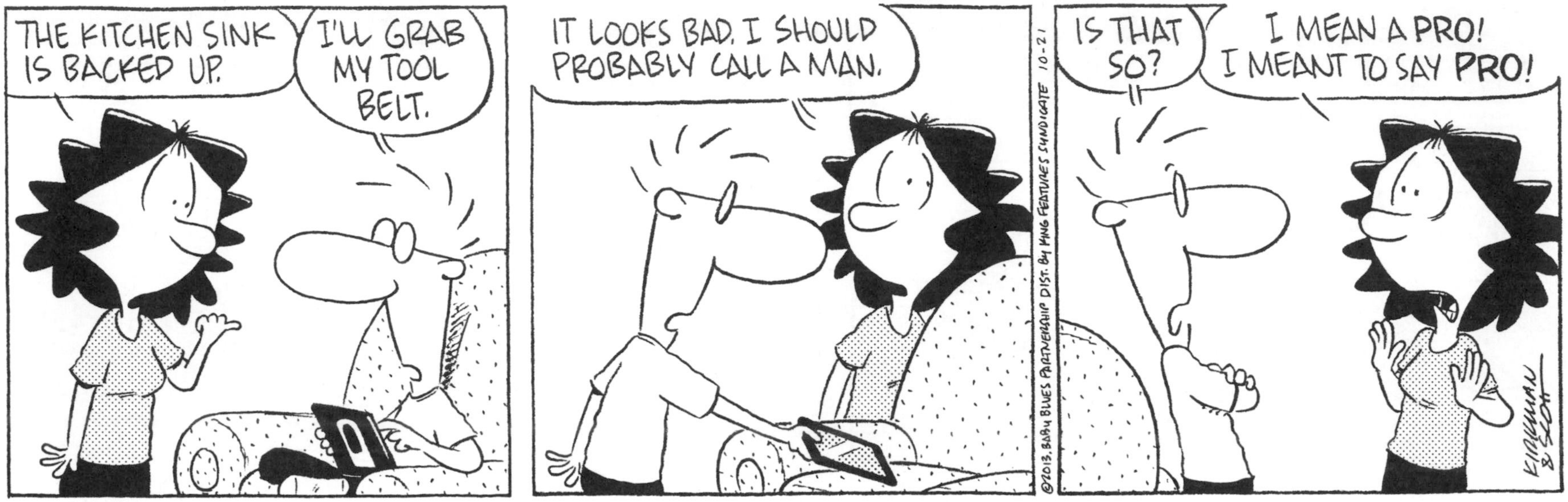
THE KITCHEN SINK IS BACKED UP.
I'LL GRAB MY TOOL BELT.
IT LOOKS BAD. I SHOULD PROBABLY CALL A MAN.
IS THAT SO?
I MEAN A PRO! I MEANT TO SAY PRO!
©2013, BABY BLUES PARTNERSHIP DIST. BY KING FEATURES SYNDICATE 10-21
KIRKMAN & SCOTT

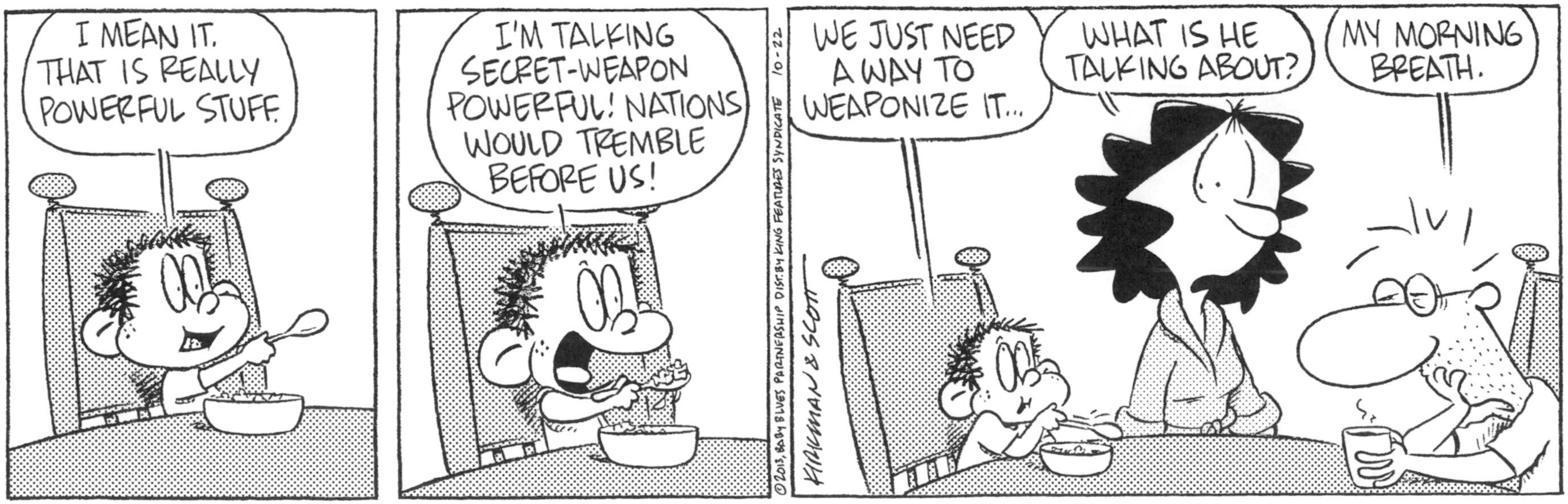
I MEAN IT. THAT IS REALLY POWERFUL STUFF.
I'M TALKING SECRET-WEAPON POWERFUL! NATIONS WOULD TREMBLE BEFORE US!
WE JUST NEED A WAY TO WEAPONIZE IT...
WHAT IS HE TALKING ABOUT?
MY MORNING BREATH.
©2013, BABY BLUES PARTNERSHIP DIST. BY KING FEATURES SYNDICATE 10-22
KIRKMAN & SCOTT

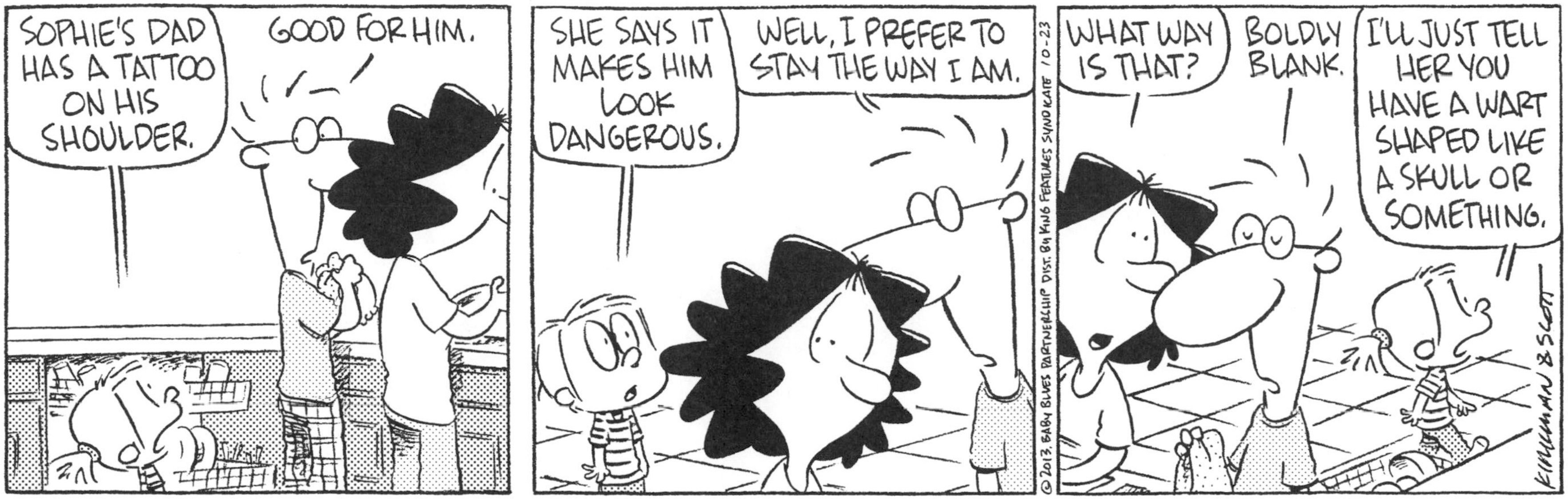
SOPHIE'S DAD HAS A TATTOO ON HIS SHOULDER.
GOOD FOR HIM.
SHE SAYS IT MAKES HIM LOOK DANGEROUS.
WELL, I PREFER TO STAY THE WAY I AM.
© 2013, BABY BLUES PARTNERSHIP DIST. BY KING FEATURES SYNDICATE 10-23
WHAT WAY IS THAT?
BOLDLY BLANK.
I'LL JUST TELL HER YOU HAVE A WART SHAPED LIKE A SKULL OR SOMETHING.
KIRKMAN & SCOTT

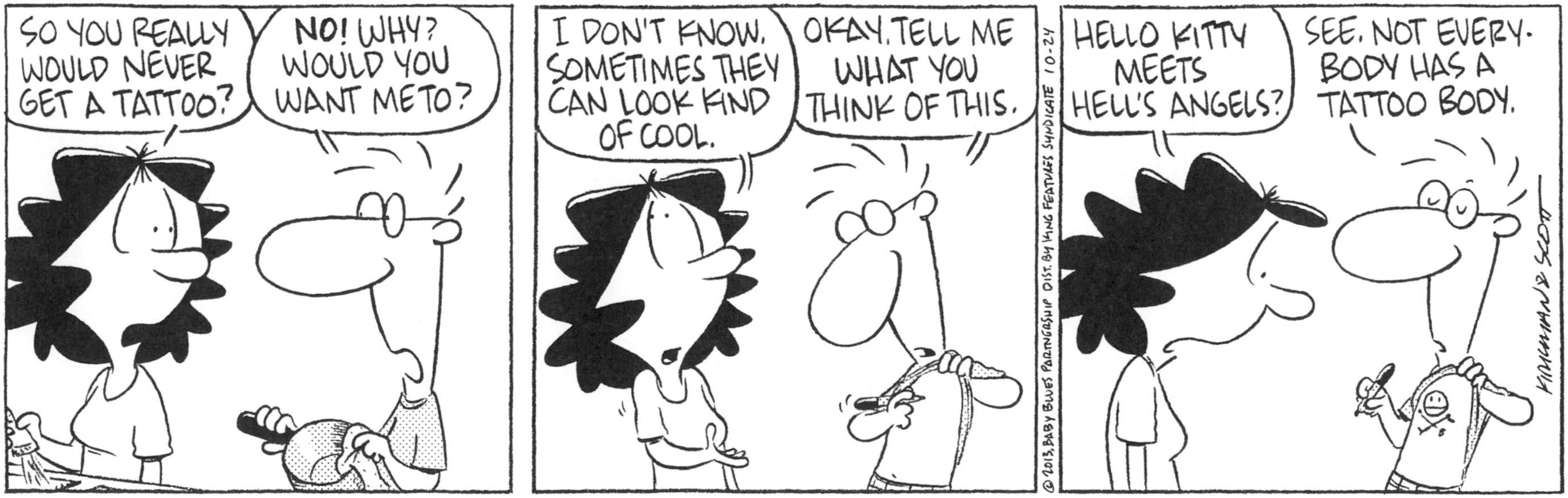
SO YOU REALLY WOULD NEVER GET A TATTOO?
NO! WHY? WOULD YOU WANT ME TO?
I DON'T KNOW. SOMETIMES THEY CAN LOOK KIND OF COOL.
OKAY. TELL ME WHAT YOU THINK OF THIS.
© 2013, BABY BLUES PARTNERSHIP DIST. BY KING FEATURES SYNDICATE 10-24
HELLO KITTY MEETS HELL'S ANGELS?
SEE. NOT EVERYBODY HAS A TATTOO BODY.
KIRKMAN & SCOTT

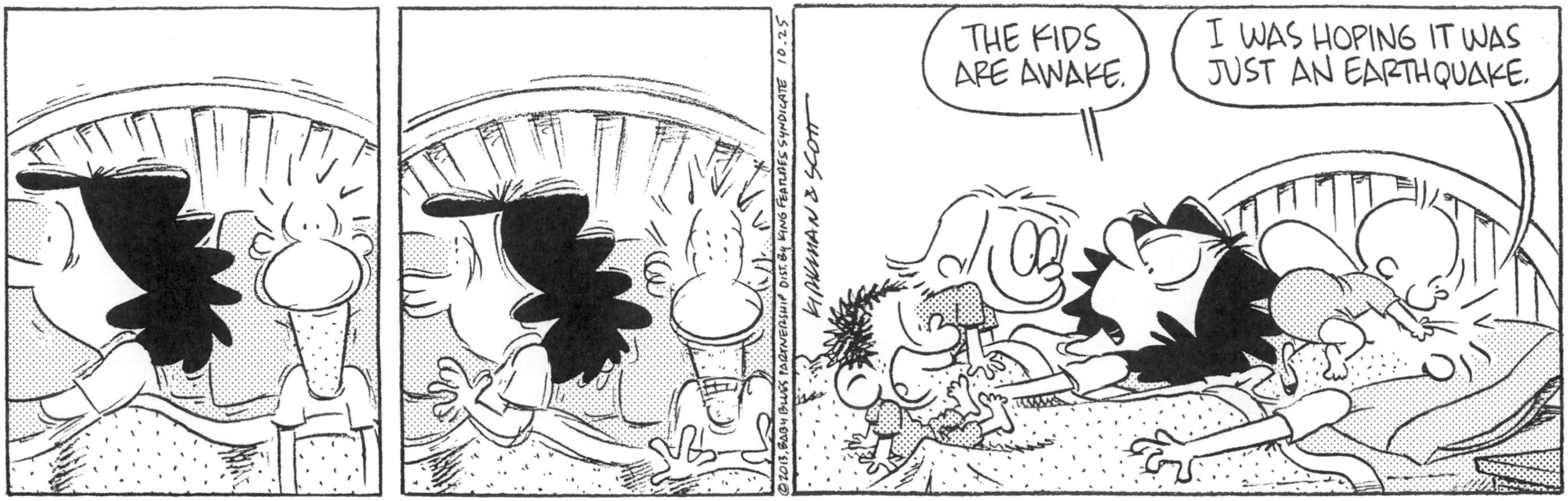

THE KIDS ARE AWAKE.
I WAS HOPING IT WAS JUST AN EARTHQUAKE.
©2013, BABY BLUES PARTNERSHIP DIST. BY KING FEATURES SYNDICATE 10.25
KIRKMAN & SCOTT

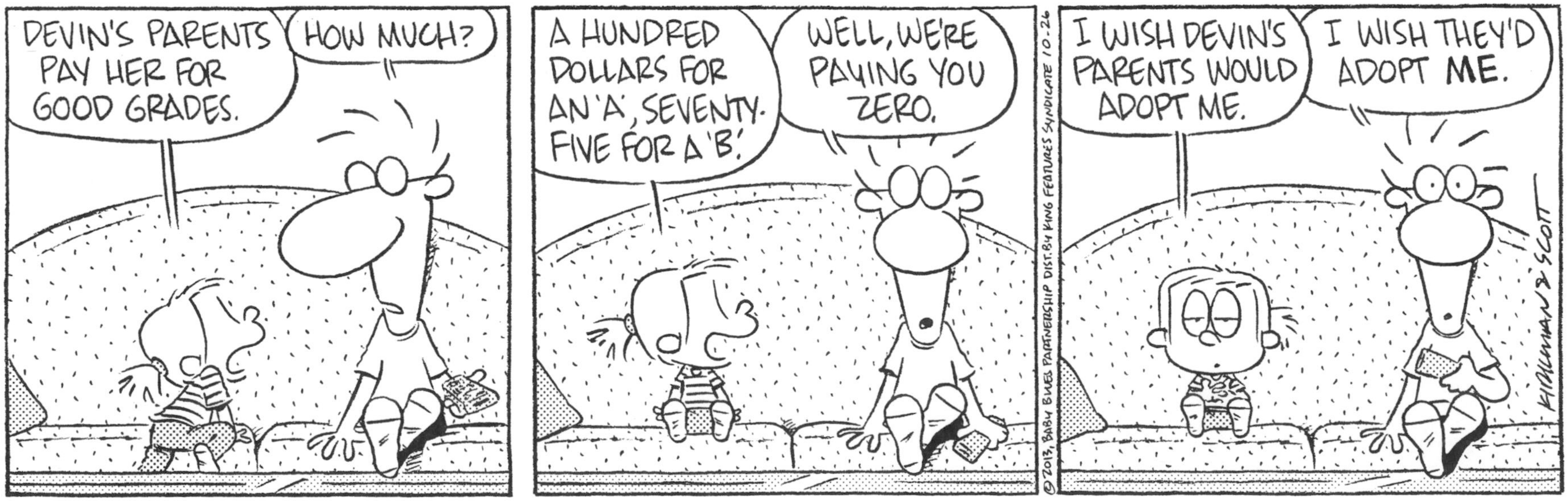

DEVIN'S PARENTS PAY HER FOR GOOD GRADES.
HOW MUCH?
A HUNDRED DOLLARS FOR AN 'A', SEVENTY-FIVE FOR A 'B'.
WELL, WE'RE PAYING YOU ZERO.
©2013, BABY BLUES PARTNERSHIP DIST. BY KING FEATURES SYNDICATE 10.26
I WISH DEVIN'S PARENTS WOULD ADOPT ME.
I WISH THEY'D ADOPT **ME**.
KIRKMAN & SCOTT

Rick: Peer pressure is not just for kids.

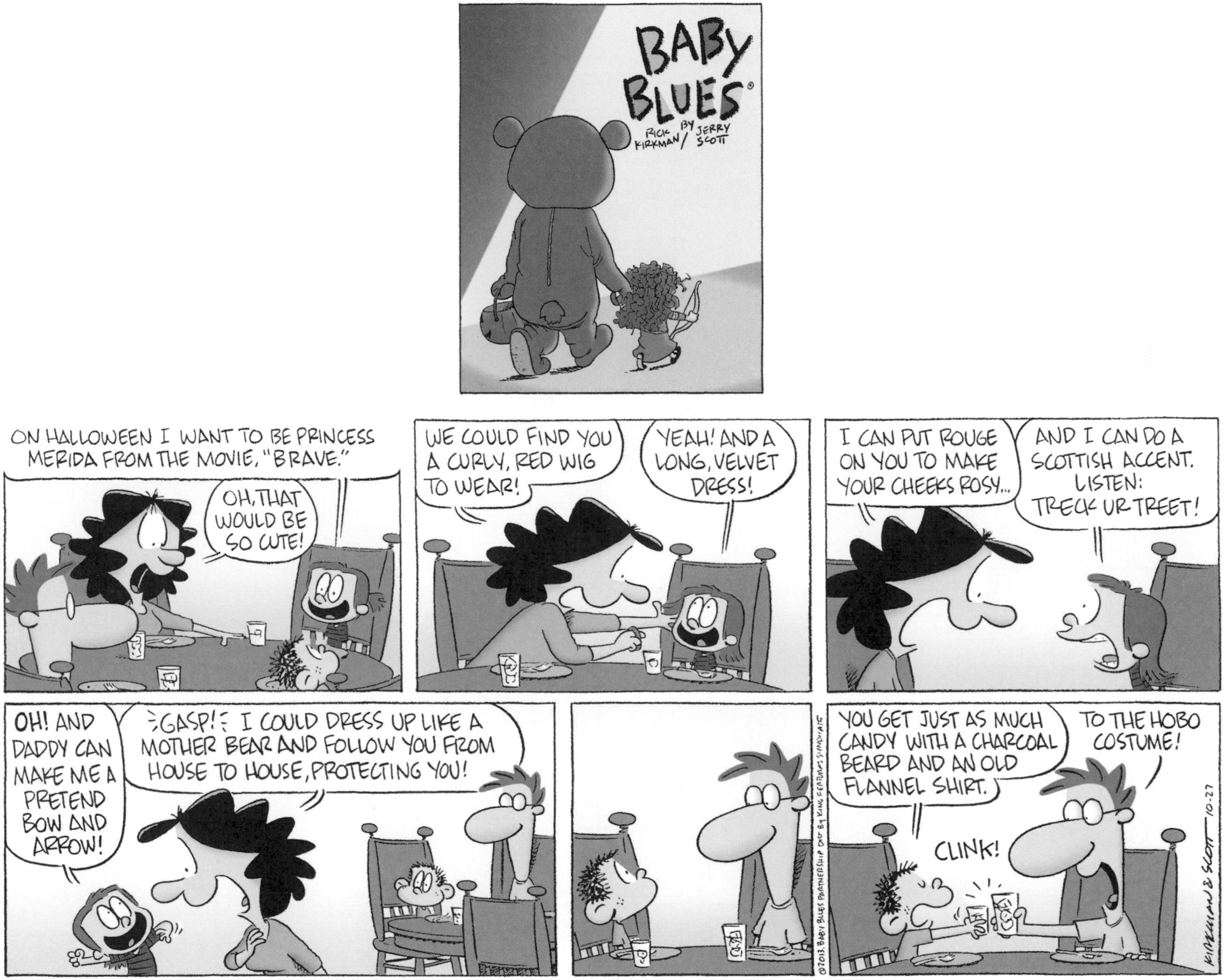
BABY BLUES®
RICK KIRKMAN / BY JERRY SCOTT
ON HALLOWEEN I WANT TO BE PRINCESS MERIDA FROM THE MOVIE, "BRAVE."
OH, THAT WOULD BE SO CUTE!
WE COULD FIND YOU A CURLY, RED WIG TO WEAR!
YEAH! AND A LONG, VELVET DRESS!
I CAN PUT ROUGE ON YOU TO MAKE YOUR CHEEKS ROSY...
AND I CAN DO A SCOTTISH ACCENT. LISTEN: TRECK UR TREET!
OH! AND DADDY CAN MAKE ME A PRETEND BOW AND ARROW!
GASP! I COULD DRESS UP LIKE A MOTHER BEAR AND FOLLOW YOU FROM HOUSE TO HOUSE, PROTECTING YOU!
YOU GET JUST AS MUCH CANDY WITH A CHARCOAL BEARD AND AN OLD FLANNEL SHIRT.
TO THE HOBO COSTUME!
CLINK!
KIRKMAN & SCOTT
10-27

Jerry: Last Halloween I shaved off the left side of my beard and mustache and went to a party. Nobody noticed. Next year, hobo again.

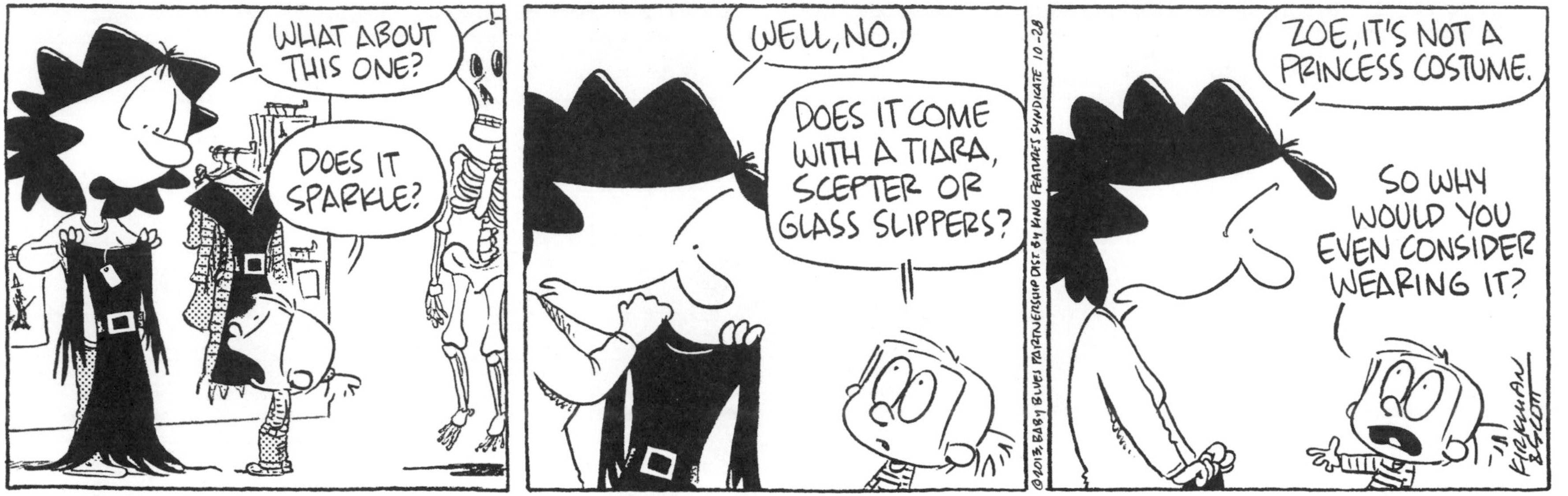
WHAT ABOUT THIS ONE?
DOES IT SPARKLE?
WELL, NO.
DOES IT COME WITH A TIARA, SCEPTER OR GLASS SLIPPERS?
ZOE, IT'S NOT A PRINCESS COSTUME.
SO WHY WOULD YOU EVEN CONSIDER WEARING IT?
©2013, BABY BLUES PARTNERSHIP DIST BY KING FEATURES SYNDICATE 10-28
KIRKMAN & SCOTT

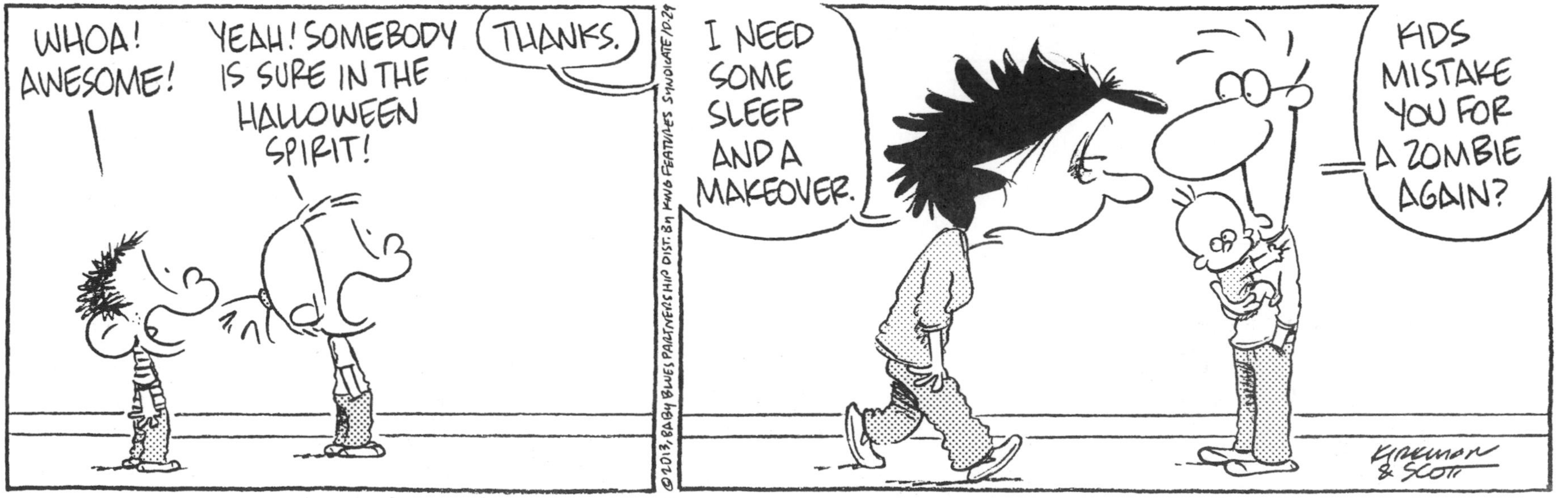
WHOA! AWESOME!
YEAH! SOMEBODY IS SURE IN THE HALLOWEEN SPIRIT!
THANKS.
I NEED SOME SLEEP AND A MAKEOVER.
KIDS MISTAKE YOU FOR A ZOMBIE AGAIN?
©2013, BABY BLUES PARTNERSHIP DIST. BY KING FEATURES SYNDICATE 10-29
KIRKMAN & SCOTT

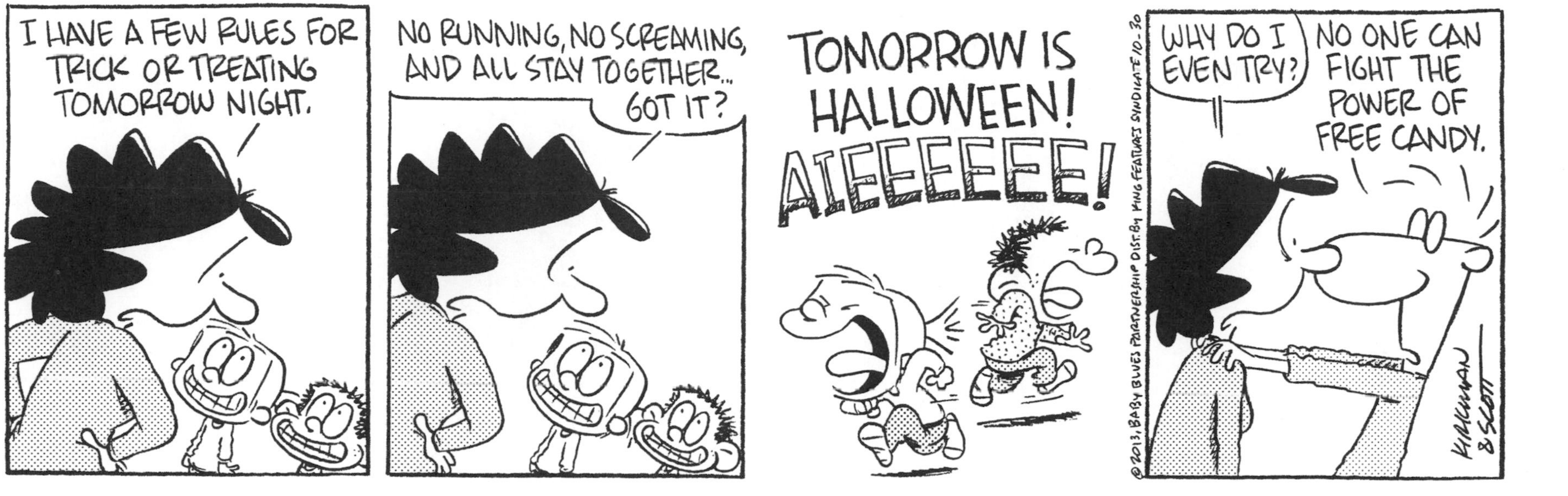
I HAVE A FEW RULES FOR TRICK OR TREATING TOMORROW NIGHT.
NO RUNNING, NO SCREAMING, AND ALL STAY TOGETHER... GOT IT?
TOMORROW IS HALLOWEEN!
AIEEEEEEE!
WHY DO I EVEN TRY?
NO ONE CAN FIGHT THE POWER OF FREE CANDY.
©2013, BABY BLUES PARTNERSHIP DIST. BY KING FEATURES SYNDICATE 10-30
KIRKMAN & SCOTT

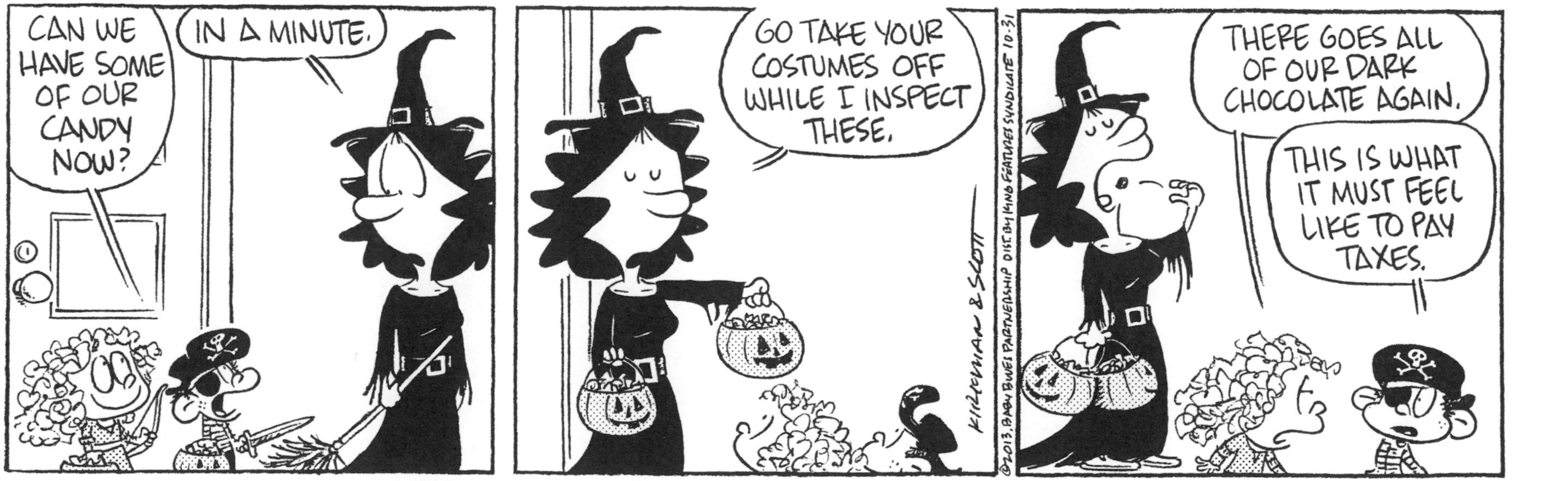
CAN WE HAVE SOME OF OUR CANDY NOW?
IN A MINUTE.
GO TAKE YOUR COSTUMES OFF WHILE I INSPECT THESE.
KIRKMAN & SCOTT
©2013, BABY BLUES PARTNERSHIP DIST. BY KING FEATURES SYNDICATE 10-31
THERE GOES ALL OF OUR DARK CHOCOLATE AGAIN.
THIS IS WHAT IT MUST FEEL LIKE TO PAY TAXES.

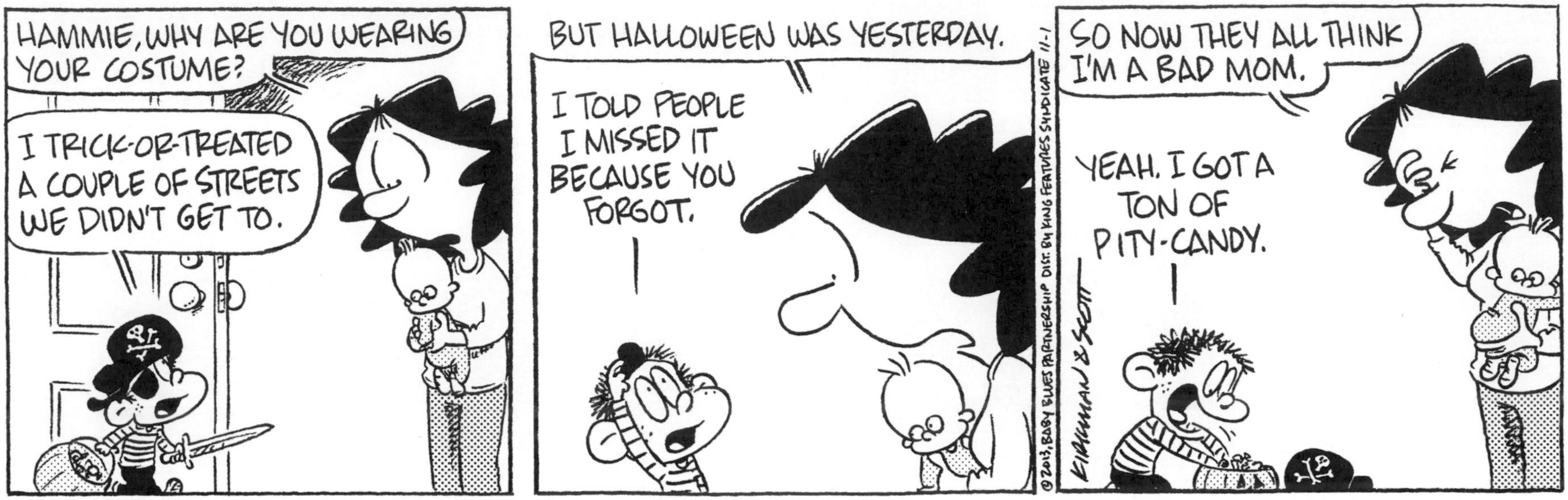
HAMMIE, WHY ARE YOU WEARING YOUR COSTUME?
I TRICK-OR-TREATED A COUPLE OF STREETS WE DIDN'T GET TO.
BUT HALLOWEEN WAS YESTERDAY.
I TOLD PEOPLE I MISSED IT BECAUSE YOU FORGOT.
©2013, BABY BLUES PARTNERSHIP DIST. BY KING FEATURES SYNDICATE 11-1
KIRKMAN & SCOTT
SO NOW THEY ALL THINK I'M A BAD MOM.
YEAH. I GOT A TON OF PITY-CANDY.

Rick: I have to admire the ingenuity of that idea. And cringe for Wanda.

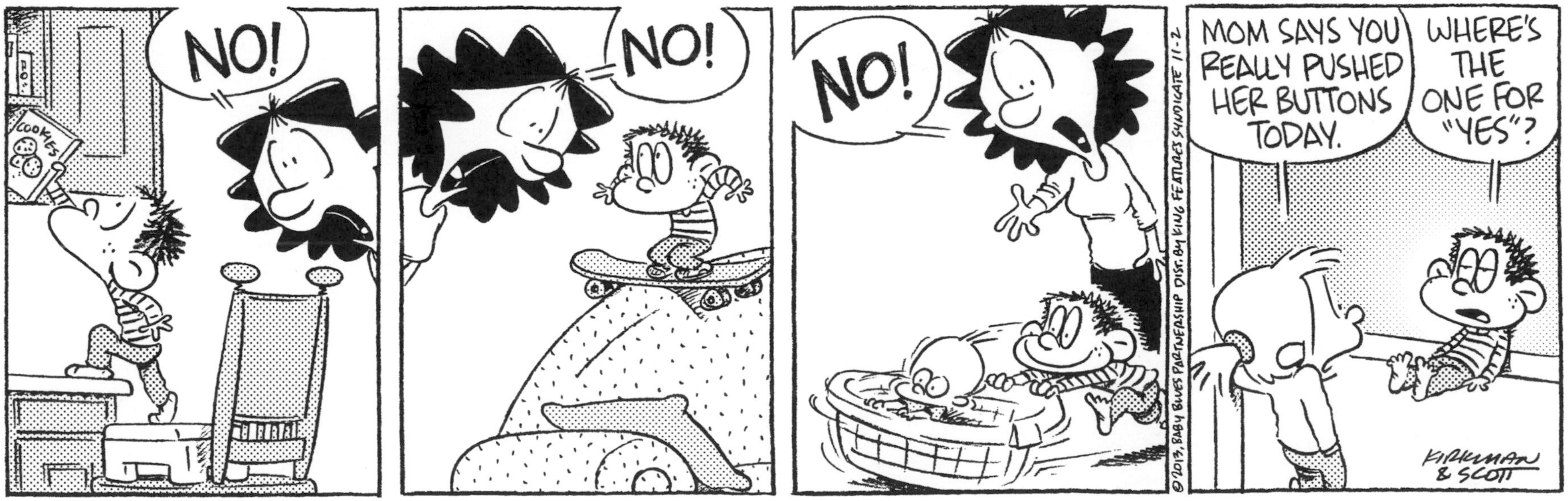
COOKIES
NO!
NO!
NO!
©2013, BABY BLUES PARTNERSHIP DIST. BY KING FEATURES SYNDICATE 11-2
MOM SAYS YOU REALLY PUSHED HER BUTTONS TODAY.
WHERE'S THE ONE FOR "YES"?
KIRKMAN & SCOTT

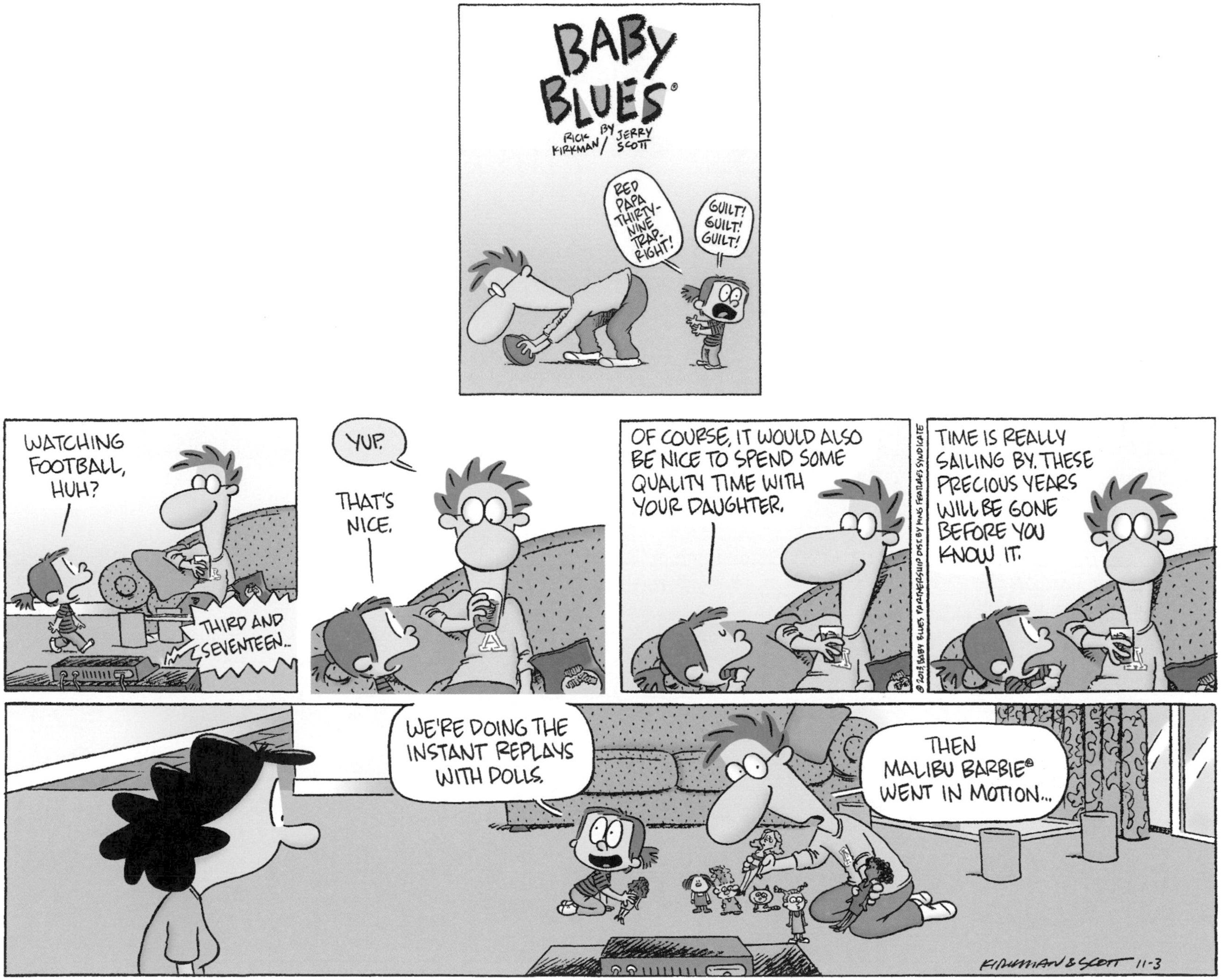
BABY BLUES®
BY RICK KIRKMAN / JERRY SCOTT
RED PAPA THIRTY-NINE TRAP. RIGHT!
GUILT! GUILT! GUILT!
WATCHING FOOTBALL, HUH?
THIRD AND SEVENTEEN..
YUP.
THAT'S NICE.
OF COURSE, IT WOULD ALSO BE NICE TO SPEND SOME QUALITY TIME WITH YOUR DAUGHTER.
© 2013, BABY BLUES PARTNERSHIP DIST. BY KING FEATURES SYNDICATE
TIME IS REALLY SAILING BY. THESE PRECIOUS YEARS WILL BE GONE BEFORE YOU KNOW IT.
WE'RE DOING THE INSTANT REPLAYS WITH DOLLS.
THEN MALIBU BARBIE® WENT IN MOTION...
KIRKMAN & SCOTT 11-3

Jerry: Successful parenting is a series of creative compromises.

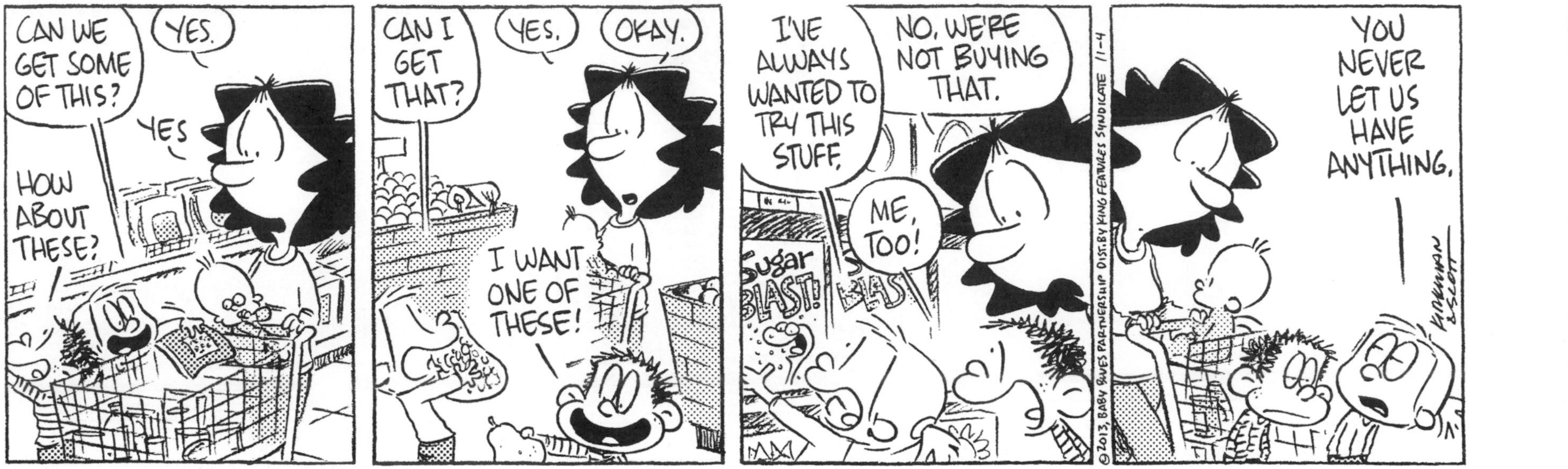
CAN WE GET SOME OF THIS?
YES.
HOW ABOUT THESE?
YES
CAN I GET THAT?
YES.
I WANT ONE OF THESE!
OKAY.
I'VE ALWAYS WANTED TO TRY THIS STUFF.
Sugar BLAST!
NO, WE'RE NOT BUYING THAT.
ME, TOO!
YOU NEVER LET US HAVE ANYTHING.
KIRKMAN & SCOTT
© 2013, BABY BLUES PARTNERSHIP DIST. BY KING FEATURES SYNDICATE 11-4

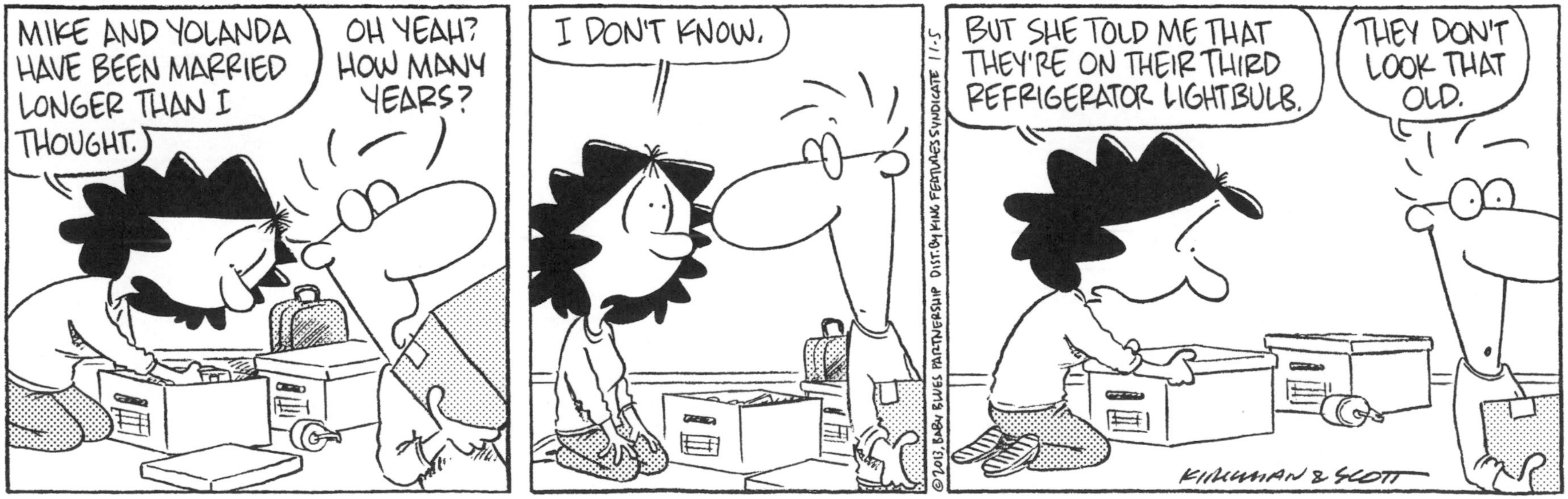
MIKE AND YOLANDA HAVE BEEN MARRIED LONGER THAN I THOUGHT.
OH YEAH? HOW MANY YEARS?
I DON'T KNOW.
BUT SHE TOLD ME THAT THEY'RE ON THEIR THIRD REFRIGERATOR LIGHTBULB.
THEY DON'T LOOK THAT OLD.
KIRKMAN & SCOTT
© 2013, BABY BLUES PARTNERSHIP DIST. BY KING FEATURES SYNDICATE 11-5

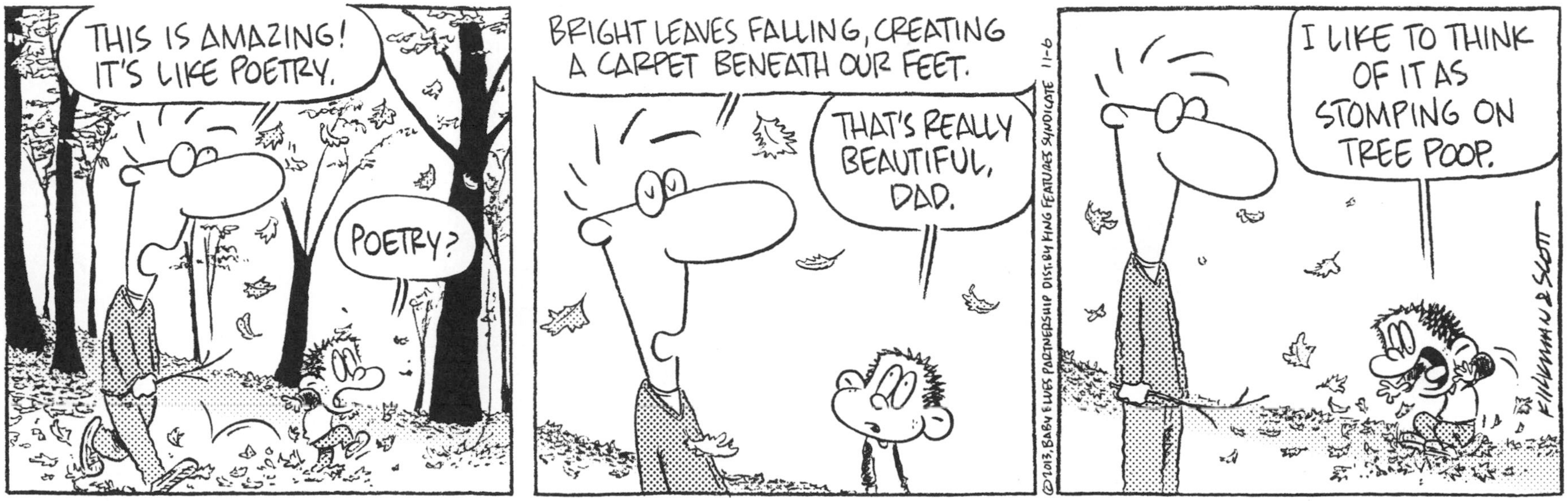
THIS IS AMAZING! IT'S LIKE POETRY.
POETRY?
BRIGHT LEAVES FALLING, CREATING A CARPET BENEATH OUR FEET.
THAT'S REALLY BEAUTIFUL, DAD.
11-6
©2013, BABY BLUES PARTNERSHIP DIST. BY KING FEATURES SYNDICATE
I LIKE TO THINK OF IT AS STOMPING ON TREE POOP.
KIRKMAN & SCOTT

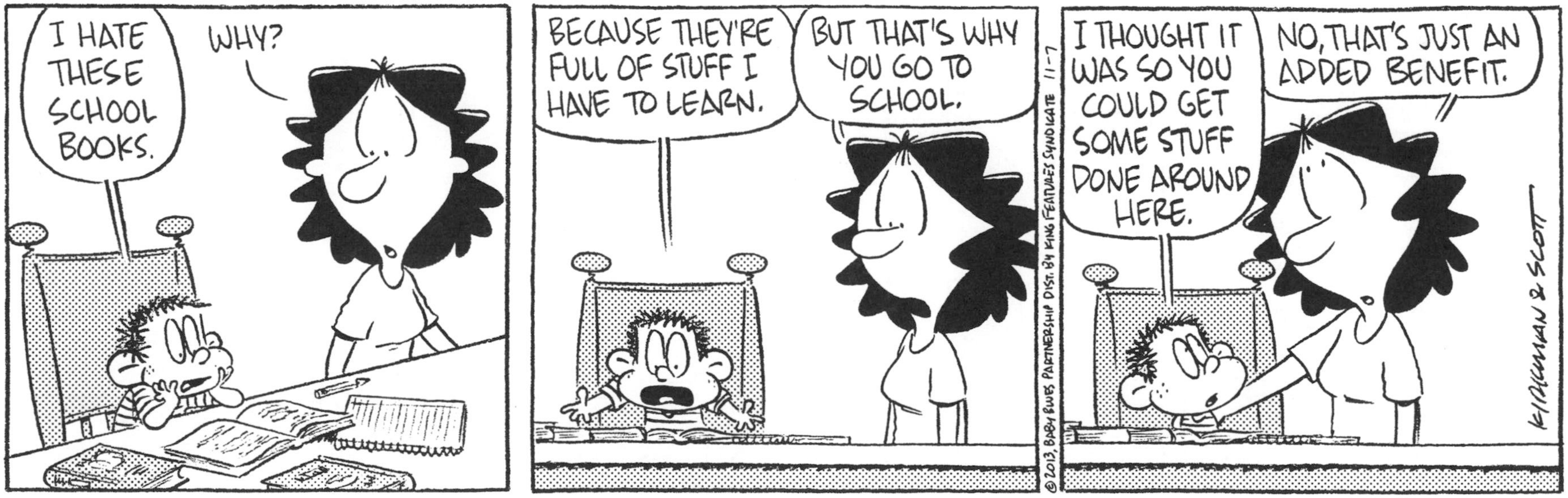
I HATE THESE SCHOOL BOOKS.
WHY?
BECAUSE THEY'RE FULL OF STUFF I HAVE TO LEARN.
BUT THAT'S WHY YOU GO TO SCHOOL.
11-7
©2013, BABY BLUES PARTNERSHIP DIST. BY KING FEATURES SYNDICATE
I THOUGHT IT WAS SO YOU COULD GET SOME STUFF DONE AROUND HERE.
NO, THAT'S JUST AN ADDED BENEFIT.
KIRKMAN & SCOTT

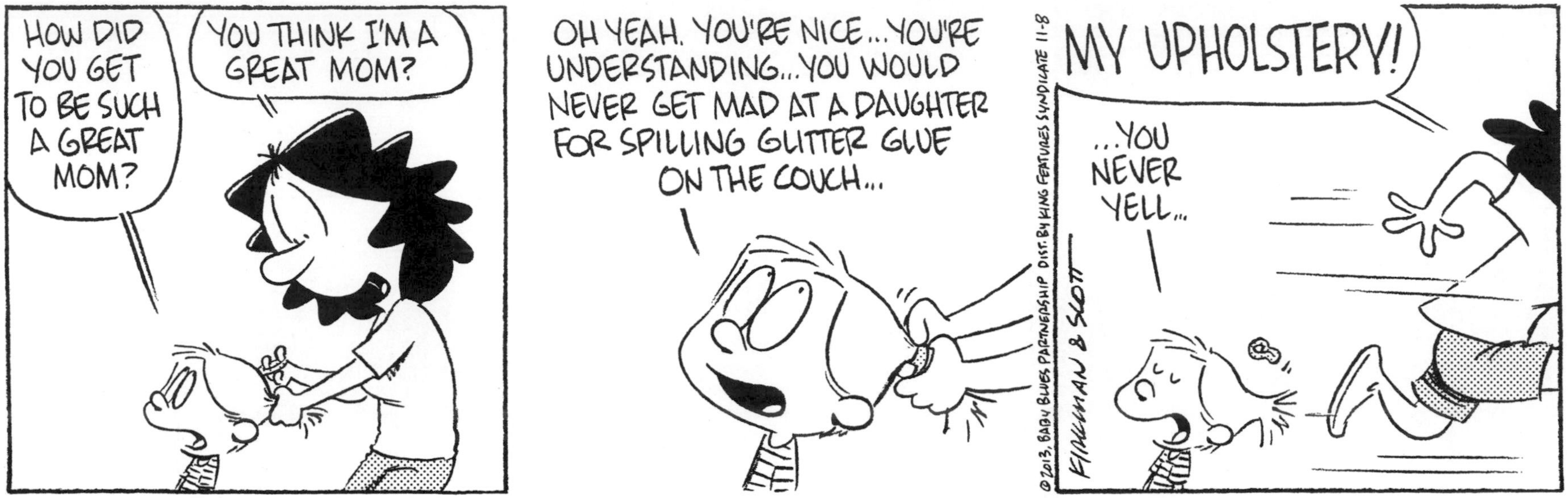
HOW DID YOU GET TO BE SUCH A GREAT MOM?
YOU THINK I'M A GREAT MOM?
OH YEAH. YOU'RE NICE... YOU'RE UNDERSTANDING... YOU WOULD NEVER GET MAD AT A DAUGHTER FOR SPILLING GLITTER GLUE ON THE COUCH...
©2013, BABY BLUES PARTNERSHIP DIST. BY KING FEATURES SYNDICATE 11-8
KIRKMAN & SCOTT
...YOU NEVER YELL...
MY UPHOLSTERY!

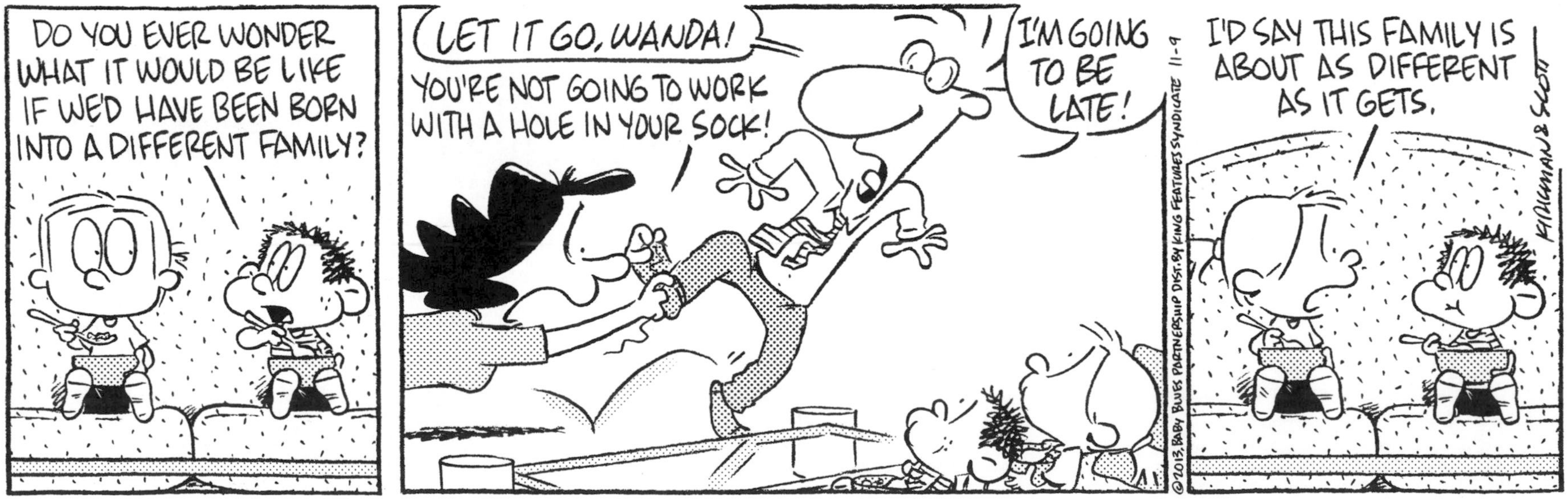
DO YOU EVER WONDER WHAT IT WOULD BE LIKE IF WE'D HAVE BEEN BORN INTO A DIFFERENT FAMILY?
LET IT GO, WANDA!
YOU'RE NOT GOING TO WORK WITH A HOLE IN YOUR SOCK!
I'M GOING TO BE LATE!
©2013, BABY BLUES PARTNERSHIP DIST. BY KING FEATURES SYNDICATE 11-9
I'D SAY THIS FAMILY IS ABOUT AS DIFFERENT AS IT GETS.
KIRKMAN & SCOTT

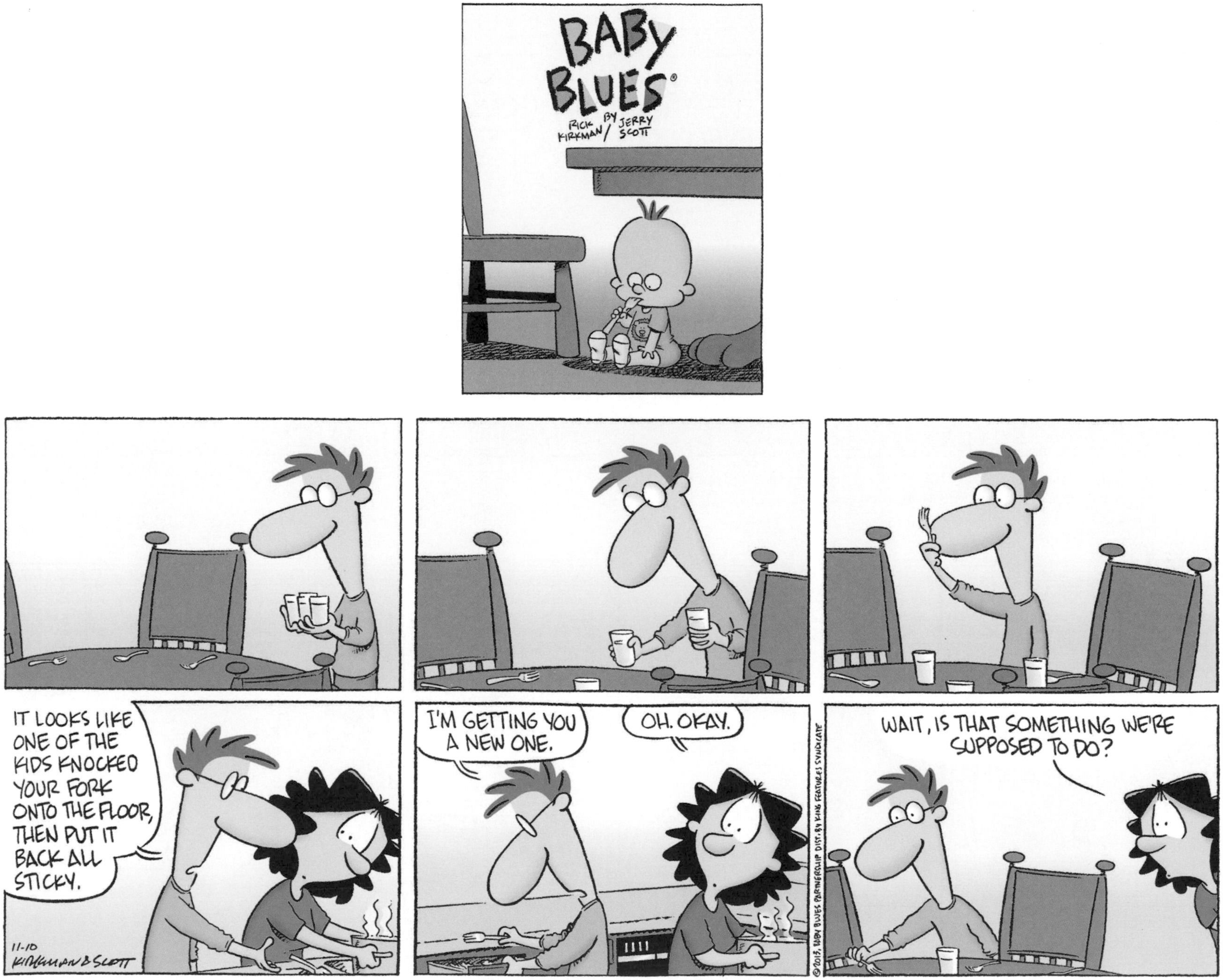
BABY BLUES®
BY RICK KIRKMAN/ JERRY SCOTT
IT LOOKS LIKE ONE OF THE KIDS KNOCKED YOUR FORK ONTO THE FLOOR, THEN PUT IT BACK ALL STICKY.
11-10 KIRKMAN & SCOTT
I'M GETTING YOU A NEW ONE.
OH. OKAY.
©2013, BABY BLUES PARTNERSHIP DIST. BY KING FEATURES SYNDICATE
WAIT, IS THAT SOMETHING WE'RE SUPPOSED TO DO?

Rick: This was based on an actual situation in our house. Except our kids were grown and had moved away. So it was a cat instead of a kid. Hey, you get your gags where you can.

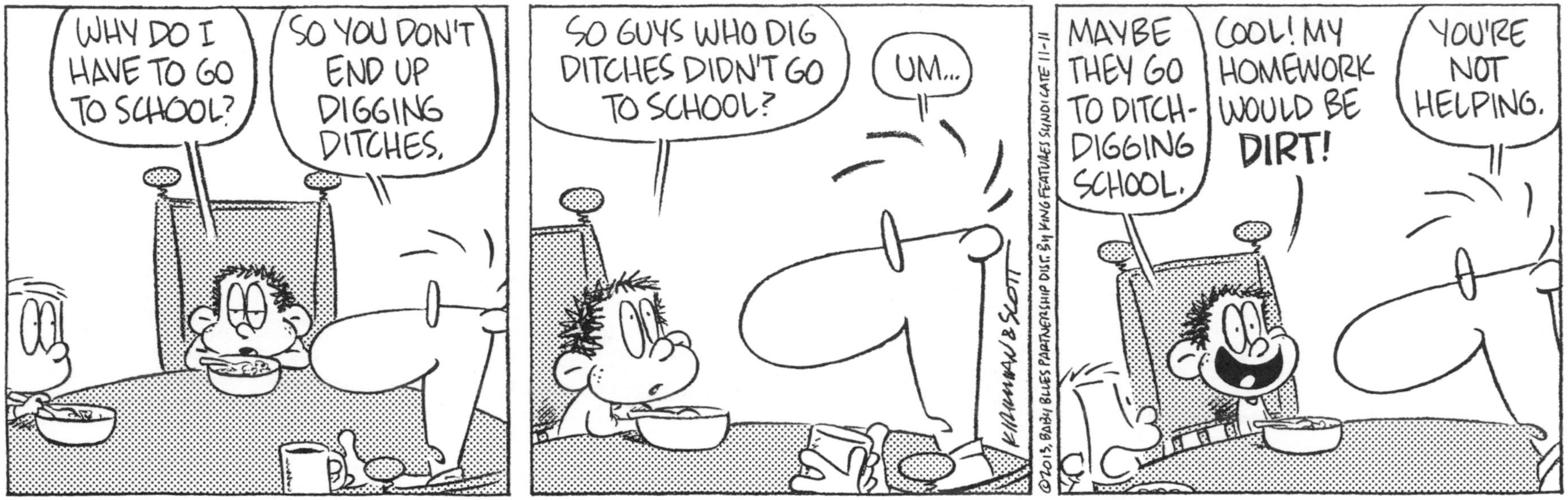
WHY DO I HAVE TO GO TO SCHOOL?
SO YOU DON'T END UP DIGGING DITCHES.
SO GUYS WHO DIG DITCHES DIDN'T GO TO SCHOOL?
UM...
KIRKMAN & SCOTT
©2013, BABY BLUES PARTNERSHIP DIST. BY KING FEATURES SYNDICATE 11-11
MAYBE THEY GO TO DITCH-DIGGING SCHOOL.
COOL! MY HOMEWORK WOULD BE **DIRT!**
YOU'RE NOT HELPING.

Jerry: A lot of ditches these days are dug by wealthy contracting companies. Thanks for warning me away from all that success, Mom and Dad.

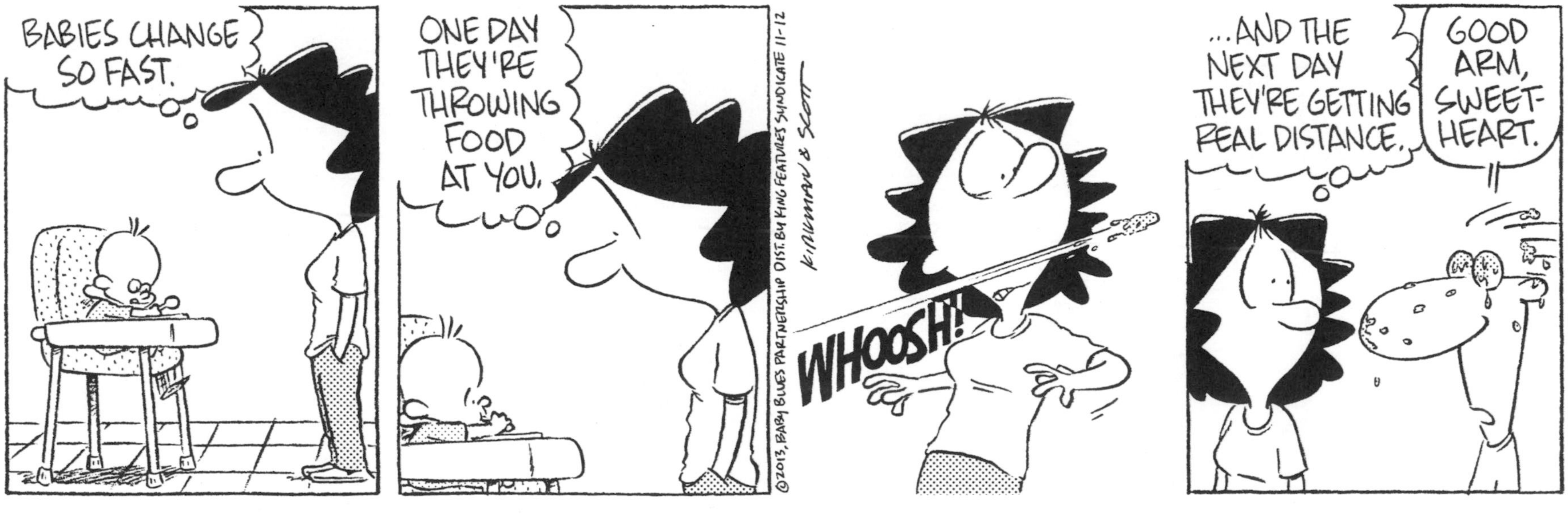
BABIES CHANGE SO FAST.
ONE DAY THEY'RE THROWING FOOD AT YOU.
©2013, BABY BLUES PARTNERSHIP DIST. BY KING FEATURES SYNDICATE 11-12
KIRKMAN & SCOTT
WHOOSH!
...AND THE NEXT DAY THEY'RE GETTING REAL DISTANCE.
GOOD ARM, SWEET-HEART.

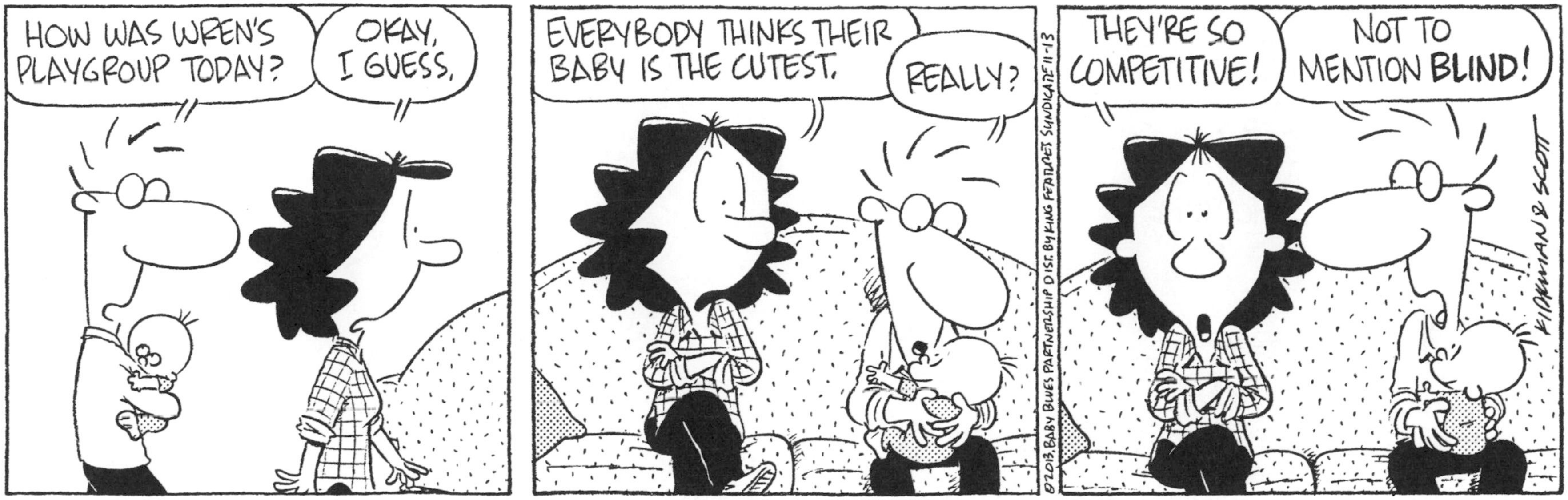
HOW WAS WREN'S PLAYGROUP TODAY?
OKAY, I GUESS.
EVERYBODY THINKS THEIR BABY IS THE CUTEST.
REALLY?
©2013, BABY BLUES PARTNERSHIP DIST. BY KING FEATURES SYNDICATE 11-13
THEY'RE SO COMPETITIVE!
NOT TO MENTION **BLIND**!
KIRKMAN & SCOTT

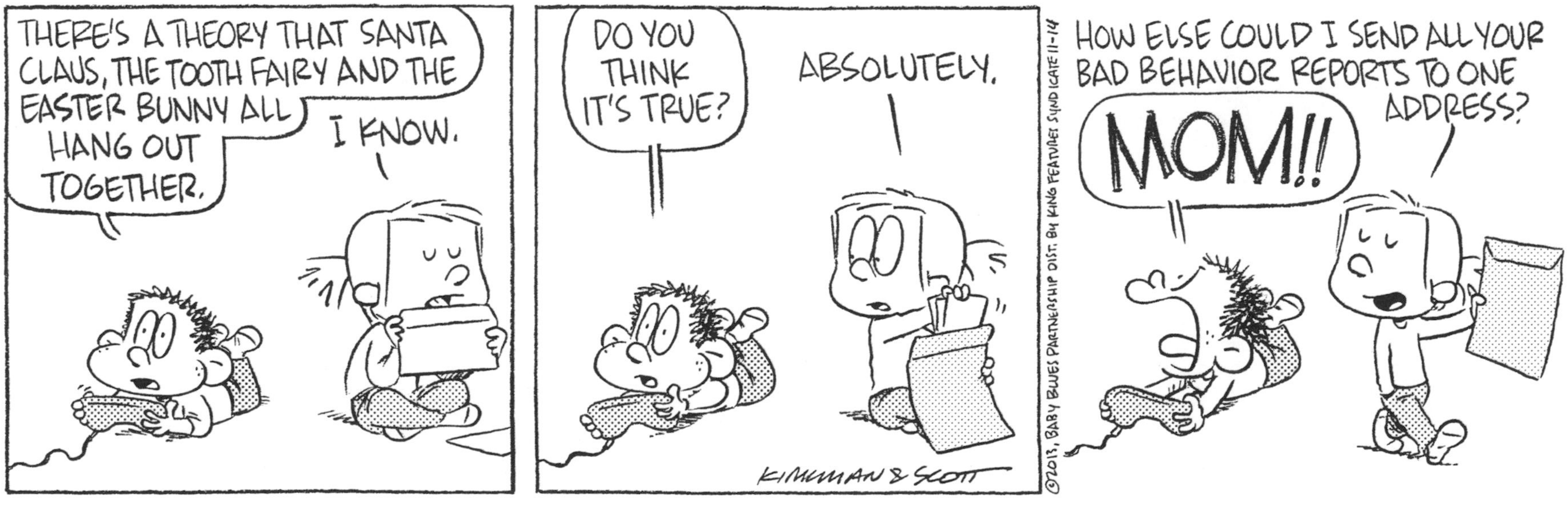
THERE'S A THEORY THAT SANTA CLAUS, THE TOOTH FAIRY AND THE EASTER BUNNY ALL HANG OUT TOGETHER.
I KNOW.
DO YOU THINK IT'S TRUE?
ABSOLUTELY.
KIRKMAN & SCOTT
©2013, BABY BLUES PARTNERSHIP DIST. BY KING FEATURES SYNDICATE 11-14
HOW ELSE COULD I SEND ALL YOUR BAD BEHAVIOR REPORTS TO ONE ADDRESS?
MOM!!

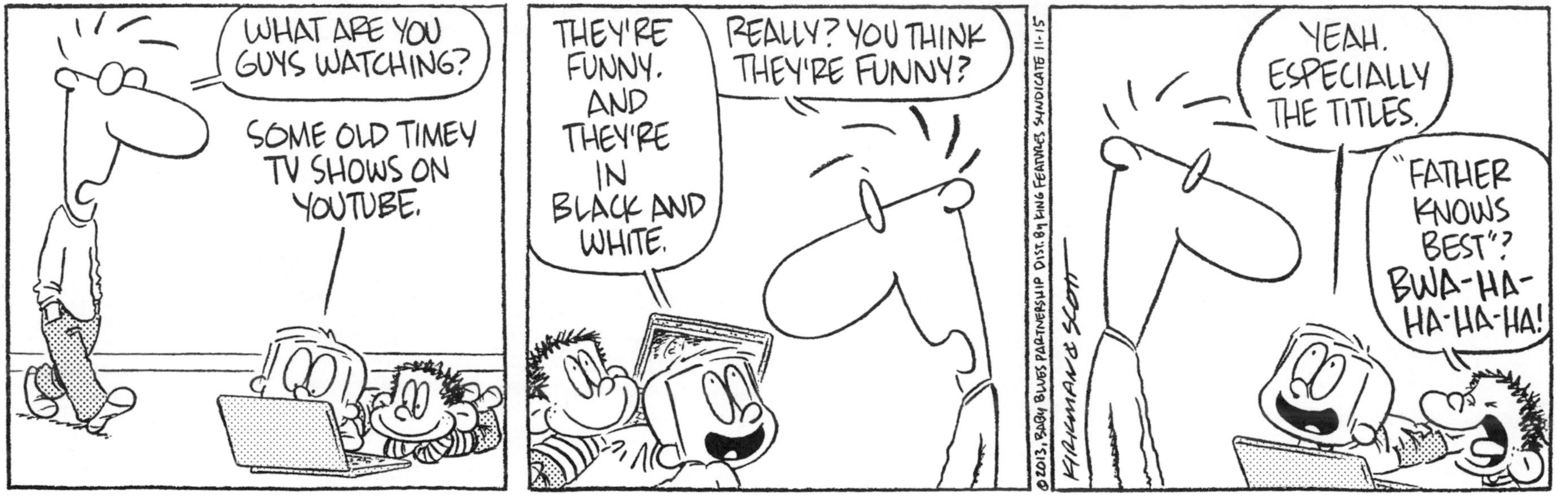
WHAT ARE YOU GUYS WATCHING?
SOME OLD TIMEY TV SHOWS ON YOUTUBE.
THEY'RE FUNNY. AND THEY'RE IN BLACK AND WHITE.
REALLY? YOU THINK THEY'RE FUNNY?
©2013, BABY BLUES PARTNERSHIP DIST. BY KING FEATURES SYNDICATE 11-15
KIRKMAN & SCOTT
YEAH. ESPECIALLY THE TITLES.
"FATHER KNOWS BEST"? BWA-HA-HA-HA-HA!

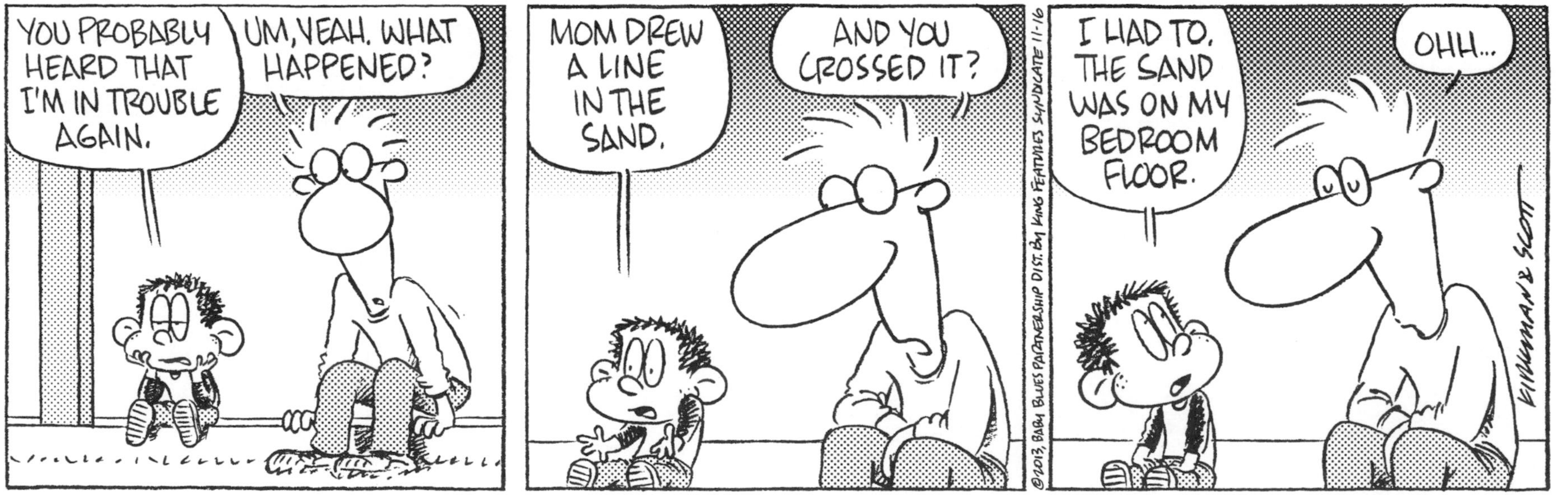
YOU PROBABLY HEARD THAT I'M IN TROUBLE AGAIN.
UM, YEAH. WHAT HAPPENED?
MOM DREW A LINE IN THE SAND.
AND YOU CROSSED IT?
©2013, BABY BLUES PARTNERSHIP DIST. BY KING FEATURES SYNDICATE 11-16
I HAD TO. THE SAND WAS ON MY BEDROOM FLOOR.
OHH...
KIRKMAN & SCOTT

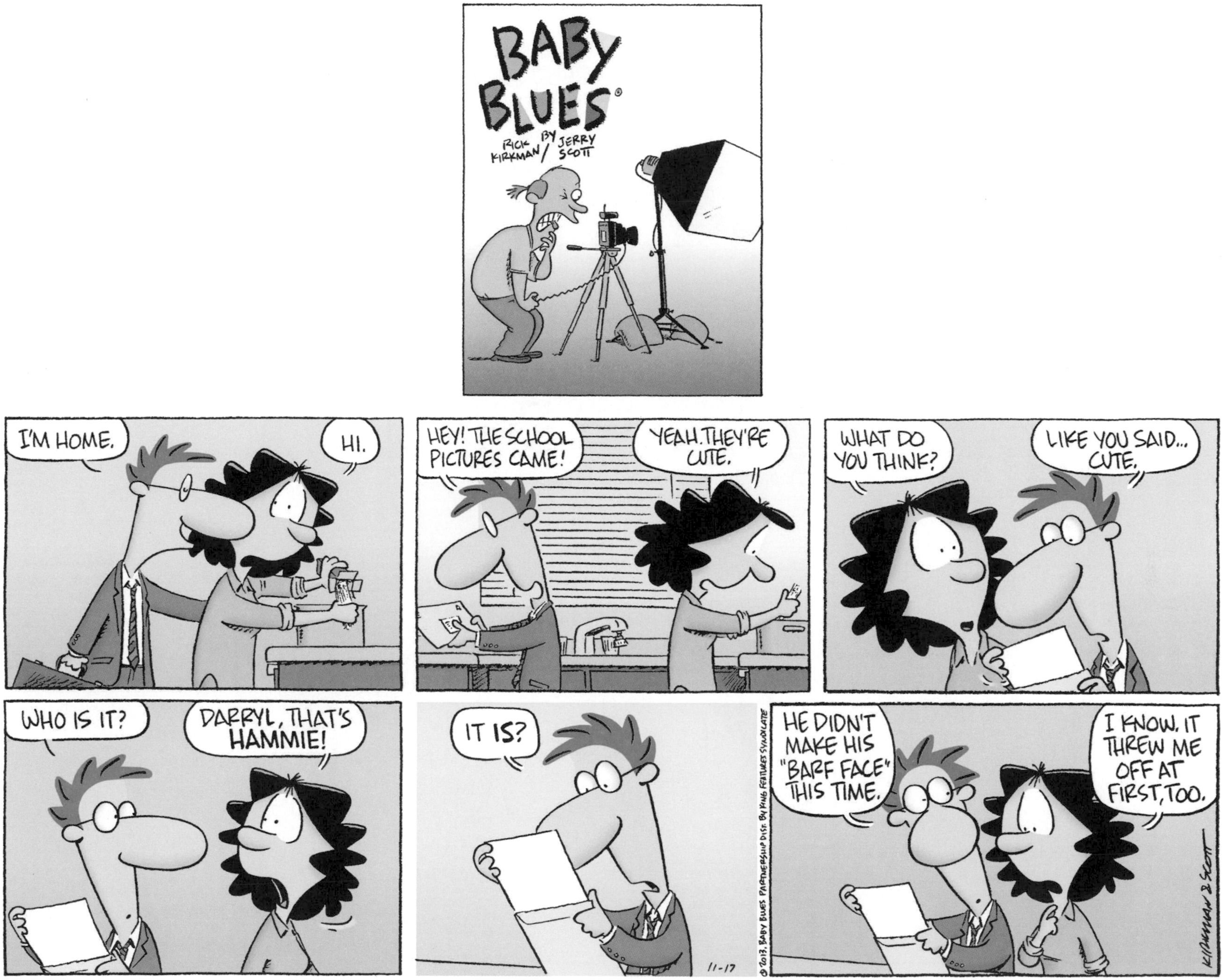
BABY BLUES®
BY RICK KIRKMAN / JERRY SCOTT
I'M HOME.
HI.
HEY! THE SCHOOL PICTURES CAME!
YEAH. THEY'RE CUTE.
WHAT DO YOU THINK?
LIKE YOU SAID... CUTE.
WHO IS IT?
DARRYL, THAT'S HAMMIE!
IT IS?
11-17
© 2013, BABY BLUES PARTNERSHIP DIST. BY KING FEATURES SYNDICATE
HE DIDN'T MAKE HIS "BARF FACE" THIS TIME.
I KNOW. IT THREW ME OFF AT FIRST, TOO.
KIRKMAN & SCOTT

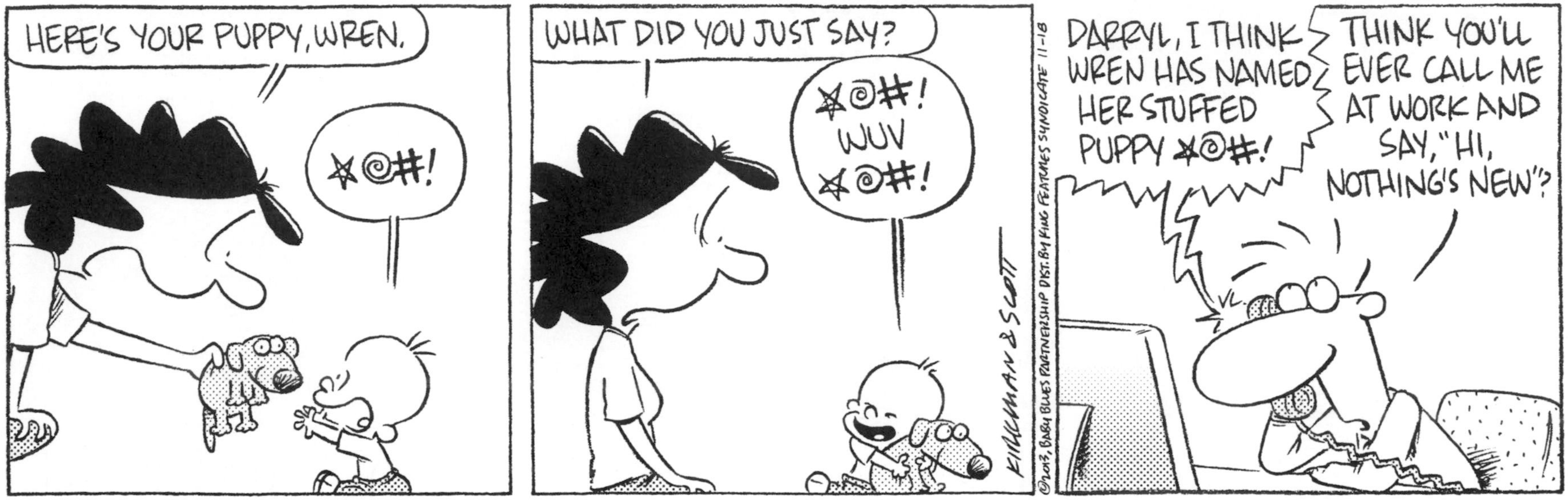
HERE'S YOUR PUPPY, WREN.
✱@#!
WHAT DID YOU JUST SAY?
✱@#! WUV ✱@#!
KIRKMAN & SCOTT
©2013, BABY BLUES PARTNERSHIP DIST. BY KING FEATURES SYNDICATE 11-18
DARRYL, I THINK WREN HAS NAMED HER STUFFED PUPPY ✱@#!
THINK YOU'LL EVER CALL ME AT WORK AND SAY, "HI, NOTHING'S NEW"?

Jerry: This series was based on my niece's son. I wish I could tell you what he innocently named his stuffed puppy, but this is a family comic strip.

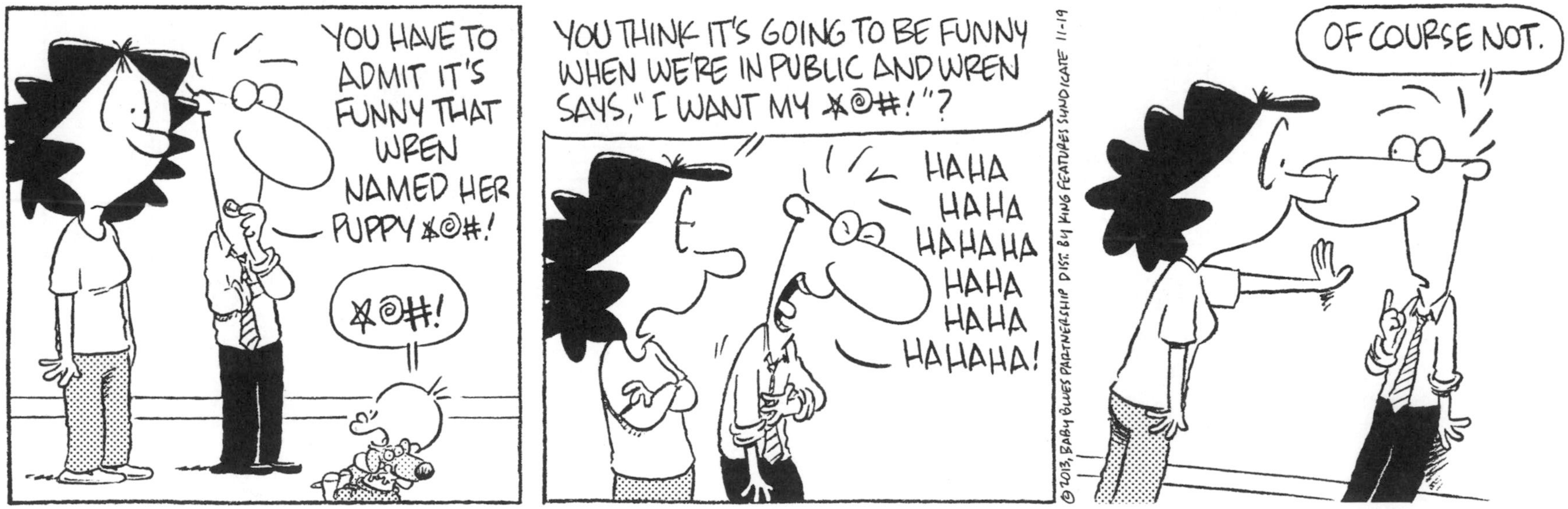
YOU HAVE TO ADMIT IT'S FUNNY THAT WREN NAMED HER PUPPY ✱@#!
✱@#!
YOU THINK IT'S GOING TO BE FUNNY WHEN WE'RE IN PUBLIC AND WREN SAYS, "I WANT MY ✱@#!"?
HAHA HAHA HAHAHA HAHA HAHA HAHAHA!
©2013, BABY BLUES PARTNERSHIP DIST. BY KING FEATURES SYNDICATE 11-19
OF COURSE NOT.

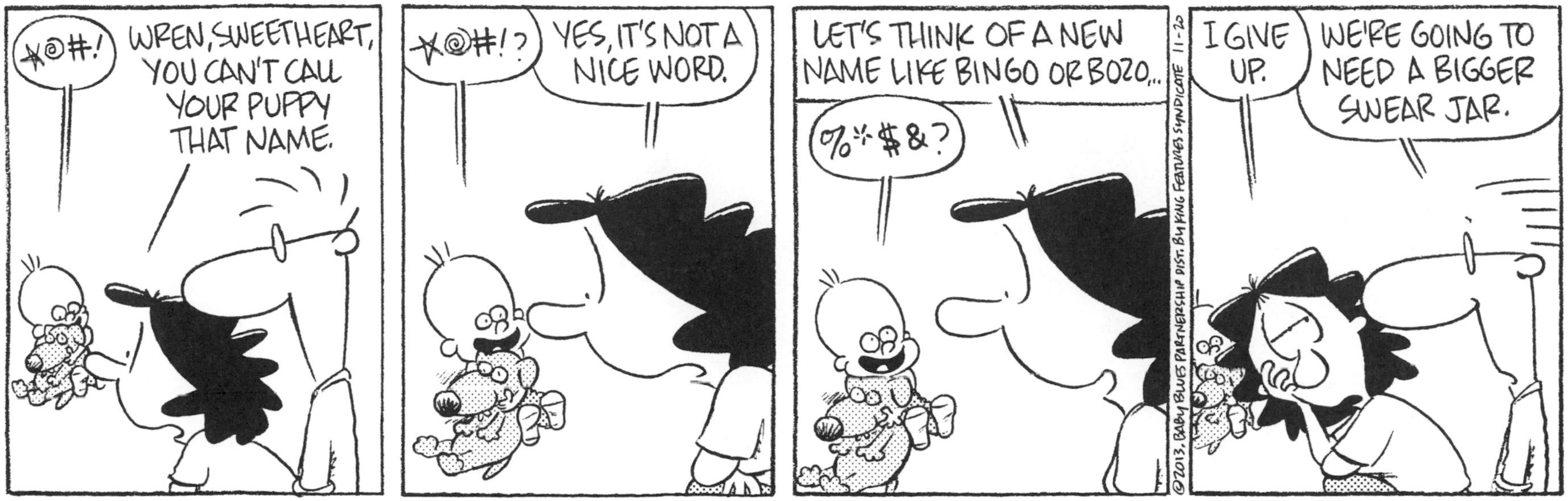
*@#!
WREN, SWEETHEART, YOU CAN'T CALL YOUR PUPPY THAT NAME.
*@#!?
YES, IT'S NOT A NICE WORD.
LET'S THINK OF A NEW NAME LIKE BINGO OR BOZO...
%*$&?
I GIVE UP.
WE'RE GOING TO NEED A BIGGER SWEAR JAR.
©2013, BABY BLUES PARTNERSHIP DIST. BY KING FEATURES SYNDICATE 11-20

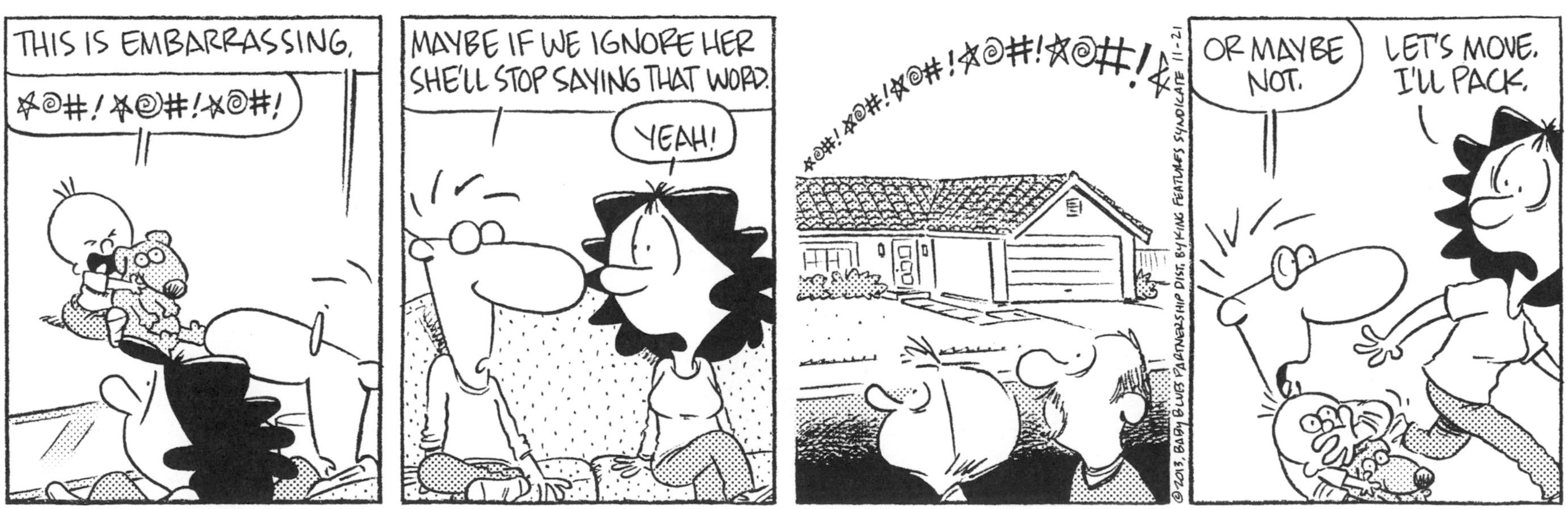
THIS IS EMBARRASSING.
*@#! *@#! *@#!
MAYBE IF WE IGNORE HER SHE'LL STOP SAYING THAT WORD.
YEAH!
*@#! *@#! *@#! *@#! *@#! *
©2013, BABY BLUES PARTNERSHIP DIST. BY KING FEATURES SYNDICATE 11-21
OR MAYBE NOT.
LET'S MOVE. I'LL PACK.

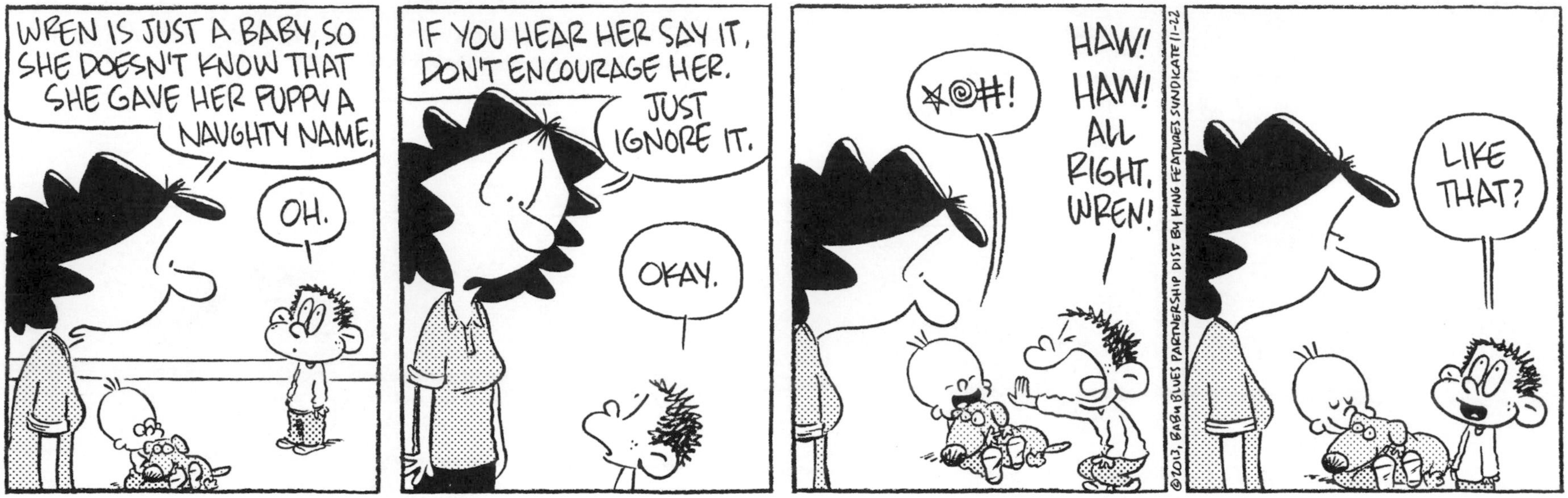
WREN IS JUST A BABY, SO SHE DOESN'T KNOW THAT SHE GAVE HER PUPPY A NAUGHTY NAME.
OH.
IF YOU HEAR HER SAY IT, DON'T ENCOURAGE HER.
JUST IGNORE IT.
OKAY.
★◎#!
HAW! HAW! ALL RIGHT, WREN!
©2013, BABY BLUES PARTNERSHIP DIST BY KING FEATURES SYNDICATE 11-22
LIKE THAT?

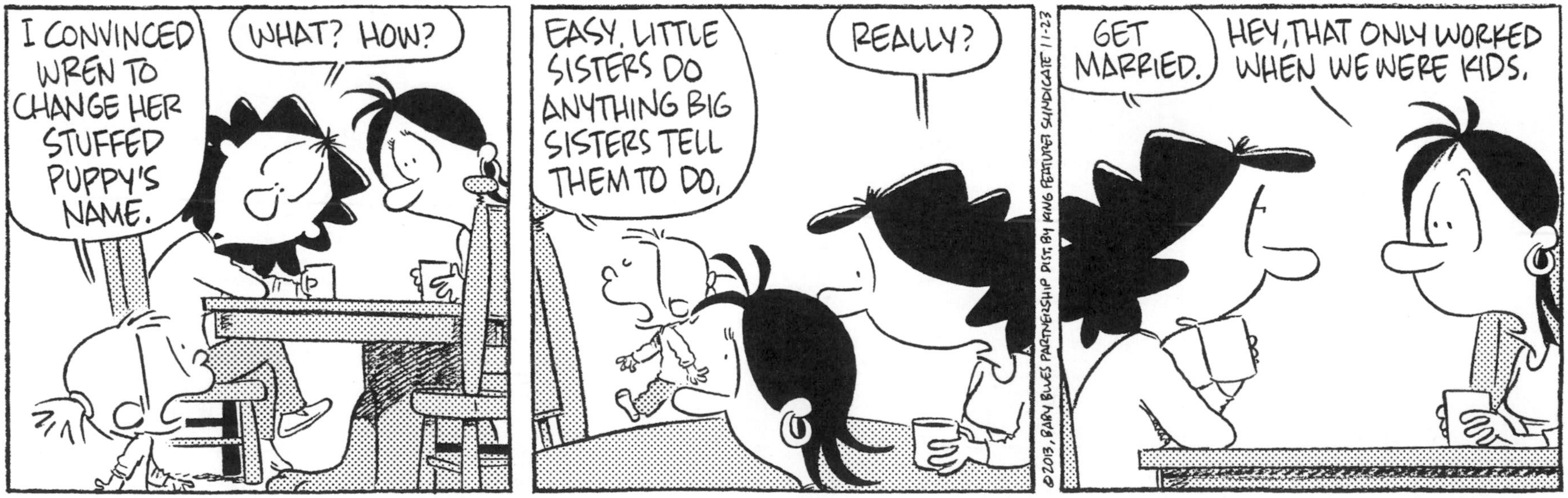
I CONVINCED WREN TO CHANGE HER STUFFED PUPPY'S NAME.
WHAT? HOW?
EASY. LITTLE SISTERS DO ANYTHING BIG SISTERS TELL THEM TO DO.
REALLY?
©2013, BABY BLUES PARTNERSHIP DIST. BY KING FEATURES SYNDICATE 11-23
GET MARRIED.
HEY, THAT ONLY WORKED WHEN WE WERE KIDS.

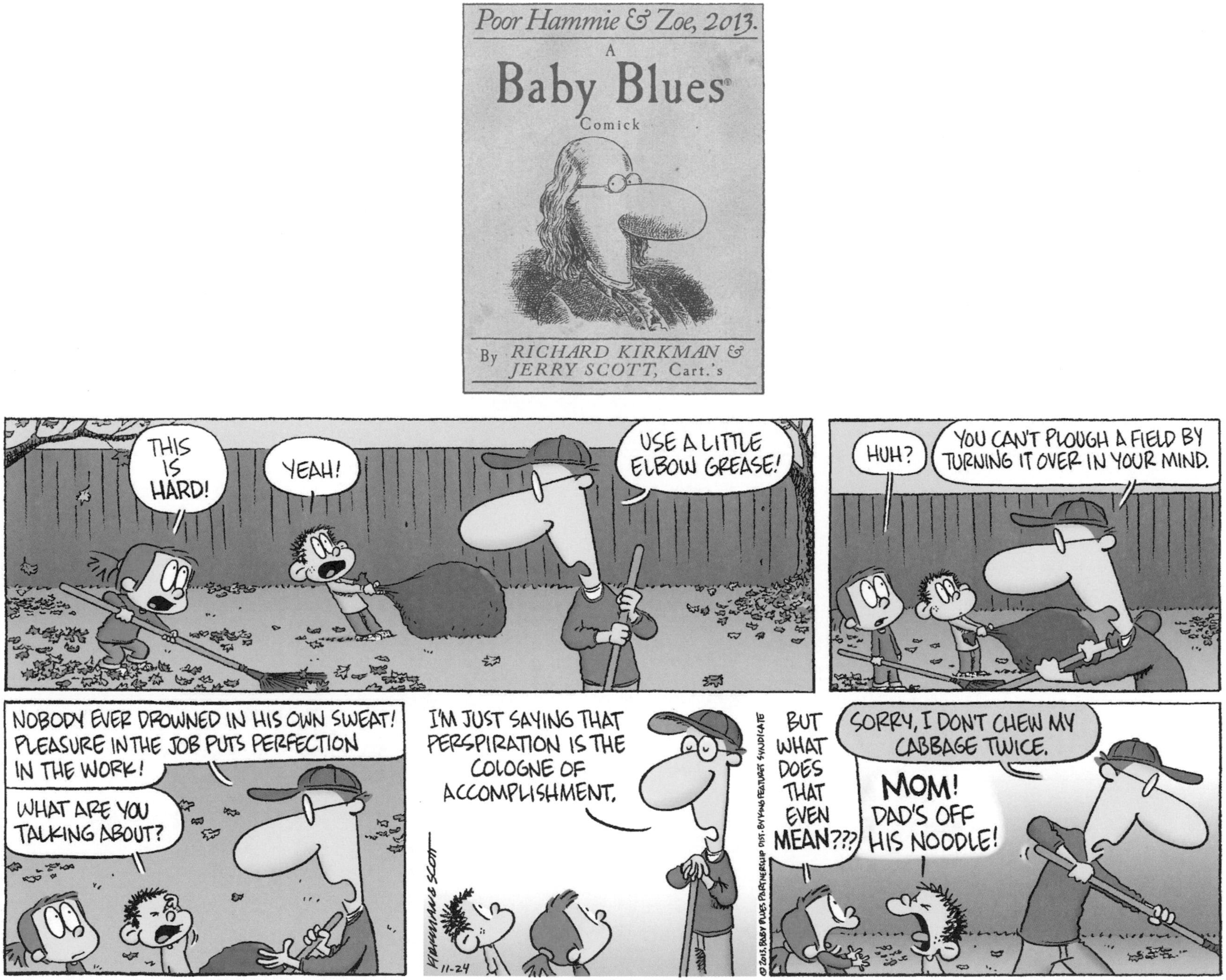
Poor Hammie & Zoe, 2013.
A
Baby Blues®
Comick
By RICHARD KIRKMAN & JERRY SCOTT, Cart.'s
THIS IS HARD!
YEAH!
USE A LITTLE ELBOW GREASE!
HUH?
YOU CAN'T PLOUGH A FIELD BY TURNING IT OVER IN YOUR MIND.
NOBODY EVER DROWNED IN HIS OWN SWEAT! PLEASURE IN THE JOB PUTS PERFECTION IN THE WORK!
WHAT ARE YOU TALKING ABOUT?
I'M JUST SAYING THAT PERSPIRATION IS THE COLOGNE OF ACCOMPLISHMENT.
KIRKMAN & SCOTT
11-24
BUT WHAT DOES THAT EVEN MEAN???
SORRY, I DON'T CHEW MY CABBAGE TWICE.
MOM! DAD'S OFF HIS NOODLE!

Rick: I like this gag a lot, with all the strange idioms—just how Jerry talks in real life. Of course, Ben Franklin and *Poor Richard's Almanack* were perfect for the title panel. The Internet comes to the rescue again with reference photos of one of the original almanacs.

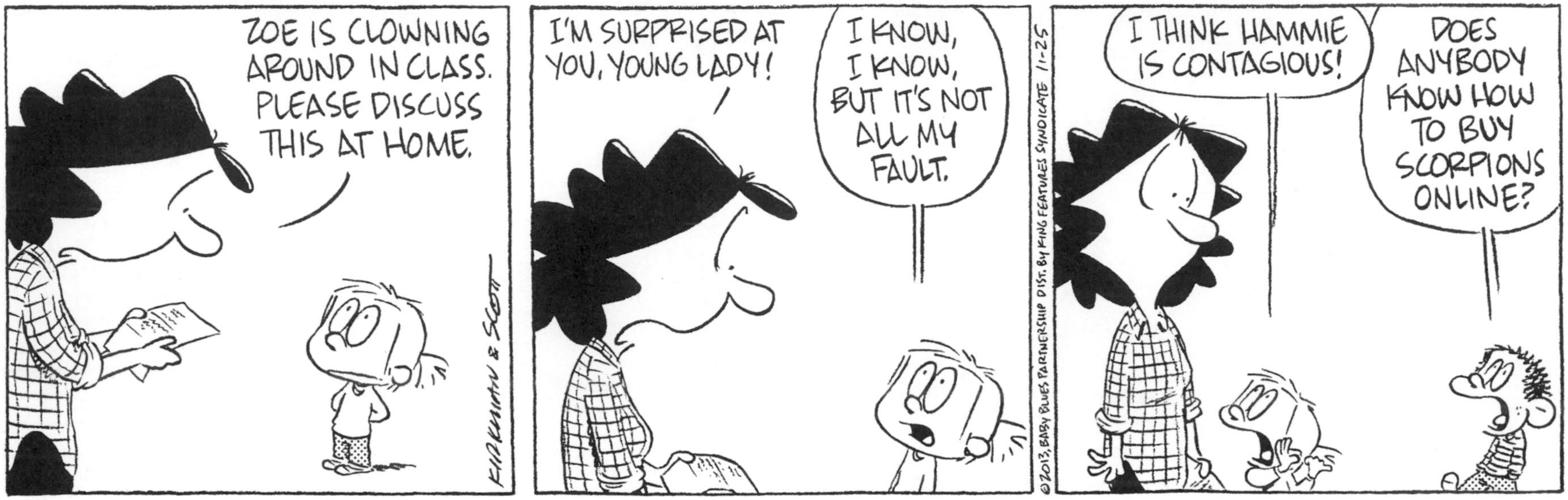
ZOE IS CLOWNING AROUND IN CLASS. PLEASE DISCUSS THIS AT HOME.
KIRKMAN & SCOTT
I'M SURPRISED AT YOU, YOUNG LADY!
I KNOW, I KNOW, BUT IT'S NOT ALL MY FAULT.
11-25
©2013, BABY BLUES PARTNERSHIP DIST. BY KING FEATURES SYNDICATE
I THINK HAMMIE IS CONTAGIOUS!
DOES ANYBODY KNOW HOW TO BUY SCORPIONS ONLINE?

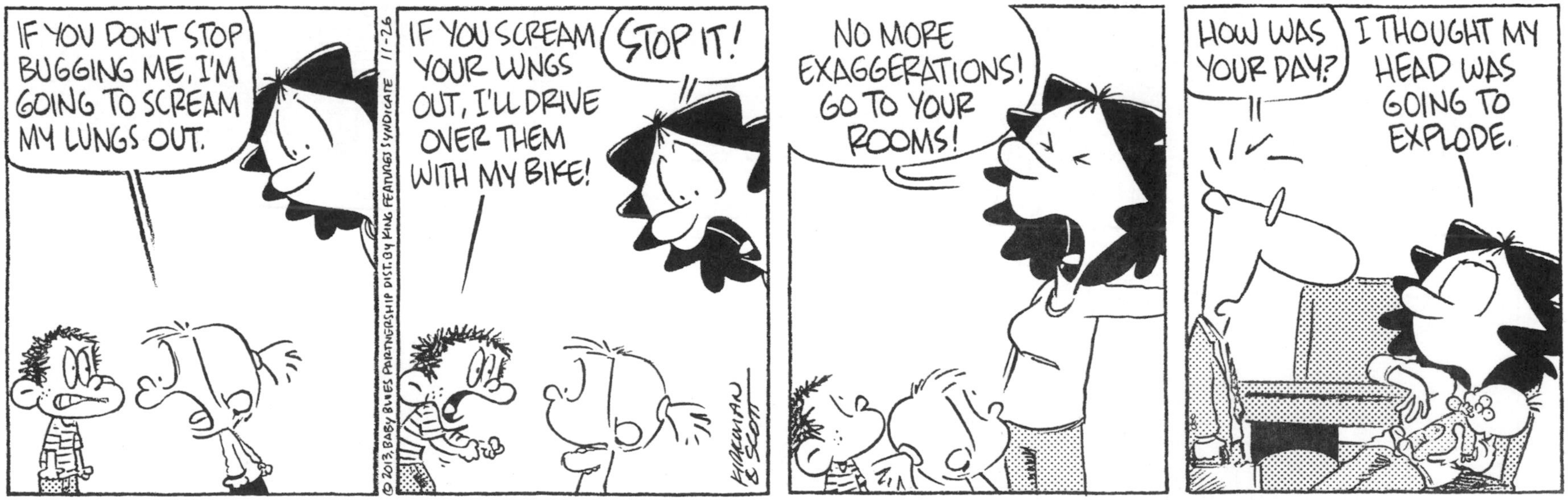
IF YOU DON'T STOP BUGGING ME, I'M GOING TO SCREAM MY LUNGS OUT.
11-26
©2013, BABY BLUES PARTNERSHIP DIST. BY KING FEATURES SYNDICATE
IF YOU SCREAM YOUR LUNGS OUT, I'LL DRIVE OVER THEM WITH MY BIKE!
STOP IT!
KIRKMAN & SCOTT
NO MORE EXAGGERATIONS! GO TO YOUR ROOMS!
HOW WAS YOUR DAY?
I THOUGHT MY HEAD WAS GOING TO EXPLODE.

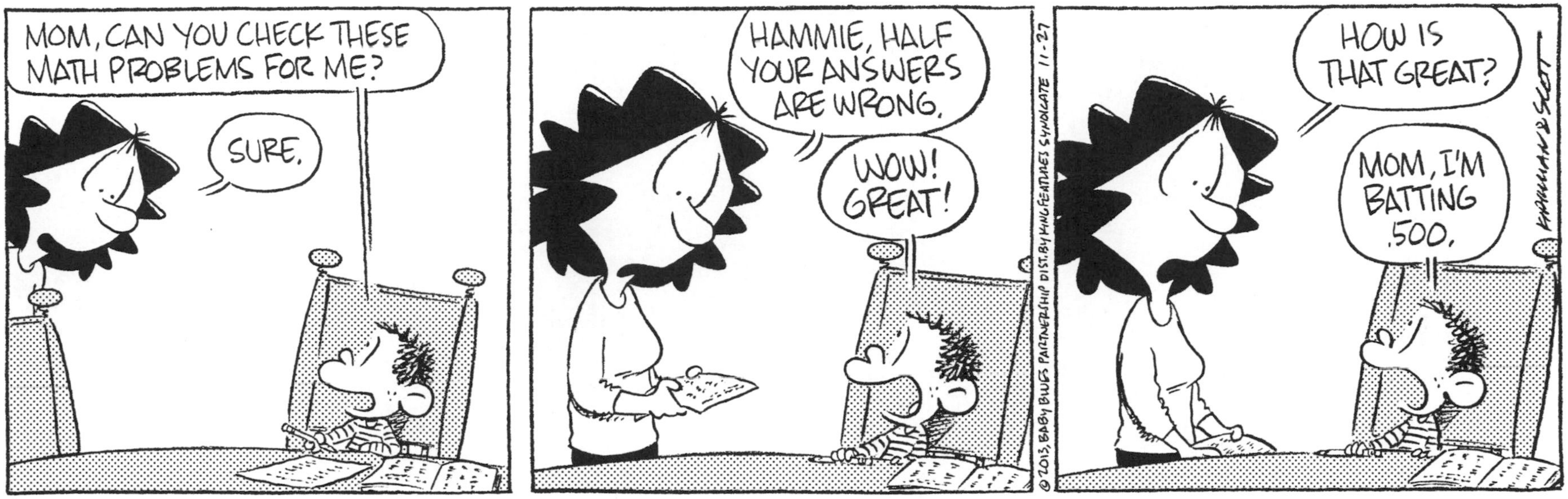
MOM, CAN YOU CHECK THESE MATH PROBLEMS FOR ME?
SURE.
HAMMIE, HALF YOUR ANSWERS ARE WRONG.
WOW! GREAT!
© 2013, BABY BLUES PARTNERSHIP DIST. BY KING FEATURES SYNDICATE 11-27
HOW IS THAT GREAT?
MOM, I'M BATTING .500.
KIRKMAN & SCOTT

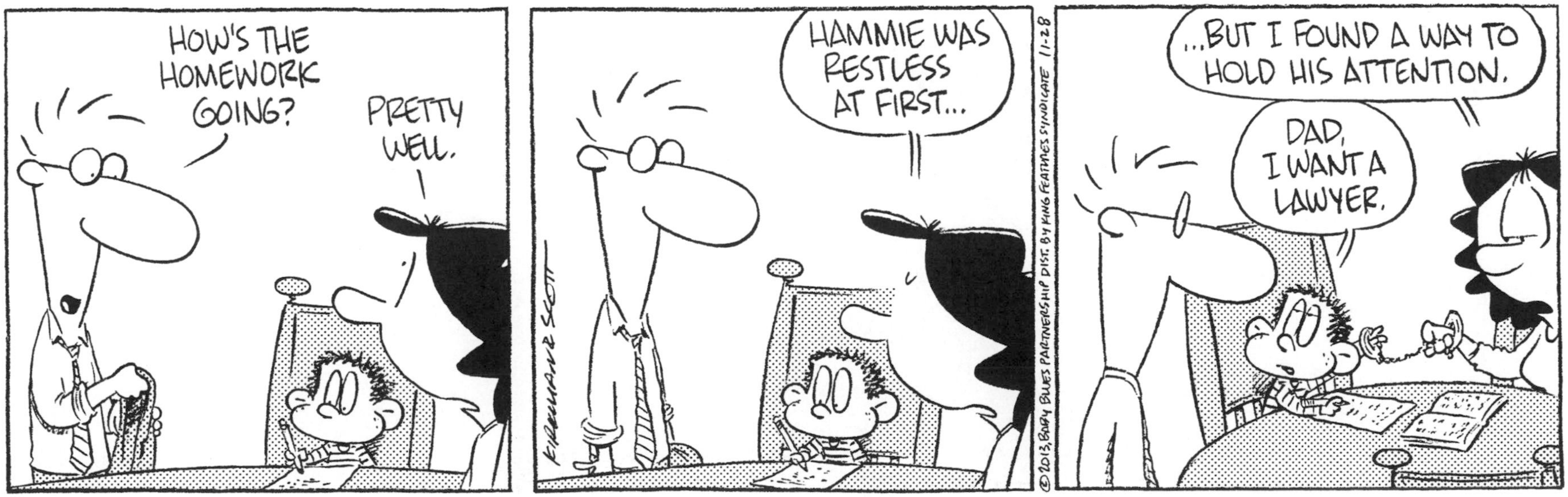
HOW'S THE HOMEWORK GOING?
PRETTY WELL.
KIRKMAN & SCOTT
HAMMIE WAS RESTLESS AT FIRST...
© 2013, BABY BLUES PARTNERSHIP DIST. BY KING FEATURES SYNDICATE 11-28
...BUT I FOUND A WAY TO HOLD HIS ATTENTION.
DAD, I WANT A LAWYER.

Jerry: My daughter got a pair of toy handcuffs as a gift and wore them around for weeks. The neighbors are keeping a closer eye on us nowadays.

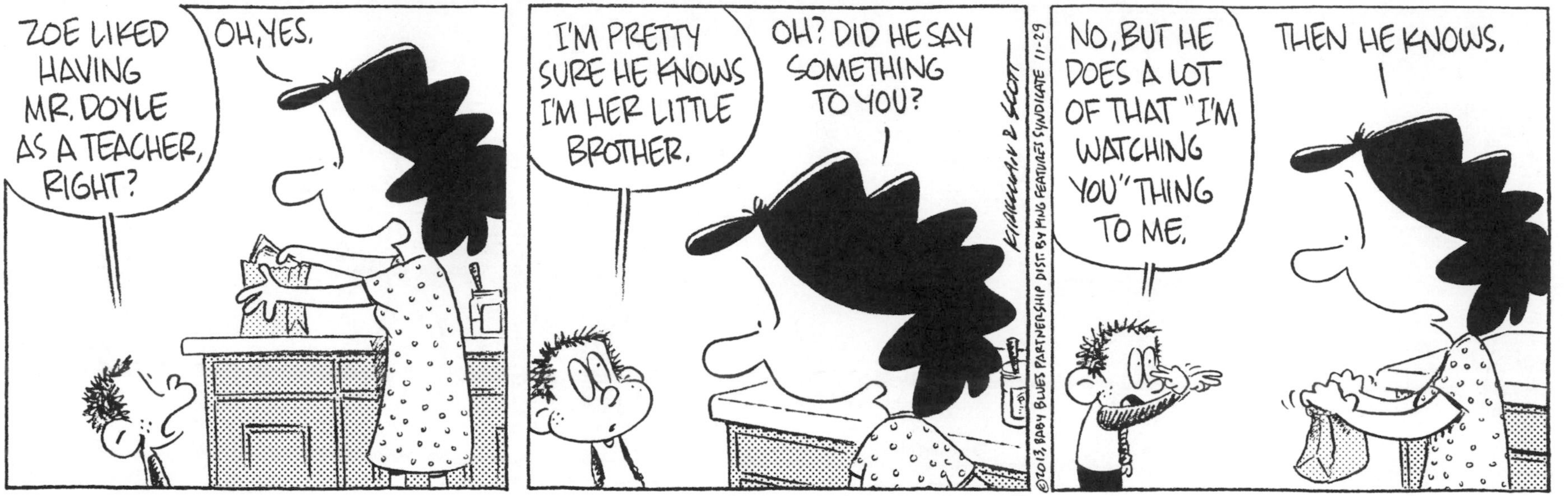
ZOE LIKED HAVING MR. DOYLE AS A TEACHER, RIGHT?
OH, YES.
I'M PRETTY SURE HE KNOWS I'M HER LITTLE BROTHER.
OH? DID HE SAY SOMETHING TO YOU?
KIRKMAN & SCOTT
©2013, BABY BLUES PARTNERSHIP DIST. BY KING FEATURES SYNDICATE 11-29
NO, BUT HE DOES A LOT OF THAT "I'M WATCHING YOU" THING TO ME.
THEN HE KNOWS.

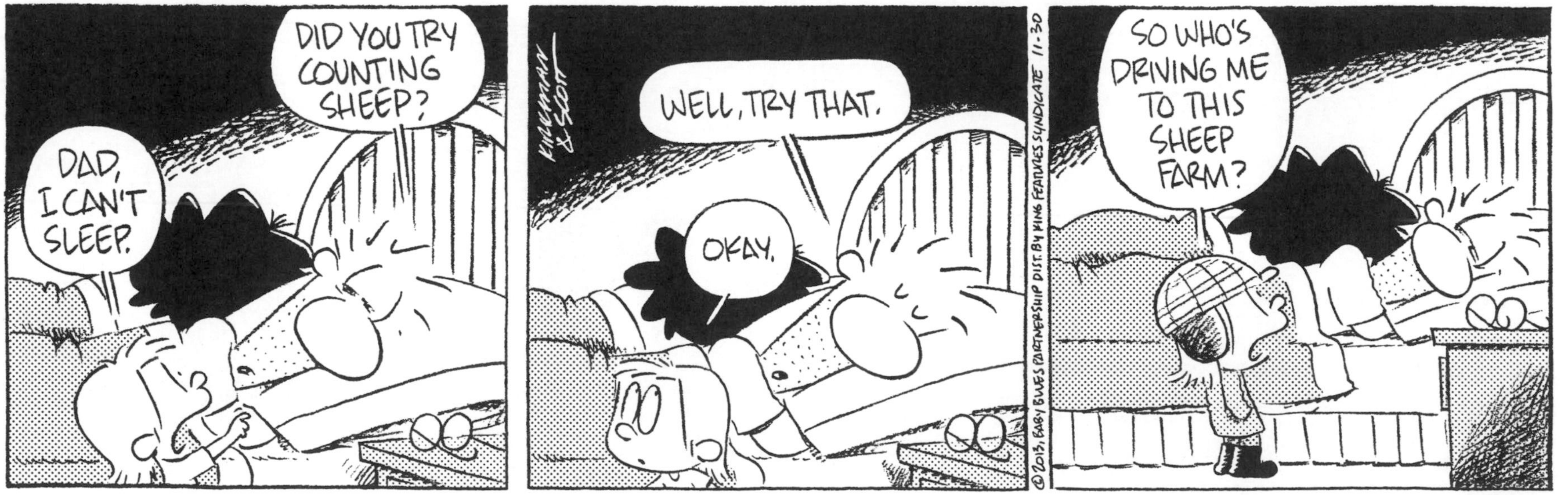
DAD, I CAN'T SLEEP.
DID YOU TRY COUNTING SHEEP?
KIRKMAN & SCOTT
WELL, TRY THAT.
OKAY.
©2013, BABY BLUES PARTNERSHIP DIST. BY KING FEATURES SYNDICATE 11-30
SO WHO'S DRIVING ME TO THIS SHEEP FARM?

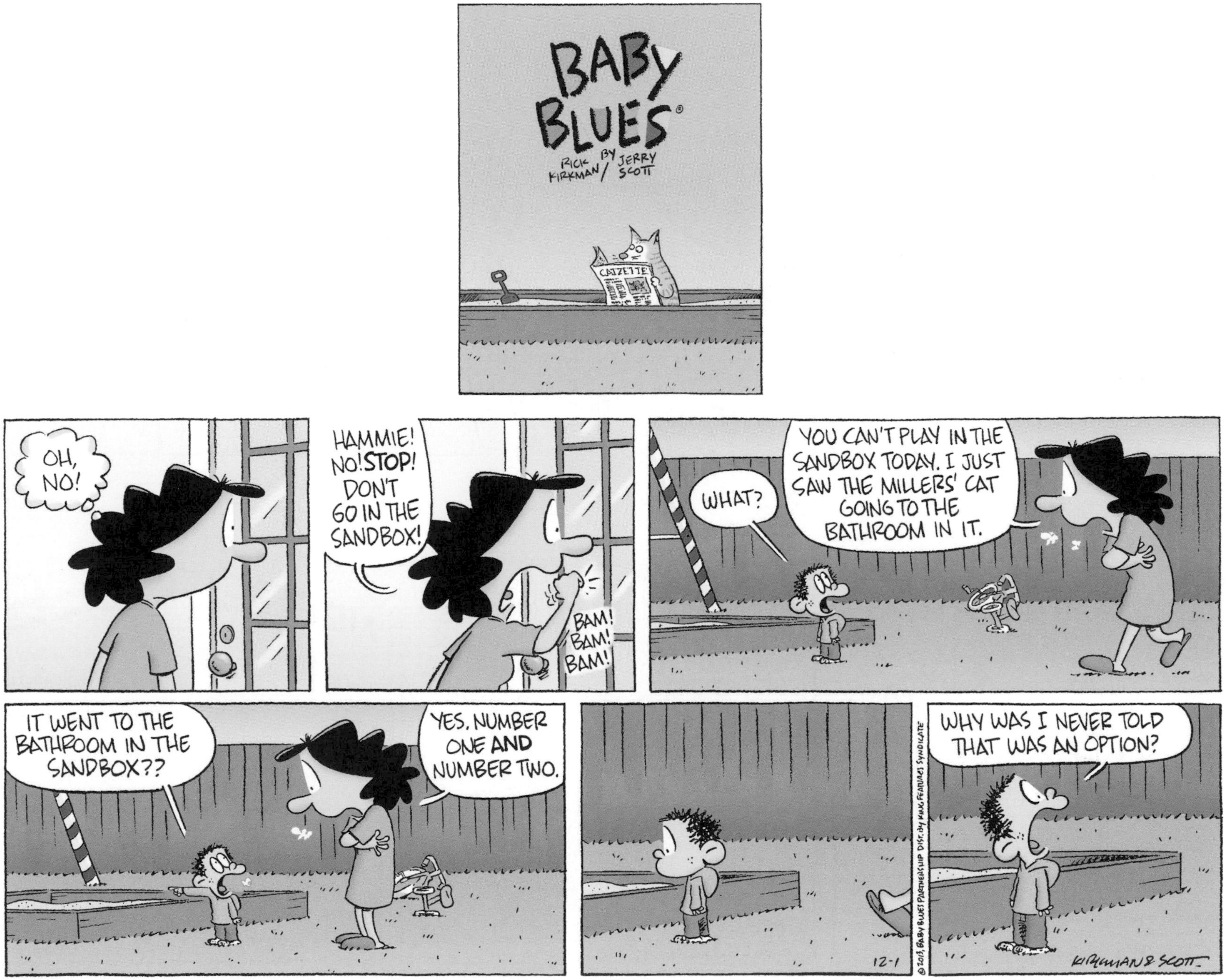
BABY BLUES®
RICK KIRKMAN / BY JERRY SCOTT
CATZETTE
OH, NO!
HAMMIE! NO! **STOP!** DON'T GO IN THE SANDBOX!
BAM! BAM! BAM!
WHAT?
YOU CAN'T PLAY IN THE SANDBOX TODAY. I JUST SAW THE MILLERS' CAT GOING TO THE BATHROOM IN IT.
IT WENT TO THE BATHROOM IN THE SANDBOX??
YES. NUMBER ONE **AND** NUMBER TWO.
12-1
WHY WAS I NEVER TOLD THAT WAS AN OPTION?
KIRKMAN & SCOTT

Rick: A new favorite of mine.

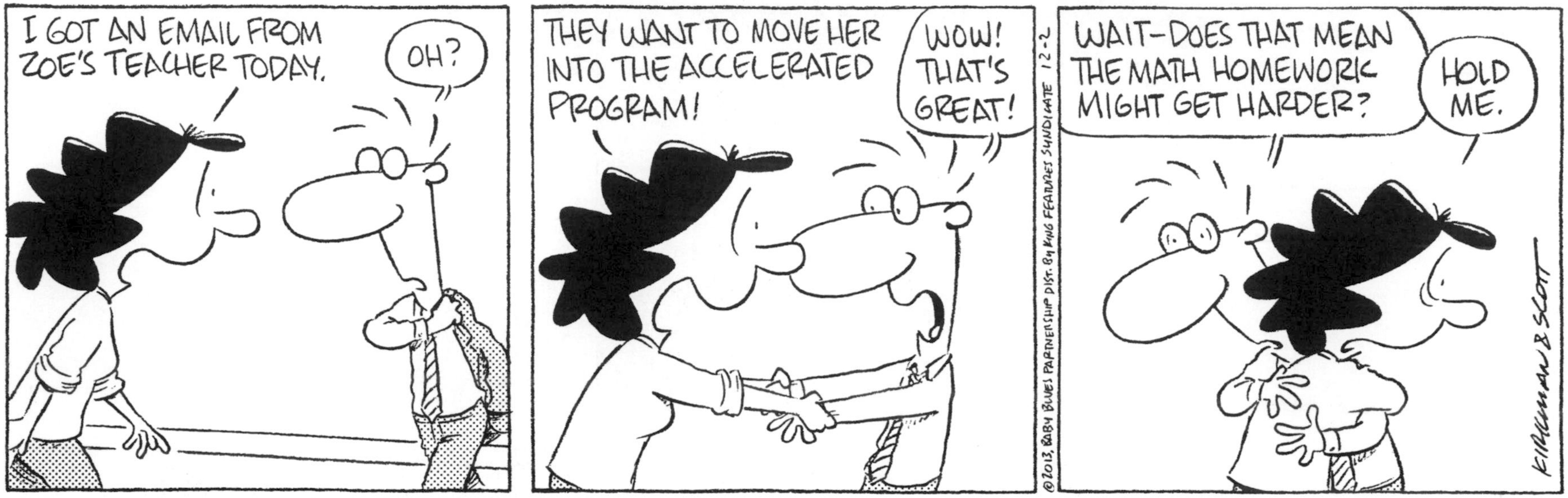
I GOT AN EMAIL FROM ZOE'S TEACHER TODAY.
OH?
THEY WANT TO MOVE HER INTO THE ACCELERATED PROGRAM!
WOW! THAT'S GREAT!
©2013, BABY BLUES PARTNERSHIP DIST. BY KING FEATURES SYNDICATE 12-2
WAIT–DOES THAT MEAN THE MATH HOMEWORK MIGHT GET HARDER?
HOLD ME.
KIRKMAN & SCOTT

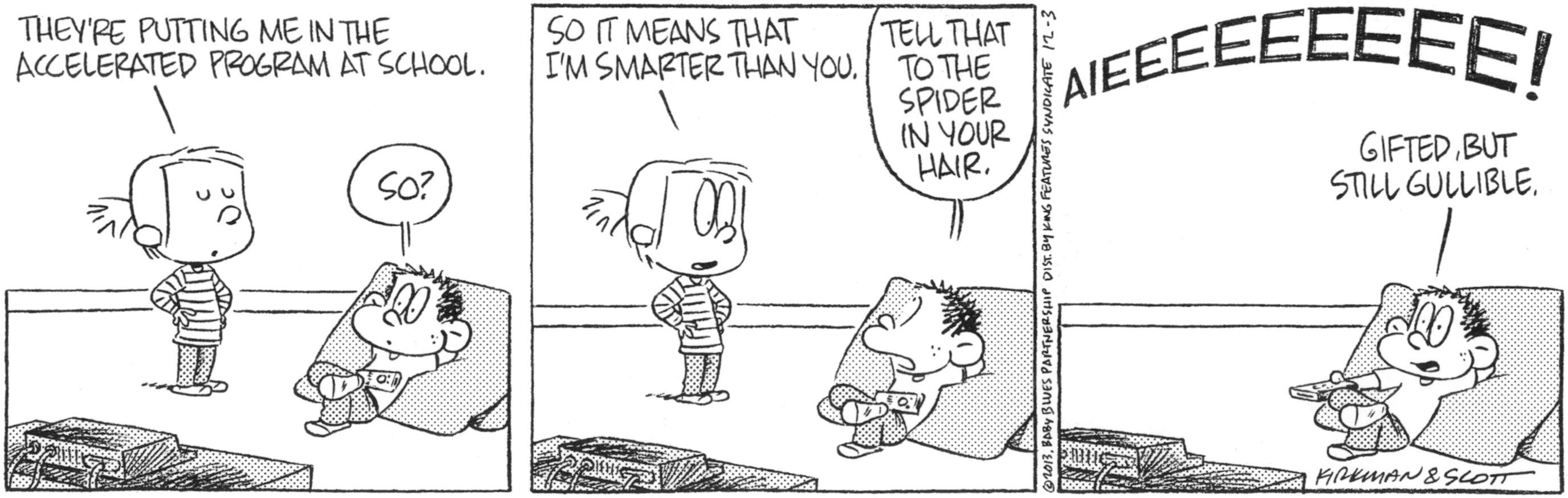
THEY'RE PUTTING ME IN THE ACCELERATED PROGRAM AT SCHOOL.
SO?
SO IT MEANS THAT I'M SMARTER THAN YOU.
TELL THAT TO THE SPIDER IN YOUR HAIR.
©2013, BABY BLUES PARTNERSHIP DIST. BY KING FEATURES SYNDICATE 12-3
AIEEEEEEEEEEE!
GIFTED, BUT STILL GULLIBLE.
KIRKMAN & SCOTT

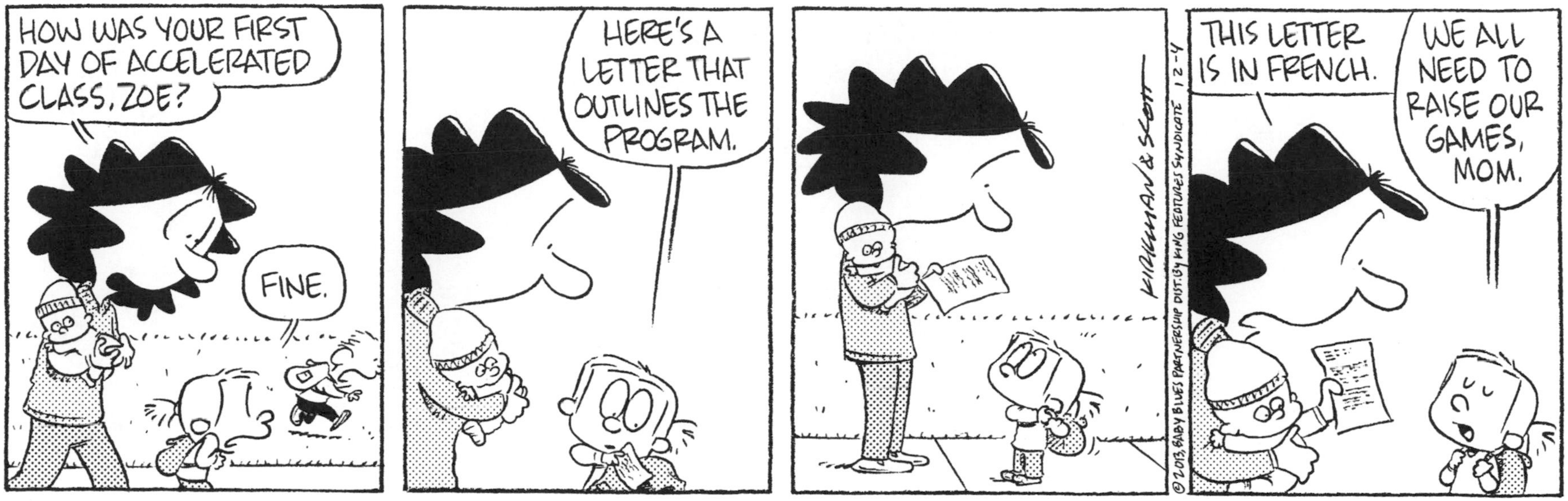

HOW WAS YOUR FIRST DAY OF ACCELERATED CLASS, ZOE?
FINE.
HERE'S A LETTER THAT OUTLINES THE PROGRAM.
KIRKMAN & SCOTT
© 2013, BABY BLUES PARTNERSHIP DIST. BY KING FEATURES SYNDICATE 12-4
THIS LETTER IS IN FRENCH.
WE ALL NEED TO RAISE OUR GAMES, MOM.

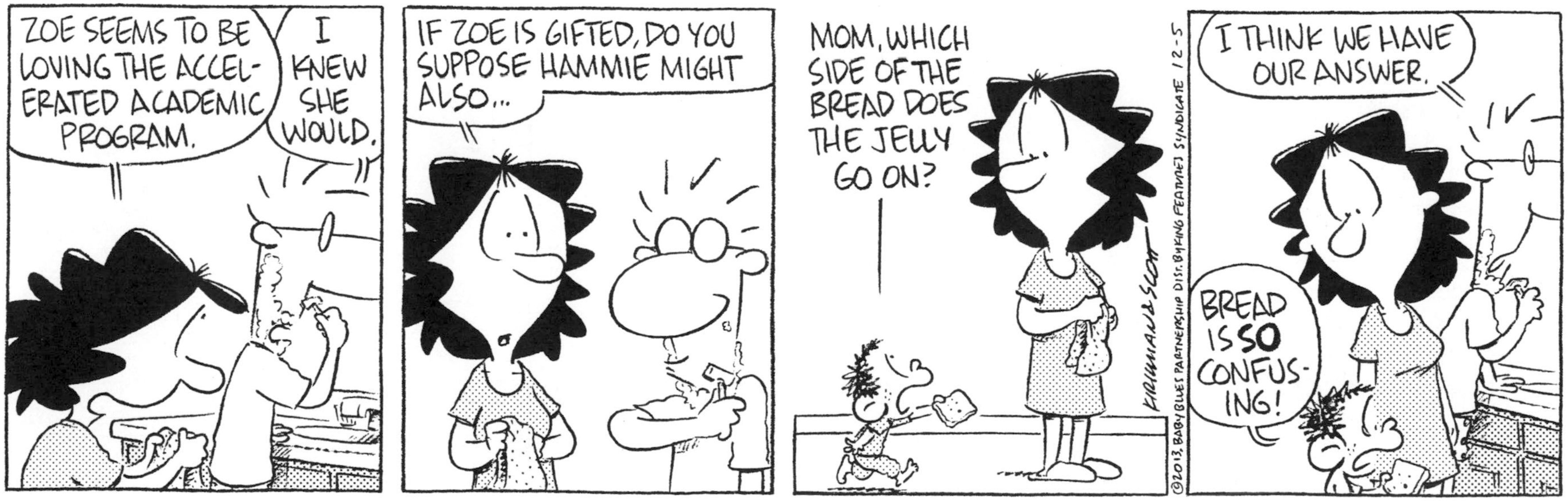

ZOE SEEMS TO BE LOVING THE ACCEL-ERATED ACADEMIC PROGRAM.
I KNEW SHE WOULD.
IF ZOE IS GIFTED, DO YOU SUPPOSE HAMMIE MIGHT ALSO...
MOM, WHICH SIDE OF THE BREAD DOES THE JELLY GO ON?
KIRKMAN & SCOTT
© 2013, BABY BLUES PARTNERSHIP DIST. BY KING FEATURES SYNDICATE 12-5
I THINK WE HAVE OUR ANSWER.
BREAD IS **SO** CONFUS-ING!

Rick: A teacher wrote us at the beginning of this series about how she'd already pegged Hammie as gifted. I wonder what she thought after this strip.

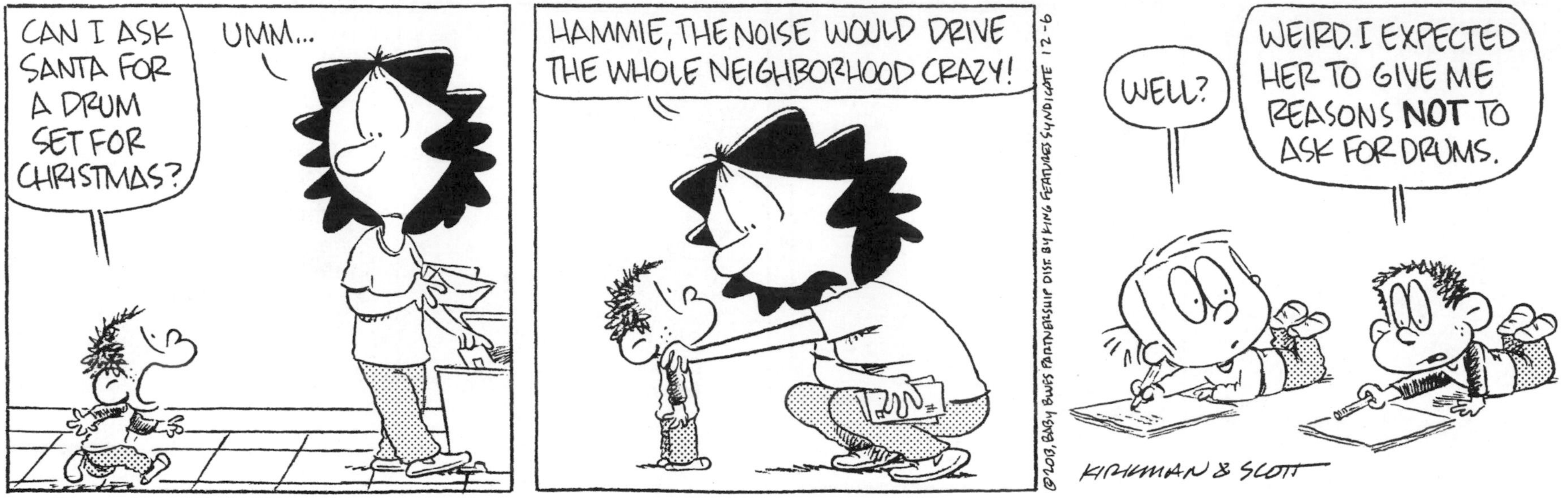
CAN I ASK SANTA FOR A DRUM SET FOR CHRISTMAS?
UMM...
HAMMIE, THE NOISE WOULD DRIVE THE WHOLE NEIGHBORHOOD CRAZY!
WELL?
WEIRD. I EXPECTED HER TO GIVE ME REASONS NOT TO ASK FOR DRUMS.
©2013, BABY BLUES PARTNERSHIP DIST. BY KING FEATURES SYNDICATE 12-6
KIRKMAN & SCOTT

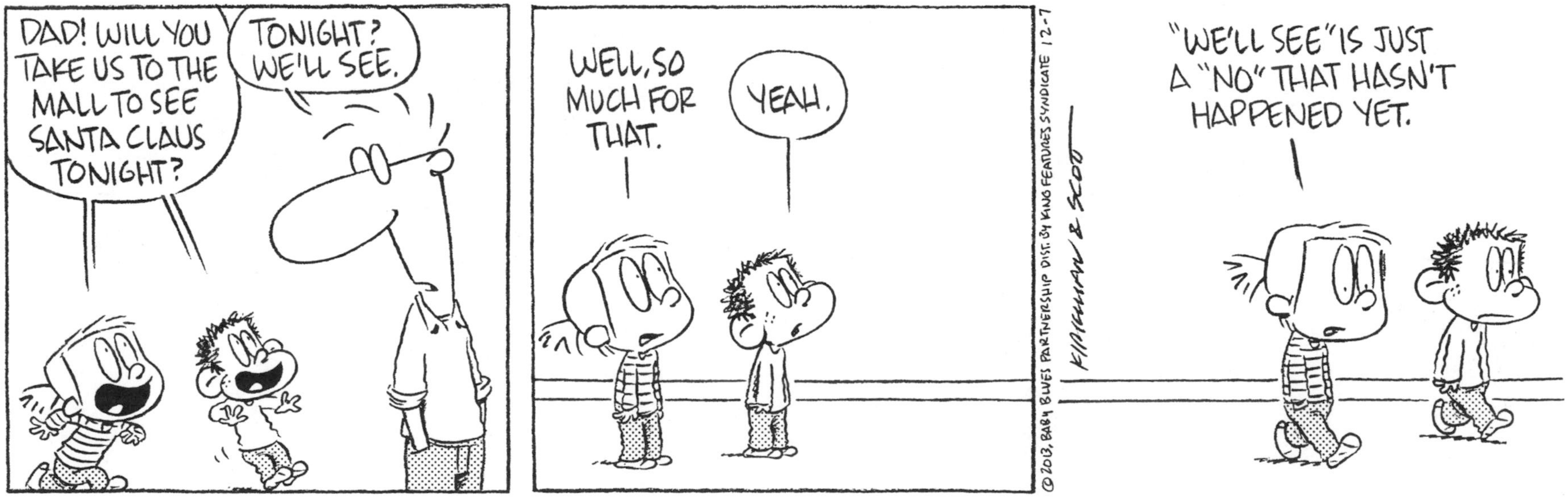
DAD! WILL YOU TAKE US TO THE MALL TO SEE SANTA CLAUS TONIGHT?
TONIGHT? WE'LL SEE.
WELL, SO MUCH FOR THAT.
YEAH.
"WE'LL SEE" IS JUST A "NO" THAT HASN'T HAPPENED YET.
©2013, BABY BLUES PARTNERSHIP DIST. BY KING FEATURES SYNDICATE 12-7
KIRKMAN & SCOTT

Jerry: Somehow, I knew this life fact early on.

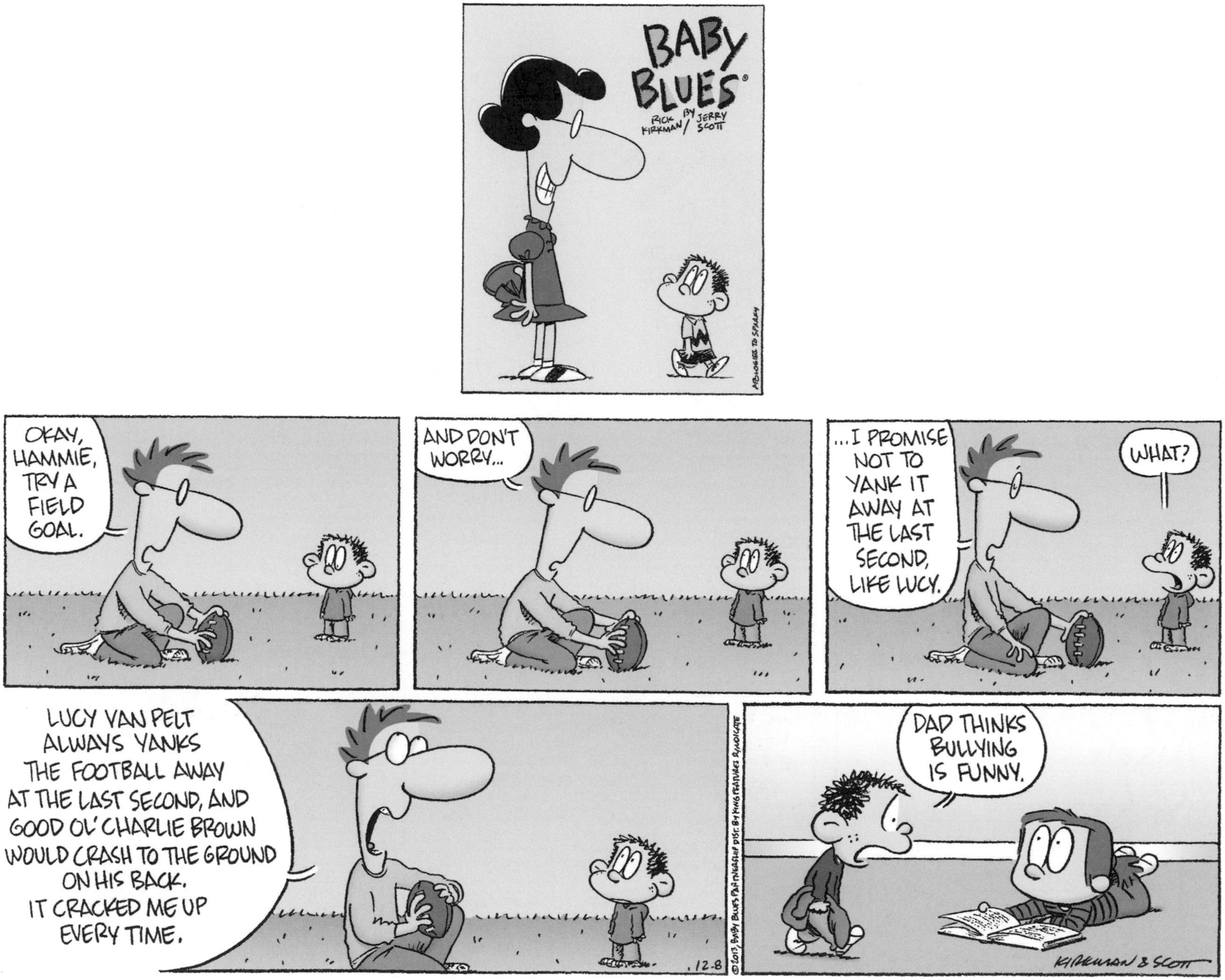
BABY BLUES®
RICK KIRKMAN / BY / JERRY SCOTT
OKAY, HAMMIE, TRY A FIELD GOAL.
AND DON'T WORRY...
...I PROMISE NOT TO YANK IT AWAY AT THE LAST SECOND, LIKE LUCY.
WHAT?
LUCY VAN PELT ALWAYS YANKS THE FOOTBALL AWAY AT THE LAST SECOND, AND GOOD OL' CHARLIE BROWN WOULD CRASH TO THE GROUND ON HIS BACK. IT CRACKED ME UP EVERY TIME.
12-8
DAD THINKS BULLYING IS FUNNY.
KIRKMAN & SCOTT

Rick: Wow. That's a spin on it I never thought of. It was fun turning Darryl and Hammie into Lucy and Charlie Brown.

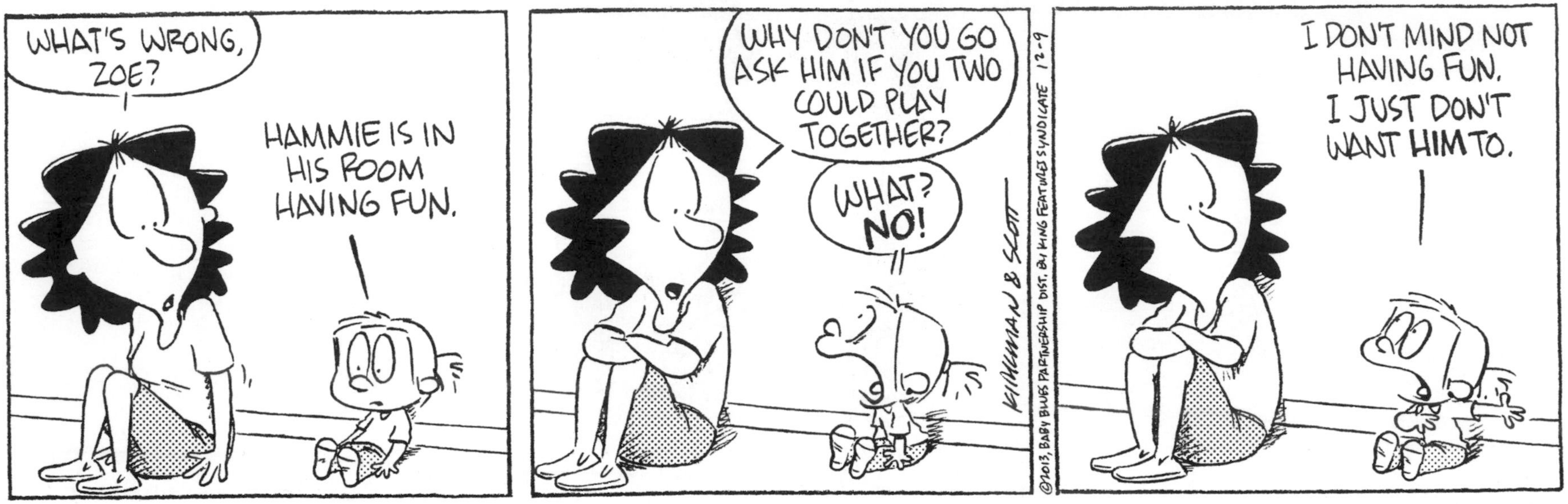
WHAT'S WRONG, ZOE?
HAMMIE IS IN HIS ROOM HAVING FUN.
WHY DON'T YOU GO ASK HIM IF YOU TWO COULD PLAY TOGETHER?
WHAT? NO!
KIRKMAN & SCOTT
©2013, BABY BLUES PARTNERSHIP DIST. BY KING FEATURES SYNDICATE 12-9
I DON'T MIND NOT HAVING FUN. I JUST DON'T WANT HIM TO.

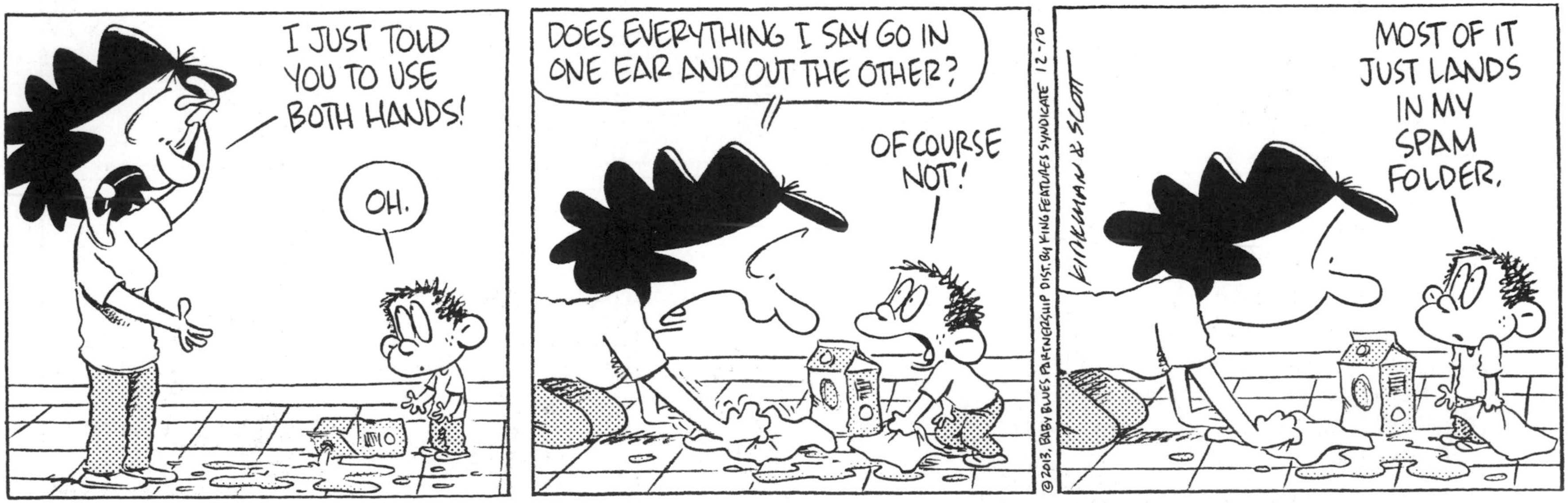
I JUST TOLD YOU TO USE BOTH HANDS!
OH.
DOES EVERYTHING I SAY GO IN ONE EAR AND OUT THE OTHER?
OF COURSE NOT!
©2013, BABY BLUES PARTNERSHIP DIST. BY KING FEATURES SYNDICATE 12-10
KIRKMAN & SCOTT
MOST OF IT JUST LANDS IN MY SPAM FOLDER.

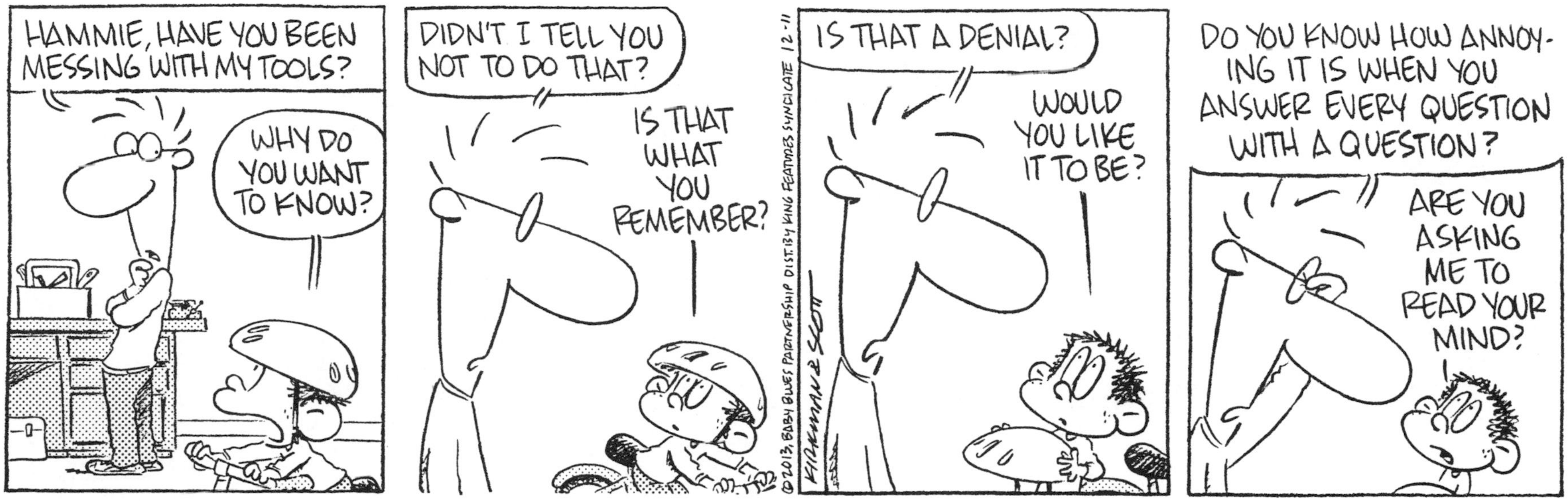
HAMMIE, HAVE YOU BEEN MESSING WITH MY TOOLS?
WHY DO YOU WANT TO KNOW?
DIDN'T I TELL YOU NOT TO DO THAT?
IS THAT WHAT YOU REMEMBER?
©2013, BABY BLUES PARTNERSHIP DIST. BY KING FEATURES SYNDICATE 12-11
KIRKMAN & SCOTT
IS THAT A DENIAL?
WOULD YOU LIKE IT TO BE?
DO YOU KNOW HOW ANNOYING IT IS WHEN YOU ANSWER EVERY QUESTION WITH A QUESTION?
ARE YOU ASKING ME TO READ YOUR MIND?

Rick: Despite all evidence to the contrary, I think Hammie might have a future as a lawyer. Or a psychotherapist.

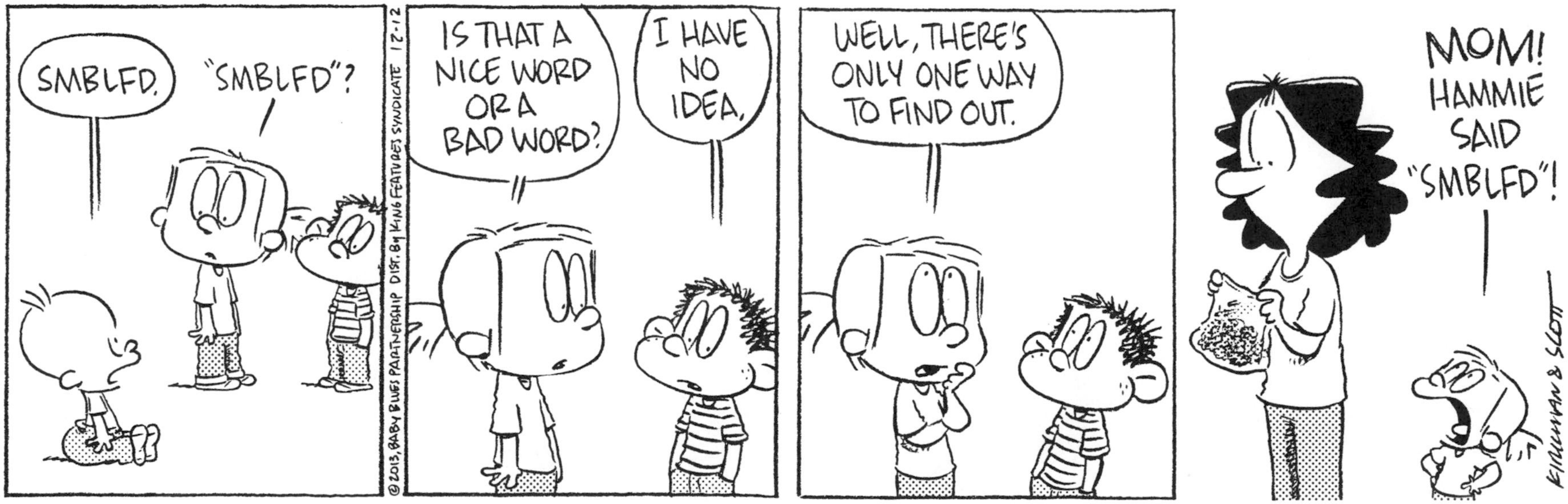
SMBLFD.
"SMBLFD"?
©2013, BABY BLUES PARTNERSHIP DIST. BY KING FEATURES SYNDICATE 12-12
IS THAT A NICE WORD OR A BAD WORD?
I HAVE NO IDEA.
WELL, THERE'S ONLY ONE WAY TO FIND OUT.
MOM! HAMMIE SAID "SMBLFD"!
KIRKMAN & SCOTT

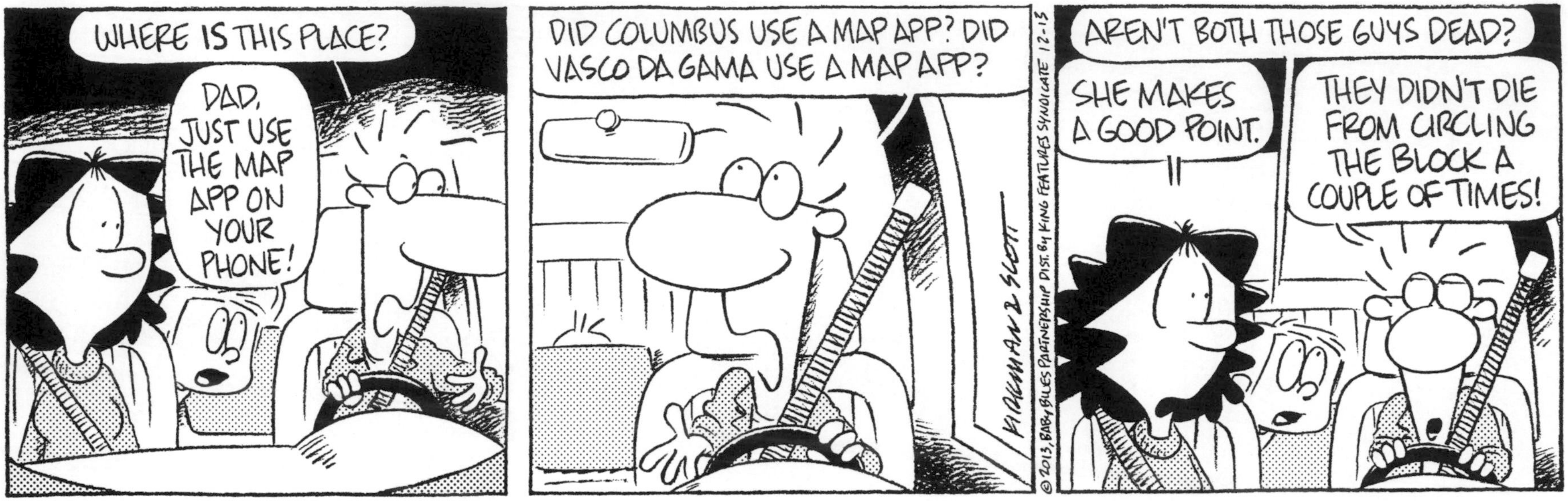
WHERE IS THIS PLACE?
DAD, JUST USE THE MAP APP ON YOUR PHONE!
DID COLUMBUS USE A MAP APP? DID VASCO DA GAMA USE A MAP APP?
KIRKMAN & SCOTT
© 2013, BABY BLUES PARTNERSHIP DIST. BY KING FEATURES SYNDICATE 12-13
AREN'T BOTH THOSE GUYS DEAD?
SHE MAKES A GOOD POINT.
THEY DIDN'T DIE FROM CIRCLING THE BLOCK A COUPLE OF TIMES!

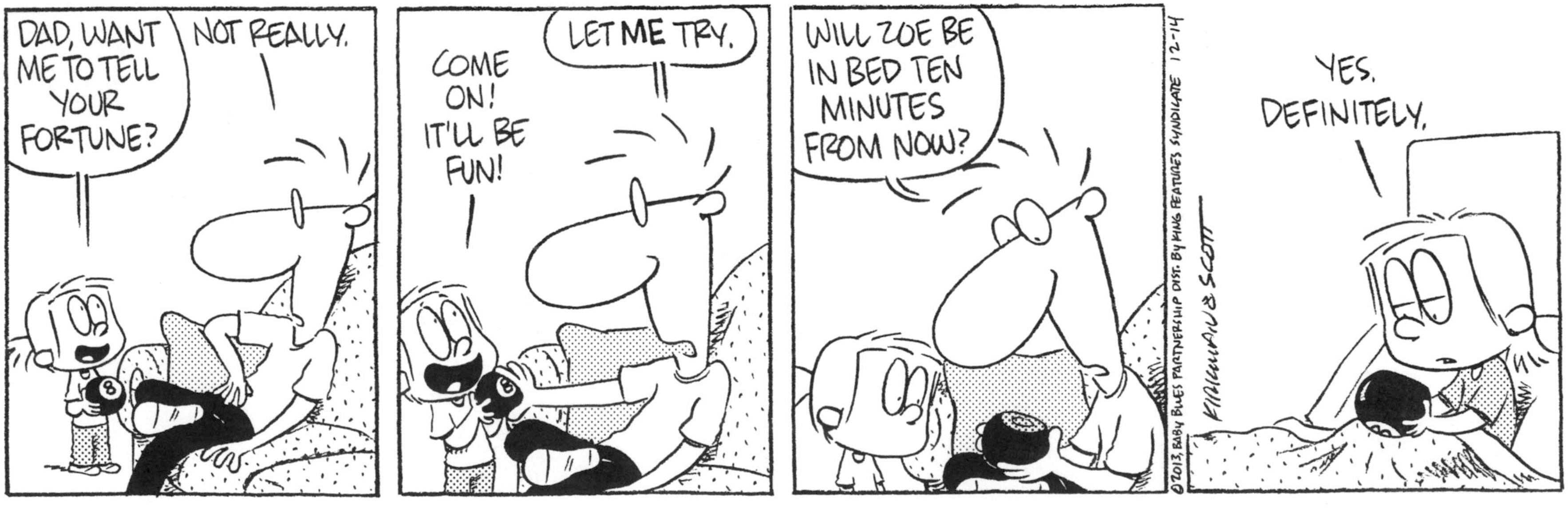
DAD, WANT ME TO TELL YOUR FORTUNE?
NOT REALLY.
COME ON! IT'LL BE FUN!
LET ME TRY.
WILL ZOE BE IN BED TEN MINUTES FROM NOW?
© 2013, BABY BLUES PARTNERSHIP DIST. BY KING FEATURES SYNDICATE 12-14
KIRKMAN & SCOTT
YES. DEFINITELY.

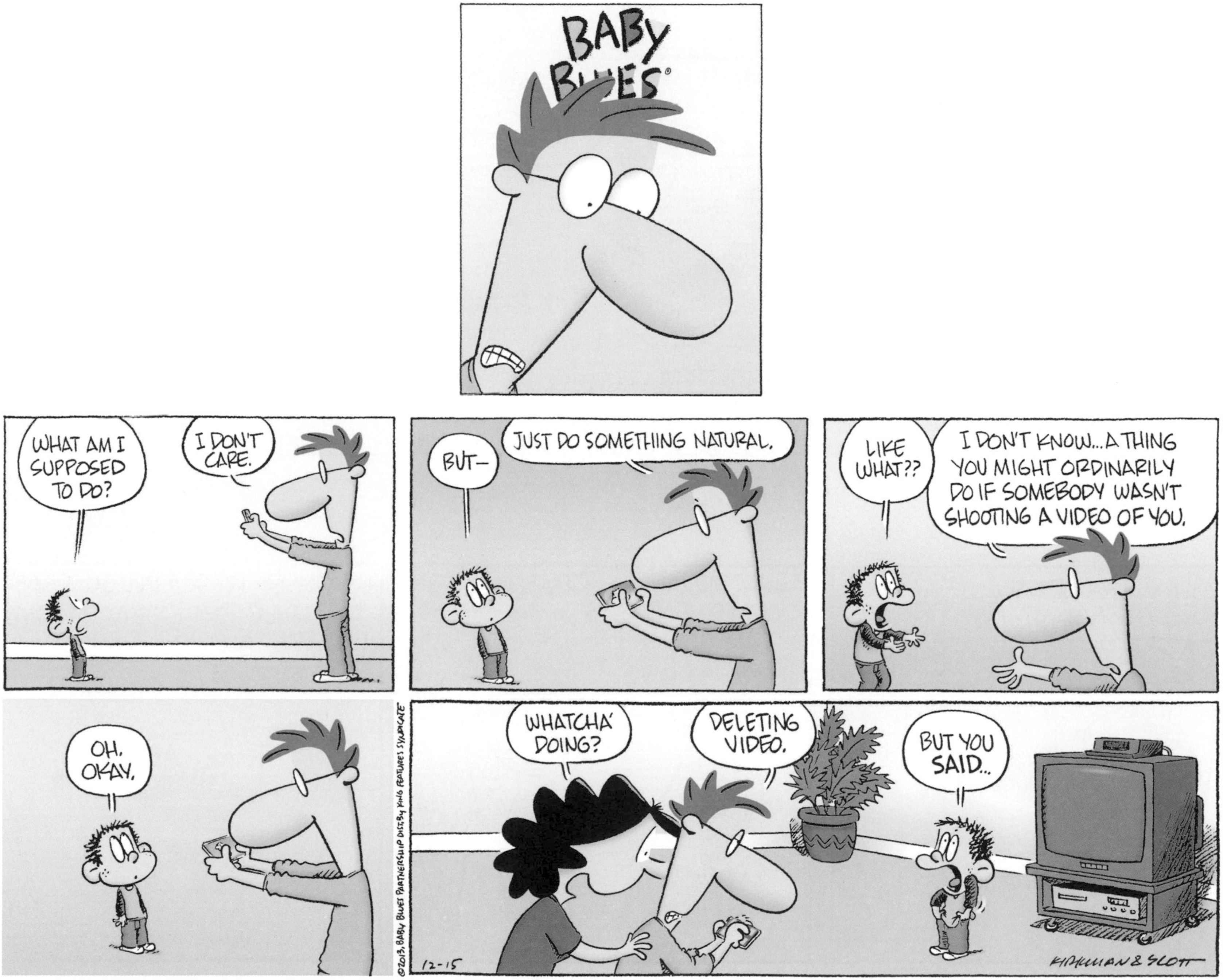
BABY BLUES®
WHAT AM I SUPPOSED TO DO?
I DON'T CARE.
BUT–
JUST DO SOMETHING NATURAL.
LIKE WHAT??
I DON'T KNOW... A THING YOU MIGHT ORDINARILY DO IF SOMEBODY WASN'T SHOOTING A VIDEO OF YOU.
OH. OKAY.
©2013, BABY BLUES PARTNERSHIP DIST. BY KING FEATURES SYNDICATE
WHATCHA' DOING?
DELETING VIDEO.
BUT YOU SAID...
12-15
KIRKMAN & SCOTT

Jerry: A lot happened in the space between the fourth and fifth panels in this strip. You can decide what it was.

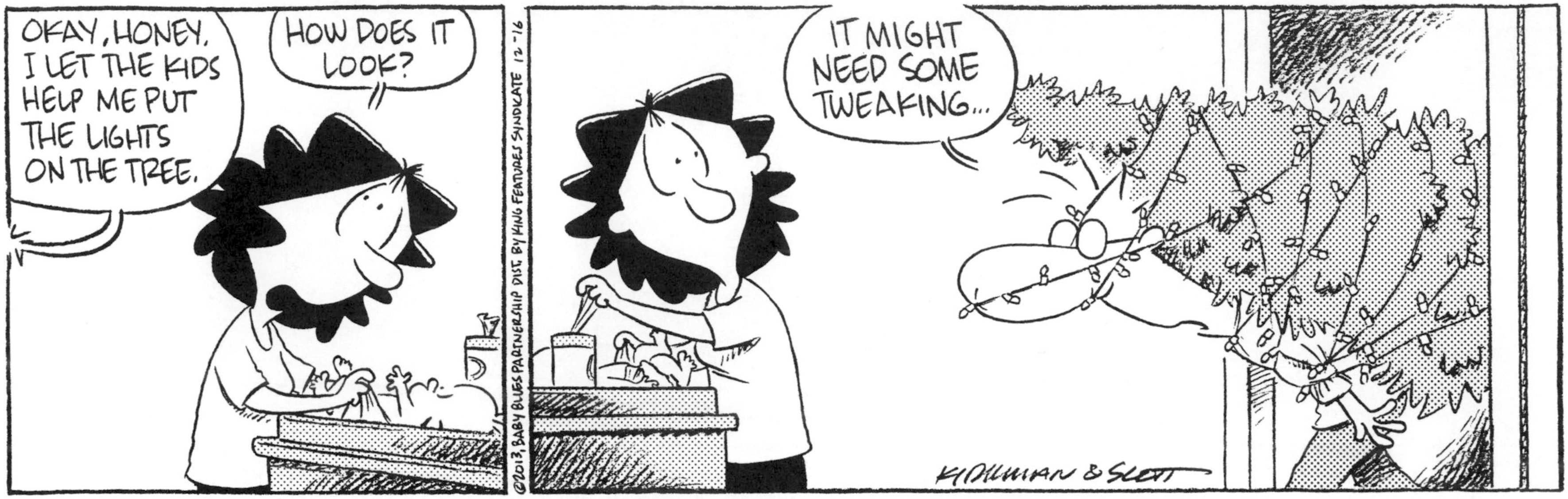
OKAY, HONEY, I LET THE KIDS HELP ME PUT THE LIGHTS ON THE TREE.
HOW DOES IT LOOK?
©2013, BABY BLUES PARTNERSHIP DIST. BY KING FEATURES SYNDICATE 12-16
IT MIGHT NEED SOME TWEAKING...
KIRKMAN & SCOTT

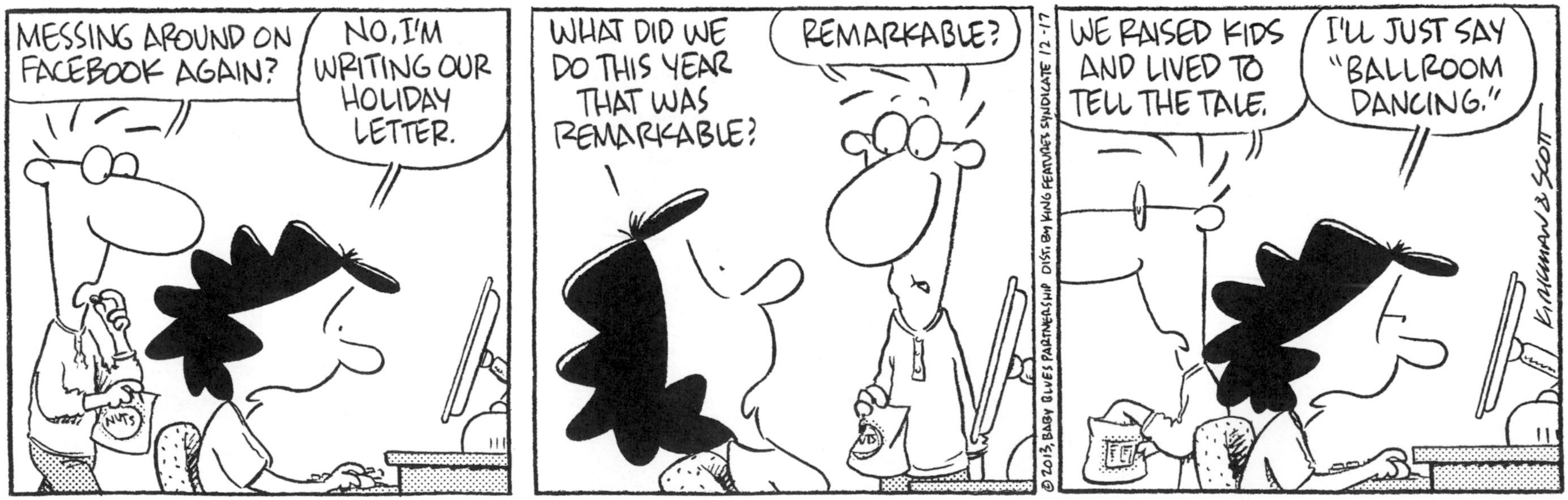
MESSING AROUND ON FACEBOOK AGAIN?
NO, I'M WRITING OUR HOLIDAY LETTER.
NUTS
WHAT DID WE DO THIS YEAR THAT WAS REMARKABLE?
REMARKABLE?
©2013, BABY BLUES PARTNERSHIP DIST. BY KING FEATURES SYNDICATE 12-17
WE RAISED KIDS AND LIVED TO TELL THE TALE.
I'LL JUST SAY "BALLROOM DANCING."
KIRKMAN & SCOTT

Jerry: I've always considered the holiday letter semifictional.

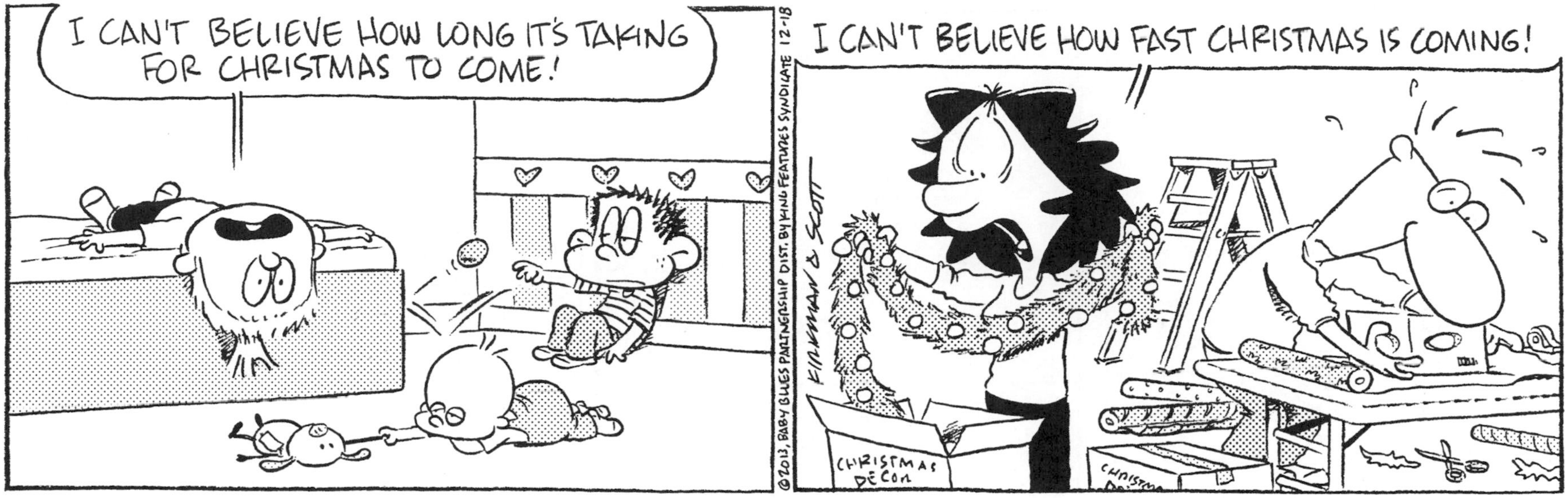

I CAN'T BELIEVE HOW LONG IT'S TAKING FOR CHRISTMAS TO COME!
©2013, BABY BLUES PARTNERSHIP DIST. BY KING FEATURES SYNDICATE 12-18
KIRKMAN & SCOTT
I CAN'T BELIEVE HOW FAST CHRISTMAS IS COMING!
CHRISTMAS DECOR

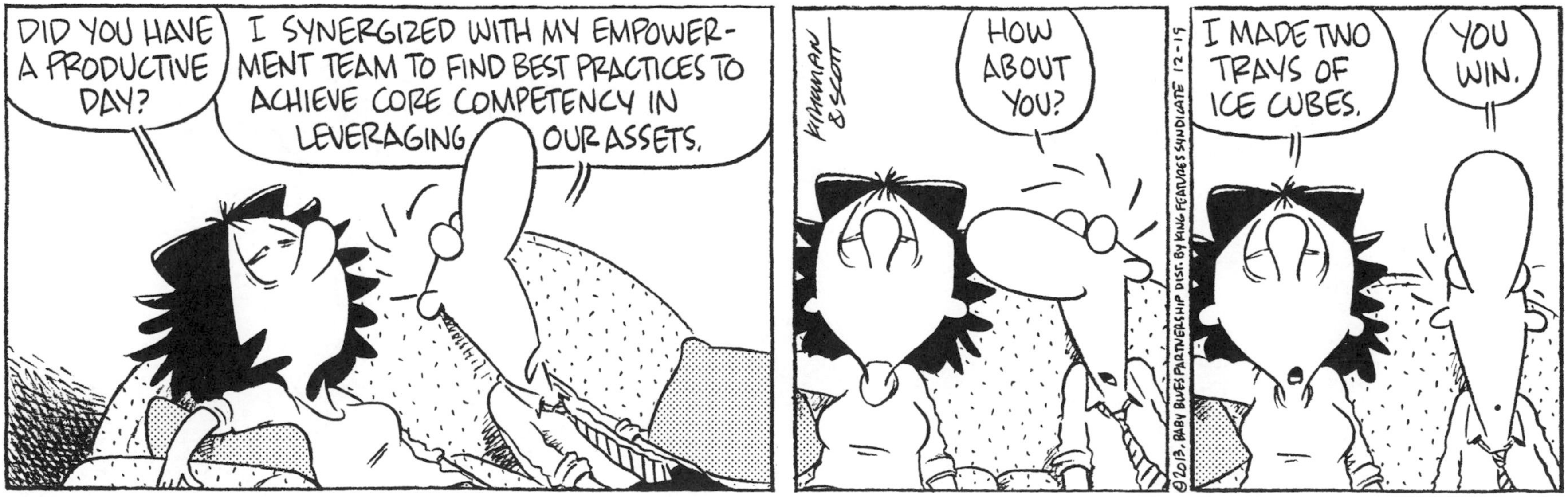

DID YOU HAVE A PRODUCTIVE DAY?
I SYNERGIZED WITH MY EMPOWERMENT TEAM TO FIND BEST PRACTICES TO ACHIEVE CORE COMPETENCY IN LEVERAGING OUR ASSETS.
KIRKMAN & SCOTT
HOW ABOUT YOU?
©2013, BABY BLUES PARTNERSHIP DIST. BY KING FEATURES SYNDICATE 12-19
I MADE TWO TRAYS OF ICE CUBES.
YOU WIN.

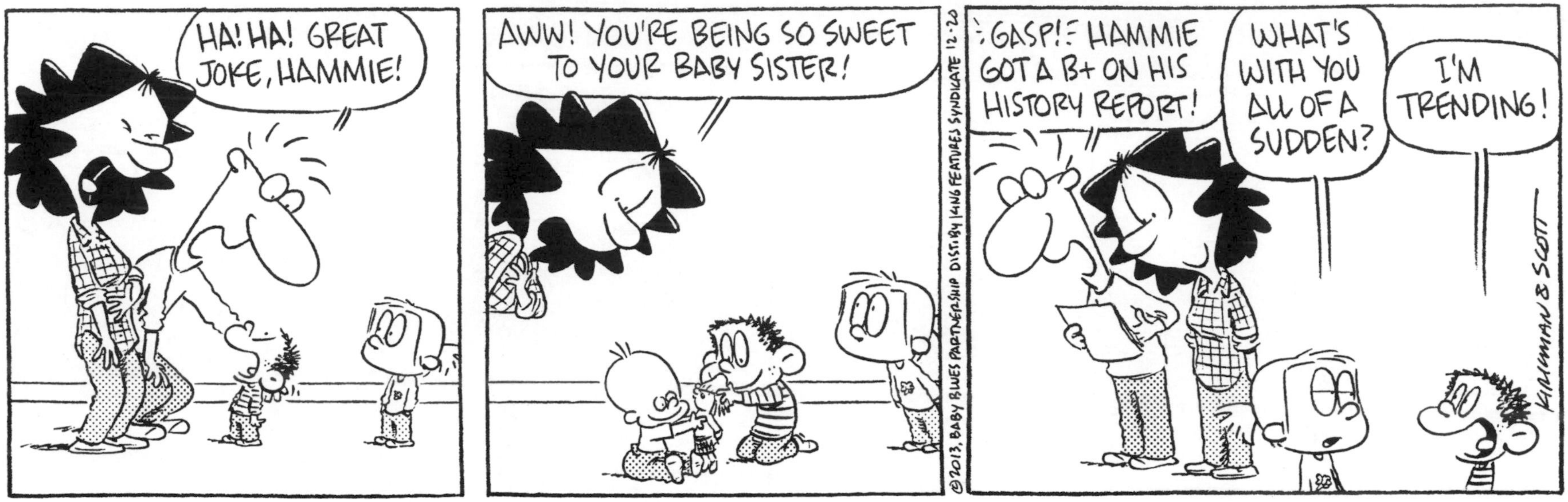
HA! HA! GREAT JOKE, HAMMIE!
AWW! YOU'RE BEING SO SWEET TO YOUR BABY SISTER!
12-20
©2013, BABY BLUES PARTNERSHIP DIST. BY KING FEATURES SYNDICATE
:GASP!: HAMMIE GOT A B+ ON HIS HISTORY REPORT!
WHAT'S WITH YOU ALL OF A SUDDEN?
I'M TRENDING!
KIRKMAN & SCOTT

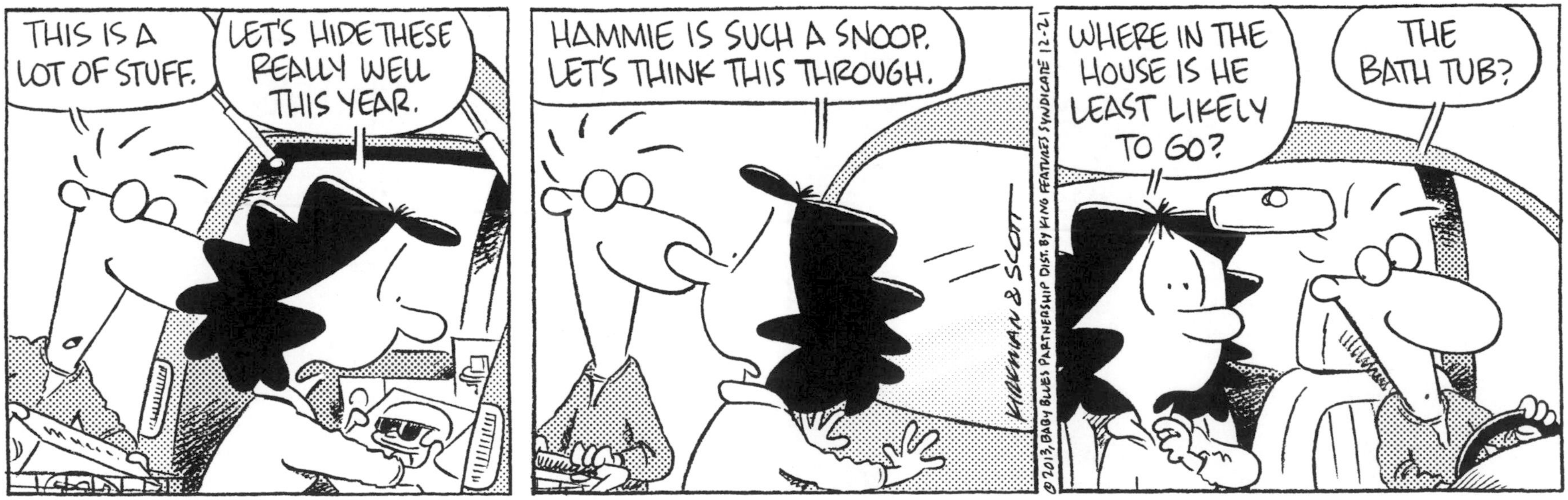
THIS IS A LOT OF STUFF.
LET'S HIDE THESE REALLY WELL THIS YEAR.
HAMMIE IS SUCH A SNOOP. LET'S THINK THIS THROUGH.
KIRKMAN & SCOTT
12-21
©2013, BABY BLUES PARTNERSHIP DIST. BY KING FEATURES SYNDICATE
WHERE IN THE HOUSE IS HE LEAST LIKELY TO GO?
THE BATH TUB?

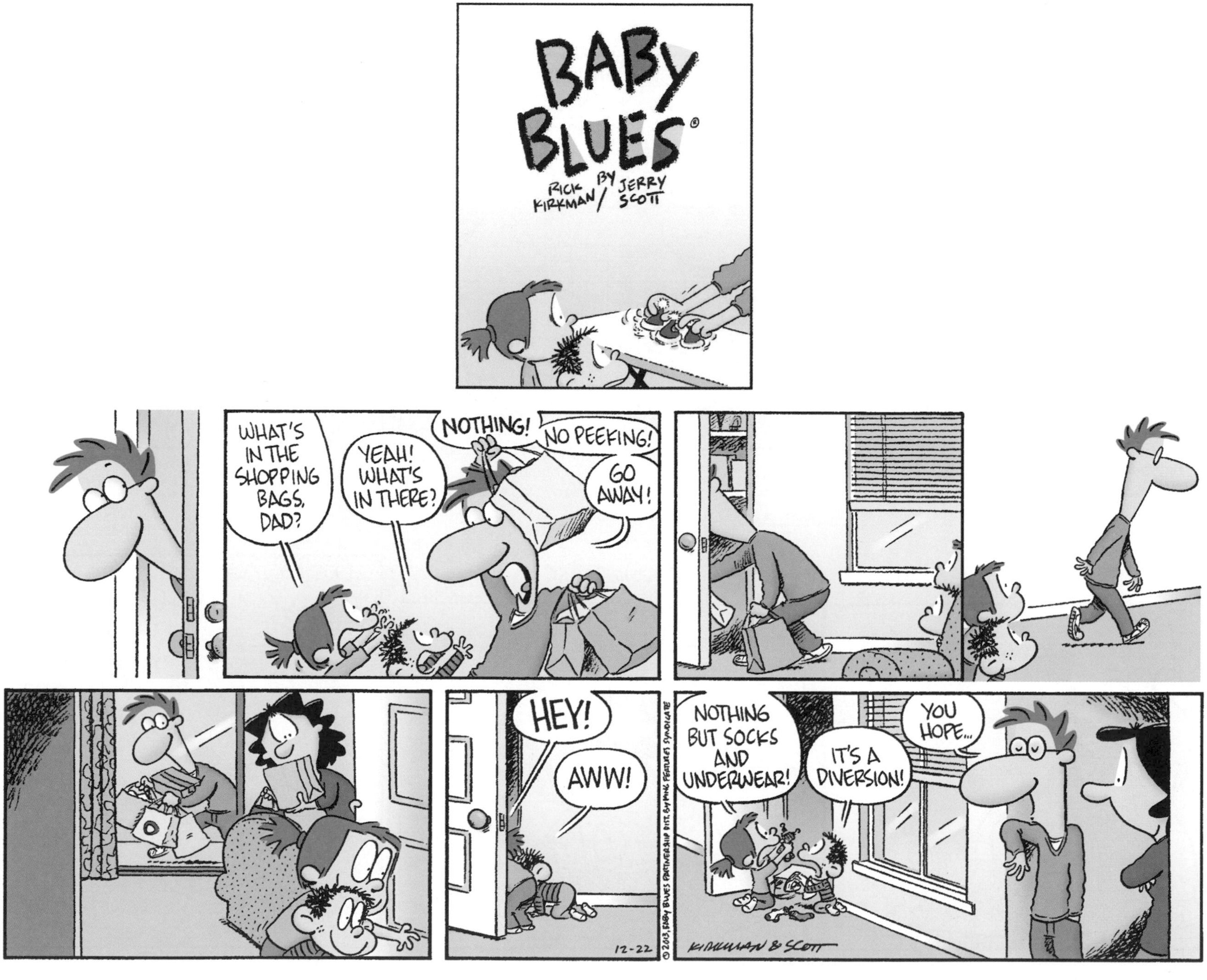
BABY BLUES®
BY RICK KIRKMAN / JERRY SCOTT
WHAT'S IN THE SHOPPING BAGS, DAD?
YEAH! WHAT'S IN THERE?
NOTHING!
NO PEEKING!
GO AWAY!
HEY!
AWW!
© 2013, BABY BLUES PARTNERSHIP DIST. BY KING FEATURES SYNDICATE
12-22
NOTHING BUT SOCKS AND UNDERWEAR!
IT'S A DIVERSION!
YOU HOPE...
KIRKMAN & SCOTT

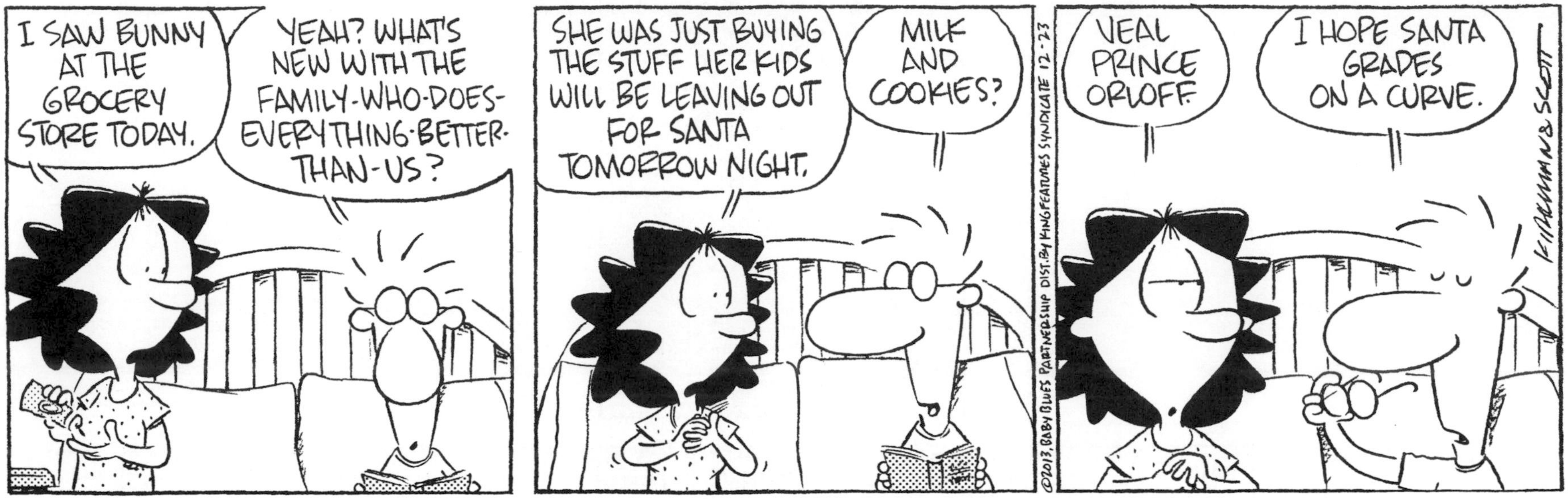
I SAW BUNNY AT THE GROCERY STORE TODAY.
YEAH? WHAT'S NEW WITH THE FAMILY-WHO-DOES-EVERYTHING-BETTER-THAN-US?
SHE WAS JUST BUYING THE STUFF HER KIDS WILL BE LEAVING OUT FOR SANTA TOMORROW NIGHT.
MILK AND COOKIES?
©2013, BABY BLUES PARTNERSHIP DIST. BY KING FEATURES SYNDICATE 12-23
VEAL PRINCE ORLOFF.
I HOPE SANTA GRADES ON A CURVE.
KIRKMAN & SCOTT

Jerry: We always leave cookies. Okay, sometimes they're not exactly homemade, but by the time Santa gets down the alphabet to the Scotts on the list, is he really paying all that much attention?

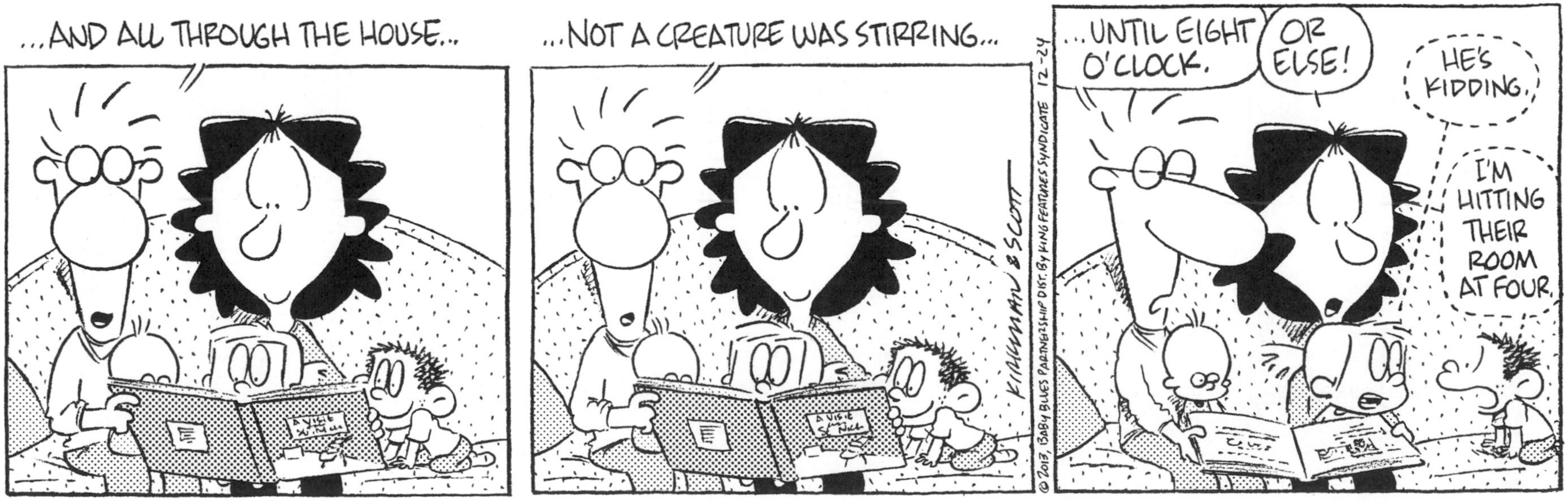
...AND ALL THROUGH THE HOUSE...
...NOT A CREATURE WAS STIRRING...
KIRKMAN & SCOTT
©2013, BABY BLUES PARTNERSHIP DIST. BY KING FEATURES SYNDICATE 12-24
...UNTIL EIGHT O'CLOCK.
OR ELSE!
HE'S KIDDING.
I'M HITTING THEIR ROOM AT FOUR.

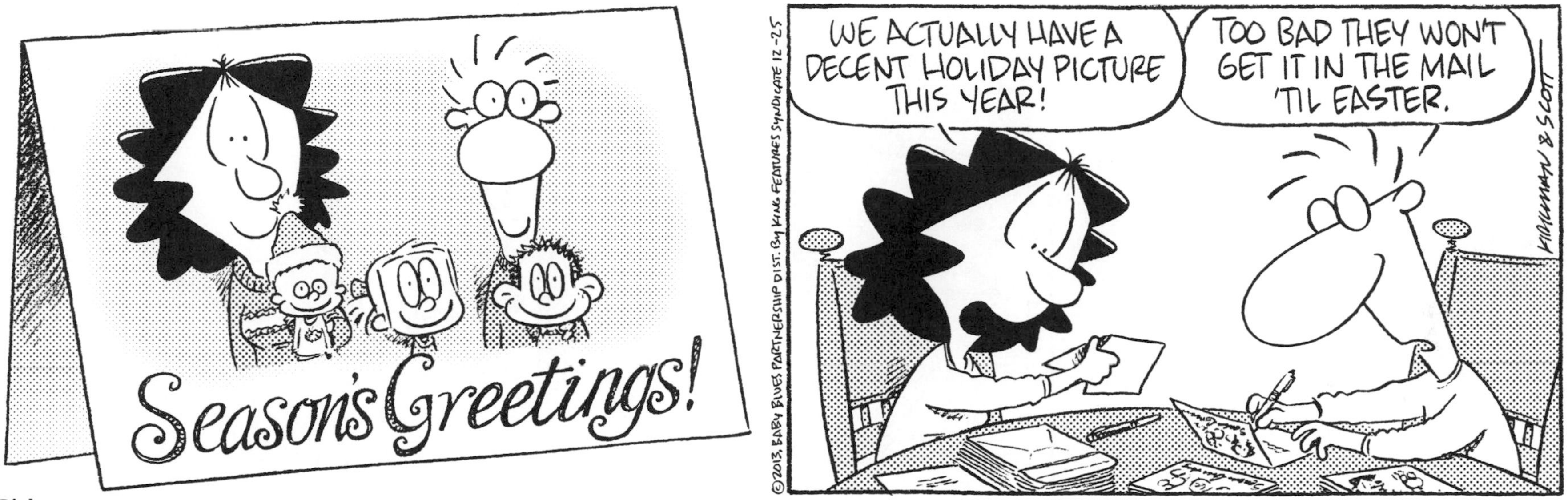
Season's Greetings!
©2013, Baby Blues Partnership Dist. By King Features Syndicate 12-25
WE ACTUALLY HAVE A DECENT HOLIDAY PICTURE THIS YEAR!
TOO BAD THEY WON'T GET IT IN THE MAIL 'TIL EASTER.
KIRKMAN & SCOTT

Rick: This strip prompted the following e-mail:

Sir — You must think I'm an idiot. In no way does it do anything but imply otherwise - it's clear as gin that they are suggesting that the postal service will not get their cards to there [sic] destination before Easter.

As a 40 year veteran of the Postal Service I am offended by this strip, and if I didn't enjoy it I would probably treat it like 'XXXXXXX' - and never read it."

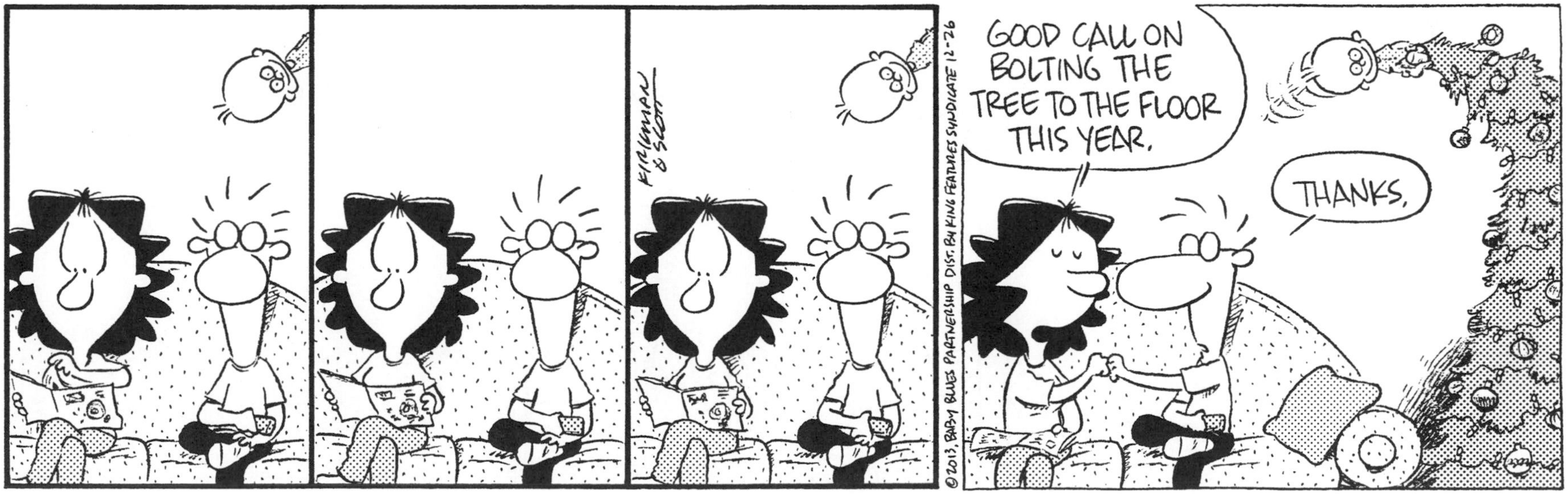
KIRKMAN & SCOTT
©2013, Baby Blues Partnership Dist. By King Features Syndicate 12-26
GOOD CALL ON BOLTING THE TREE TO THE FLOOR THIS YEAR.
THANKS.

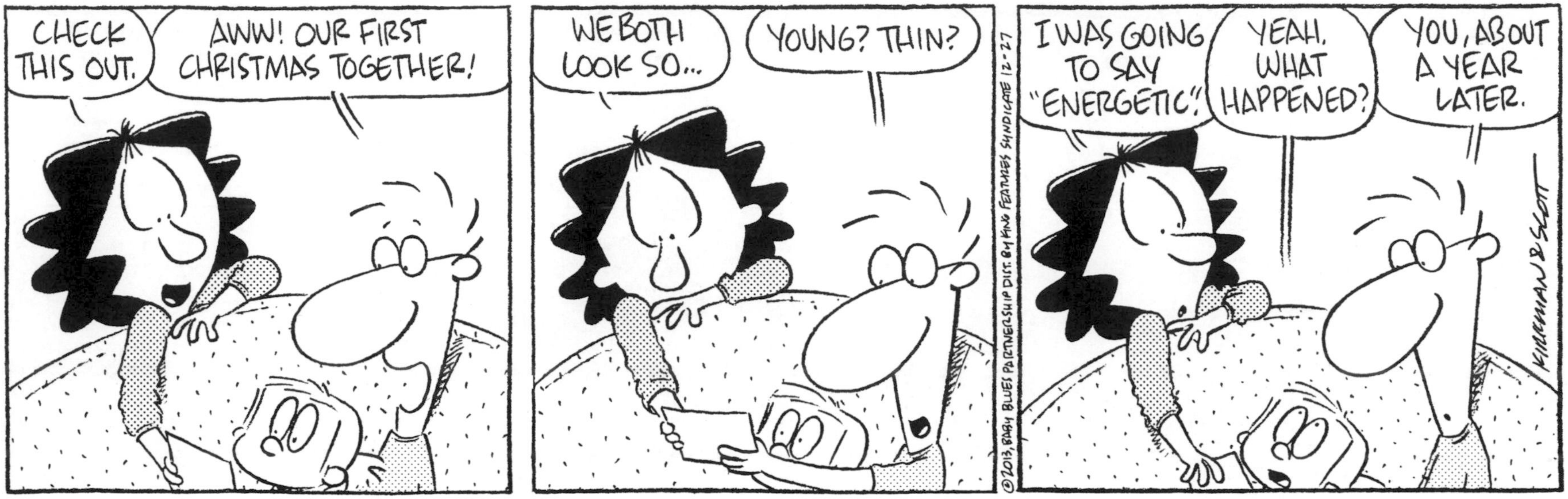
CHECK THIS OUT.
AWW! OUR FIRST CHRISTMAS TOGETHER!
WE BOTH LOOK SO...
YOUNG? THIN?
I WAS GOING TO SAY "ENERGETIC."
YEAH. WHAT HAPPENED?
YOU, ABOUT A YEAR LATER.
©2013, BABY BLUES PARTNERSHIP DIST. BY KING FEATURES SYNDICATE 12-27
KIRKMAN & SCOTT

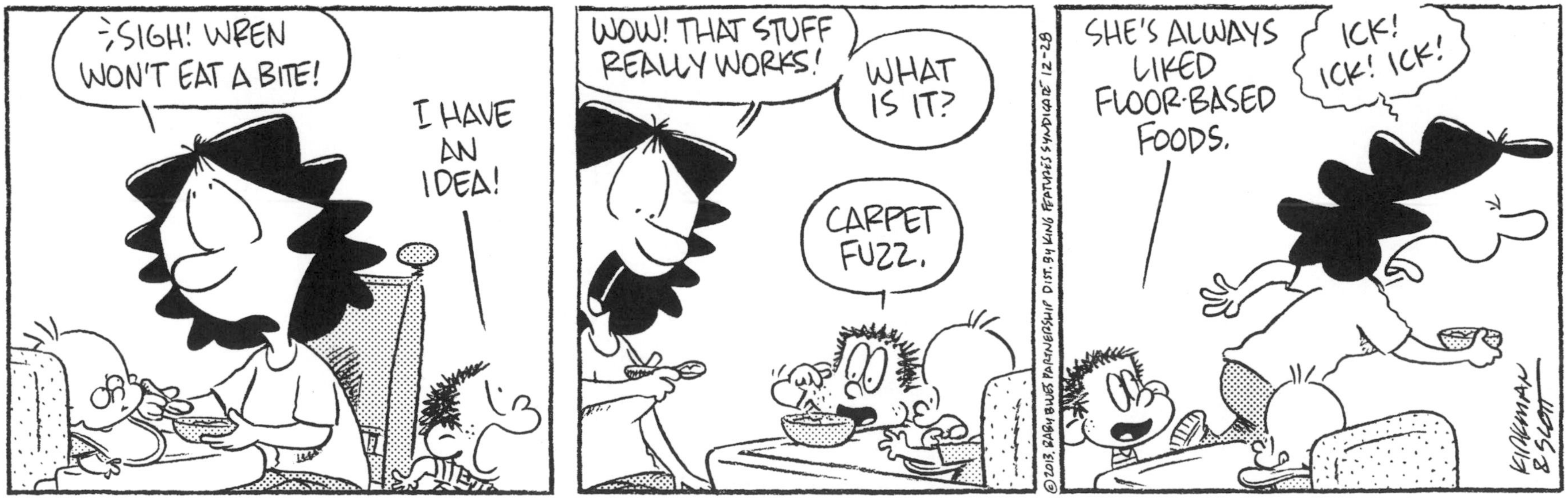
SIGH! WREN WON'T EAT A BITE!
I HAVE AN IDEA!
WOW! THAT STUFF REALLY WORKS!
WHAT IS IT?
CARPET FUZZ.
SHE'S ALWAYS LIKED FLOOR-BASED FOODS.
ICK! ICK! ICK!
©2013, BABY BLUES PARTNERSHIP DIST. BY KING FEATURES SYNDICATE 12-28
KIRKMAN & SCOTT

Jerry: Best that we parents don't know every single detail about every single detail.

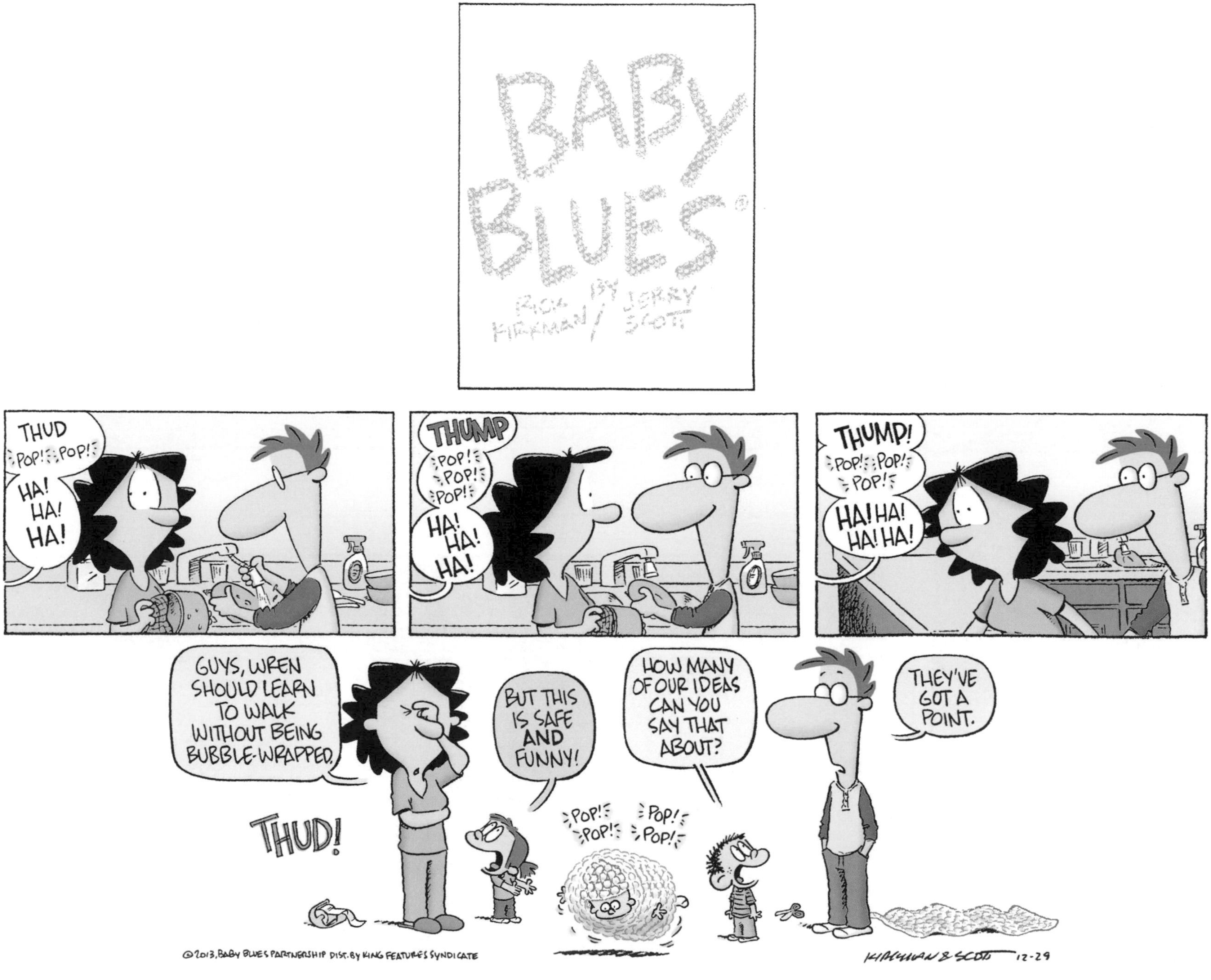

BABY BLUES®
BY RICK KIRKMAN / JERRY SCOTT
THUD
POP! POP!
HA! HA! HA!
THUMP
POP! POP! POP!
HA! HA! HA!
THUMP!
POP! POP! POP!
HA! HA! HA! HA!
GUYS, WREN SHOULD LEARN TO WALK WITHOUT BEING BUBBLE-WRAPPED.
BUT THIS IS SAFE AND FUNNY!
HOW MANY OF OUR IDEAS CAN YOU SAY THAT ABOUT?
THEY'VE GOT A POINT.
THUD!
POP! POP! POP! POP!
©2013, BABY BLUES PARTNERSHIP DIST. BY KING FEATURES SYNDICATE
KIRKMAN & SCOTT 12-29

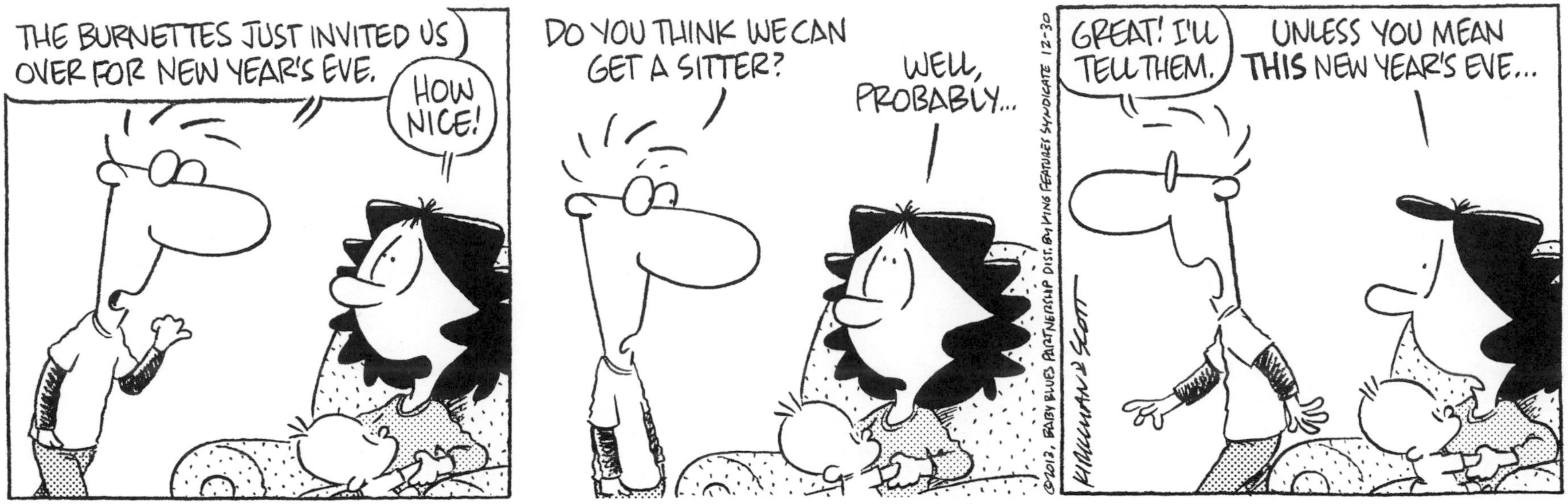
THE BURNETTES JUST INVITED US OVER FOR NEW YEAR'S EVE.
HOW NICE!
DO YOU THINK WE CAN GET A SITTER?
WELL, PROBABLY...
GREAT! I'LL TELL THEM.
UNLESS YOU MEAN THIS NEW YEAR'S EVE...
©2012, BABY BLUES PARTNERSHIP DIST. BY KING FEATURES SYNDICATE 12-30
KIRKMAN & SCOTT

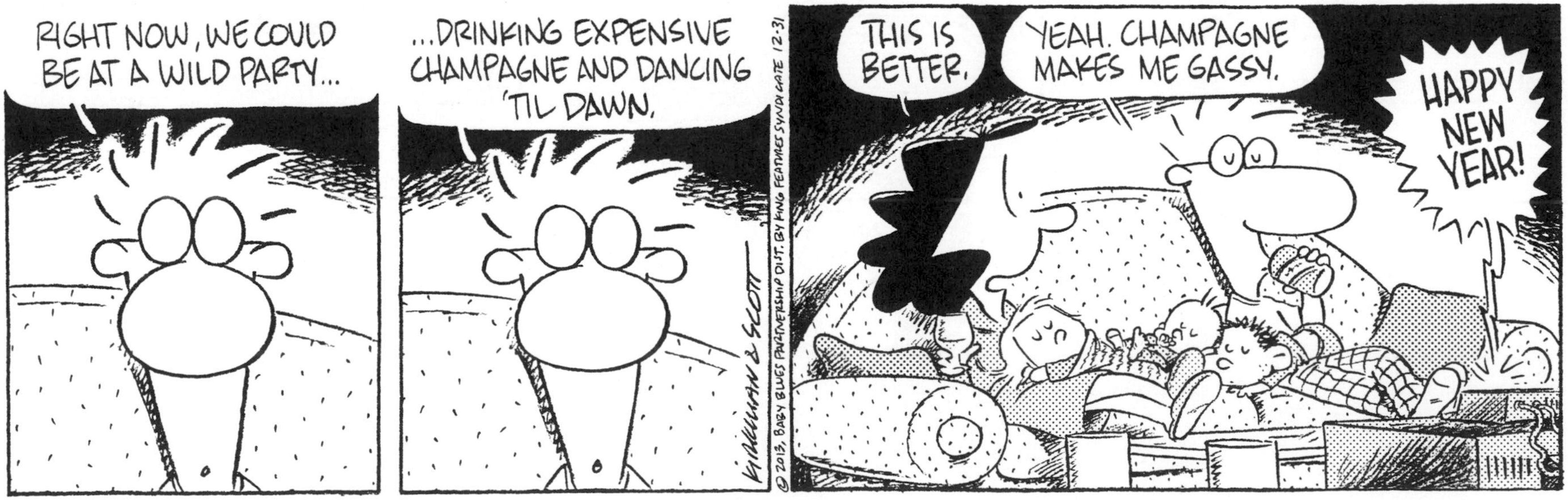
RIGHT NOW, WE COULD BE AT A WILD PARTY...
...DRINKING EXPENSIVE CHAMPAGNE AND DANCING 'TIL DAWN.
©2013, BABY BLUES PARTNERSHIP DIST. BY KING FEATURES SYNDICATE 12-31
KIRKMAN & SCOTT
THIS IS BETTER.
YEAH. CHAMPAGNE MAKES ME GASSY.
HAPPY NEW YEAR!

Rick: The drawing in the last panel is one of my favorites of them all together. It feels like I remember that time of life.

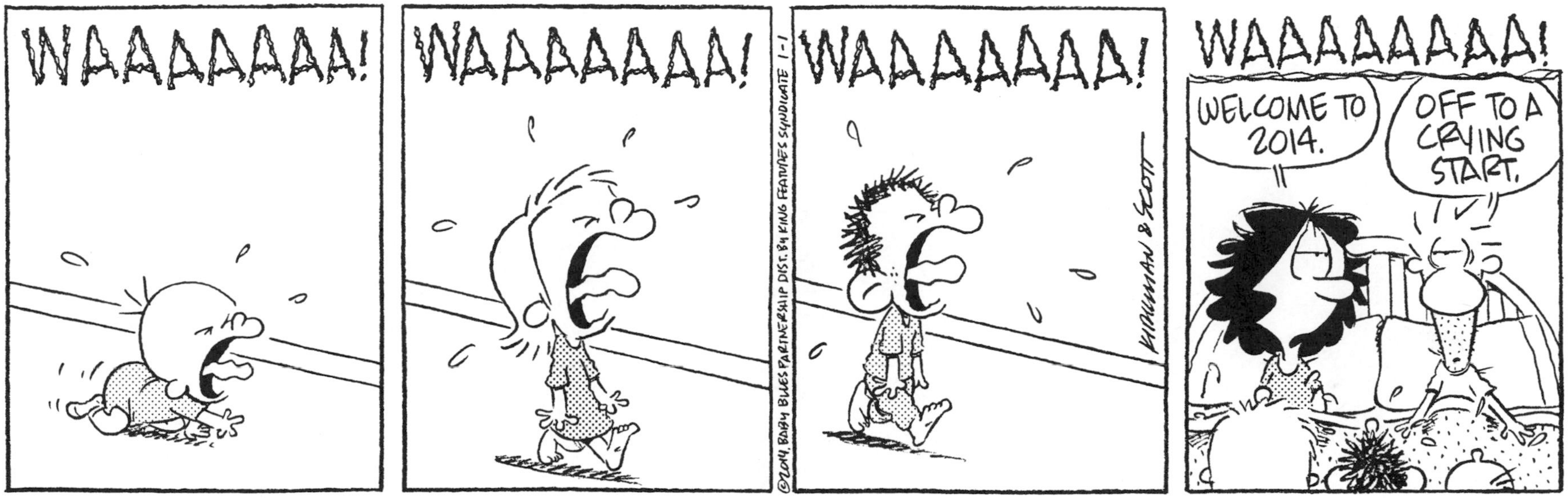
WAAAAAAA!
WAAAAAAAA!
©2014, Baby Blues Partnership Dist. By King Features Syndicate 1-1
WAAAAAAAA!
Kirkman & Scott
WAAAAAAAAA!
WELCOME TO 2014.
OFF TO A CRYING START.

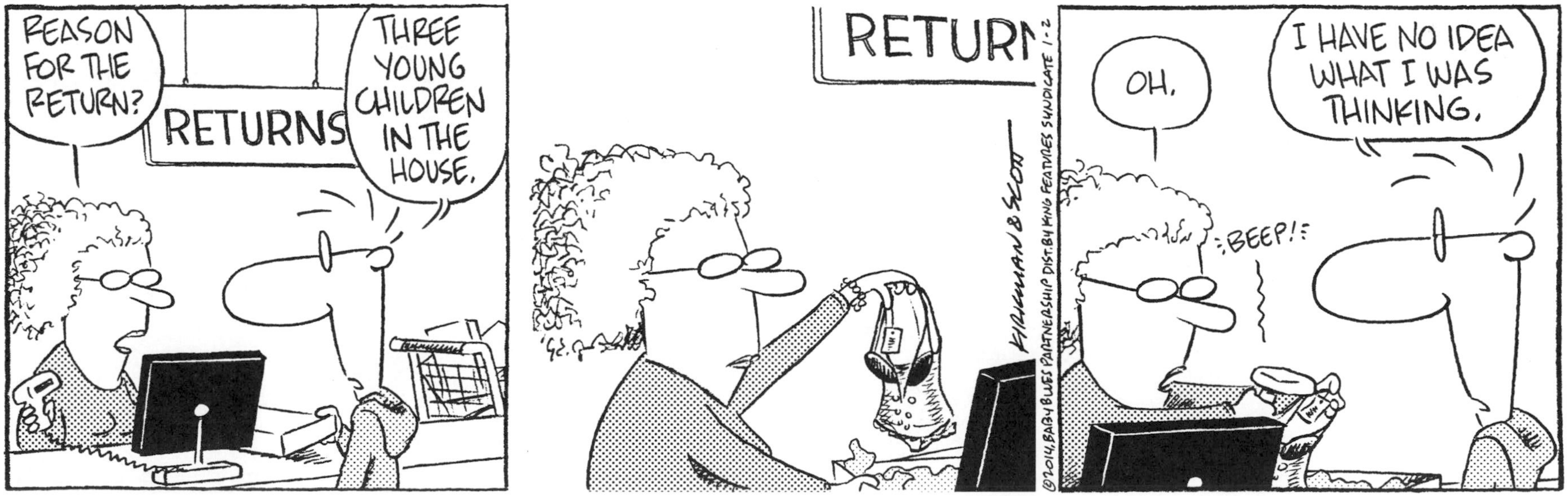
REASON FOR THE RETURN?
RETURNS
THREE YOUNG CHILDREN IN THE HOUSE.
RETURN
©2014, Baby Blues Partnership Dist. By King Features Syndicate 1-2
Kirkman & Scott
OH.
BEEP!
I HAVE NO IDEA WHAT I WAS THINKING.

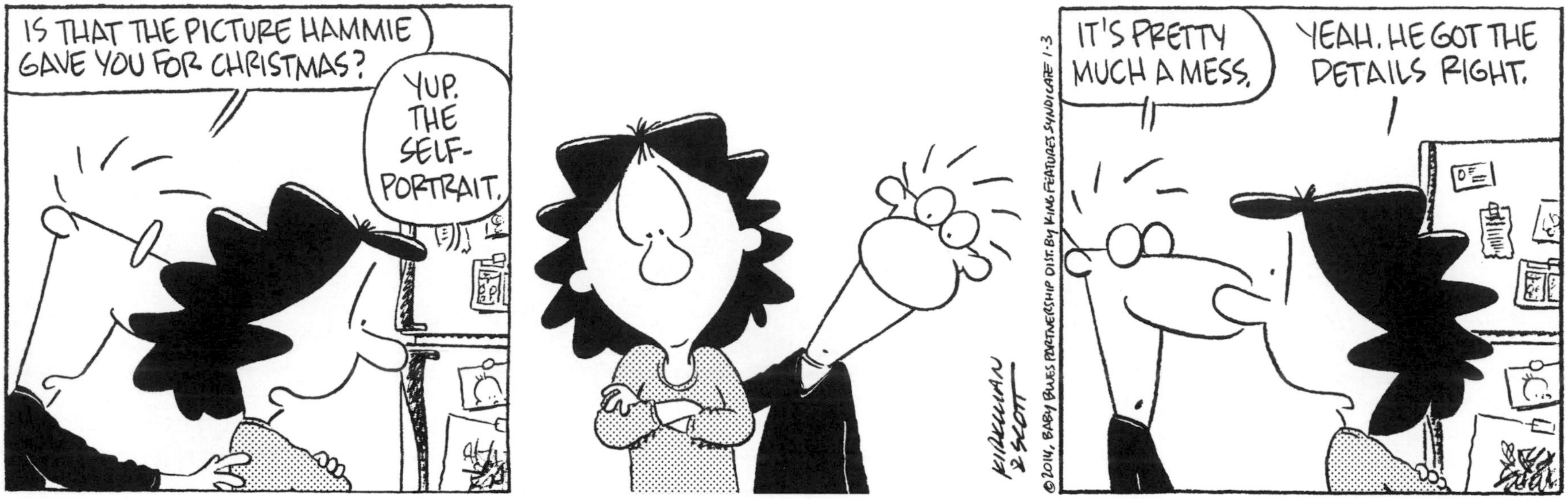
IS THAT THE PICTURE HAMMIE GAVE YOU FOR CHRISTMAS?
YUP. THE SELF-PORTRAIT.
IT'S PRETTY MUCH A MESS.
YEAH. HE GOT THE DETAILS RIGHT.
KIRKMAN & SCOTT
©2014, BABY BLUES PARTNERSHIP DIST. BY KING FEATURES SYNDICATE 1-3

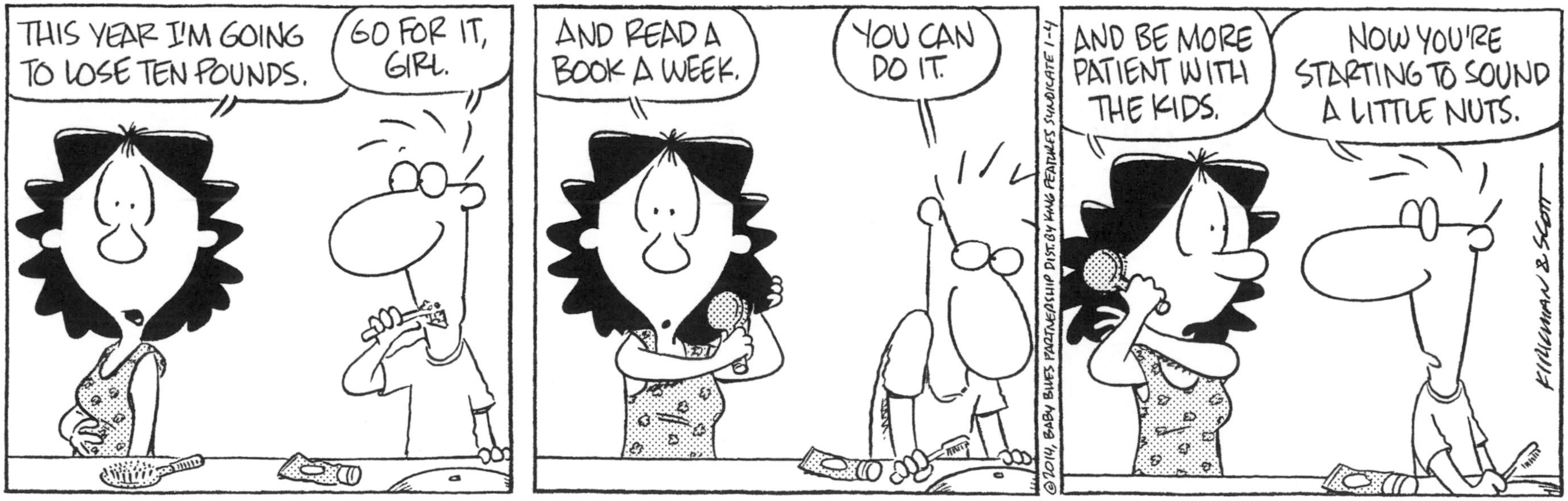
THIS YEAR I'M GOING TO LOSE TEN POUNDS.
GO FOR IT, GIRL.
AND READ A BOOK A WEEK.
YOU CAN DO IT.
AND BE MORE PATIENT WITH THE KIDS.
NOW YOU'RE STARTING TO SOUND A LITTLE NUTS.
©2014, BABY BLUES PARTNERSHIP DIST. BY KING FEATURES SYNDICATE 1-4
KIRKMAN & SCOTT

Jerry: That's been my New Year's Resolution for a long time. One of these years it's gonna stick.

Baby Blues® is syndicated internationally by King Features Syndicate, Inc.
For information, write King Features Syndicate, Inc.,
300 West Fifty-Seventh Street, New York, New York 10019.

Andrews McMeel Publishing, LLC
an Andrews McMeel Universal company
1130 Walnut Street, Kansas City, Missouri 64106
www.andrewsmcmeel.com

15 16 17 18 SDB 10 9 8 7 6 5 4 3 2

ISBN: 978-1-4494-5825-6

Library of Congress Control Number: 2014935612

Find *Baby Blues*® on the Web at www.babyblues.com.

ATTENTION: SCHOOLS AND BUSINESSES
Andrews McMeel books are available at quantity discounts with bulk purchase for educational,
business, or sales promotional use. For information, please e-mail the Andrews McMeel Publishing
Special Sales Department: specialsales@amuniversal.com.